AF375449

TSIMSHIAN EAGLE

A CULTURE BEARER'S JOURNEY

Book and cover design by Dan D Shafer
Cover photo by Steve Quinn *(top)* and courtesy of the National Museum of the American Indian *(bottom)*

ISBN: 9781634050524
Library of Congress Control Number: 2023944192

Published by Chin Music Press
1501 Pike Place #329
Seattle, WA 98101-1542
www.chinmusicpress.com

FIRST PRINTING

TSIMSHIAN EAGLE
A CULTURE BEARER'S JOURNEY

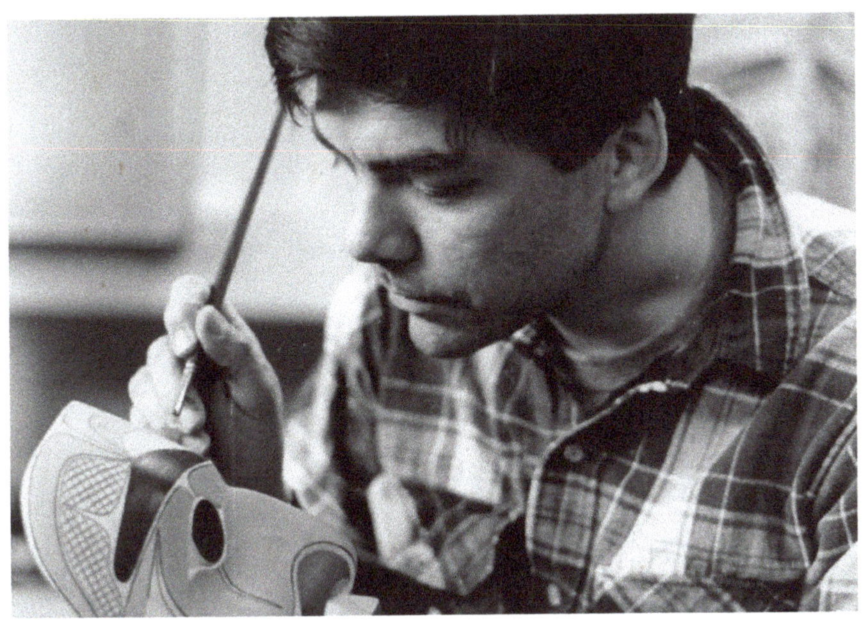

David A. Boxley
with STEVE QUINN

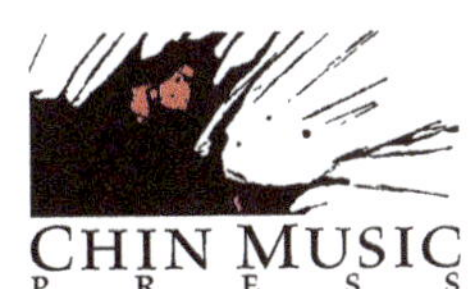

CHIN MUSIC PRESS

TABLE OF CONTENTS

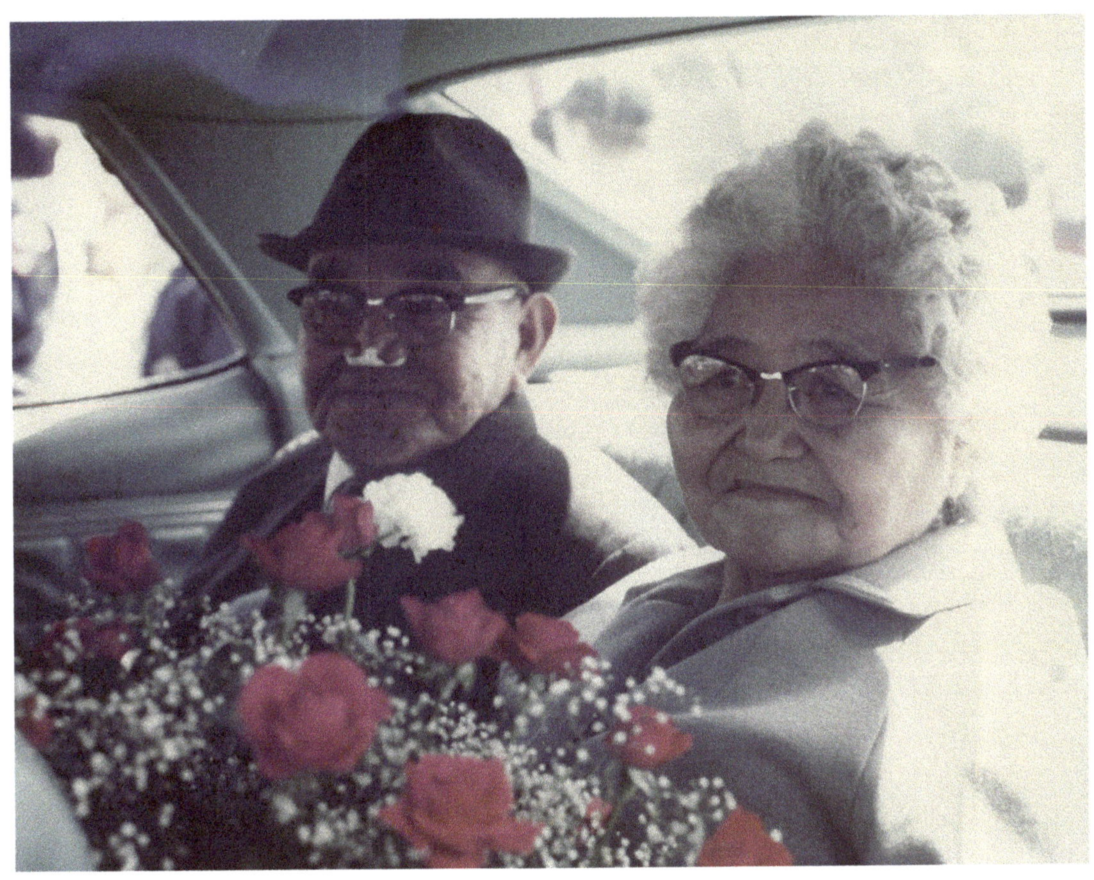

for YAYA *and* GIGI

Everything I am is because of them.

MEASURE OF A MAN / *Wilat nii goo da'axɫga 'yuuta*

BY GYIBAAWM LAXHA — DAVID ROBERT BOXLEY

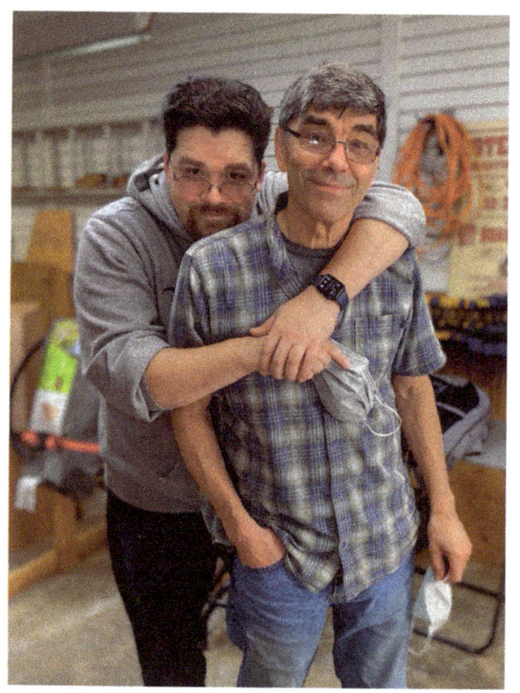

"Do what you say you're going to do. That is the measure of a man." This lesson was repeated to me often as I was growing up, and it's this phrase that reminds me most of my dad, David Albert Boxley. I still hear him say it in my head in the moments when I fail to live up to his advice. And while no one is perfect, the weight of always trying to do what is right is a good weight to bear.

My dad grew up not knowing his father, a selfish enigma of a man from Oklahoma, who left my grandmother before Dad was born. My grandma, due to the impacts of the government school and a major injury to her face in her childhood, struggled with alcohol and was an inconsistent presence in Dad's life.

I thank his grandparents, my yaya and gigi, for giving me a father who—desperate to do better for my brother and me than his parents did for him—gives everything he can for his children. Albert and Dora Bolton gave him love, stability, and access to the bits and pieces of our culture that survived in Metlakatla, setting the foundation for who and what he would become.

"Back rim, arch, follow through." Few would know it anymore if they didn't know him back then, but my dad was a school teacher and a basketball coach—a really good coach, actually. Every team he ever coached went to the championship of their league or division, even the little league teams my brother and I played on.

He was demanding as a coach, as he is in life, running his players hard, expecting their best. He has always had a quick temper. He once held the record for the most technical fouls in a season. I'm not sure if that record still stands. I'll never forget my teammates and me holding him down on the bench during a little league game to stop him from yelling at a referee. My teammates still say he's the best coach they ever had.

Dad was an only child and was spoiled by his grandparents. That hasn't always prepared him for the disappointments of life. The trauma of absentee parents, being teased and bullied when he was young, and being criticized when attempting to practice our culture, have stayed with him. Those pains burden him, but they have also driven him to succeed.

"Pride in heritage." I was a baby in my dad's first workshop as he carved his grandmother's memorial totem pole, the first pole in Metlakatla. I danced on his shoulders for the potlatch when it was raised. The smell of red cedar is the smell of my childhood and is filled with memories of countless hours spent with my dad and of learning what it is to be Ts'msyen.* In many cases, I have learned right along with him.

The history of our people is complicated and full of beauty, tragedy, and resilience. That I could grow up in the shadow of totem poles is a testament to the power of Ts'msyen culture and the stubborn willpower of my dad. His decision to retire from teaching to be a carver was driven not only out of passion for the art itself, but also by the desire to ensure our people were proud of being Ts'msyen.

Our art and culture are inextricably intertwined. I was always taught, by Dad's instruction and by his example, that we must give back to our people. I was with him as he was writing the first new songs for the first adult dance group in Metlakatla. He had never written songs before but it's what was needed for our people to begin our path back to our cultural identity.

"I want to be just like you when I grow up." He says this to me when I have successes in my life or when I give him good advice. I can count on him no matter what, even in my adolescence when I didn't want him around quite so much. We argued a lot as I was becoming an adult, mostly because I am also spoiled and we both wanted our way. But he also struggled with the switch from father to friend.

The reality is that I always wanted to be like him when I grew up, or at least the best parts of him: his dedication and commitment to everything he decides to do; his absolute devotion to his family and our people; and, though sometimes shrouded in an intimidating frown or in words he should've thought more about before he said them, his profound generosity and kindness of heart. I will be chasing those goals for the rest of my life.

No one is perfect. But we can overcome the pain and trauma in our lives. We can make choices that will leave a mark on this world for the better. I think that's what I want everyone to take from the story of Dad's life and work. That it's up to you to make your corner of the world a better place. To do what you say you will and be glad to bear the weight. ❖

* **NOTE:** The spelling of our tribal name is most commonly rendered Tsimshian, which is used in the title of this book. The alternative, Ts'msyen, reflects someone who speaks our traditional language.

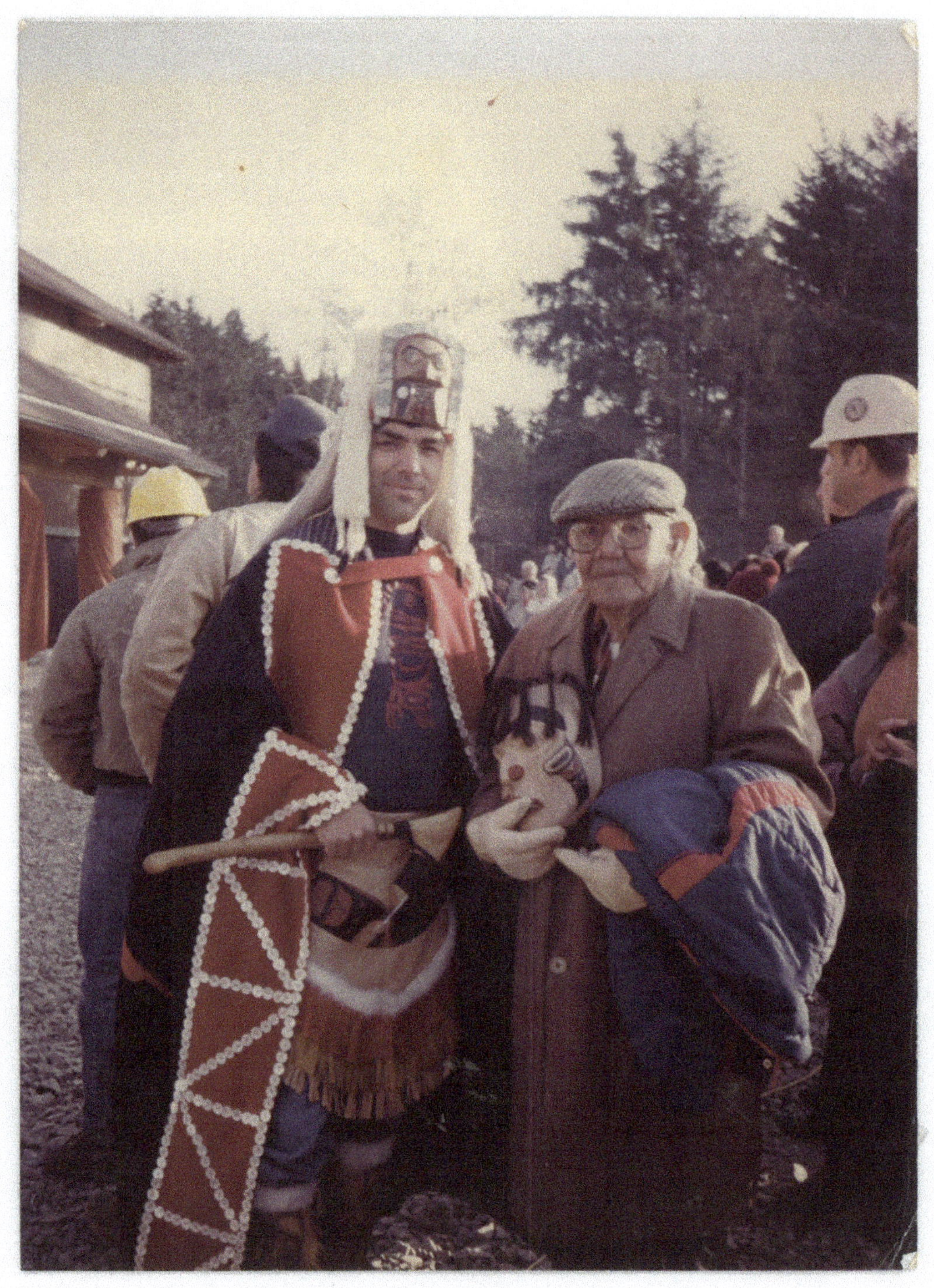

my Hero... my Grandfather

There's not a day that goes by
that his voice, his love, is not
with me. for that I am grateful.

NEW PURSUITS / *Su goo dm dzabit*

Another school year had ended in Metlakatla, Alaska, and I was about to make the toughest decision of my life and certainly my professional career: I decided to leave Metlakatla—this time for good—and move to Seattle. There, I would pursue a passion and ultimately embark on a cultural mission to be a full-time artist.

That day in 1986, I dropped my school keys on my principal's desk and said, "I'm leaving. I'm not going to be school teaching anymore."

I was leaving a solid career and the certainty of health insurance and retirement within the next ten to fifteen years; if I didn't do it then, I'm sure I would not have the chance to do it later.

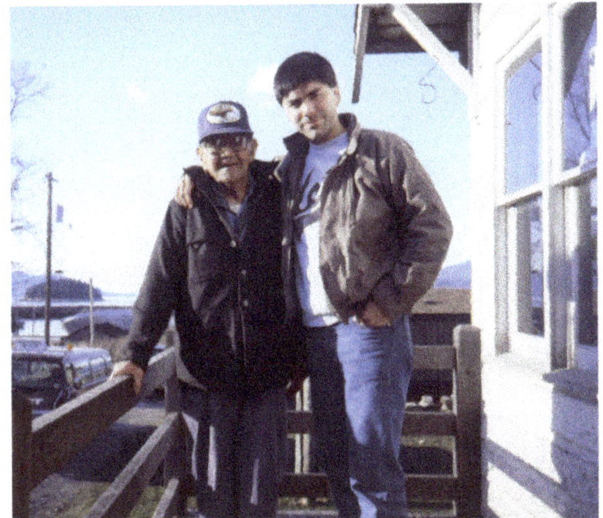

But it was really a lot more than changing careers and finding a new home for my family. I also wound up making a very painful decision to leave my grandfather, Albert Bolton—and, man, that was hard—but I wanted to see what I could do, how much I could accomplish.

My grandfather, who had already been alone without my grandmother for six years, was my teacher, my hero, and he supported my decision. When I was starting to become involved with carving and the Tsimshian culture, he got to see that, and I got to share it with him.

Looking back, it's really strange, maybe even ironic. I realize now that I had to move away from my traditional village to become a traditional carver and cultural leader. ❖

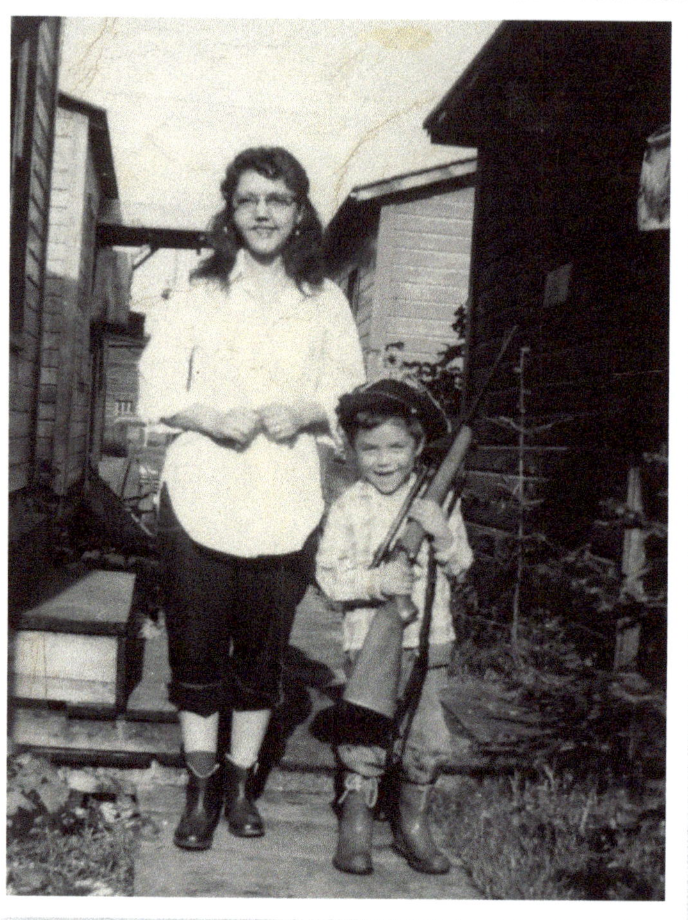

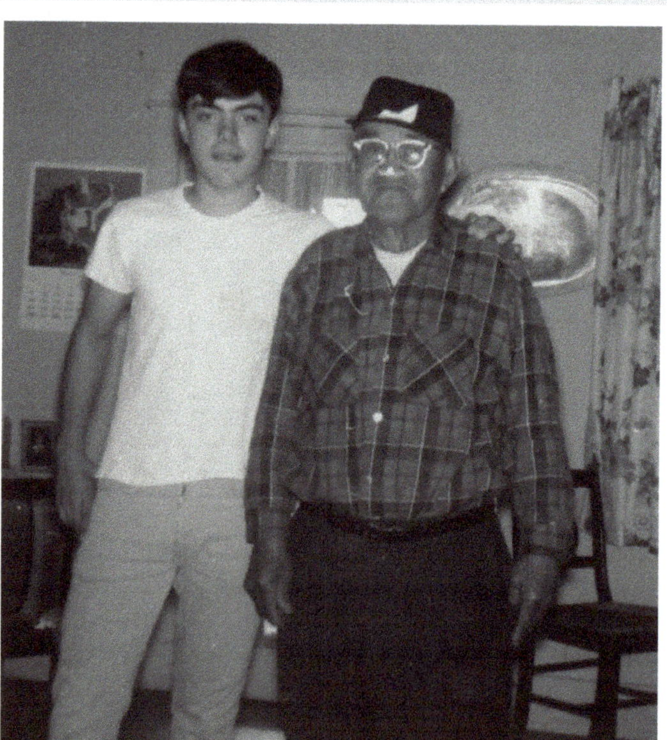

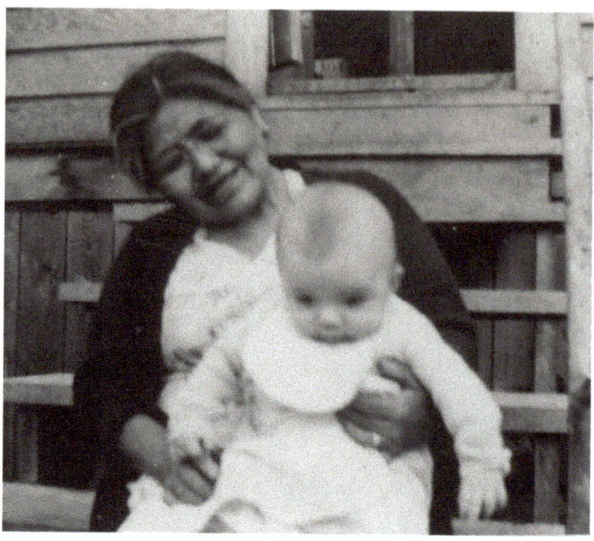

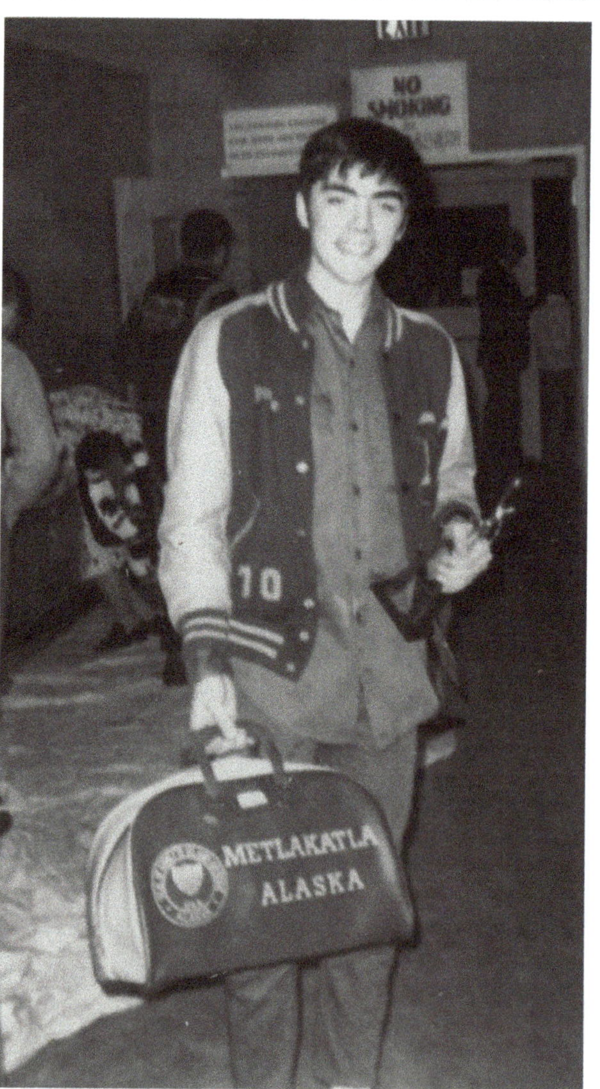
NO SMOKING
METLAKATLA
ALASKA

CHAPTER ONE

BEGINNINGS / *Sit'aatgm*

I've been in the Seattle area for nearly forty years producing Tsimshian art—totem poles, masks, and bentwood boxes among other items.

My work has been placed in galleries, people's homes, and museums worldwide. But any success I've had traces to my childhood home, Metlakatla, Alaska, and to the people who raised me, my grandparents Albert and Dora Bolton. I still see them every day; their portrait hangs prominently in my shop, near the adze my grandfather helped me craft nearly four decades ago.

My attachment and ties to Metlakatla, Alaska's lone federal reserve on Annette Island in the state's southeast region, and those who influenced my life remain as strong today as the day I left. The house in which I grew up still stands a hundred years after my grandfather built it. We had three bedrooms downstairs, a big room upstairs, and a tiny, little bathroom. Now I own that house and my son Davey lives there. The three totem poles he and I carved stand in front of the house. And we expanded and remodeled the once tiny bathroom.

That house is a foundation for me and all of my memories: so many family members have gone in and out of that same house. It is a reflection of our cultural history.

Back then people were living in what we called a longhouse. There were sometimes two or three generations living in one house. That's how it was in our house. My grandparents, my uncles and my mom, my cousins. Not all at once, of course. They came and went; the house was there when they needed it.

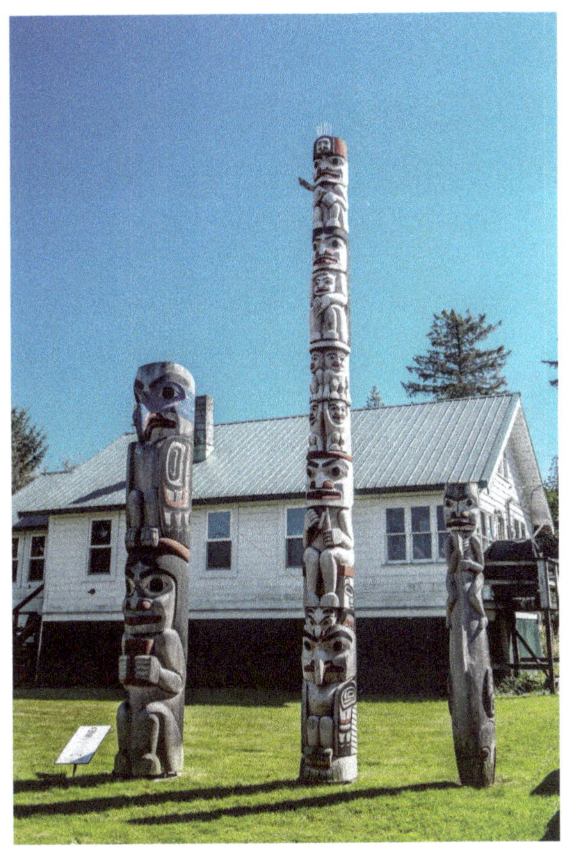

My childhood home (and now the home of my son Davey) in Metlakatla, Alaska.

The door was always open to visit, and there was always food to share. I remember lots of times when I was a kid, people from British Columbia would come to visit my grandparents. I can still see them in my mind. I could hear our traditional language, Sm'algyax, and see all the food being brought out. It was quite a big deal.

My uncles—Uncle Frank, Uncle Don, and Uncle Alex, all of whom lived with us at different times—and their friends would visit. They would just know somehow that my grandmother was baking bread or pie. She made this great apple pie, and her homemade bread was really delicious. The door would be open in the springtime. You could smell the bread through the house and the pies cooking in the oven. People would just come running up the steps.

It was a safe house. No alcohol. No abuse. Just a safe place. To grow up in Metlakatla in those days, the Fifties and early Sixties, you could go anywhere, climb a mountain, go to the beach, and not worry about anybody hurting you. It was a wonderful time to be a kid, fishing and hunting and playing in the woods. The reason I stress this is a friend of mine grew up in an opposite situation where there was a lot of abuse and alcohol. The stories he told me still scare me.

I was born on January 19, 1952, in Ketchikan, located immediately north of Metlakatla. My grandparents brought me home two days later. My mother, Laverne Bolton Welcome, struggled with alcoholism, and my father left her six months before I was born. She married my stepfather after I was born. He was abusive when he drank and he left my mother when I was six. So, my grandparents took me into their home.

I grew up in a village that was losing its Tsimshian identity: cultural ceremonies no longer took place; totems poles, which stood in other villages, didn't exist there; and Sm'algyax, our centuries-old language, was not being spoken the way it was when the founders arrived in 1887. What awaited me was a chance to embark on a cultural journey.

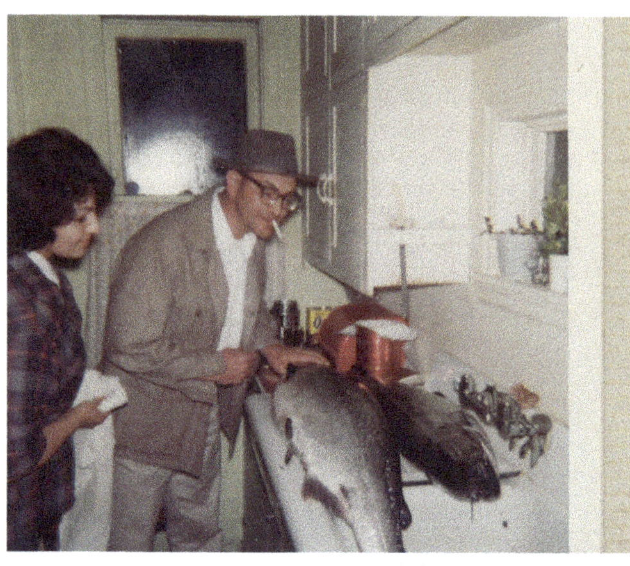

TOP: Uncle Don Bolton would visit to inspect yaya's salmon catch. He would tease yaya about how small it was, but we knew better.

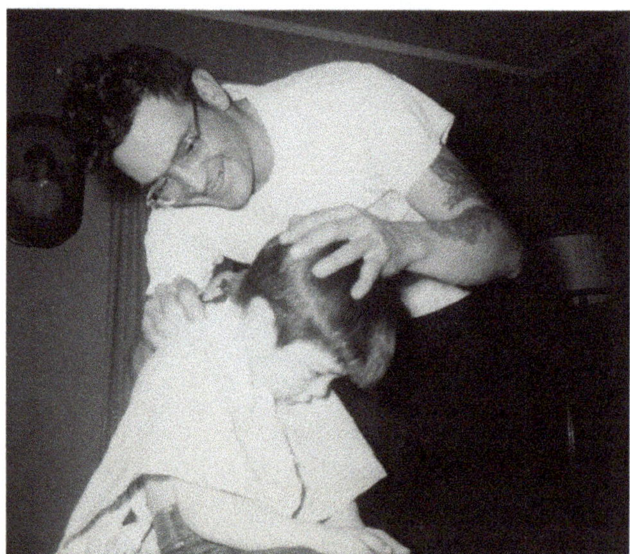

BOTTOM: Uncle Don gave me most of my haircuts while growing up. He would always cut my hair too short.

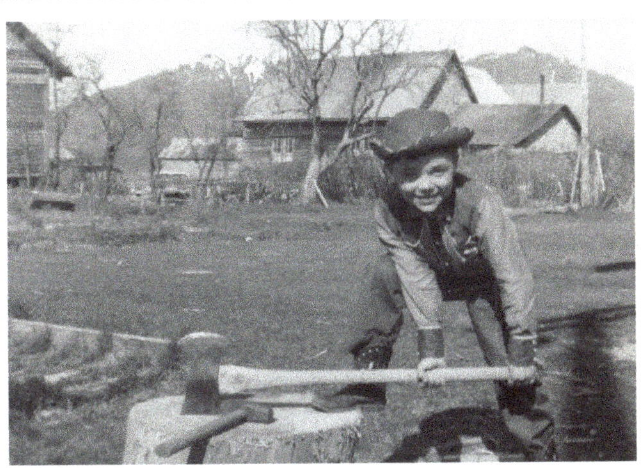

My grandfather really did all of the chopping, but I
enjoyed carrying and stacking the wood.

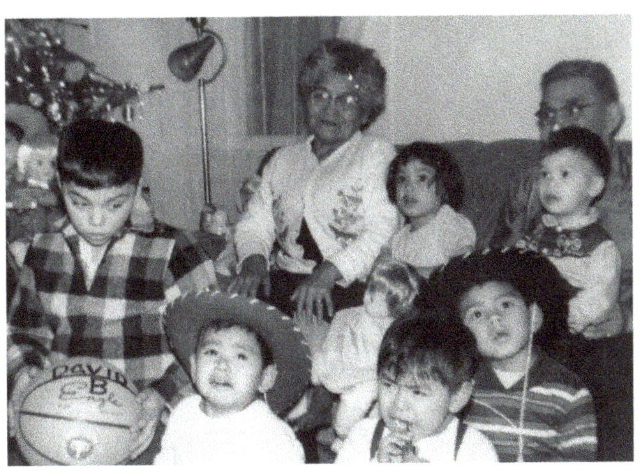

My first basketball. Who would have thought
it would be such a big part of my life?

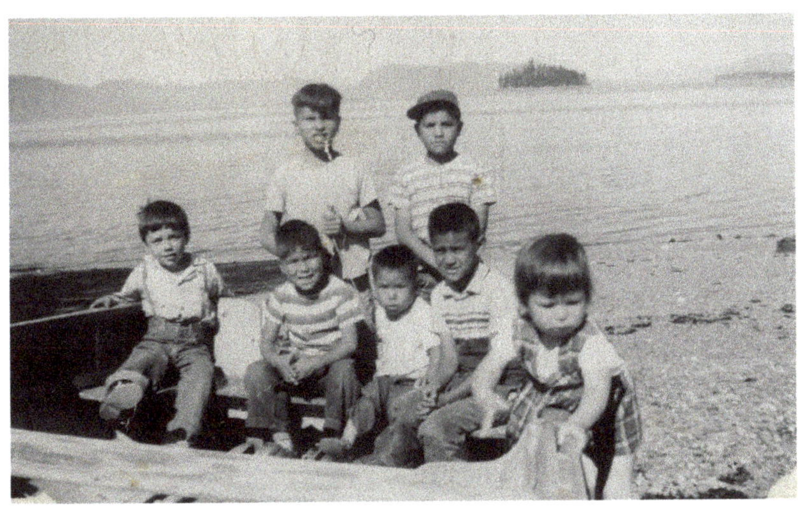

Metlakatla was a cool place to grow up—the beaches and the woods were our playgrounds.
Kids had a different way of life than they do now. Being outdoors was just a natural thing
to do. Yaya made this boat. He built it right where the photo was taken. I remember sitting
in the bow of the boat and seeing porpoises swimming on both sides.

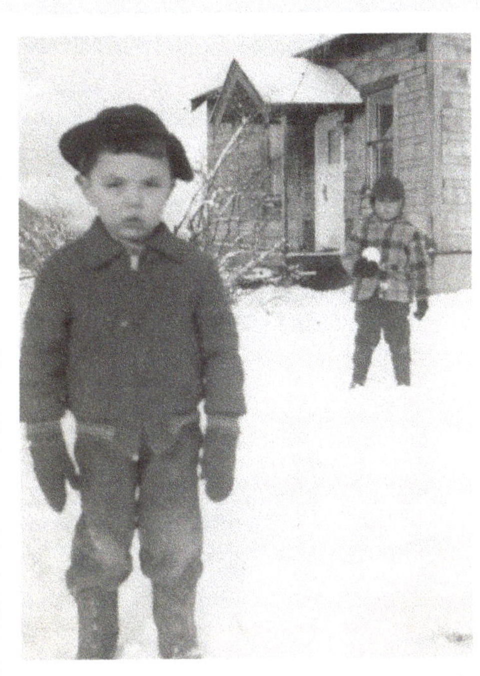

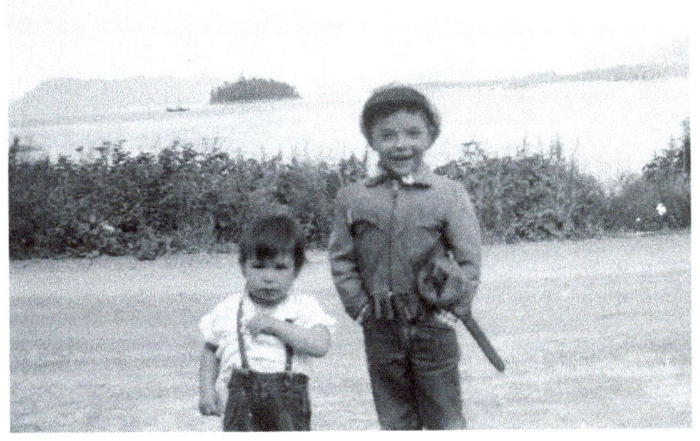

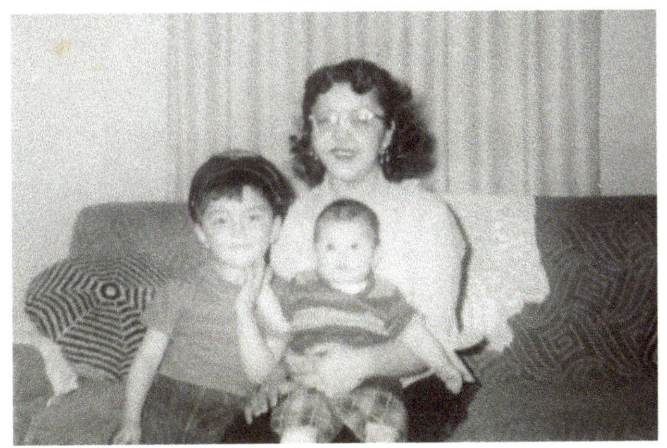

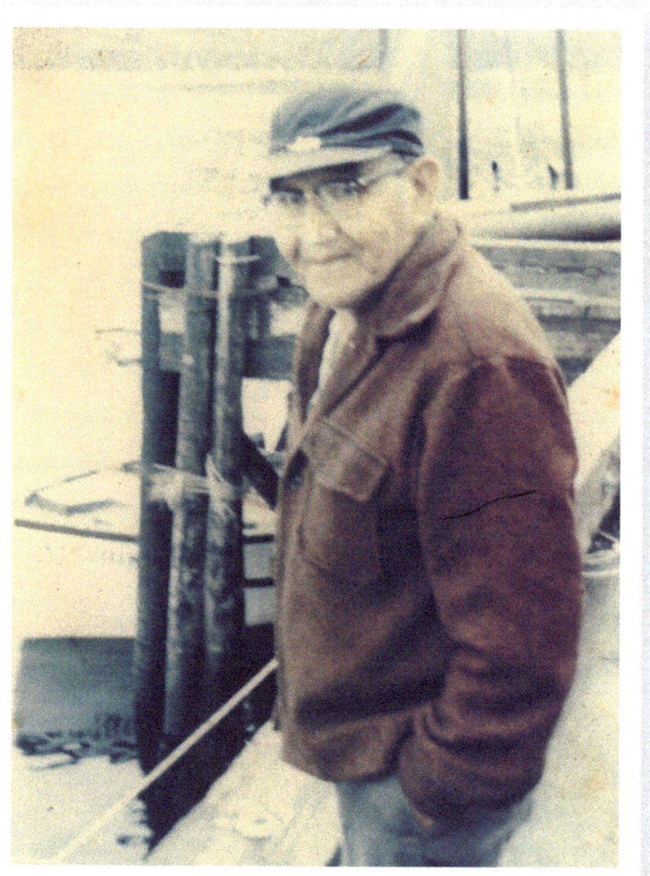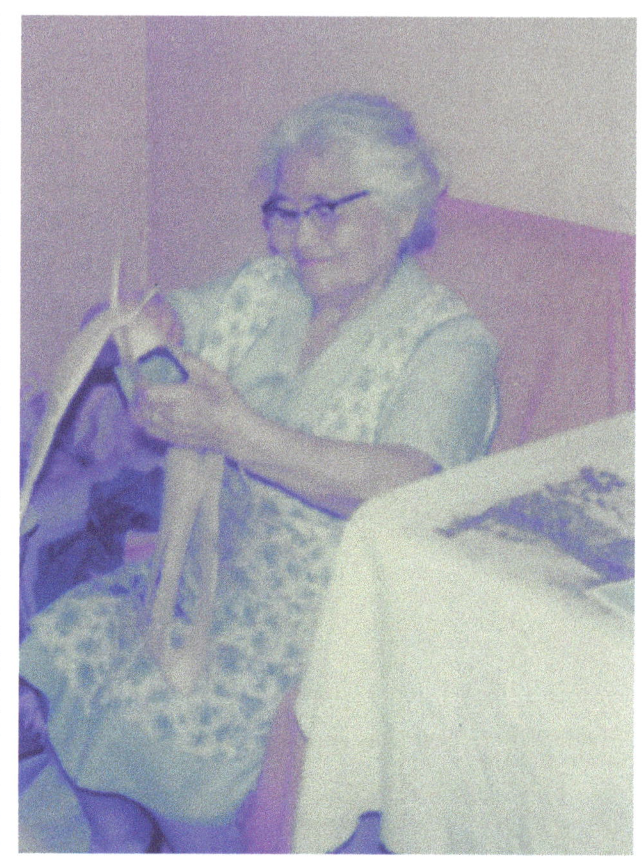

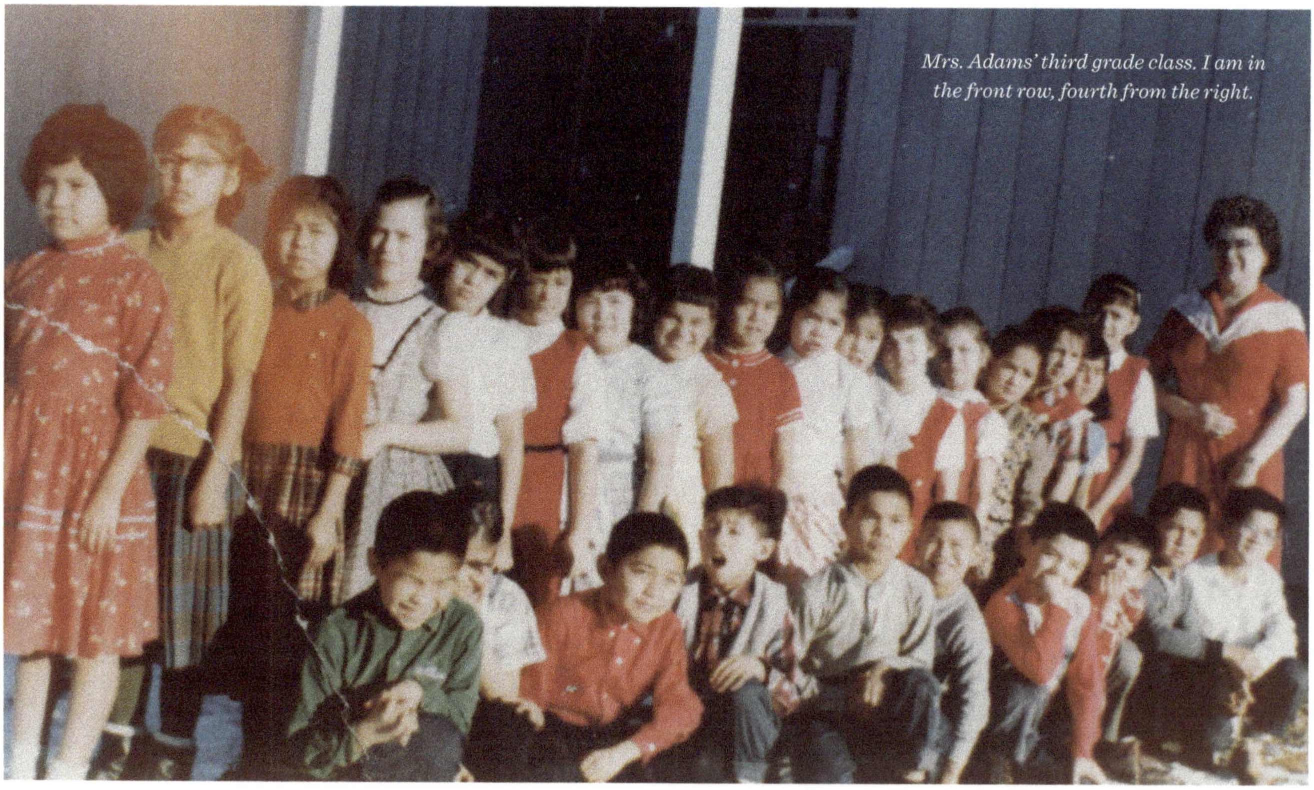

Mrs. Adams' third grade class. I am in the front row, fourth from the right.

My grandparents are also my link to our village's founders, who were led by missionary William Duncan in their August 7, 1887, journey from British Columbia. They were a connection for me to the old people, the people before there was a Metlakatla. Neither one of them went past the third grade because their families would always take them out of Mr. Duncan's school in the fall to go salmon fishing and then halibut fishing. That's just the way it was. Everybody had to help. They had to work together to gather food for the winter.

My grandfather's ancestors were Gitwilgyoots, the People of the Kelp. They came from the British Columbia coast, south of the Nass River. My grandmother's family came from Gitḵ'a'ata, the People of the Cane.

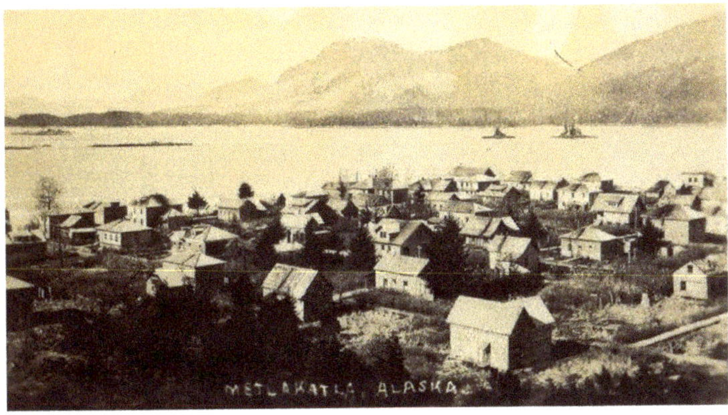

ABOVE: Metlakatla, Alaska, circa early 1900s.

BELOW: My grandparents, Albert and Dora Bolton, were married in 1918, the same year missionary William Duncan died.

They were married in August of 1918. That's the same time that Duncan passed away. He died of a cerebral hemorrhage around the same time they got married. My grandmother had a short marriage before she met my grandfather. Her husband died. That was a mini controversy at that time, too, because some people didn't think the mourning period had been long enough. Things were different back then.

My grandmother was so tiny. She was 4′9″ or 4′10″. You see pictures on my wall and in my books. She was just this round, little lady with a great smile and great laugh. She didn't speak English that well. Her first language was Sm'algyax. I give her all the credit for what I know of our language because she was the one talking to me all the time.

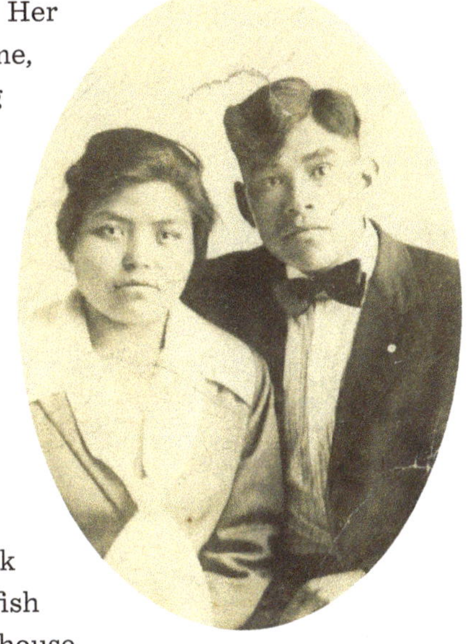

Despite her size, she could do everything her ancestors used to do: filet, salt, and smoke fish; pick berries; dig for cockles. I helped her pack a lot of the fish after she fileted it all behind our house at the smoke house. She and I would go berry picking.

We would go down to the beach, visit different parts of the island, then get in the boat and go out to dig for cockles or clams. I remember once my grandmother found a sea urchin when we were digging for clams. She broke it open and ate it. She broke open another one and said, "Here, eat it." Boy, I had a hard time with that, being a little kid.

I spent all my time with my grandparents: hunting, fishing, picking berries, digging for clams. My grandfather would help her get bark for her baskets. We would go camping all the time. I had some great adventures with them. One night when we were camping on one of the Percy Islands, my grandmother woke me up. One of our boats had gotten loose and was way out on the water. It was pitch black. I was about thirteen or fourteen then, and she told me to go get the boat.

My grandfather held the rope. I stripped down and waded out to the boat, then grabbed the rope and fastened it to the boat.

The very next morning, my grandmother said, "Davey, there's a deer outside." All of the tide had gone down, and there it was, right outside the cabin. I grabbed my .22, and I shot and hit it in the antler.

The deer started running down the beach. I grabbed my grandfather's .30-30 and went running down the beach after it. I didn't know what to do, so I just said, "Hey!" The deer turned around and looked at me, and I shot it. My grandmother was so happy.

This kind of subsistence living was really the most visible sign of our Native culture.

When I was a little boy, I would follow my grandmother around. She would take me with her when she would visit elder friends or relatives. They would give me ice cream and set me off on the side while they visited. They always spoke in our language. I soaked it up.

I was teased too about how much I hung out with my grandmother. I used to be embarrassed about it. But today I'm grateful that I was able to follow her around and listen to

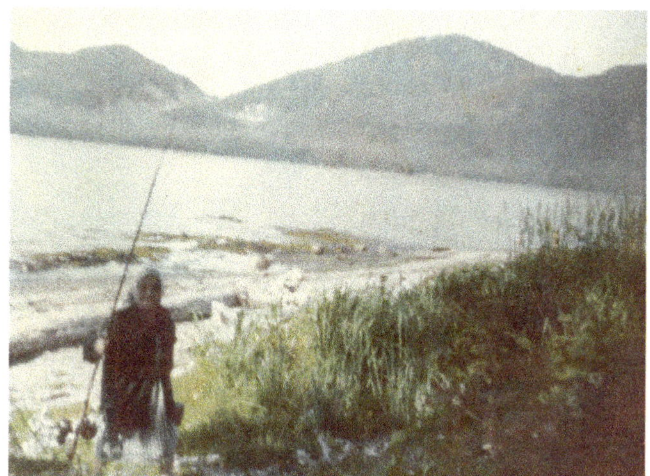

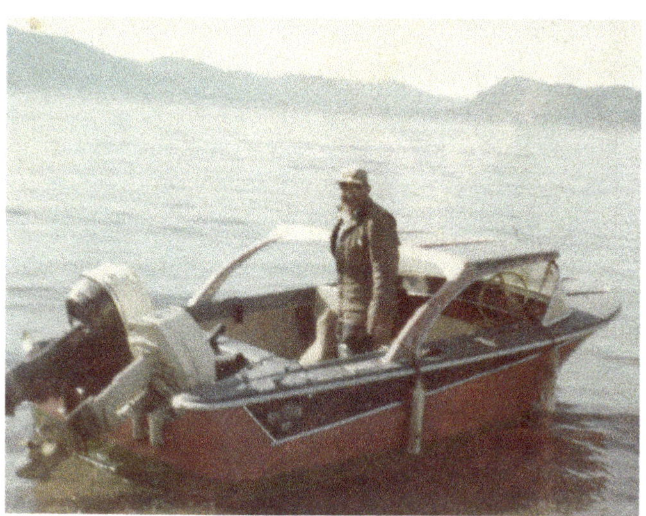

I spent a lot of time with yaya and gigi fishing, hunting, gathering seafood. They were my focus growing up. We took the boat to other parts of the island to hunt.

them talk. Otherwise, I would not have learned a language that was disappearing right before our eyes.

I had a good life with them. I have so many good memories of hunting and fishing and camping. Berry picking. Helping them dry seaweed. Helping my grandmother hang her fish when she smoked salmon. My grandmother would usually go if we were harvesting seaweed. We had this wooden box. It was really old. My grandfather used it for years, probably since before I was born.

When I got be old enough to help, my job was to make sure the food box that my grandmother packed was delivered to my

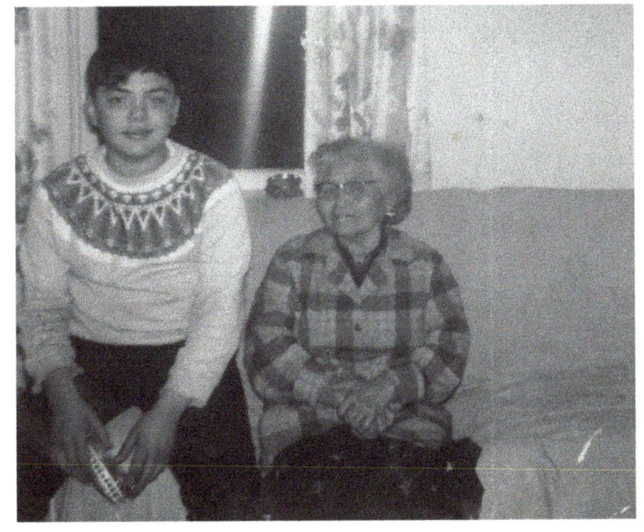

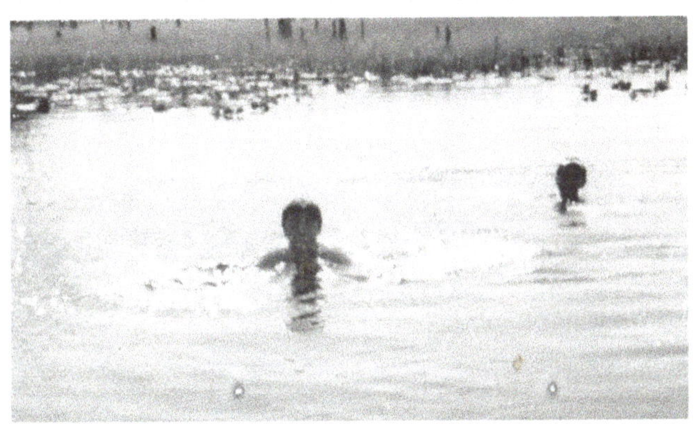

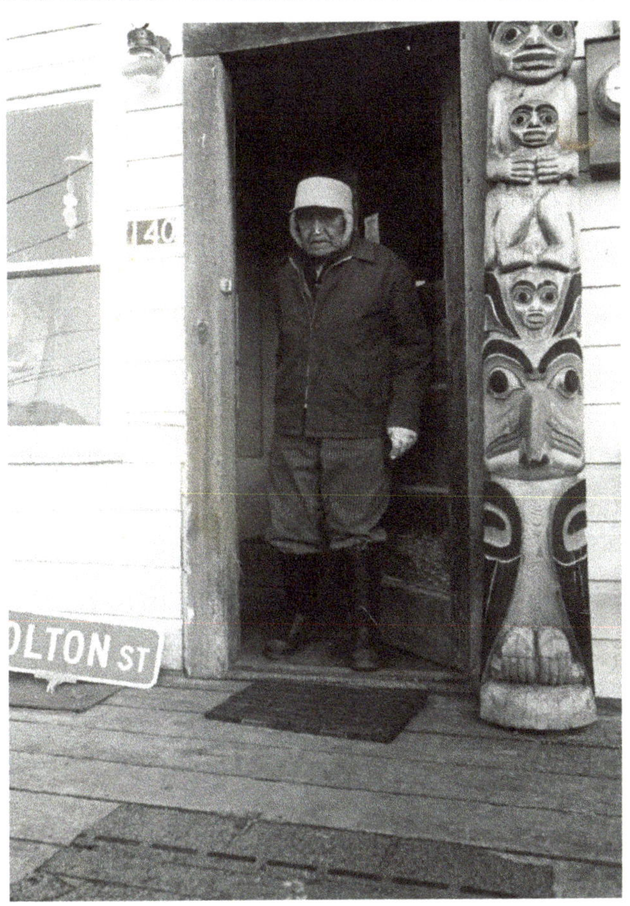

Yaya standing next to the first pole I carved.
I carved it right after my gigi died.

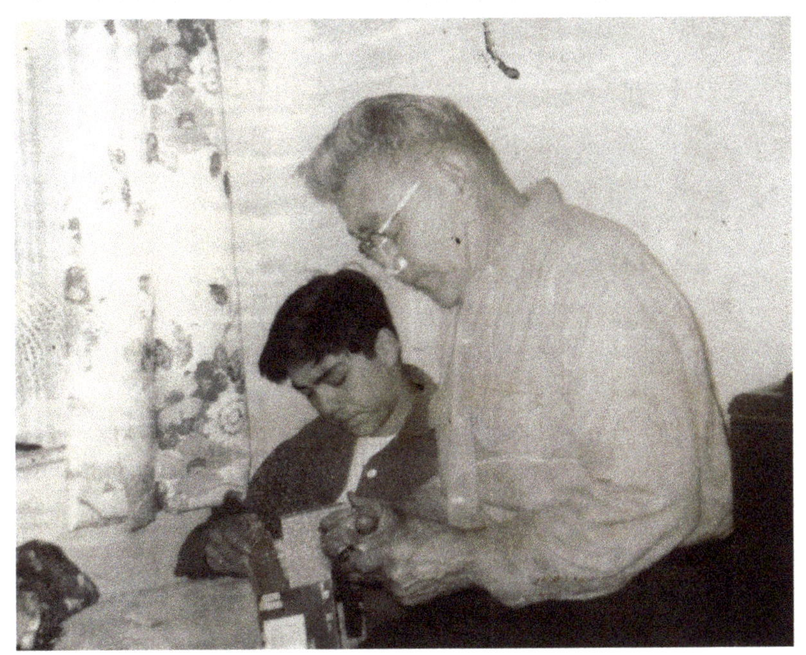

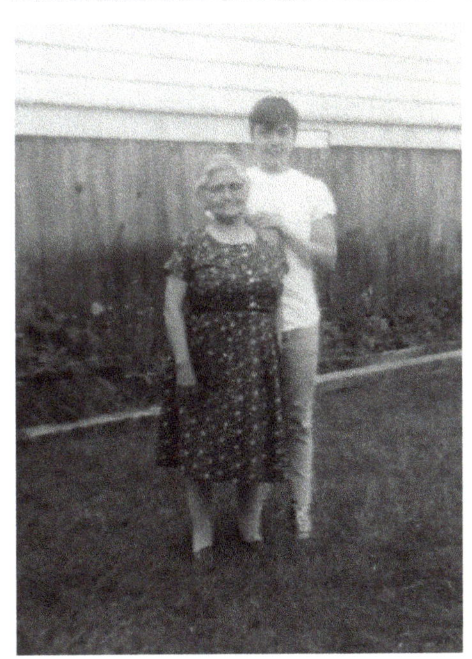

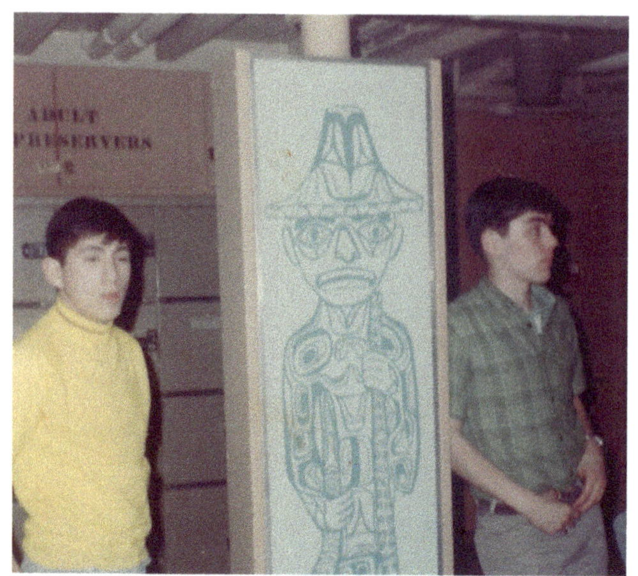

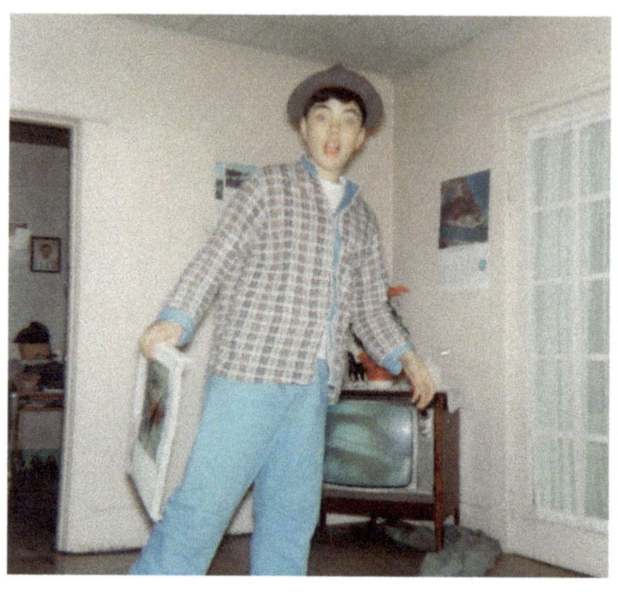

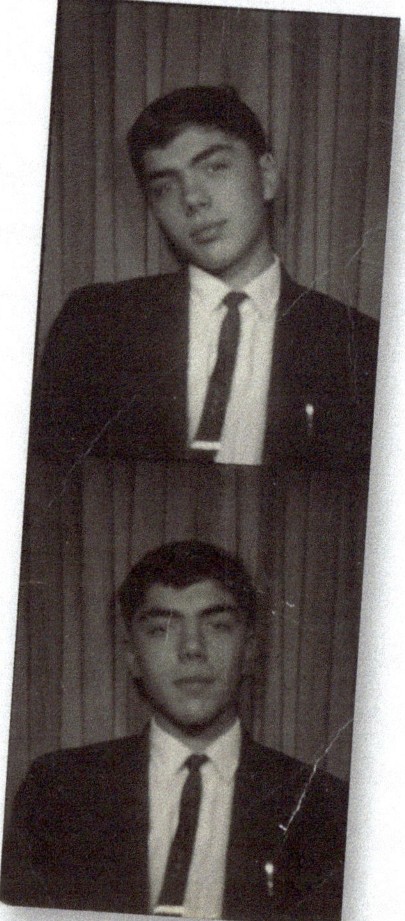

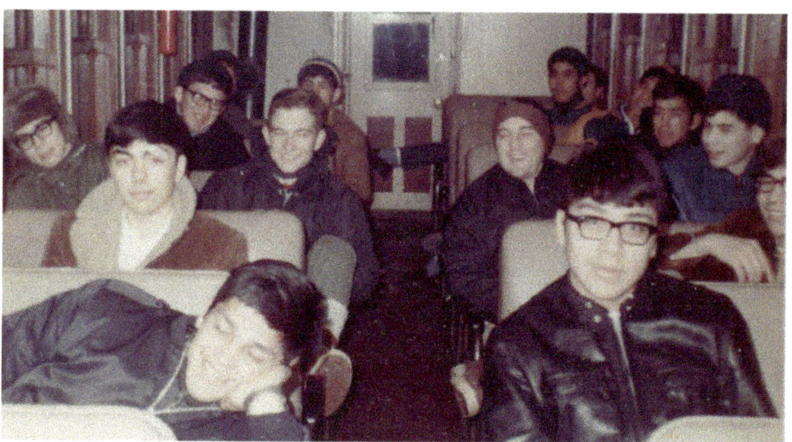

In Southeast Alaska, you would travel 12 hours on a seine boat to another village, then play four games in a week, unlike city kids who took a bus to another part of town, then returned home that afternoon. The host villages would house and feed us. It was normal to miss a week of school for games.

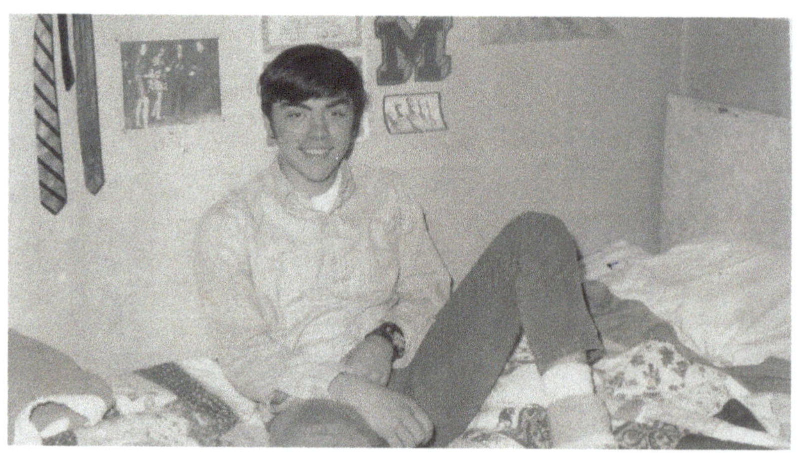

grandfather. She packed Sailor Boy crackers, jarred fish, and she made sure we had other things that we would need for camping.

My job was to make sure that box went from our house to yaya's boat and from the boat to wherever we were camping and then back. I still have that box in my shop and use it for tools.

My grandfather ran the boilers at the cannery. All the equipment was run by steam. He ran the boilers for fifty years. When he was a young man, he pitched fish. He unloaded the fish barges. He became a union member. He was the only family member I knew of who belonged to a union—the AFL-CIO. He was one of the few Natives who belonged and he was really proud of that.

My grandparents were both excellent providers. They come from that time when you couldn't just go buy things; you had to make everything pretty much, even our clothes. They smoked and dried and canned and froze the food. I am one hundred percent sure I never tasted a steak until I went to college.

Our community didn't have a lot of big stores but we'd get frozen food: chicken, pork, hamburgers. The majority of the things we ate, my grandfather provided: salmon, halibut, clams, cockles, deer.

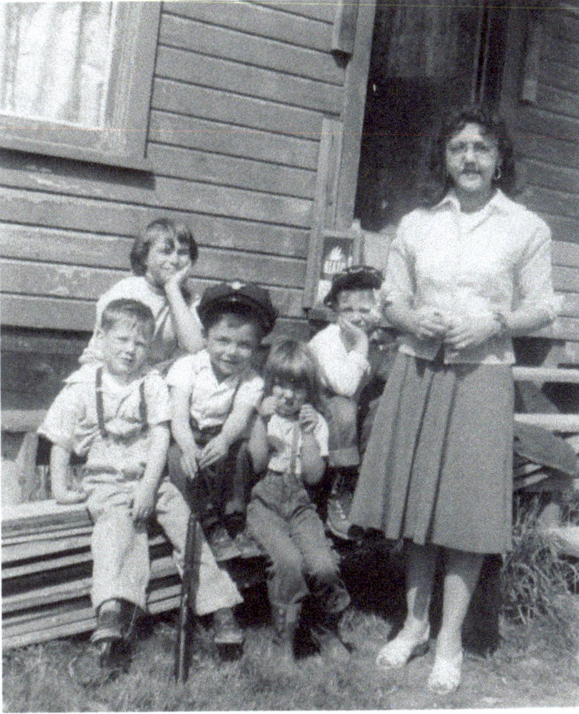

This is in Edna Bay logging camp with my mother when I was five years old. Years later, when I was coaching, I took a team to play against Thorne Bay. The girl in the back still lived there at the time and, reunited as adults, she took me hunting.

In some people's eyes, I was that square peg trying to fit into a round hole because of how much time I spent with my grandparents. When other kids were out being crazy at night, getting into trouble, I was usually with yaya and gigi. I took heat for it from other kids, especially in high school, for being so square as they put it, but as I look back on my life with them, I was fortunate. My grandparents literally saved my life.

All of my life, it never occurred to me that they would be gone one day. I wish that I had done more with them, even though we did so much together. I wish I had been more insistent on them speaking our language with me. That's one of the few regrets in my life.

My mom wasn't around much because of her alcohol problems. She had a really hard life. She had an accident when she was in puberty, about eleven or twelve years old. She was accidentally hit in the mouth by the swing of a baseball bat, which damaged all of her glands. She was in the hospital in Juneau for a year. They didn't have penicillin in those days.

It affected her for the rest of her life. Her self-image took a really big hit. She wanted to be a schoolteacher when she was younger. But she never graduated, never finished school.

One day, just in passing when I was in junior high, I asked my mother, "Who's my dad? What happened to him? I'd sure like to meet him." She didn't say anything. What I didn't know was, she had hired a private detective, who found my dad living in Reno. My mom and my dad met in 1948, four years before I was born. He was working for the U.S. geological survey, making maps. They met and got married. When she got pregnant with me, he didn't believe it. Eventually, he left.

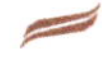

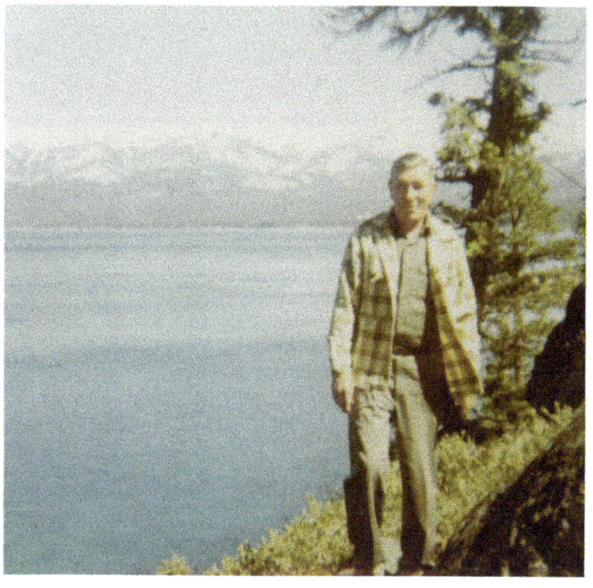

My father Clifford Boxley standing near Lake Tahoe. He may have been my father, but the man who raised and supported my cultural journey was my yaya, Albert Bolton.

On July 4, after my freshman year in high school, I was in Ketchikan. A lot of times we would go there to watch the parade and buy fireworks. I was with my friend, Ernest Leask, who we called Binky. He came up to me and said, "Hey, David, there's a guy walking around here, says he's your dad."

I said, "What are you talking about?"

Some time after that, this guy comes walking toward me on the dock in Ketchikan. He's not a very big guy. He's wearing this heavy coat on the fourth of July, cowboy boots and this bolo tie. All he needed was a cowboy hat. I don't remember any of the conversation we had except me asking him, "Are you my dad?"

My dad, Clifford Boxley, took Binky and me to a soda fountain and bought us a milkshake. We talked for a while. I found out he had moved to Ketchikan. He got a job at the spruce mill in downtown Ketchikan. He lived there until I graduated from high school. I would go over to the trailer park where he lived about once a month and stay for the weekend.

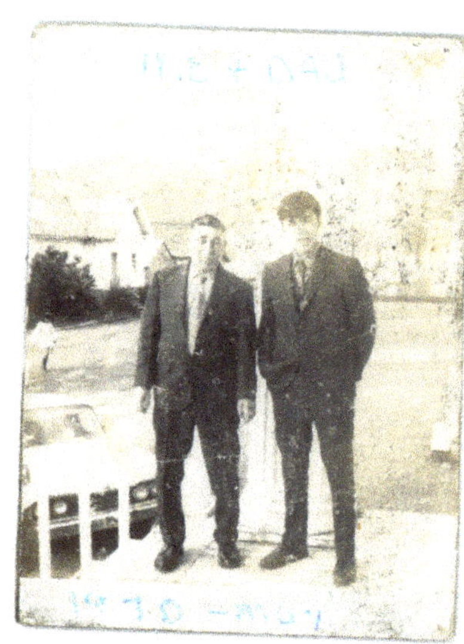

But, without any notice, he left. The day I finished high school, he showed up at my graduation. I gave the senior class president's welcome speech. He was there for that. He had set up his trailer and two cars at the Alaska state ferry before he came over to my graduation. He was gone before the graduation was over.

He was a guy who didn't want to talk about his past. He never would tell me about his family.

Later, I found out I had a brother, Robert, from another marriage. That brother told me that Dad had gotten into some illegal things. He was married two other times that I know of before he married my mom. And I had three siblings from him. I met one sister, Barbara. The other sister passed away before I could meet her.

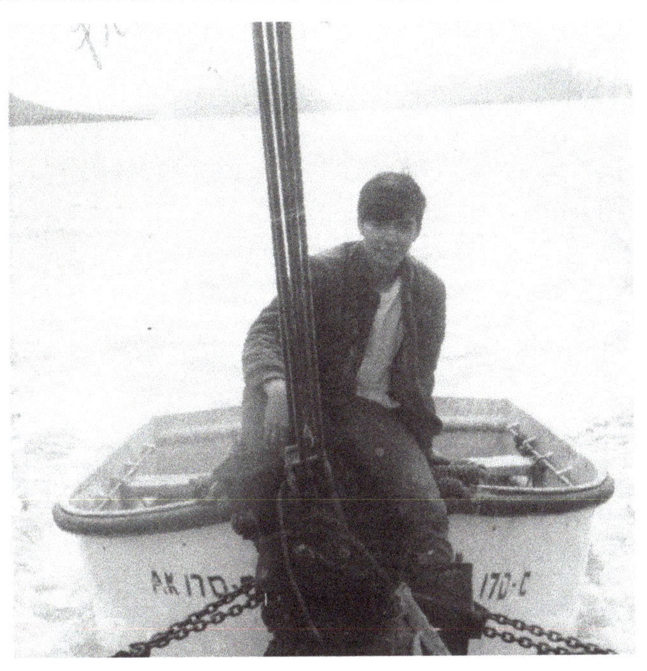

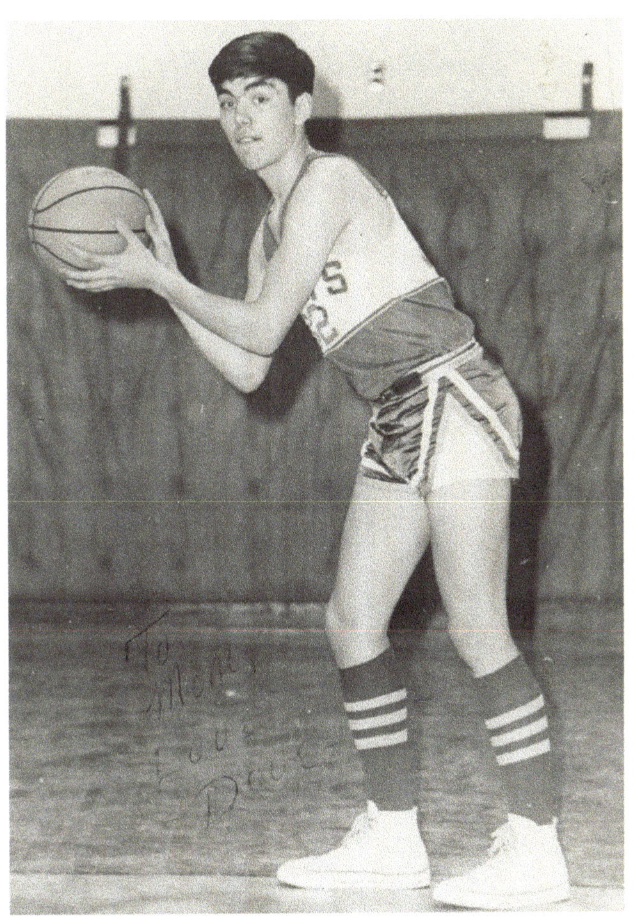

I enjoyed being outdoors and I loved fishing with my childhood friend Bob Leask and his family on the Sea Lad. After leaving for school, my love for the outdoors continued with some backpacking.

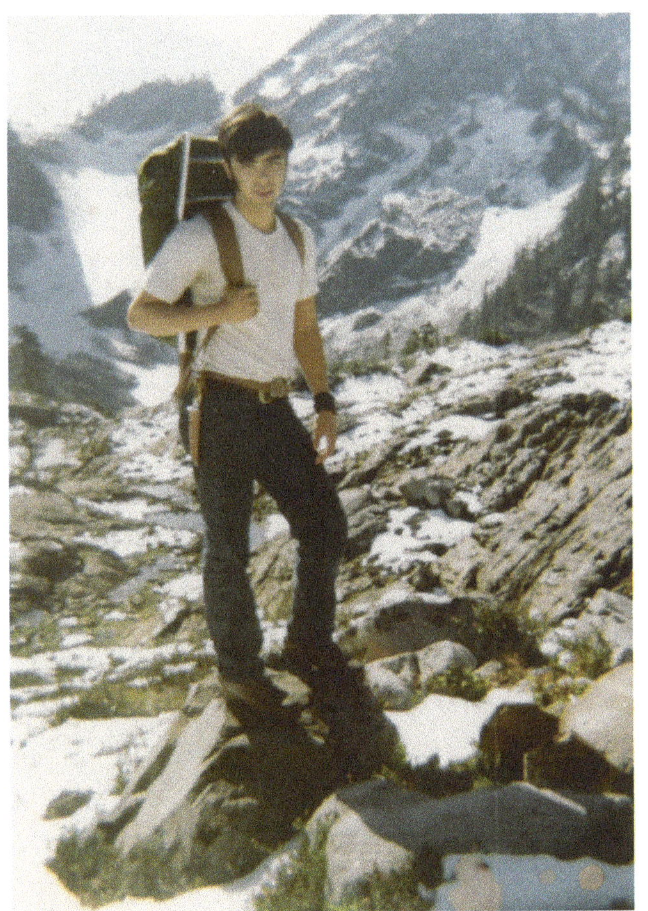

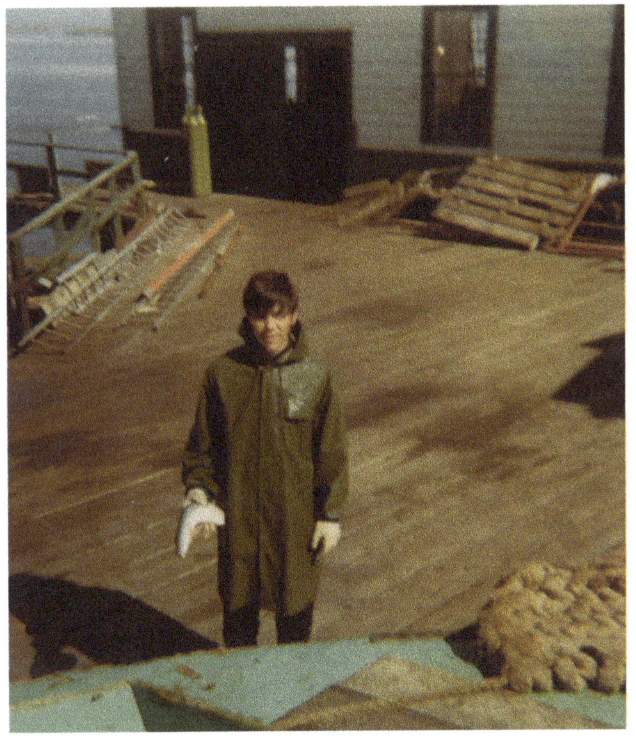

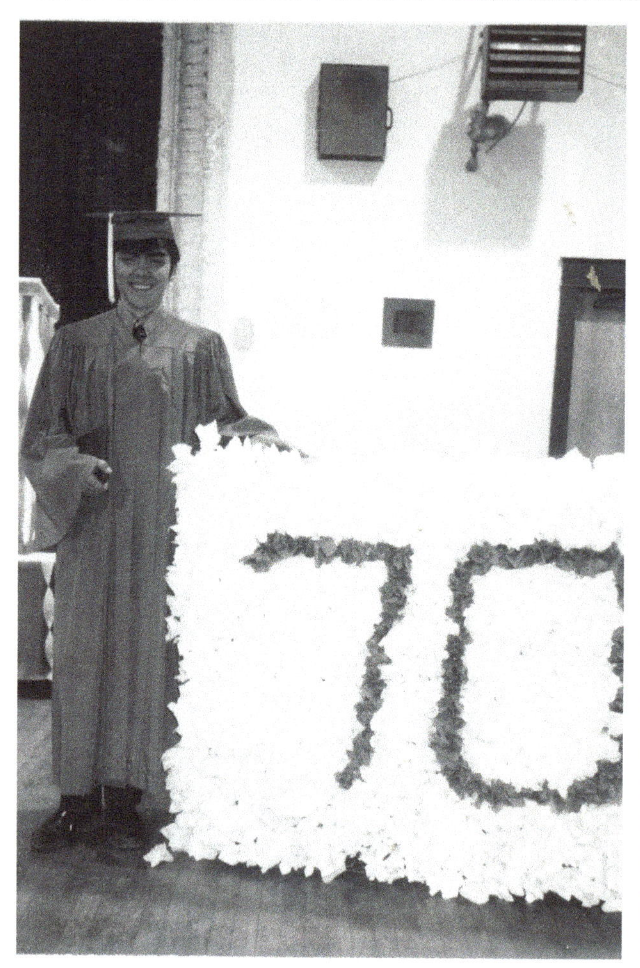

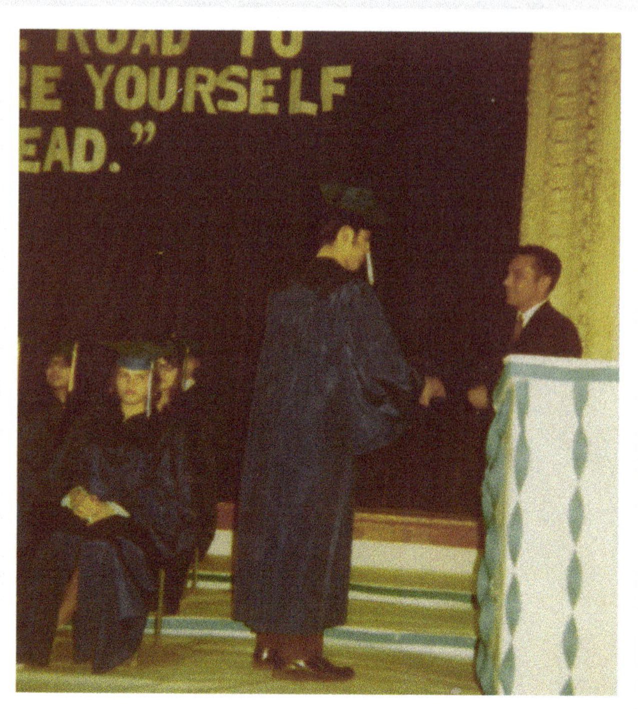
ROAD TO
E YOURSELF
EAD."

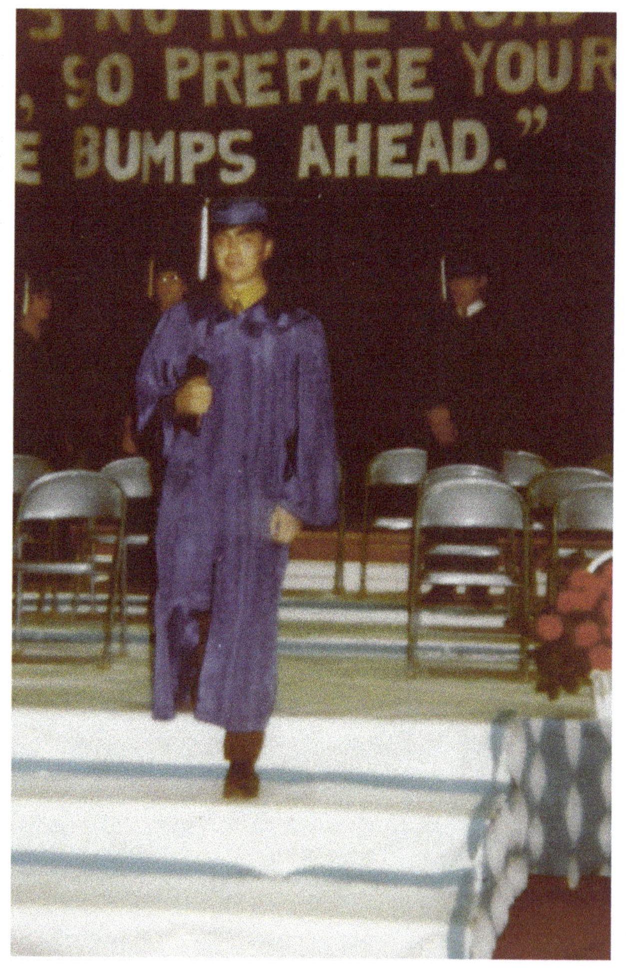
NO ROYAL ROAD
SO PREPARE YOUR
E BUMPS AHEAD."

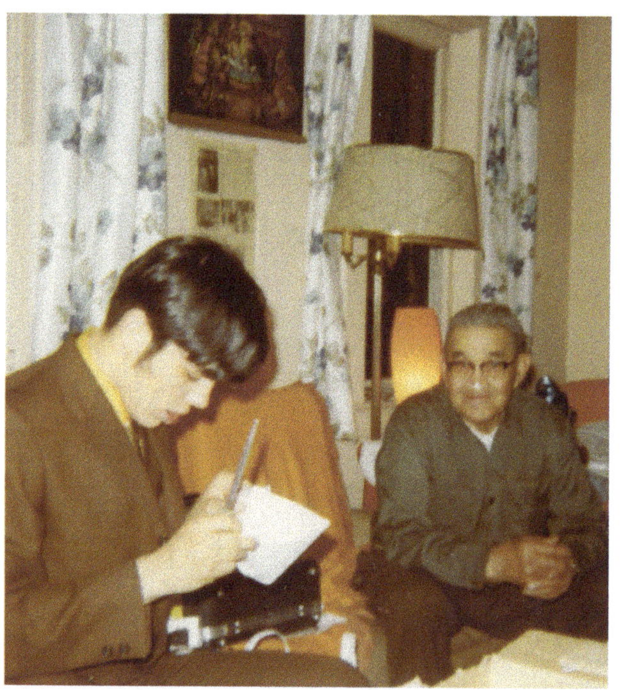

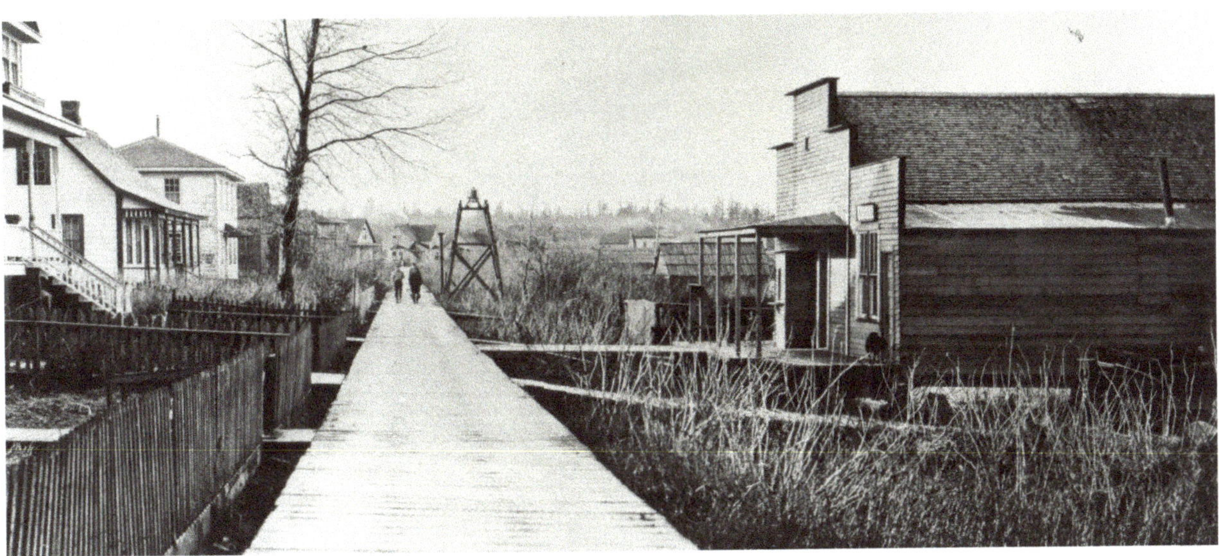

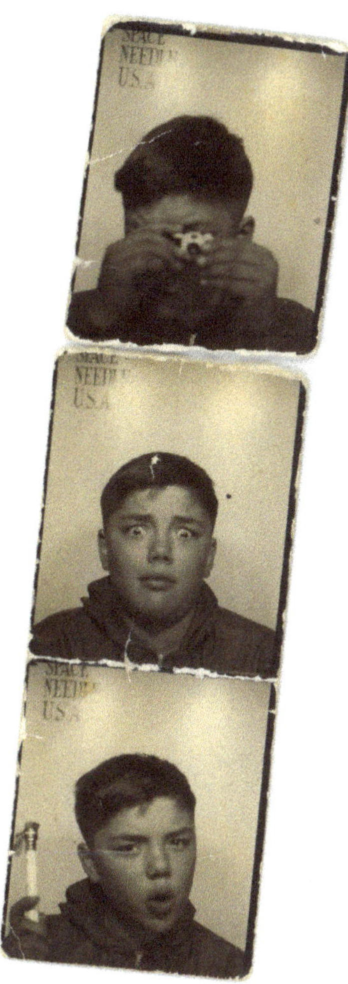

When I was growing up, Metlakatla still had the boardwalk streets that were built back in the original days of the town. I remember seeing cars drive on those boardwalk streets. I remember running to school in the western end of town on those boardwalk streets. The main roads were gravel roads back then.

When I started school, there was no kindergarten, so I had to wait till first grade. I was one of the youngest students in my grade.

One day in third grade really stands out. The teacher put a picture of a horse—the head and neck—on a blackboard. She passed out pieces of blank paper and pencils or pens. She said, OK everybody I want you to draw this horse. I guess mine was the best one. That's what the teacher said anyway. That was the first time I realized I had some kind of ability as an artist.

Looking back, as a kid, I never saw any kind of Native art in our village. There were some guys who were tourist carvers. They would do assembly line totem poles, cut them out on a band saw, sand them up, and paint them. That was about it. But I can't say their work had anything to do with our culture. There were no high-quality formline Northwest coast style art designs back then. No regalia. No totem poles. Nothing at all. Back then, I also wasn't aware of these voids. That's because the missionaries had done their best to erase all that. Later, in 1982, when I was planning Metlakatla's first potlatch—a cultural ceremony—I realized there was almost no one who could help me.

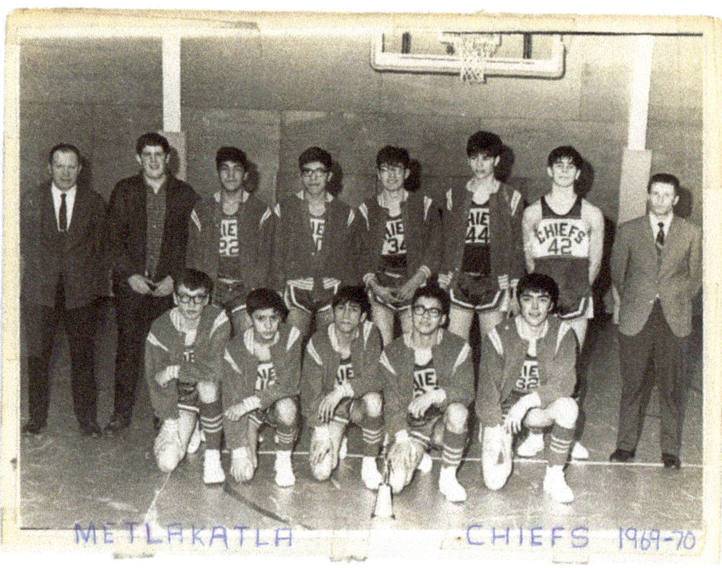

We had just lost the Class B championship to Hoonah during my senior year. While we were at this tournament in Skagway, my high school burned down.

My *grandparents used* to take me to Seattle every fall to visit my aunts and other family members living in the lower forty eight. We first came down on a steamer, then later on, we would fly down. We would be gone sometimes for a month. One of the trips took place when I was a freshman and I missed basketball tryouts. I played junior varsity and became the manager of the varsity team. We didn't have a lot of success the years that I played, but every once in a while, three or four times in my lifetime, Metlakatla had some extraordinary athletes who could beat the big schools.

While we were playing in a Southeast Alaska B Tournament in Skagway during my senior year, my high school burned down. We finished the year taking classes in the church, the Salvation Army hall, and the community gymnasium. I gave my senior welcome speech in high school in Sm'algyax. I don't think anyone has done that since. But I had to ask my grandfather, my uncle Frank Hayward, and honored elder Alfred Eaton, to listen to my speech and help me fine tune it. It was a pretty simple speech, but it was important because it had been a long time since our language had been heard in that setting, and I'm not sure it has since.

I didn't know it at the time, but it would be the first small step toward immersing myself in our Tsimshian culture. ❖

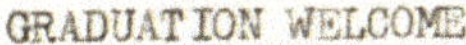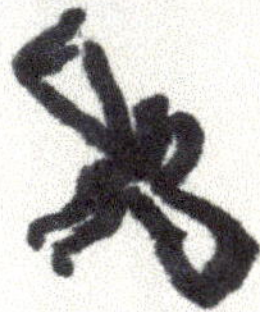

GRADUATION WELCOME

    Ladies and Gentlemen, honored guests, faculty parents, friends and fellow students. As president of the Senior Class of 1970, I am pleased and honored to welcome you all to our commencement exsersises.

    This occasion marks the end of one very important, enjoyable, and meaningfull phase of our lives. We are grateful for all the help given to us while we were on the sometimes rocky road leading to this moment, from the first good mark in grade school to the good-byes as we depart for what ever lies in front of us, the helping hand we recieved from you will never be forgotten

    Now with the great opportunities that lie in front of us, but also the tests of the outer world, we feel confident that we have the support of the people we think the world of, you our past, will be the stepping stones of our future.

    Again I thank each of you all for taking the time to witness the final product of 12 years of patient but steadfast manufacturing.....thank you.

                        David Boxley. SR. PRESIDENT

Ha-aliagh-en Da-aapsh   Speak slowly!

Dela-waan weelaakshim, aada shu-pushum-get.

Lu-aama-goadu da-wilgut-goikshim da hoople ga-uun.

Gwa-ah aama-pushim-get geetsa gowty shu-waalksh,

Tse-gaown shetaama sha-up-yaan.

 Wha...,gum-goalth-walshim sha-iet thla-maam-en,

quinee-wila-goiksh.

Ukim-deem thla-gowty shu-pushum get...Eyuta, ada

Hanna-ah da-geeloan thla-moamen.

Ukin-dee hatugh, ai-en! Aam-get!

Gidi-gaan haal-um shimhoun. Sha-maagth hatugh-kin

tul-goilshk.

Geeloh-lawuntha-goadshim......dim-al-aam.

Lukel Gun-goalth-waalshim

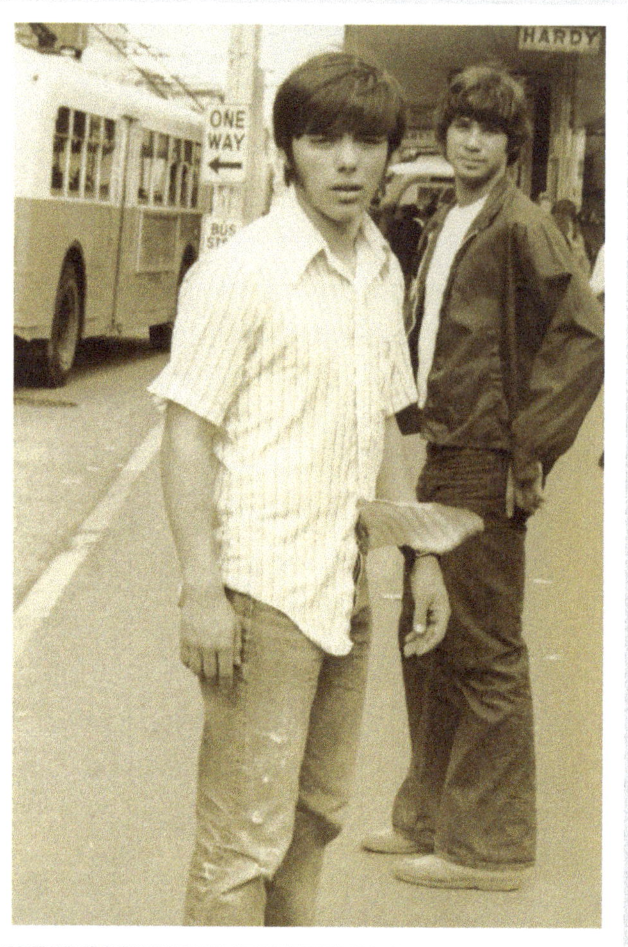

ONE WAY
BUS STOP
HARDY

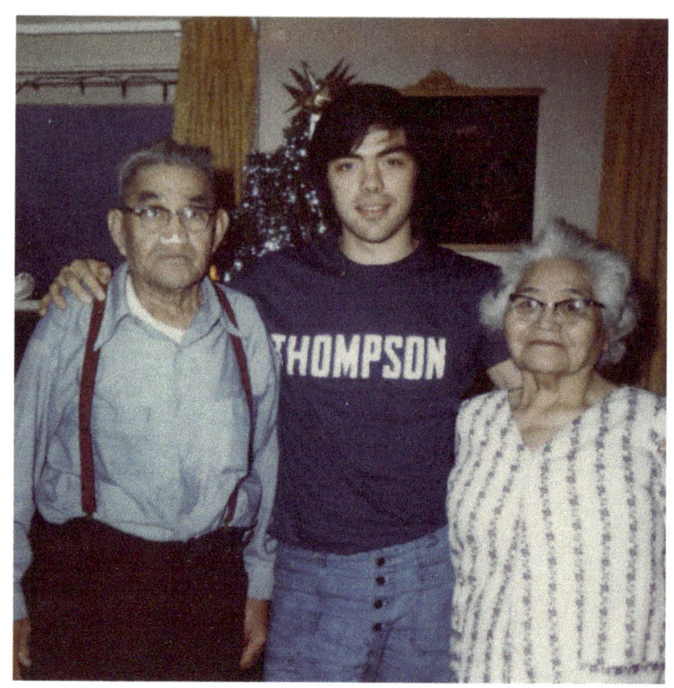

THOMPSON

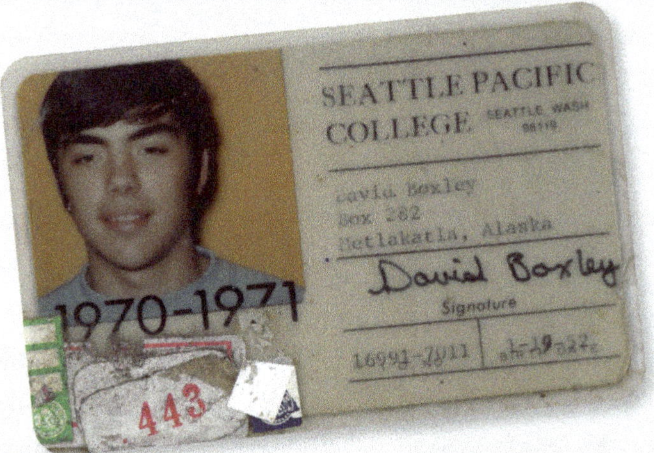

SEATTLE PACIFIC
COLLEGE SEATTLE, WASH.
David Boxley
Box 262
Metlakatla, Alaska
David Boxley
Signature
1970-1971
443

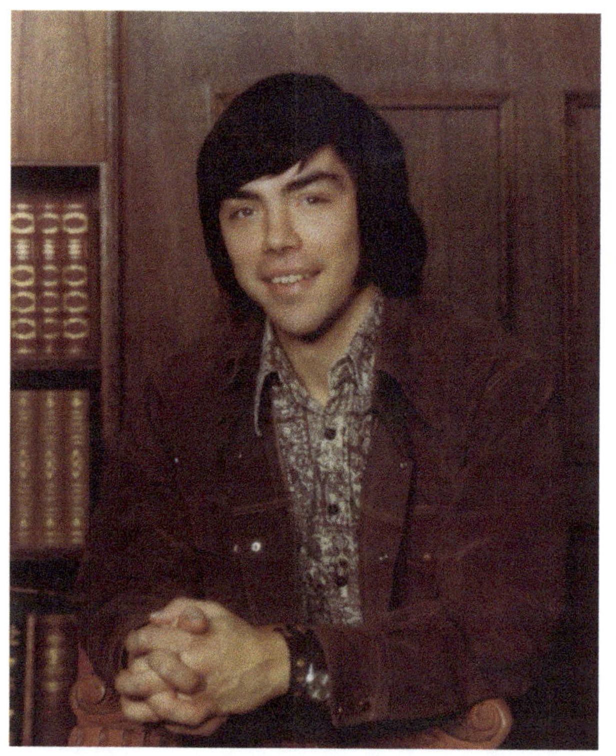

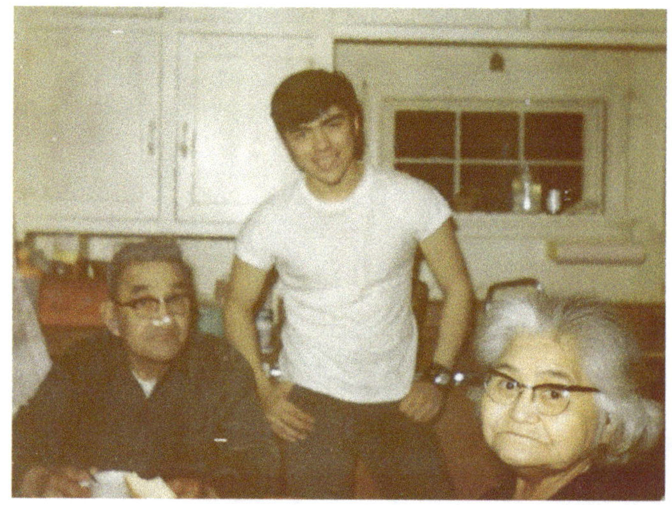

CHAPTER TWO

THE JOURNEY BEGINS / *Sit'aatga tgu'waayt*

For years, I never thought art was going to be my career. I thought I would be a teacher and a basketball coach because I was very influenced by the schoolteachers I had.

When I was growing up, our ferry boat was really a seine boat, a fish packer, but it was our community's ferry at the time. We used to go down to the docks in late August and earn a dime, maybe a quarter, helping people with their luggage or freight they brought over from Ketchikan. I remember going down there and sitting on the floating dock watching these teachers come off the boat carrying their suitcases. They were wide-eyed looking at the Indians and the village, wondering what they had gotten themselves into. I used to think, geez, these people are the smartest people in the world. They come to teach us. They must know everything.

When I became a school teacher and I'd sit in the teachers' lounge—a place I never really felt comfortable in—I'd listen to them complain, and I found out they weren't so perfect after all. But I wanted to be a basketball coach, and the only way for me to be a basketball coach was to be a teacher.

So, in the fall of 1970, I left Metlakatla to attend Seattle Pacific University.

When I got there, I was sitting with a counselor and planning out my classes. This counselor asked what foreign language do I want to take? Everybody takes Spanish, but I didn't want to take Spanish. She asked, "Aren't you Alaska Native? Do you know your language?" I never thought about what I knew because I never used it outside of the house or at least away from my grandparents.

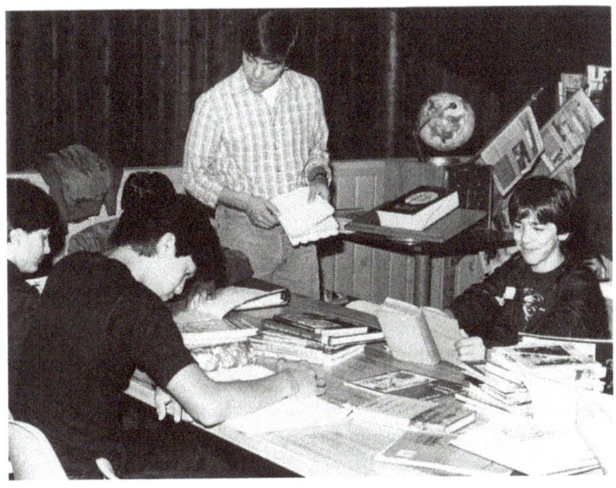

I developed a ninth-grade Native studies history class, taught normally at the school. This time, however, we held class at the village's longhouse.

My uncles and my mom all spoke English even though they knew Sm'algyax. Their whole generation was not encouraged to speak it. They are kind of like a lost generation.

So the counselor said, "We'll put in a petition and you can skip having to take these foreign language classes because you speak your own language."

I asked, "How are you going to test me to see if I know this language?"

She just smiled and said, "I'm not going to test you."

I met my future college roommate by chance while wandering around the student union. I heard this guy playing rock music on a piano, which was strange for a Christian college. A bunch of students crowded around him, This guy was amazing. I asked if he could play "Love Potion No. 9," and he said, "Of course." His name was Randy McMillan, and he was blind since birth. He would become my roommate for my last three years in school. He still performs and, for a while, was known as Seattle's lone blind radio sports reporter.

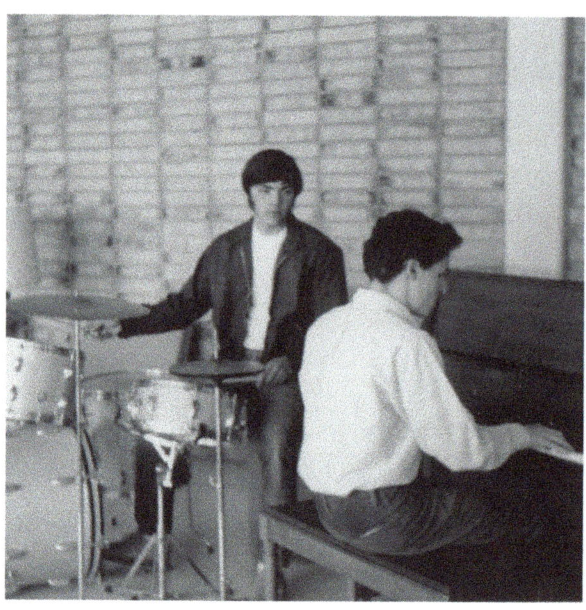

My roommate of three years, Randy McMillan, was a magnificent piano player. He could play three or four instruments. He was the only blind sportscaster in Seattle. He would listen to the game then he would type on his braille machine, then read it over the air.

=

Ultimately, *I was* not prepared for college. There were all kinds of distractions. Also, I didn't have the discipline or education from high school to take care of my grades. My first quarter was a disaster grade wise. It took me another two years to restore my grade point average and build it back to where I could be accepted into the school of education. I worked hard for it, and I took more credits than I needed to, then I got accepted to the school of education, and in the end, it worked out really well.

I was the first one in my class to be hired by Seattle Public Schools, which assigned me to Thompson Junior High, where I could teach as many different sports as I wanted. I'm proud of that especially because one of my counselors told me a couple of years earlier, "You're not going to make it."

You can't tell me something like that. It just makes me work harder. I took the letter from Seattle schools offering me a job and went to that same counselor's office. I knocked on his door and went into his office.

"What can I do for you?" the counselor asked. It was clear he didn't remember me. I put that letter in front of him, tapped it and said, "Read that," and walked out of his office.

Dr. Ken Foreman, the coach of the women's Olympic track and field team and the dean of students for the athletic department, had a really big influence on me. I had been sleeping through morning classes and didn't have good grades. One day, he called me into his office and bawled me out for a half hour or more. To this day, I still don't like being late for anything. He gave me such a hard time for that, and I never forgot it. I admire the guy. He was an amazing athlete himself. I ran into him years later when I was living in Kingston. I told him how big an influence he had been in my life, and he cried. He was so grateful to hear that. He basically changed the direction of my life. I didn't really understand what it was like to go to college until I sat in his office and he read me the riot act, saying I'd better shape up or I wasn't going to make it.

When I wasn't working on recovering from a poor first quarter, I began producing oil paintings with Native themes. Art was becoming a hobby. Eventually I added an art minor to my physical education degree.

I played a lot of Native basketball mostly with Alaskans and those who lived on Washington reservations when I lived in Seattle. One of my teammates was a Tlingit man from Angoon, Alaska, named Albert Kookesh, who became a lawyer, a fierce advocate for Alaska Natives, and an Alaska state senator. He remained a close friend who would show up at my house with herring eggs, salmon, and deer meat. I miss him dearly.

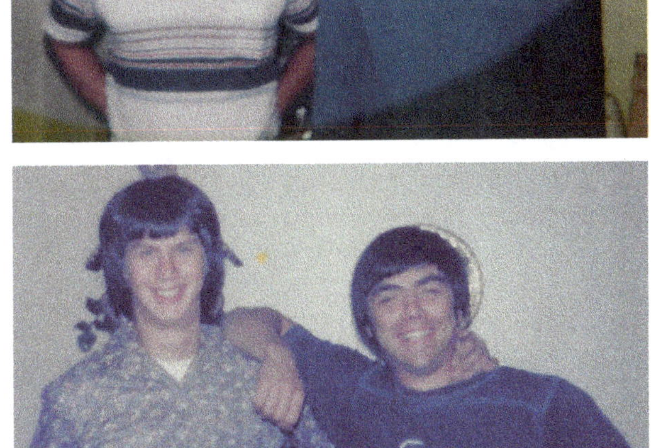

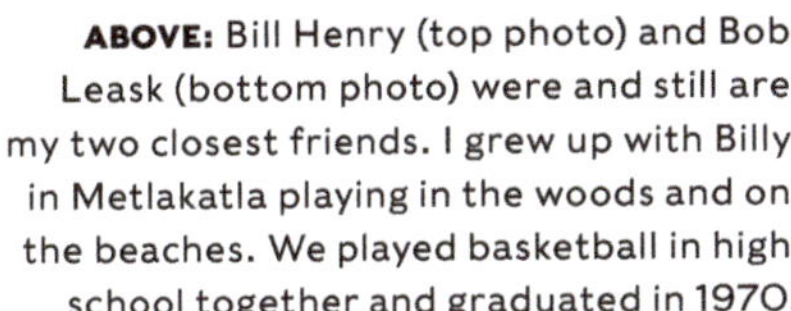

ABOVE: Bill Henry (top photo) and Bob Leask (bottom photo) were and still are my two closest friends. I grew up with Billy in Metlakatla playing in the woods and on the beaches. We played basketball in high school together and graduated in 1970.

BELOW: After moving to Seattle, Bob still returned with his family to fish in Metlakatla's waters on his father's boat, the Sea Lad. Bob and I played Native basketball and carved together in Seattle.

I *spent the* next five years coaching a game I love. Basketball was and is still the biggest thing back home. Except for maybe cross country and wrestling once in a while, basketball has always been the major sport in many Native villages. It has been this way for generations of men and women, boys and girls, even as far back as when girls were only playing half court games. When I was a kid, we even had the Harlem Globetrotters come to play our all-stars. We really didn't have anything else; we didn't have the money for football or the sports facilities. We ran cross country, but it was mainly a way to get conditioned for basketball. I could play pretty well for my talent level. For years I was a gym rat. I loved to play basketball.

The disappointing part of my whole experience as a basketball player was when I was in high school, we had four coaches in

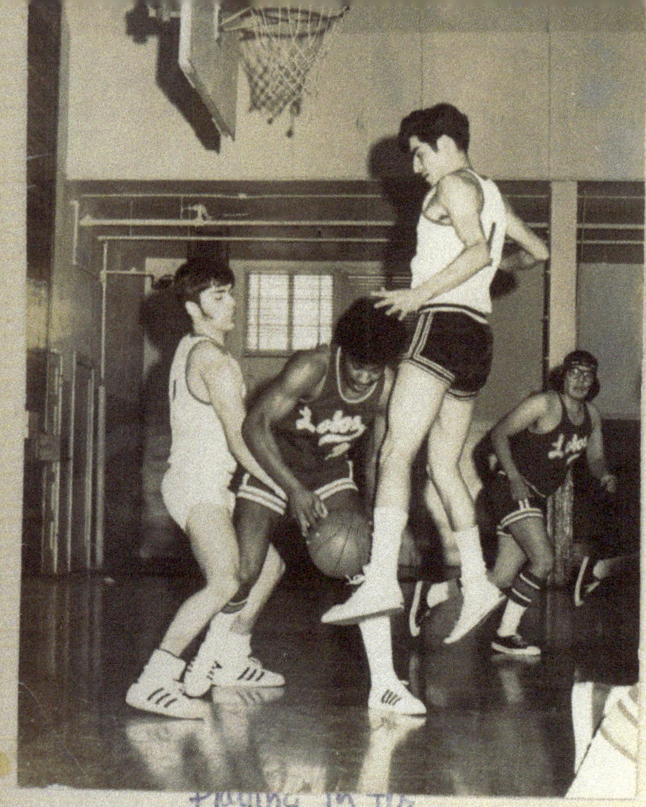

Playing in the
All-Native League in Seattle
Tillicum & Naggets

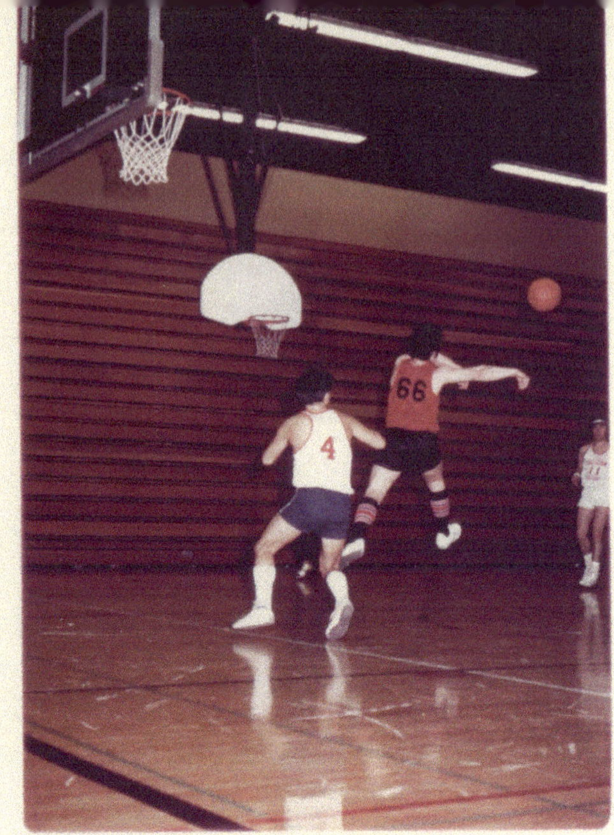

ALL NATIVE
BASKET-BALL 1971-72

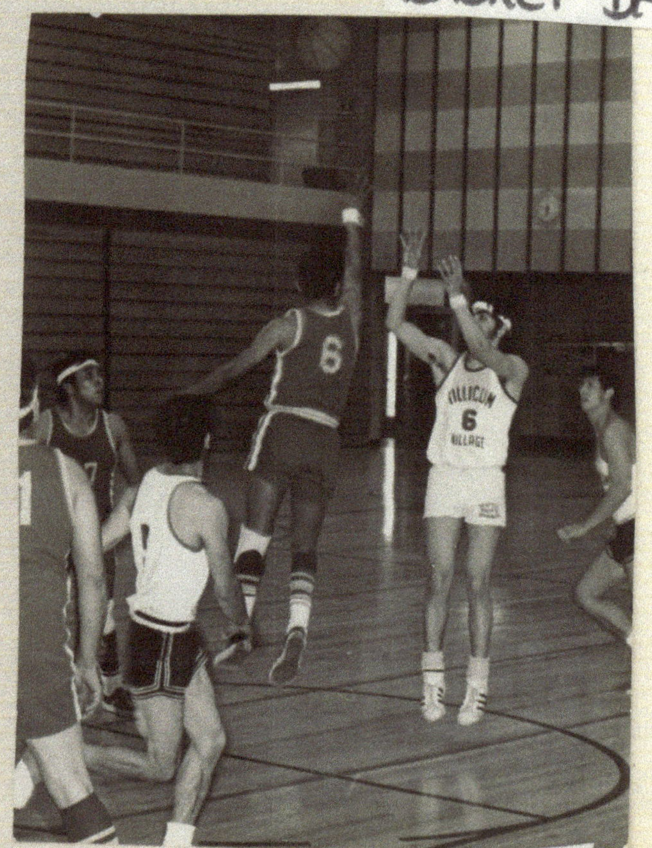

SEATTLE

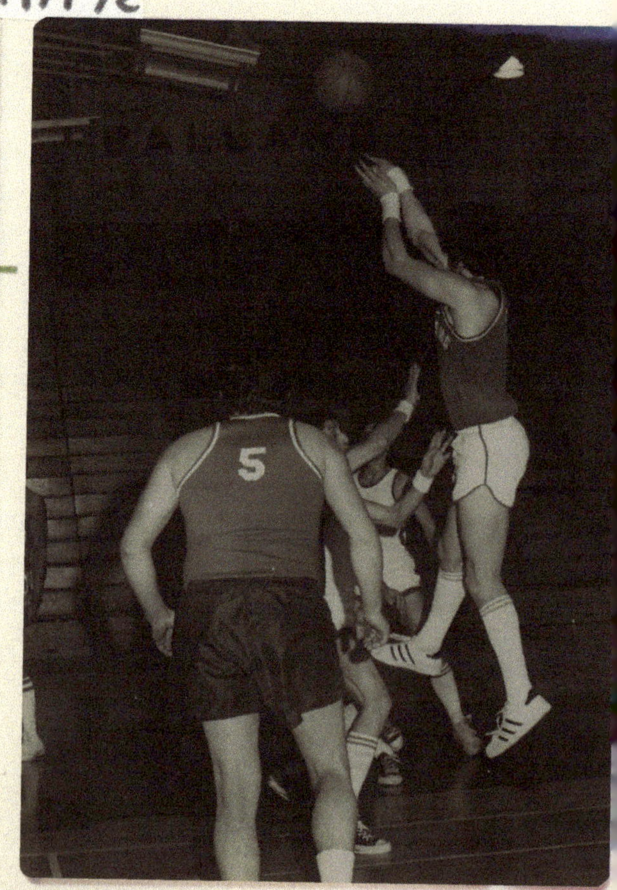

four years. One year a coach got fired in the middle of the season. In those days there were no opportunities to go to basketball camps.

The resurgence of our culture, which I've been in the middle of, provided a healthy outlet for our people. Sports does the same kind of thing—it provides a healthy outlet. You feel like you belong to something.

While at Seattle Pacific, I was a student teacher at Magnolia Junior High and was able to coach the basketball team. Then, after I graduated I coached the Thompson Junior High team. After coaching at Thompson, the levy failed to fund the school district at a certain level. Me and thousands of other schoolteachers lost their jobs. I could have stayed and waited to be re-hired. If you were white, you had to have eleven years' experience to be re-hired. If you were African-American, you had to have six years. If you were Native, it was three years. If I had stayed in Seattle, I probably could have been re-hired, but I decided to take a head coaching job in Metlakatla and become head of the physical education department. In three years, I had a 57–3 regular season record. We didn't have state tournaments then for our classification, but we did win Class B runner up in 1977 and won the region the next year.

I went to basketball camps every summer at Washington State University. George Raveling was the coach at the time. He was the assistant coach on the Dream Team (1992 Olympics), so I learned a lot about technique, tricks to coaching, drills—lots of drills. I always liked practice more than the games because I liked teaching, and that's where most of the teaching took place. I really enjoyed that part of the game. In three years of coaching in Metlakatla, winning the Class B championship in 1978 was the highlight of my coaching career. I'll never forget those boys.

I realized I came back to Metlakatla too soon. I needed to learn more and be a better coach, so I wanted more competition. I wanted to step into the fire, so, after we won the B Division championship, I resigned and applied for a couple of different positions. I got hired in Forks, Washington.

It was a terrible experience except for the basketball. My cousin, Doug Bolton, was in the seventh grade at the time and I talked his folks into letting him come down to live with me. He became my basketball manager just so I could have him around. He needed a positive role model. He lost like fifty pounds living with me. For a seventh grader, that's a big deal. We ran into a lot of bad

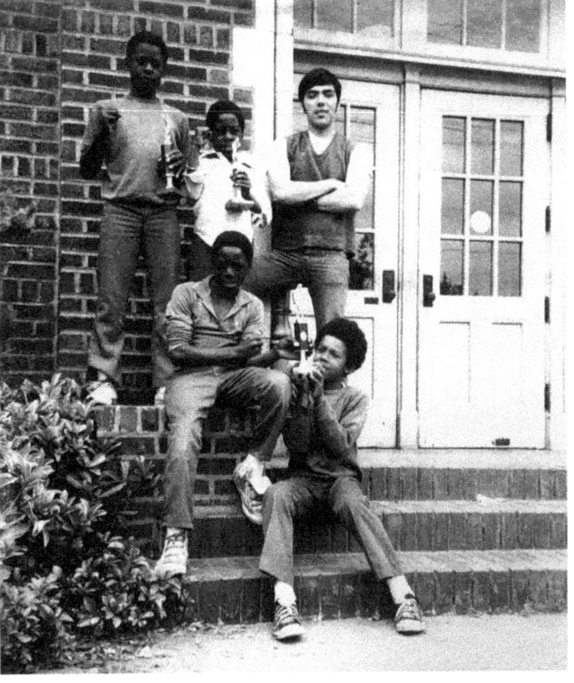

As a sophomore student teacher I organized a one-on-one tournament for third through sixth grades. This photo is at Bailey Gatzert Elementary. These players were the division champs and just great kids.

FACING PAGE: Almost every weekend I was playing Native basketball with friends.

stuff including racism. Lots of it. There was just a lot of disrespect of teachers and authorities. I had rocks thrown at my apartment house. We'd go to a movie and get names yelled at us.

The varsity basketball team was great; I had a good bunch of kids playing for me, and I learned a lot. We lost the regional tournament by two points. If we had won, then we would have gone to the state tournament. That was hard. I'd rather lose by twenty than by two any day. It makes you feel like you made a few wrong decisions, and it could have gone the other way. Eventually I just had enough living in Forks, so I went to Seattle and was hired to be head basketball coach at Ballard High School.

I was really a competitor. I hated to lose. I wanted the very best out of the kids who I coached. Every team I ever coached won most of its games. Part of it was the way I coached. But I enjoyed practice more than the games. Games were hard on me emotionally at Ballard. I probably led the league in technical fouls the first half of the season in Seattle, but the second half I calmed down.

My goal at the time was to be a college coach. I wanted to learn how to be a better coach. Then I would go home and give the kids from my village the benefit of what I had learned.

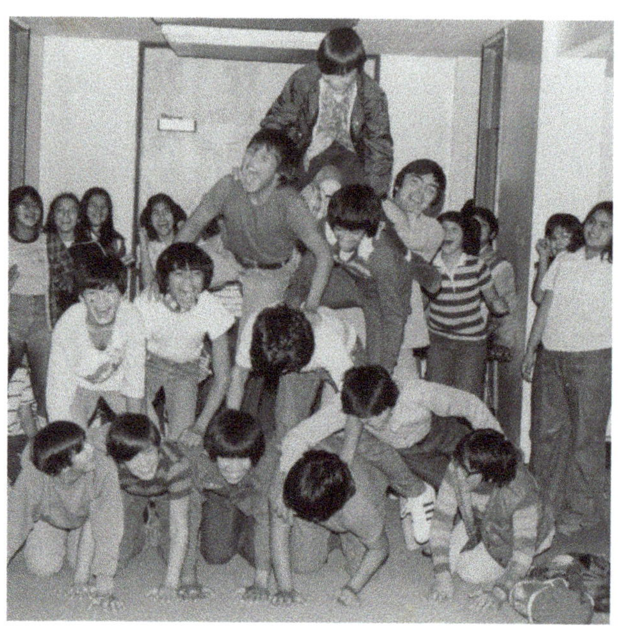

We had a power outage during physical education class. We came out into the hall where the sunlight came into the windows. The kids decided to build a human pyramid. The photo was taken just as the pyramid collapsed.

But, in 1980—six years after graduating and embarking on a circuitous coaching path—I decided to return to Metlakatla for a teaching position. What I didn't know at the time was my cultural journey had already begun.

—

I *moved back* because I wanted to be around my grandmother. There was a physical education teaching job available, but no basketball coaching position, just cross country. The crazy thing is, if there were a coaching position, I would have accepted it and I probably wouldn't have become a full-time artist. I would have continued art as a hobby.

The next six years would be among the most pivotal and hectic. I married my first wife, Liz Duryea, and welcomed sons Davey and Zach into the world. I built and opened a sweet shoppe that served ice cream and baked goods. I was becoming a full-time artist, studying the works of others while taking what few classes were available. I created my first totem pole, carved in honor of my grandmother who died six months after I returned.

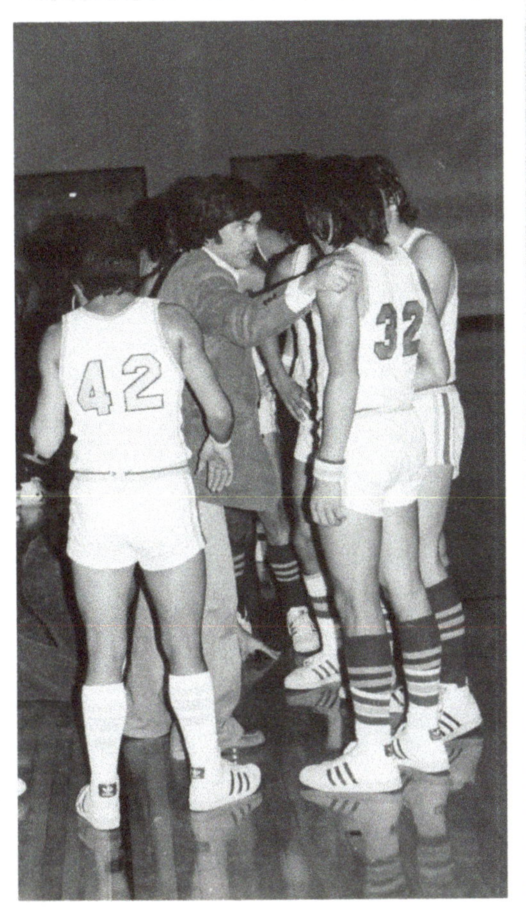

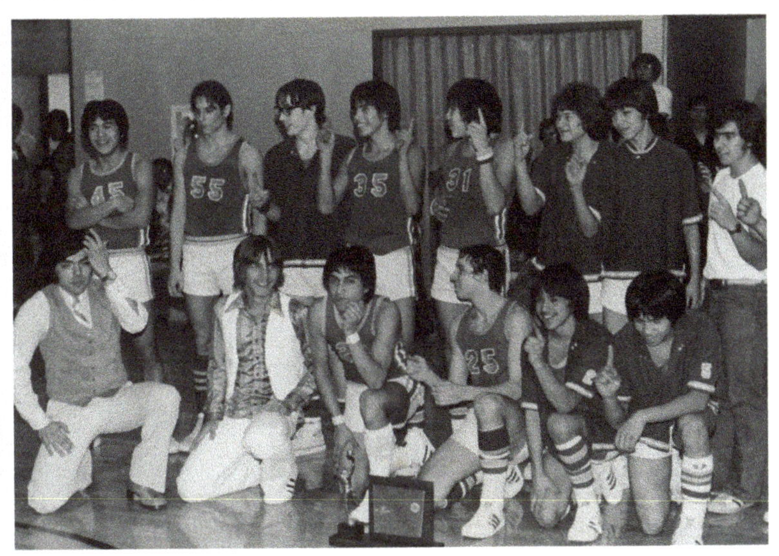

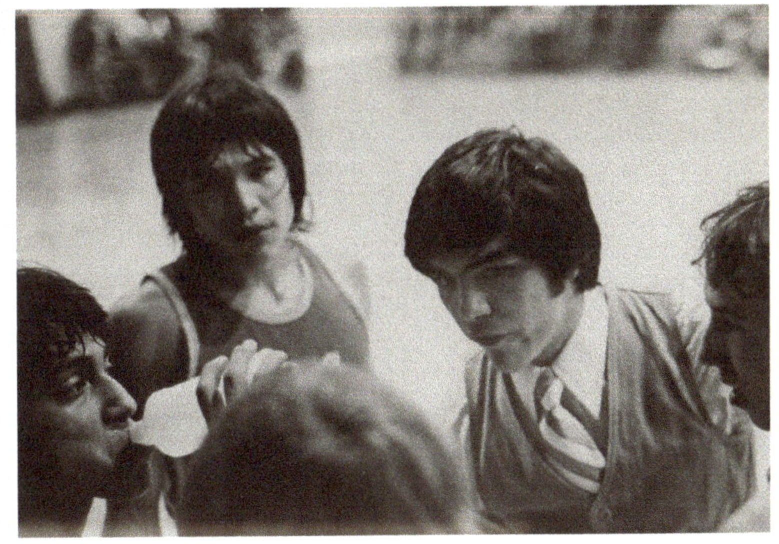

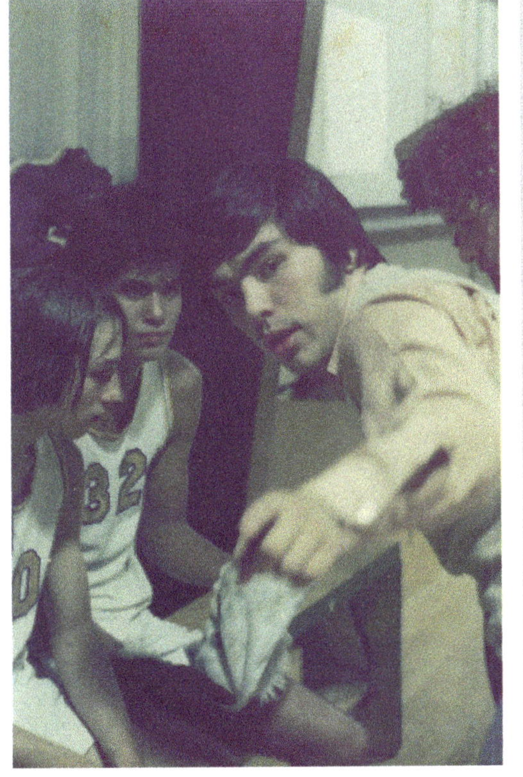

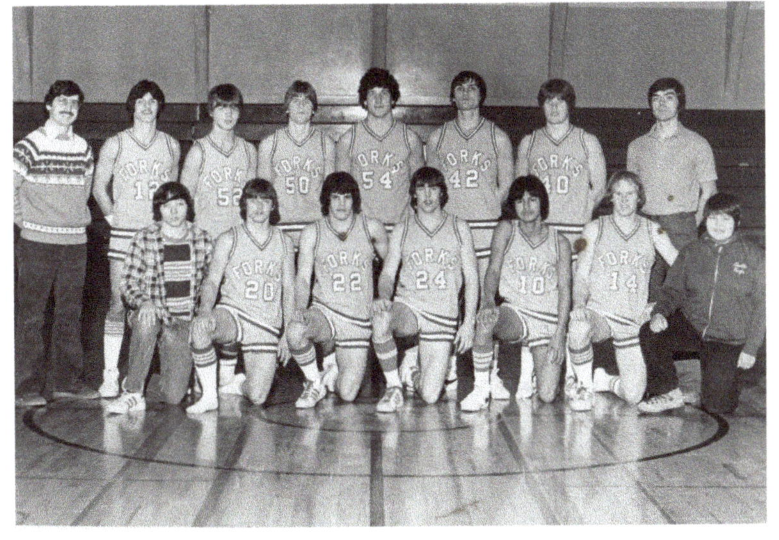

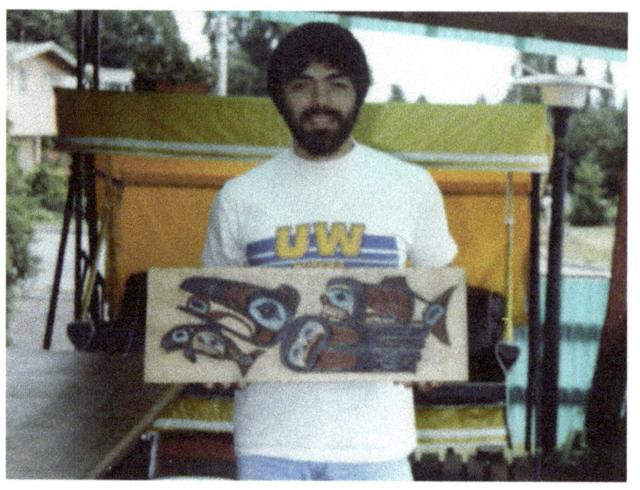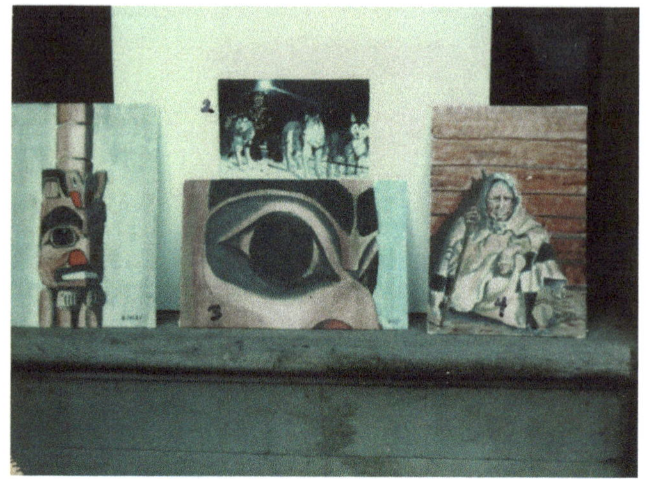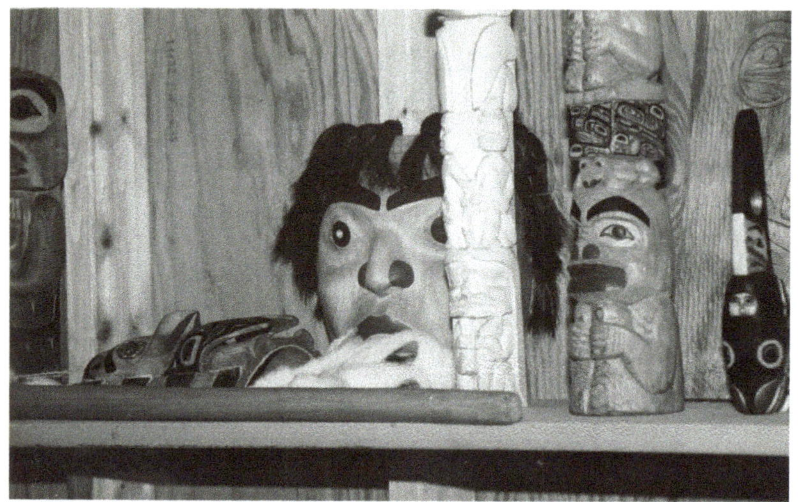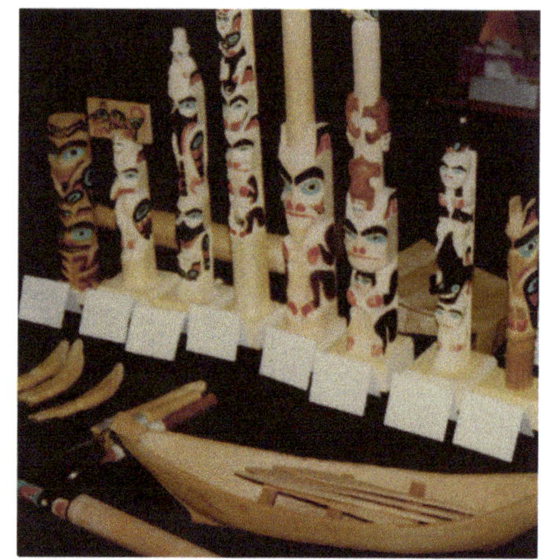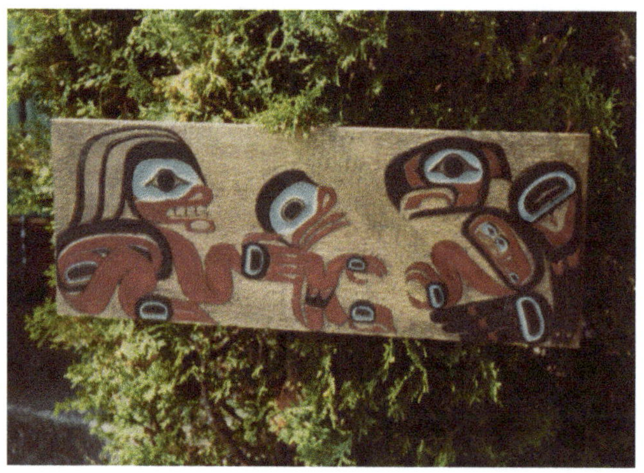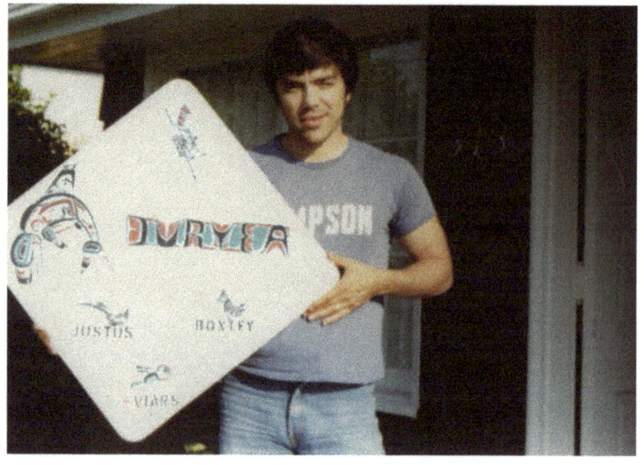

Some of my earliest work, even before I committed to become a full-time artist, is reflected on this page. Before I began carving, I produced a lot of paintings, like those on the top right. Some of my first panels are at the top and lower left, which portrayed my first wife announcing the arrival of Davey. The model poles in the middle right were part of my first show at Daybreak Star in Seattle. The mask in the middle I carved during a class taught by Jack Hudson.

I was hungry for any teaching I could get, and I took classes from Jack Hudson, who started teaching after I left for college and taught for many years after that. I had a pretty horrific accident. I dropped a blade and clapped my legs together to grab the blade. I drove the blade into my thigh. It caused all kinds of consternation and confusion in the class. I went into a little shock. He said, "This is a sign. You're either going to be really good or you had better quit now."

Everybody quit after a while. Pretty soon, it got down to just me and maybe a few other people. Guys dropped out of the class, and then he cancelled the class. But I still made three things with him: a mask, a bentwood box, and some paintings.

In the summer of 1983, I took classes with Seattle-area artist Duane Pasco. I was still teaching school, so that summer, I stayed with my in-laws and commuted every day to his house. The timing wasn't that great. He was getting ready for a one-man show, and I was getting ready to be in a show at Sacred Circle Gallery. I made a number of things with him. I made a paddle, a mask, a bentwood box, and a panel.

Some of the things I made with Pasco I put in my show. I don't think he was too happy with that. I just didn't get it at the time. I thought I did the work. But as a teacher now, I tell my students, if I work on your piece, if my hands are on your piece, it's not yours. When you carve something all by yourself, then you can do what you want with it. I didn't really understand that at the time.

Eventually, I had three full-time jobs: PE teacher, business owner, carver. I had to make one of the toughest decisions ever: to leave Metlakatla and my grandfather again. I embarked on my cultural jouney which would go on for the next four decades.

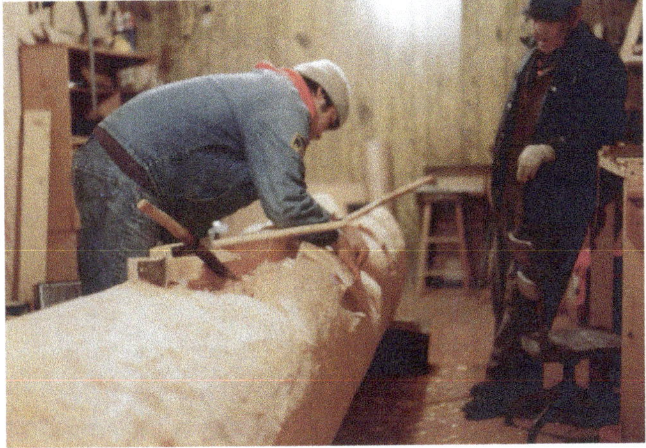

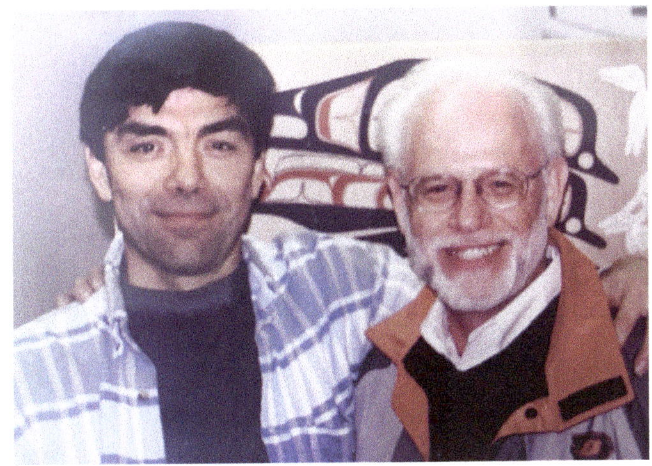

ABOVE: My first carving shop in Metlakatla with grandfather. I'm really glad I got to share this with him.

BELOW: After leaving in 1986, I found a new home in Kingston. That's where I met neighbor Mike Ruelle. He was willing to help with things around my new home, even getting on the roof. I was lucky in that I was getting one commission after another. He was there to share the early part of the journey with me.

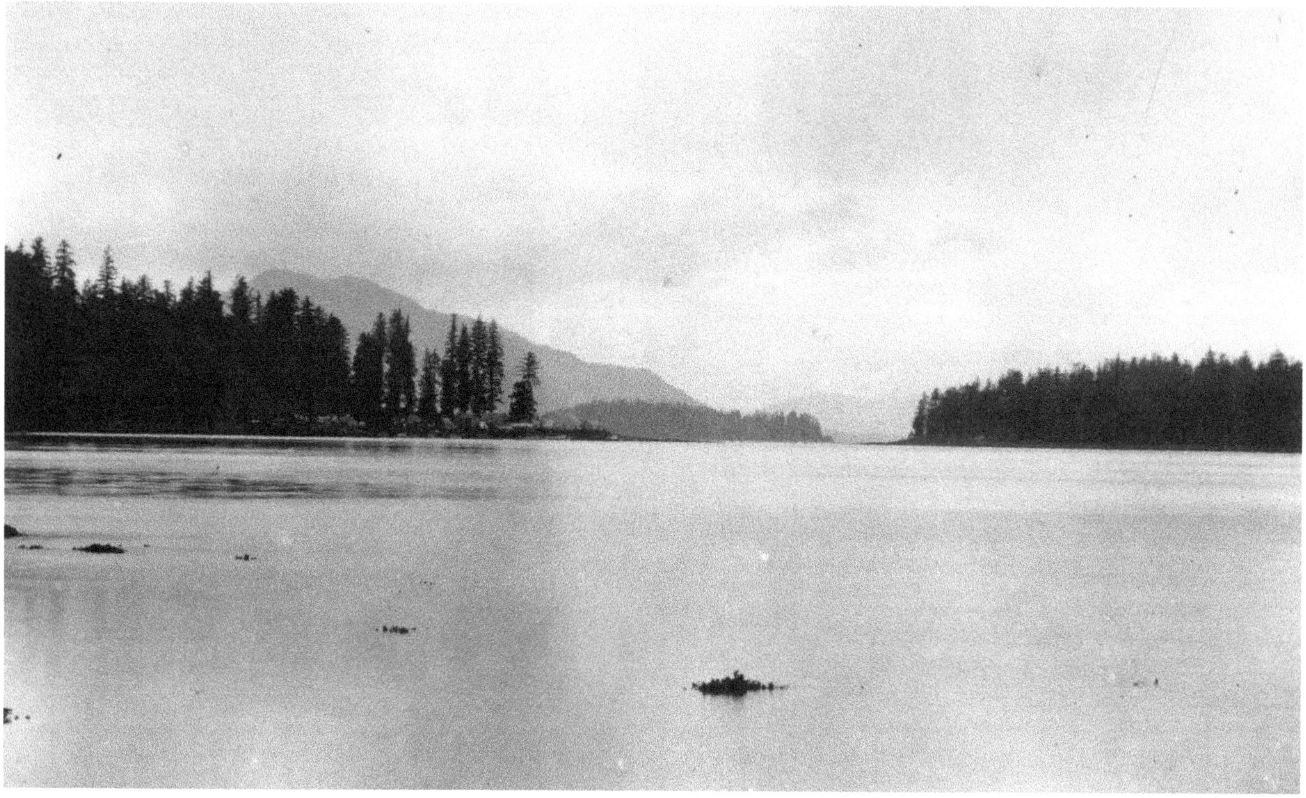

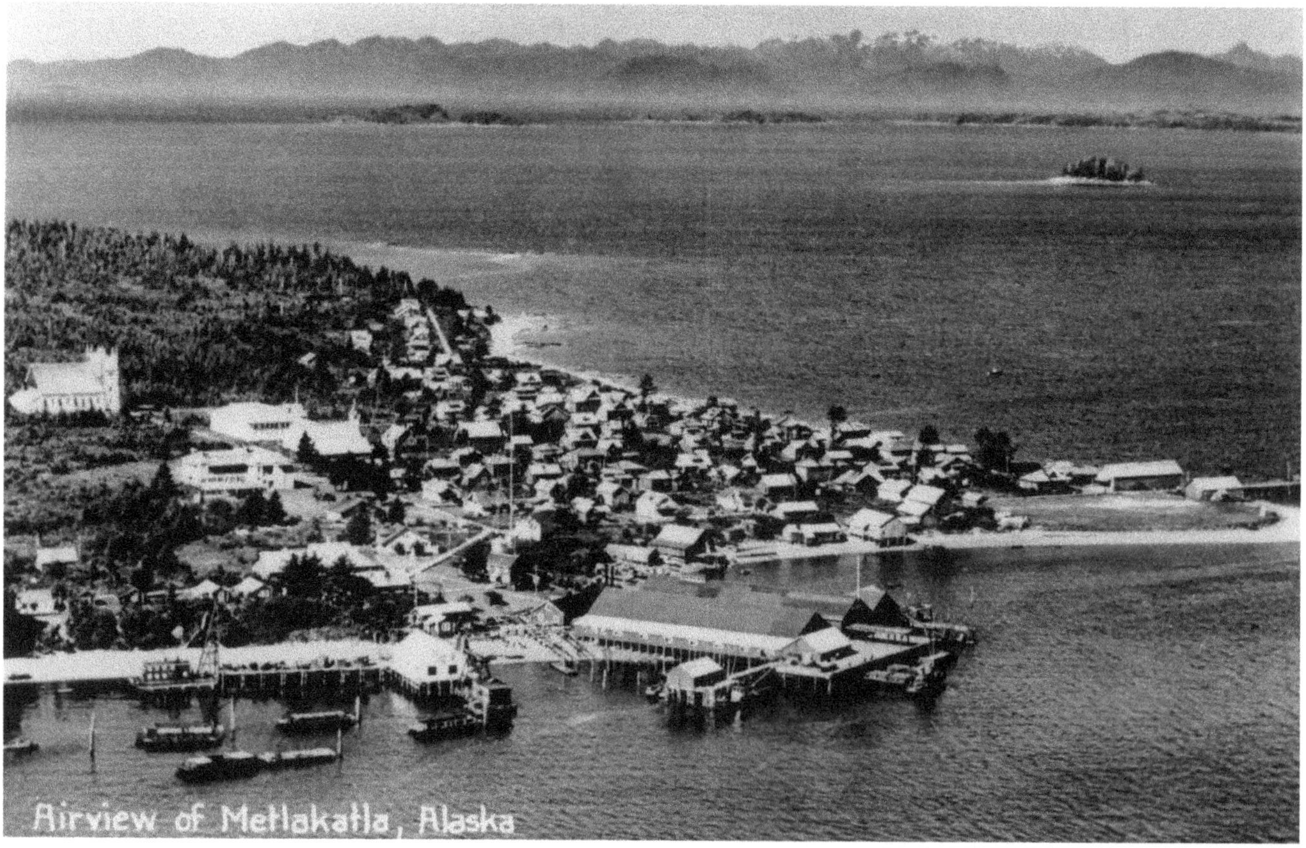

Airview of Metlakatla, Alaska

I *try returning* home as often as I can, sometimes in early August to celebrate Metlakatla's Founders' Day. Reconnecting with friends and recalling memories with my grandparents always produces a smile. I get to watch dance groups perform in cultural ceremonies called potlatches.

But what I enjoy most is watching my son Davey and his friends work daily to instill Tsimshian pride into the community through Sm'algyax language lessons, discussions on art and dance, and stories of the village's history.

Davey has told some memorable stories about our village and our people. So, on some nights, I would sit back, relax, and listen to him engage visitors and residents, sharing with them Metlakatla's young but rich history. Here is one story he recently shared:

OUR STORY IS unique and beautiful. It belongs to each and every one of us. It's the reason we're here. It's a big world and we come from a small corner of it. Tsimshian people, along with the Nisga'a and Gitxsan, originate at the headwaters of the Skeena water. According to our oral history, after the flood, the people dispersed down the rivers, establishing villages all the way to the coast.

Each village would take on a name to call themselves based on either an event that happened around the creation of the community or something about the land that's special.

Our community is 130 years old. Tsimshian history is much, much older. Our people lived in villages that faced water to make sure that we could see people arriving. There would be mountains and forests behind our villages to protect from raids or attacks.

WE ARE A PEOPLE of the cedar. Our culture is based around the cedar tree. Our homes, our clothes, our canoe, our clothing, our ceremonial objects are from the cedar. Even baby diapers were made out of cedar.

The techniques of using cedar were the same for our people as the Haida. Our canoes allowed us to travel to the Aleutian Islands and even down to California and northern Mexico. We had a very advanced trading system up and down the coast.

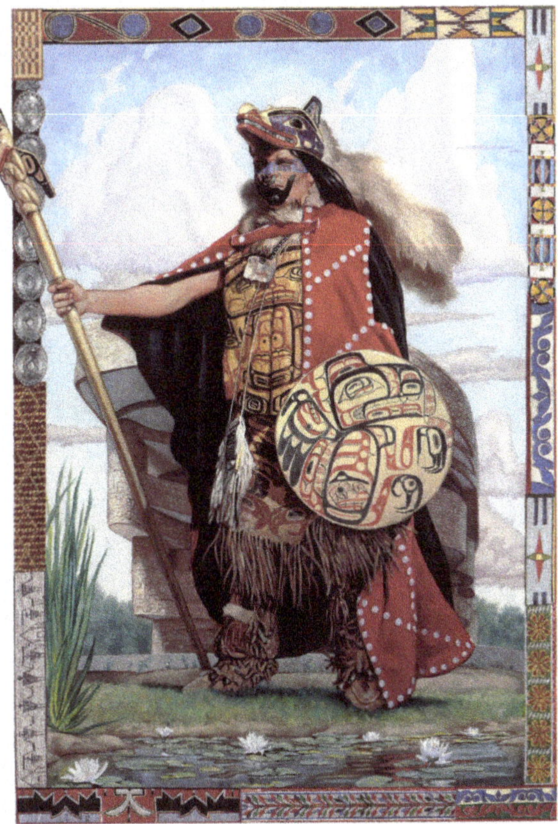

My good friend Chris Hopkins has produced dozens of paintings of my family and dance group. This is Davey and it represents a new generation of cultural leaders.

If you go east from Haida Gwaii to the mainland, you have to go through Tsimshian country. If you go south from Southeast Alaska, you hit Tsimshian country. If you go north from Washington and B.C., you have to go through Tsimshian country.

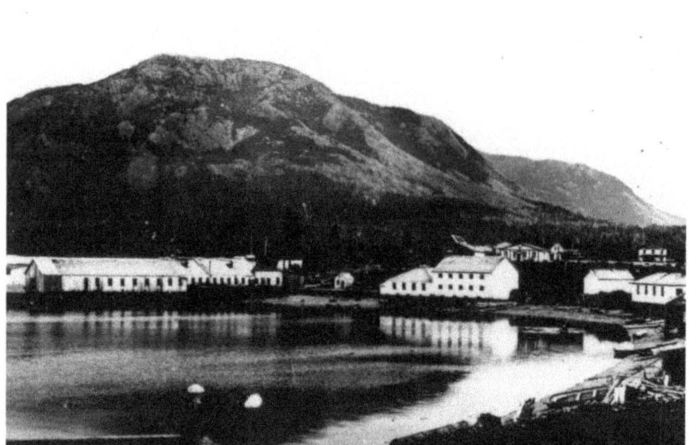

Tsimshians created a very advanced trade system and a trade language that's rooted in Washington state with the Chinook people. Some of our elders could write in that language. Many Natives would know words from it. One of the most famous words is "skookum," which means strong.

It's said that Sm'algyax speaking people are the originators of the Chilkat blanket. It's called the Chilkat blanket because the last weavers of it were found in the Chilkat territory of southeast Alaska. We call the blanket Gwishalaayt. We call the raven rattle Smhalaayt. The chief's headdress is called Amhalaayt.

NORTHWEST COAST CULTURE, up and down the coast, was a rich culture. We developed a system of gathering the food we needed in the summer, then in the winter, our people had the time to create incredible art that stands on its own right with ancient Egyptian art and ancient Roman art. People who are struggling to find food don't have time to create such wonders.

We are a matrilineal society. Everything we are comes from our mothers. Tsimshian people are divided into four matrilineal groups: the Laxsgyiik (eagle clan), Ganhada (raven clan), Gisbutwada (killer whale clan), and the Laxgyibuu (wolf clan). We wear those crests when we feast. We still display the four crests on our flag.

Our people were innovators. It's amusing when I hear us talk about "traditional" button blankets. They are only several hundred years old in the scheme of our many-thousand year history. We use the buttons to reflect firelight and show our crests.

The potlatch feasts serve as our system of notary public. You invite guests, feed them, and you pay them for witnessing your claims. They accept your food and gifts, and make legal the

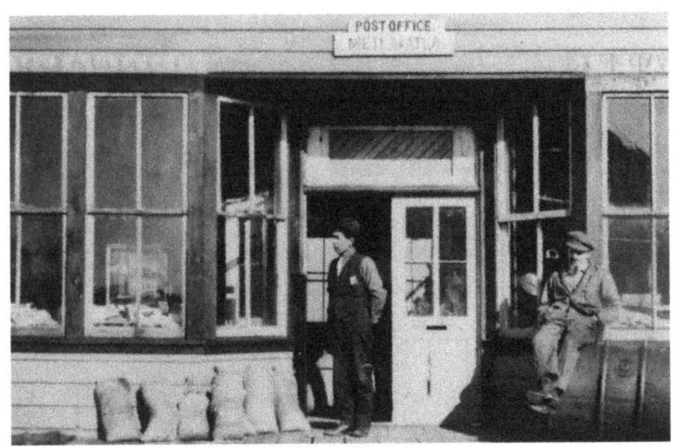

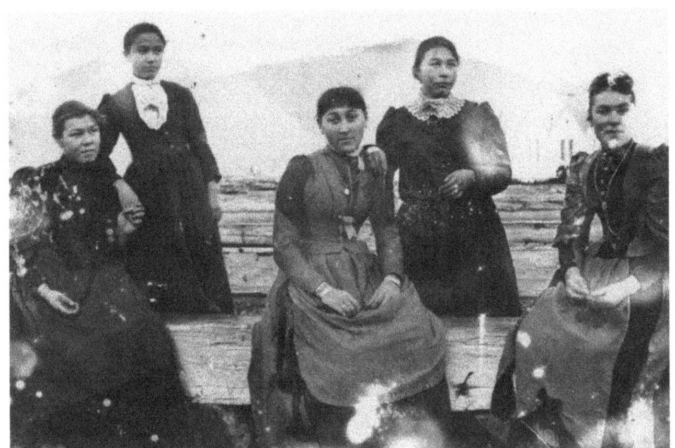

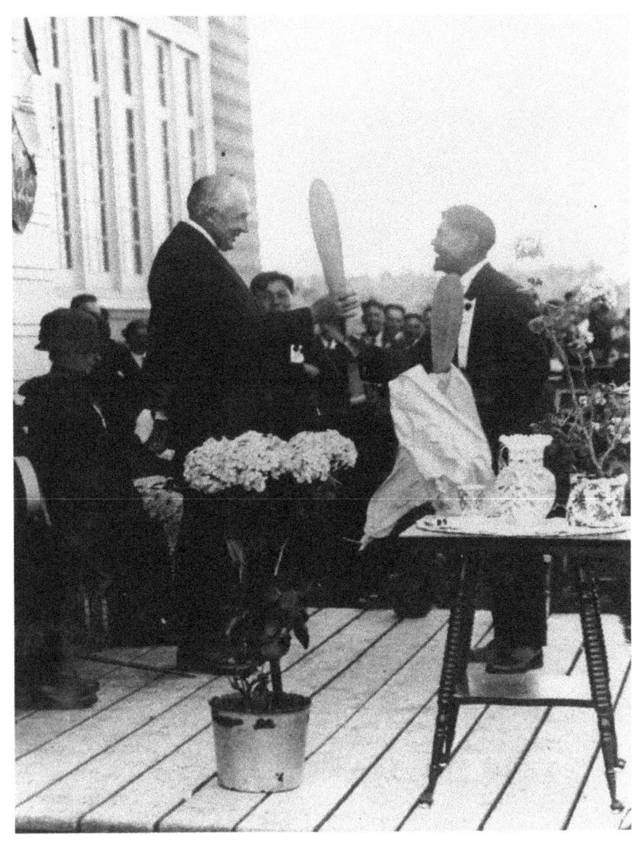

President Warren G. Harding visited Metlakatla and was presented with a traditional paddle.

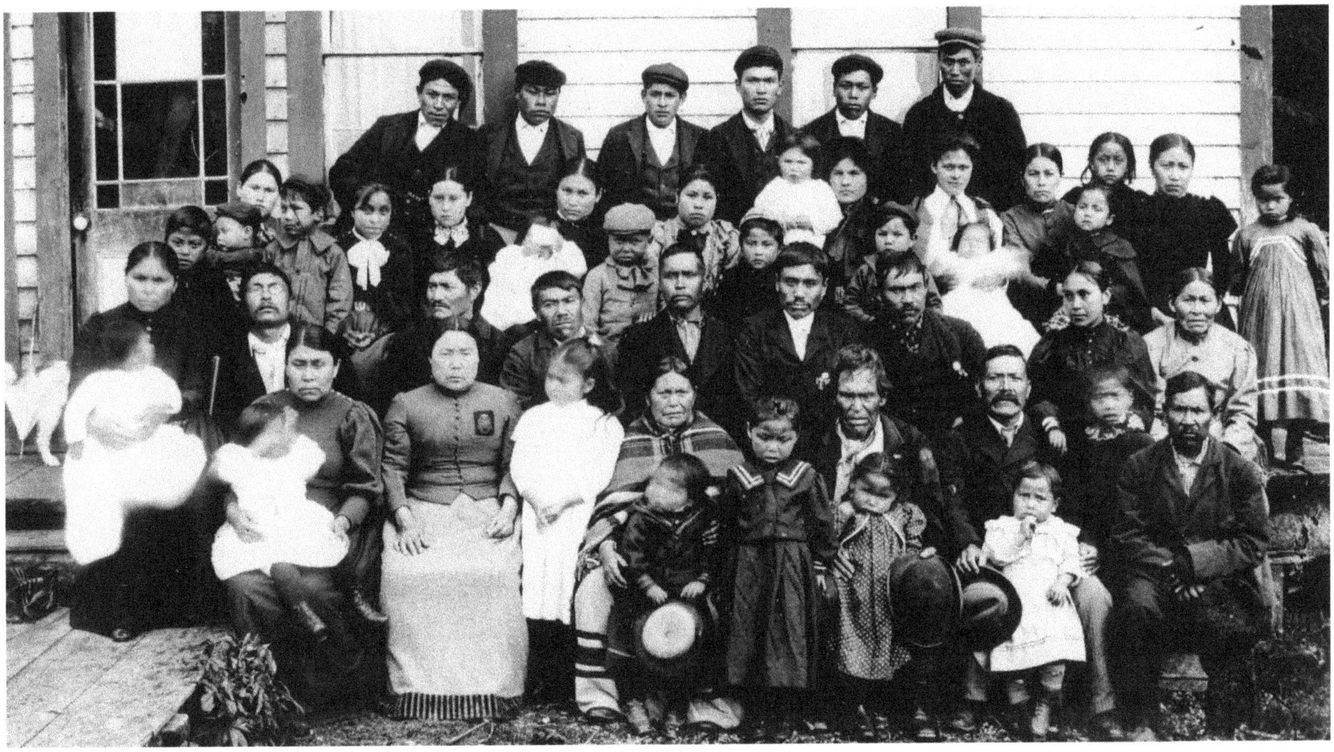

marriages, memorials, chiefships, et cetera. Everything that was important to our people happened through potlatches.

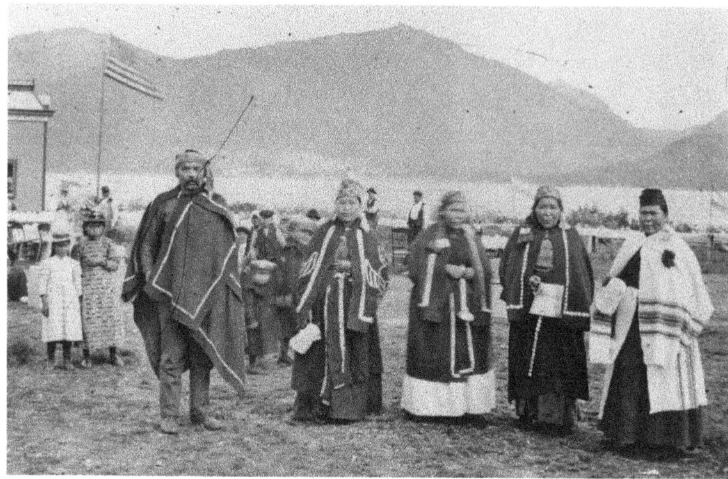

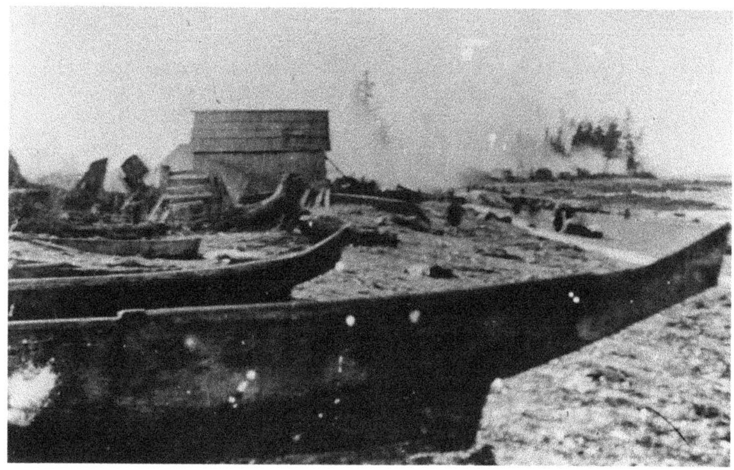

The more you give at a feast, the wealthier you are. That was something the Europeans greatly misunderstood about us.

Totem poles are an iconic symbol of northwest coast people and oddly have become a symbol of Native American people in general. Despite the cowboy-and-Indian totem pole toys, totem poles are unique to the northwest coast.

Totem poles are like a signpost and a picture book combined. They stand in front of your home and let people know where you lived and the history of your family. They were never, ever—*ever*—worshiped. That was also a great misunderstanding.

The name Tsimshian wasn't even something we would have all considered ourselves prior to contact with the Europeans. We would have only identified ourselves by our village and tribe, like Gitxaała or Gitlaan or Gispaxlo'ots.

IN 1831, A TRADING company named Hudson Bay Company tried and failed to establish a fort near the Nass River. Several years later, they built a fort on the mainland side that our people called Lax łgu k'alaams and they named the fort, Fort Simpson. To our people, this was somewhat of an intrusion not only into our land, but our people. A number of chiefs had become very powerful because of trade and were not prepared to allow a foreign fort to come in and take over their territory.

Ligeex became the first chief of chiefs. He was powerful enough to become chief of all the Tsimshian people. He decided he would move his tribe, the Gispaxlo'ots, to Fort Simpson. Not to be out done, the chiefs of the other eight tribes that lived in another area called Maxłaxaała also decided to move. Maxłaxaała is where those nine villages had wintered and potlatched for thousands of years. There were also other villages that didn't move. A ship captain came to the fort for a visit and saw the conditions of the fort. What happened was we were introduced to poor trading practices, but we were also introduced to alcohol, firearms, and disease. Our potlatches, which had been these very strict and important events for our people, descended into "whisky feasts." I feel bad these people had to come and see what the effects of contact had done and judge us on that rather than what we had been before they gave us all of that.

The ship captain went back to England and told the church missionaries that they had to send someone to Christianize and civilize these poor people at Fort Simpson. So they sent a man named William Duncan. He was twenty-four years old from Beverly, England. He was born out of wedlock. That was a strike against you in English and European society. He worked all of his life to prove he was better than the circumstances of his birth.

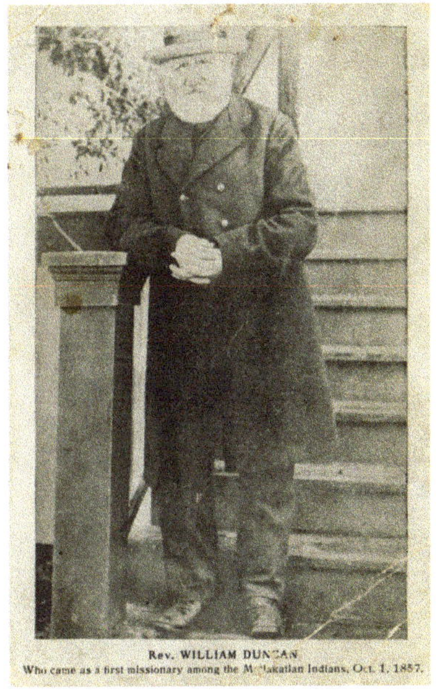

William Duncan was the missionary who led a migration from British Columbia to Alaska. He died in 1918.

Duncan arrived in Fort Simpson in 1857. There was a Tsimshian man who had become friendly with the people of the fort, and they asked this man to come teach the new missionary our language. He spent six months to a year learning our language and in turn taught this man English. The Tsimshian man would eventually be baptized and given the name Arthur Wellington. After Duncan learned our language, he gave an address to the nine chiefs who lived there and told them why he had come.

He built a church and school house at the fort, and over five years, converted many of our people. But Duncan knew he couldn't do what he had come to do with the potlatching being done around the fort. From his perspective, he needed to get us away from our old traditions so we could focus on becoming Christian. So the missionaries decided to make a move. They decided to pick this old village site called Łpuunm G̱alts'ap—meaning the village of plenty—and they created a village and called it Metlakatla.

OVER THE NEXT twenty-five years, they built an incredibly famous community. It was a symbol of what could be done to modernize and "civilize" Native people. We built the largest church north of San Francisco and west of Chicago. We had a cannery, a sawmill, a blacksmith shop, and a trading post.

Mr. Duncan made us sign a piece of paper to move to Metlakatla. We were to give up things like potlatch and our traditional medicine. But he never took away our

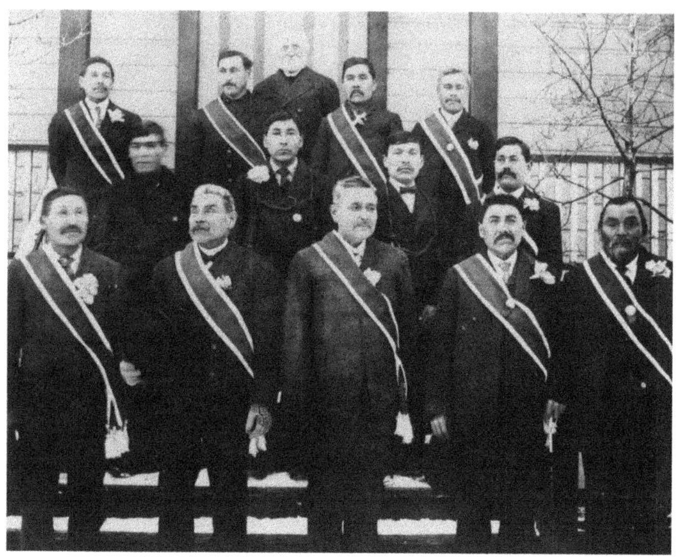

language. He preached to us in our language. It's said he spoke it so much that he dreamt in our language. In order to move to Metlakatla, chiefs had to give up their positions. Everyone was to be equal. That's something our elders still express to me: we are all equal. But Duncan gave those men powerful positions in the community like councilman and captain of the fire brigade.

Metlakatla prospered. There are people who will question why we went with the missionary. Shortly after we moved to Metlakatla, a smallpox epidemic swept through the coast and killed many thousands of people. It hit Fort Simpson and devastated Haida Gwaii. But we missed it at Metlakatla and Mr. Duncan had medicine for us. Our people made a choice. They decided to give their hearts to God because the world they lived in all of the sudden didn't belong to them anymore. Duncan showed a way we could make it through a very hard time. He offered us safety and an education in the new world.

The church, though, did not care for how Mr. Duncan ran the mission. He didn't serve wine at the communion. He was a minimalist as far as Anglican religion goes. He removed ceremonies of the Anglican religion, so we did not compare our traditional ceremonies with theirs. The church didn't care for that. At the same time, Duncan was fighting the Canadian government. He argued that we deserved the right to our land, and they shouldn't be able to come here and do whatever they wanted with it.

So they sent a man named Bishop Ridley, and he tried to take over the mission. It caused a great division. A majority stayed loyal to Mr. Duncan. Quite a few sided with Bishop Ridley. Rather than fight the church and the Canadian government, which were more or less one in the same, we decided it would be best to move. I do say "we." Another misunderstanding is that we were blind followers who were told what to do and where to go. Our people made every decision. Our people chose to move to Metlakatla. We chose to move to Alaska. We believed in the leadership of Mr. Duncan.

In early 1887, Mr. Duncan left Metlakatla, B.C., and headed for Washington, D.C. He met with government agencies, members of Congress, and finally President Cleveland. He asked permission for us to move to Alaska. At the same time, a canoe with seven men, including a white doctor, headed north to find a suitable location for a new community.

THERE ARE DIFFERENT stories as to how the location was picked. There were beautiful sandy beaches, a waterfall to provide fresh water, an abundance of traditional food, and a flat area to build our community. The men went back and told everyone they found a good place. About fifty men were sent ahead to begin building temporary homes.

On August 7, 1887, Mr. Duncan arrived with some officials from Washington D.C. The advance party met them with great joy, raised the American flag, and had an evening church service on the beach. They chimed the church bell they had taken from the church in Metlakatla. That bell sits in the Duncan church today.

Over the rest of August, 823 of our people would make their way here to what used to be a Tlingit village called T'aakwAani. And that is where the Sm'algyax pronunciation, Tak'waan comes from.

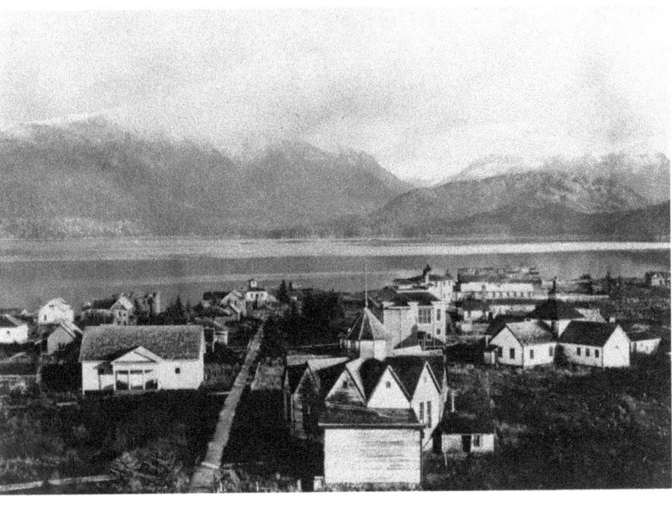

These are some of the old mission community buildings: town hall, school, girls dorms.

SO WE STARTED OVER. Our people were willing to work so hard to be in charge of our own destiny. We lived on the beach for two winters in makeshift homes. Some of the people moved to Ketchikan. There is still a strong community of Tsimshian in Ketchikan. Some but not many of our people returned to British Columbia. There was a Tlingit totem pole when we arrived and Mr. Duncan had it sent to Sitka. It's now part of the Sheldon Jackson Museum.

Even though our people descended from every single Tsimshian tribe—there are fourteen of them on the B.C. side—they became, we became, one people, a new tribe of Tsimshian people.

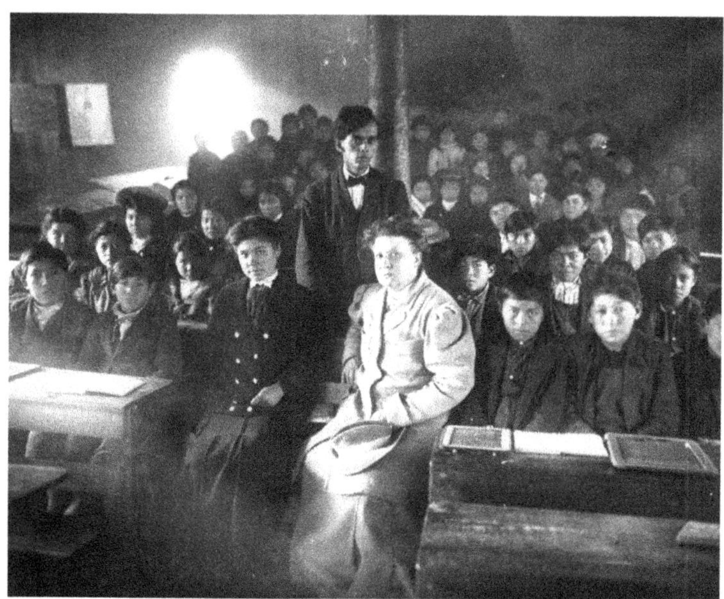

We rebuilt the church. It was not quite as big as the one in Metlakatla, but it could hold a thousand people. Mr. Duncan learned to play many instruments and he taught our people. Mr. Duncan was with us for sixty-one years.

Toward the end of his life, our people noticed the school only went to eighth grade. They petitioned the government to build a new school. Until then, our classes were taught in Sm'algyax and English. When the government agreed to come in, our school was torn down, and they built a new school.

From then on Sm'algyax was no longer allowed in school and our people were punished for it in many different ways. Some of them were forced to chop wood if they were caught speaking it; some had their mouths washed out with soap; some were beaten.

We were made to feel ashamed. There was a little girl who lived with her grandmother and she answered her grandmother in Sm'algyax. Her grandmother asked her a question and she said "Oo," which means yes. A teacher walking by heard her say that, and even though the girl wasn't on school property, she took her up to the school and spanked her.

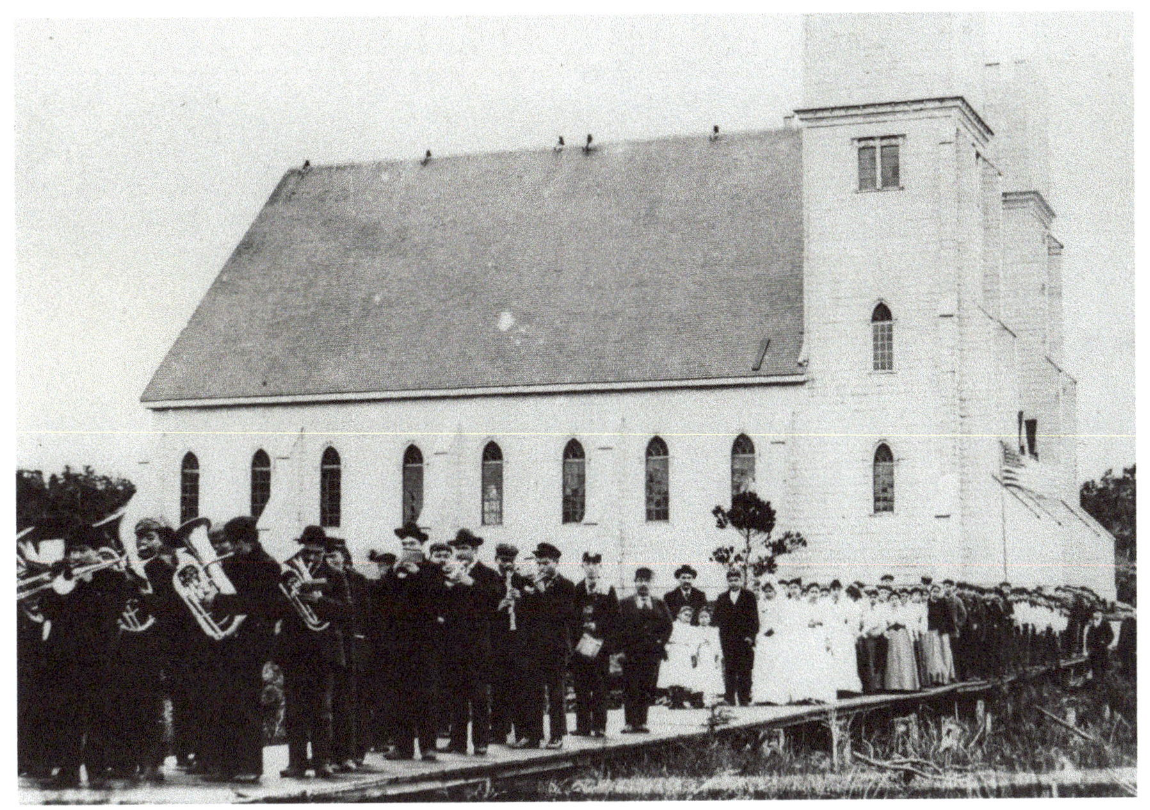

She brought her back and her grandmother asked her
in Sm'algyax if she was spanked. "Oo." The teacher took
her right back up and spanked her again.

The impacts of that cannot be overstated. When land
is taken from you, when your language, your very
identity is taken from you, that leaves a scar that can
cause genetic injury. Genes can be turned off and on
from trauma and that's passed on from generation to
generation.

Mr. Duncan passed away in 1918. No matter what you
may think of him, the more you read of our history the
more you have to recognize, he was a man of his time
and he did what he felt was best for our people. I believe
he loved us. We have this beautiful island thanks to him.
So, no matter how we feel today about him, we have to
at least be grateful for that. ❖

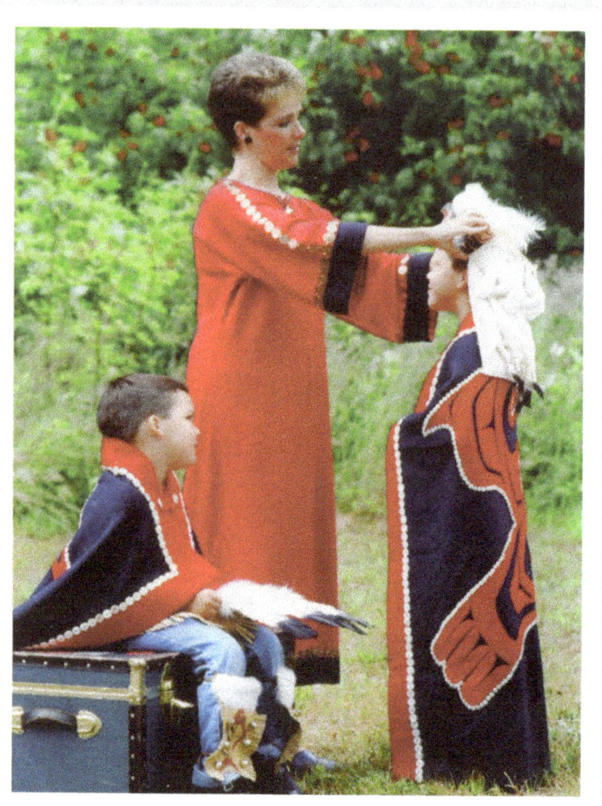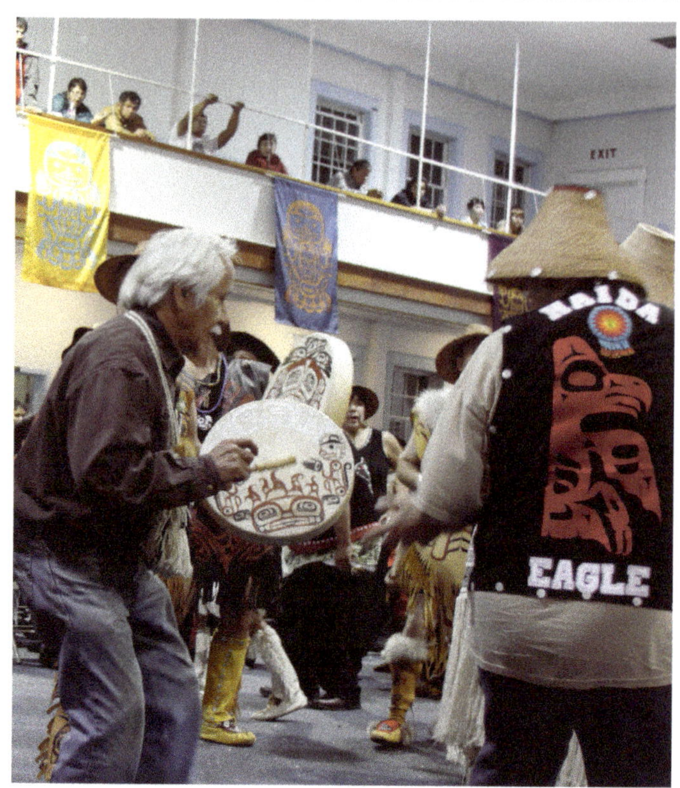

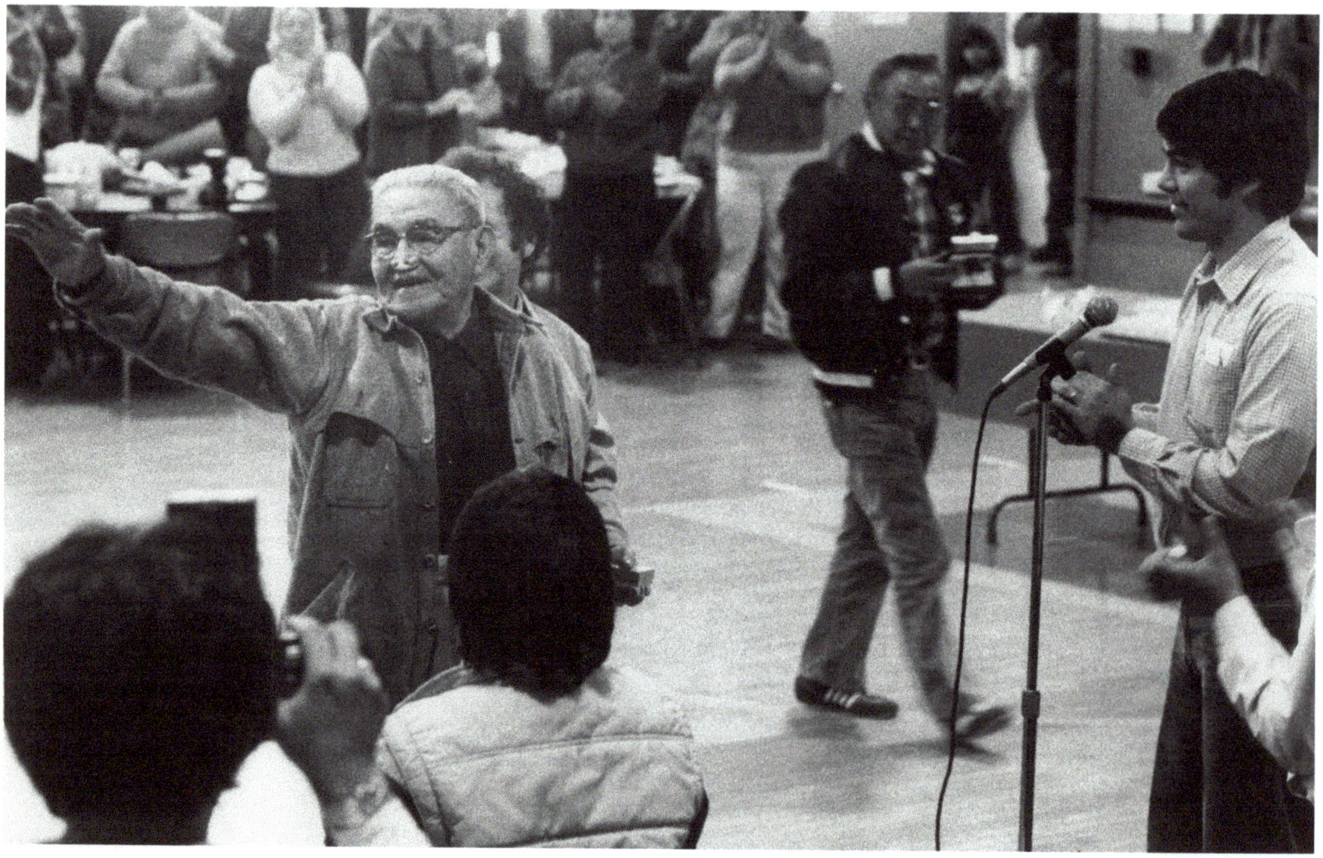

CHAPTER THREE

FIRST TO POTLATCH

Ksgooga Yaawk

When some people hear the word "potlatch," they think we mean a potluck. But I view this common mistake as a chance for us to share what a potlatch really is and why it's so important to our culture. I tell people to think of the potlatch as being the cultural hub of our wheel.

It's the center, and everything radiates out from the potlatch: names, chiefs, rules of feasts, regalia, songs, dance, carvings, the stories, the oral tradition. That's why the potlatch was—and still is—important to our people.

Dancing for the sake of dancing isn't something my son is a fan of because a potlatch is directly connected to why we dance and why we are performing our clan's dances. I agree with him; we always must remember why we do the things we do culturally, otherwise it gets lost in the shuffle.

A potlatch is our way of saying, "This is who we are. These are the things that are important to us. This is the way we pass on our history, our stories, our names, the important events of our lives." The word "potlatch" is a Chinook jargon word, which means "to give." Our words for potlatch are "luugyit" and "yaawk."

This system of potlatch is a reciprocal system. There is the host and there is the guest. The host prepares the potlatch for extended periods, makes or gathers up all the items that will be given out. The three basic rules are: public witness; gifting, paying the witnesses; and feeding guests.

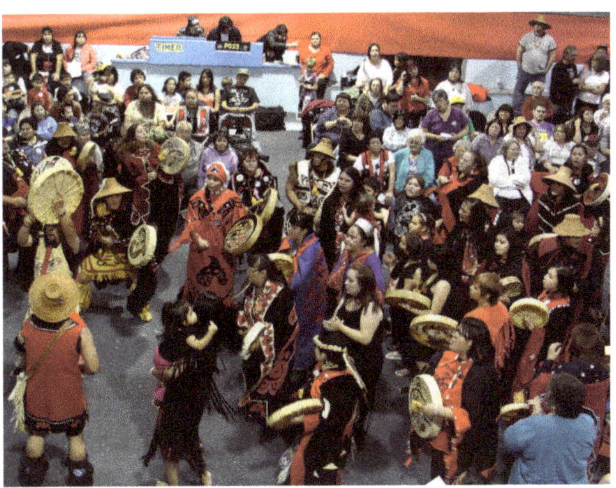

A potlatch is the cultural hub that brings friends and relatives together.

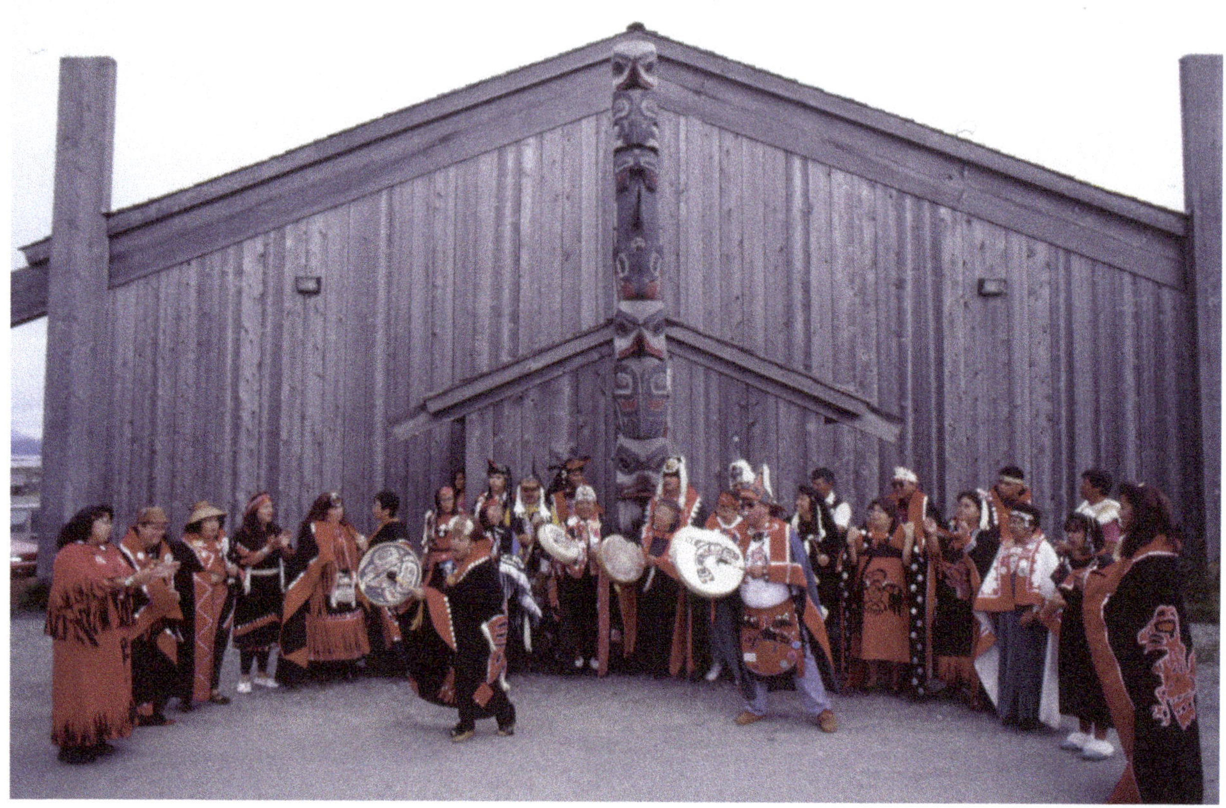

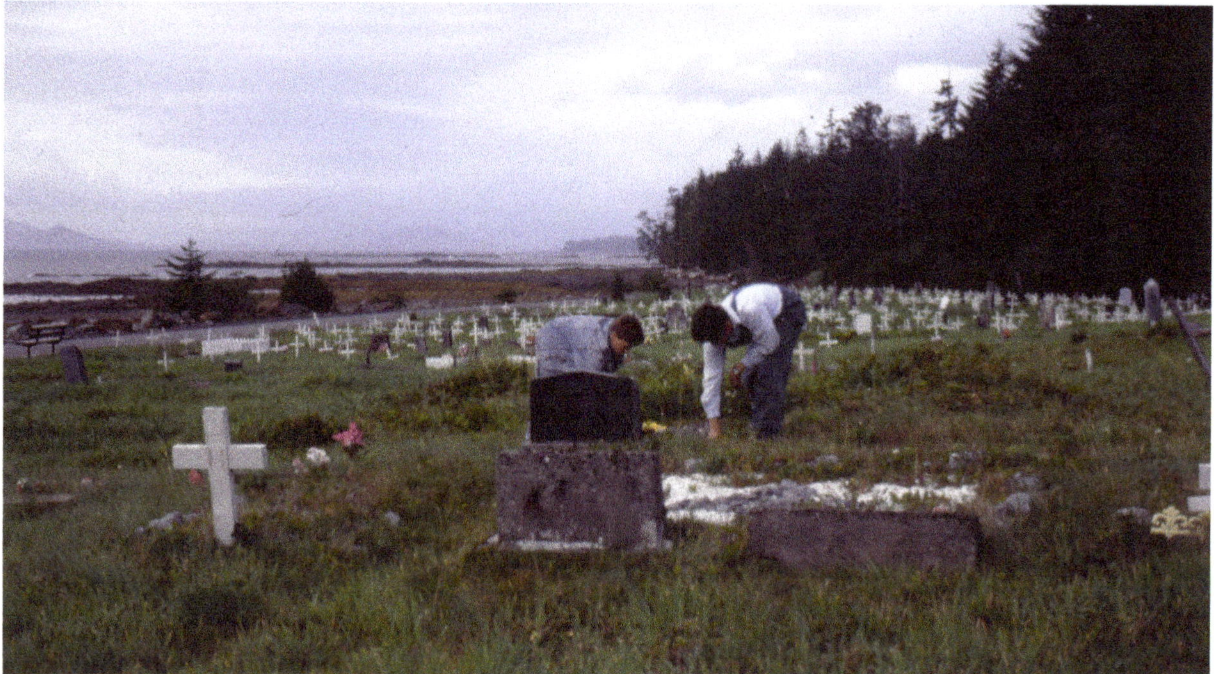

ABOVE: This is the 4th Generation Dancers singing a welcome song to the potlatch guests during the 1987 gathering to celebrate Metlakatla's 100th anniversary of settlers arriving from British Columbia. The group was formed as a direct result of the potlatch. I carved the totem pole standing behind them. Unfortunately a storm took it down. It represents all four clans and was commissioned by the village's senior citizens center.

BELOW: Davey and I cleaned my grandfather's grave in advance of the 1994 potlatch.

You need to invite guests who witness your claims, the totem pole raising, and the naming. Then you pay the witnesses with gifts. The gifts reflect the status of the guests or the importance of their contributions. When they accept those gifts, they're saying, "I agree with you." You try to give as much as possible to make your claims honest and true.

One of the most important things to witness is someone receiving a Tsimshian name. To have a name, it puts you above, it makes you a member, it makes you real. Unfortunately, there are so many of my own people who don't have names because of their birth or because they were raised away from the culture—say their mother is not Native—and they don't have a clan unless they are adopted into one. I'm a proponent of every single Native person belonging to a clan, and having a Native name as well as their English name. It is a way to be part of something that was taken from us.

At a potlatch you feed everybody. The hosts eat last. They make sure everyone gets more than enough food, including food to take home with them as well as their gifts. You charge the guests with the responsibility of remembering what happened: the stories that are told, the songs that they hear, the story of the totem pole.

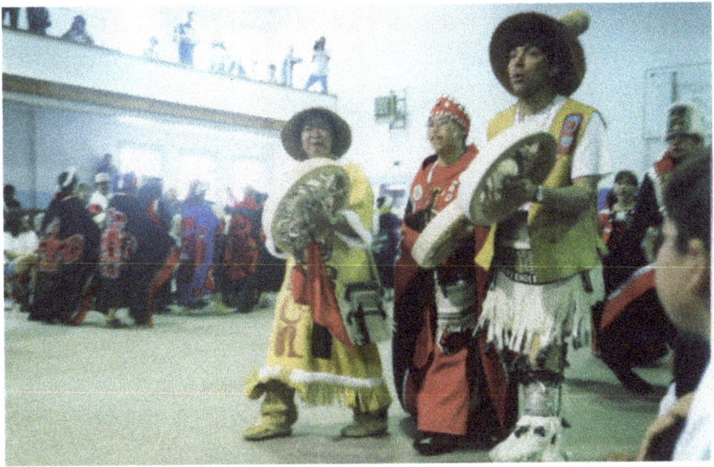

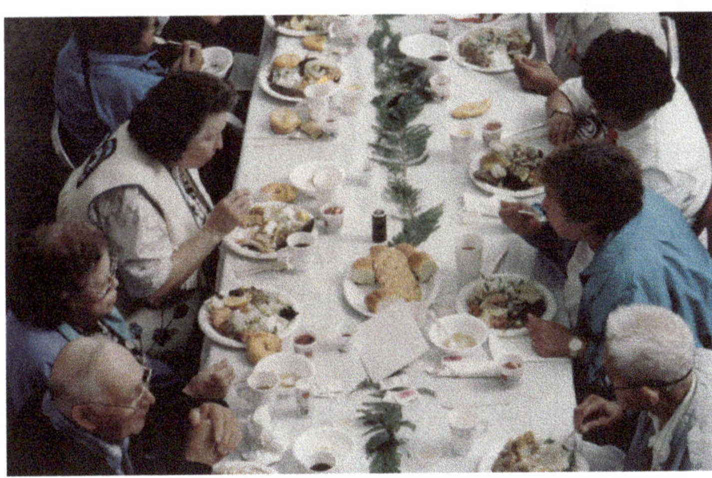

In the 1994 potlatch, Theo Bayou and her daughter Marcella Asiksik gave me incredible support.

We went through a period when the government and churches took the potlatch away. They made it illegal. People went to jail for putting on a potlatch. People went to jail for dancing, giving gifts. Things were confiscated. There are a lot of artifacts in museums that were confiscated. It's crazy to think of that happening.

I *developed the* idea for the first potlatch in Metlakatla during a Native history class I was teaching in the eighties. That potlatch was in 1982, which was still four years before I would make the most difficult decision of my life to leave Metlakatla. At the time, I had received permission from the school to develop and teach a Native history class. I did a lot of research. It was a half semester class for ninth graders. There were a lot of cultural things taught there besides history. But I had to be careful about stepping into Jack Hudson's area as the Native arts teacher. He was my first Native arts teacher, and I needed to respect his work.

I learned more about the potlatch as I researched. I knew the tenets and I knew the rules but I had never been to one. I also thought this is a good opportunity to do something to honor my grandmother. I also wanted to do something that would show my grandfather how grateful I am that he raised me.

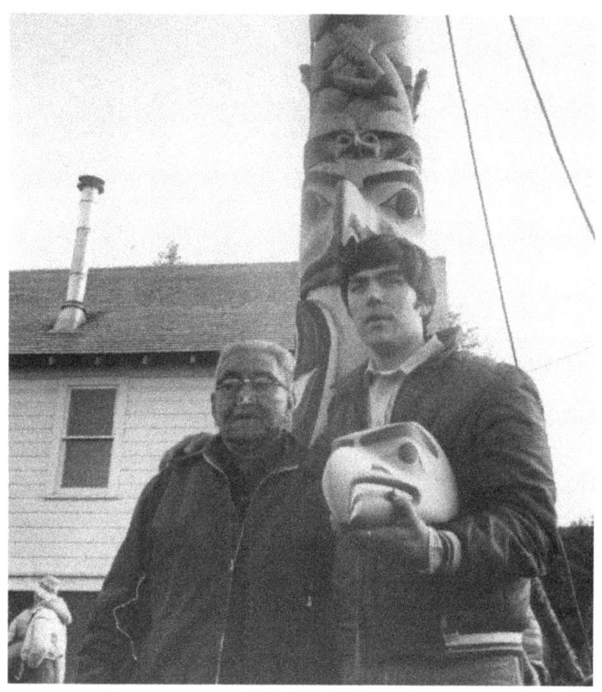

In 1982, my grandfather stood by my side after the pole was raised for grandmother in front of the house he built in Metlakatla. I could not have done any of it without him.

This was around the time I carved my first big totem pole. It was a twenty-three footer for my grandmother's memorial. It was supposed to be twenty-four feet, but I couldn't get the entire log in the shop, so I cut off a foot. I still had to put the pole in on an angle because it couldn't go straight in.

My grandfather helped me select the log. He and I went in the woods on the west side of the island and found a red cedar tree. He showed me what it takes to cut it down. It wasn't a very large tree, but it was exciting to take it down with my grandfather's help. I learned a lot that day about cutting down smaller trees.

We dropped the tree down. It was just the two of us in the woods. Basically, because it was downhill in this creek area, we were able to move the pole on these other little tree branches that we had placed across its path. We got it down to a point where we couldn't move it anymore. I asked Jim Gilmur, a construction man from town, to help us move the log. He brought in an earth mover with a winch attached to it. We pulled it up over a hill and then down to the road, then a couple of guys who worked for Metlakatla Power and Light put it on a trailer like they would utility poles.

The community let me use a warehouse at the cannery. That's where I did most of the carving through the winter. As it got closer to being finished, we moved it to the carving shop that my neighbor and friend, Ben Eaton, helped me build. Not long after that, Ben also built the Sweet Shoppe, the ice cream parlor and bakery my wife Liz and I opened.

I had no one I could go to when it came to the culture. The missionaries were so successful in stripping the previous generation of our identity. Poles were intricately connected with potlatches. Although there were still many who were fluent speakers of our language when I was a kid, there was no cultural life in the village. Nothing at all. There was a lot of racism in Ketchikan and other communities back then. Even when I was

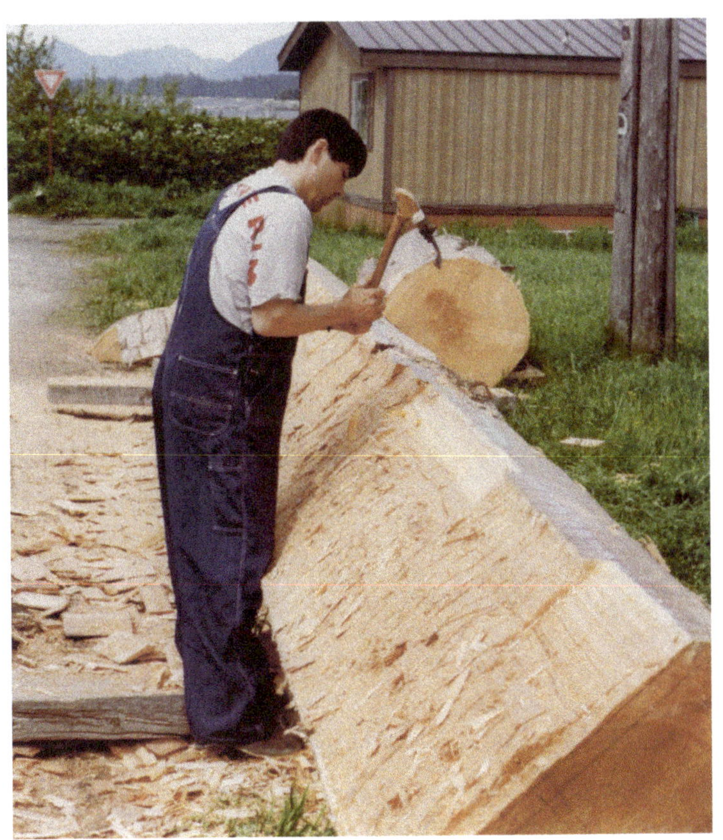

PREPARING FOR POTLATCH

Getting ready for a potlatch can take up to a year. Here, I'm preparing my grandfather's totem pole in the 1994 potlatch. The log came from Prince of Wales Island.

I made hundreds of soup spoons for as gifts for those who witnessed potlatches. I grew up using these type of spoons for the salmon soup that my grandmother used to make. I still have them, but we don't use them anymore.

These were for the 1994 potlatch. I made even more for my mother's potlatch in 2011. I kept a list of anyone who helped my mother when she was alive and even after she passed away.

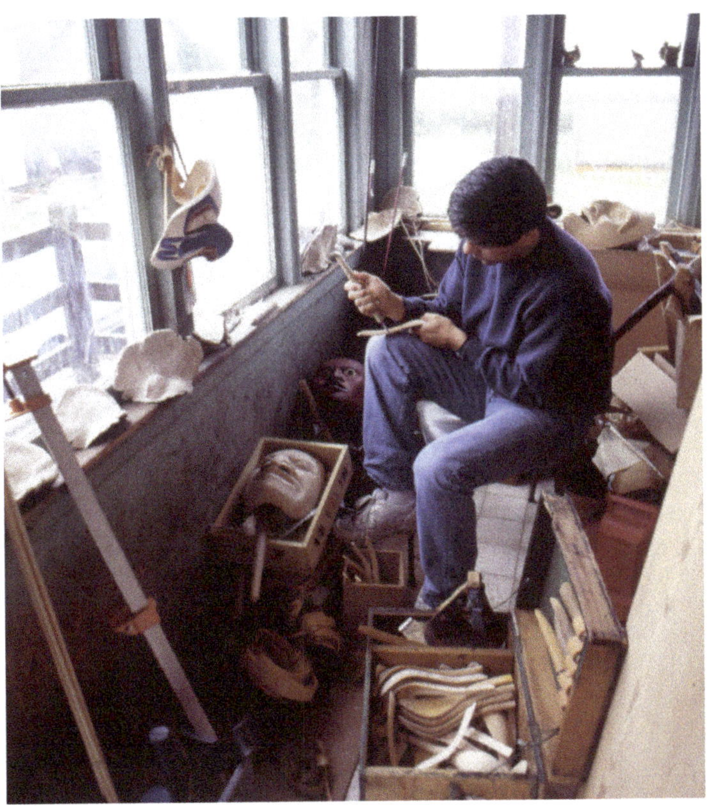

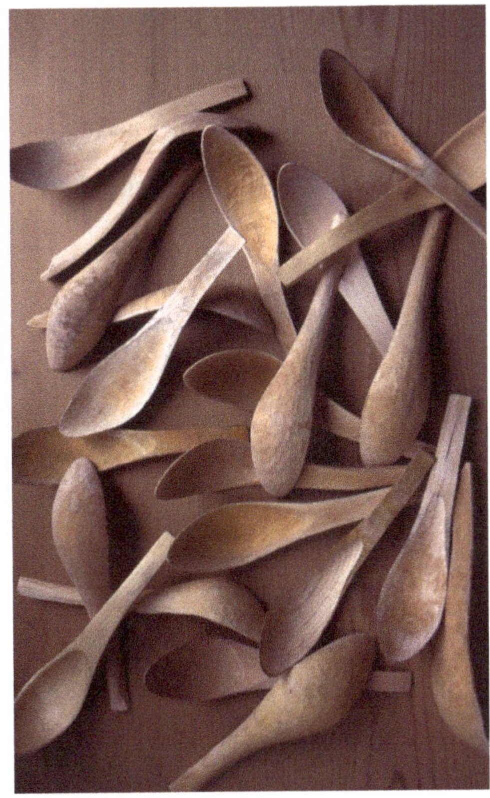

Reviving a Forgotten Tradition

Honoring my grandmother

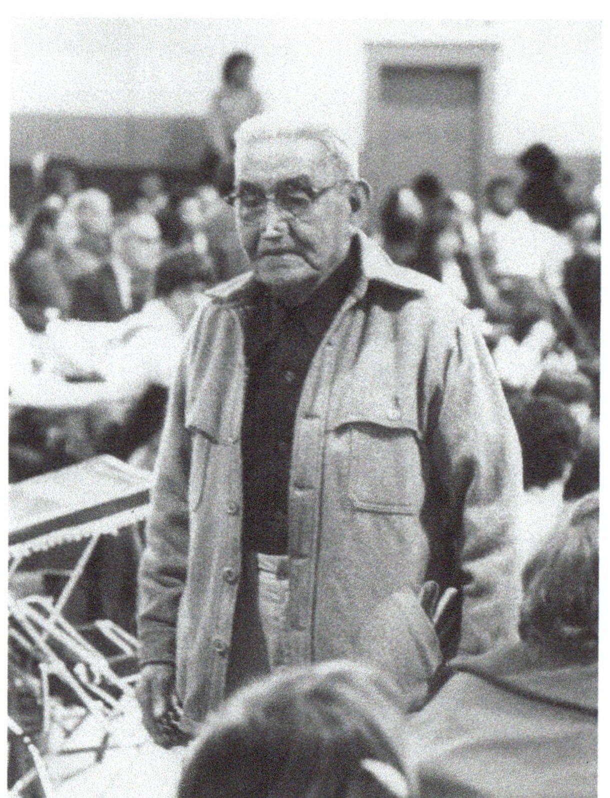

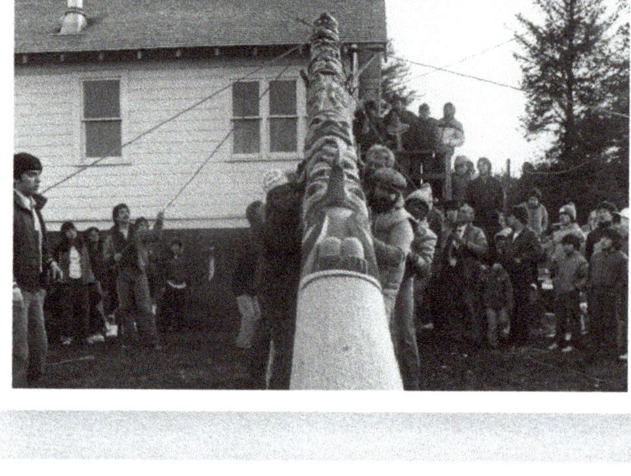

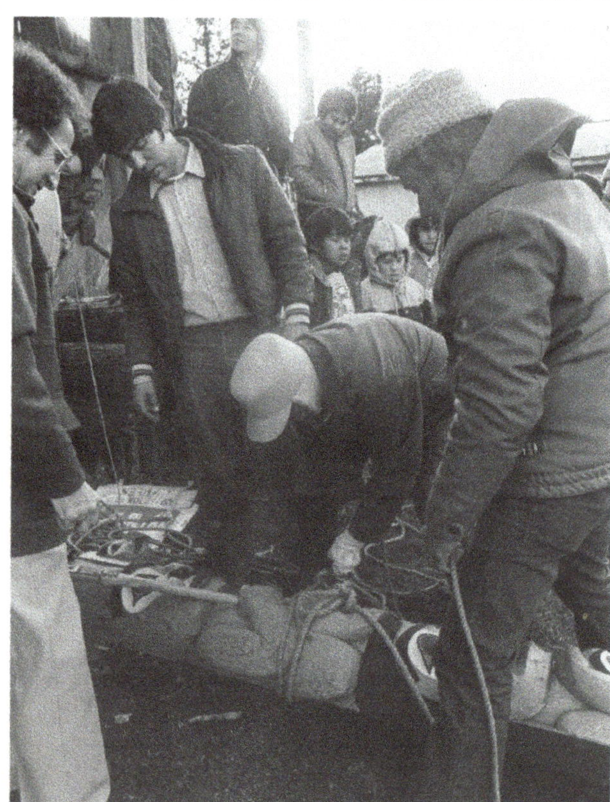

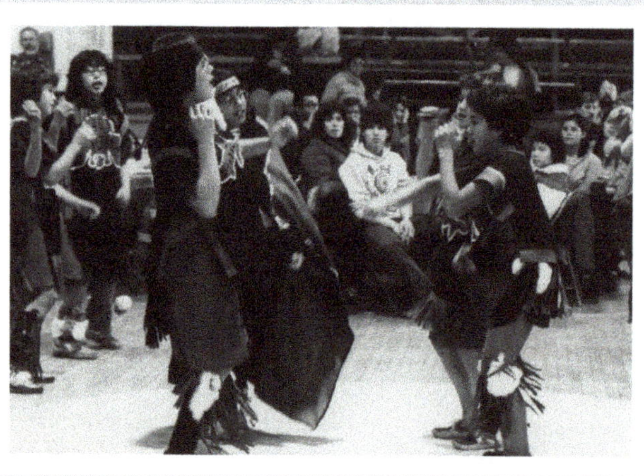

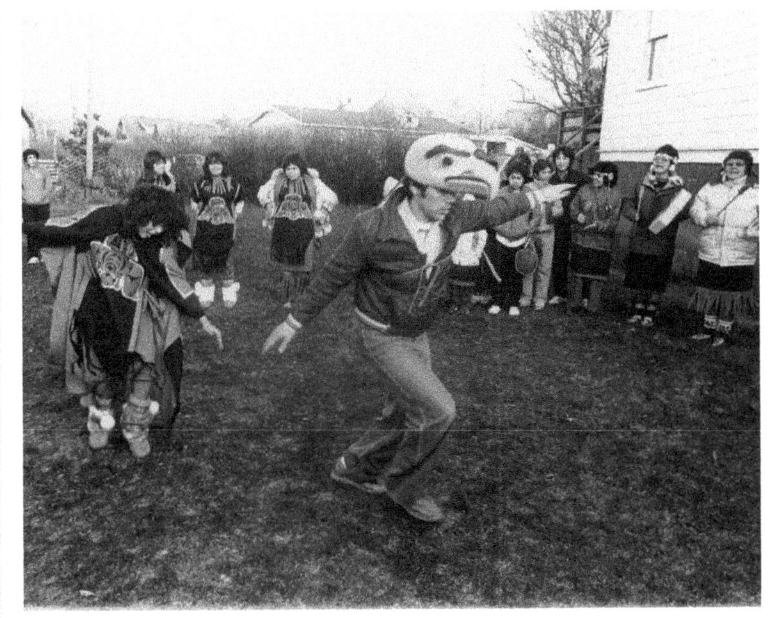
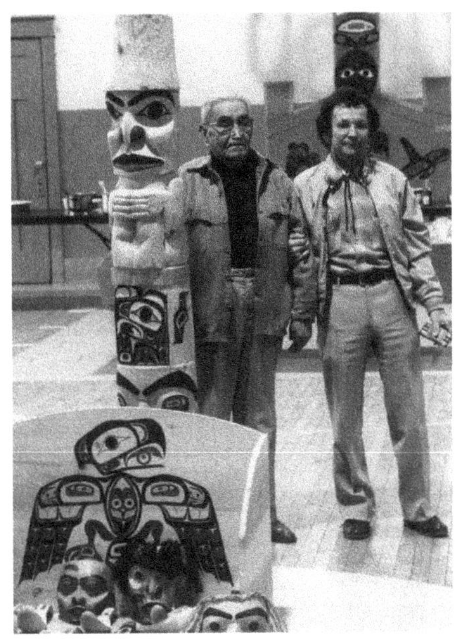
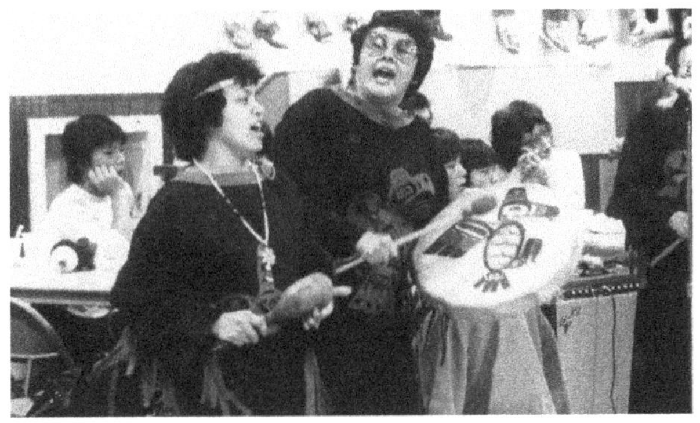
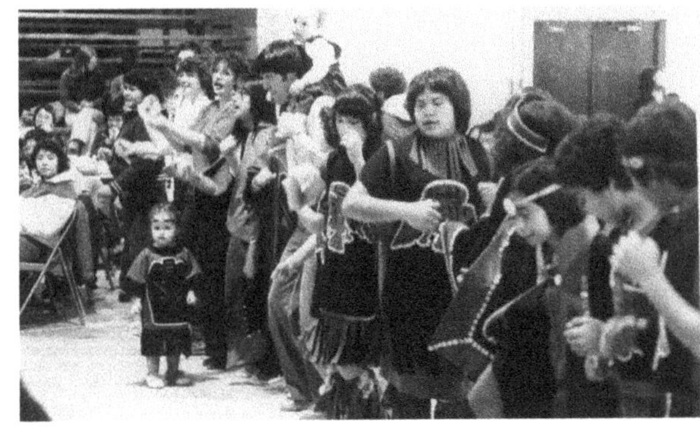
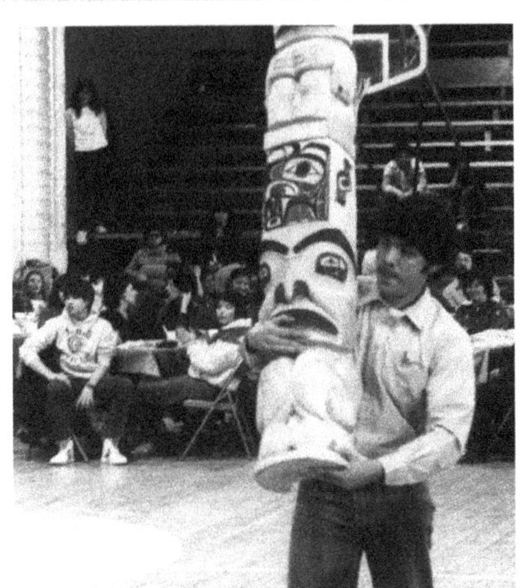
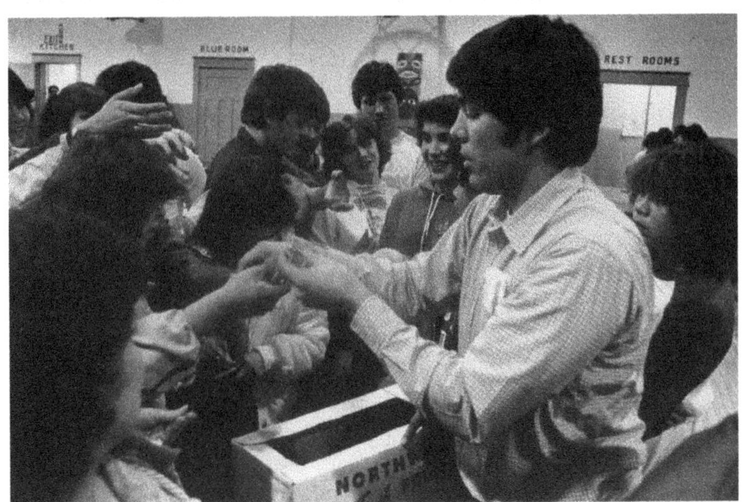

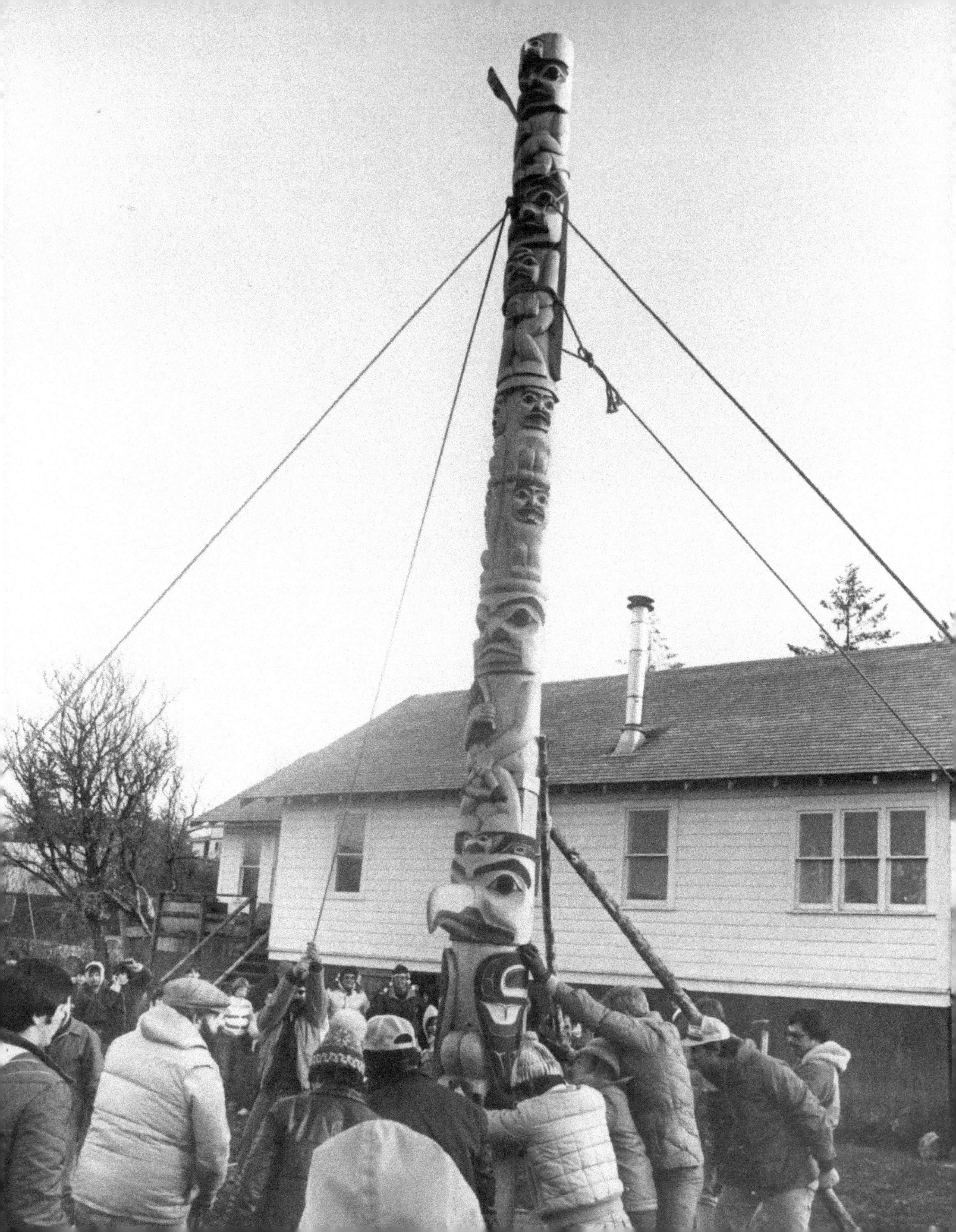

growing up, you could feel it. Our people spent all our money over there in Ketchikan. There were Native people there, too. "Indian town" is what they called it. Tlingits, Haidas, and Tsimshians lived there, too. It was a different time. I never saw any of our culture at home. There weren't dance groups like there are now. The Tlingits in Ketchikan had a lot of things going on—feasts and potlatches and things like that. In the seventies, things started to ramp up.

Trying to resurrect the potlatch was a real task. It's hard to bring something back when there's nearly nothing left. It's hard to re-establish something when there's a vacuum. There's nobody to ask. At that time, the elders were the children of those who stopped doing the potlatches and focused on being good Christians.

In 1982, planning that first potlatch, it was hard to get anybody to help. At times, it was just me and my first wife, Liz, doing everything. It was really hard. Maybe people just didn't know how to help. I did have a few people say, "Why do you want to do that?" and that was tough to take. We had a couple of meetings with the Laxsgyiik (eagle clan), but I could never get more than five or six people to come to a meeting, and that would be considered a big meeting.

I could rely on a few people from different clans: my aunt Johanna, a raven and my dear friend; Theo Bayou, also a raven. Those were the people who helped me plan. When you plan a potlatch, the first thing you have to do is decide where to get the food, but the other thing is the gifting. I just laugh now as I didn't know what I was doing. I was just feeling my way through it.

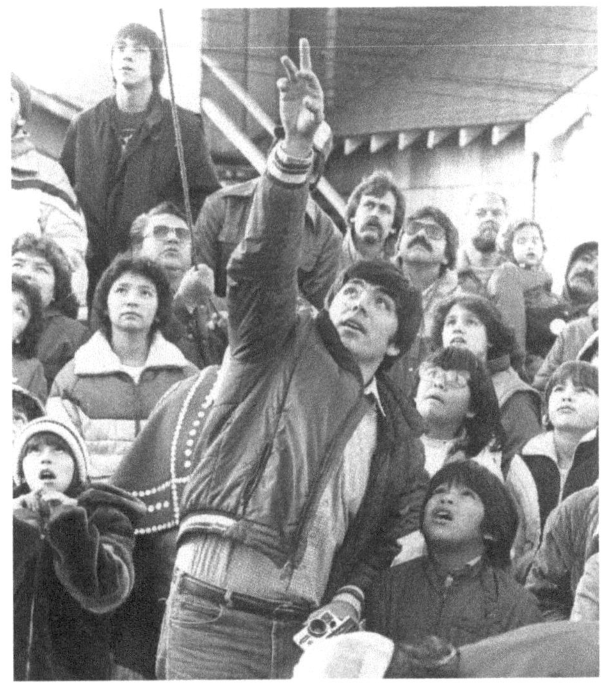

I'm describing the figures on the pole to the students I taught in school. I never thought how important that day was and how it changed everything, paving the way for cultural advancements that took place afterward.

The stuff that I gave away was modest. I gave away dollar bills. Lighters. Bumper stickers. Handmade pouches. My first silkscreen print. It was really amazing what I didn't know compared to what I have done in recent potlatches. It was a beginning.

I had asked the high school band to come and play the Star-Spangled Banner to open the event. There were very few people in the Town Hall. Almost all the chairs sat empty. I remember we had thirty-seven tables. It was supposed to start at noon, but no one was there, and I was getting nervous. You could hear a pin drop, it was so quiet and empty. Most of the people there were kids, maybe a dozen of them. After they played the national anthem, I asked them to play a couple more songs. They did while I held my breath.

Not long after that, it seemed like the doors to the town hall burst open and all of the sudden there was close to five hundred people.

They came through the door with big pots of food, cases of soda, stuff like that. All my worries were for nothing. If you look at the photos, the town hall was full of people. There were quite a few speakers. All of them are gone now.

There was spontaneous applause, a standing ovation for my grandfather. I felt like someone was stuffing my pockets with gold when all those people stood up and my grandfather waved to everybody. That was amazing. That paid me for all that effort and all that worry.

Eagle clan Elder Albert Eaton decided to give me a name at the end of the potlatch. Ksgooga Yaawk, First to Potlatch. I didn't fully understand the honor of it at the time.

We did things a little differently that day. It was the first ever pole raising and potlatch in my village. We raised the pole after the potlatch. Normally you put the pole up first. My grandfather was out there trying to help rig up the ropes. So many people came to see the pole.

There are a lot of feelings going through me when a pole gets raised, including the fear that something can go wrong. After all of these years and carving as many poles as I have, it's still amazing to see a pole get raised. If you look at a pole as it's being carved, it's laying there two or three feet off the ground for months, then all of a sudden when it goes up, it goes up and up and up, and you realize just how big it is. If I look at a pole laying there, I can take it all in with one look, but when it goes up, it's an entirely different thing. Even a relatively short one is awesome.

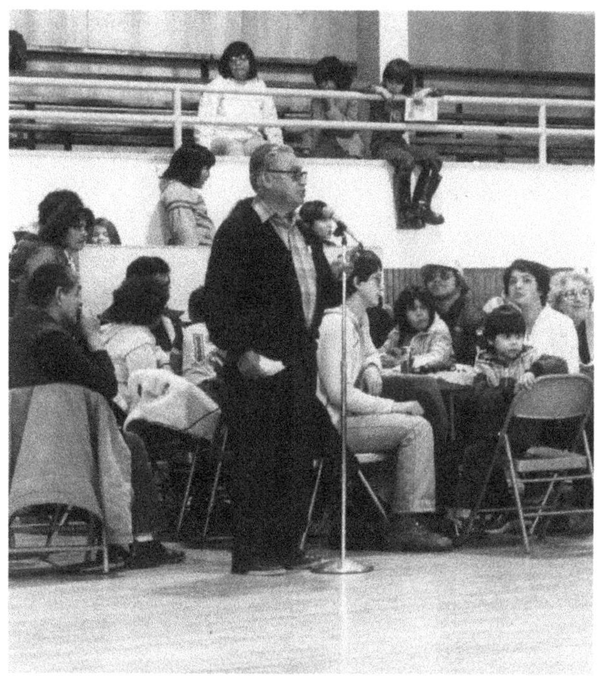

Alfred Eaton was a fluent Sm'algyax speaker. His daughter, Sarah Booth, became vital in helping my son Davey, along with his friends, and ultimately all of Metlakatla in the revitalization of the Sm'algyax language.

When we raised my grandmother's pole in 1982, it never occurred to me that I was starting something. I just wanted to say thank you to her, but she was gone by then. I wanted to say thank you to my grandfather. I just wanted to do it as much in the old way as I could.

The next big one I was involved with was 1994—that was supposed to be for my grandfather's hundredth birthday. I asked if I could give him a potlatch for his birthday. I thought he was going to make it. He was ninety-six when I was talking to him about it. Unfortunately, he passed away on Christmas Day just before he was ninety-eight. I decided to include all of the clans: Laxsgyiik (eagle clan), Gispwutwada (killer whale

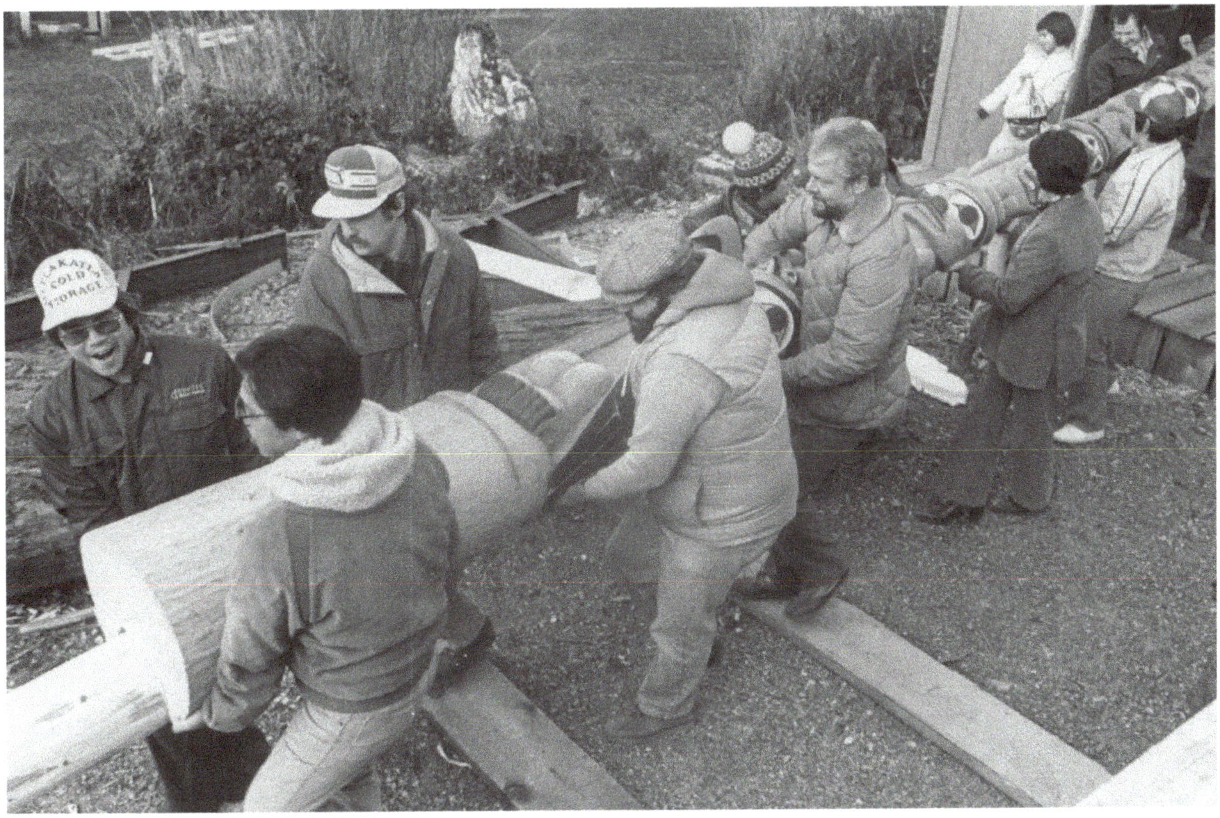

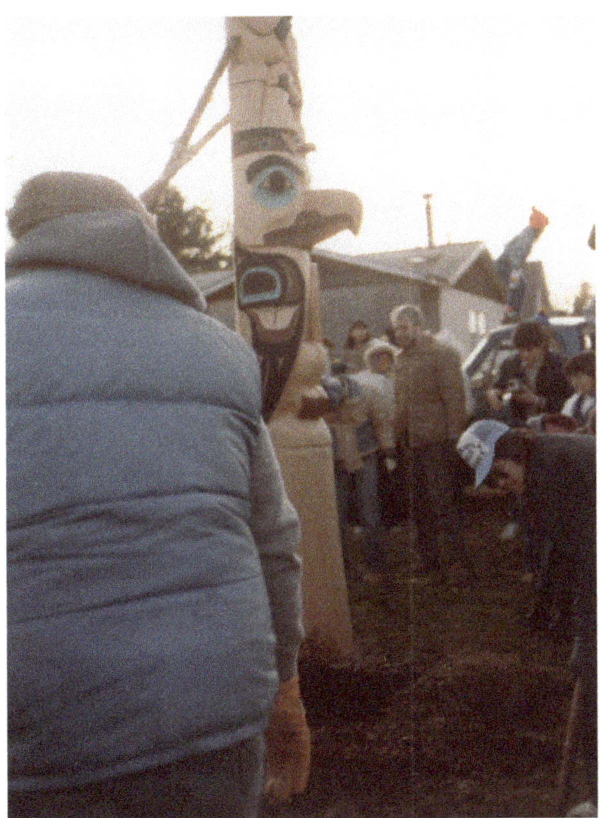

POLE-RAISING AT POTLATCH

These are guys hand-picked to be pole carriers. They carried it out of the carving shop in front of my grandfather's house. Some of them become principle pole raisers, too. I tried to get people who are not eagles, members of my clan. In this case, two or three are non-Native, the rest are killer whale clan members. The pole ended up being 23 feet—it was too long for the carving shed, so we had to cut off one foot. Later, Davey and I carved a replica, and the original is in a museum in Ketchikan, Alaska.

Four clans coming together

Honoring my grandfather

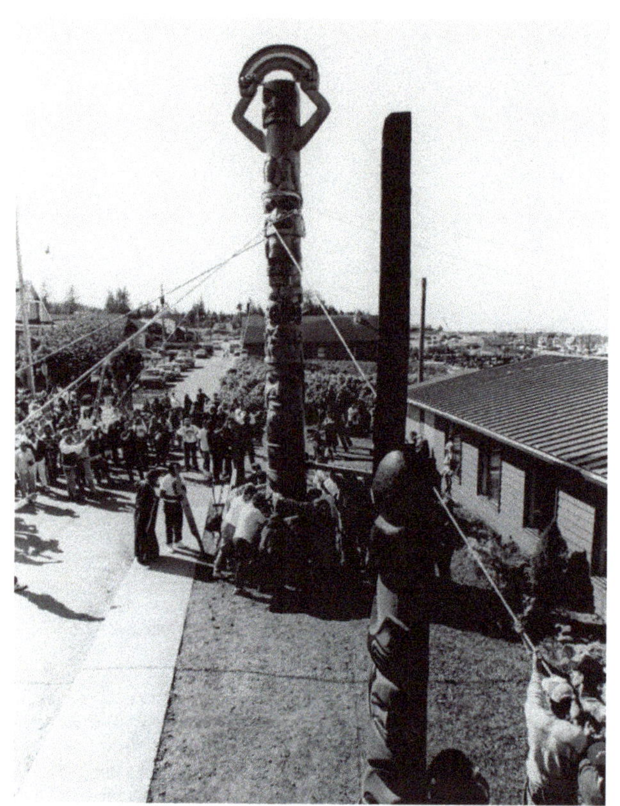

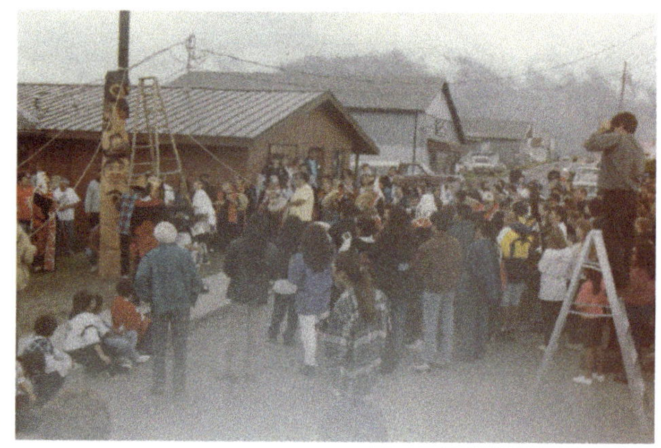

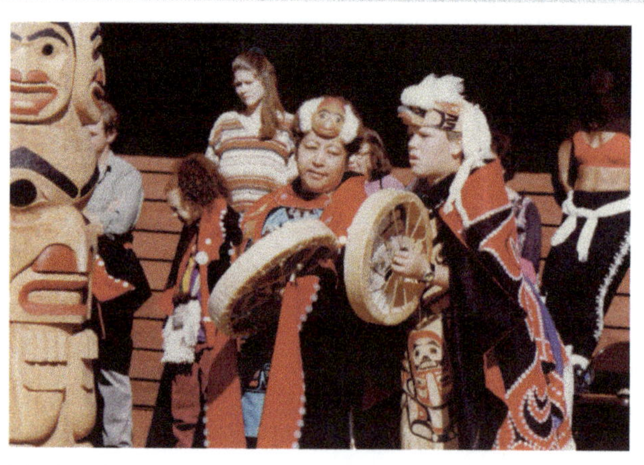

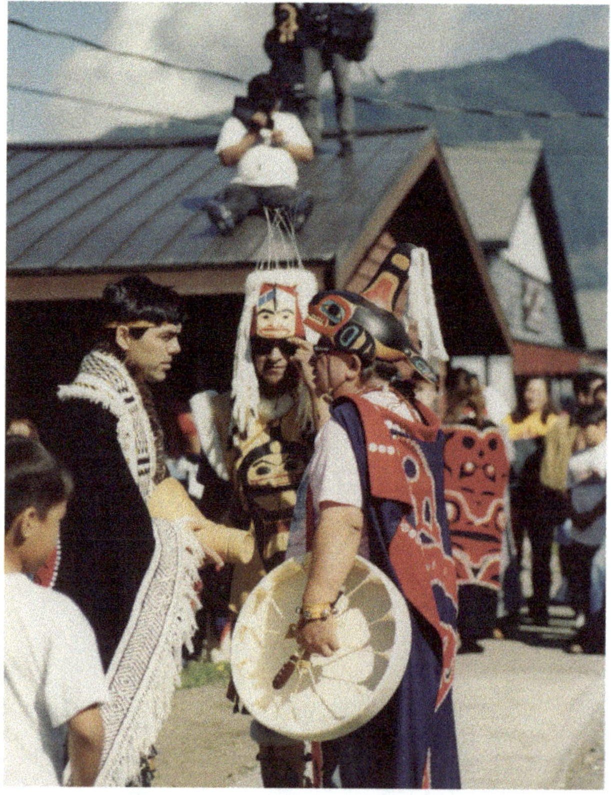

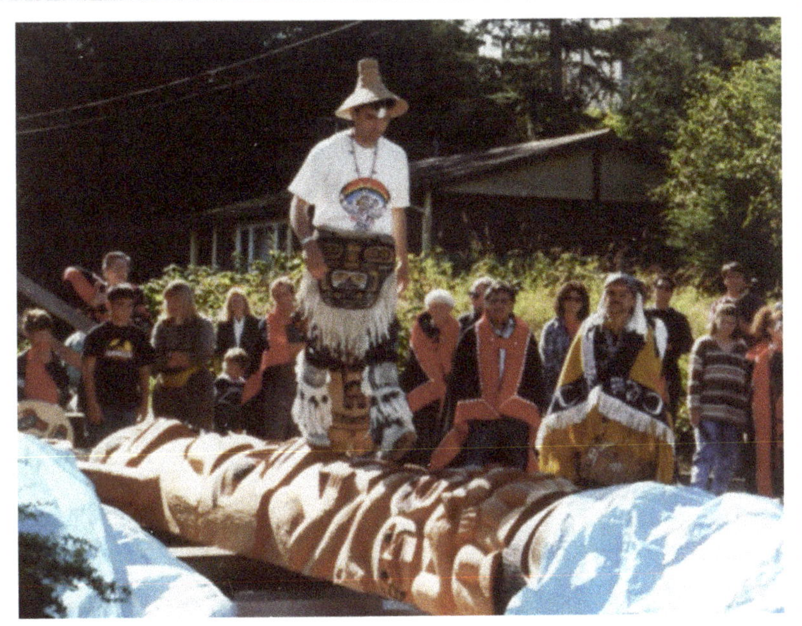
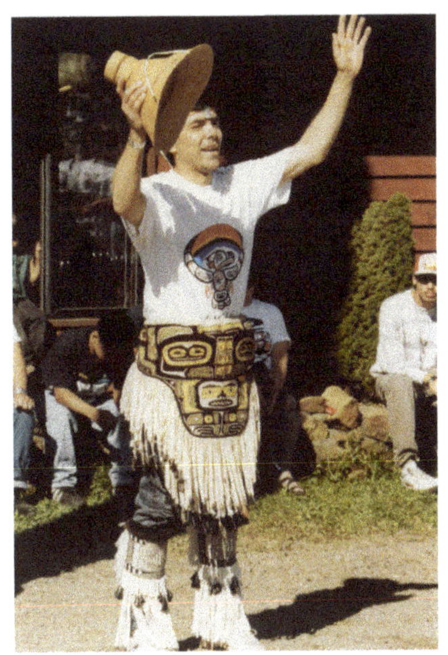
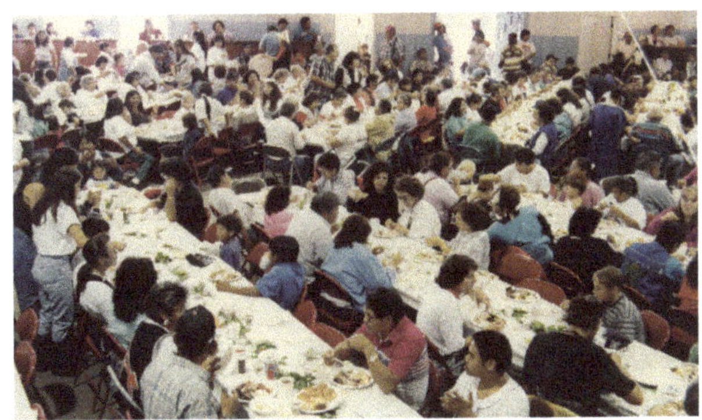
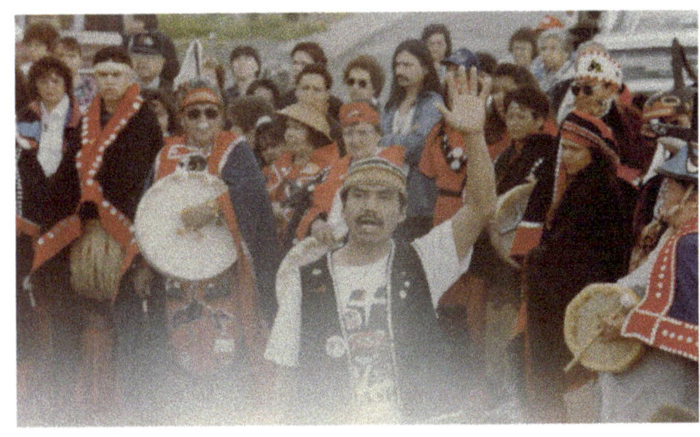
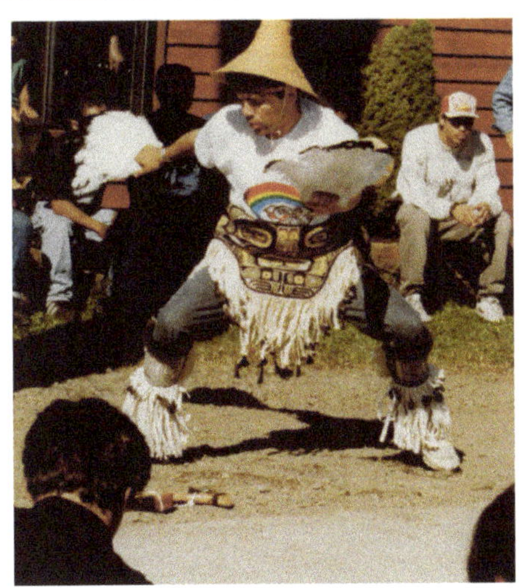
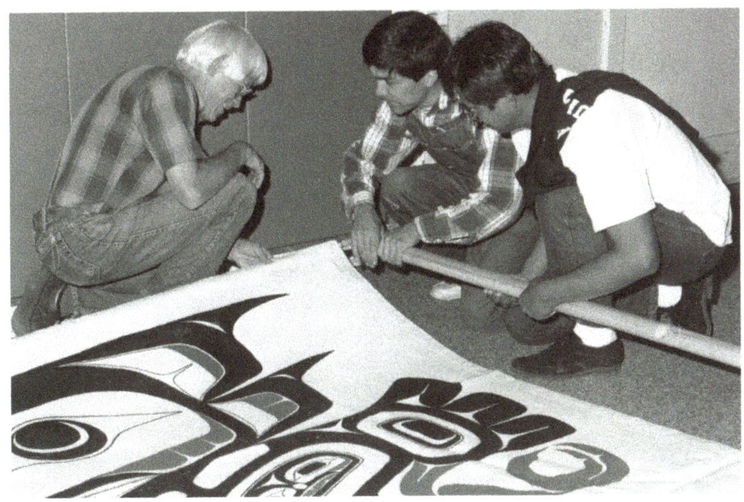

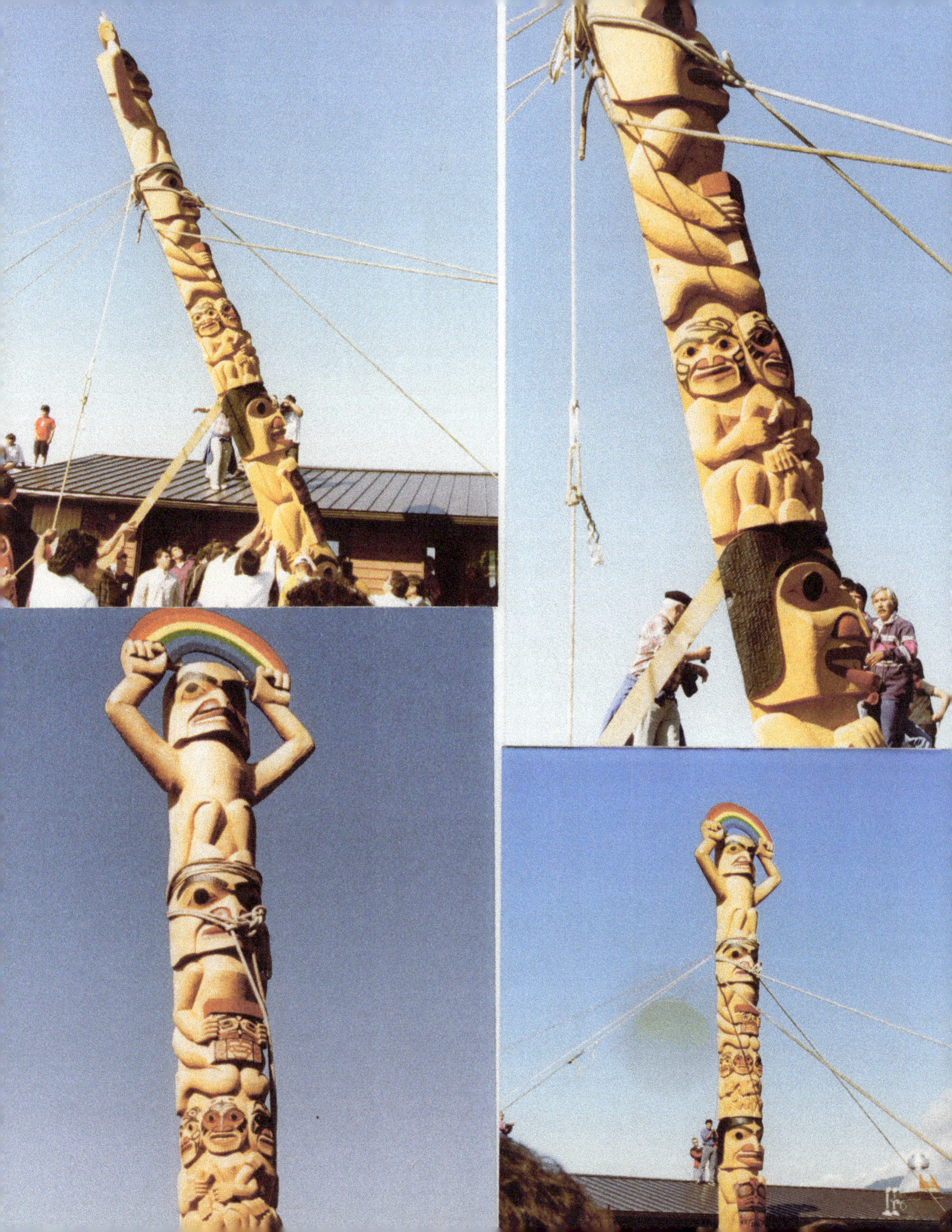

clan), G̱anhada (raven clan), and Laxgyibuu (wolf clan). It turned into this huge event. I had meetings in Seattle, Ketchikan, and Metlakatla.

I wrote a letter to the community in advance of an October meeting in Metlakatla.

Over the past dozen years, many changes have occurred culturally in Metlakatla. There has been a renewed interest in Tsimshian heritage and a rebirth of pride which surprised a lot of people not only at home but outside too. Time has flown by (since the 1982 and 1987 potlatches) and as you all know, many changes have occurred. The biggest change being that this birthday party has now become a memorial potlatch to honor my grandfather Albert Bolton.

Why am I doing this? Here are three main reasons: Number one, I loved my grandfather. He was my best friend, he was always there for me, and without his love, guidance, and protection, my life would have been drastically different. Through his example, I learned to have pride in my heritage. It is apparent to me that this is the best way to say, "Yaya, thank you."

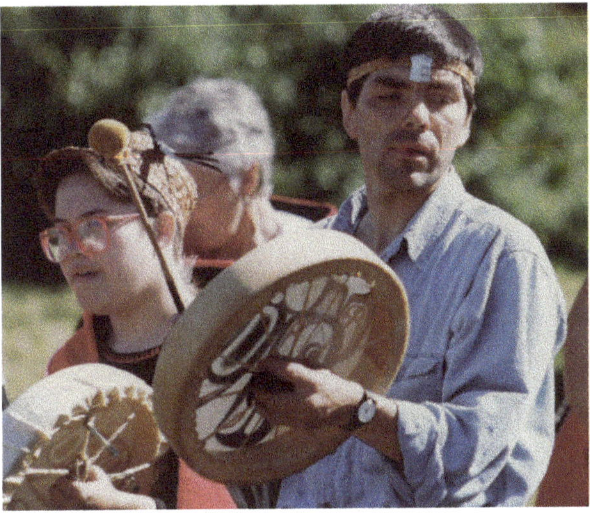

At age 13, Davey was in charge of raising the salmon pole during the potlatch. While he was doing that, I led the singing for the carver's dance.

My second reason for taking on this project is the children. The future of our people in the next century. The outside influences they are exposed to are so strong. Those influences have a way of diluting and assimilating our culture. Like a carpenter building a house, the foundation comes first, and the experiences a child has become the structure for his/her life. So, these four days in November will be unforgettable and a positive experience. The pride in who they are as Native people will help to build a generation of strong, positive, forward-looking young men and women.

The third reason is you, the people of Metlakatla. As you know, the plan is to have the potlatch spread out over four days. Why? No one individual can or should put on a traditional event like this alone. I wish to give all four clans the opportunity to share the event. In addition to remembering Albert Bolton, the people of Metlakatla can take this opportunity to commemorate loved ones, celebrate their families, clans, and individual cultural pride.

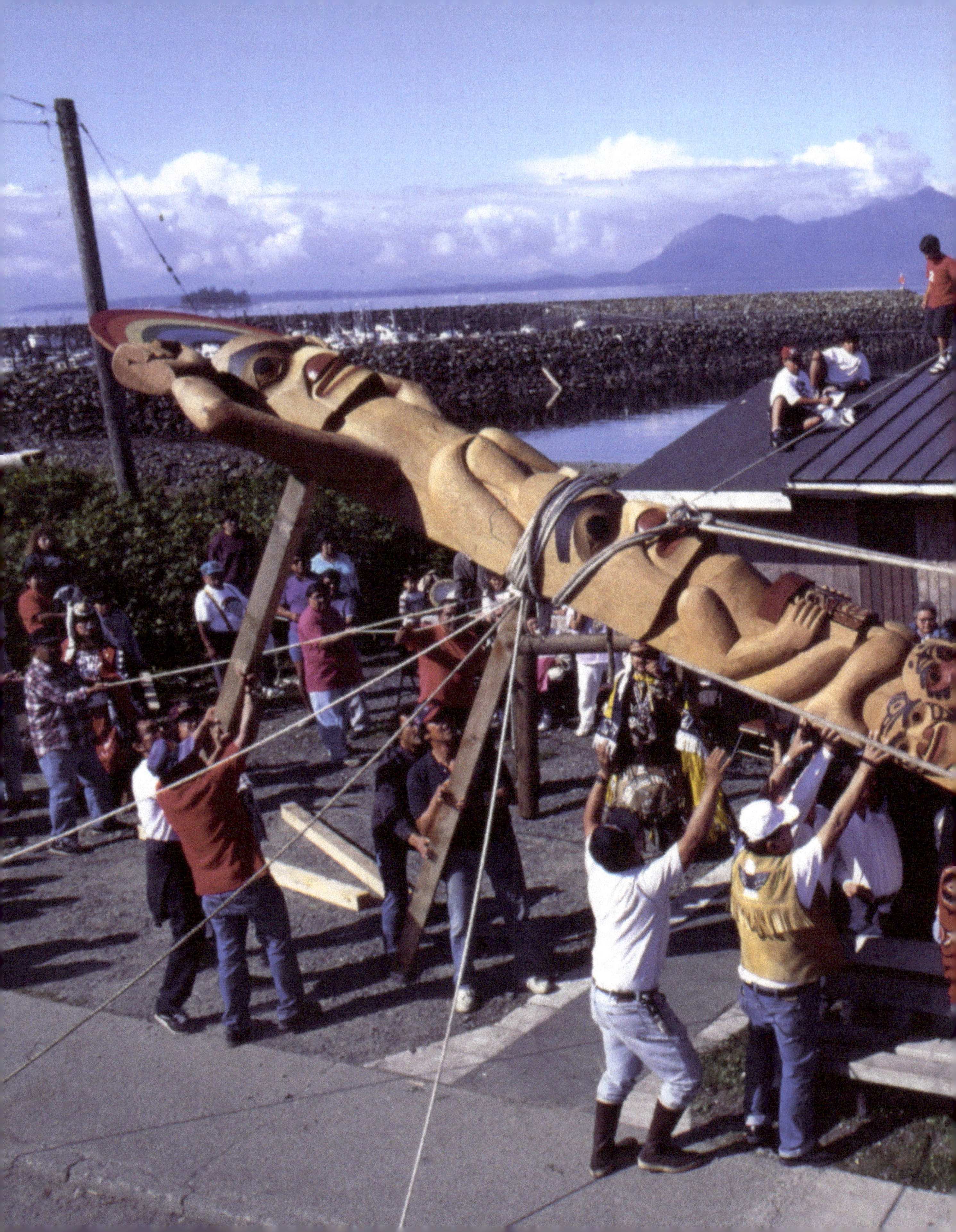

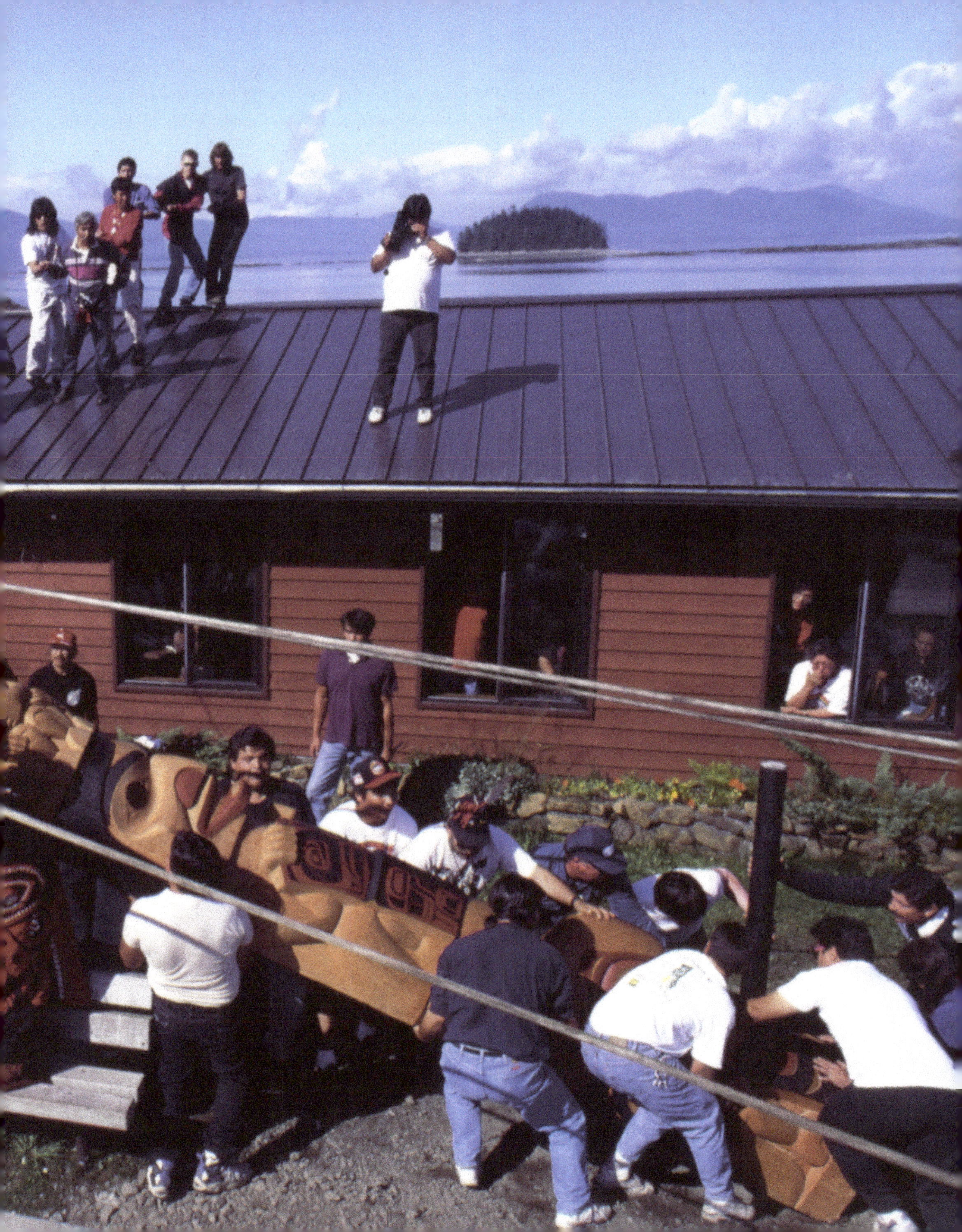

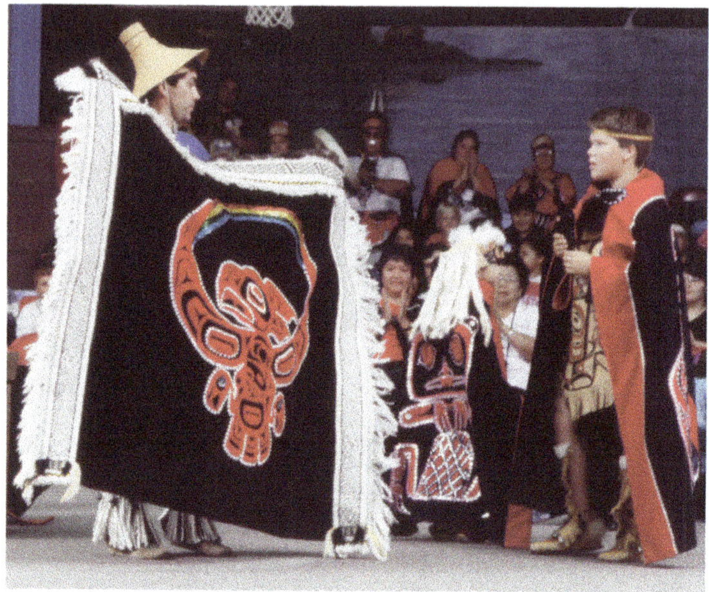

Evelyn Vanderhoop made this magnificent robe for me for the 1994 potlatch. It's a button robe with raven's tail trim, the fringe around the sides. It was her first raven's tail robe. Evelyn has become one of the most prominent Haida chilkat weavers. I had Davey help me with putting it on me. Even at age 13, he was a big part of this potlatch. He was also in charge of raising of the shorter pole, one of three raised during the potlatch.

This was the first of four nights, and we used that night to bring out all 54 robes presented. The design on my robe reflects the pole that I carved to honor my grandfather, Albert Bolton.

When I got to Metlakatla, I was challenged for my approach. Even as I had a better understanding of potlatches than a decade prior, I was still really innocent at that time. I laid out the four days: raven clan was going to be first, then the wolf clan, then killer whale clan, then my clan, the eagles, were going to be on the last day. I'm sure that were I to do this today, I would not need to be so controlling, as my people are knowledgeable about how to put on a potlatch.

There was a bit of a storm that night, and people came down to the senior center. I explained what I was laying out. I told the groups what was expected of them. Like I said before, I innocently wanted this to happen, thinking that everyone would jump on board.

One lady stood up—I didn't expect this, but I should have—and she pointed her fingers at me and said, "Why should we help you put on a potlatch for your grandfather?" And she was right. I didn't realize I was probably coming across as telling these clans what to do. That's not really the smartest thing to do.

I wanted to include the whole community. It was like a light bulb went on over my head. I said, "OK you guys find your own emcee and do whatever you want. But this is what I'm asking you to serve for the dinners." I stuck to that. And I stuck to the idea that we'd have memorials—each clan would be in charge of their own memorials. We'd have the button robes dedicated on the first night, so people could have their regalia.

I learned that our own people are tough on each other. People were really hard on me. People always think you have some ulterior motive, you want to get rich off of something. I was doing things because I wanted them to happen. I wanted to bring my own people with me. I was really innocent and naïve about that. I thought everybody would just jump on the bandwagon. It was heart breaking to hear the insults second- or third-hand. It was hurtful.

But after that woman challenged me, the potlatch caught on. They all went off on their secret meetings. They had their own headquarters. They looked to certain people who became leaders of each clan. It was amazing. When the potlatch happened, every day was unique. Every day was special. Every clan hit home runs with what they did. Lots of folks came. Dance groups came from all over Southeast Alaska and Canada. It was beautiful.

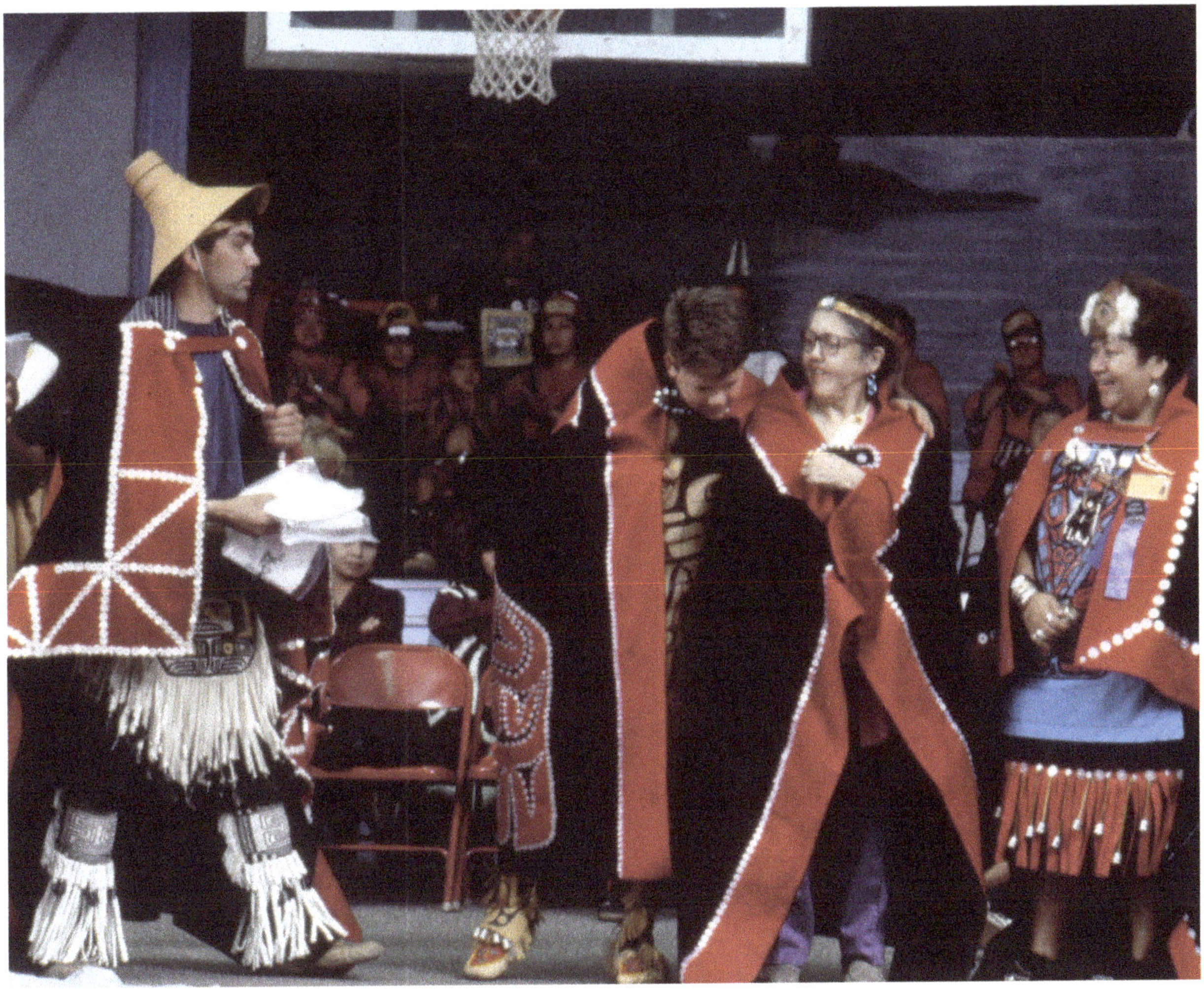

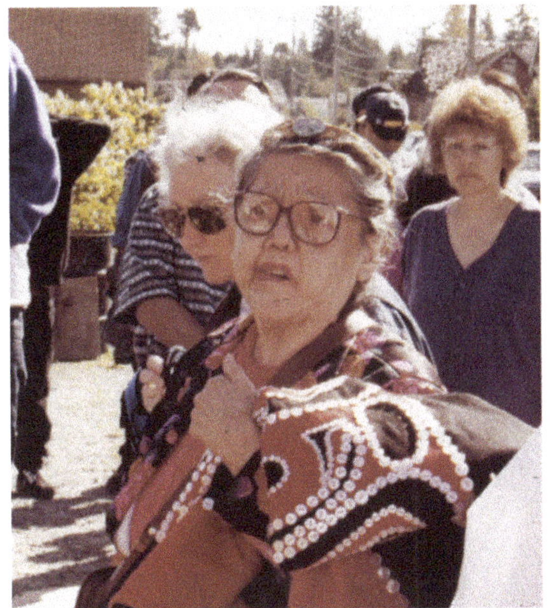

This photo carries a lot of memories. I surprised my mother with her one and only robe, and Davey helped present it to her. My good friend Theo Bayou is there because she is one of the people who made the robe. It was the first night of the potlatch and there were 55 button robes dedicated that night by various people of different clans.

When my mother's presentation was done, they all danced to a button robe song that I wrote. It was the first and only time that she danced in her life. She never wore it again.

Seventeen years later, at my mom's potlatch, I gave that robe to Floyd Guthrie. That headdress that Theo's wearing I made for her in 1982. The hat I'm wearing belongs to Haida weaver Delores Churchill, but she let me borrow it for the potlatch.

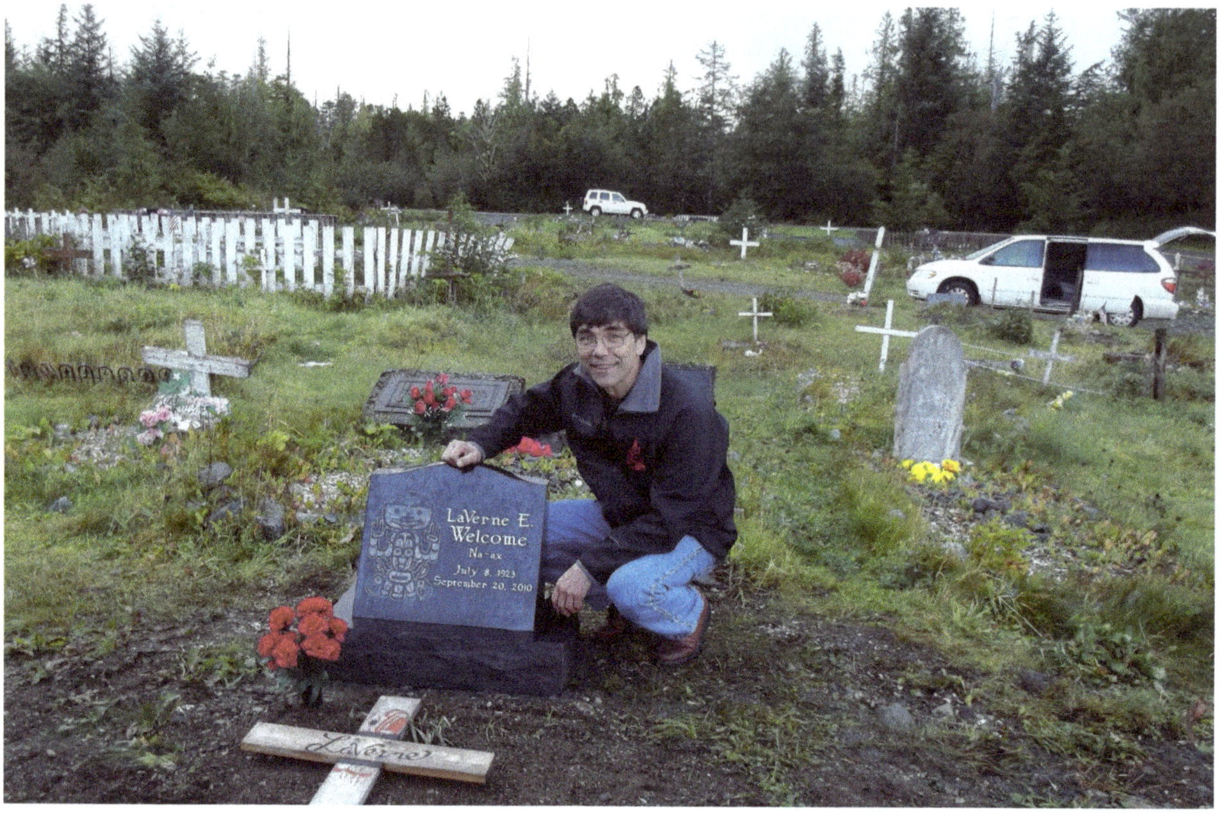

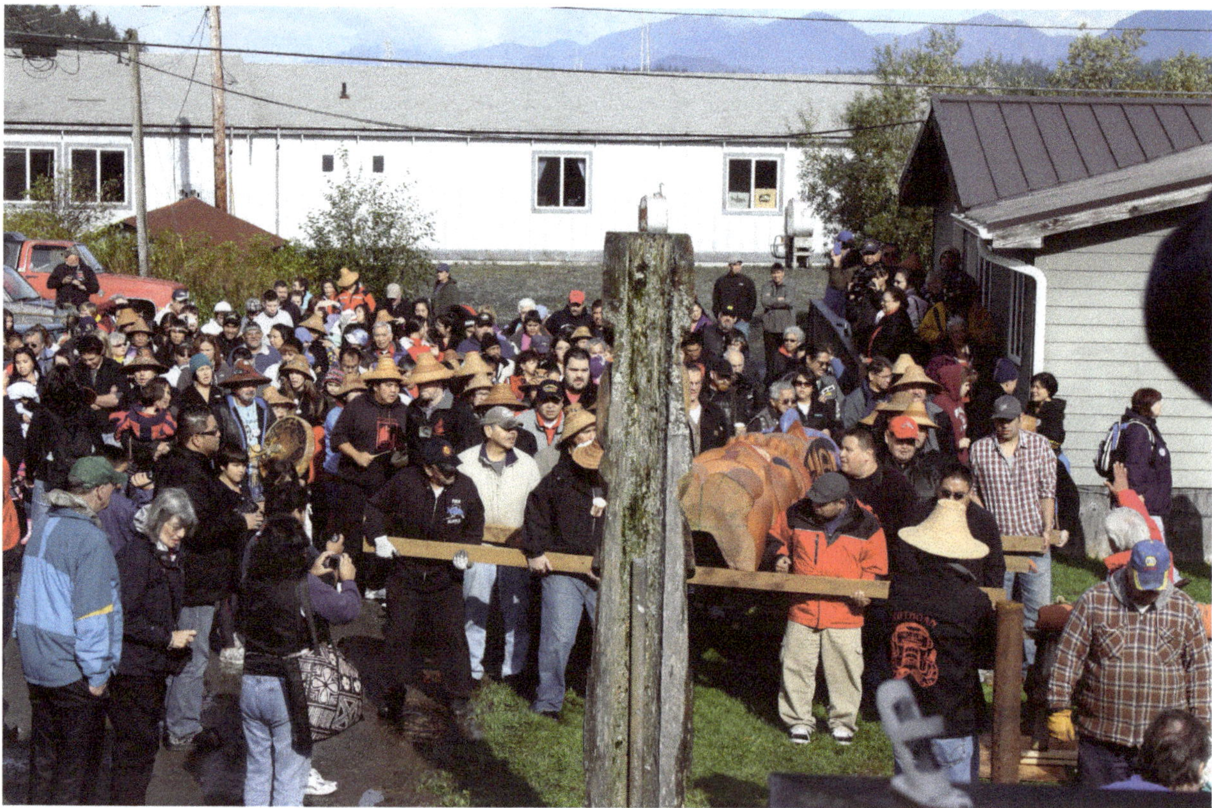

All I had to worry about were the totem poles and to help the eagles with the last day. We raised three poles that weekend. I got some help from my late friend, Wayne Hewson, who died suddenly in 2022 and whose work with me becomes increasingly more significant to me. Since the potlatch, he worked with me on ten or twelve poles. We did a couple in Metlakatla. We did two for a park near Issaquah. He would always tell people, "I've got to go bail out Boxley again."

We grew up in two different worlds in Metlakatla. Mine was a real safe environment because my grandparents were very protective of me. I didn't know a lot of things that were happening to some people in my village with alcohol and drugs.

But Wayne saw and experienced it all. You couldn't have two more different guys than Wayne and me. But we just liked each other's company. He was extremely open and honest about his life. I realized how I grew up in a different world, this safe world my grandparents created for me. He didn't have that.

When I went home for his memorial, I brought a letter from him that he wrote in 1987 when Metlakatla celebrated its centennial. It was a week after the Fourth Generation dancers first performed. When we had started practicing, he had come with his two sons to watch. I called out to him, saying we needed more guys to be dancers. He wasn't sure about that, but he joined them, and he eventually became a very important part of that dance group and one of its leaders.

He said in the letter, "I've always wanted to be a Tsimshian. Now I really feel like one." I've kept that letter all these years.

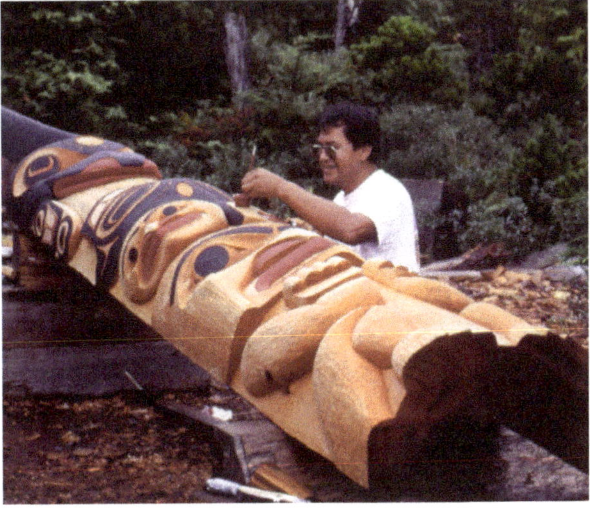

Wayne Hewson finishes painting his first pole for the 1994 potlatch. It was on the third day of the potlatch. I helped him with the carving and design, but it was mostly his work. He carved a bunch of poles after that. He's got more than a dozen poles standing in Ketchikan, where he carved in a workshop so tourists could watch poles being carved. Carving and dancing changed the direction of his life dramatically, and he began to make a living as a carver.

Thirty years after Metlakatla's first potlatch, it was time to organize one for my mother. She wasn't a high-ranking person. She was my mom. I wanted to do something to honor her because of the hard life she had. Some of it was the fault of her struggle with alcoholism. Some of it wasn't. She had terrible things happen to her when she was young, an accident that disfigured her face. She had a lot of health problems because of that. That was a turning point in her life, and I'm sure it affected her in more ways than one.

She worked hard for the community. She was very involved. She would give kids a hard time for dropping trash on the street.

Celebrating Community

Honoring my mother

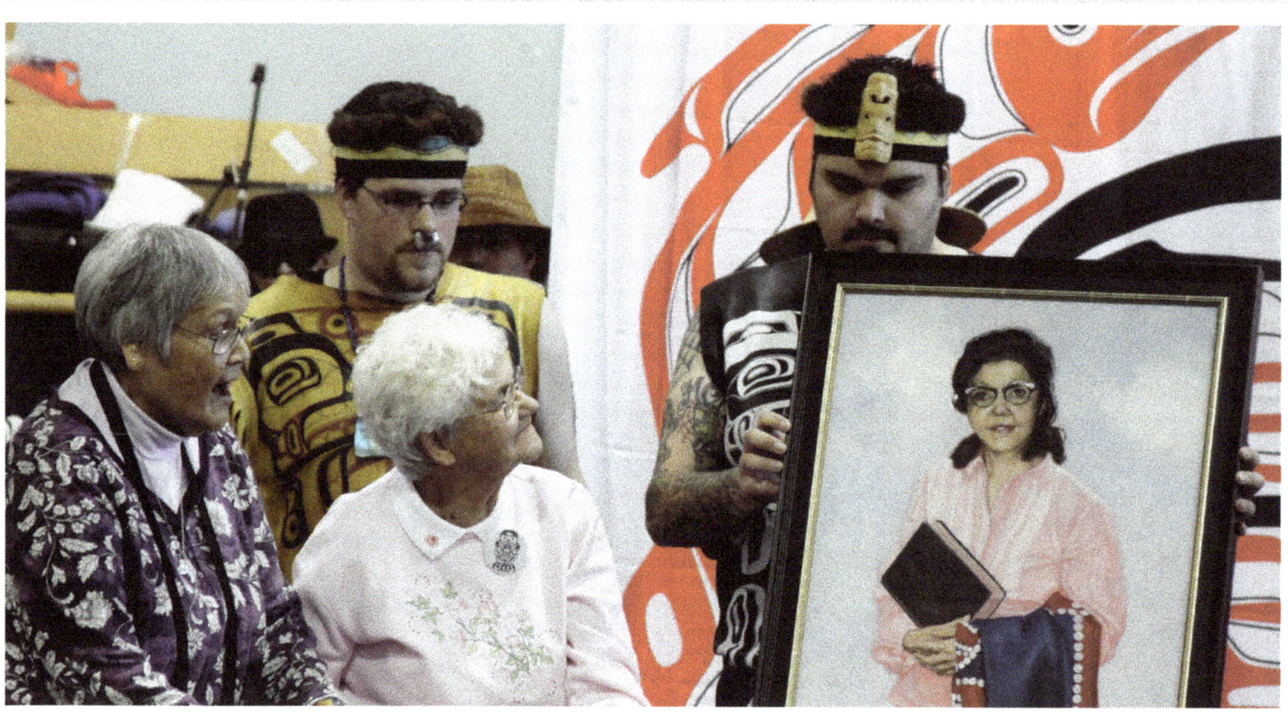

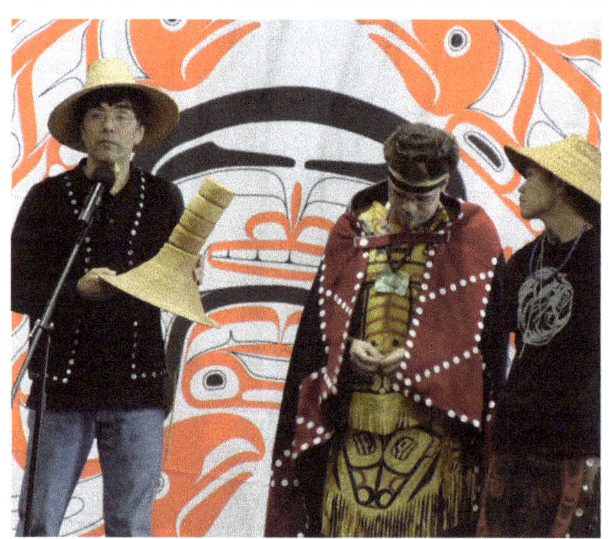

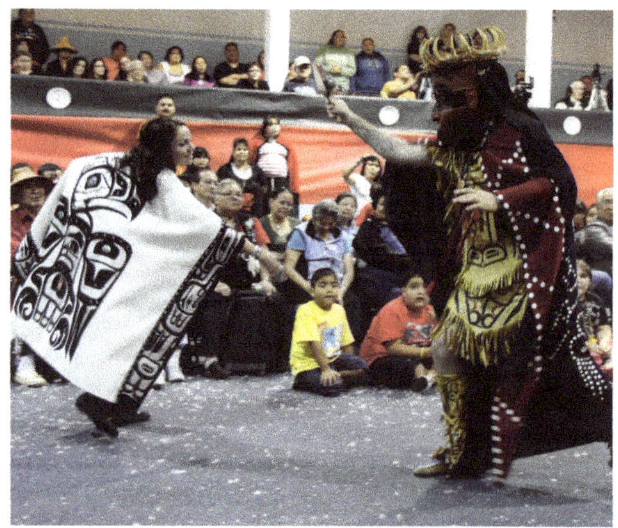

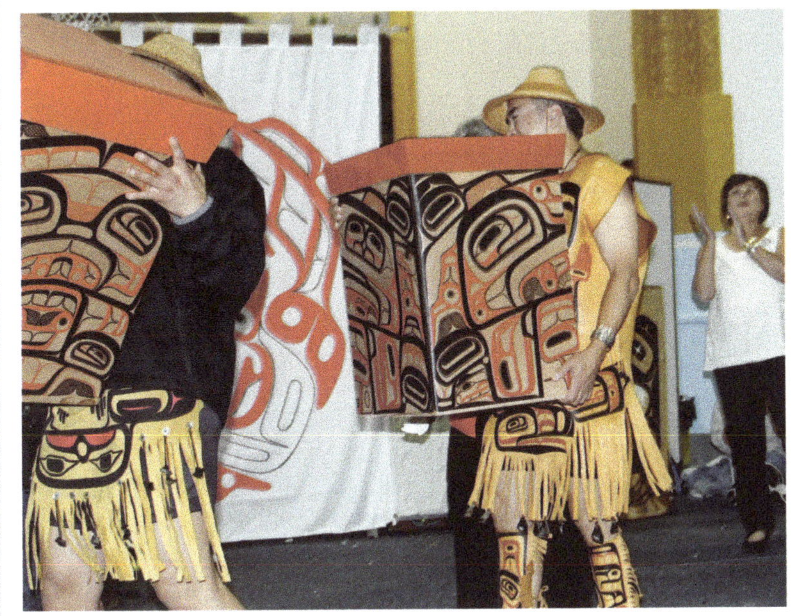
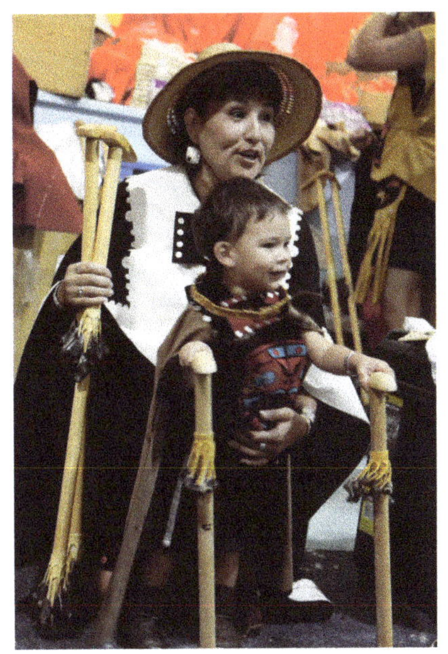
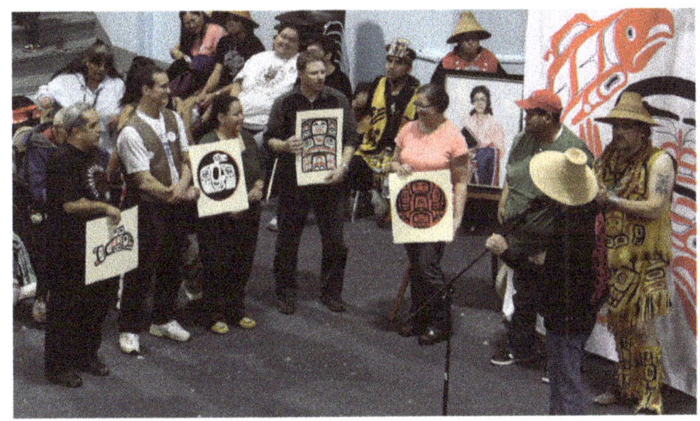
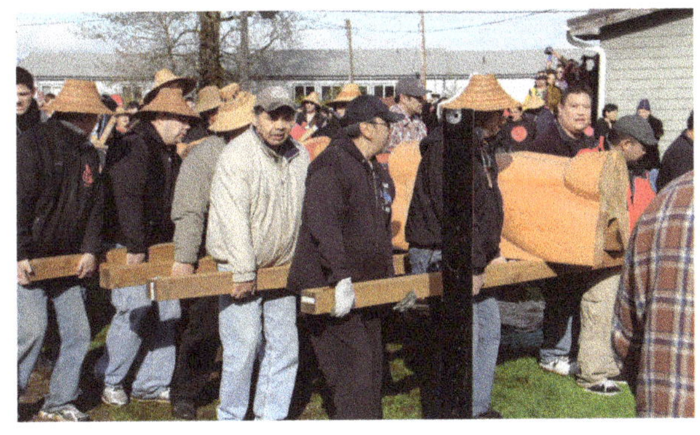
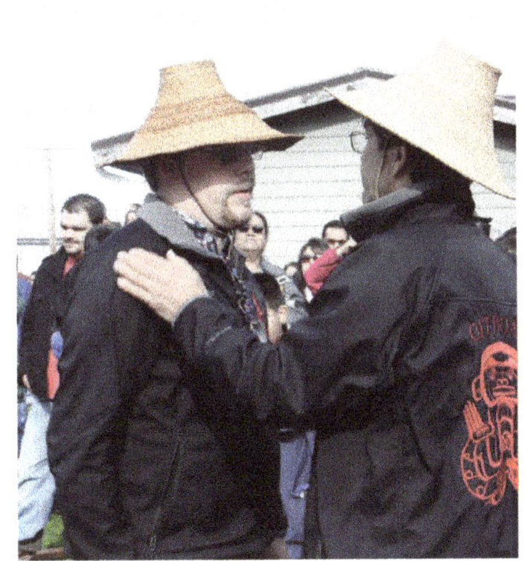
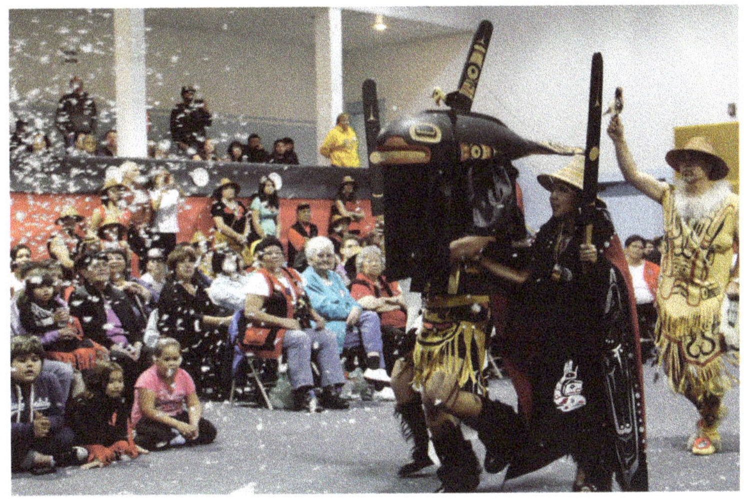

Later on, the schools had a trash pick-up day around town in her honor. Those significant things that she did for the community—the work she did at the museum and the community-wide clean up—it all needed to be talked about.

But I didn't carve the pole for this one. I had Davey carve it. He is Laxgyibuu wolf clan, and I commissioned him to carve the pole. It was an honor for me that he would do it. He did all the work. I didn't touch it at all. It was quite a day when he raised that pole.

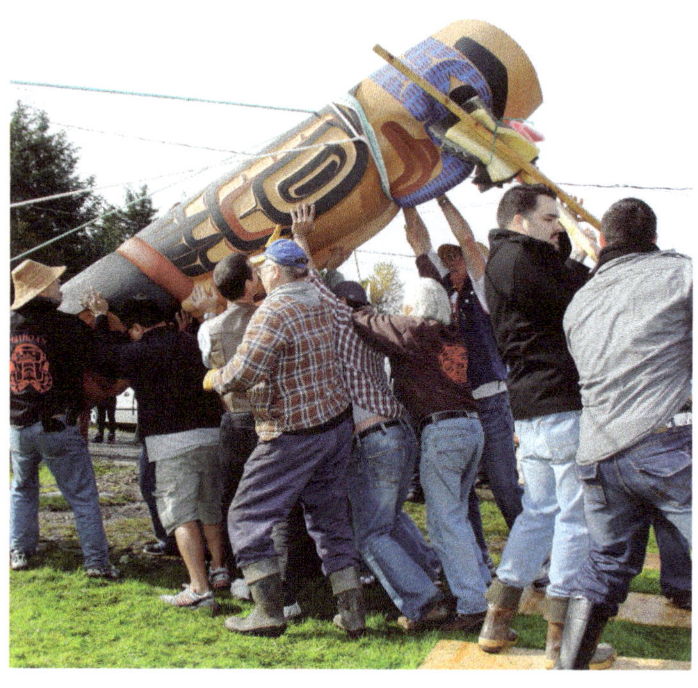

I asked my good friend, Tlingit carver and culture bearer Nathan Jackson, to lead the pole raising at my grandmother's potlatch in 1982. Then, thirty years later, he directed the raising of my son's pole at my mother's potlatch. Nathan was not just a fabulous artist; he was a culture bearer. There are not many people like that.

Nathan had a lot of struggles and illness when he was young that kept him from being a fisherman. But I saw the influence he had on so many other artists and Tlingit people in general.

I had nothing to go by when I was trying to revive Tsimshian culture. I could see what the Tlingits were doing because they were right across the water in Ketchikan. I could see what the Haida were doing too. They were ahead of us. They had dance groups. They had artists who were making things all the time. In Metlakatla, in the fifties and sixties, we had guys making band saw totem poles, like you see in the curio shops.

Nathan was a connection to the old people. He knew about the old style of dancing. He's really solid when it comes to Tlingit culture. Robert Davidson is the same way with the Haida.

Before I made my first chief's headdress, I went to Nathan's house to ask him how to do it. He has a very different kind of teaching style. He put his headdress down on the table in front of me and said, "Look at it." I looked around at his artwork, and I watched him and what he did over the years. It was very impressive to me. I wanted to be like that. I realized that I wanted to have an influence, not only just by what I did, but also by the way I live. ❖

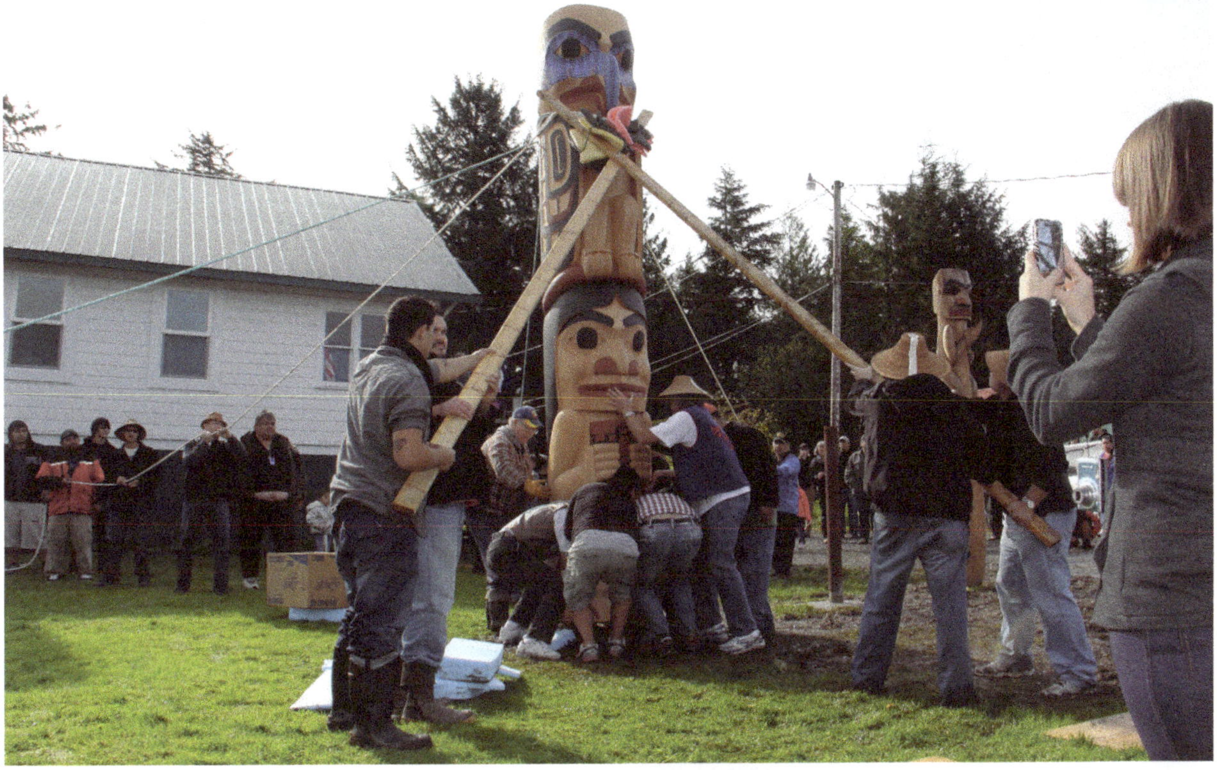

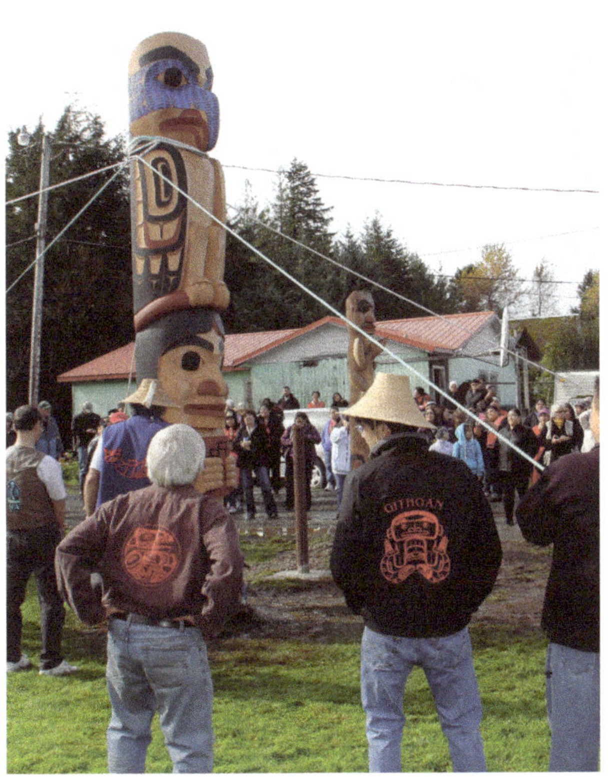

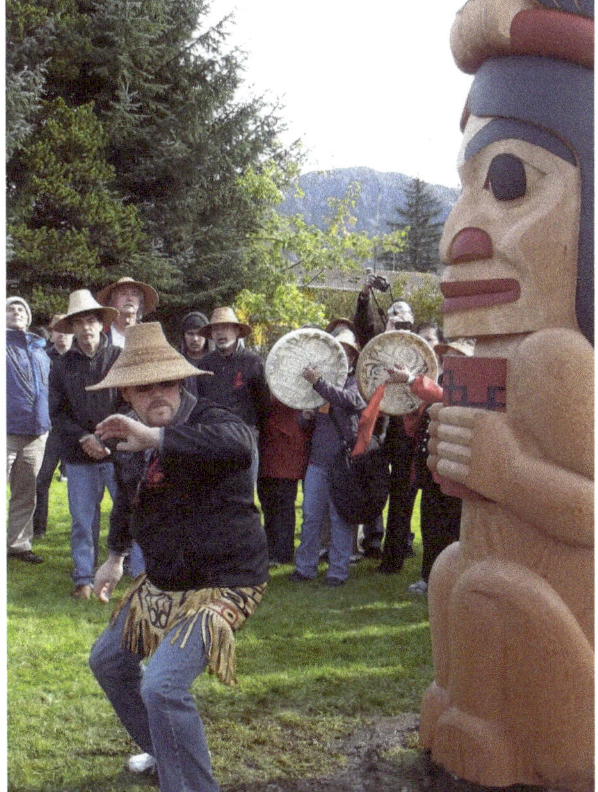

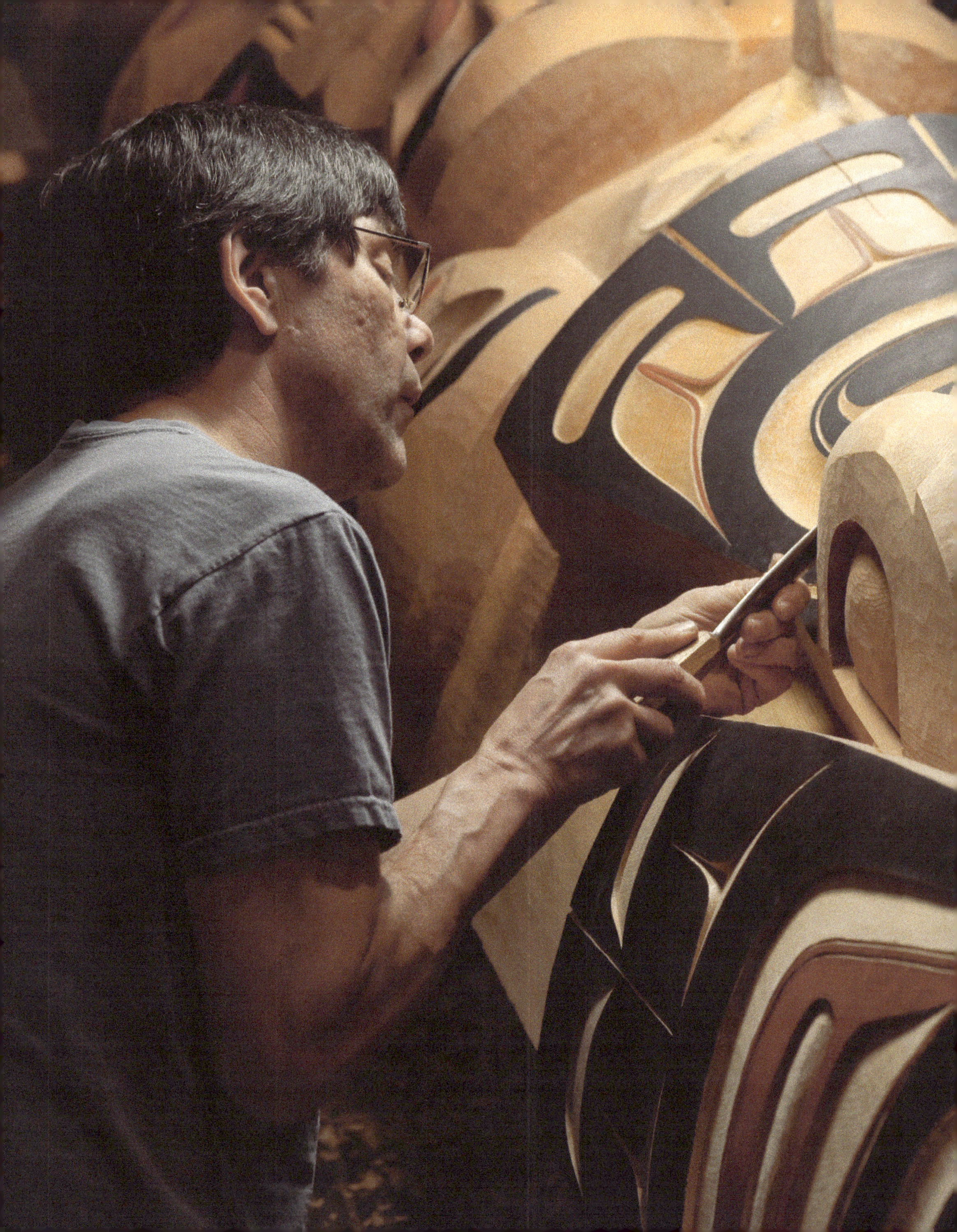

CHAPTER FOUR

GRANDFATHER OF TOTEM POLES / *Niis Bupts'aan*

There's been an amazing rebirth of totem poles for all the Southeast Alaska tribes: Tlingit, Haida, and Tsimshian. Everybody is carving poles full blast now, even though it's getting harder and harder to find more cedar.

Poles stand in villages where there were once none, and I mean some of these places had nothing for years. Now, some villages have entire cultural parks where several poles stand. That revival is all connected to celebration and ceremony—the potlatches.

We aren't just producing art; we're also leading the way in the use of our ceremonies. They are directly connected: the pole raising; the payments and the public witness in the potlatches. All of it. It's all so tightly linked.

These poles are a critical statement of sovereignty. What carvers are producing today are statements, not just of the strength of the Southeast Alaska Native culture but also of the endurance through many decades of being treated poorly. They are a living art form that is of central importance to Native culture on the Northwest coast.

We, as artists, also get hired to carve totem poles for non-Native clients, but there are an awful lot being made for villages and Native functions. One of the things I bring up every time regardless of whether non-Natives accept it or not, is that the ceremony makes the pole real, giving life back to the tree. If I'm doing the pole for Natives, they know that's what I want to do.

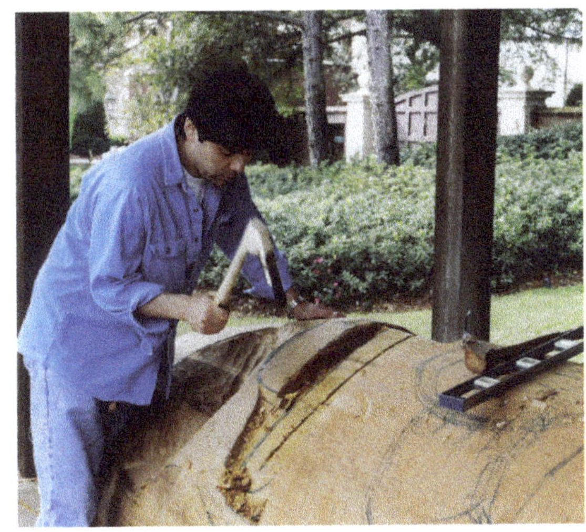

I spent three months working at Epcot in Orlando, FL. It was ultimately the first of three poles I would carve for Disney World.

I tell the people who are not Native, "This is what we do, and it's up to you." I tell them, "You don't have to. You own it, but this is what we do, and it makes it more real." Most of them have said, "Let's do it." They invite their friends over, have something to give away, and feed everybody.

This rebirth is a double-edged sword for me. On one hand, it's really exciting to see other folks putting up poles with potlatches and ceremonies. It means our culture is surviving and stronger than it was for a period. On the other hand, that old growth red cedar is going away.

You know, the Sm'algyax word for red cedar is "am ga̲n." It means, "good wood." That's because our ancestors used it for everything: houses, canoes, totem poles, bentwood boxes, bark for clothing and hats. All the tribes in the Northwest coast used red cedar. All of them. Red cedar is just a perfect tree.

It breaks my heart because it's really difficult to find the wood now, even from the few guys left who run the mills. I've lost numerous sources for that wood. It's cool seeing the next generation get involved; but as someone who is right next to this change, it's scary.

I want to do this for at least another ten years. If I can get the right commissions and if I ever get a chance to buy an extra log—as long as it's reasonably priced—I'll buy two or three logs and store them. Those days may be done. I feel sorry for Davey and Clifton Guthrie, one of my apprentices. They may not have the opportunities I have had.

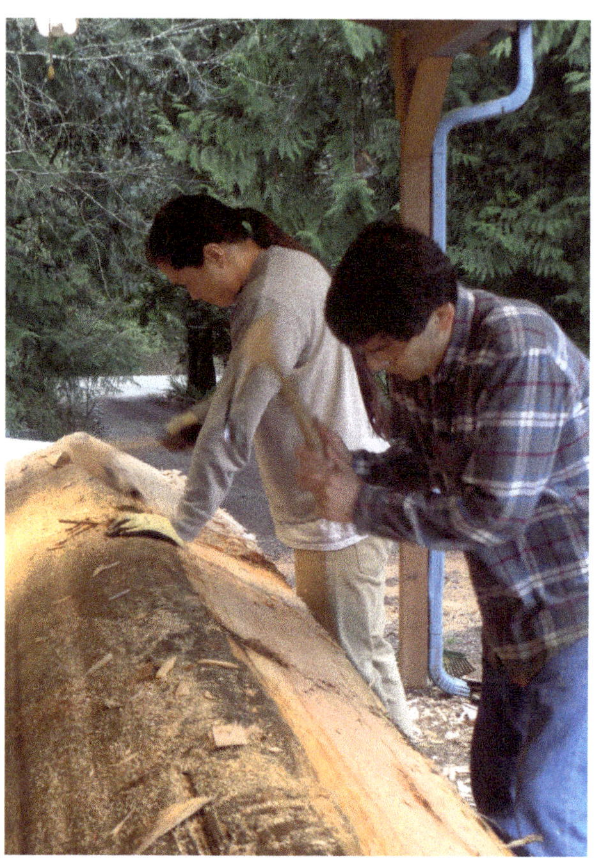

Here I'm working wth Dylan Sanidad in my Kingston shop prepping a log. Dylan went on to become one of my apprentices, producing his own art.

If I'm lucky—and I've always stressed how fortunate I really am—I could find myself carving a hundred totem poles before I retire—and my grandfather will have been with me for each pole. That's because the first time I strike a log to begin carving a new totem pole, I use an adze that my grandfather and I made more than forty years ago. I look at the adze hanging with others in my workshop and recall the effort behind making that tool.

Yaya and I went out to another part of the island in Metlakatla, and we brought a hacksaw with us. He took me to a car junk yard with a bunch of old wrecks. He looked around and he said, "Right there, right there." He was pointing to a Volkswagen Beetle lying upside down. It was really old. I didn't know what he was talking about.

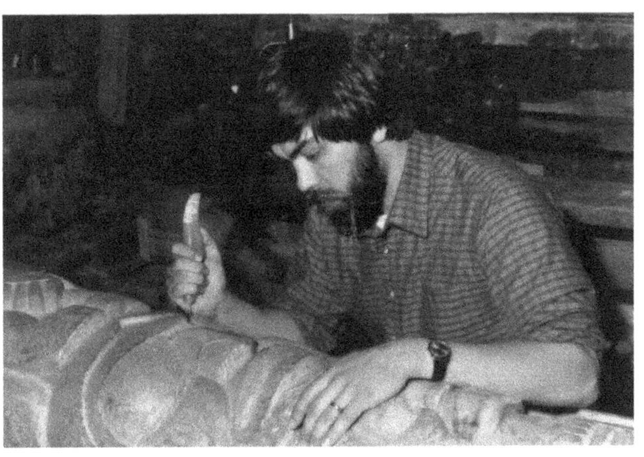

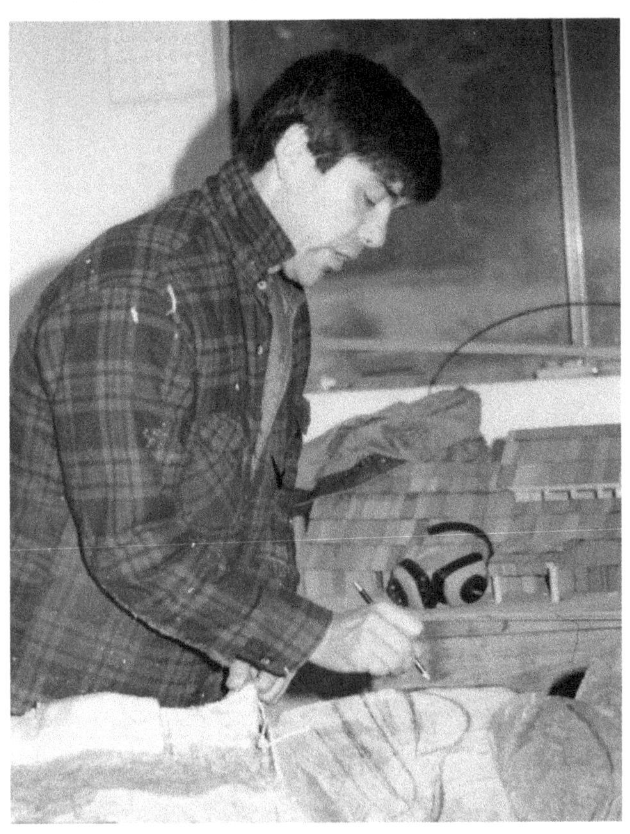

These are some of the earlier days of my carving in Metlakatla and Kingston, 1982–86.

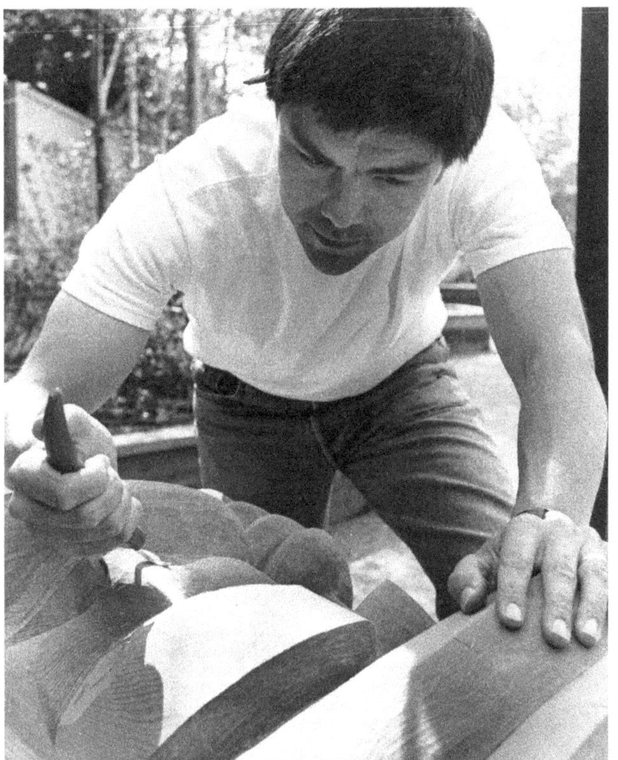

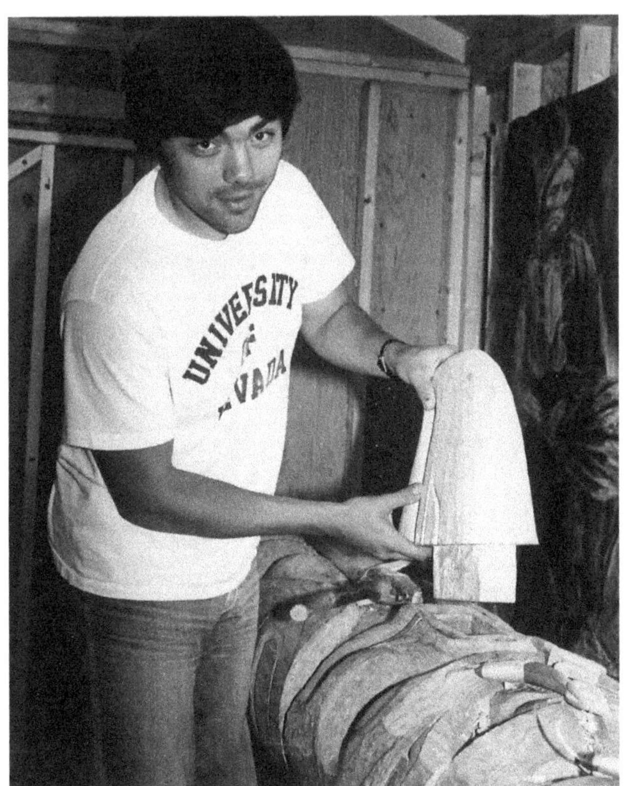

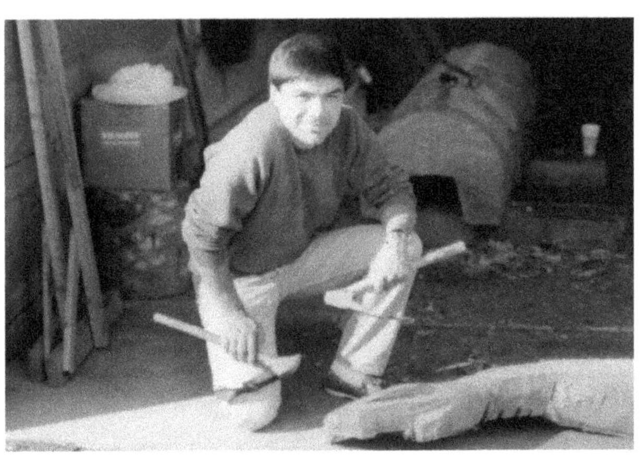

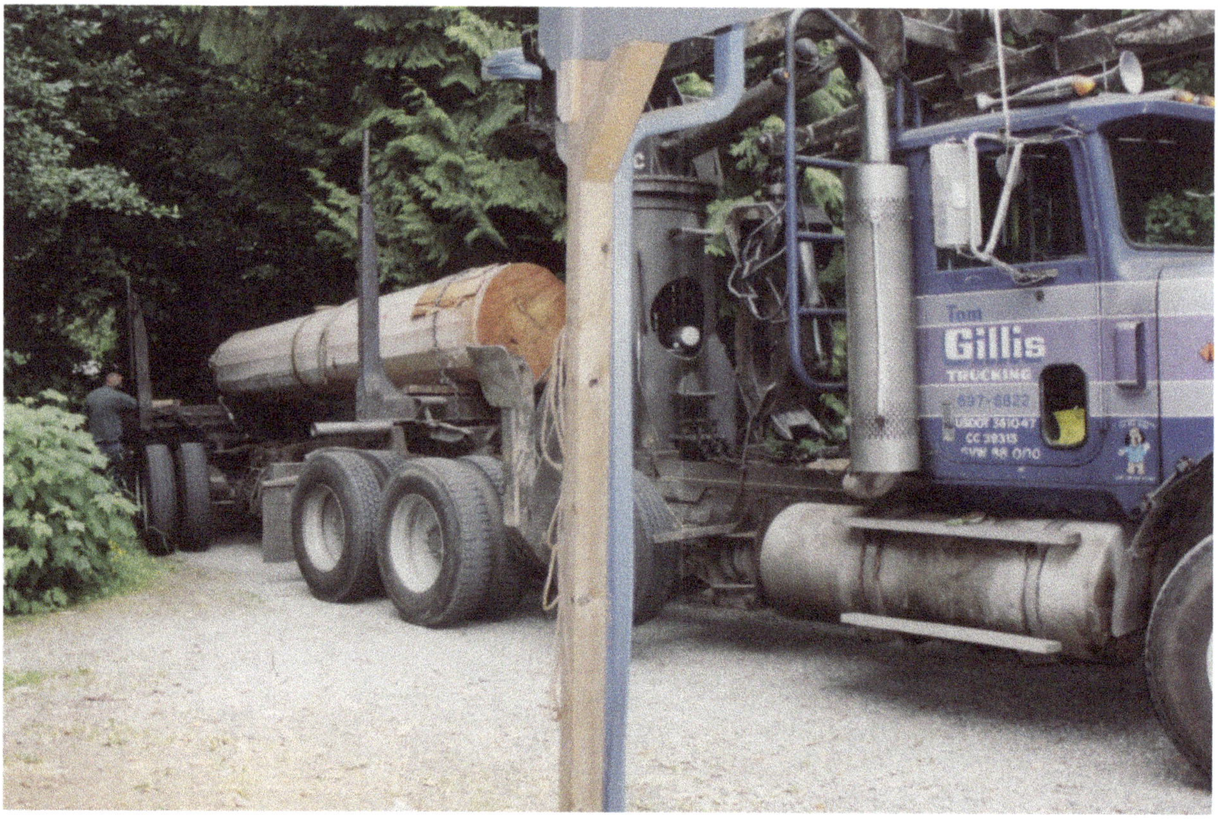

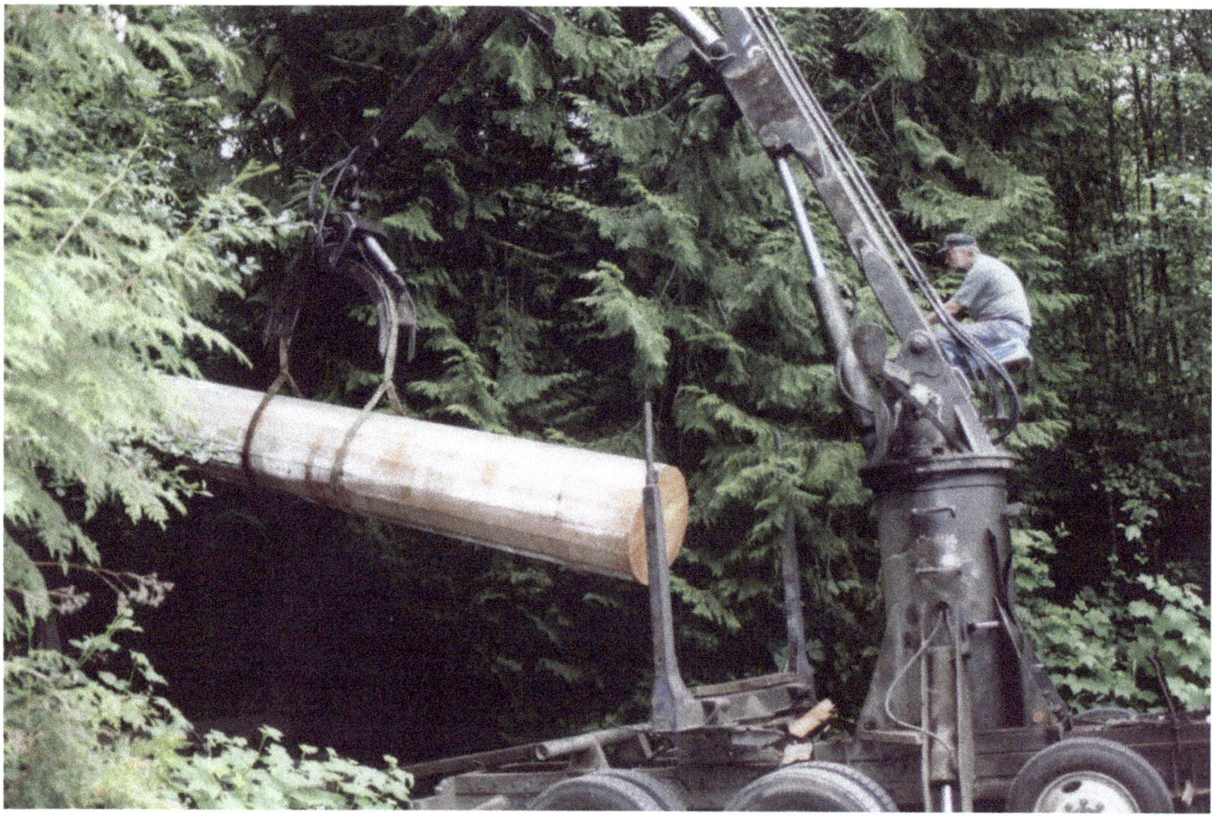

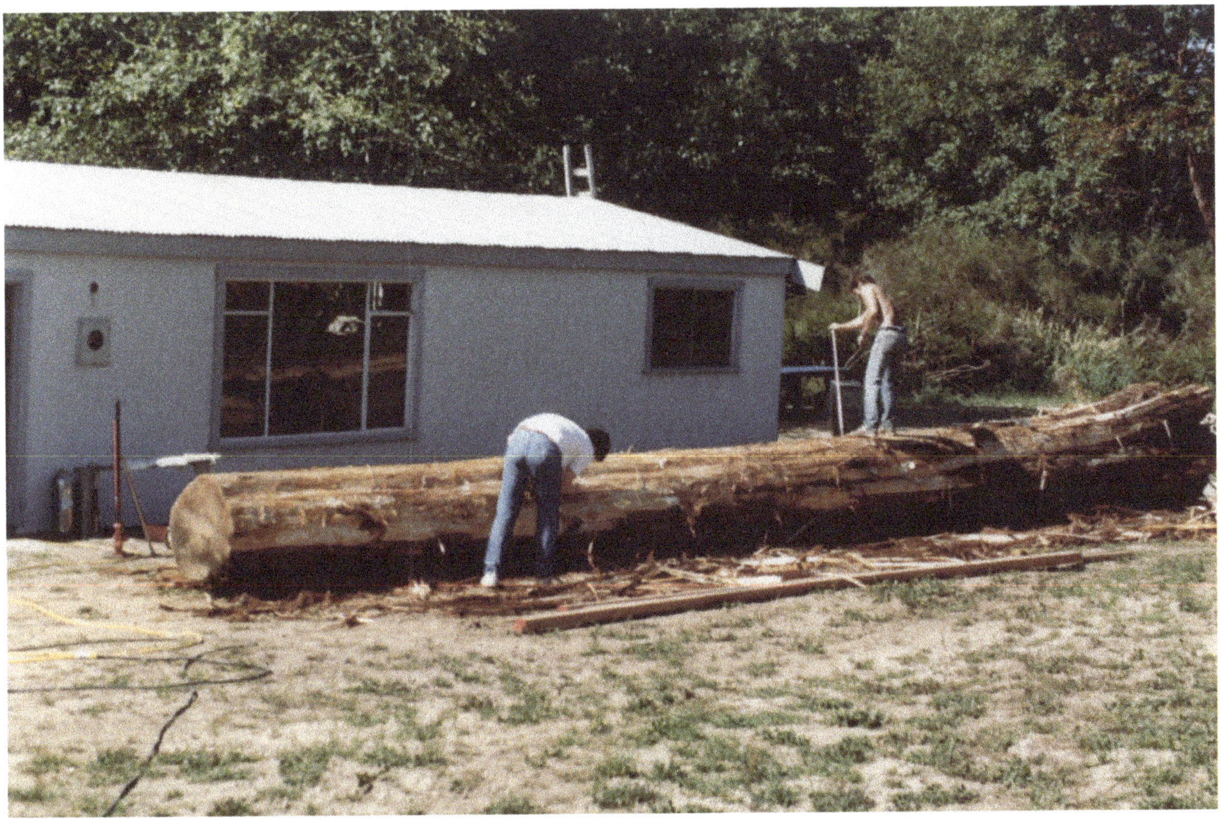

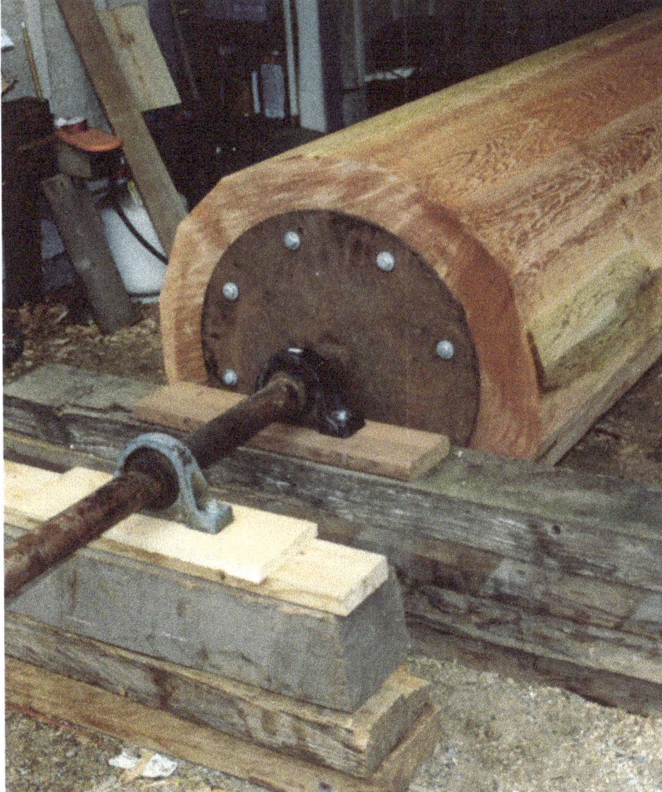

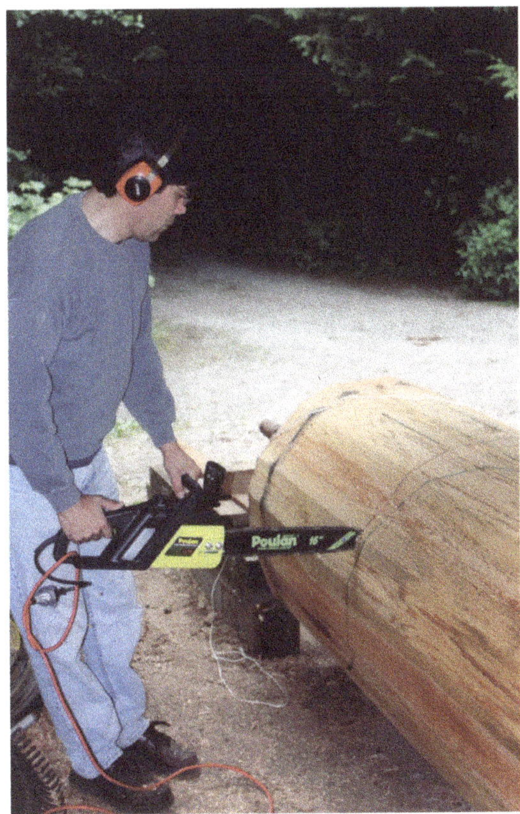

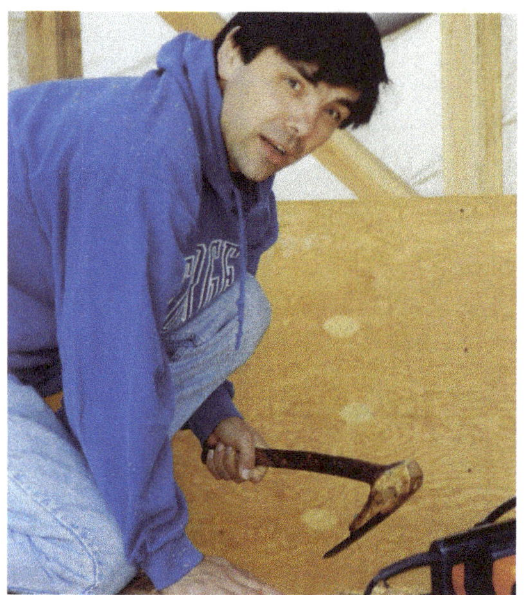

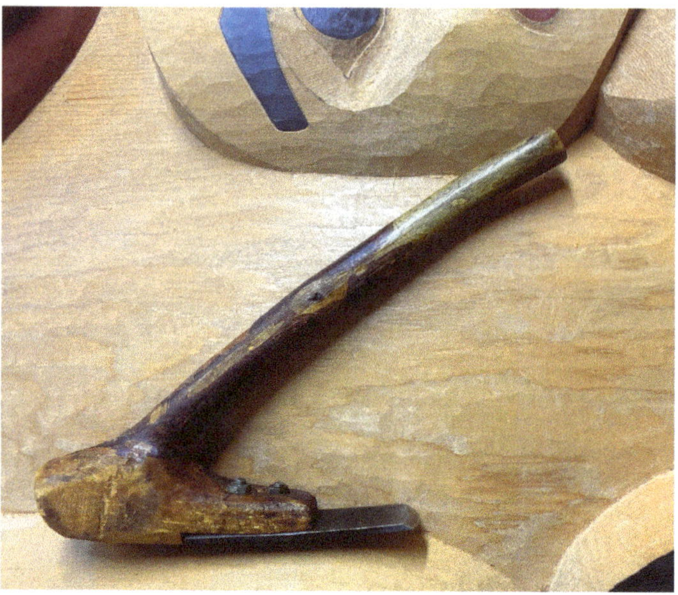

Though I'm right handed, I'm somehow holding the adze I made with my grandfather's help in my left hand. Regardless if which hand holds the adze, I treasure it and still use is almost 40 years since making it.

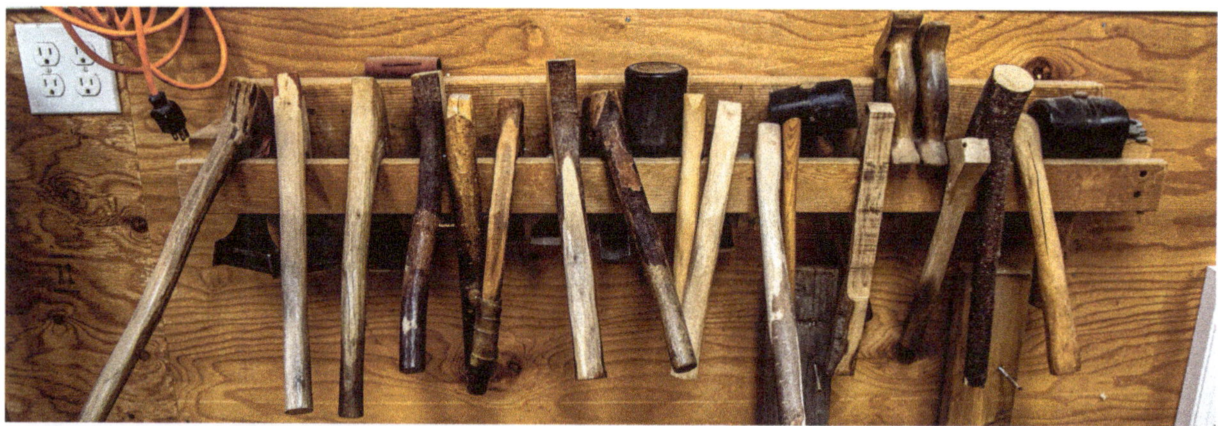

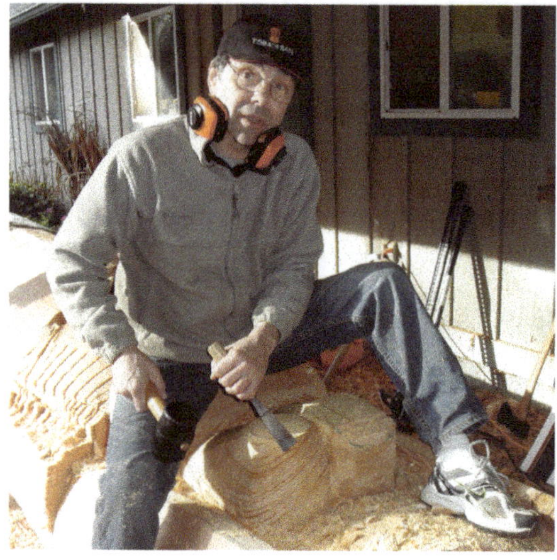

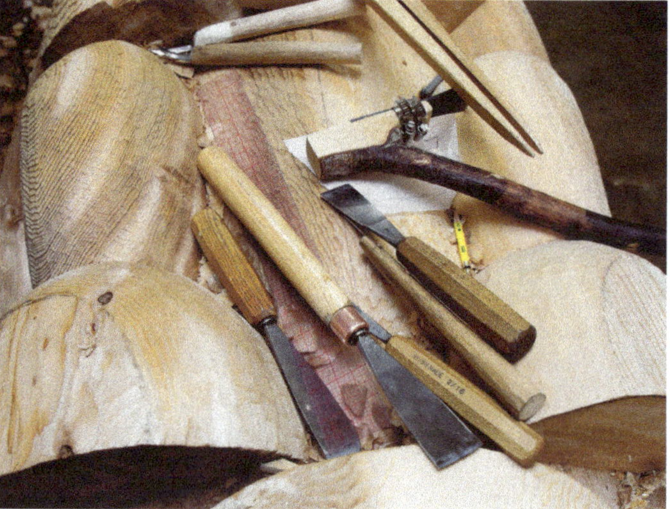

But he was pointing to a leaf spring. A Volkswagen Beetle's leaf spring has a curve in it that's perfect for adzes. It's not flat. It has just a slight curve. He pointed to it, then picked up a rock and he scratched where he wanted me to cut, then he said, "OK, cut that off." It took three hours to cut through it.

We cut it off and then we went into town to the metal shop in the high school. My grandfather knew so much about working in a shop and working with tools. So he drilled a couple of holes and he found some screws. Then we went back out. That was the first time I ever saw anybody choose an adze handle.

Where you hold the adze has everything to do with the efficiency of cutting with it. The old people somehow figured out that ninety degrees from the tip of the blade is where your thumb should be. If that works, then the motion is just effortless for the carving.

I've never made another adze blade. I bought all the other adze blades that I own except for this one. This one means the most to me. It means the most to me because my grandfather taught me with this adze. Every time I look for a handle for my adzes, I make sure it's the very same angle. That first strike belongs to him as much as it does to me.

When it comes to my work, you have to separate totem poles from everything else that I make because I never had a teacher or mentor to learn from. Everything I know about totem poles I taught myself by looking at old pieces in the museums, looking at photographs, and making lots of models. When I first started getting interested and discovering that I could carve, I started looking for books at bookstores and gift shops.

When I was starting, I got a bunch of yellow cedar and sugar pine. I got myself some Exacto tools. I just started copying Tlingit and Haida poles. That's all I knew. That's all I had access to.

But I was just really crazy about it. If I really like something, I go overboard. I made lots and lots of model poles, you know, eighteen to thirty inches tall. I was selling them for twenty dollars or thirty five dollars a pole. Today, I'd charge five thousand dollars. Eventually, I started making these six-foot, seven-foot, eight-foot poles. They were not Tsimshian looking totem poles, stylistically. They were kind of like bad Tlingit totem poles. All I had for examples were the poles in Ketchikan, Totem Bight, the Tlingit and Haida poles, and in Saxman. I'm not saying those poles were bad. I'm saying my interpretations were bad.

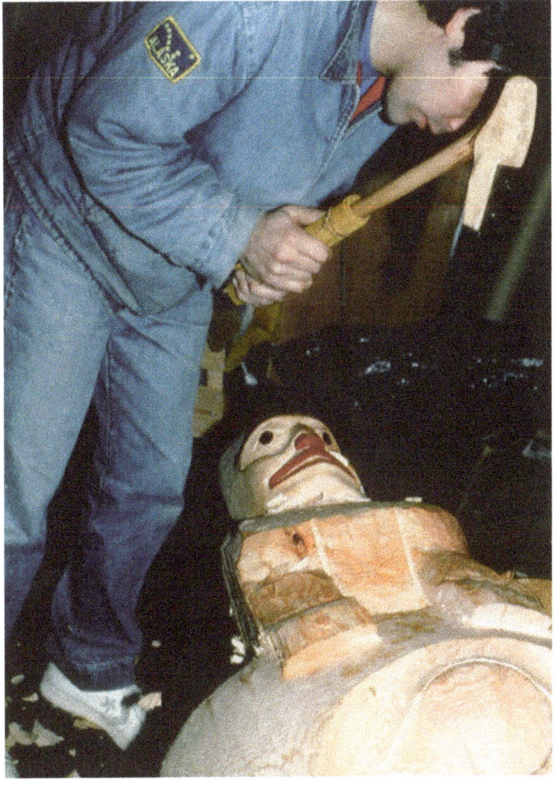

In 1983, I carved a pole for Metlakatla's swimming pool. At the time, I was making about $300 a foot. I was meeting with the principal and superintendent, and they asked Jack Hudson how much should they pay me. He said $700 a foot is the going rate, so I went from $300 a foot to $700 a foot in several seconds. The reason he was at the meeting was certainly out of respect for Jack because he was a Native arts teacher at the time. I was grateful at the time, no question.

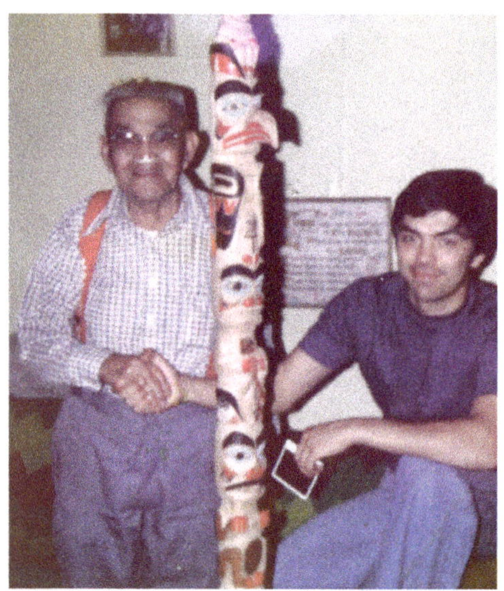

I finally began making model poles that looked Tsimshian and not Tlingit or Haida. My grandfather was with me when I carved my first large model pole.

 In the early 1990s I worked closely with childhood friend Bob Leask on this King County Arts Commission pole. The project started in Kingston and eventually moved to Issaquah where people could watch us work and ask questions about our Tsimshian culture.

started carving in Tsimshian style in the early 1980s when I visited the Royal BC Museum in Victoria, BC. The museum is dedicated to the Northwest Coast tribes, and the third floor has some totem poles. I remember sitting on a bench, trying to figure out what made the Tsimshian poles different.

I realized something about the angles and the planes—how big the eyes and cheeks were—of the Tsimshian style faces. They were different from the Tlingit and Haida poles that I had been making. My work changed after that. Even to this day I do things that have directly been influenced by those unknown carvers who put so much time into the faces and very little time into the hands and feet. There are beautifully carved faces of humans, birds, and animals. There was no one around to teach me Tsimshian carving like this, so I became self-taught. But Davey says I still learned from the masters whose art is preserved in the museums. Looking back, I see his point.

I just wanted to be a Tsimshian artist. I didn't know what that meant at the time. I knew there was more to discover. I didn't know who to ask. But Davey's right: I still had the work of the old masters to emulate.

There are a lot of things I consider when I carve. When I stand in front of a pole, and it doesn't have a mark on it, it's just a log then. I think, What have I got myself into again? There are certain things I do first. I make sure everything is symmetrical before I do any kind of details. I can't stress how important symmetry is.

I've got to make sure my drawing is done to scale. I've got to make sure everything is blown up to the size of the log. I'm constantly working on that. I measure how far things are, just to make sure everything is even. I fuss over it. I don't make a cut until I'm really sure it's going to be the right cut.

I really enjoy roughing out the pole, getting rid of large amounts of wood. I enjoy the whole process. I enjoy seeing the shapes emerge from the wood. Any doubts that I have or any nervousness goes away when I get to this point. Once I've got the measurements to where I want them to be, then I just have to do what I know how to do.

You have to really make sure you're drawing your design to scale and you know where everything is going to be. It's nerve wracking to start with. It can really be a moment of, "Uh-oh." That's because there's no room for error; you know, once you cut, you can't put the wood back. It's an expensive mistake if you cut the wrong thing. But, I've found that once I get past the initial roughing and I get rid of the main blocks of wood, then it's just art.

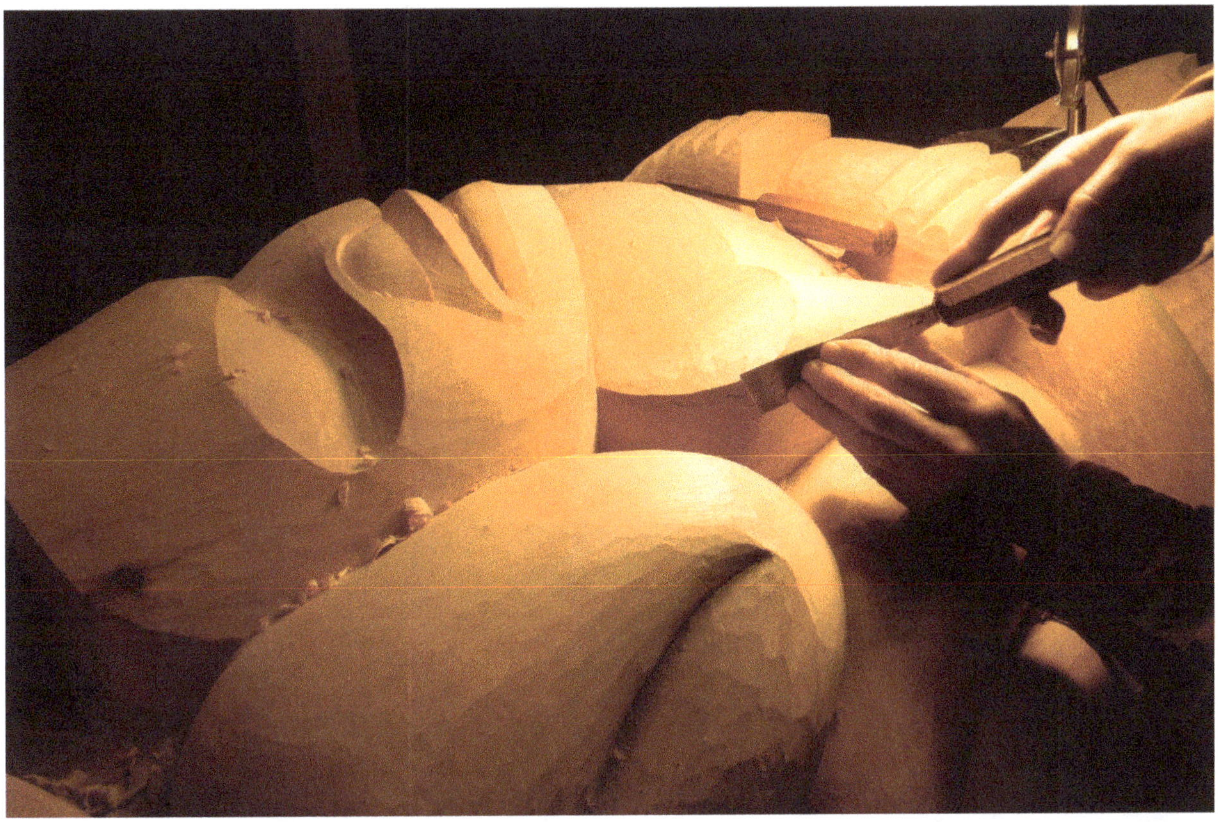

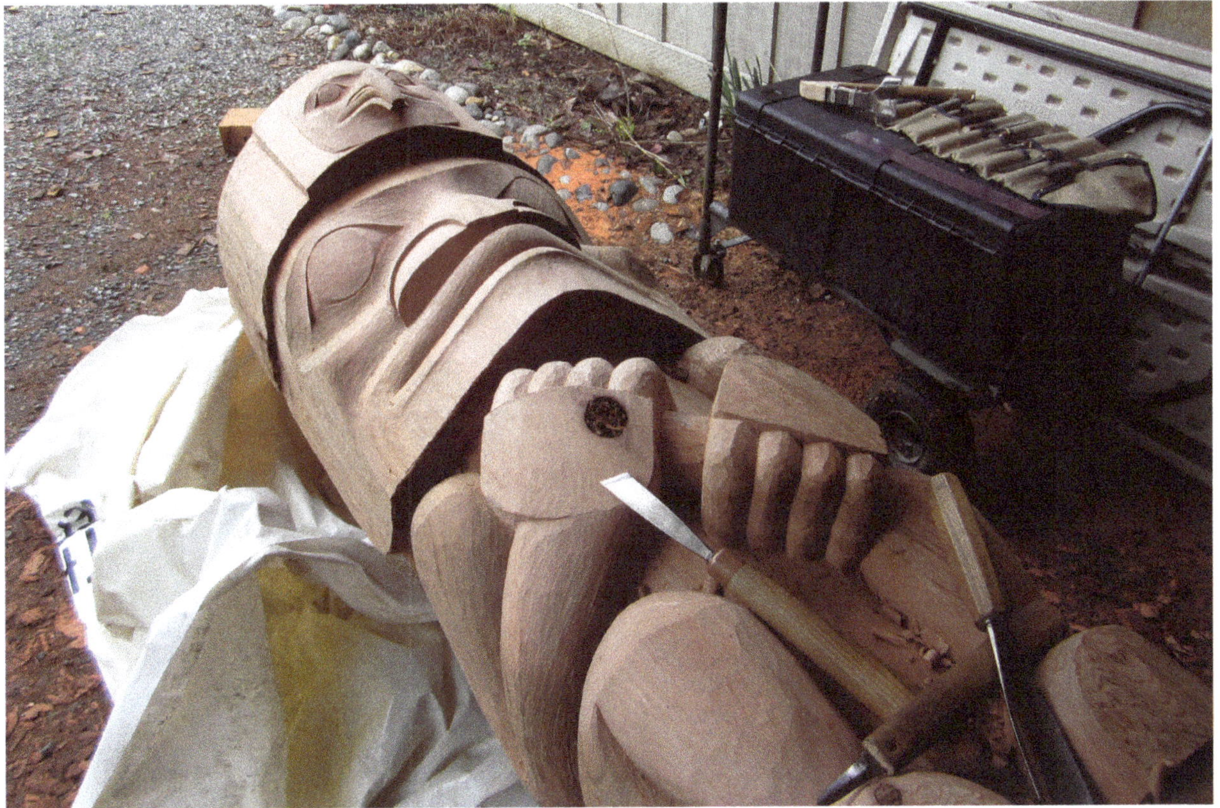

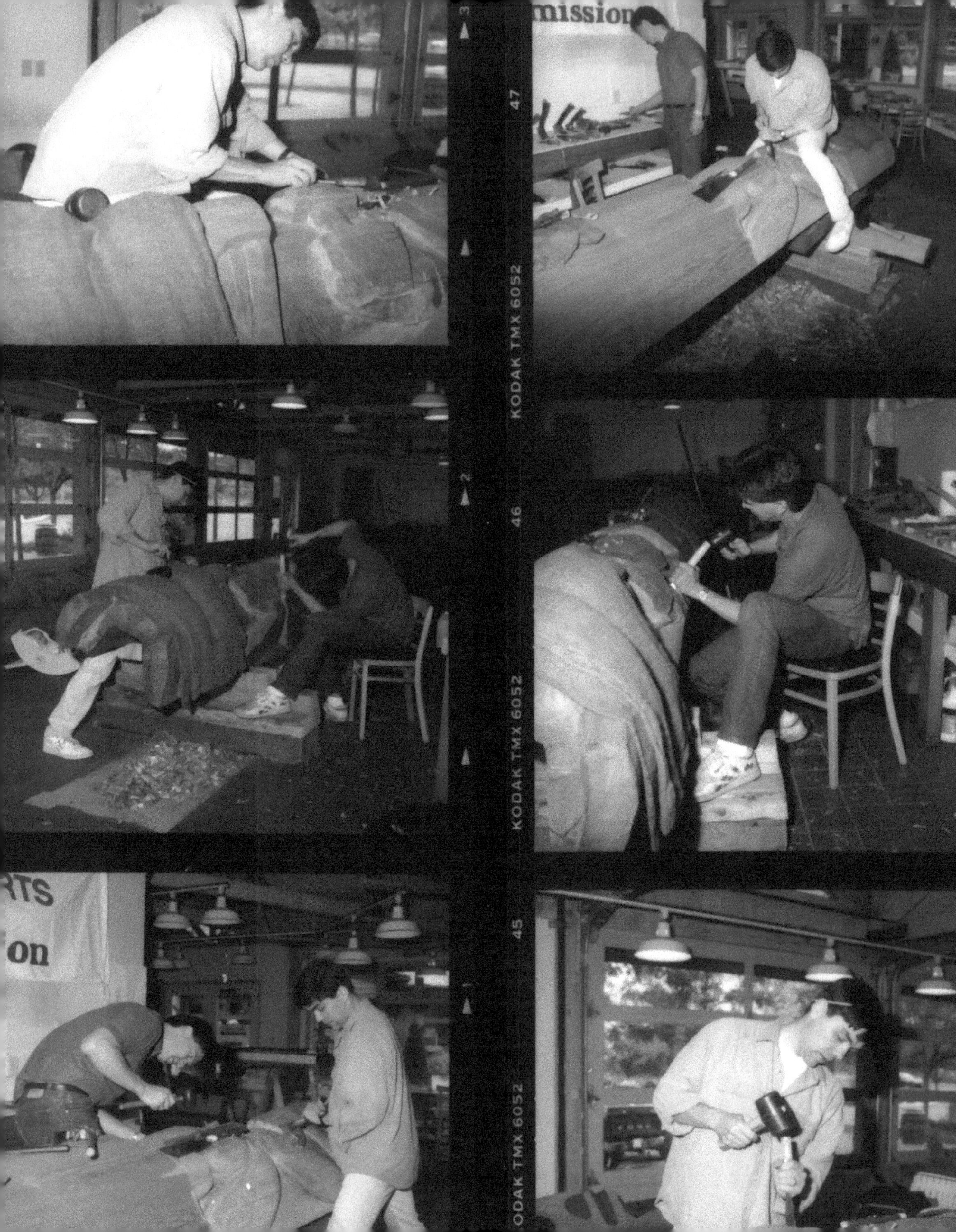

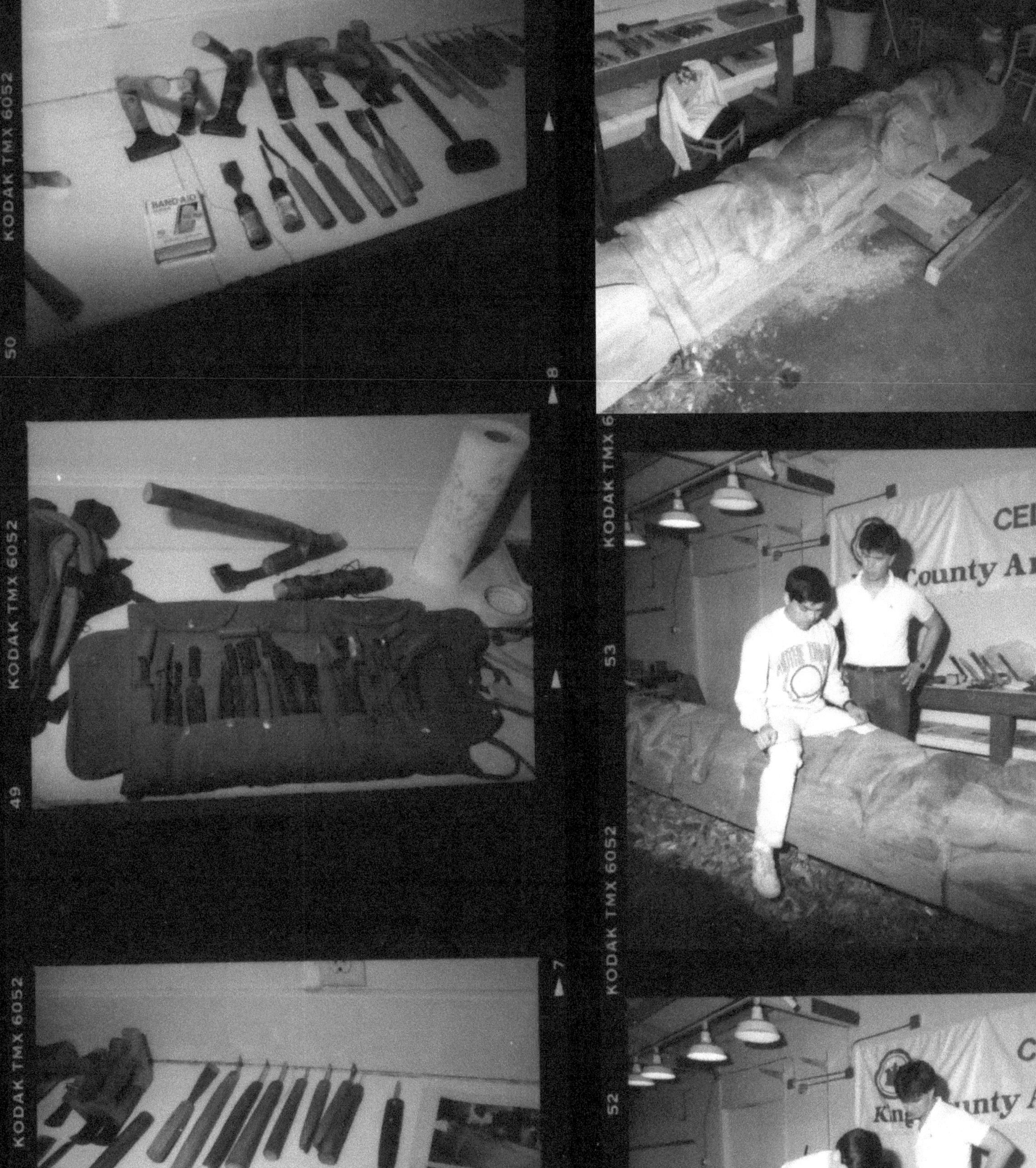

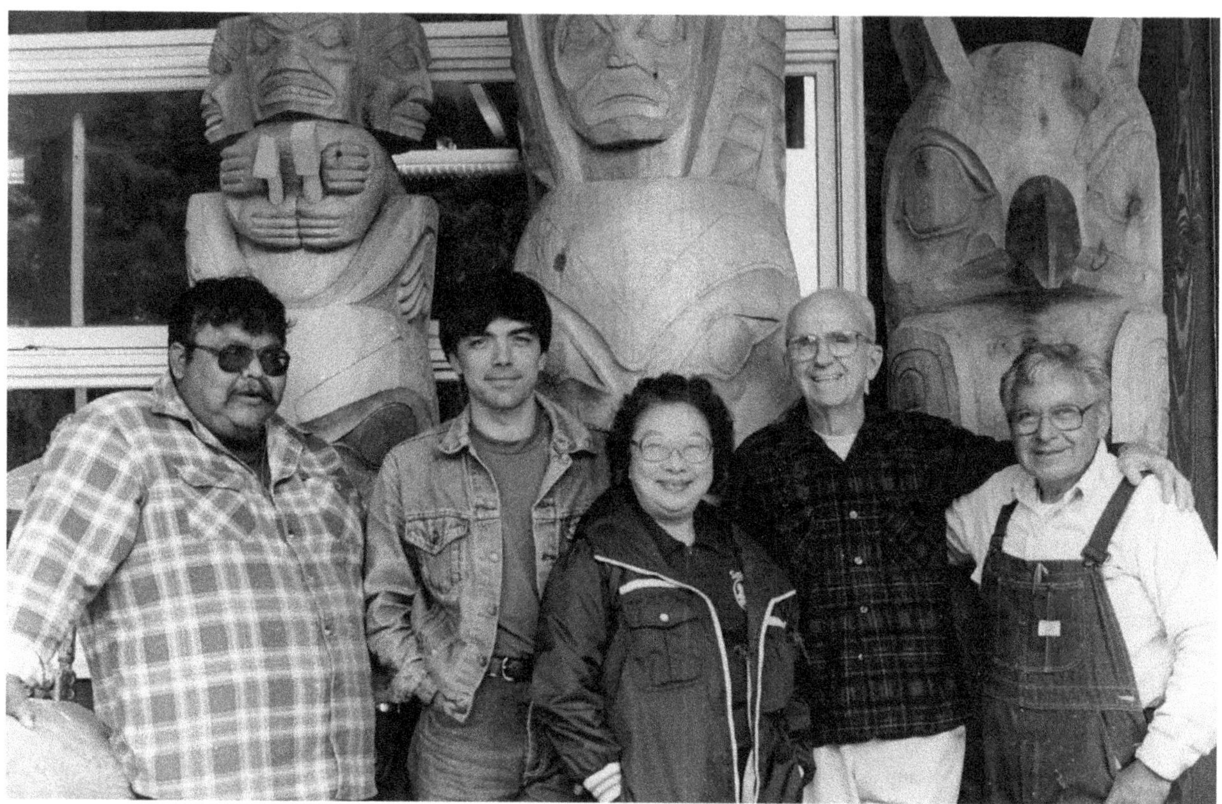

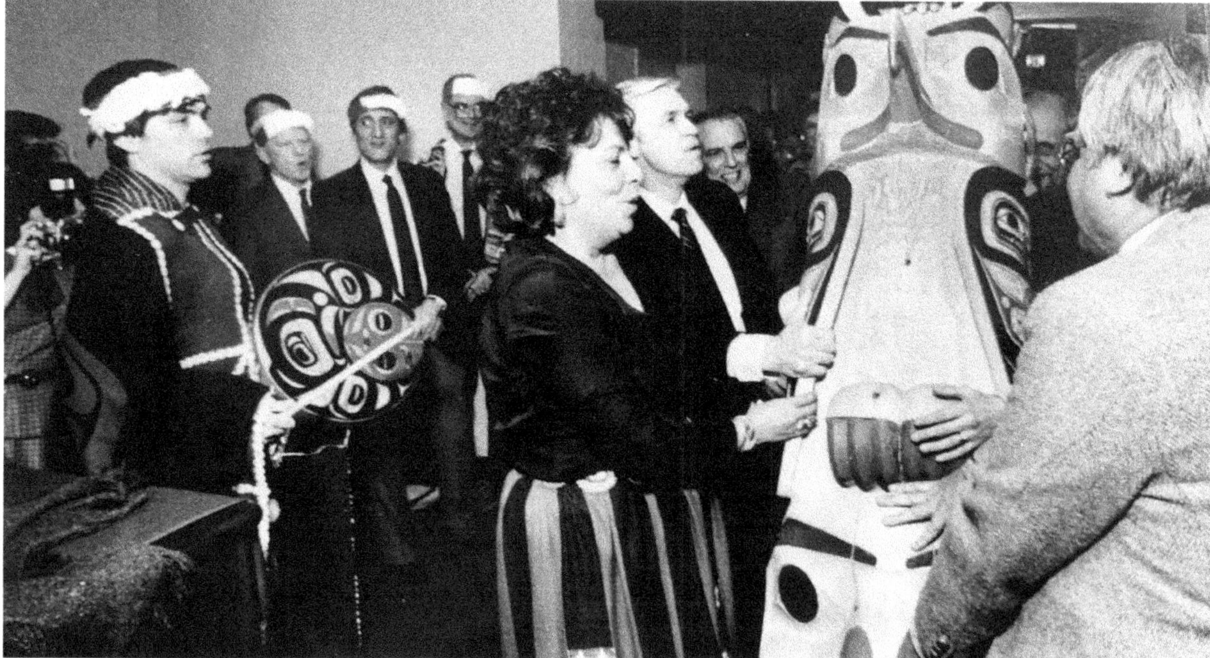

ABOVE: While on a carving assignment in Sitka, bestselling author James Michener and his wife joined me and colleagues Norman Jackson from Kake (far left) and Ernie Smeltzer (far right). The poles standing represents each of our work. We each did three poles for the Sheldon Jackson athletic complex.

BELOW: Guests at the potlatch to celebrate raising the totem pole at Washington D.C. law firm Hobbs, Straus, Dean & Walker. The pole is still standing and one of the retired partners traveled to New York with his family to watch my dance group Git Hoan perform.

Totem poles are like a photo in a book. You know the story that you're reading. Open to any page and it's got a photograph in it. That photograph is going to remind you of the story. That's what a totem pole is: it tells the story of a person, or a clan or great things that happened. Another thing I tell people, when you're looking around for something to eat and you see golden arches, what do you think? So it's kind of the same thing. You see that totem pole, and it reminds you of the story you know and you say, "I was there for that raising."

There's a prevailing myth about totem poles: that low man on the totem pole is a bad thing. It isn't. I don't like that when people say it and I still hear it to this day. I heard it on TV recently. There's no validity to that, no truth to that at all. Sometimes the figure at the bottom of the pole is the most important one. Sometimes it's the top. It depends on the order of things that are telling the story on the pole. The placement of figures on a totem pole is not a ranking system.

There is also the controversy about non-Natives doing our art. For example, there are shops with totem poles made for tourists. My first reaction is disgust. I understand that people come off those cruise ships and they aren't looking to spend ten thousand dollars they're looking to spend ten dollars. That's where that stuff fills a need. It's cheesy as anything and the quality is terrible. But you pay for what you get.

Then there's the high-end market. When someone who is non-Native is making our art it's not the same as when we do the work. There's nothing behind it. It's empty. It's almost insulting. I've heard all the excuses. "But they respect you so much." I have told people if they respected us so much, they wouldn't do our work. There are a few non-Native folks I'd give a little leeway because I know how much they have returned or given back to Native people and how they work hard to teach what they know. So much was taken from our people. It's not pleasant to see people still trying to do that.

The figures on the pole often represent a man or his family, the clan. In the old days, it was erected by the nephew of the chief. Today, poles get carved for a lot of reasons, like my mom's pole that Davey carved. She was not a chief. She was an everyday woman and I loved her, and I didn't want people to forget what she did for our community. Totem poles still say who we are. Even if it's not a Native person who is going to own it. It's important for me to ask them what's your family history. What do you want to be represented by? What's important to you?

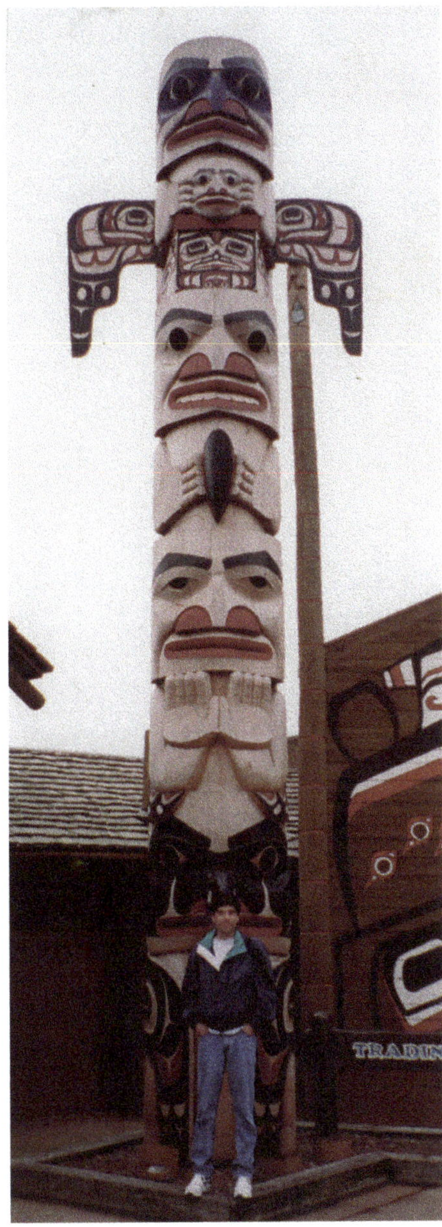

In 1996, I completed this pole, ultimately the first of three, for Disney World's Epcot.

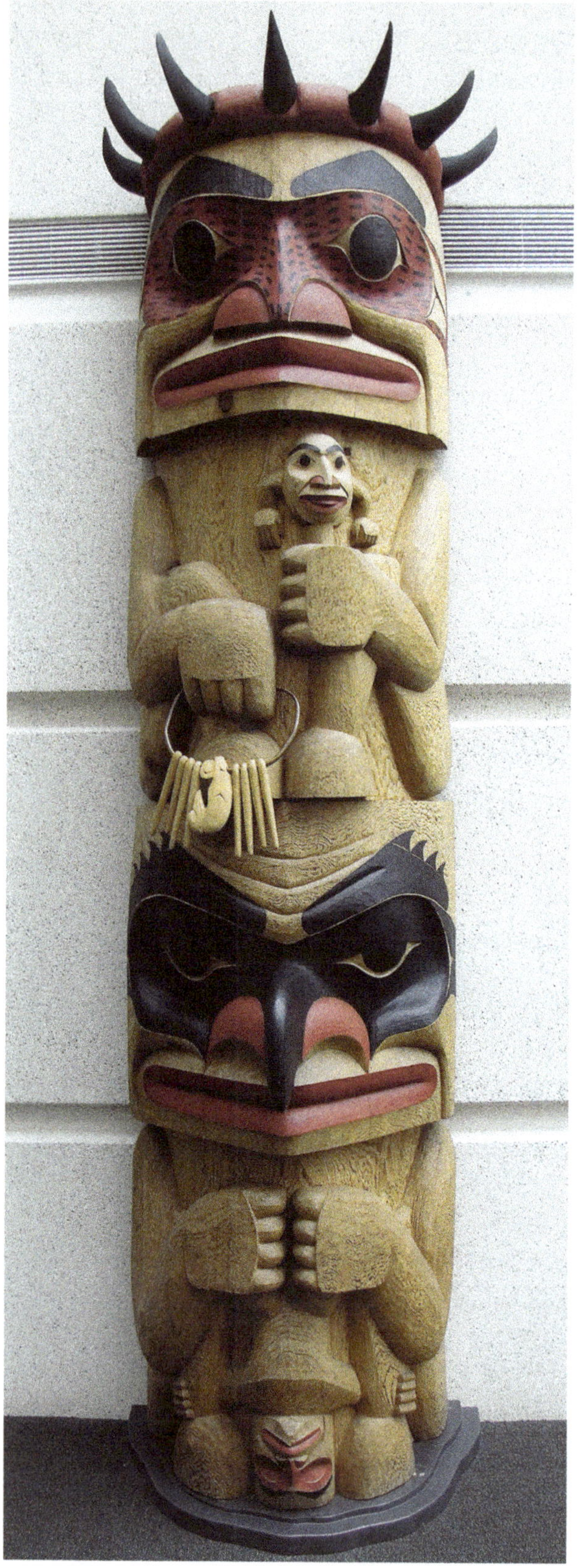

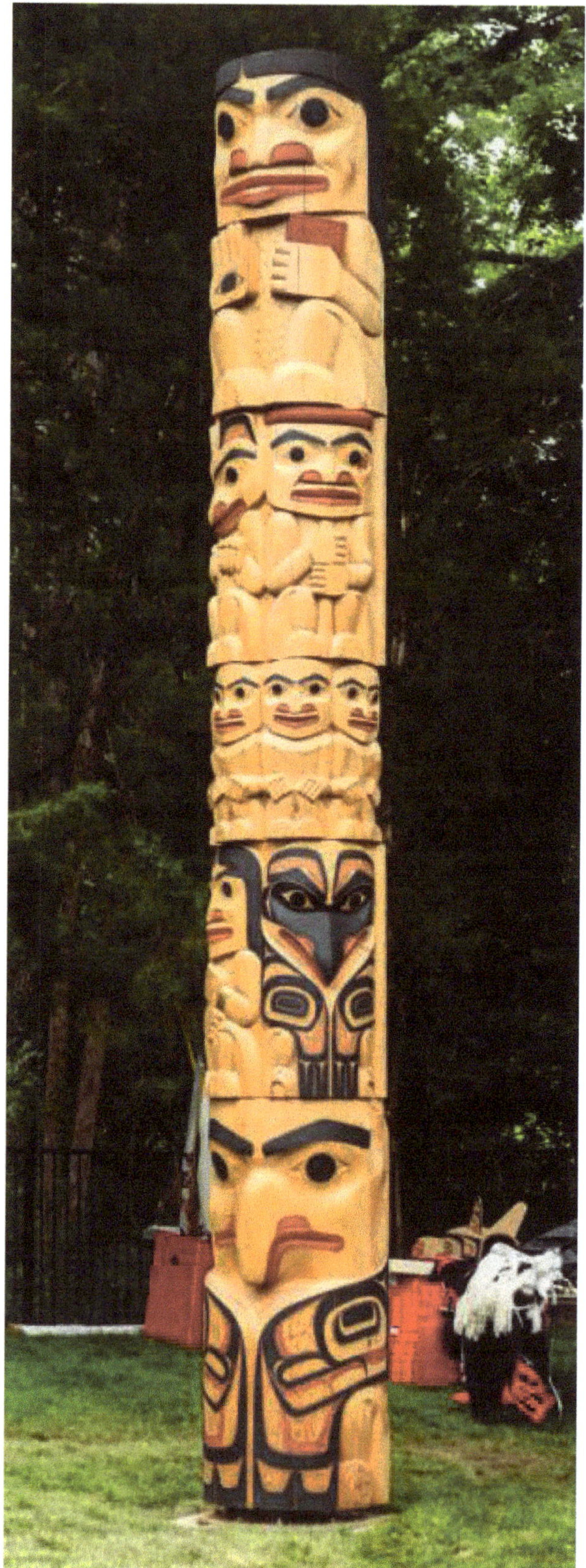

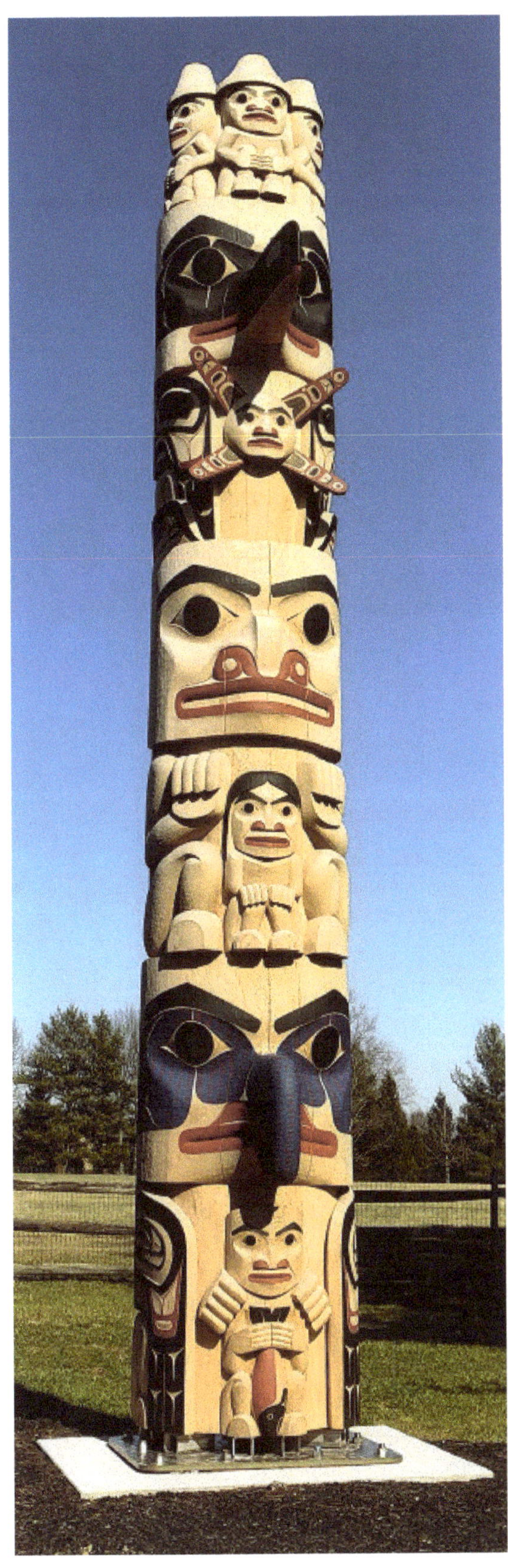

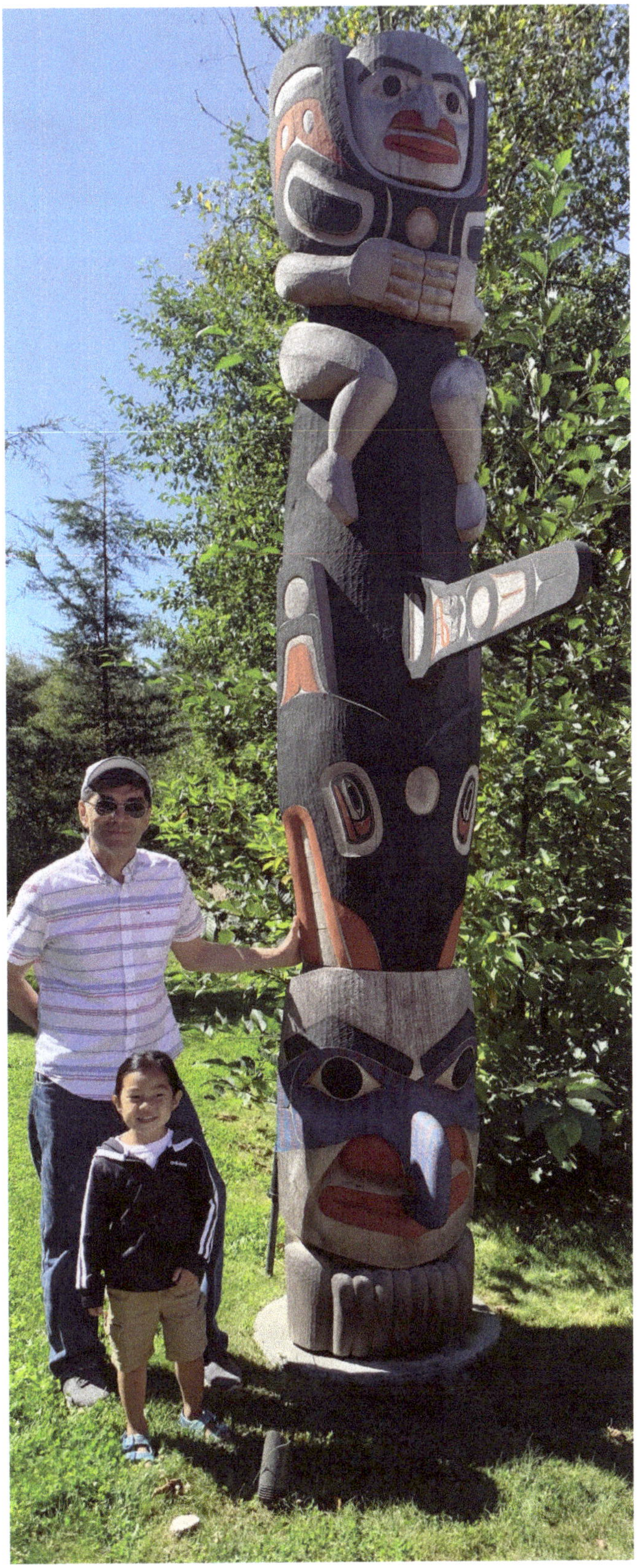

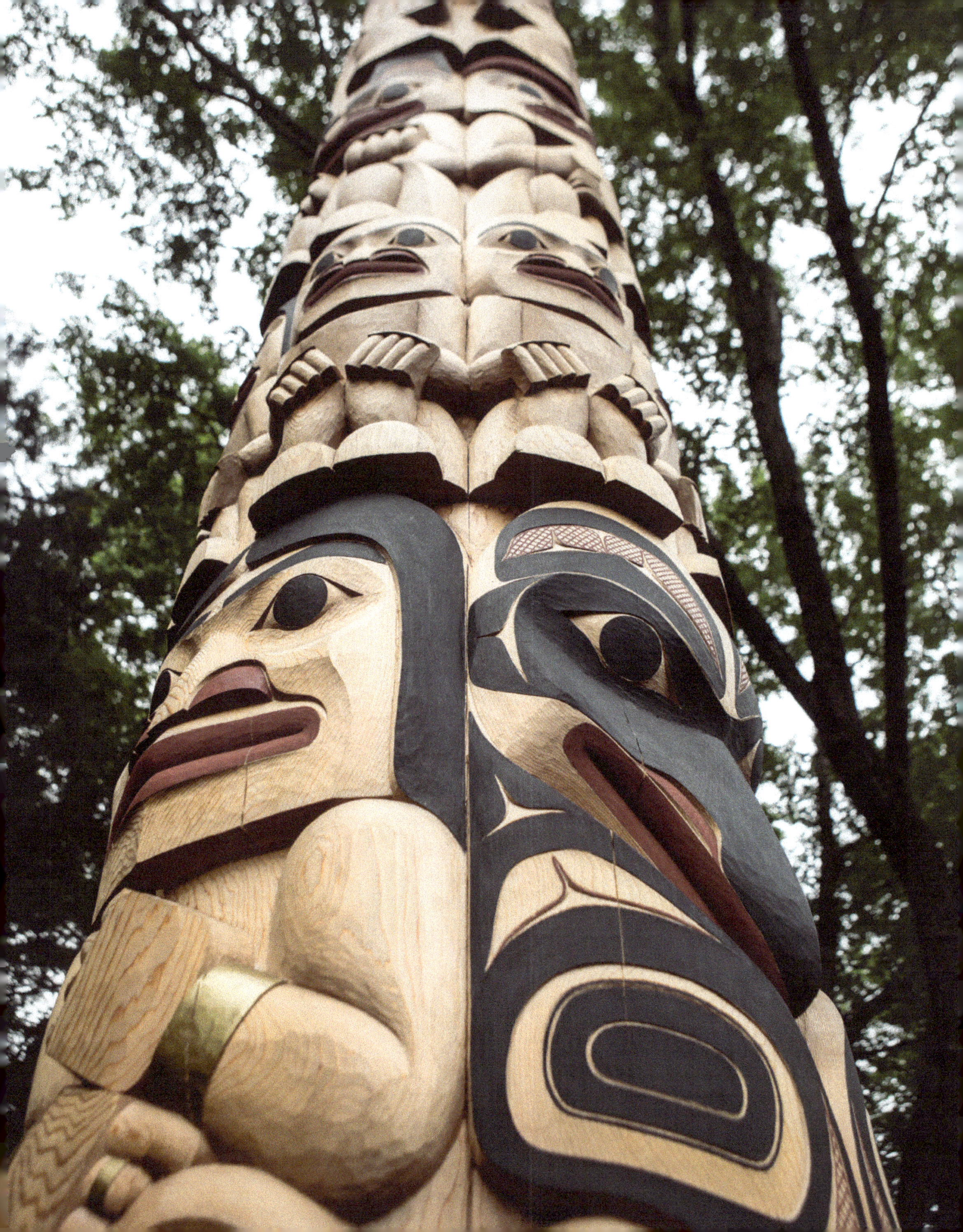

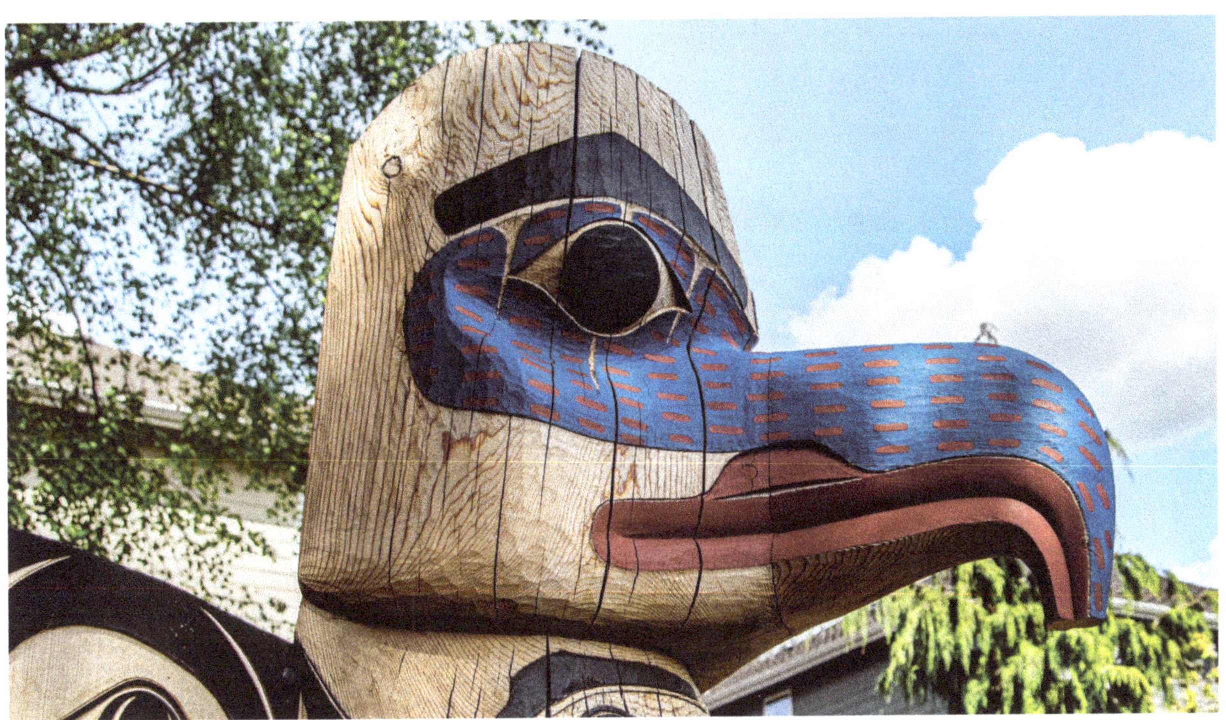

The more you crane your neck, the more magnificent the view of a pole becomes.

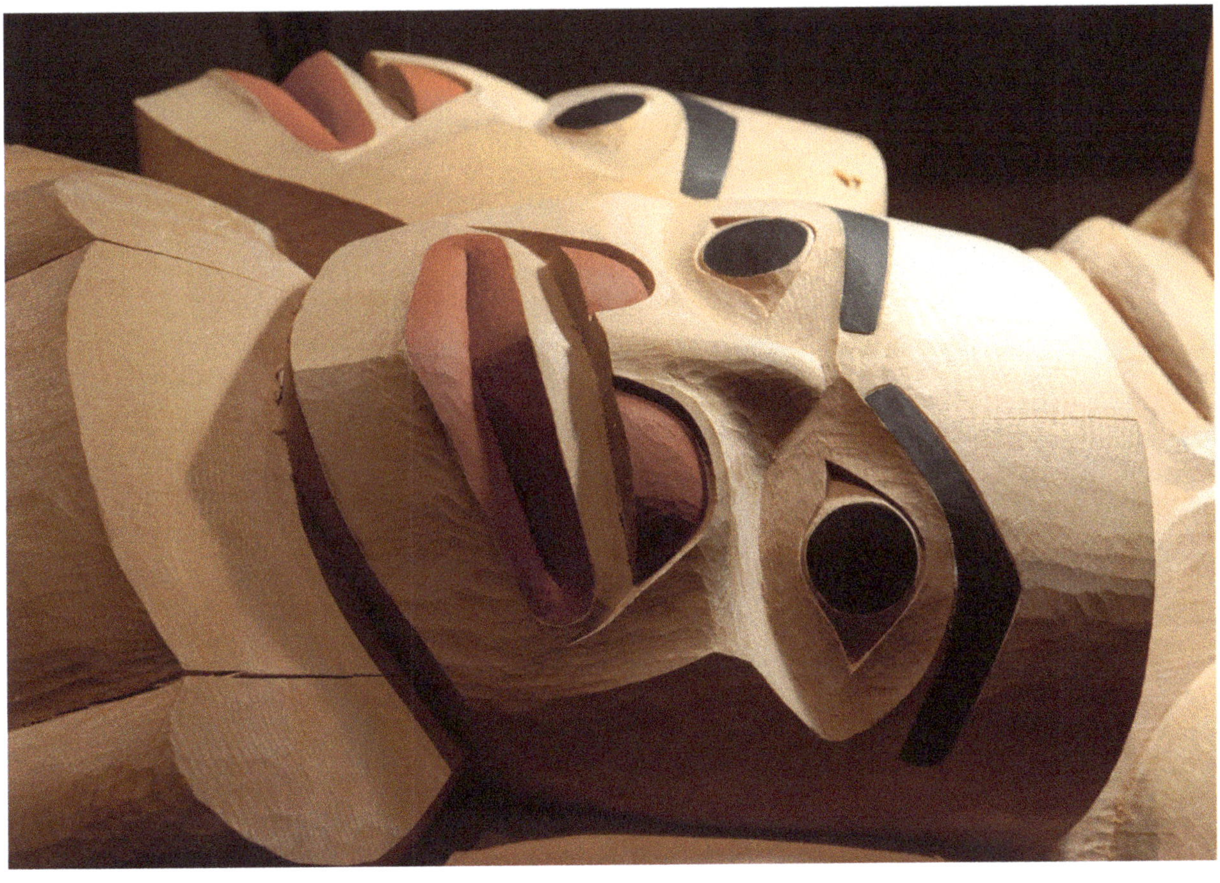

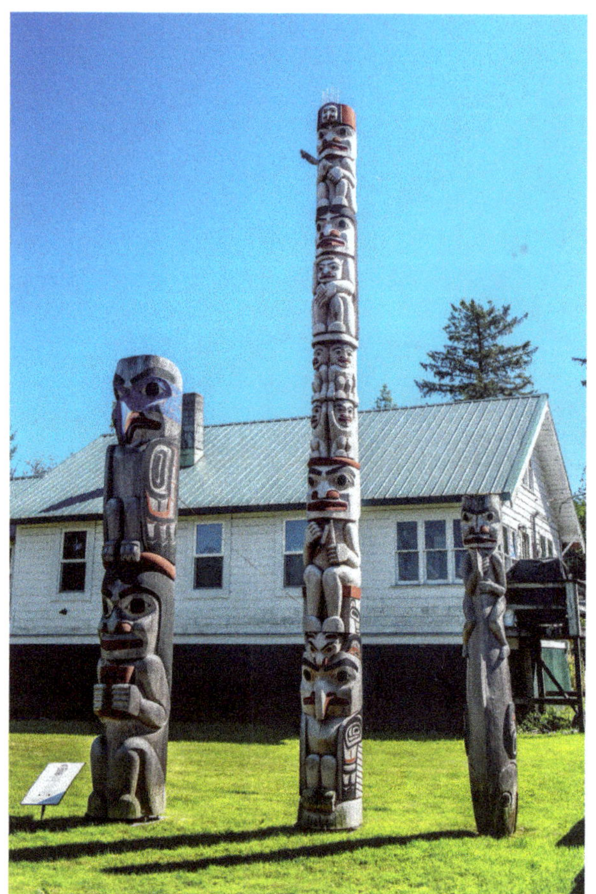

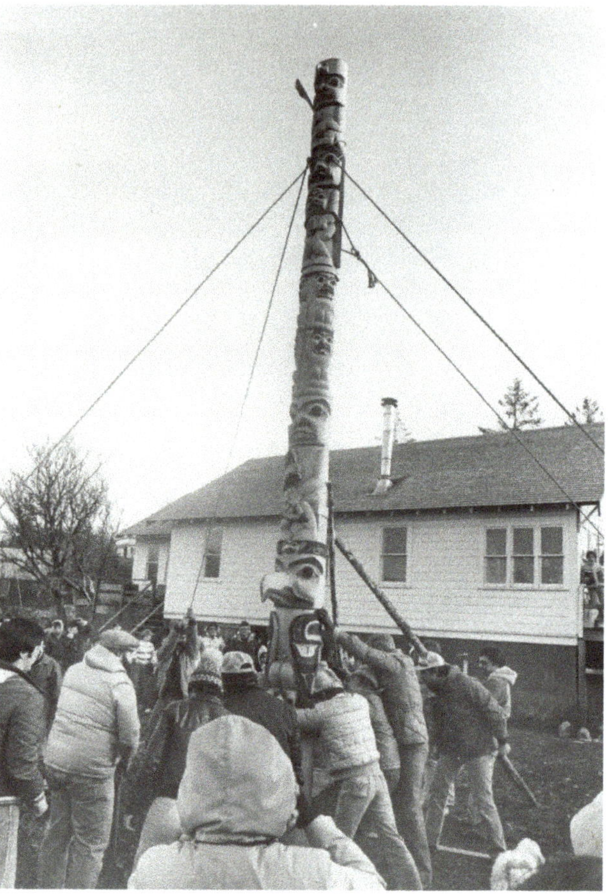

Three poles stand in front of the house where I grew up in Metlkatla. My grandfather built it 100 years ago. Now, my son Davey lives there. The center pole is a replica of my grandmother's pole (seen at right being raised in 1982 at my grandmother's potlatch at right).

I *consider my* grandmother's pole in 1982 my first major totem project. One year later, I got my first commission from Alaska's Percentage for the Arts. I'm very fortunate that commissions continued to come since I became a full-time artist and I've had Davey working shoulder-to-shoulder with me on a number of poles, including two of the three standing in Disney World *(facing page)*. We made a replica of my grandmother's pole; the original one is in a Ketchikan museum. Davey's pole for my mother is real important to me, too, but that's his pole. I commissioned him for that. He's of the wolf clan and I'm of the eagle clan, so commissioning him was the right thing to do for her. But there are two other poles he and I worked side by-side on that mean the most to me: one stands in Seattle, the other in Washington, D.C.

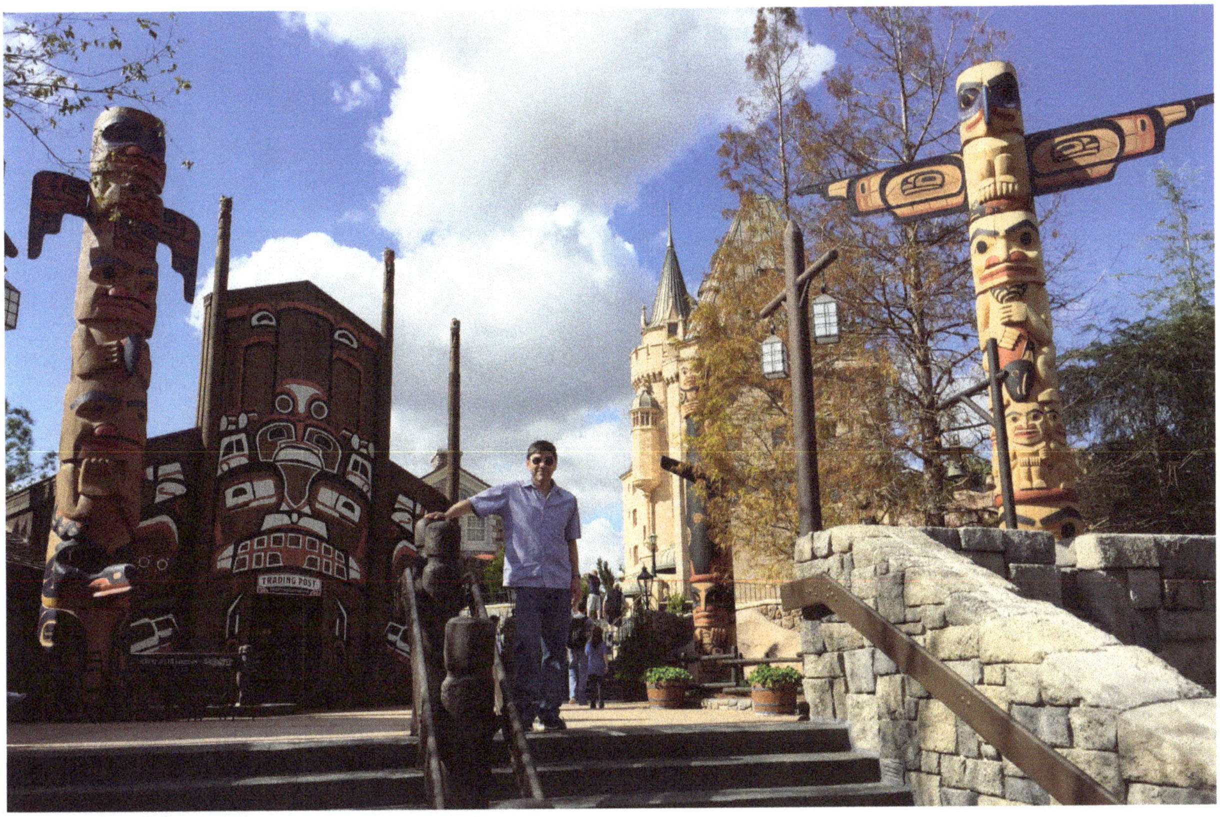

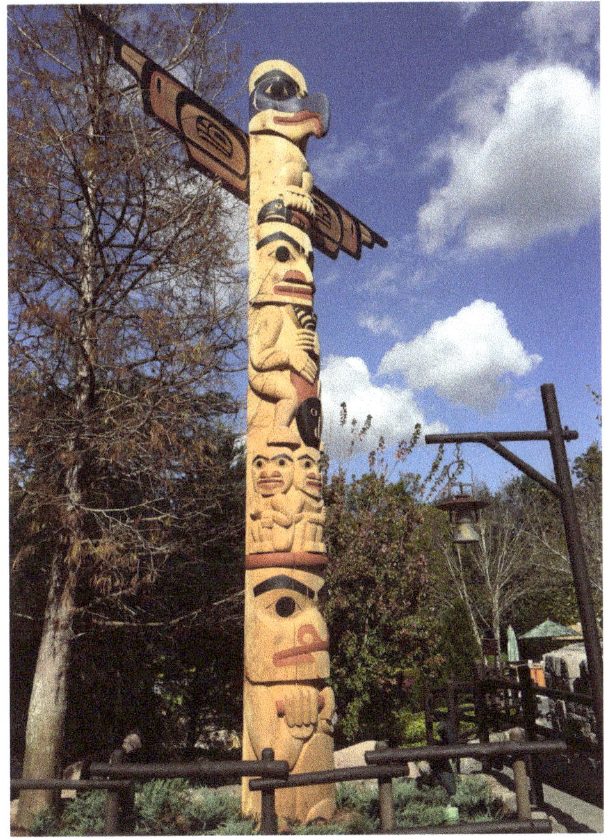

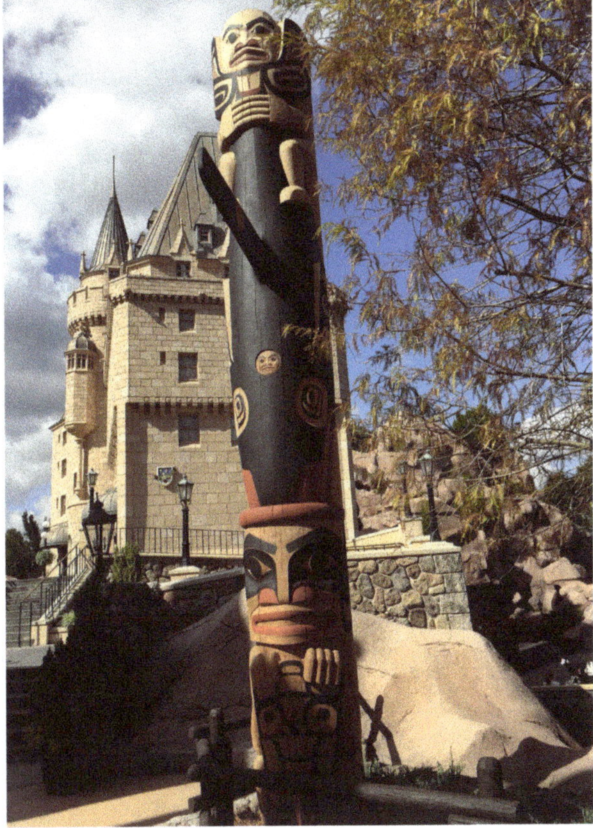

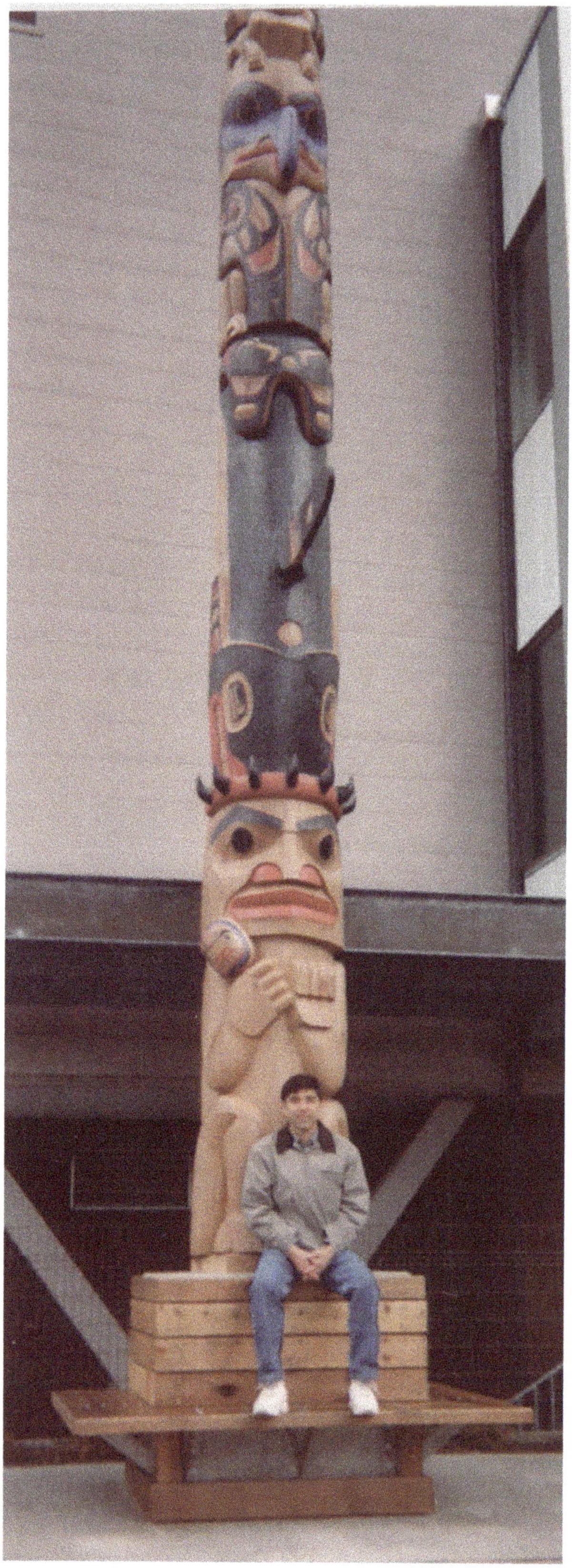

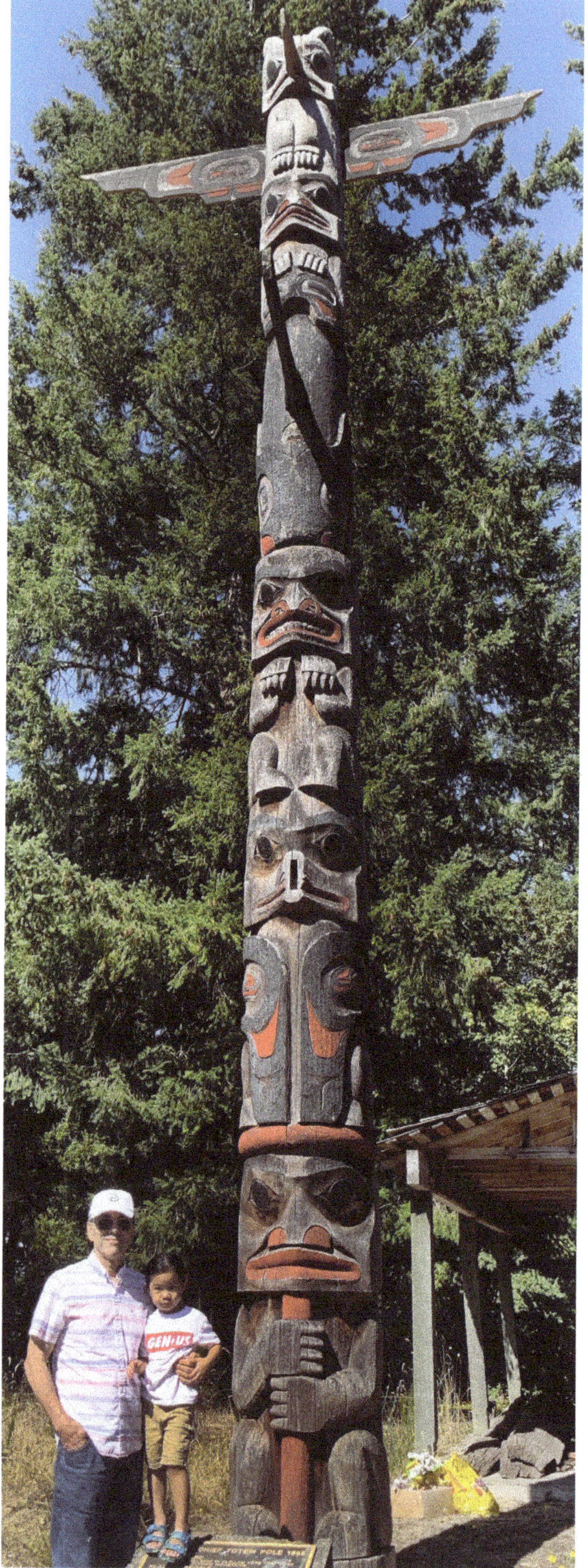

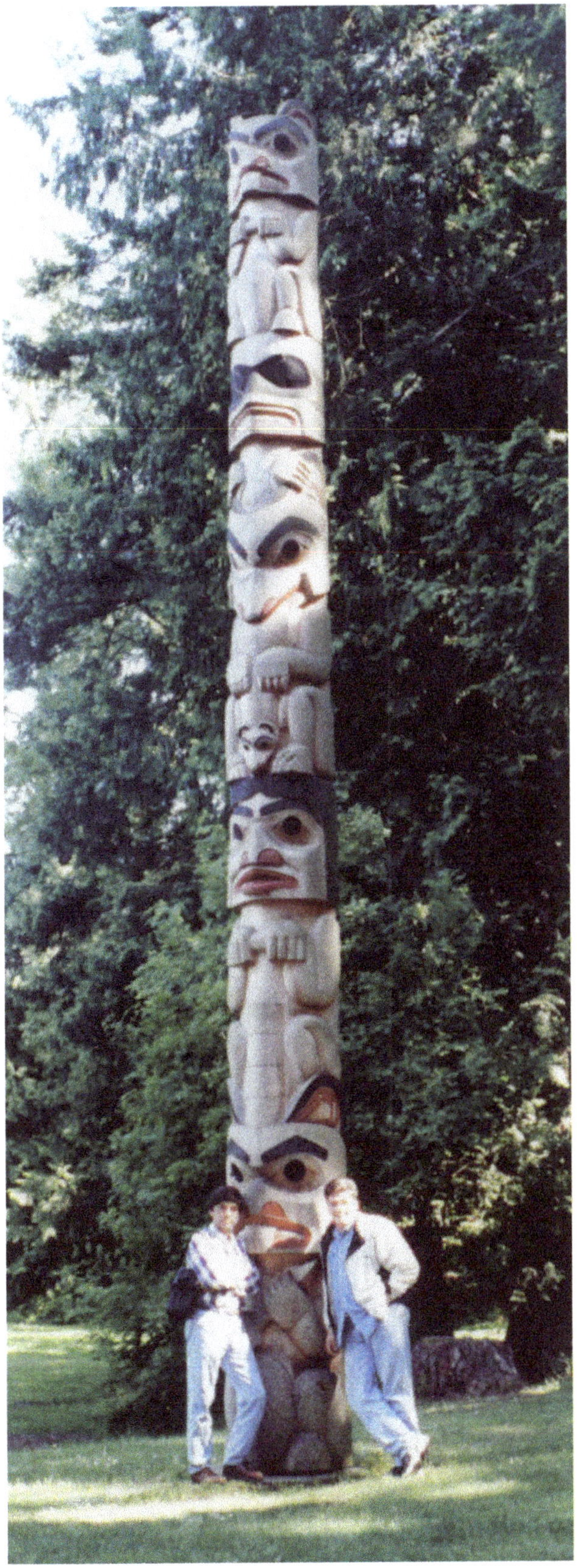

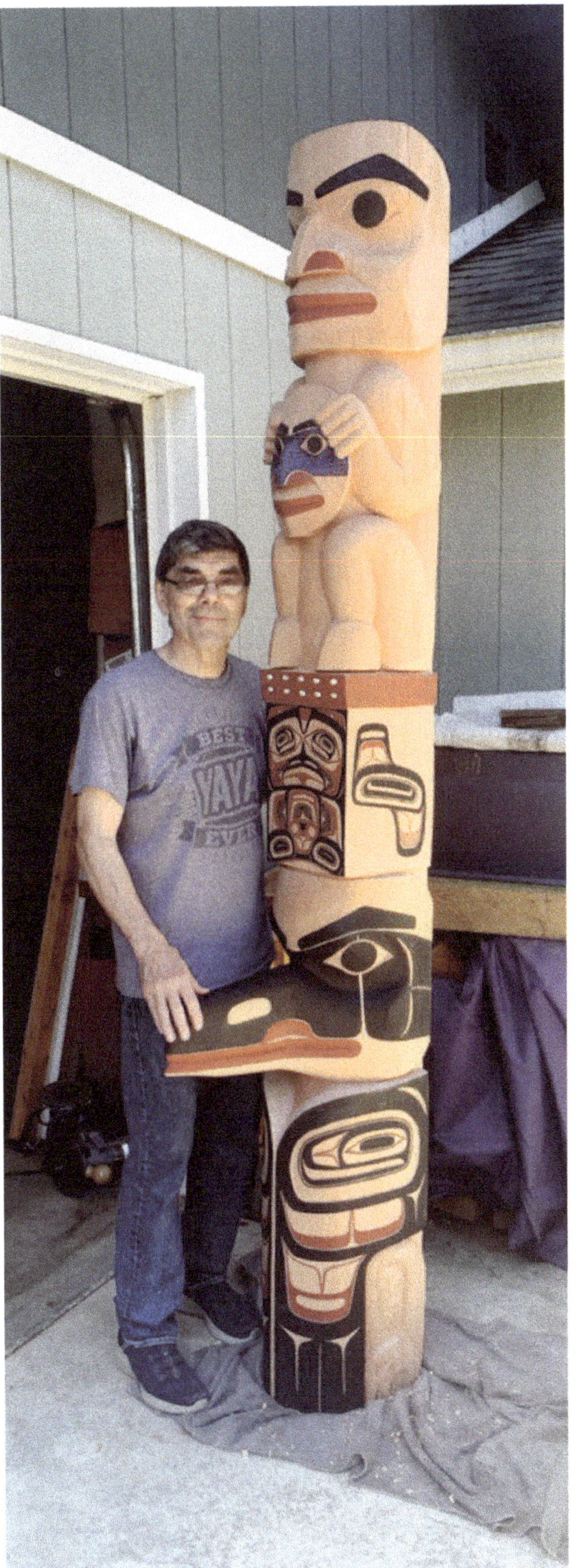

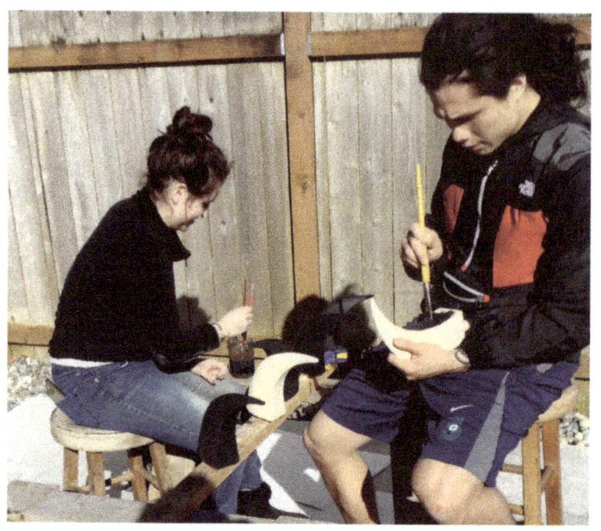
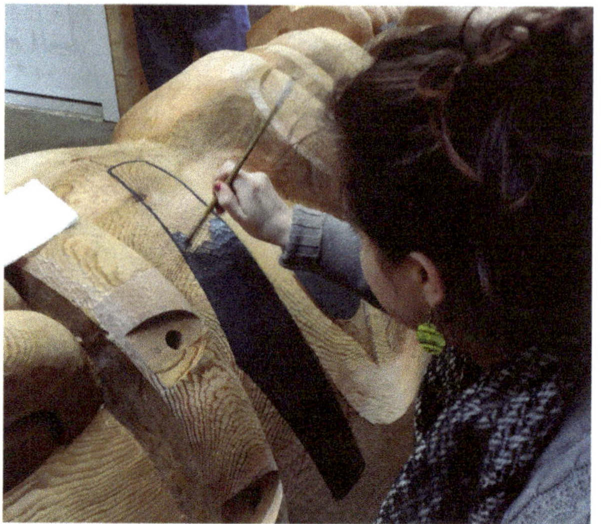
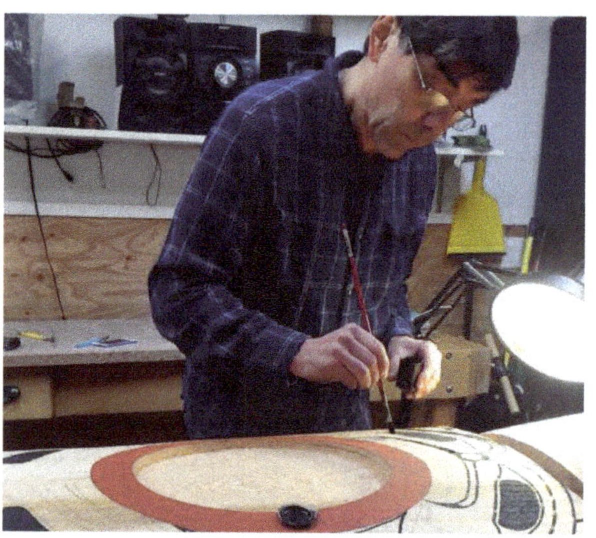
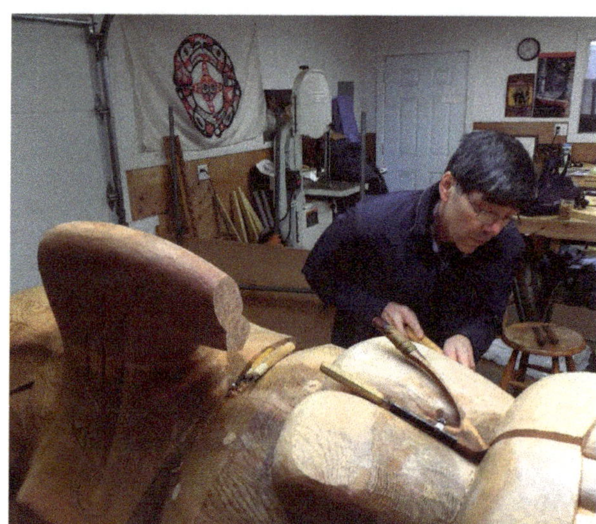
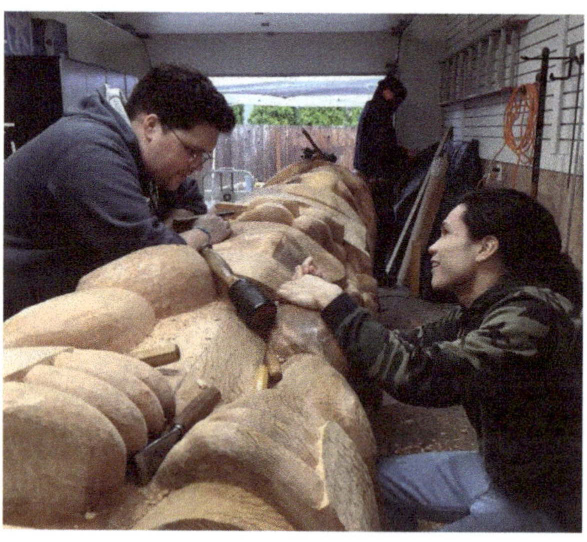
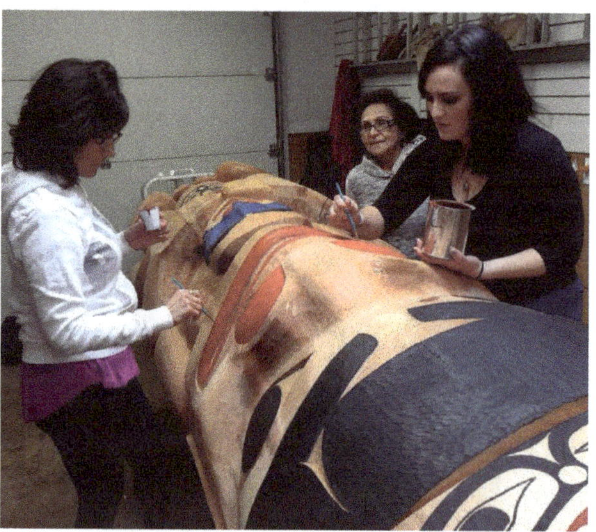

CINDY JAMES POLE | *Seattle, WA*

T*he Seattle pole* was for Cindy James, my late sister-in-law—
my wife Michelle's sister—and it stands on the grounds at
University of Washington Medical Center-Northwest. Davey's
section was the most significant. He carved the main faces on
the pole. It was really a family project. Cindy's nephews—Michelle's sons—Dylan and Darius worked on the pole; her nieces
Amanda and DeeDee did some sanding and painting.

Cindy and I were really good friends
long before Michelle and I got married. She
was the first one to come re-join my dance
group Git Hoan. She would be the first one
I would call and ask, "Do you want to go to
Florida? Do you want to go to Anchorage?
Do you want to go to New York?" Her culture meant everything to her, and helping
me with our culture was also important
to her. We lost her way too soon to ovarian
cancer.

Even though the pole was for Cindy,
there's really a larger story with this one.
The hospital had a totem pole that used to
be near what was once the front office. Over time, the campus
configurations changed, and they had a new entry way. I was
contacted a number of years before Cindy got sick to take a look
at this totem pole to see if I could repair it.

I got up on the roof. You could poke your fingers into it, it
was so rotten in some areas. The entire thing was covered with
paint. That's one of the reasons why it was in such bad shape.
When something is covered with paint, it rots from the inside
out. There's no place for the air to go. It was not done by a Native
carver. It was real cartoony looking.

I told them that the pole was in bad shape. I recommended
that they have a new one made whether it's by me or somebody
else. I guess they kept that in the back of their minds. In order
to get into Cindy's room, you had to go through the old entrance
which is right by the totem pole. Cindy and I were talking about
that pole. She talked to her main nurse and expressed her feelings about "that ugly pole," as she called it.

She talked to a nurse about the rotting pole, and the nurse
talked to somebody else, and it went up the chain. Eventually,
the hospital decided to let us replace the rotten pole with one
for Cindy. But we had to figure out how to pay for it.

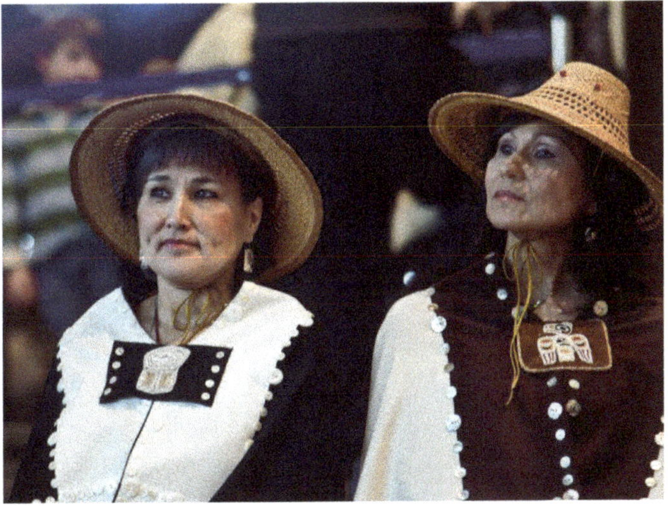

Sisters Cindy James and Michelle Boxley,
Cindy introduced me to Michelle, who would
later marry me. They were very close and
traveled all over the world together with Git
Hoan. Cindy was the first one to join my previous group Tsimshian Haayuuk. Both were
tremendously supportive of me during the
ups and downs of forming dance groups.

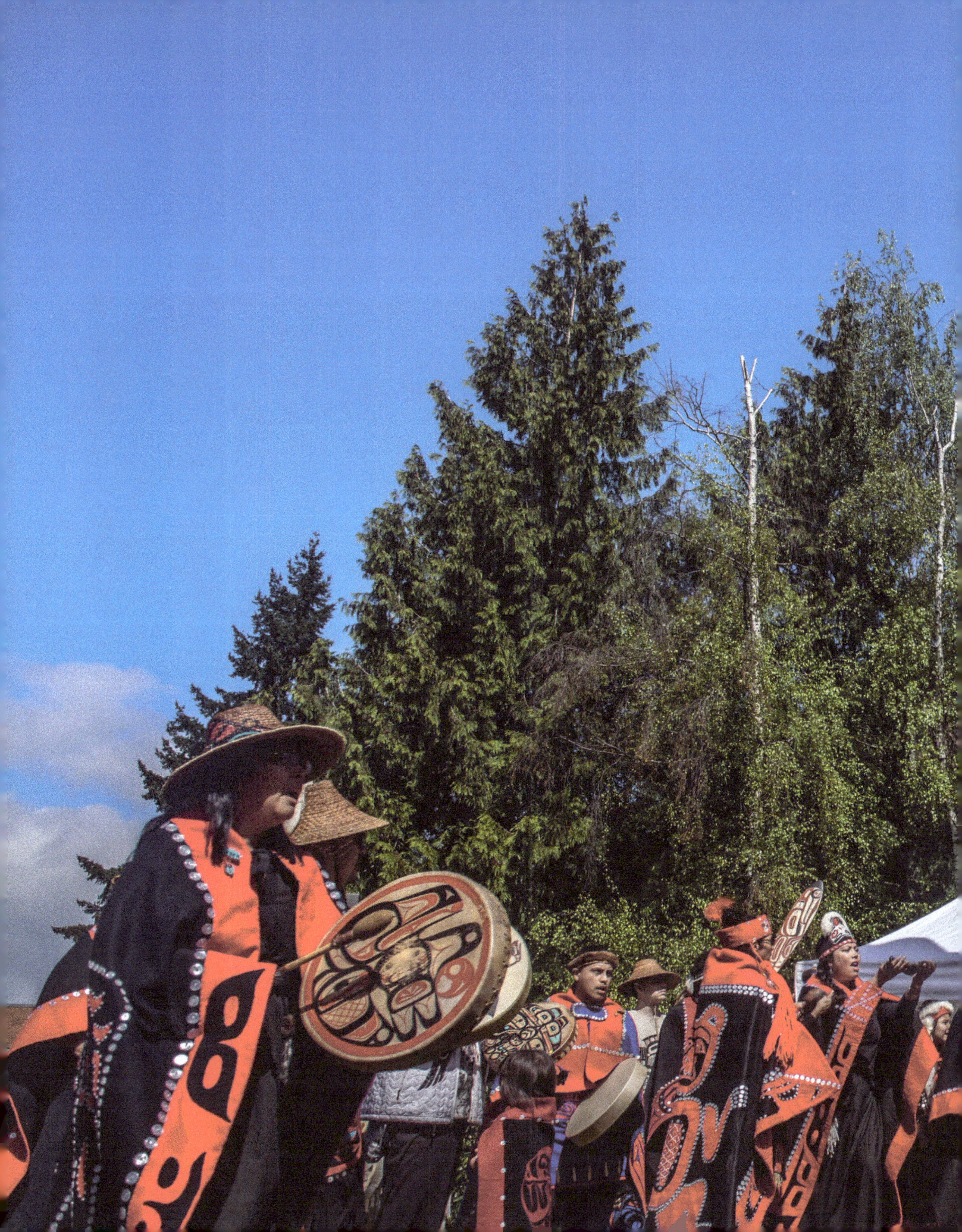

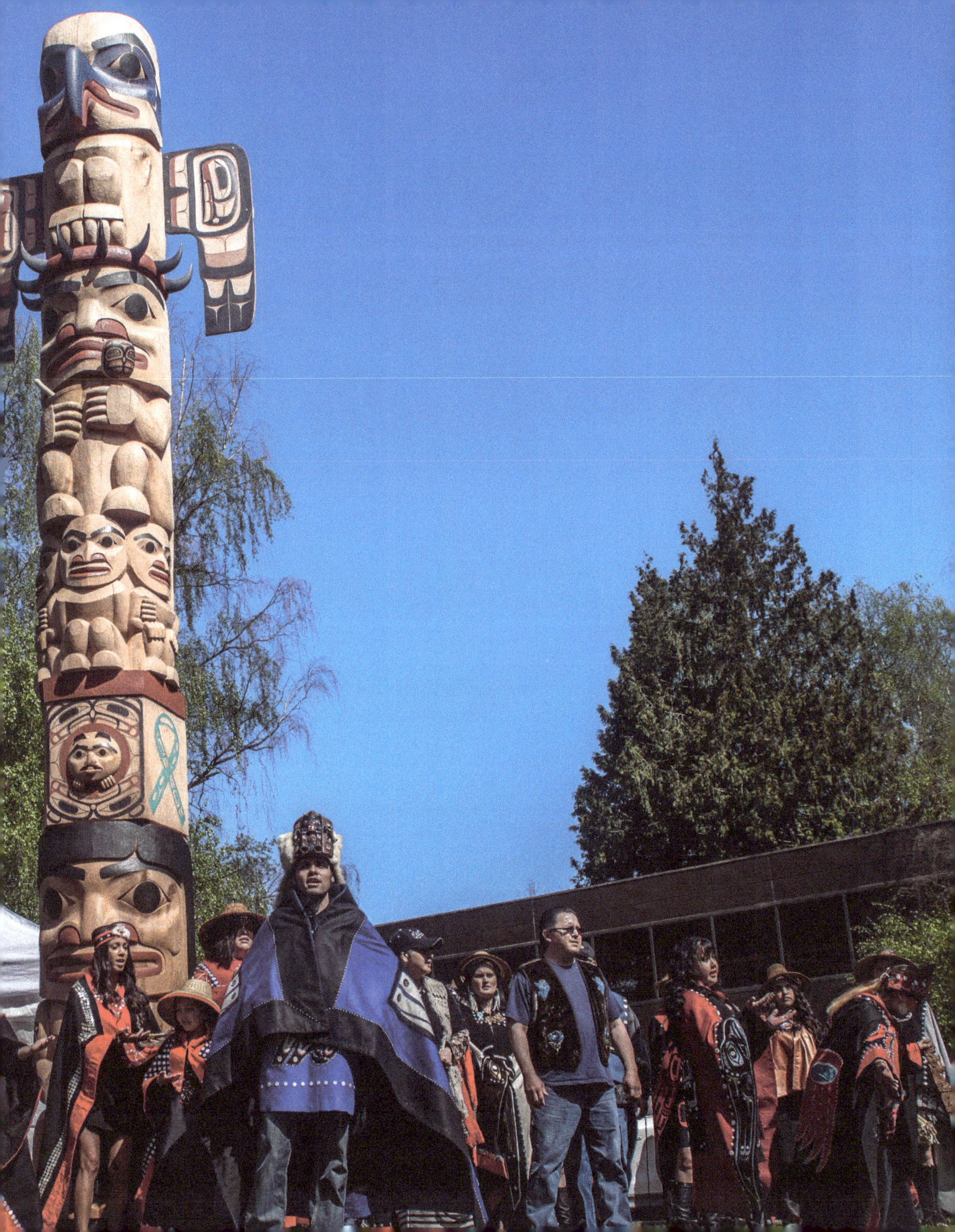

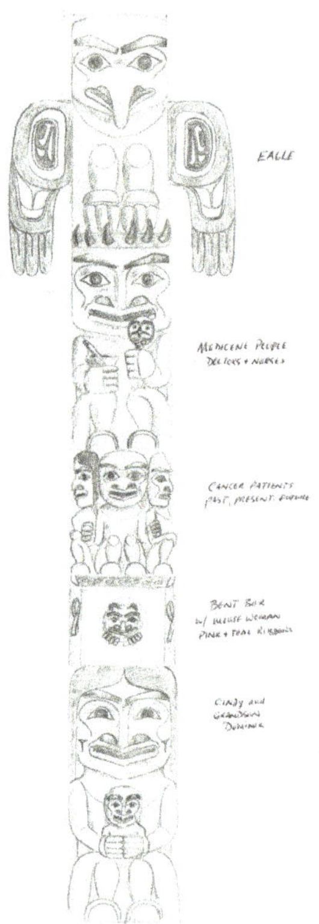

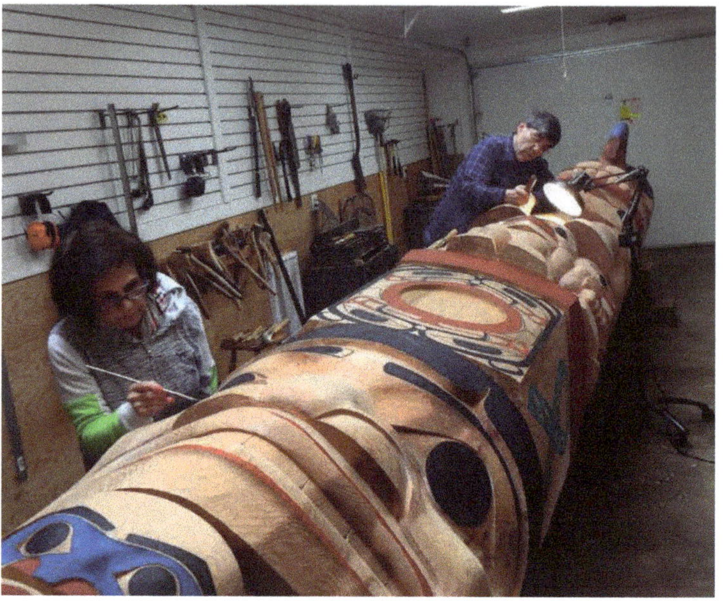

TOP LEFT: As with any project, the work on Cindy's pole started with this drawing. She and I had some really long talks about the design and what she wanted for the potlatch. We really miss her. Losing her left a big hole in our family.

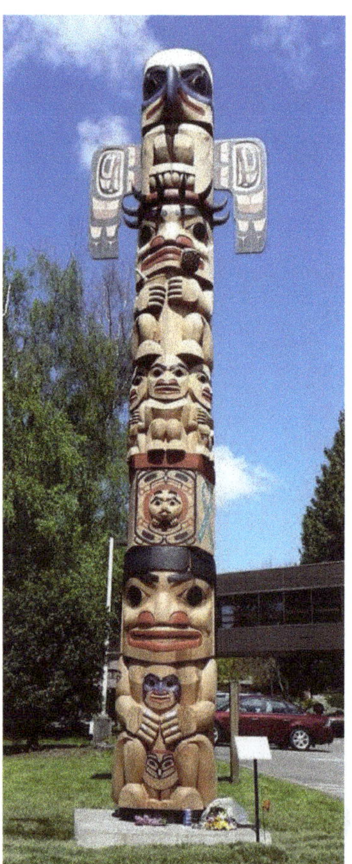

Cindy had a lot of input into that pole. She had a lot to do with the design of the pole and the potlatch. In the end, it turned into quite a day. It was beautiful weather. Lots of people came. Dance groups came from Canada, all over Washington, and Alaska. We had a gathering when she was still alive. We went outside on the lawn near her room. I gave her a Tsimshian name and she passed that name to her daughter, Amanda.

We had a potlatch after raising the pole. Everybody in the family who was local got names. Everybody in my dance group has a name. I have four names. My newest one given to me at home in Metlakatla by the Laxsgyiik (eagle clan): Niis Bupts'aan, or "grandfather of totem poles."

Cindy died in September 2016. Four years earlier, she and our whole dance group were with me and Davey for one of our most memorable pole raisings: the one in the Smithsonian's National Museum of the American Indian.

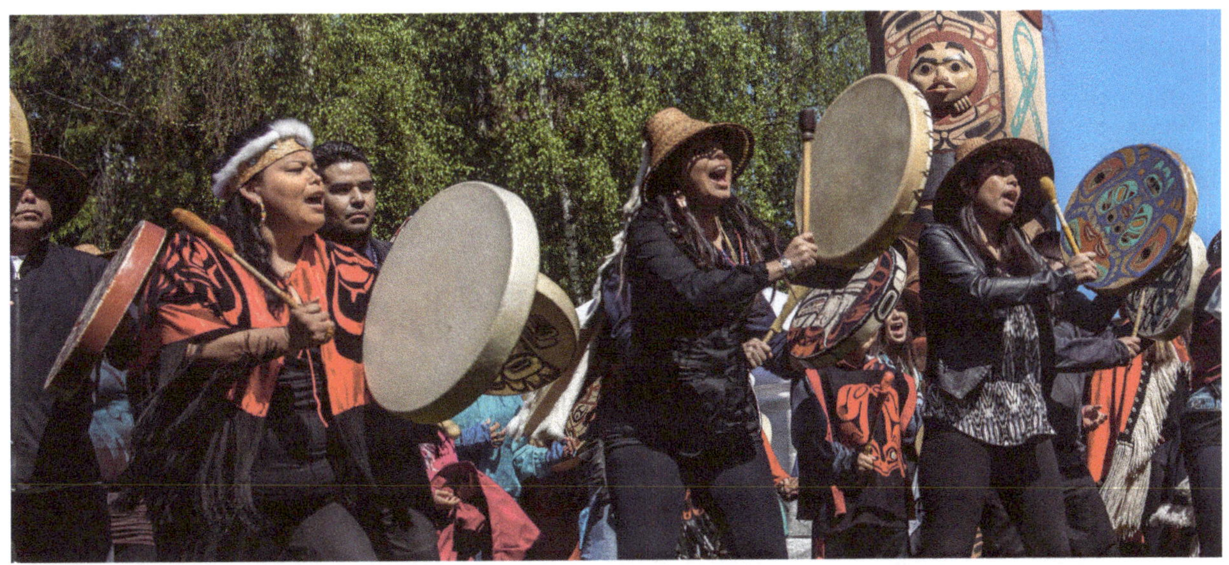

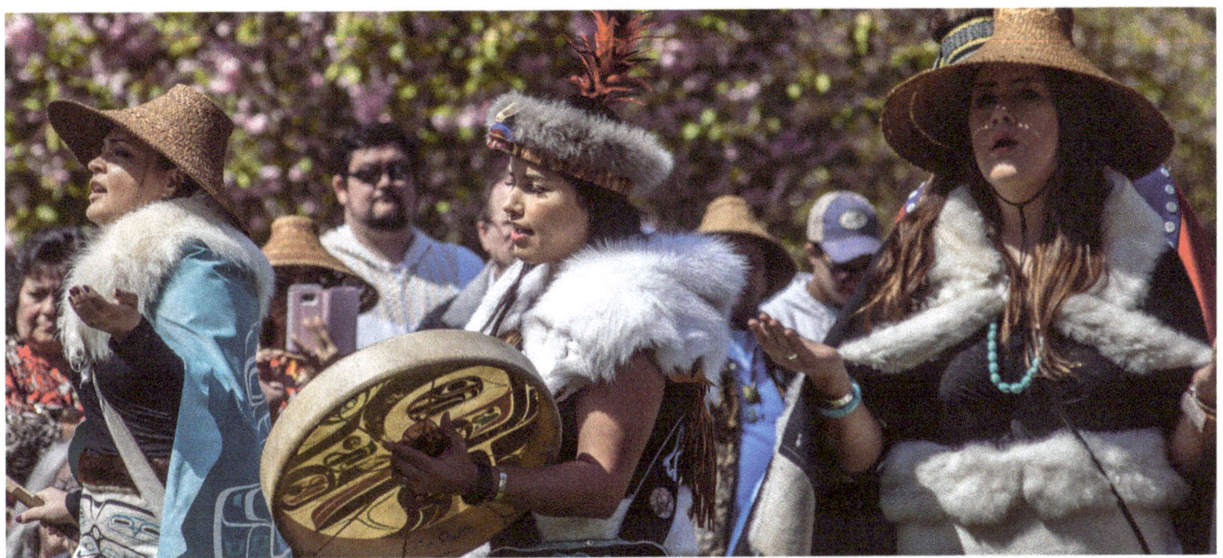

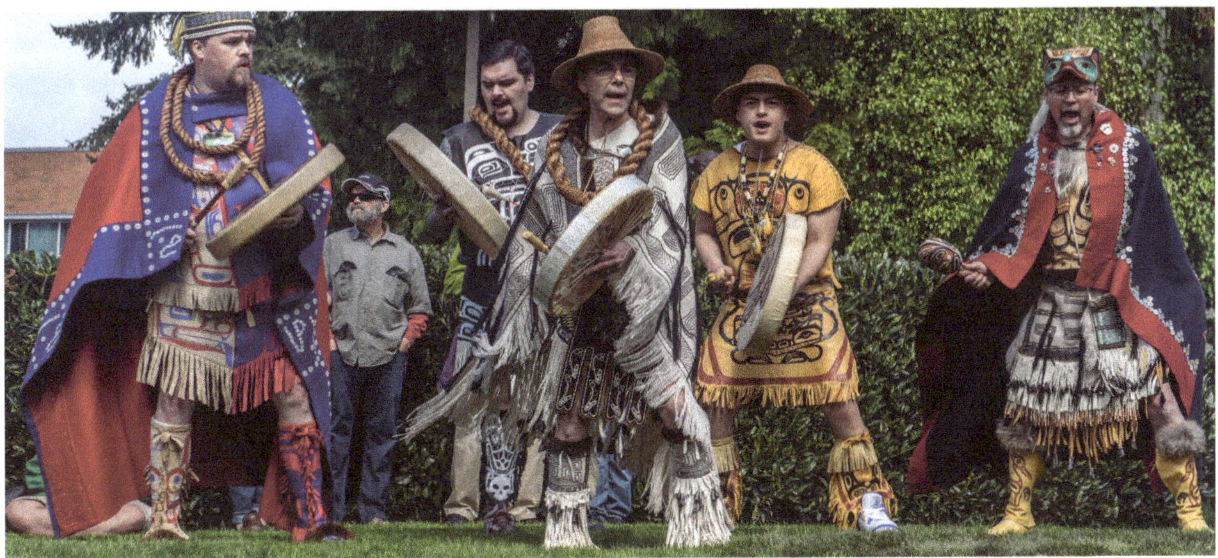

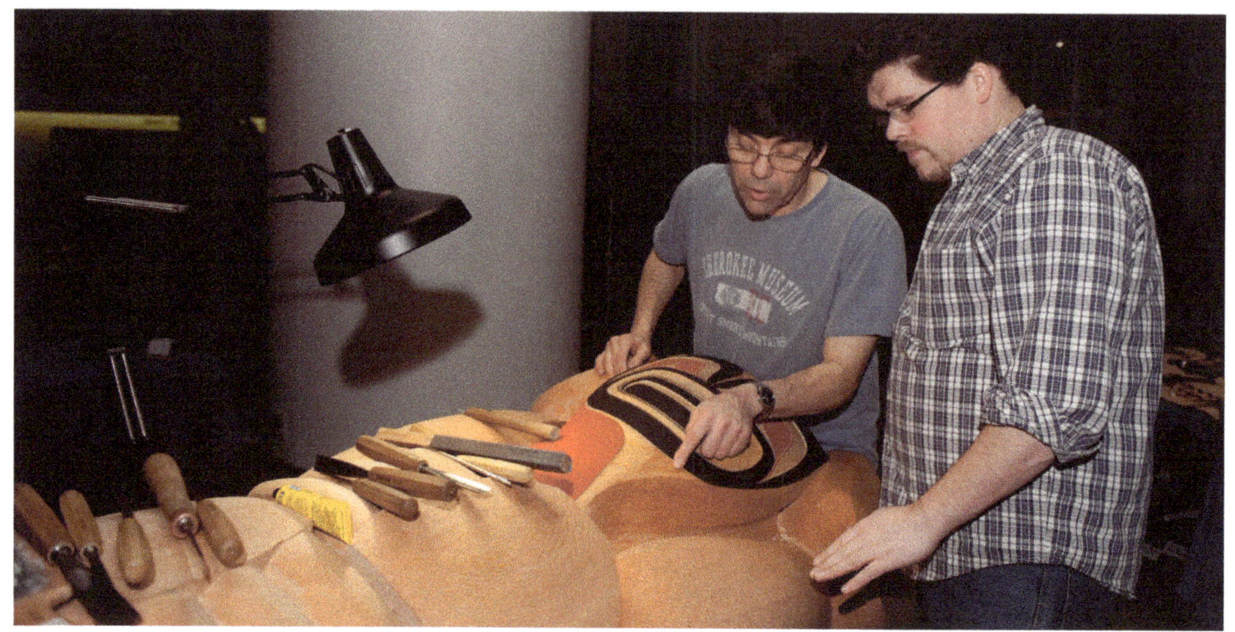

SMITHSONIAN NATIONAL MUSEUM OF THE AMERICAN INDIAN | *Washington D.C.*

Davey and I were at the selling our work at the Smithsonian National Museum of the American Indian (NMAI) and we were talking to the museum's former Chief Executive Kevin Gover. He's a Native. I made an off-handed comment, pointing to a column that was to the right of the table where all my art was. I said, "You know, a totem pole would look good right there." Nathan Jackson already had a fifteen-foot pole in what was then their gift shop. One of the reasons I said it was because it would be nice to also have a Tsimshian pole to represent our folks. Two years later, he contacted me and asked me to carve a Tsimshian pole for NMAI.

The museum has a huge rotunda, a large expansive inner space, and the pole is right there as you walk in the door, turn right, then go down the steps. It greets people as they come in. Davey and I carved the pole in my shop in Kingston. We left some things unfinished. We shipped it to D.C., then we went out there and spent a couple of weeks finishing the pole right where it was going to be raised.

I was proud to have that experience and give my people all of that publicity. When we raised the pole and we did the installation, or the unveiling, my dance group got to perform for that, and we gave gifts for the witnesses.

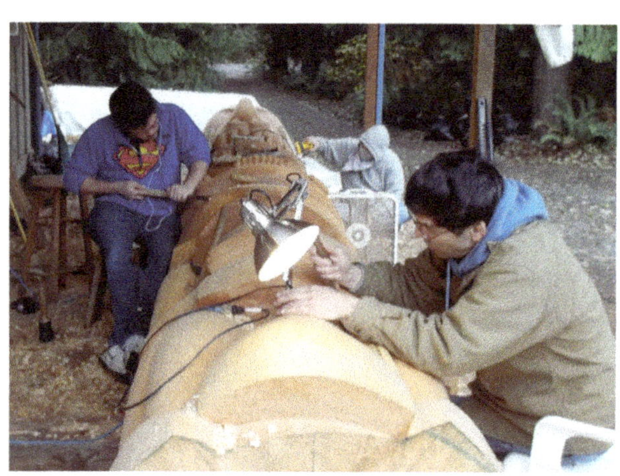

Davey, Zach and I began working on this pole in Kingston. We finished in the National Museum of the American Indian. There, people could watch us and ask questions about the pole and our culture.

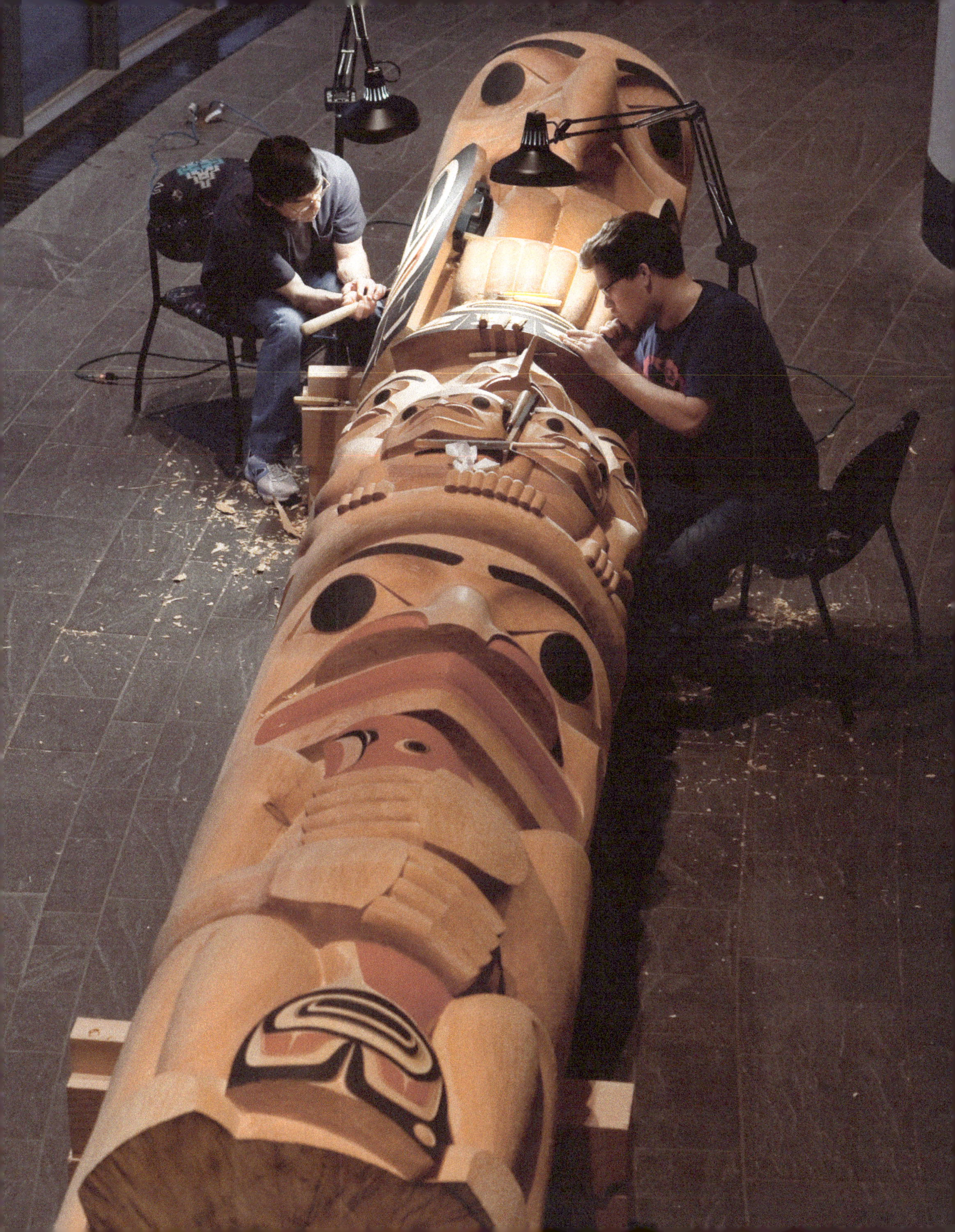

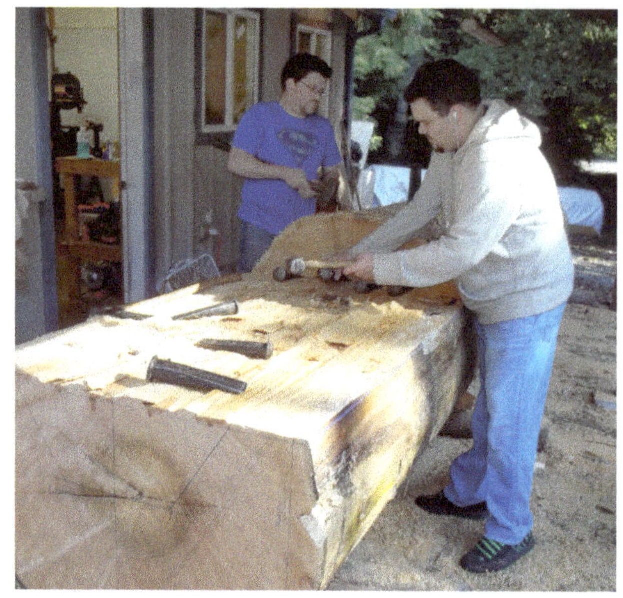
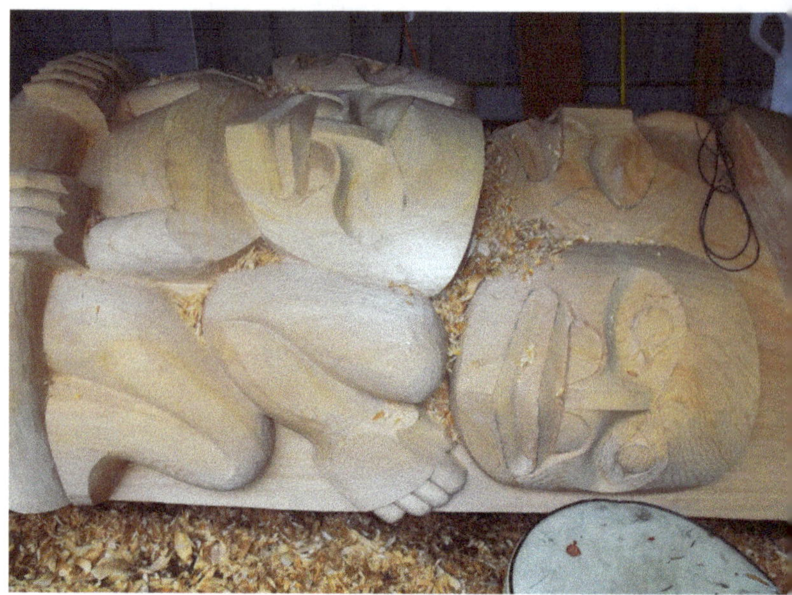
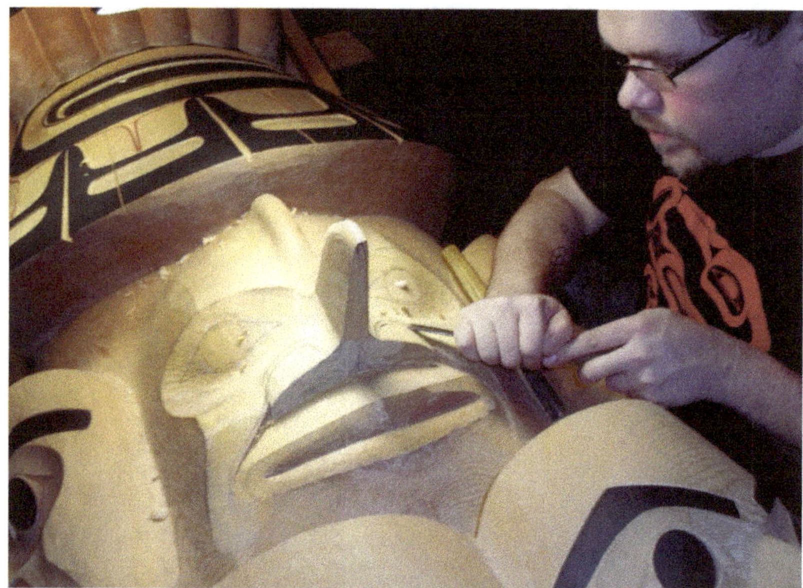
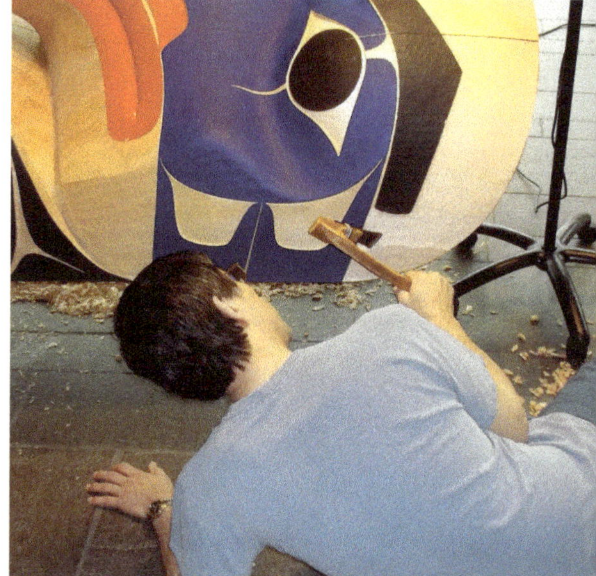
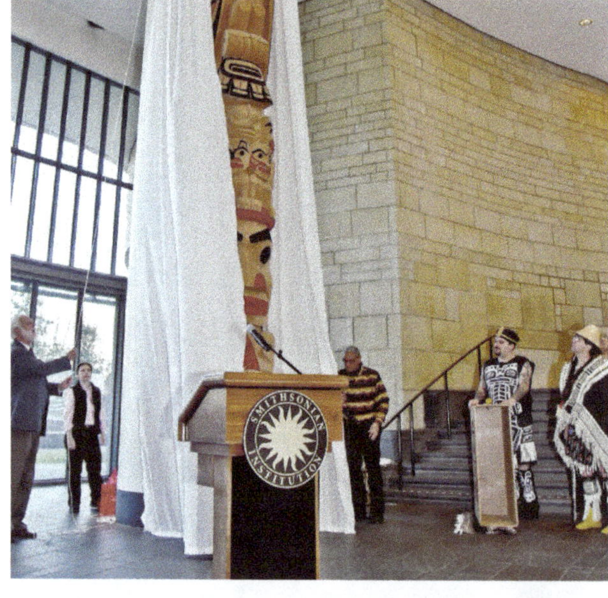
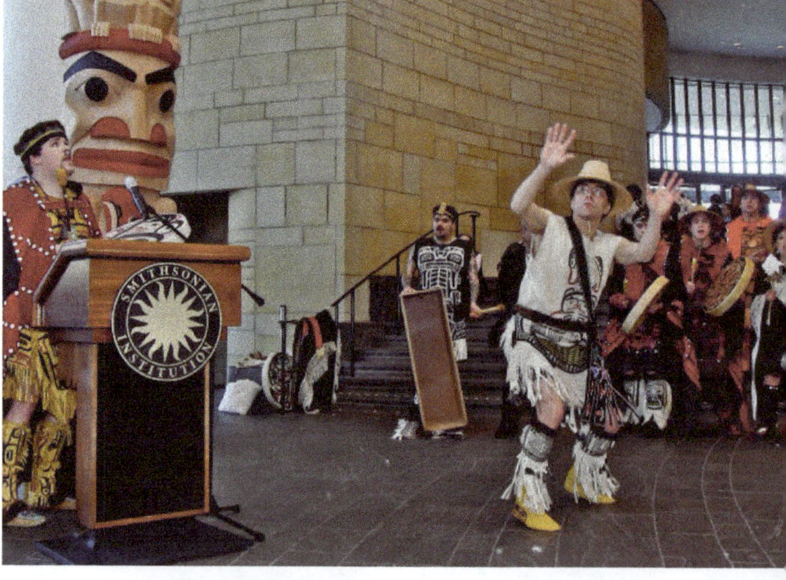

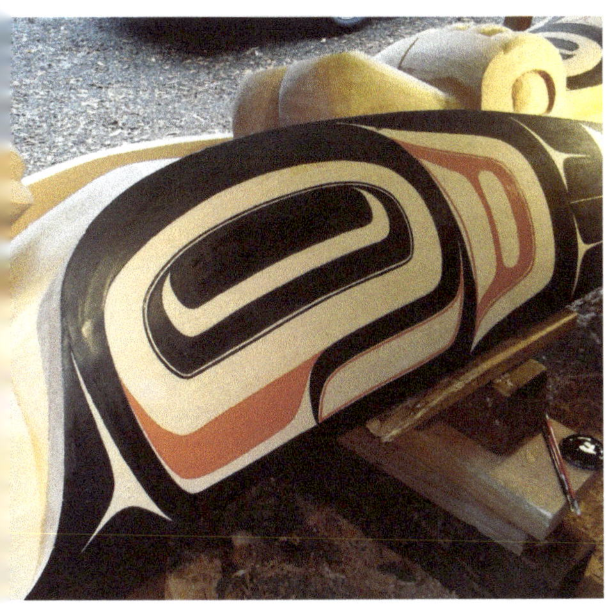
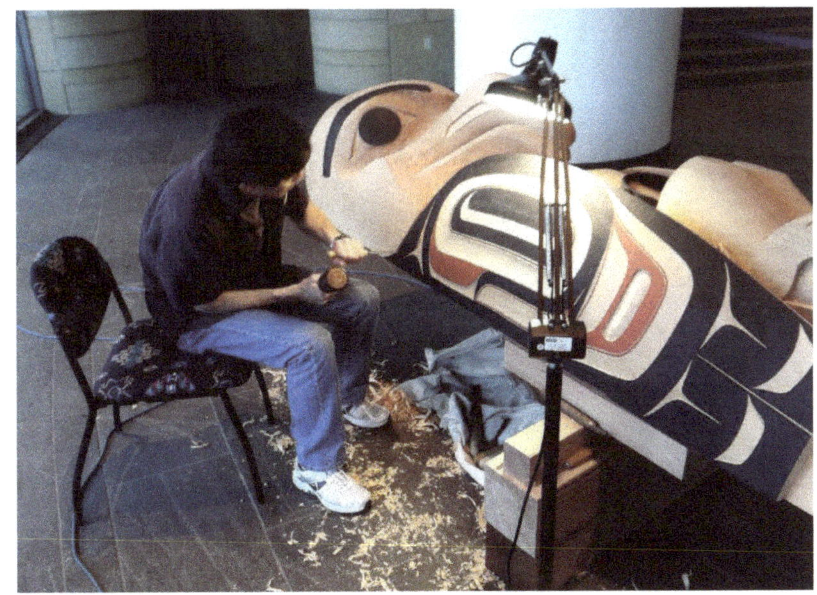
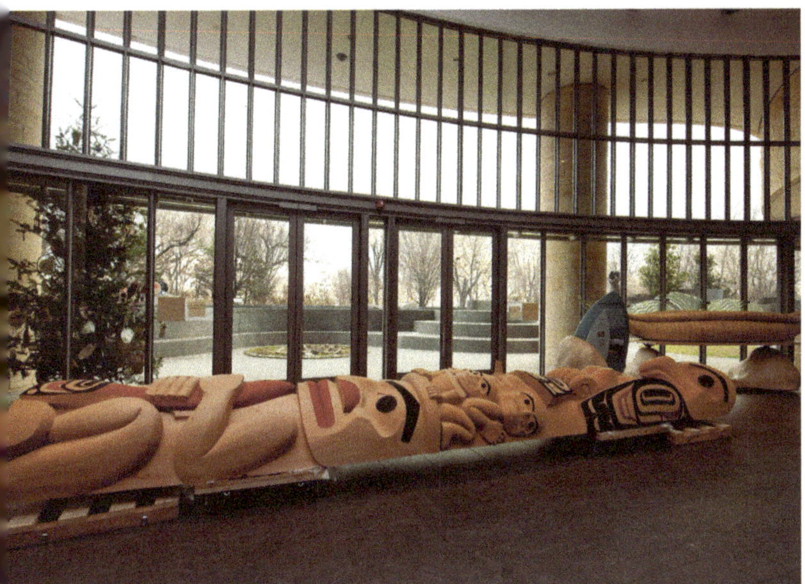
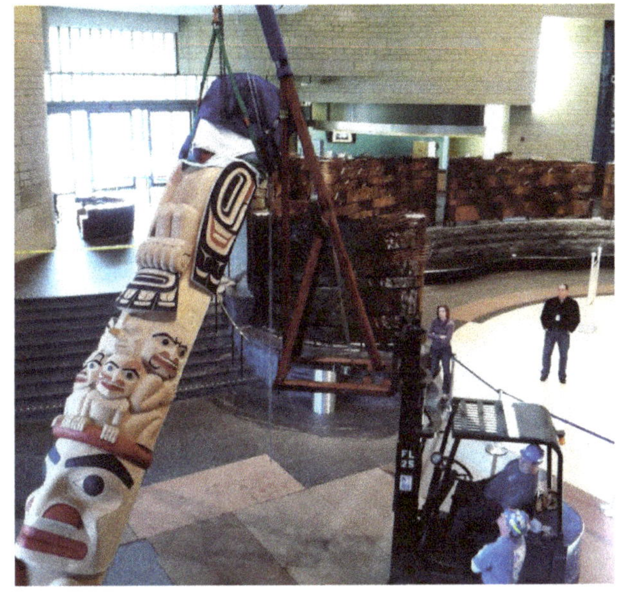
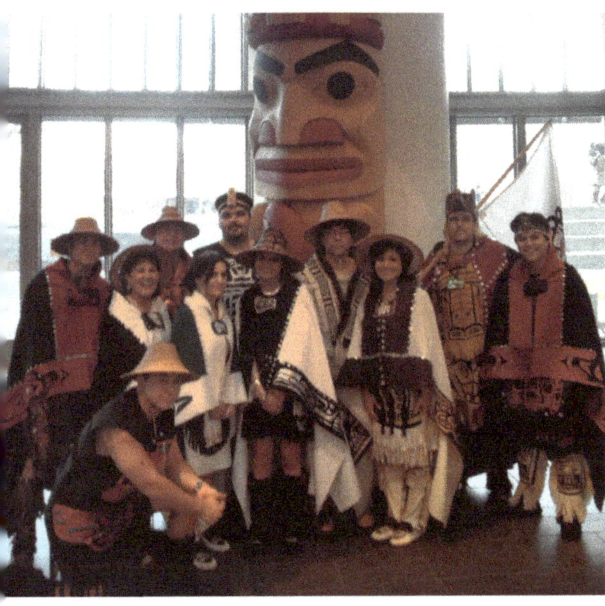
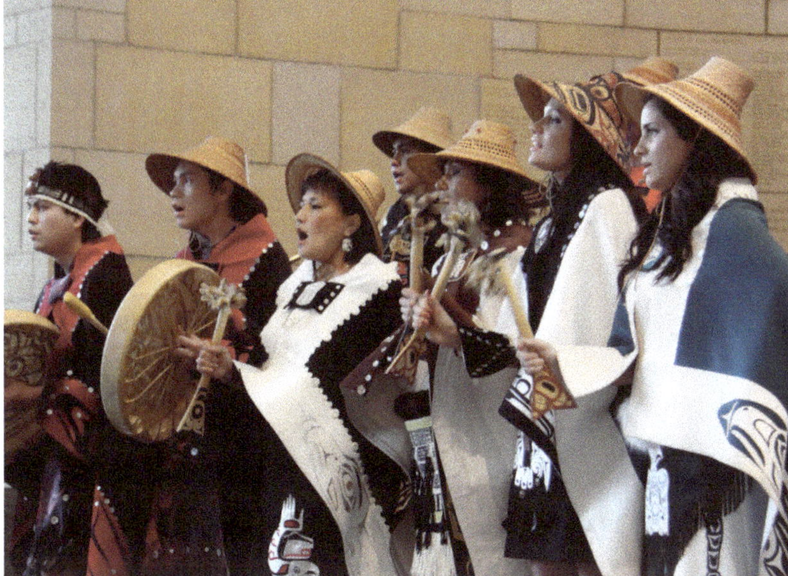

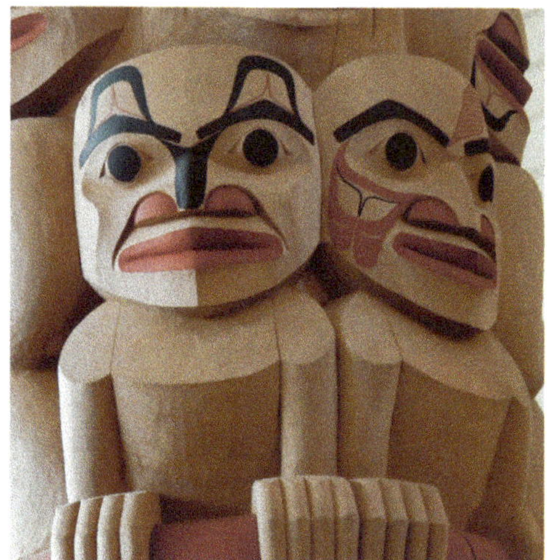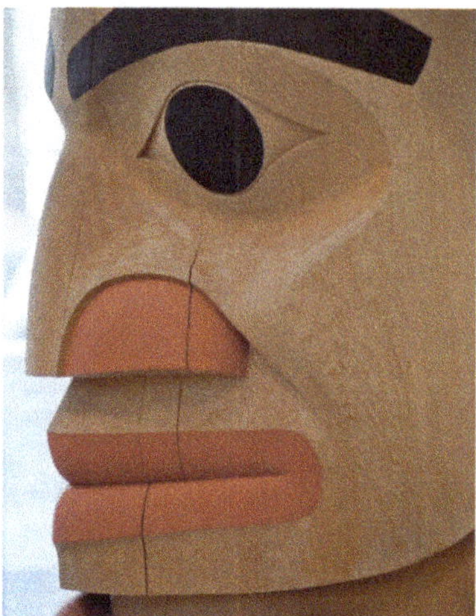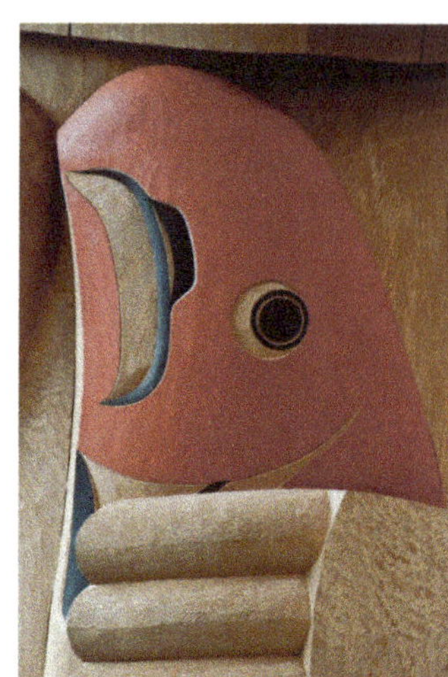

I love close-ups of my work. People seeing the art for the first time are fascinated with particular sections as much as they are the entire work.

Because it's indoors, the pole will never deteriorate. Directly across from the pole is a stained-glass window that is a number of stories tall. A certain time of the day, the sun shines through it and a kaleidoscope of colors goes right up the totem pole, as if it were planned.

It was pretty important that our little tribe, our little village was represented there. I'm proud to have that opportunity. I really wanted for our people—Northwest Coast people—to have significant representation in the museum. We accomplished that with the pole. You can't miss it; you walk in there and you can't miss it.

During those couple of weeks, we were streaming video on the Internet the whole time. There is a big-domed area and the sound is really neat. The camera was two stories up in this big, domed central area where staircases climbed upward. A couple of friends of mine who were elementary school teachers in Metlakatla were watching on their computers the whole time we were working on the pole. They would text my son to tell us to wave. We would wave at the camera. They texted back and told us the kids were happy and waving back at us.

That was one significant, happy time for us. We were doing this so far away from our little community. The other thing was we got a lot of press. *The Washington Post* was there as were several TV stations. We were interviewed by someone almost every day. Because of the Internet and the media, two words were all over the world for those two weeks: Tsimshian and Metlakatla. ❖

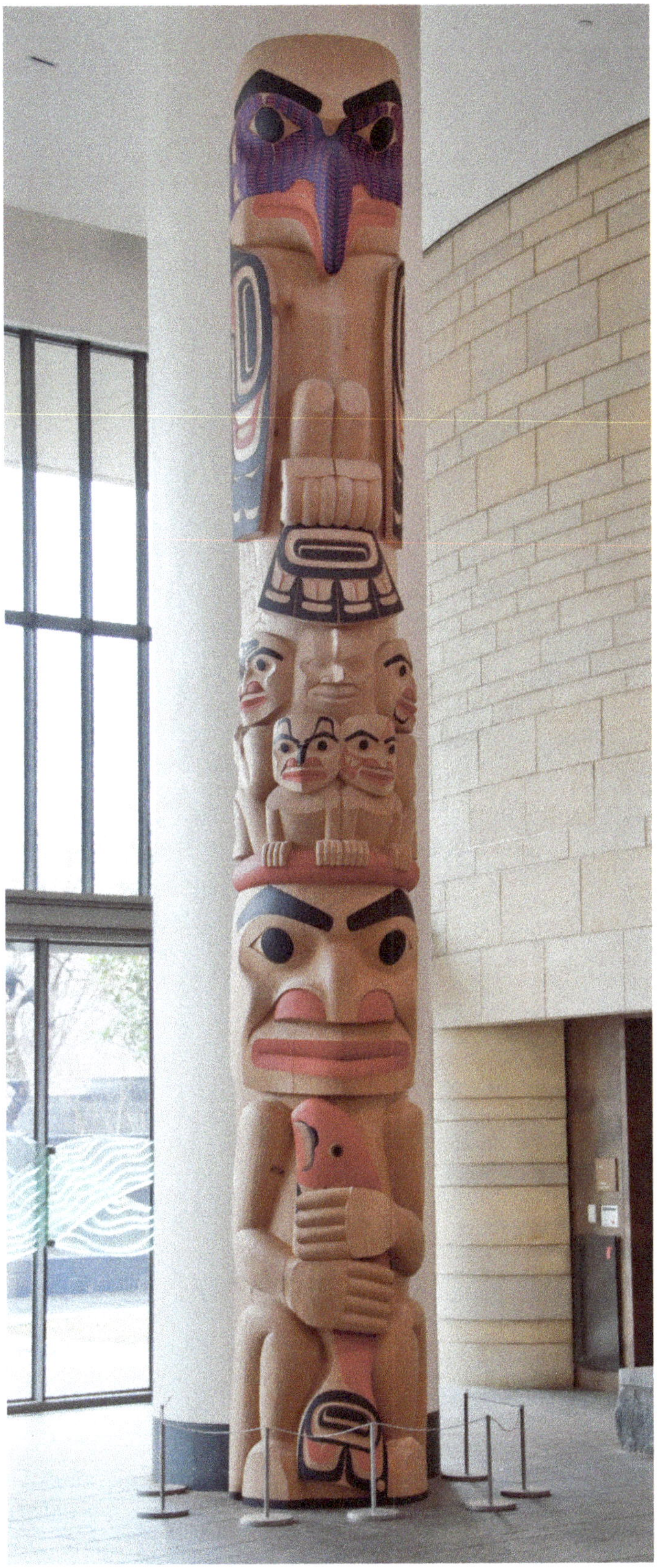

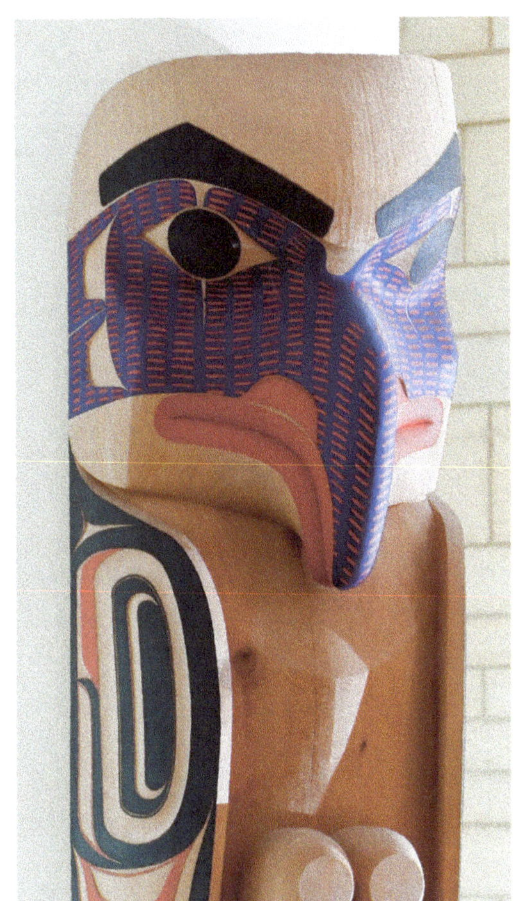

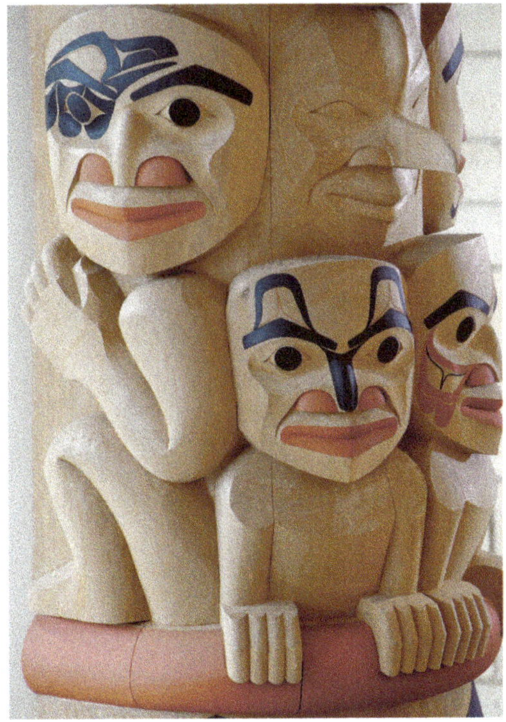

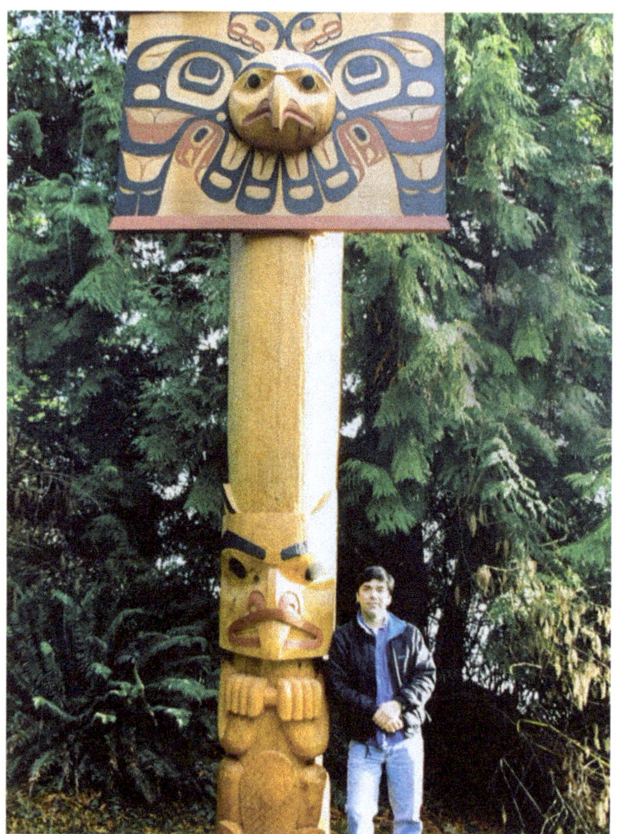

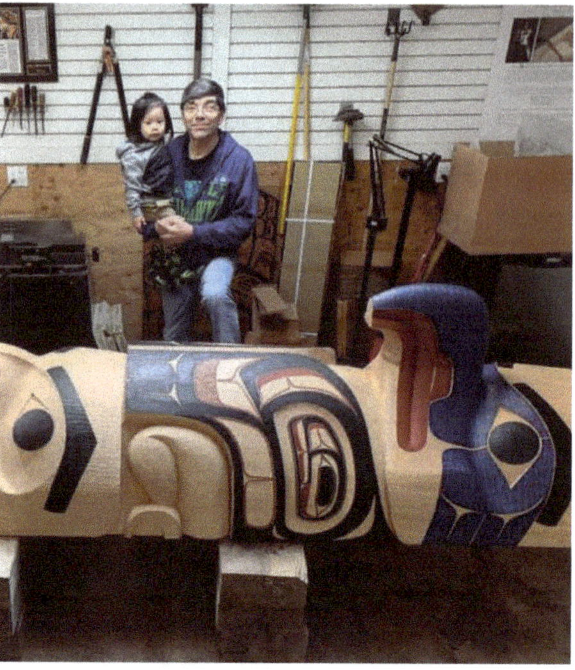

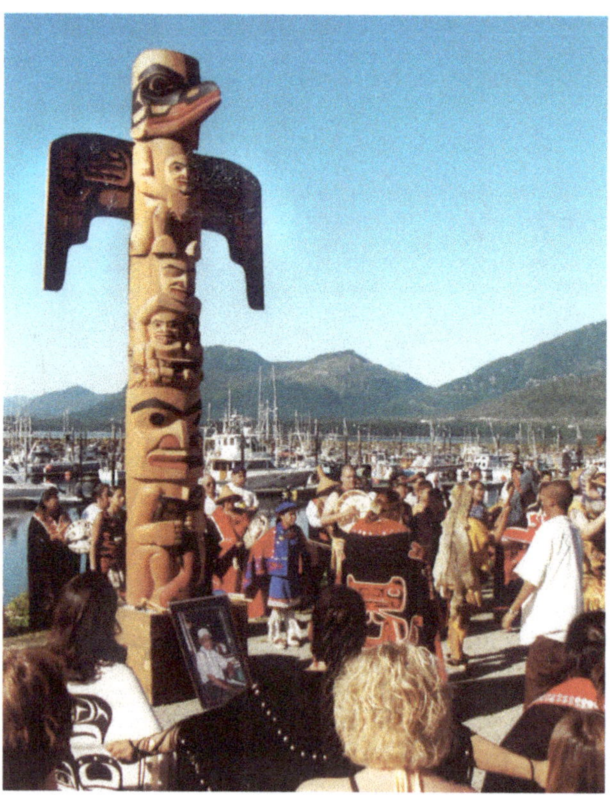

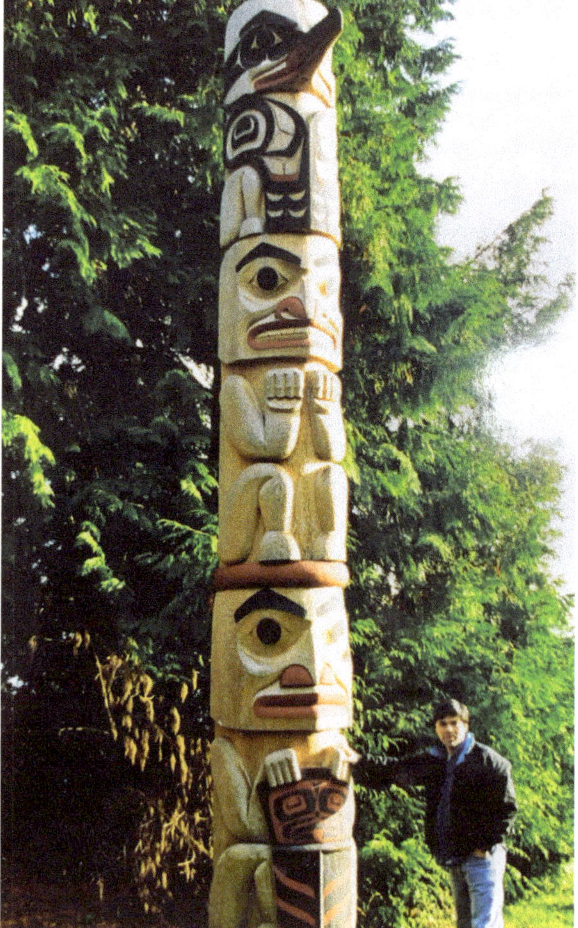

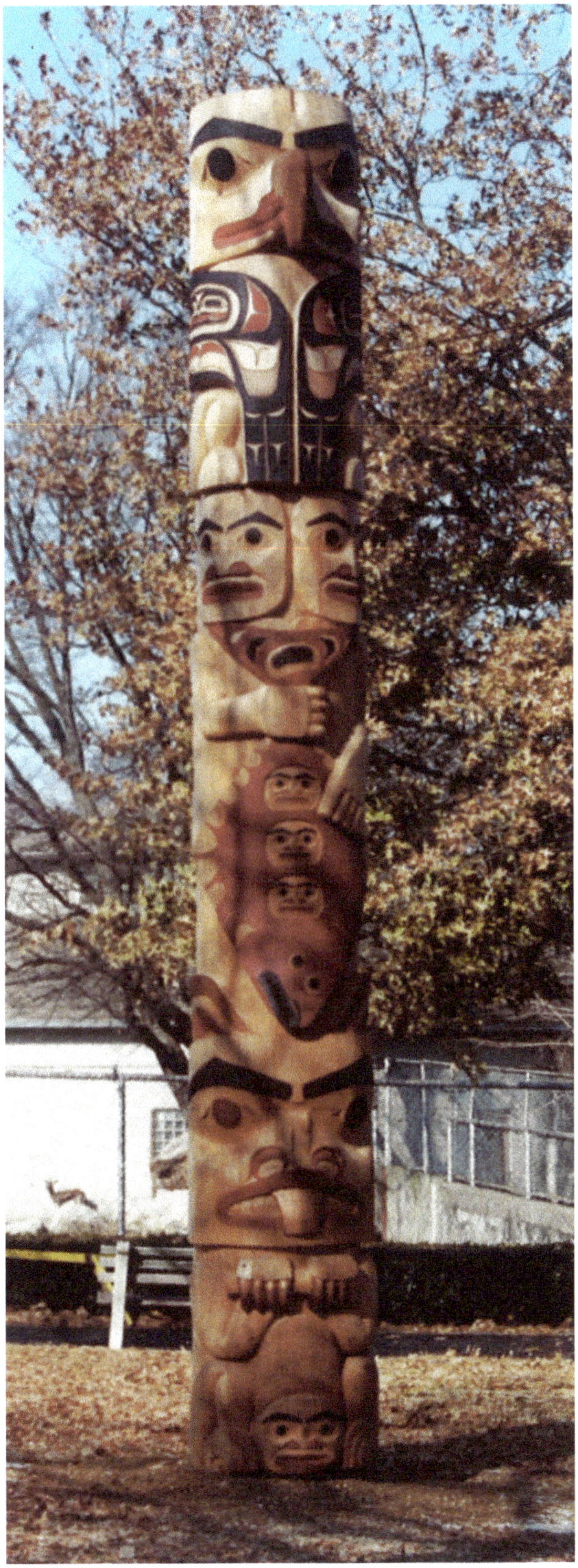

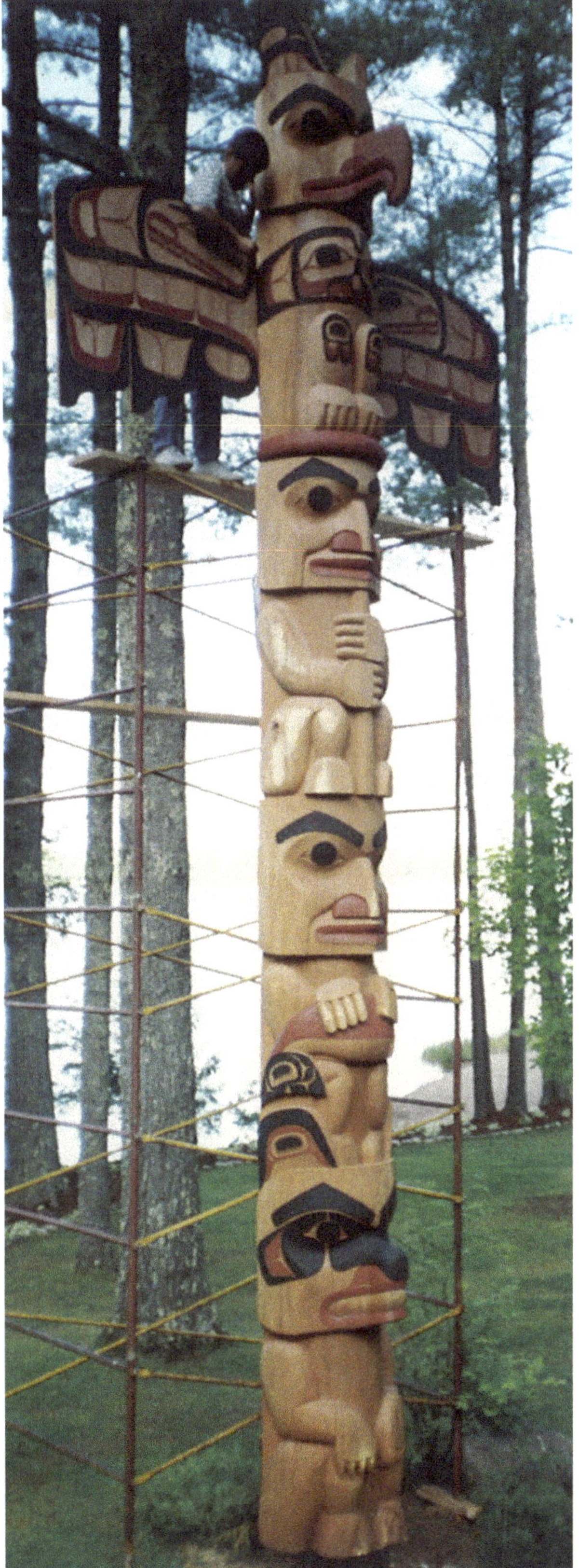

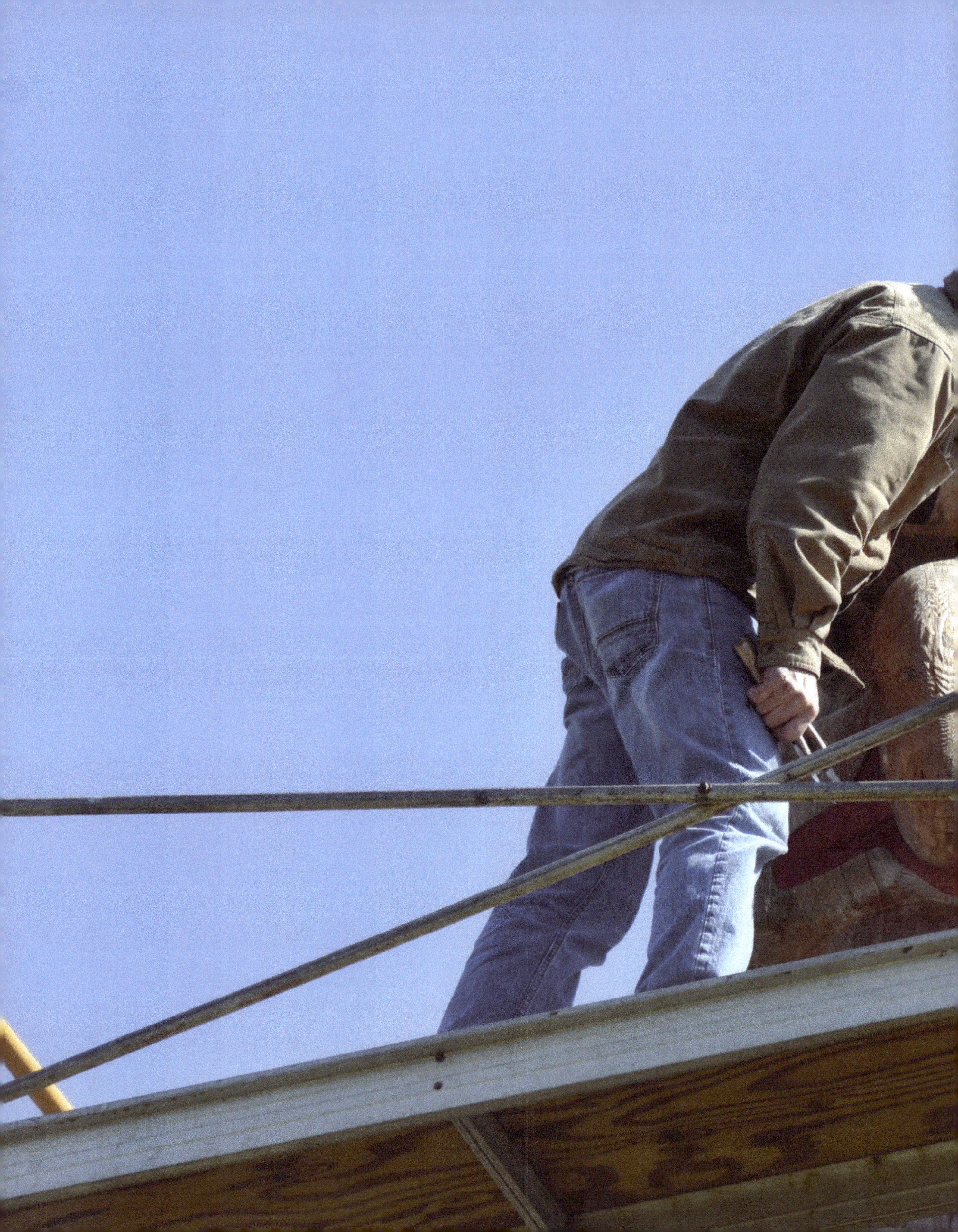

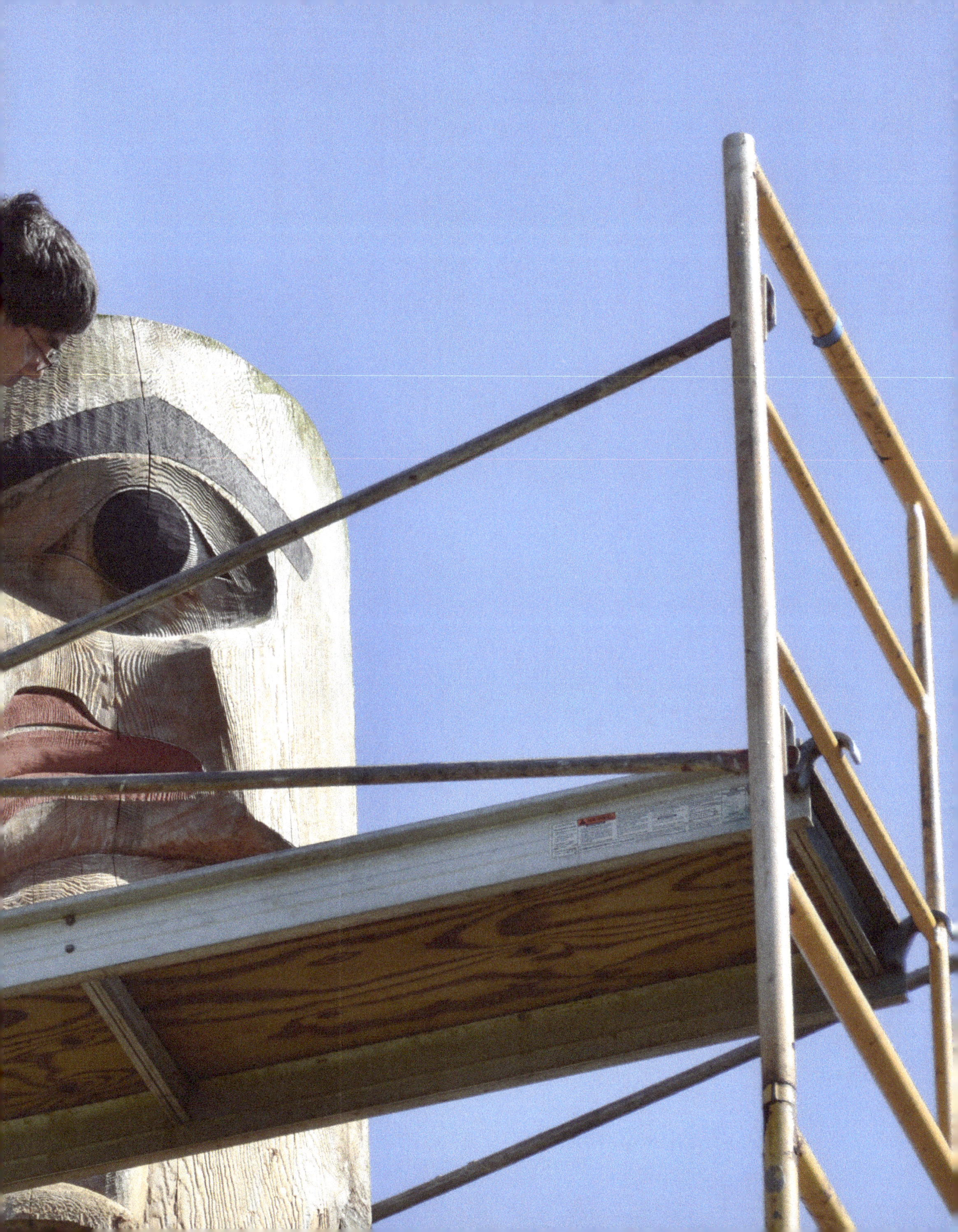

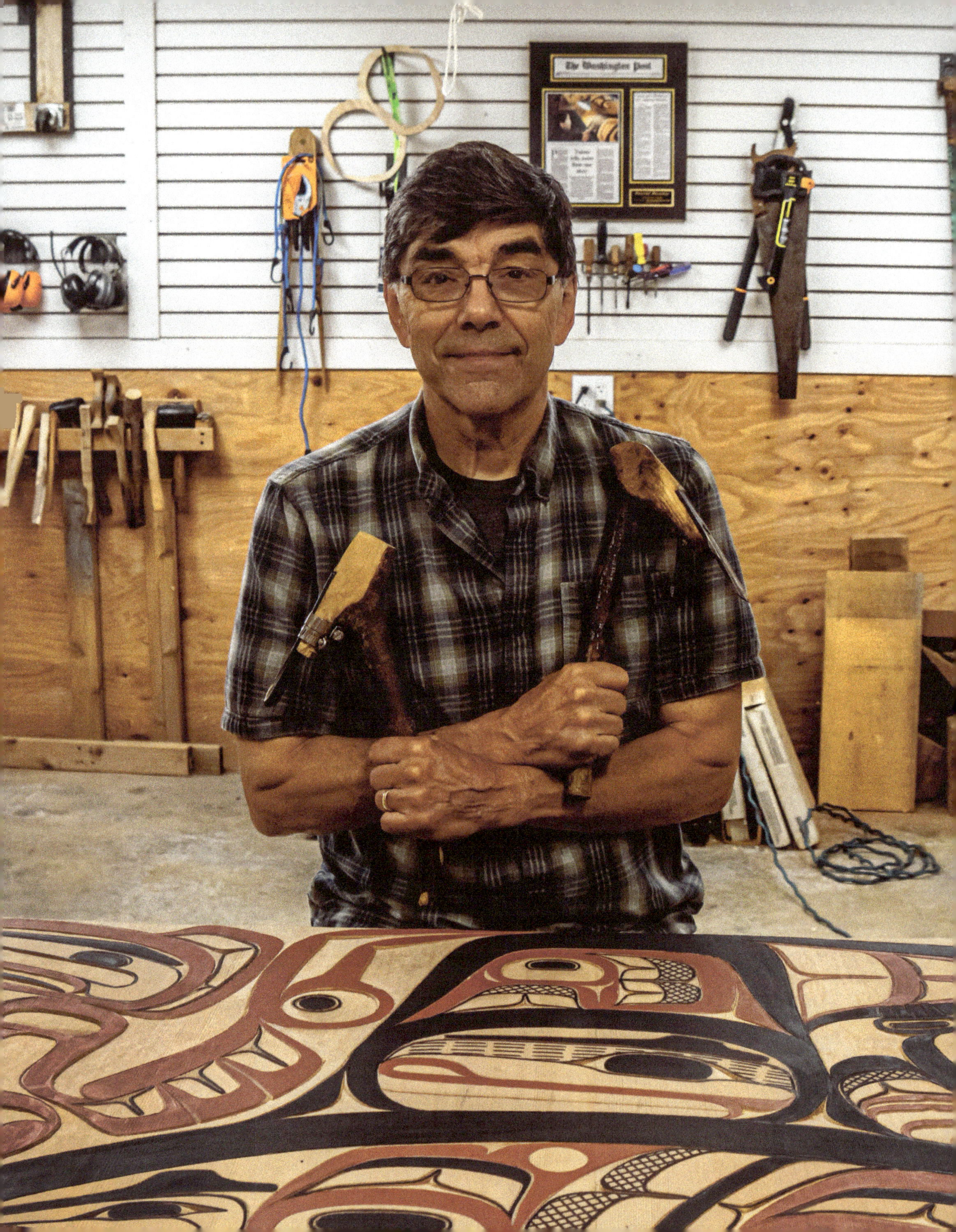

CHAPTER FIVE

OUR CULTURE IS ALIVE / *Ławila diduulsa wila loo Ts'msyen*

One of the first things I do when I come into my shop—even before I pick up an adze or paint brush—is look at photos of my grandmother and grandfather. I get a smile right away from them, even though they've been gone for years.

My grandfather's cane is up on the wall. It's a terrible piece of artwork. It's something I did when I first started. It's just awful, art wise. But it's priceless to me because both of my grandparents had their hands on it.

But it isn't just my grandparents' photos greeting me each morning. My sons, Davey and Zach, are there too. And my grandchildren. I just want to be reminded all the time of the people in my life; they tell me where I've been and who I'm sharing my life with. My shop reflects my idiosyncrasies. My wife Michelle says it's my happy place. She's right. It's the solitude and peace that I have. I love to create. I feel lucky that I have a place to work.

It's where everything happens. On a given day, I'm working on a number of pieces: panels, bowls, boxes, paddles and a totem pole. When I'm not carving or painting, I'm talking to galleries or making arrangements to get logs. I'm out here from eight or nine in the morning till ten o'clock at night just about every night. It's a good thing she's an understanding wife. I asked her a couple of times if it bothers her that I work so much. She says it doesn't. She's up until one or two in the morning herself working on regalia for somebody in the family anyway.

I've had a number of shops. The first one was my grandfather's in Metlakatla. It was an old boat shop. Actually, it was my uncle's, but my grandfather used it. It had no electricity, no

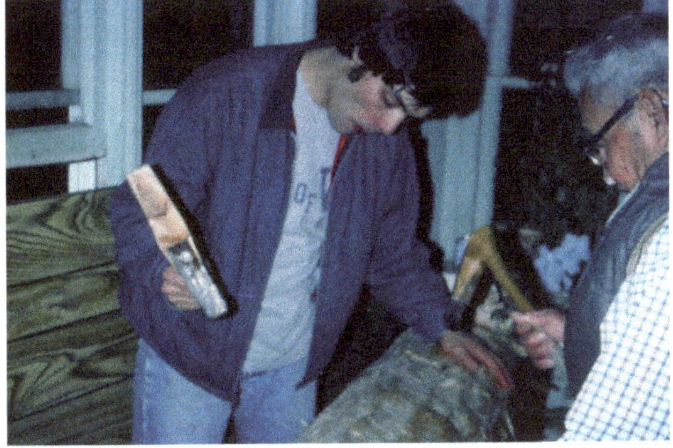

In 1981, my grandfather and I worked on the sun porch carving a small pole for my grandmother. It was right after she passed away. I made two of them for her. This was an 8-footer and it stood on my grandfather's porch for years. Now, it's in the attic.

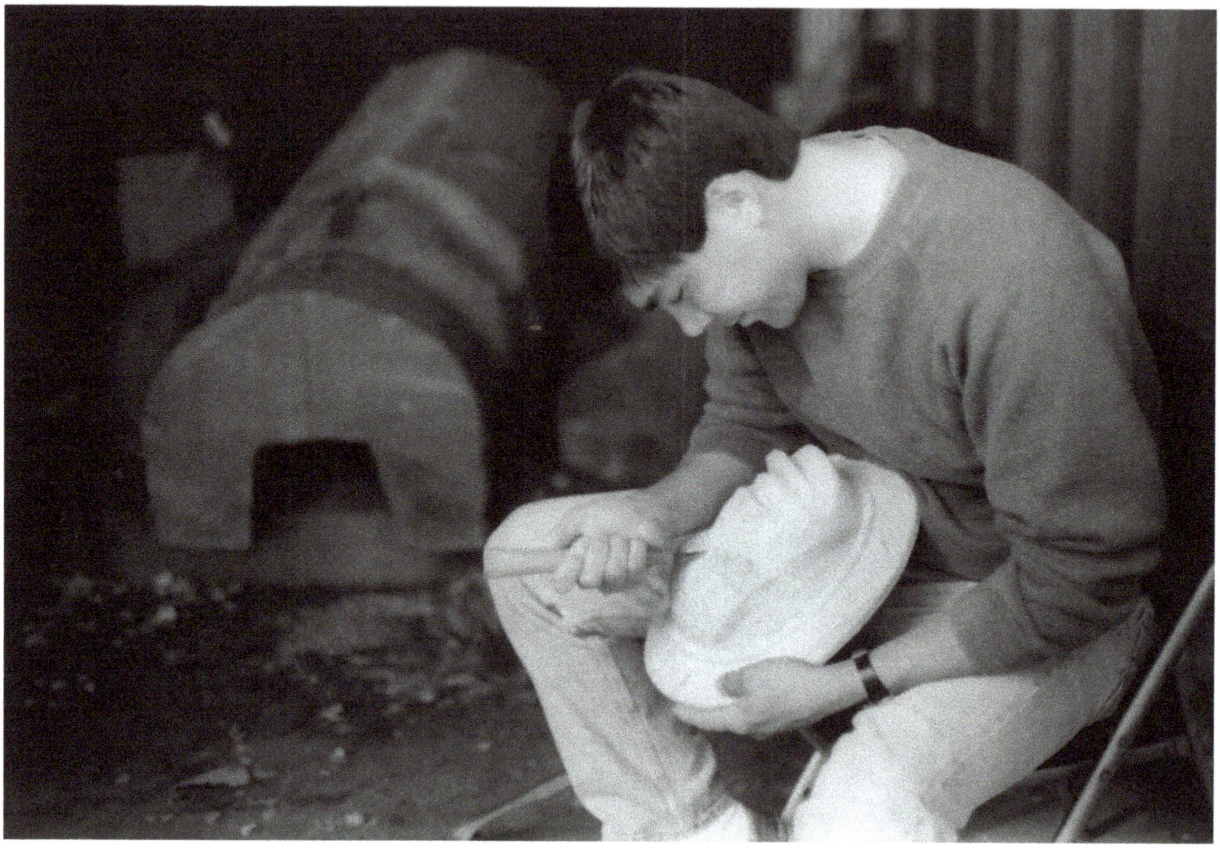

In 1986, I left Metlakatla to become a full-time artist. Here, I'm in my first shop in Kingston, WA, working on a moon mask.

water. I'd open the end doors so I had light coming in and I opened the little door facing the water. I carved my first few little poles there. All of my shops kind of look the same. They've been my refuge. I'm pretty focused on what I do. I spend a lot of time alone. When we were looking for this house we're in now, we looked for a year for a combination of a nice house and a good shop.

I made four eight-foot totem poles for the elementary school in my village—one for each clan. My grandfather happened to be visiting me in Kingston at that time. I had just finished the poles and I stood them up in a row in my shop. I opened the garage-style door and called my grandfather to take a look. I threw open the door and hit one of the totem poles, and they went down like dominos. I just saved one, it happened so fast. I grabbed the eagle. The others fell over. The killer whale broke the dorsal fin. My grandfather looked at the mess, shook his head, and said, "David, you make me cry."

I said, "Yaya, now we're going to find out how good of a carver I really am." I worked far into the night. I finished and repaired all of them. I shipped them out. They've been at the elementary school all these years.

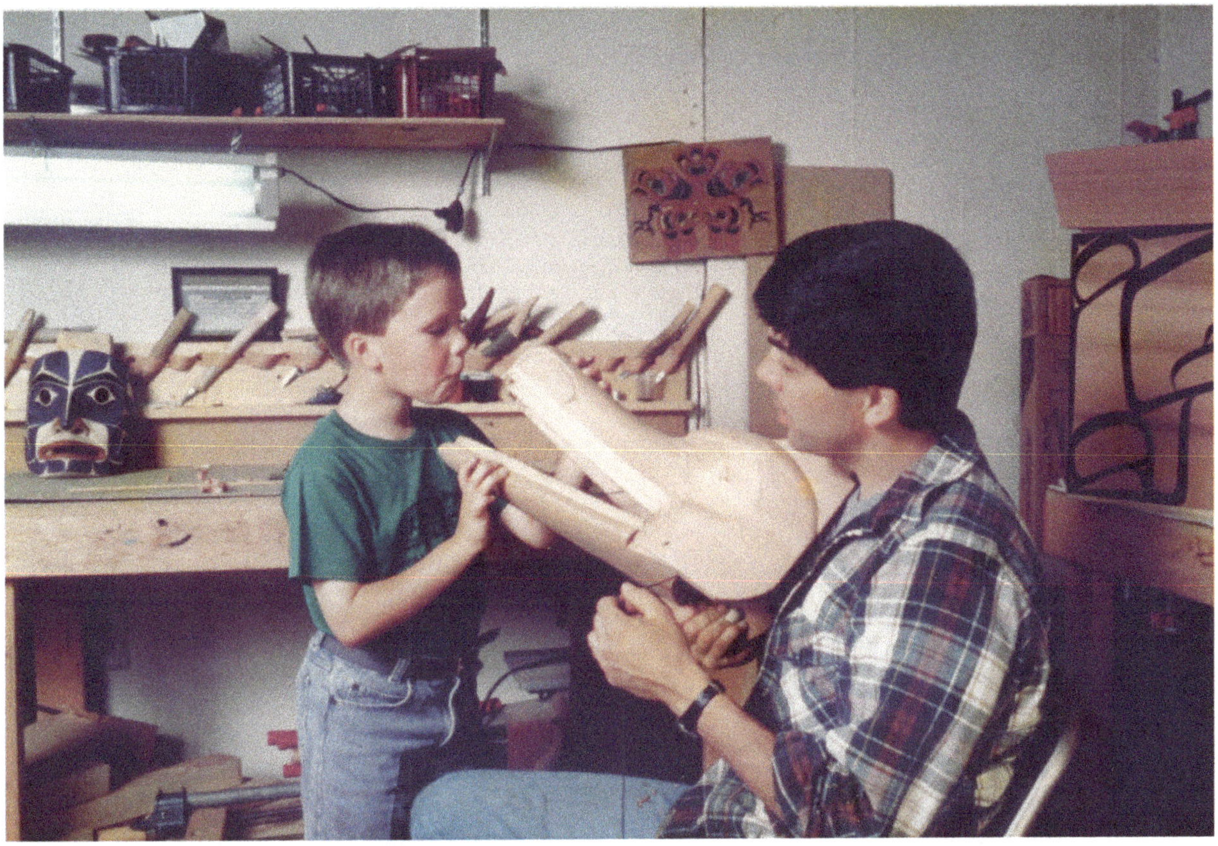

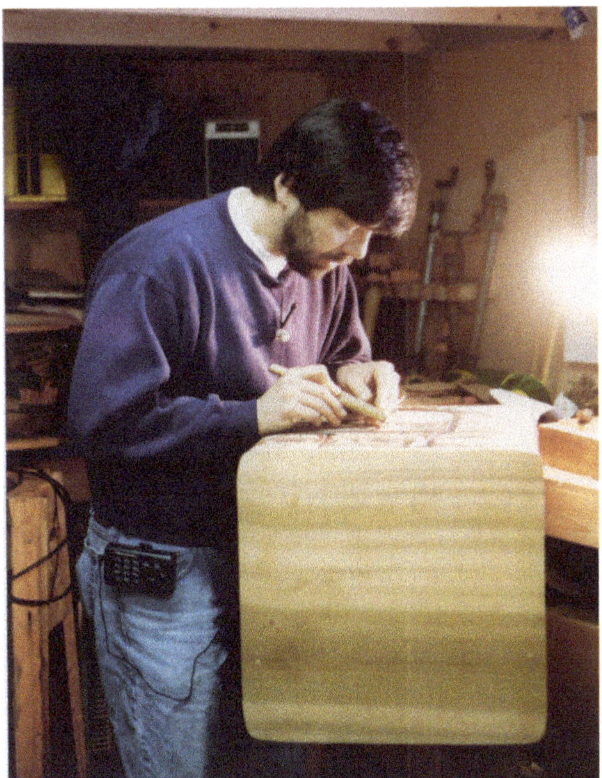

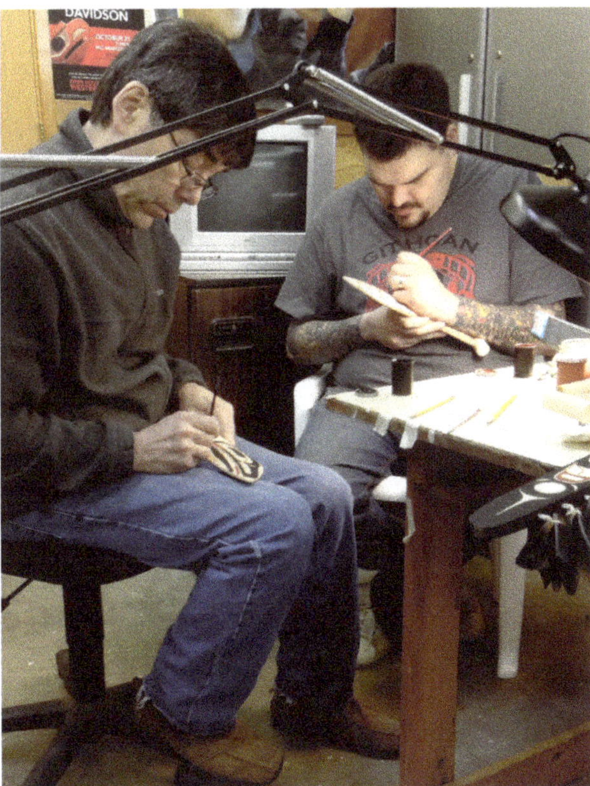

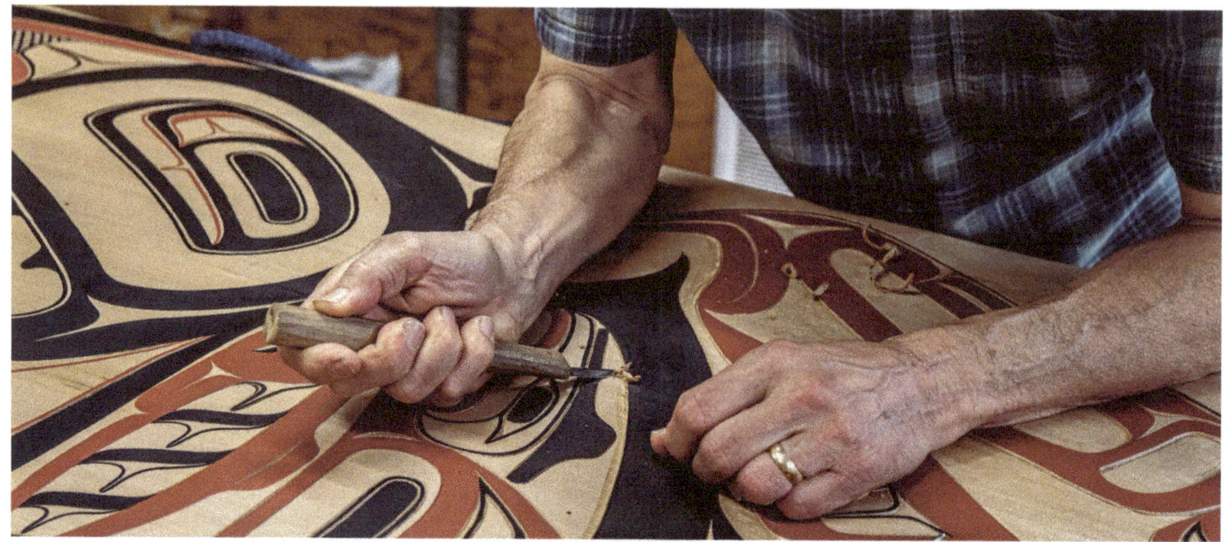

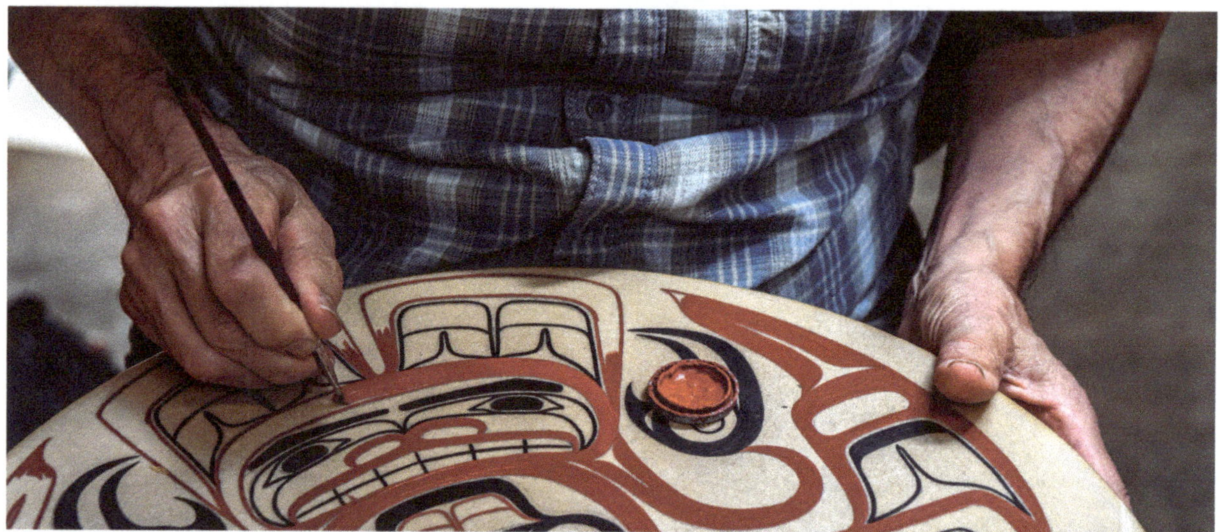

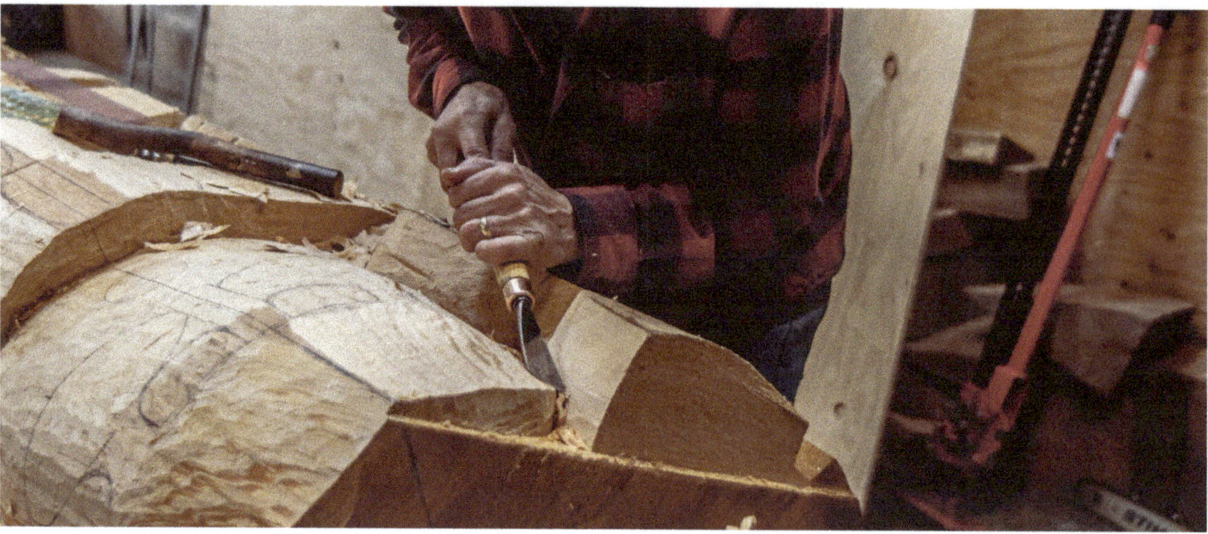

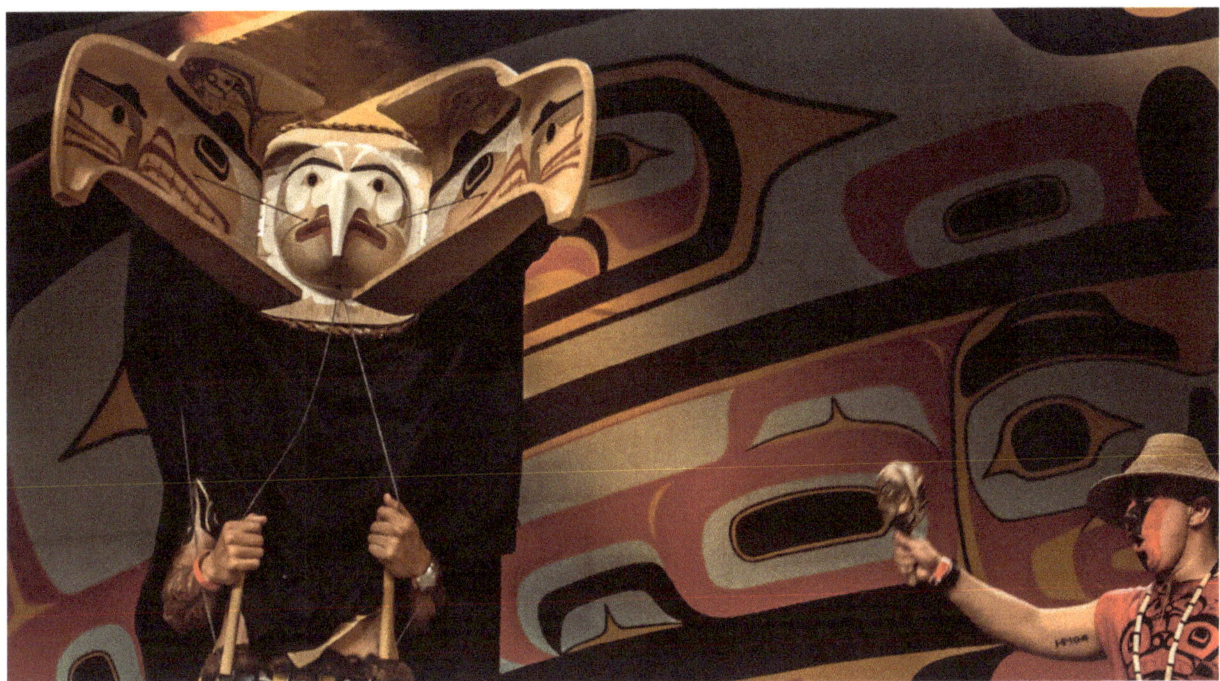

I'*m still amazed* when someone wants some of my work after all these years. It might sound phony, but it's true. I've been doing this for more than forty years, but I still worry about where my next dollar is going to come from.

What I really enjoy is carving pieces to be used in performance. That's because the pieces are being used in a traditional way, not just hanging on walls. Our culture is alive; it's not a museum curiosity. Grow up with none of it, I want it so badly and I get so excited about the culture coming back. I had to learn everything, so I could teach others. I had to reach back generations to create what is normal now.

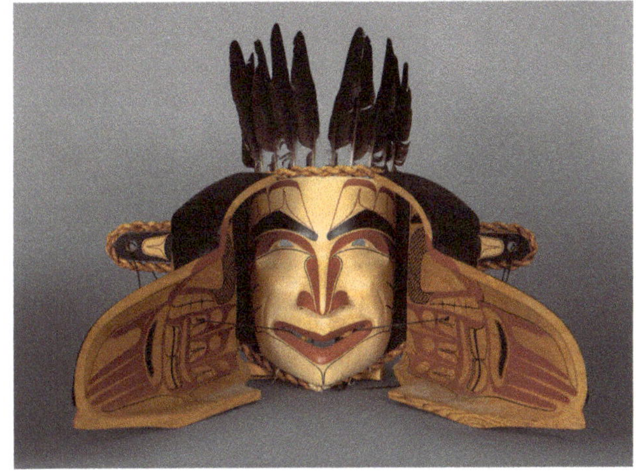

Read more about transformation masks on page 141.

We tell people to take care not to speak of our culture in the past tense. It's a living, breathing culture. It's evolving.

My favorite piece might be the transformation mask. It's that whole thing of duality of spirit. We have three big transformation masks in our show. It's an animal, usually a raven or eagle, on the outside, but when a dancer pulls a set of strings, it reveals a carved human face. Our ancestors felt there was a dual personality in all things. All animals had a human spirit. They could go back and forth between the animal and the human world.

*P*robably *the most* unusual project I produced was a house front for the inside of the Sealaska Heritage Institute Walter J. Soboleff Center in Juneau. When Davey and I finished, the work stood forty feet wide by sixteen feet high. It is the first thing people see when they enter this magnificent culture center.

It resembles the front of traditional clan houses. People who traditionally lived in the clan houses were usually the members of a specific clan, plus their spouses and children. They weren't all of the same clan. We call them longhouses; the Tlingit and Haida call them clan houses.

Davey and I created a design that represents a style and a complexity of traditional house fronts. The center tells the story of Am'ala: In Guu Man Sinyaagwa Ha'lidzog (He Who Holds up the Earth). The figure, Am'ala, is shown as a giant supernatural being who represents the land. The Tlingit, Haida, and Tsimshian people are represented across the top, and Am'ala is on his back balancing the world on a stick propped on his chest.

The small door hidden in the belly of Am'ala leads into the clan house that Sealaska Heritage, in a formal ceremony, named Shuká Hit, or Ancestors' House in Lingit.

The sides of the house front depict the four Tsimshian crests. The raven and killer whale sit on the left and eagle and wolf on the right. We carved the secondary crests—frog, grizzly bear, beaver, and black bear—in the eyes of raven, killer whale, eagle, and wolf, respectively.

Davey copied the circle design on the left side from an old photo that illustrated the remains of a Tsimshian house front from the 1800s. The circle was the only piece of the design that remained on the old front, and we placed it there to honor the ancestral Tsimshian carvers.

It was a daunting experience and a very long, detailed process, but because of Davey, it went a lot smoother than it would have without him. It began when he took the rolled-up designs, went to FedEx Kinkos and got them blown up. But once they were blown up, they were not as clean and clear as when they were small, so we had to redraw them. Then we used Exacto knives and cut them out like stencils, and we applied them to the boards. Zach sanded all the boards for us—more than forty of them. We did everything one stage at a time, building two four-by-eight tables and setting the boards end to end. We moved the boards one at a time off the table.

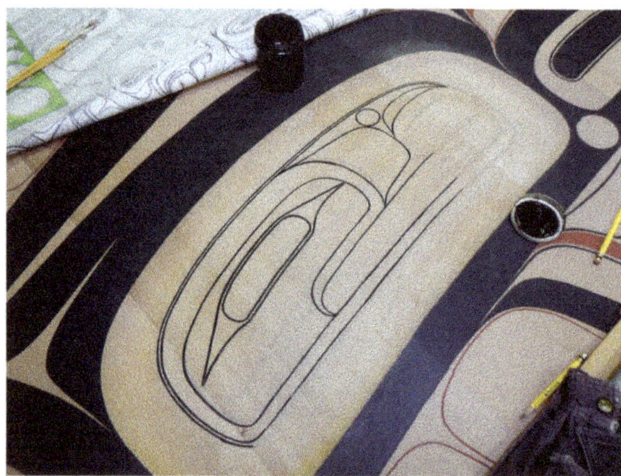

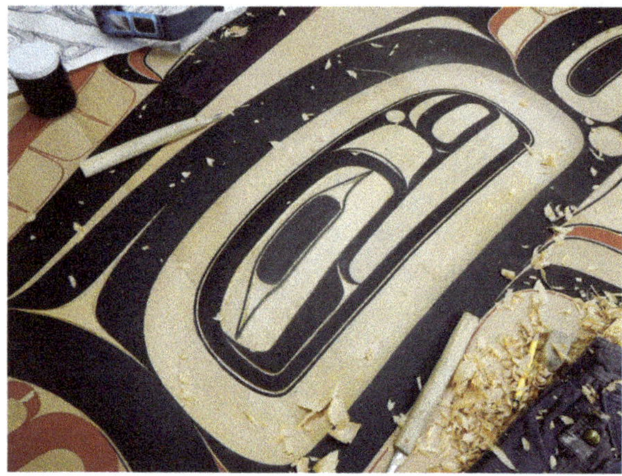

This is just one small detail of the house front Davey and I made for Sealaska Heritage Institute. We needed a variety of tools: Swiss-made knives; adzes; gouges, sometimes even an electric router to carve depths.

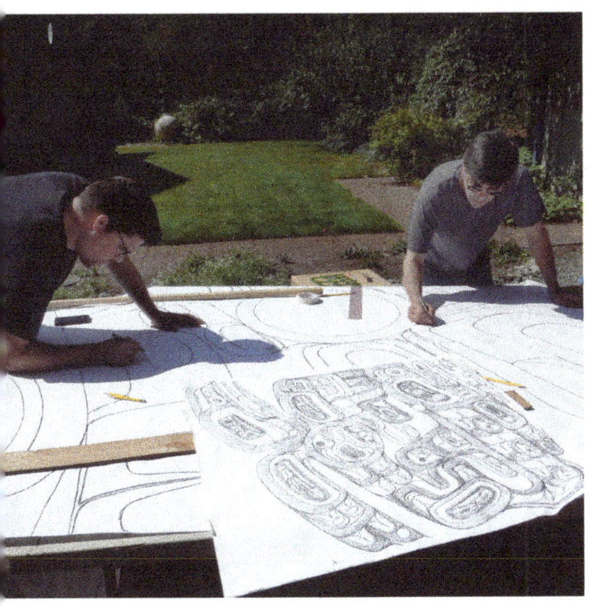
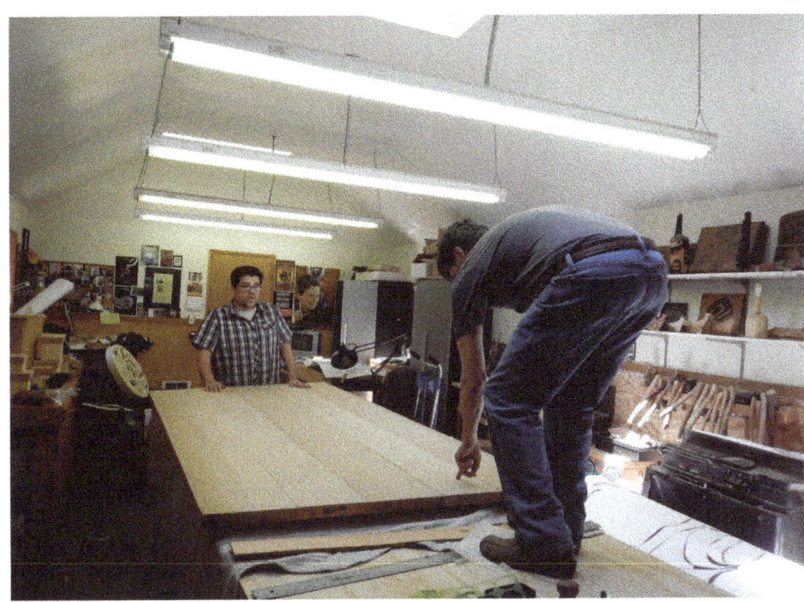
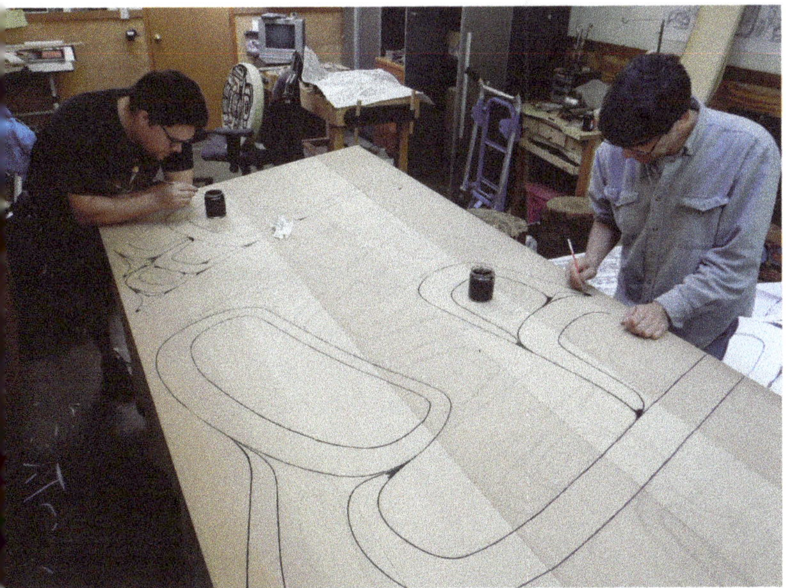
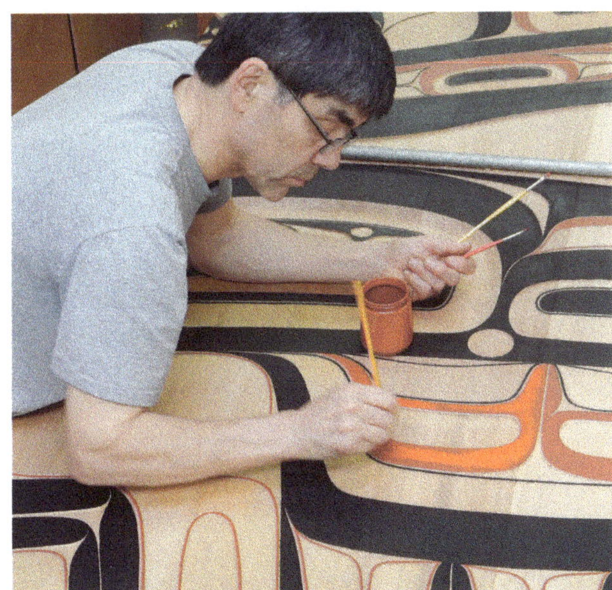
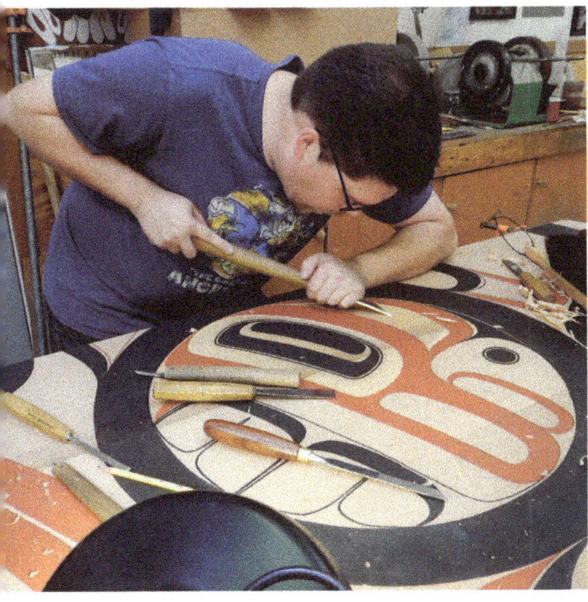
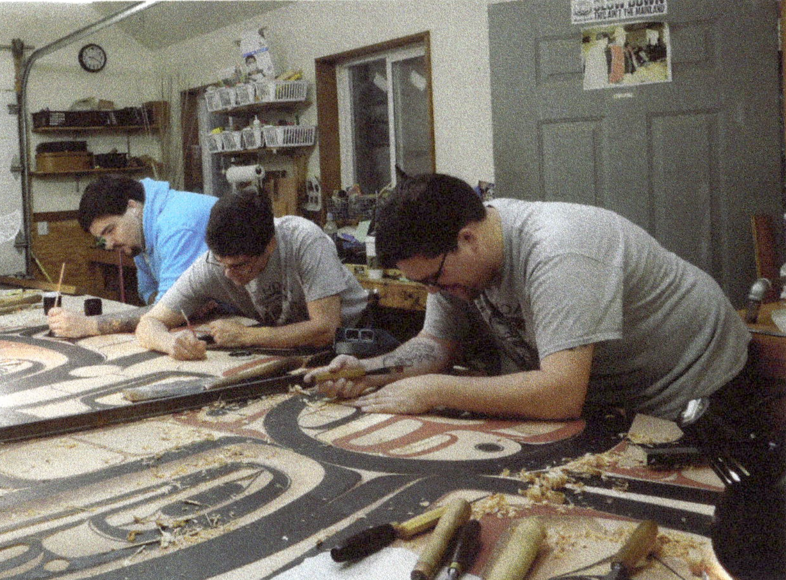

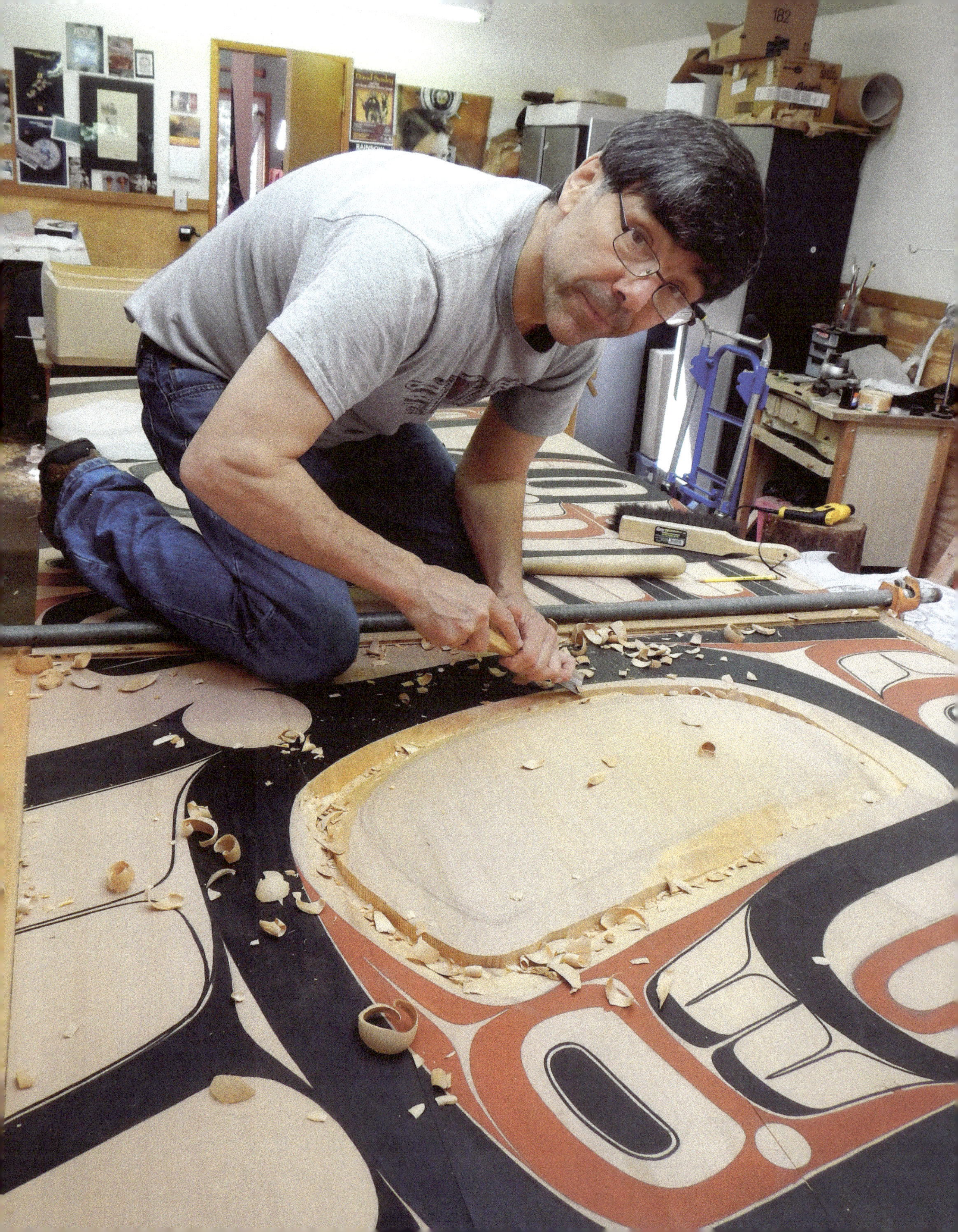

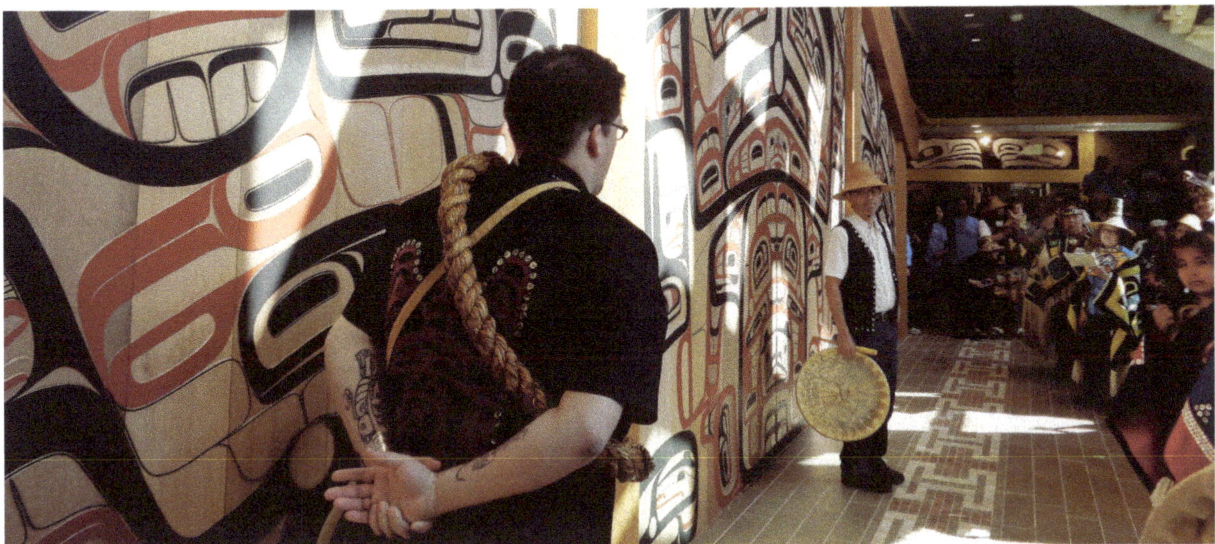

With the house front finally installed, it was truly magnificent to behold. I am glad I could share this story with Davey, who deserves a lot of the credit. It wouldn't have been the same without him.

We painted everything four boards at a time until we made it all the way across, then went back and started carving. We had to paint the black first, then the red. Some of the areas were left open.

The whole process took six months. We could put sections up against the house to see what they would look like, but we never saw it all put together until it went up in Juneau. We made sure everything fit and lined up.

It means a lot to me to tell you that it would not look as good or be done as well without Davey. I asked him to come work for me, but I also asked him to draw the design based on the old Tsimshian house front style. We wanted it to look like it was made in the 1800s. The coast Tsimshian people were known for house fronts more than totem poles even though they had totem poles.

We installed the house front in 2015. That was a once in a lifetime opportunity. I'll forever be grateful to Sealaska Heritage Institute President Rosita Worl and Chief Operating Officer Lee Kadinger for hiring me and Davey—it's important that this building and Sealaska in general includes the Tsimshian along with the Tlingit and Haida.

That house front is carved. The house fronts in the old days weren't carved. They were house fronts painted right on the house. There is historic evidence of that. A great number of them were put up temporarily, especially during potlatches, then taken down and stored, then brought out again. We understood the magnitude of our project and how fortunate we were to be able to make that house front. The nice thing is our work is indoors, so it won't be subjected to Southeast Alaska's incessant wet weather. In one hundred years, it will look the same.

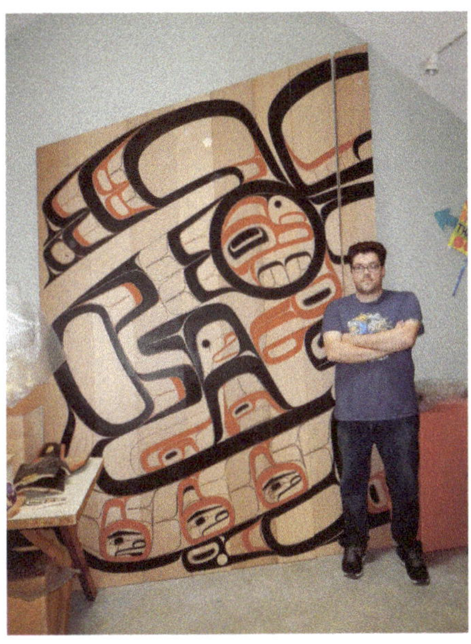

We couldn't see the entire house front until it was assembled in Juneau, but we could look at sections. Davey is 6-foot-2, so this photo tells a story of the size and scope of the project.

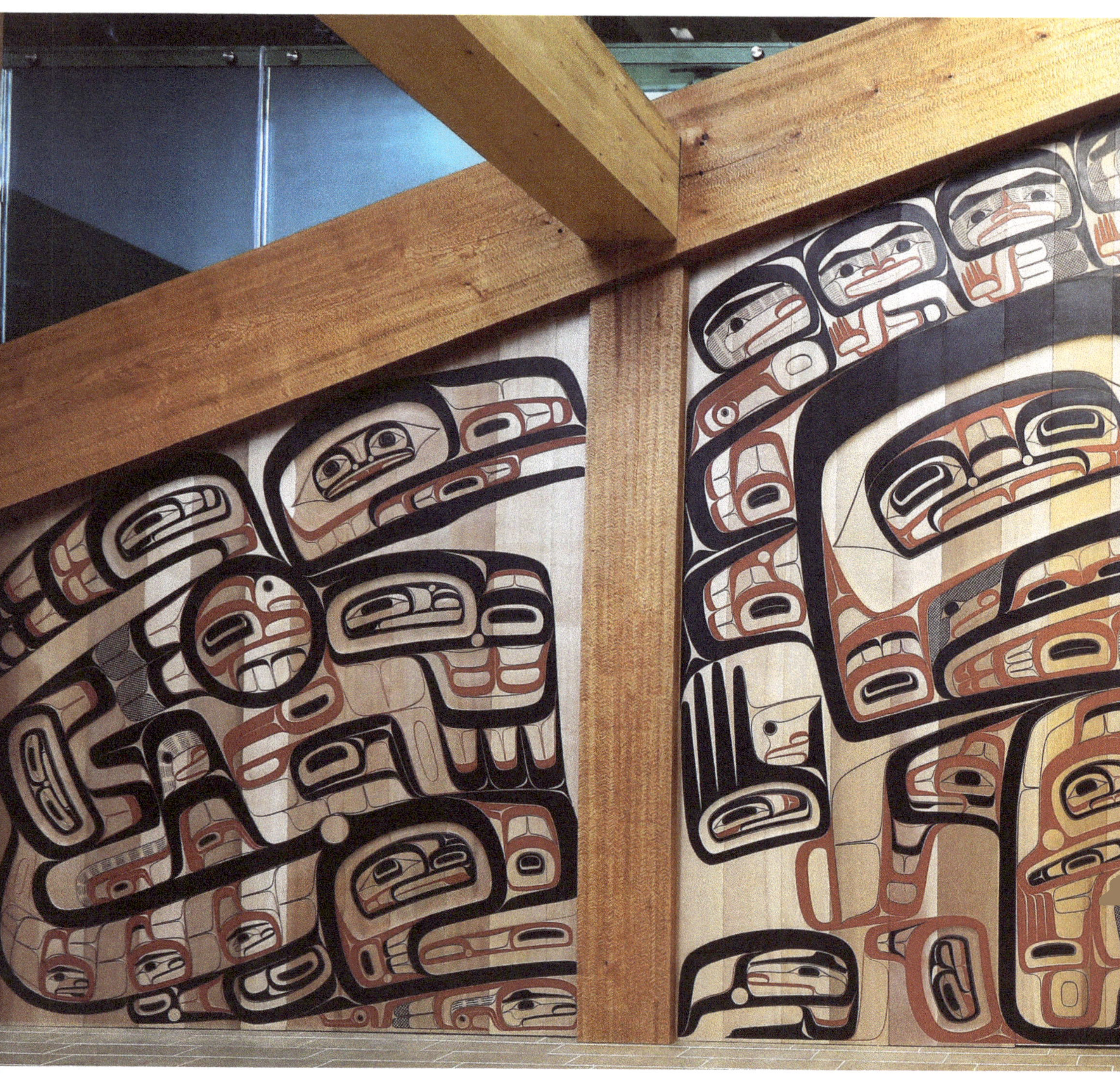

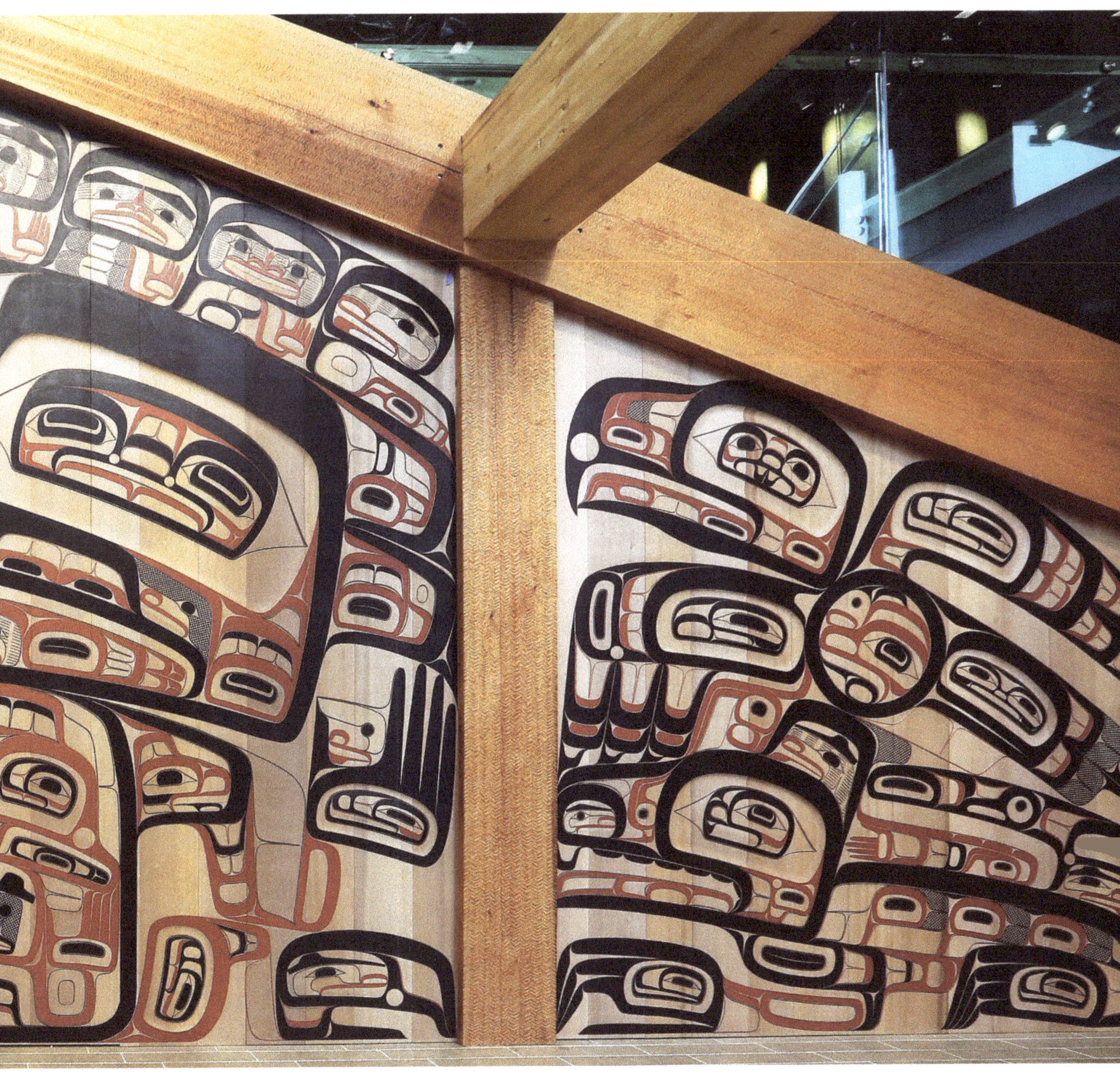

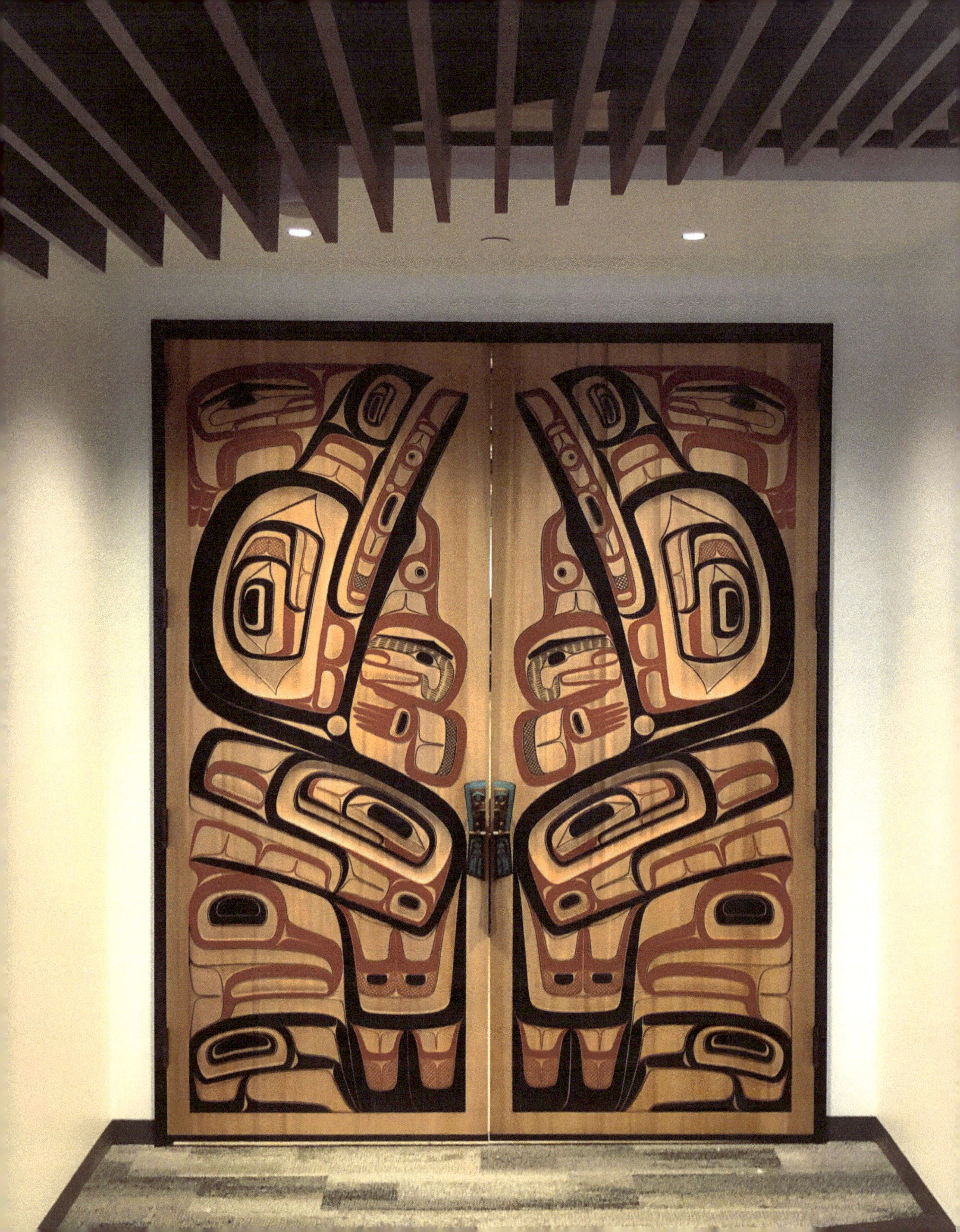

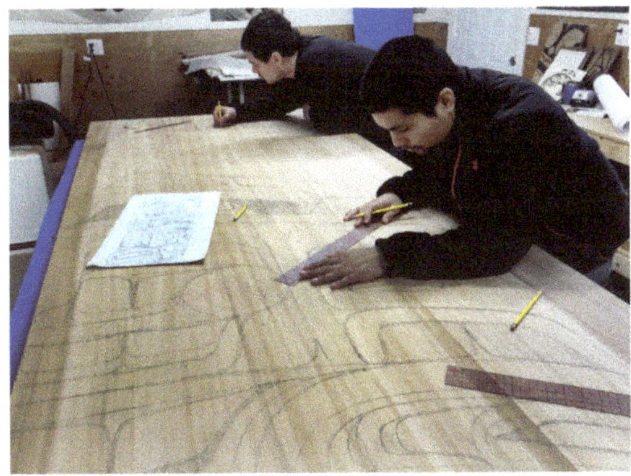

Two years after we delivered the house front, Davey and I were commissioned to build office doors carved on both sides for Sealaska Corp.'s downtown Seattle office. It was a very beautiful, tight-grained wood with a raven design on one side and eagle design on the other. Davey designed the raven side and I did the eagle side, but all four of us, including Clifton Guthrie and my step-son Darius Sanidad, carved them together. Clifton had also played a key role in carving the house front installed in Juneau.

Opportunities like this are rare because most art is displayed on a wall. The whole idea behind this one is entering the conference room, you see one design and once you're in the room, you see the other design.

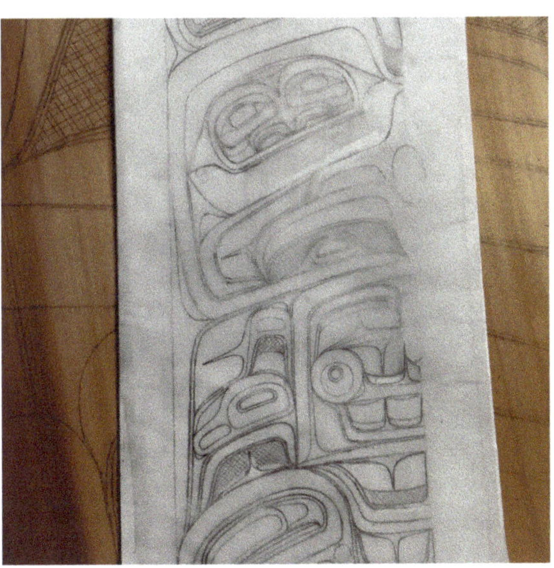

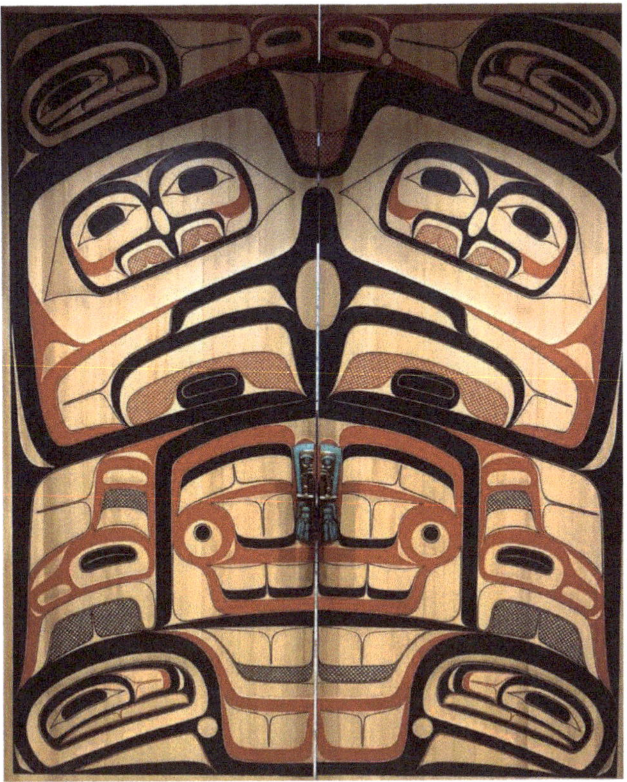

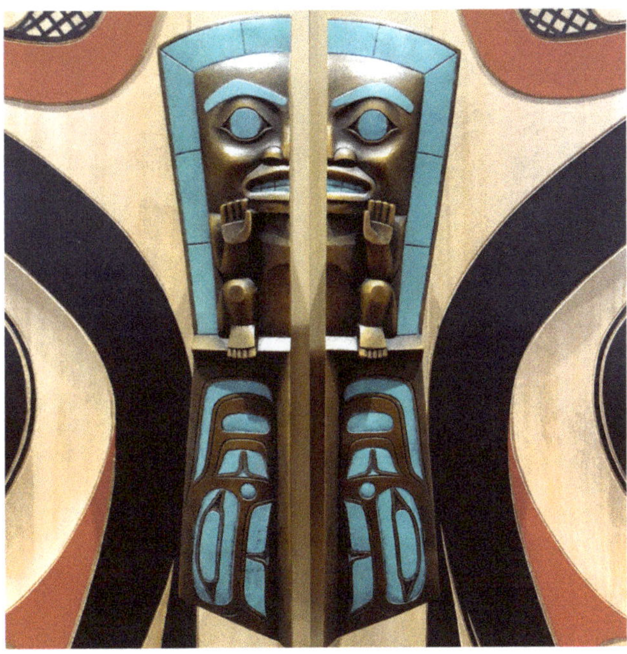

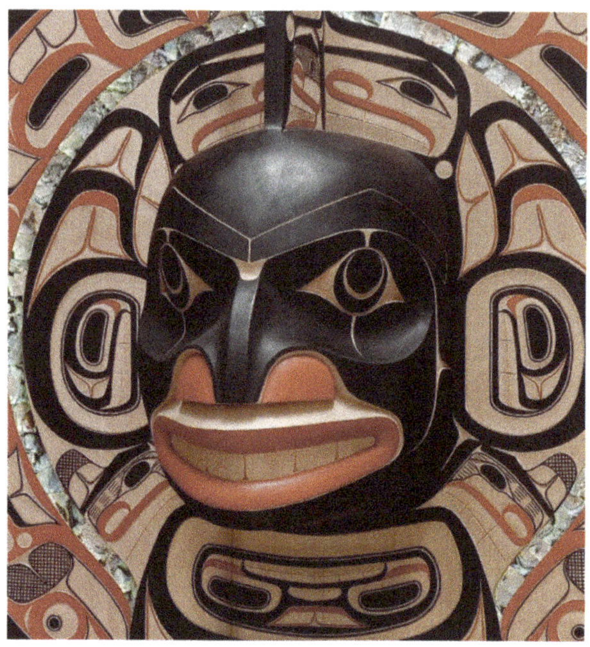

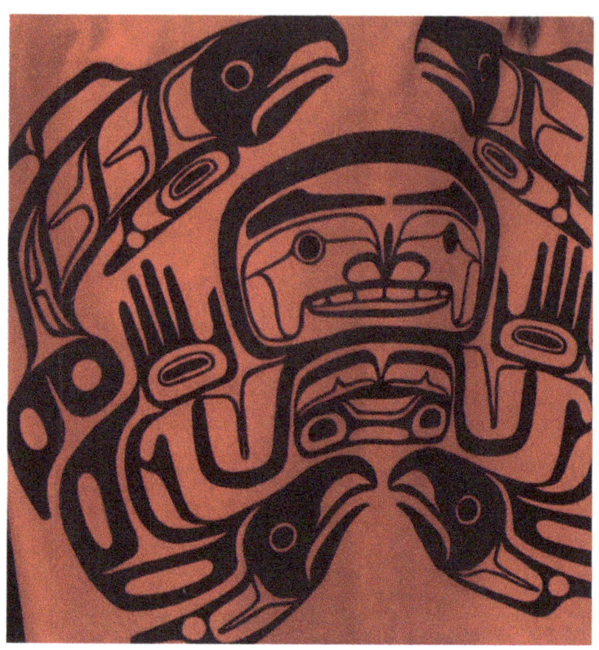

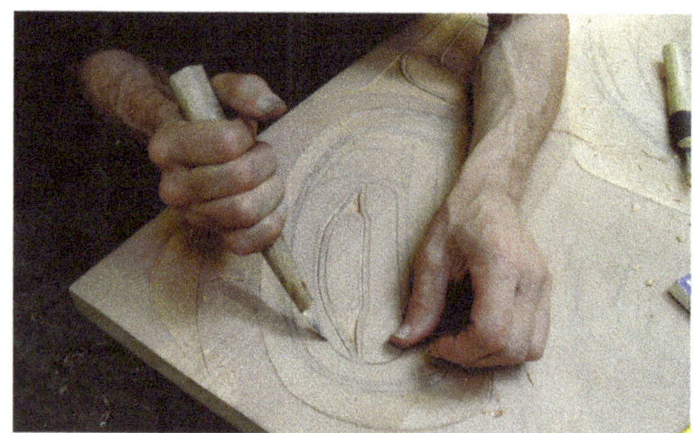

FORMLINE

The designs on the house front and the doors as well as my other work are known as formline, described as an art system where lines taper and swell, using a few foundational shapes to create designs that depict humans, animals, and supernatural beings.

It's an art that doesn't come easy and requires patience. It started long ago among all the northern people. The style's development happened over centuries. Nobody knows if it was Tsimshian, Tlingit or Haida who started it. It tells who owns things, the strength and history of a person or his family—it shows ownership.

THIS PAGE: Examples of formline in various artwork applications.

FACING PAGE: Pages from a teaching manual I use when teaching formline classes and workshops to students.

THE OVOID

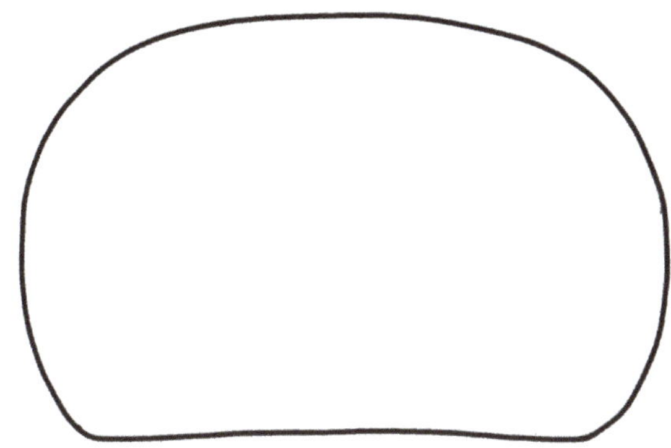

A seemingly simple bean shaped design…

The cornerstone of our art system. It looks simple enough yes, but can be a source of frustration or exhilaration, depending on your talent, your diligence in practice, and time…

In your searching through art galleries, museums, books and actually watching other artists at work you will see there are many variations on the shape of the ovoid. As with all design in general, I tell you to study carefully the old masters. But, you have some really great modern Native examples too.

Your first lesson is to imprint this ovoid on your memory …
Stare at it and know that without it … correctly done, what is produced will not be what it should be.

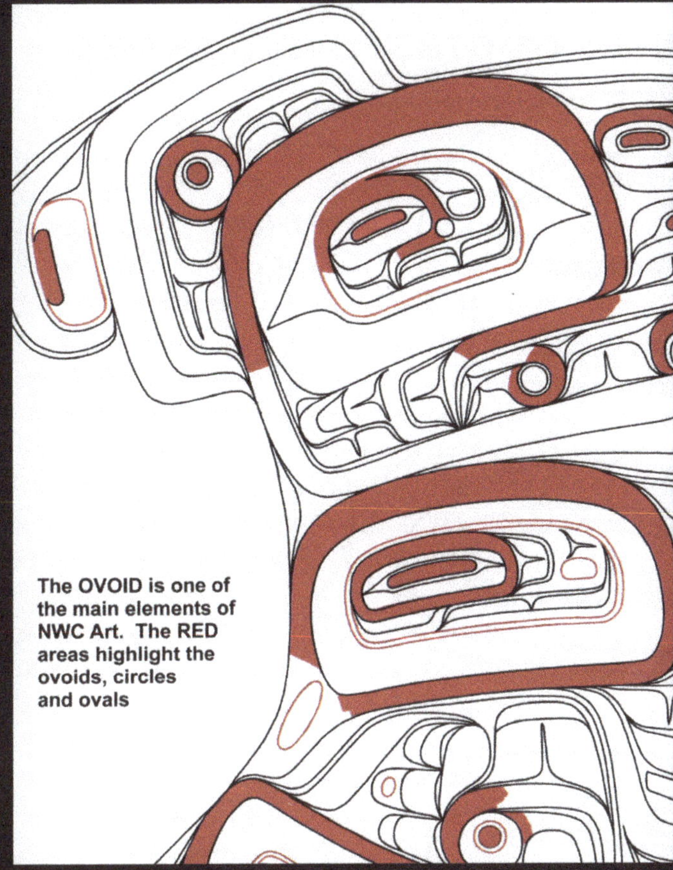

The OVOID is one of the main elements of NWC Art. The RED areas highlight the ovoids, circles and ovals

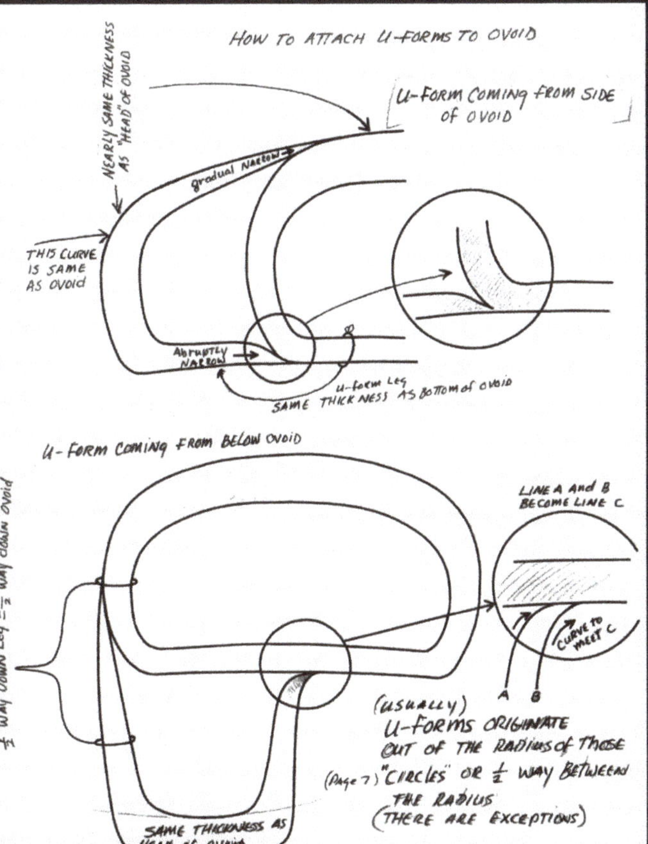

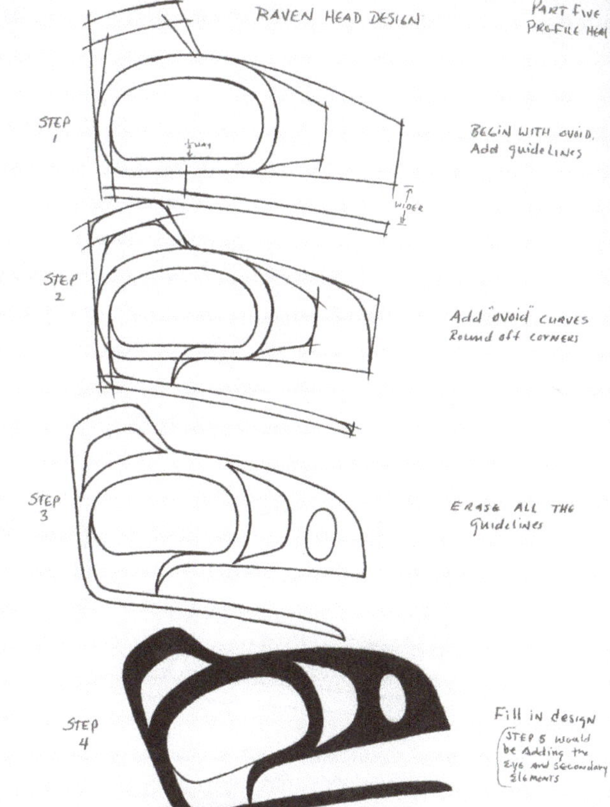

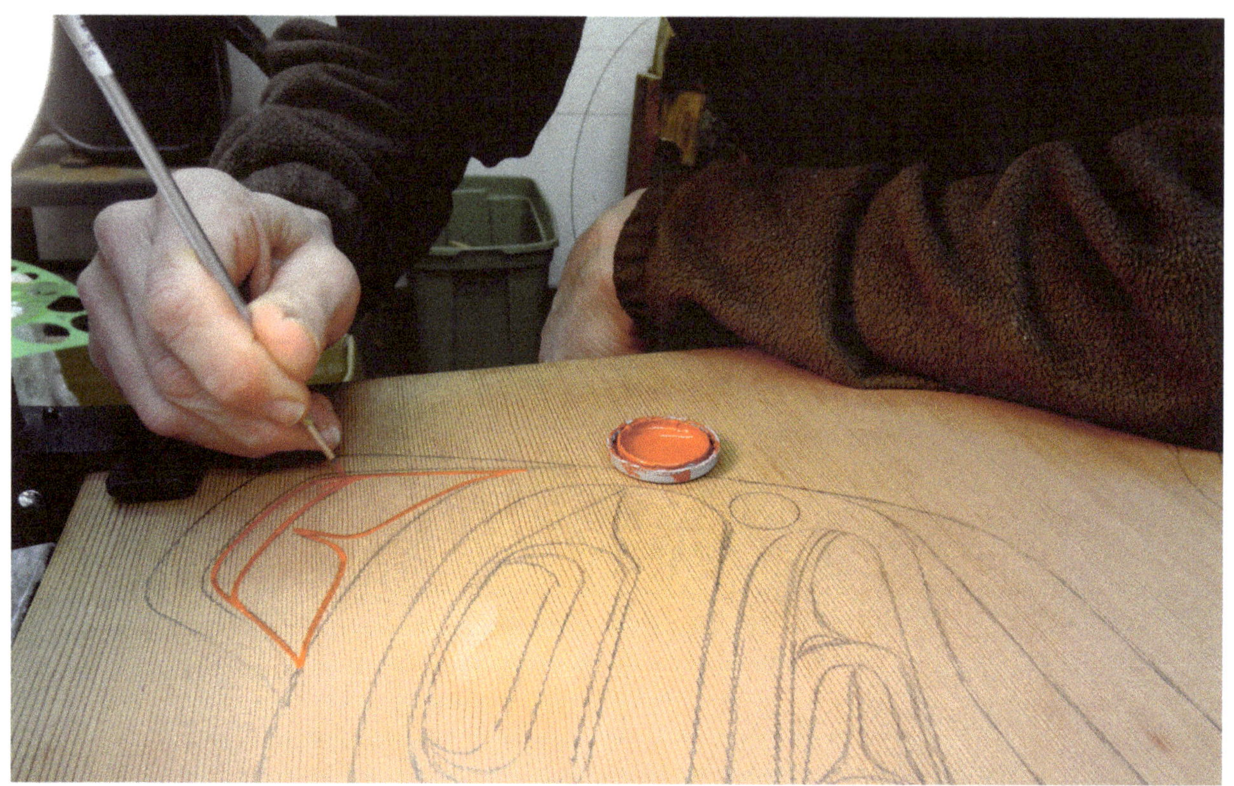

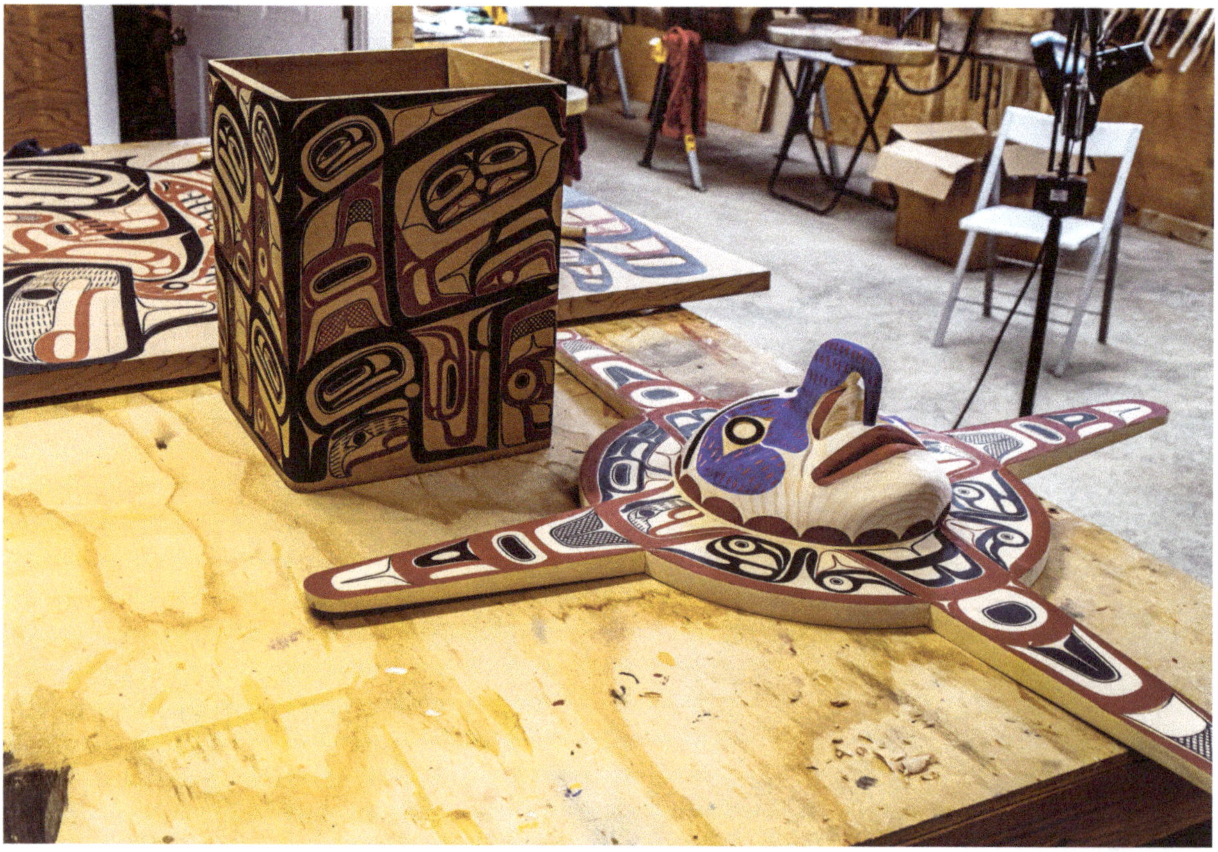

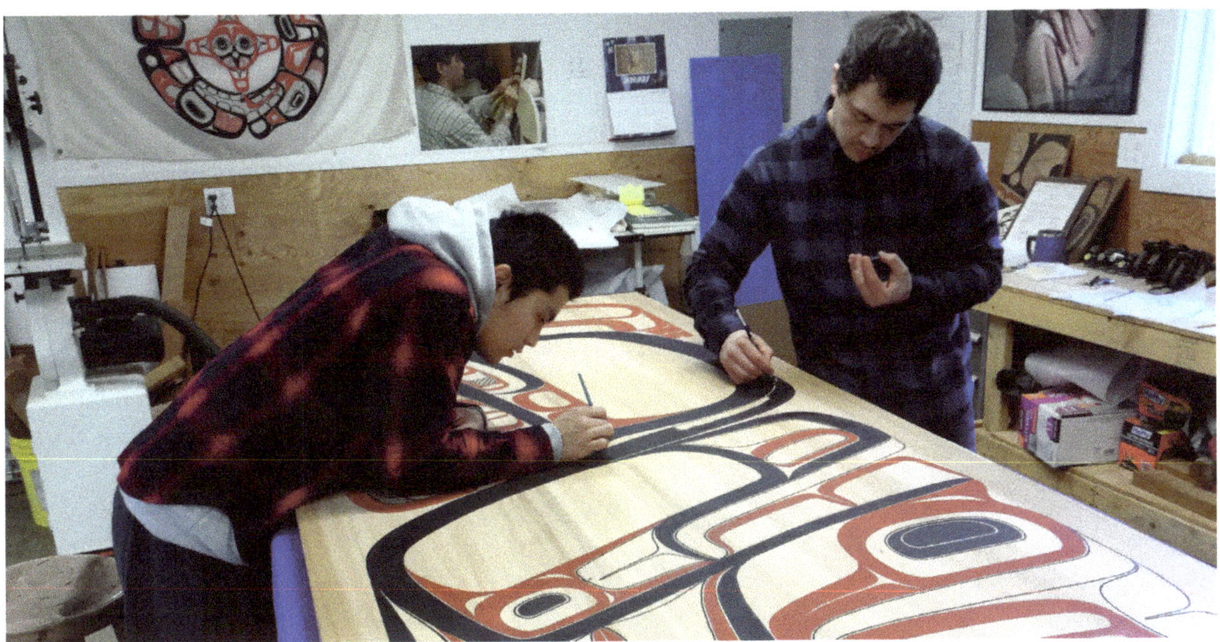

The number of active artists has probably grown tenfold during my lifetime. It's nice to be seen as one of the old guys. I don't take that for granted.

Even though I left teaching school in 1986, I've had the chance to work with lots of young artists. When I get a chance to teach them what I know how to do, it's so much more rewarding than making something to sell at a gallery. It's knowing that this work was done generations and generations ago. So many of our own people don't see the value because they are trying to make it in this modern world, and that's a struggle.

When I was teaching school, I saw that a certain percentage of kids didn't want to be there. They have their own interests. But when somebody comes to me and wants to work with me, they have a vested interest in becoming a better artist.

It's been years since I could call my son my student. I think I'm pretty good, but he's great. When he's my age, I think he's going to be thought of as one of the very best ever. People say, you say that because he's just your son. But look at his production. Look at what he does. Just the quality. He may have learned a lot from me and Robert Davidson, a Haida carver, but he had the talent all along. My younger son, Zach, might be one of the best bentwood box makers in the Pacific Northwest.

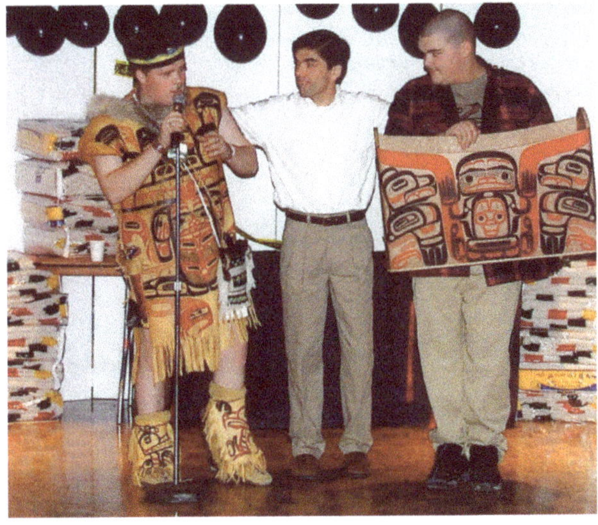

On my fiftieth birthday, Davey and Zach presented me with a bentwood box that Zach made and Davey painted.

I*'m proud of* what I've accomplished, knowing my work is in galleries, peoples' homes, and offices and in my own home. But I'm not the best carver. There's Robert Davidson. He's the best of the best. He's an innovator. He chooses to push the envelope. He's created his own style within the Haida foundation. I've already talked about Nathan Jackson and how he inspired me with his unique way of teaching me. Now, my son David, he has more skill than I could even imagine. But I worked really hard—almost too hard. People joke they are going to put on my headstone, "He should have worked harder."

I'd still like to make a canoe. I've done just about everything else, but I've never made a canoe. I've had three different opportunities to produce a canoe with other carvers, but I always had something going on in Metlakatla. Looking back, I regret that. I would have liked to work on a couple of canoes with someone who is really good at it. While I understand the concept and could make a canoe on my own, it might not be a very good one. There are certain things you have to do to make them seaworthy. If you don't make them right, they could be dangerous.

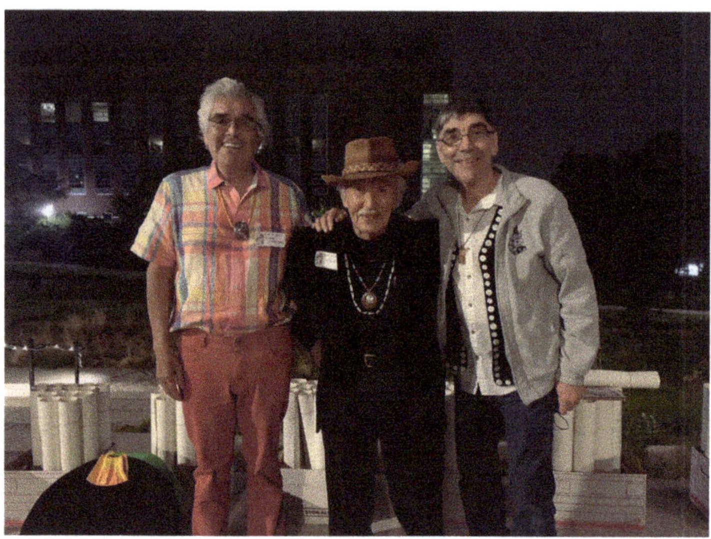

Whenever I get to spend time with Robert Davidson (**LEFT**) and Nathan Jackson (**MIDDLE**), it's a privilege. I've admired both of these men my whole career. To be thought of with them as peers is such an honor.

The people I admire are culture bearers. They have potlatches, names, hold the culture in their hands. Someone told me a long time ago that artists are like a canoe in which the culture travels. We bear that culture in that canoe. There are a lot of artists up and down the coast in different tribes. There is nothing wrong with making a living at this, but the ones who I look up to are the ones who are involved in their culture as well as making art. I've been really fortunate to be able to do things with and for my own people. That's the best part.

We call it art now, but it was once—and is now again—a way for people to say, "This is who I am. This belongs to me, this is my clan. This is my crest, this is my family history, carved and painted on wood." ❖

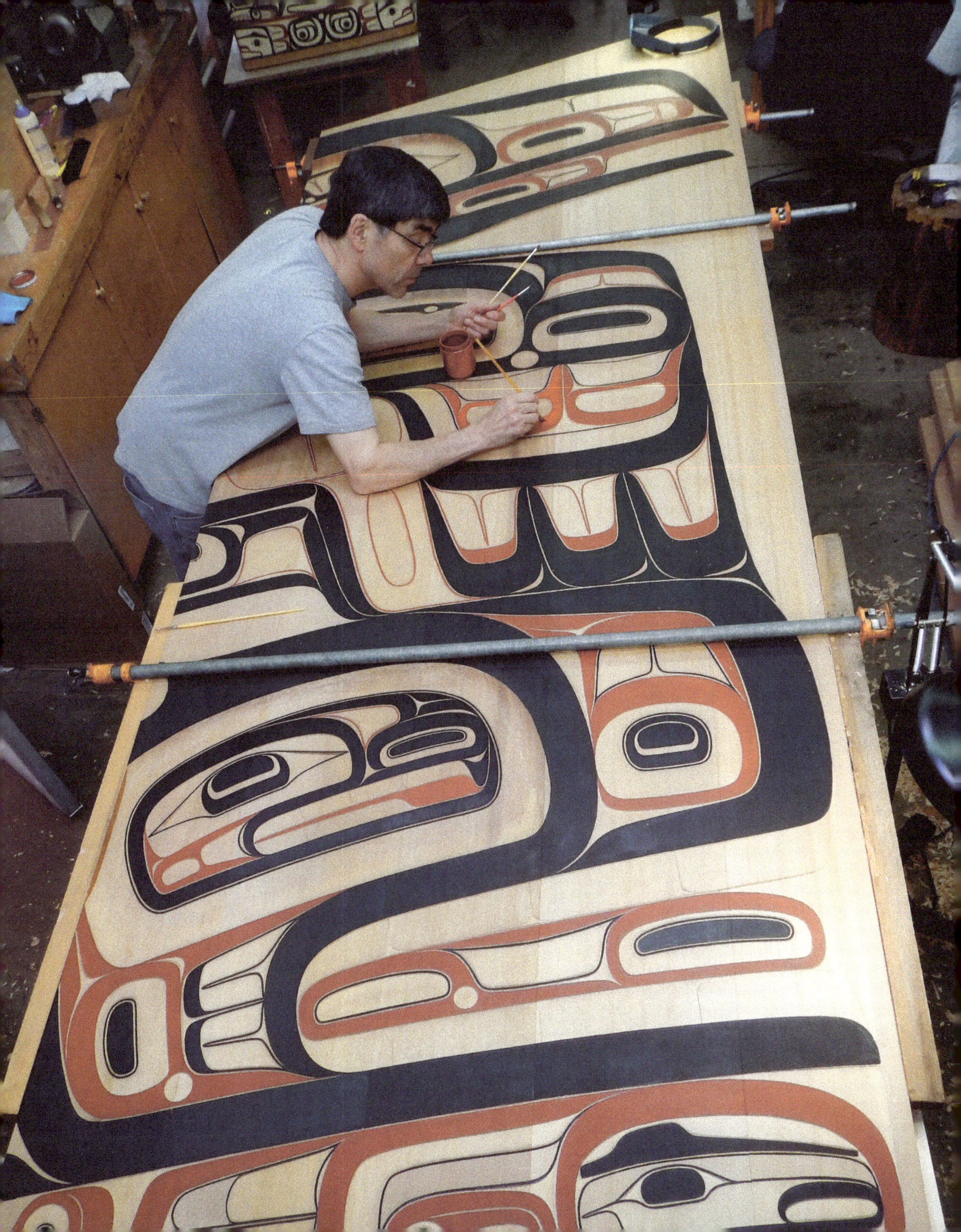

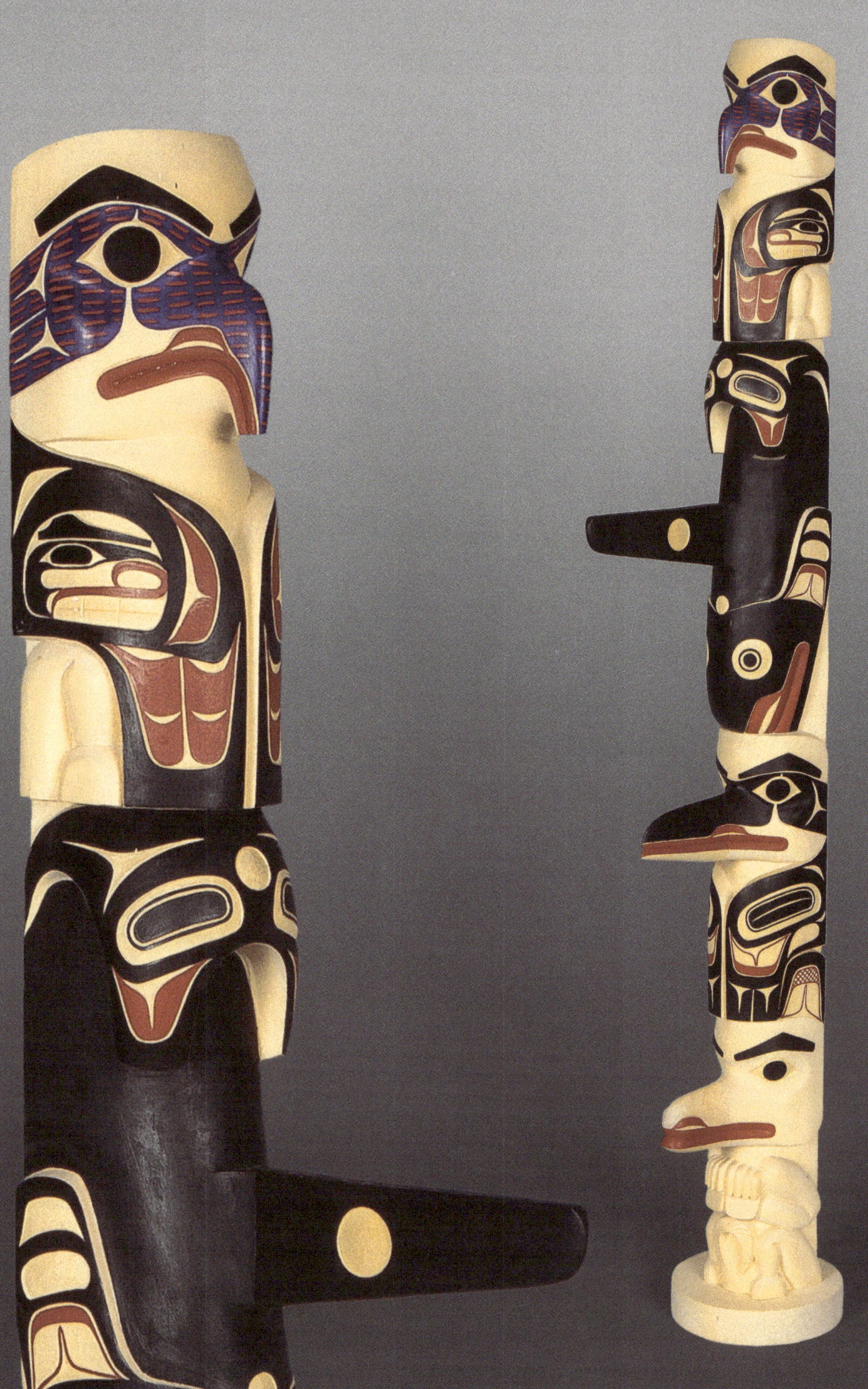

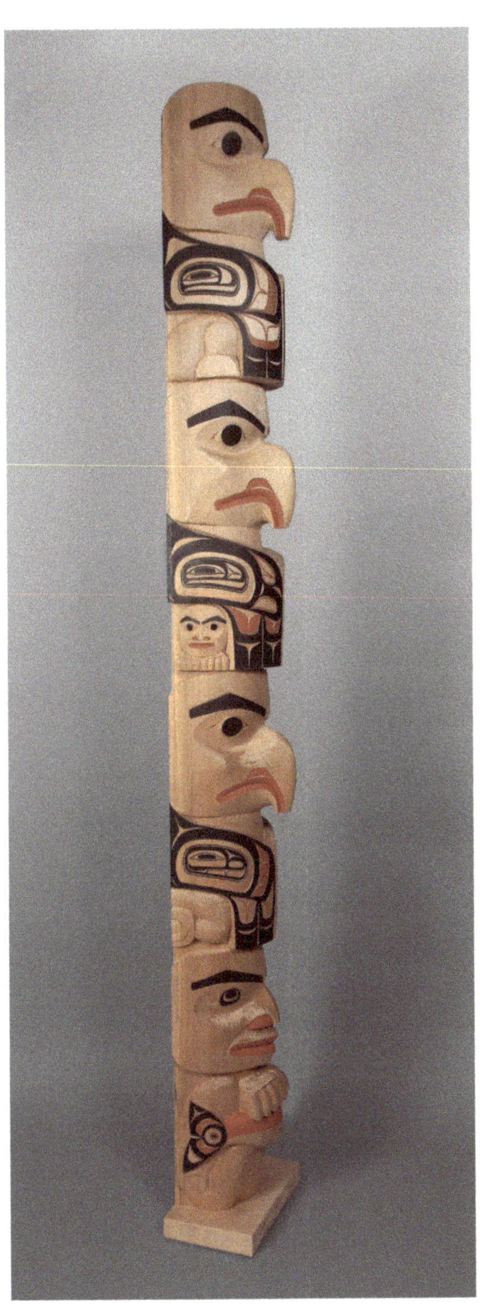

Model poles can be as tall as 8 feet like the one above or 6 feet like the one below.

MINI TOTEMS

I made dozens and dozens of models before I started doing large pieces. That helped me, especially when my work started to look Tsimshian. When I first started, I started copying Tlingit and Haida poles out of books. I didn't have anybody to teach me. After my trip to the provincial museum in Victoria, British Columbia, looking at actual Tsimshian poles affected my style. Making models is a way to prepare you for making big ones. It's the same amount of design and work but on a smaller scale.

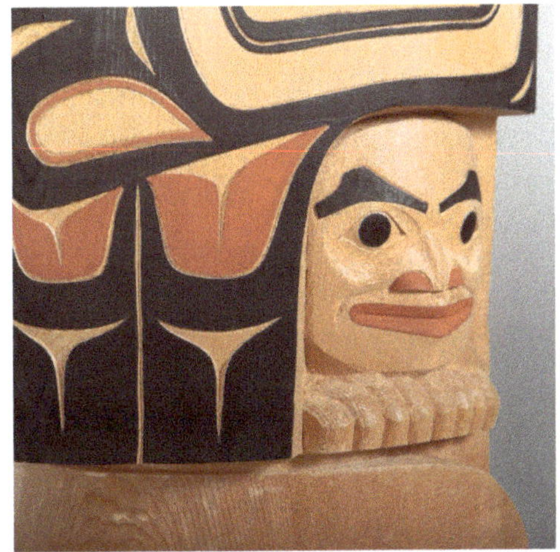

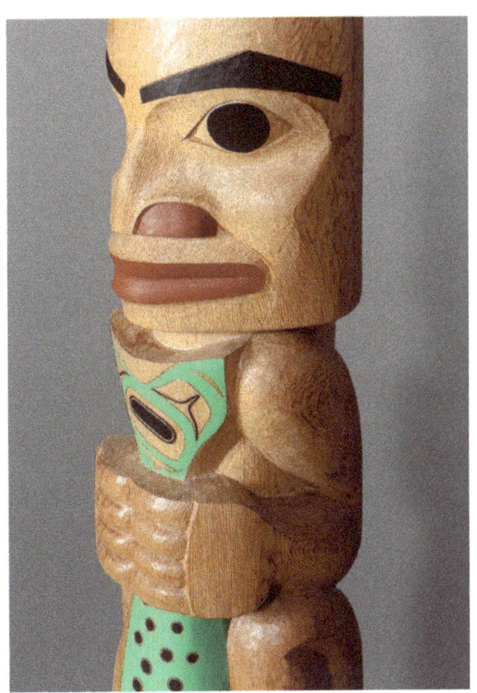

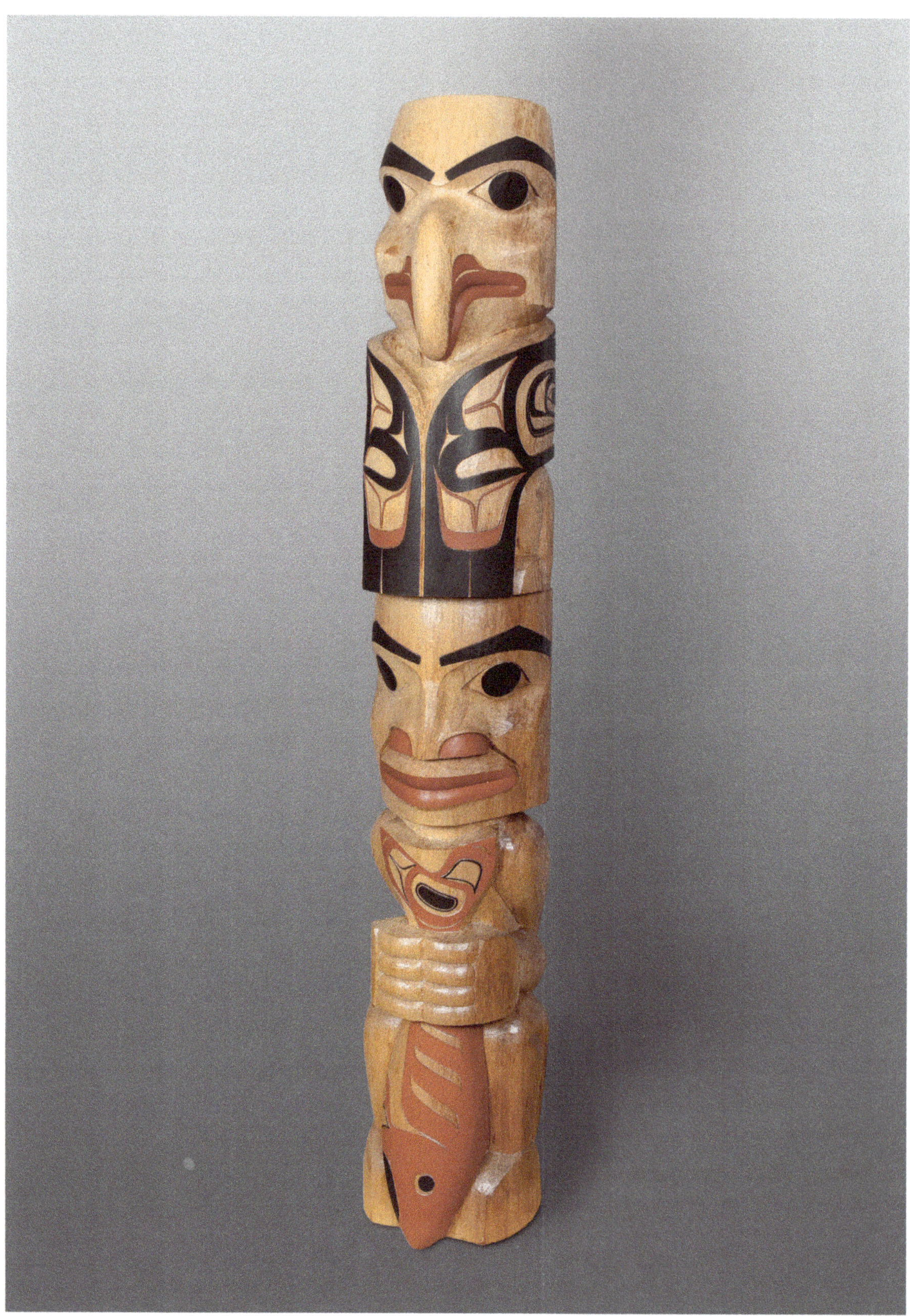

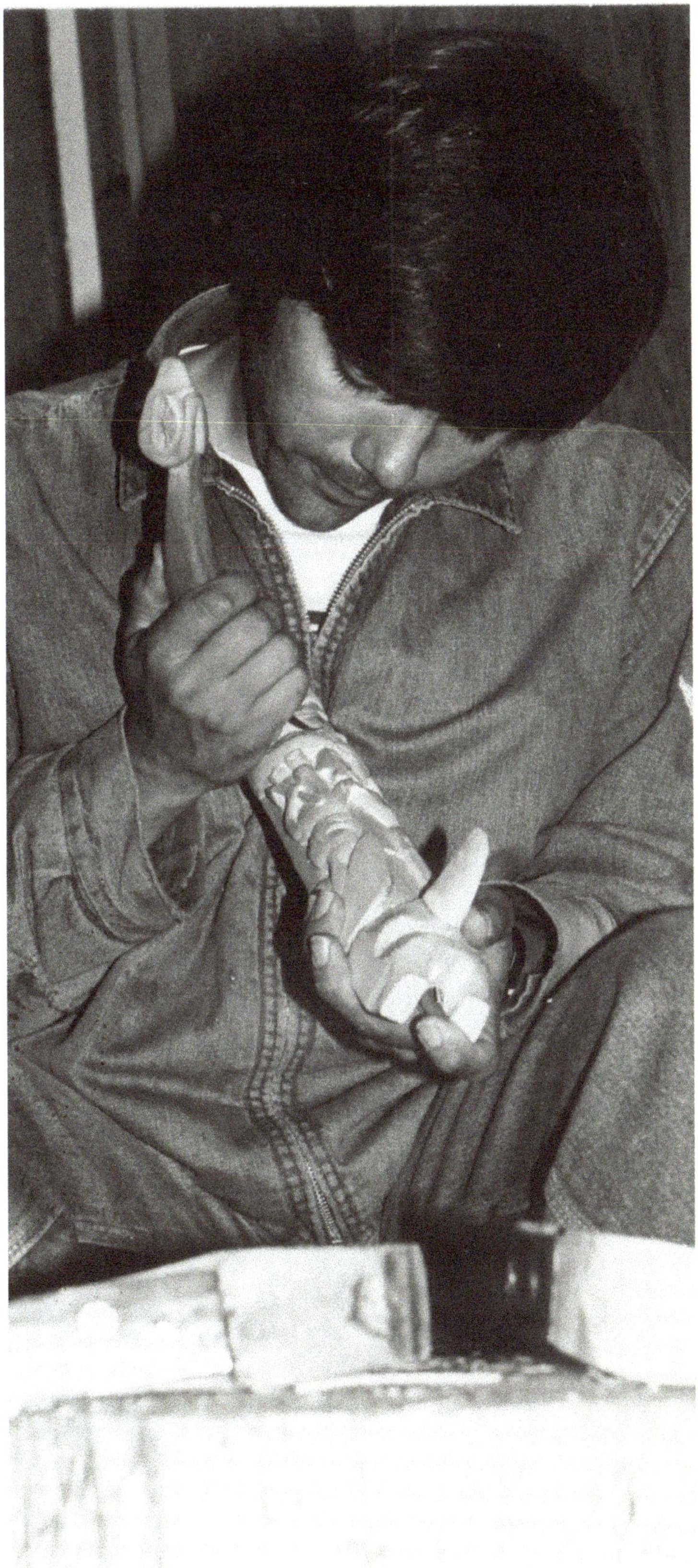

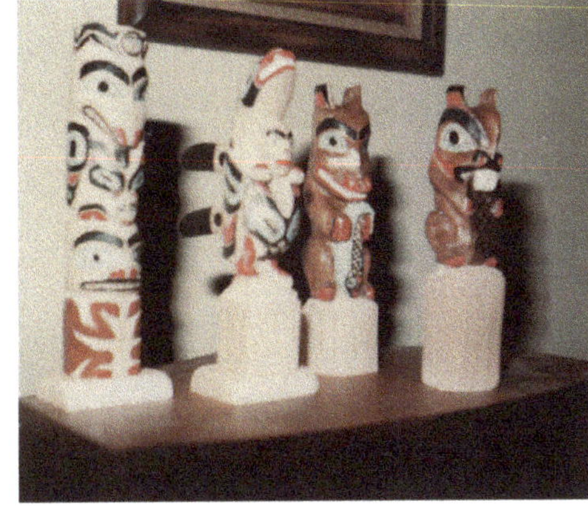

In the early 1980s, I sent these four poles to the Juneau Airport gift shop. They sent them back to me. At the time I wasn't far enough along in my career to be insulted, so I just kept working.

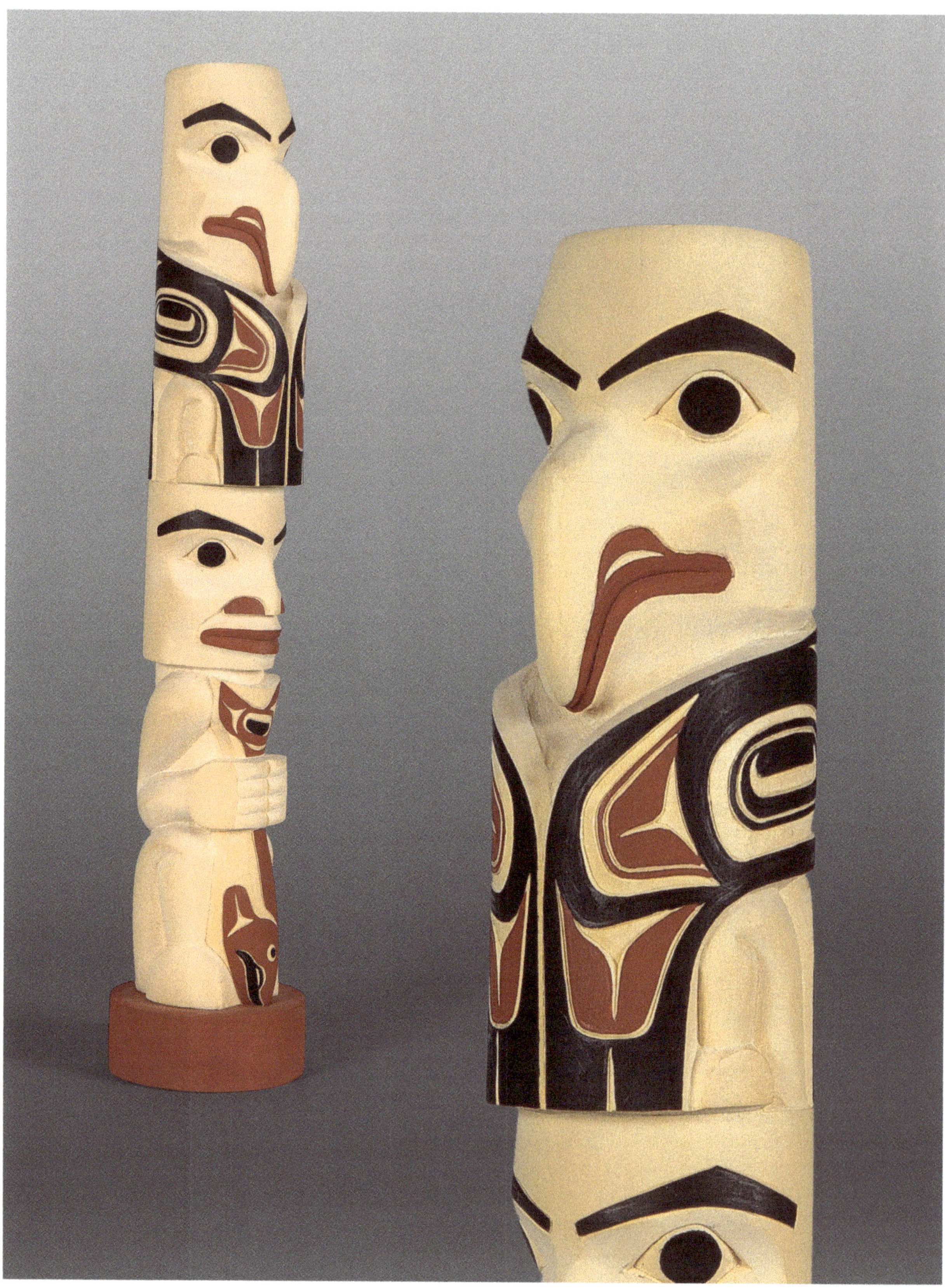

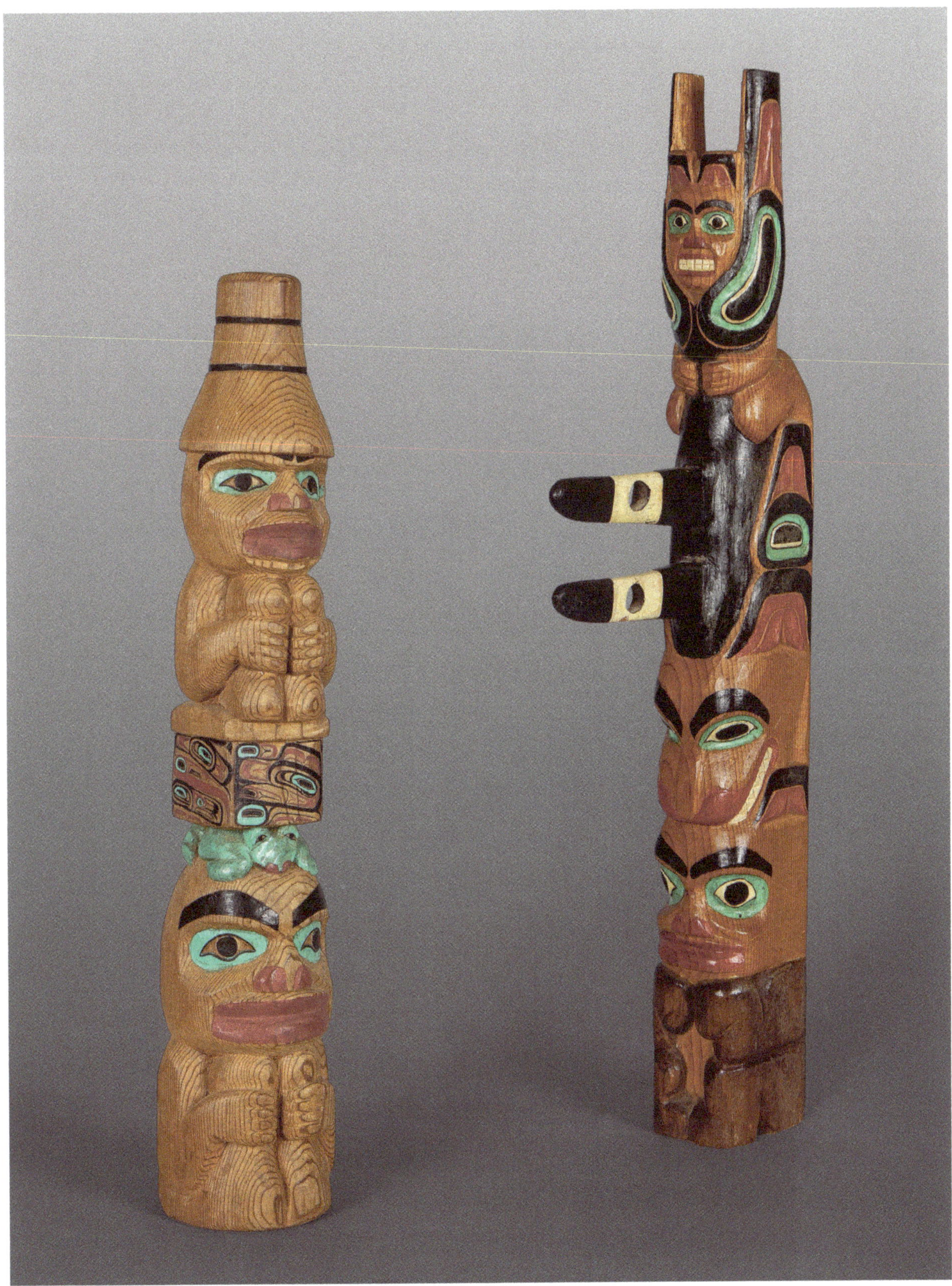

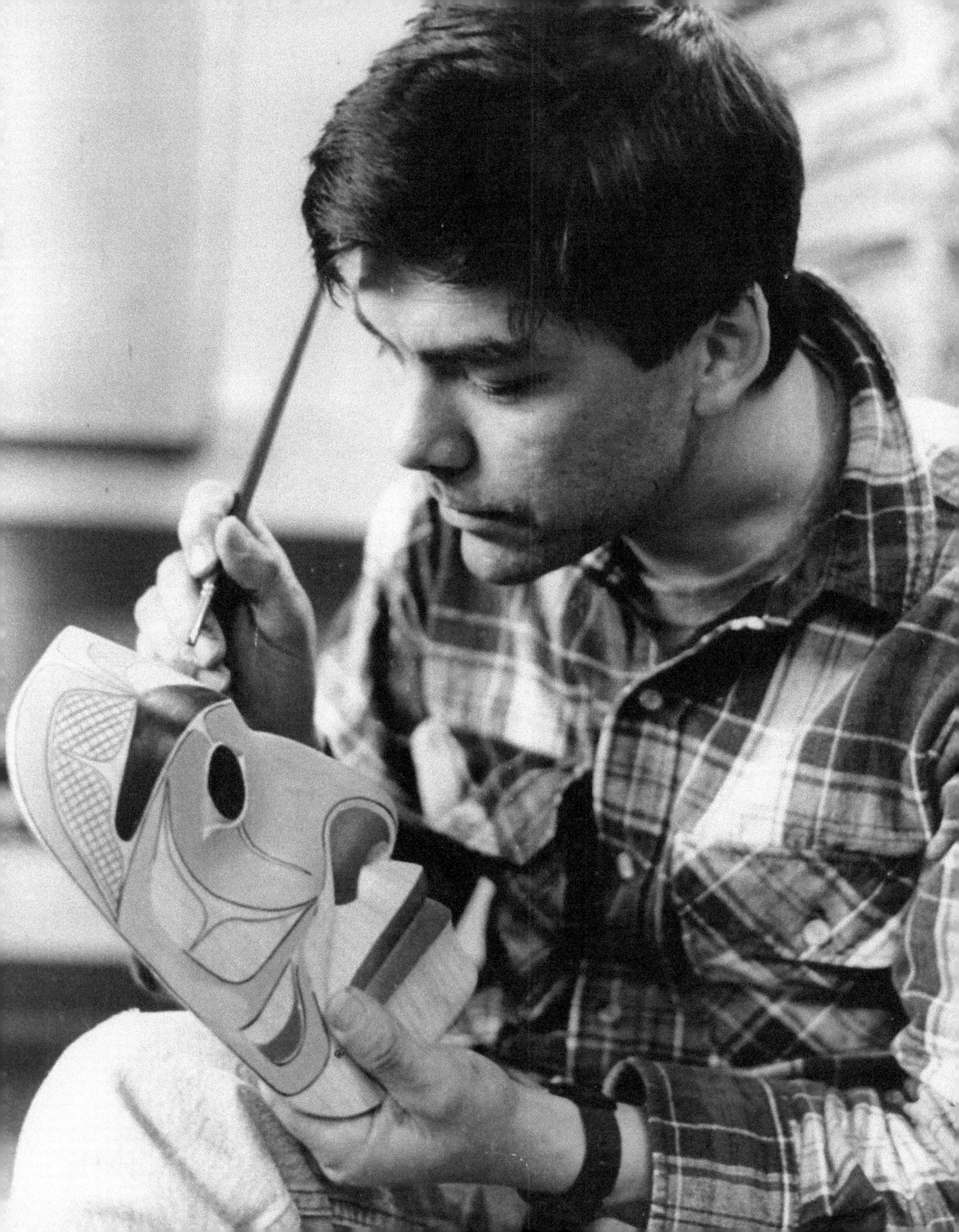

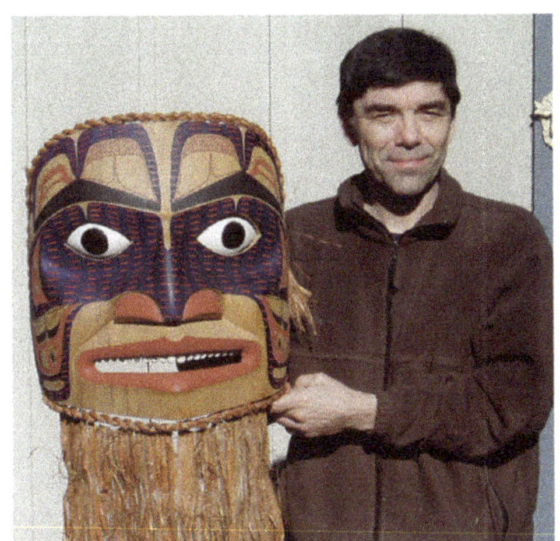

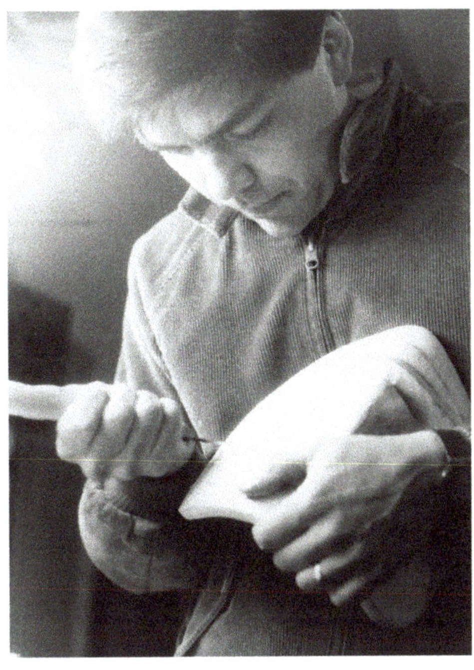

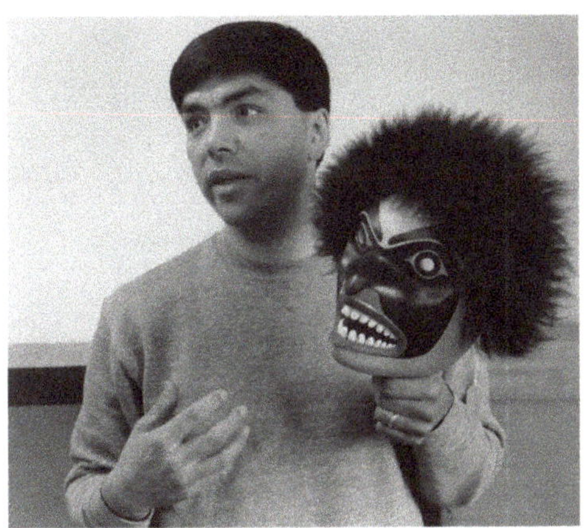

MASKS

People have varied responses to masks, ranging from fear to amazement. Some masks are simple and some are very complicated. Everyone, Tlingit and Haidas, had masks at one time, in their ceremonies. So many dance groups didn't have masks. Now many more are using them in their performances. It's such an old thing. Thousands of masks are in museums, either bought or confiscated or traded. I've made lot of masks for many other dance groups. I'm happy to do that. It means they are being used like in the old days, not just hanging on the wall. But I also don't disparage hanging them on the wall—it's how I make my living.

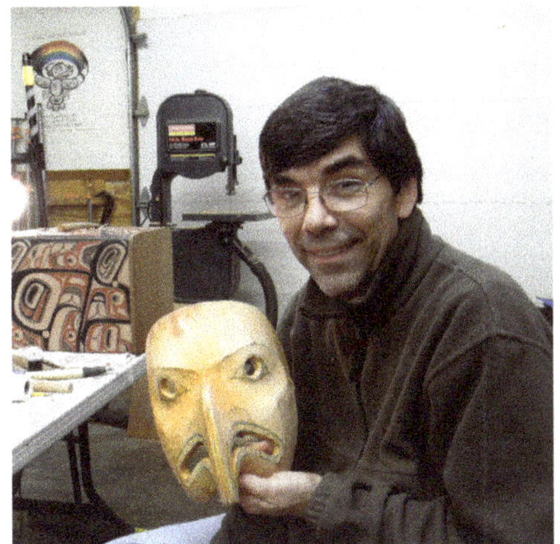

Masks vary in size, anywhere from six-inch masks to 32-inch masks that require handles to dance with.

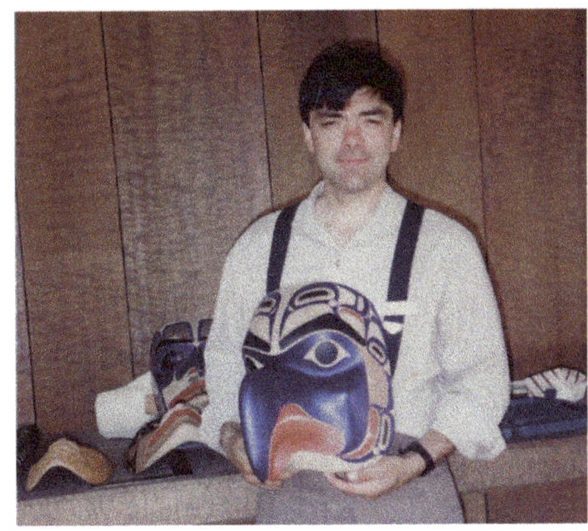

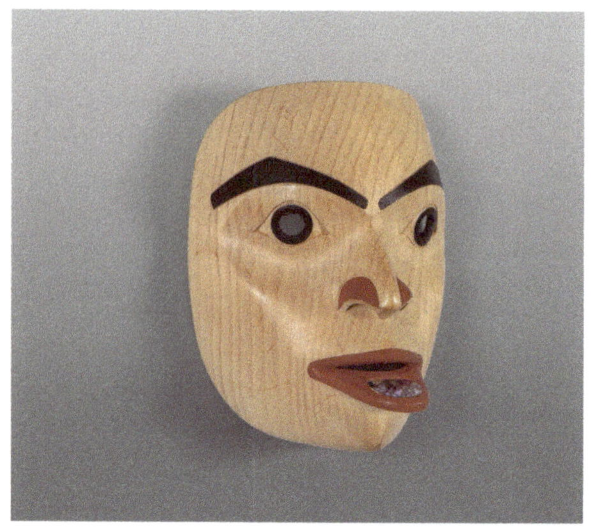

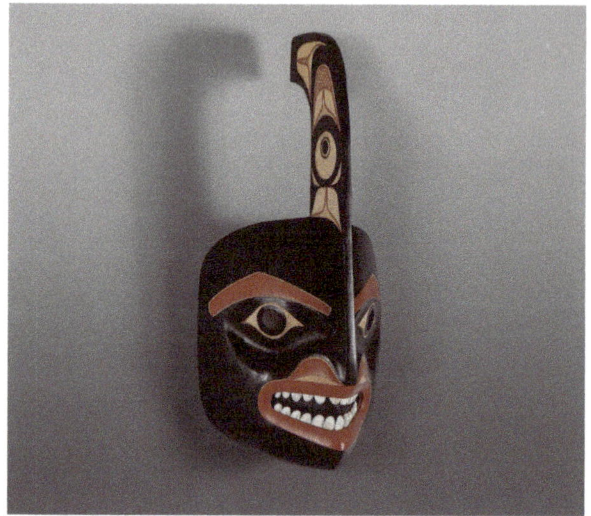

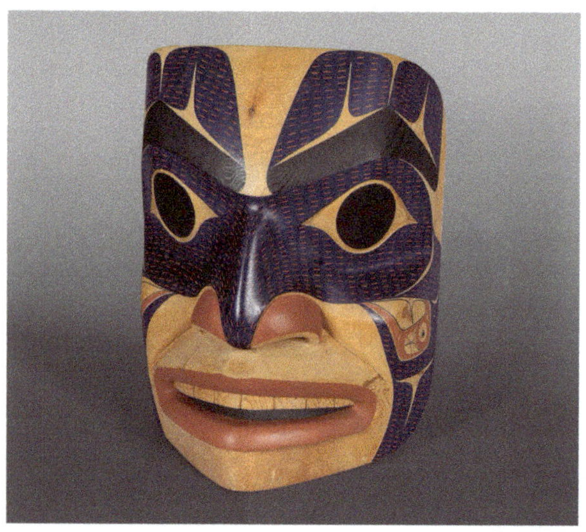

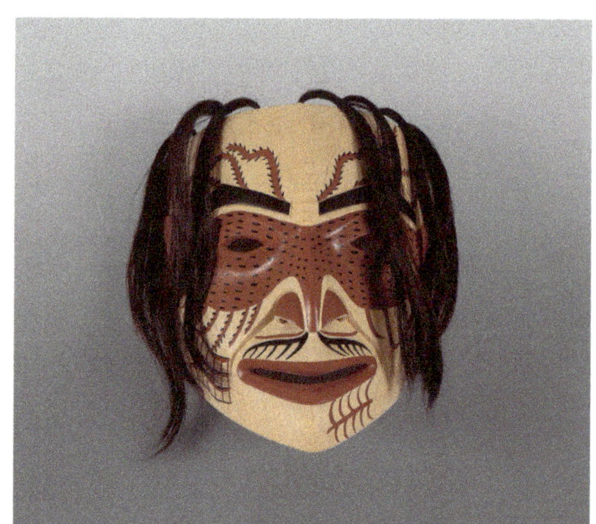

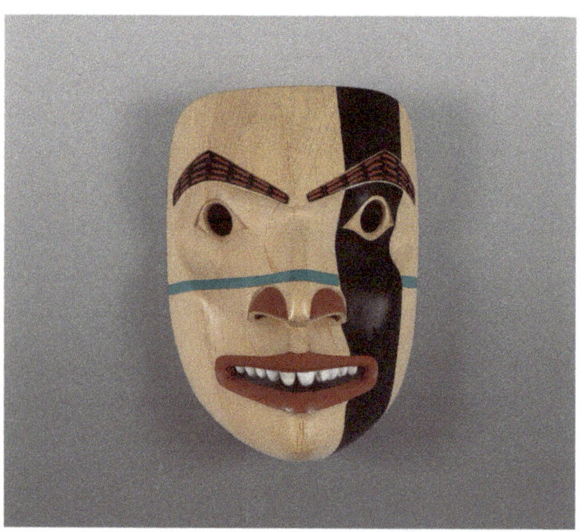

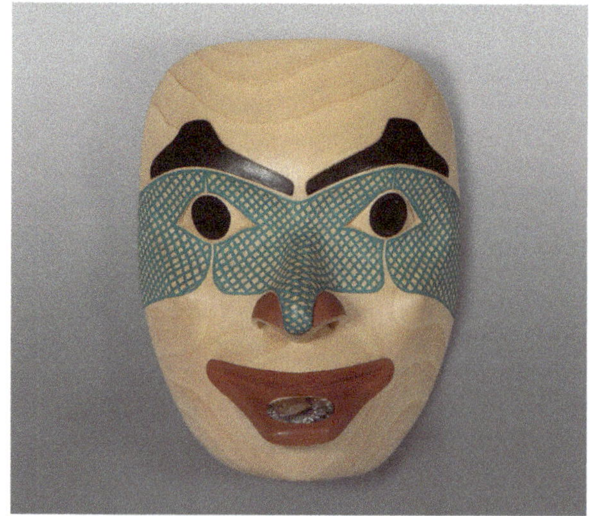

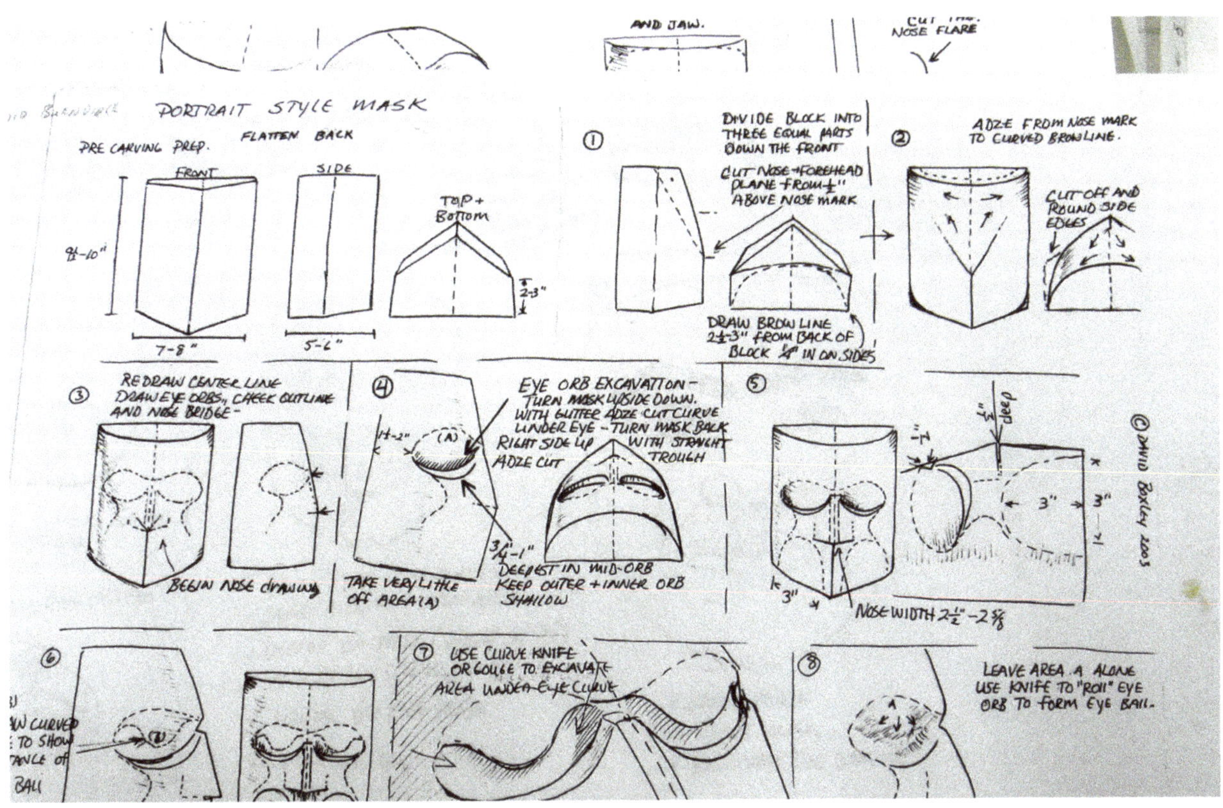

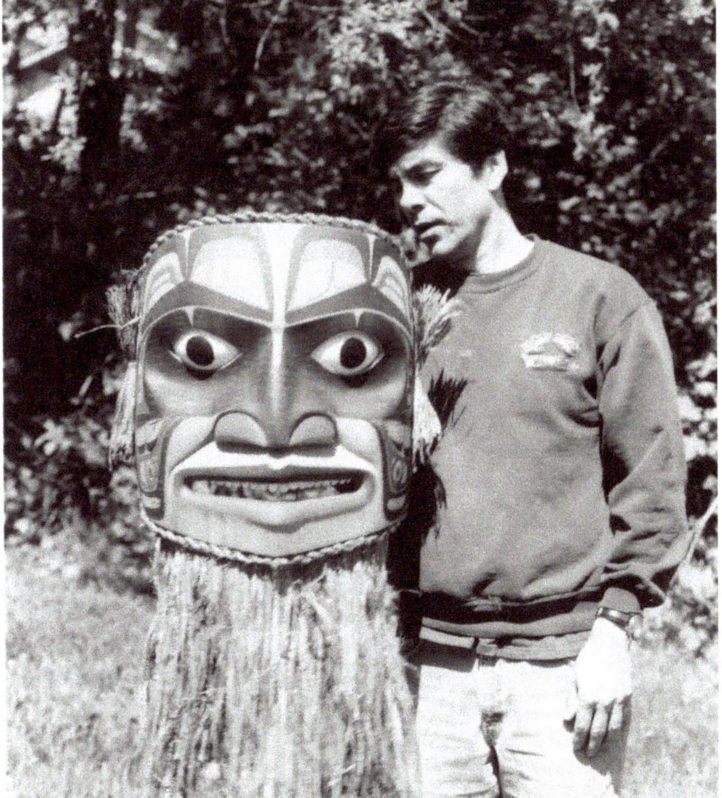

There are stages in carving a mask. Cutting planes is really important, making sure it's symmetrical. You don't want one eye here and one eye there. You want the mask to be correct tribal style as well. I draw schematics to each as well, showing them each stage. You need to finish perfectly one stage before going to the next.

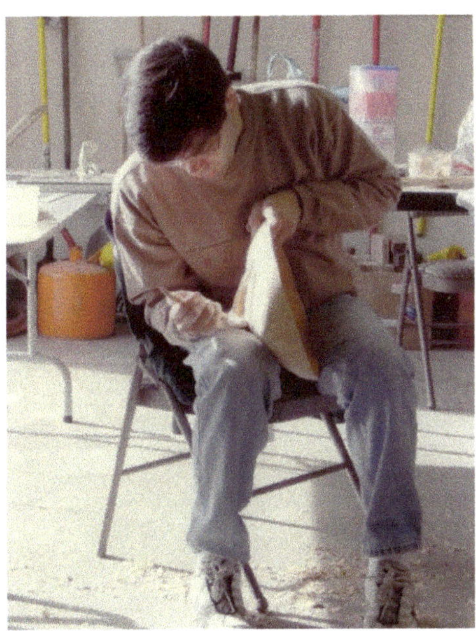

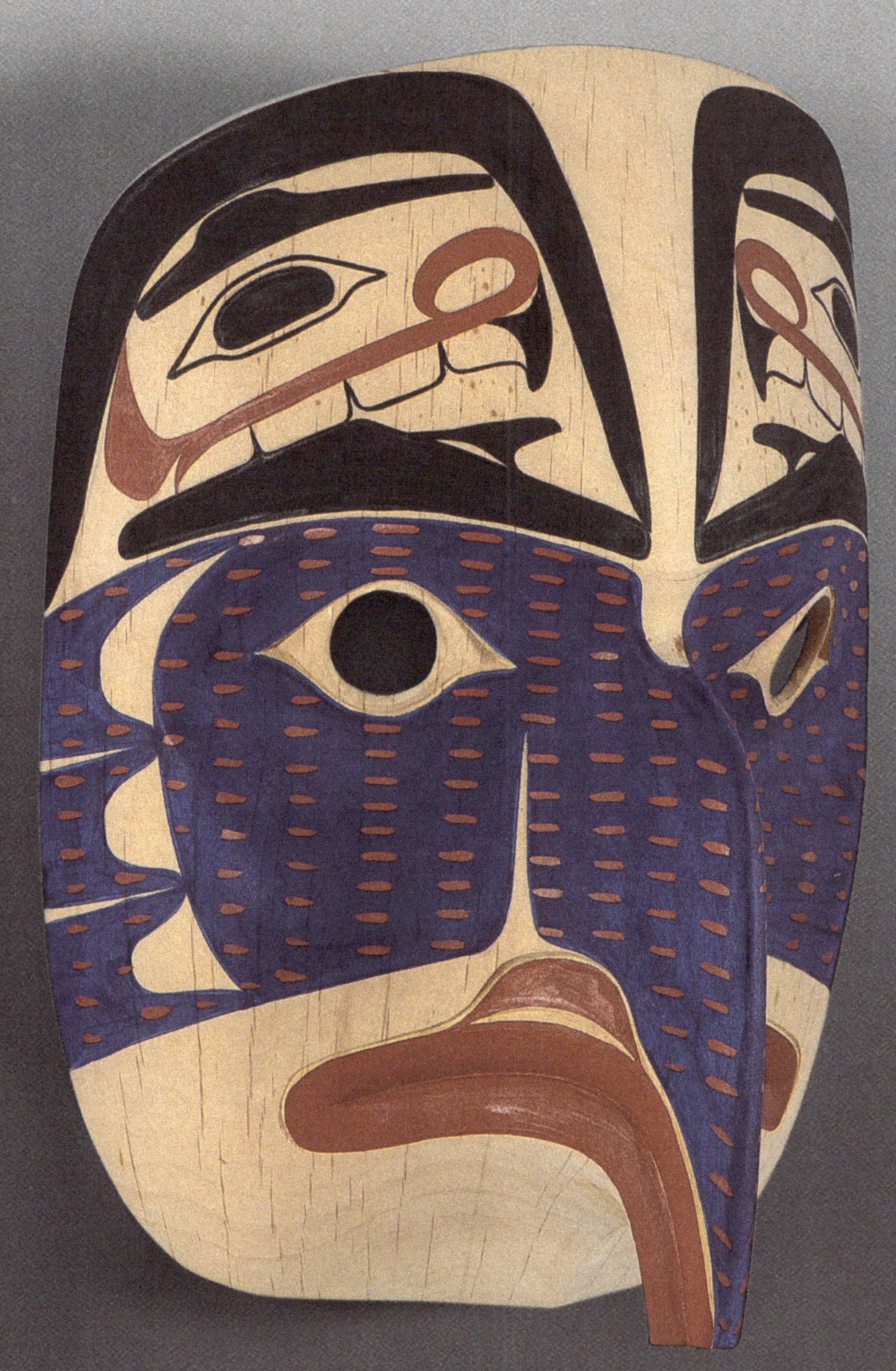

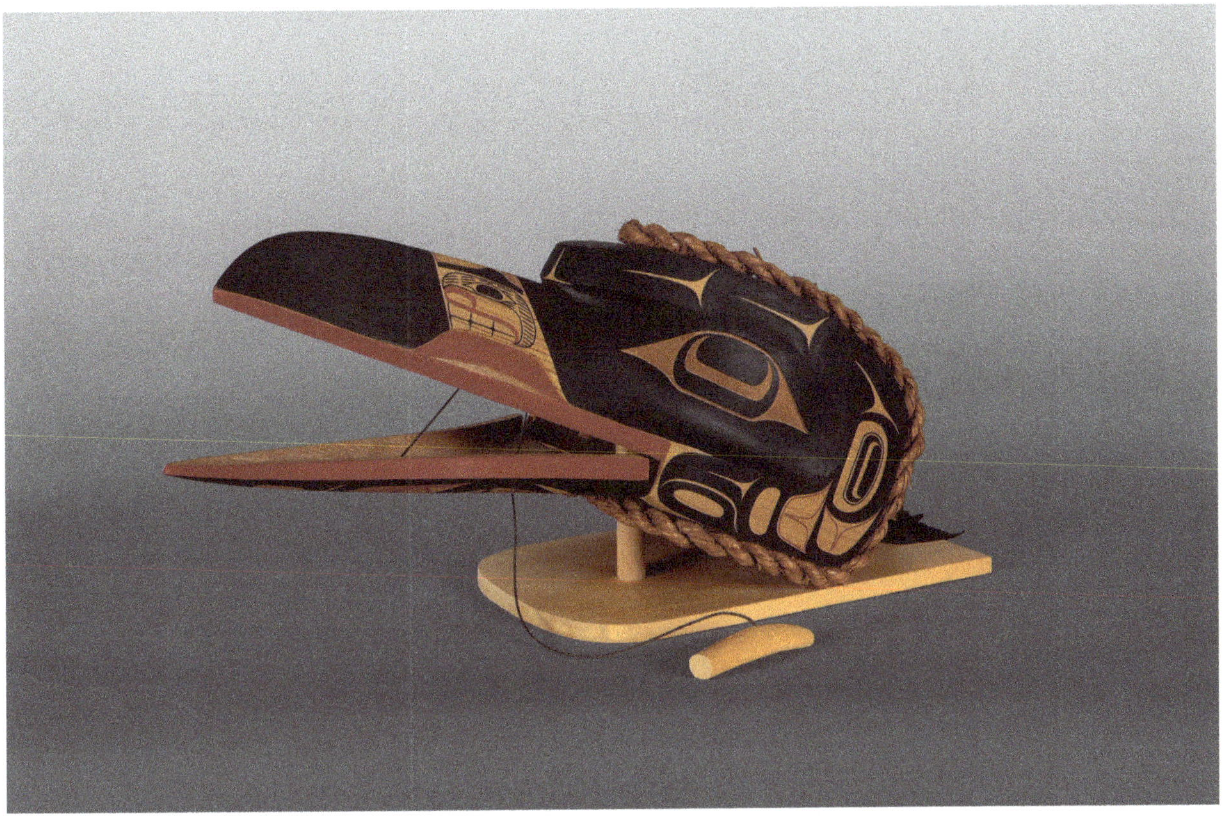

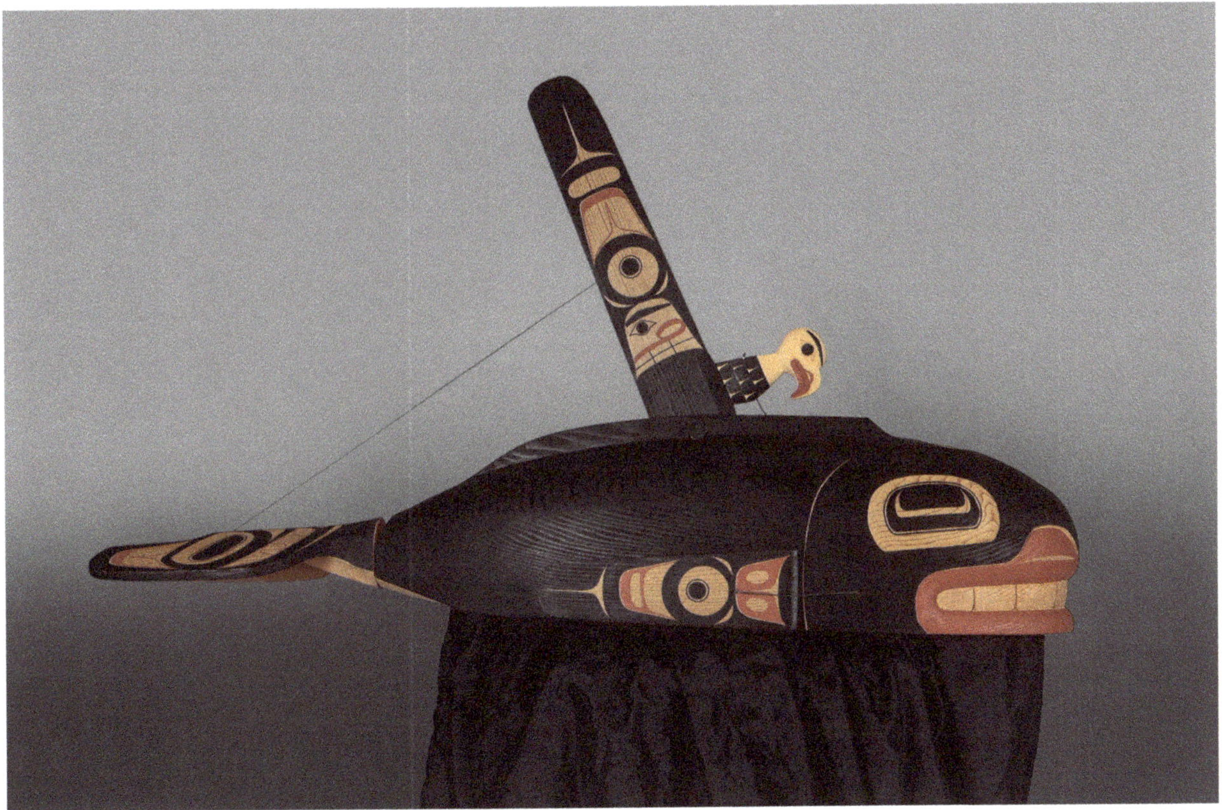

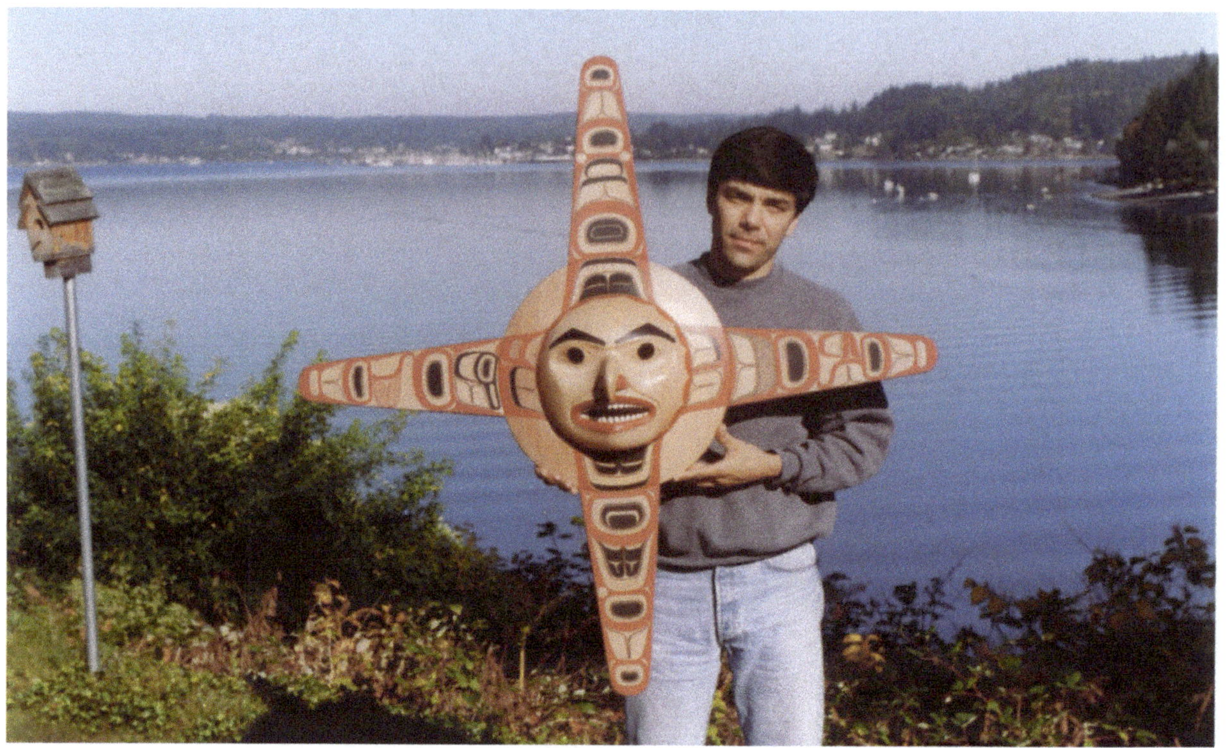

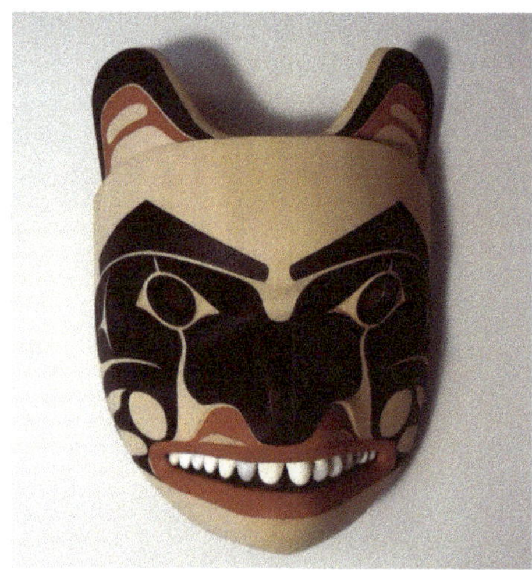

My dance group, Git Hoan, has become really well known for using masks to tell stories. People look forward to seeing what we do next. I'm lucky to have a lot of talented people who can bring these masks alive.

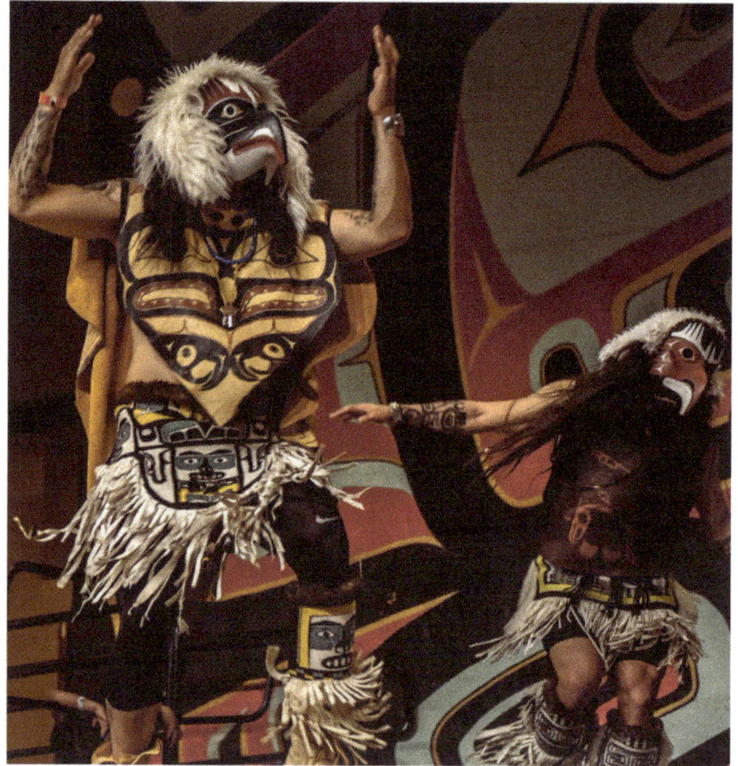

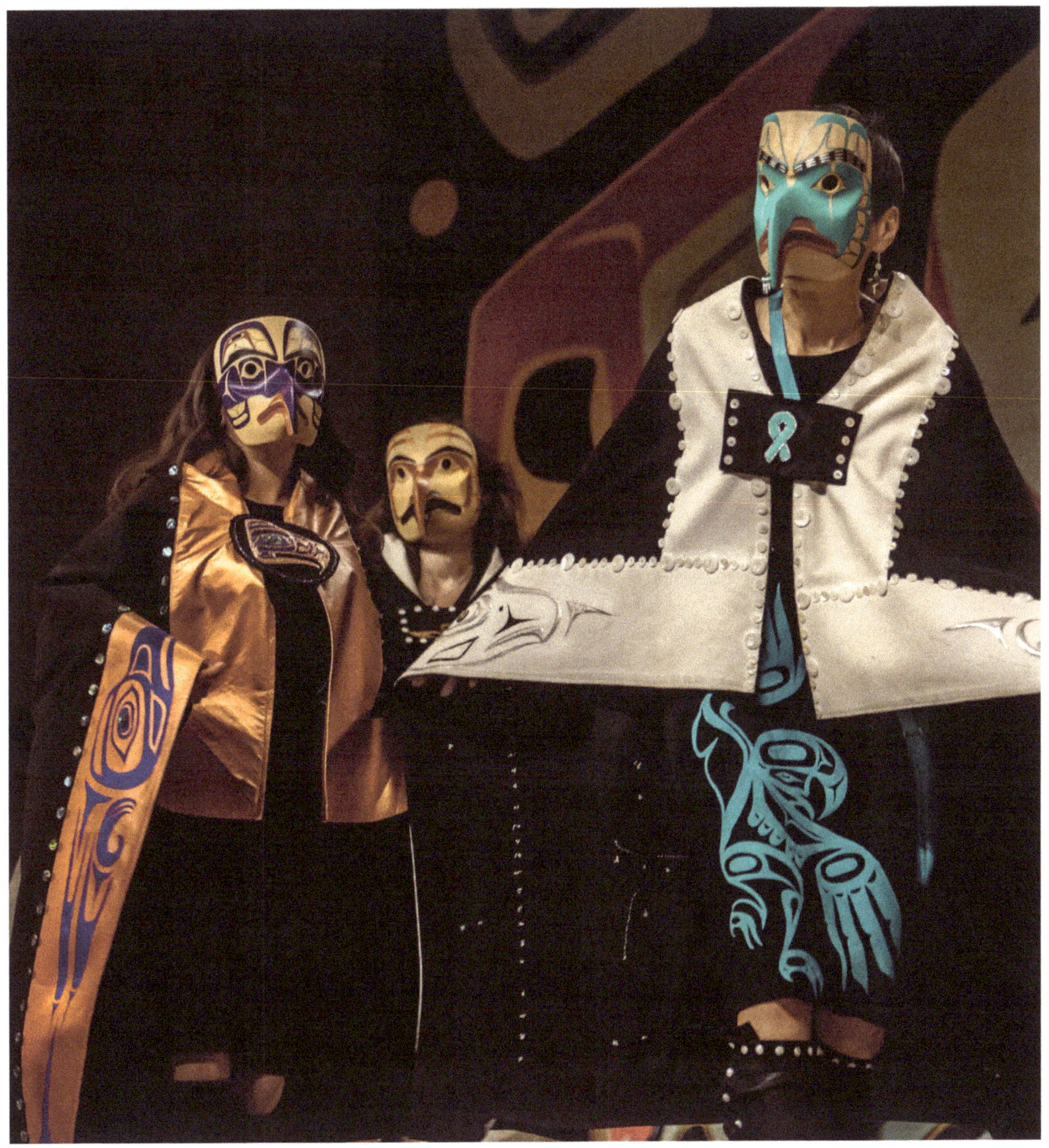

My friend Cindy (right) loved this mask. I made it for her because she was the maid-of-honor when I married her sister, Michelle. This was her last performance during the 2018 Celebration. Today her grandson, Dominic, wears the mask when he dances.

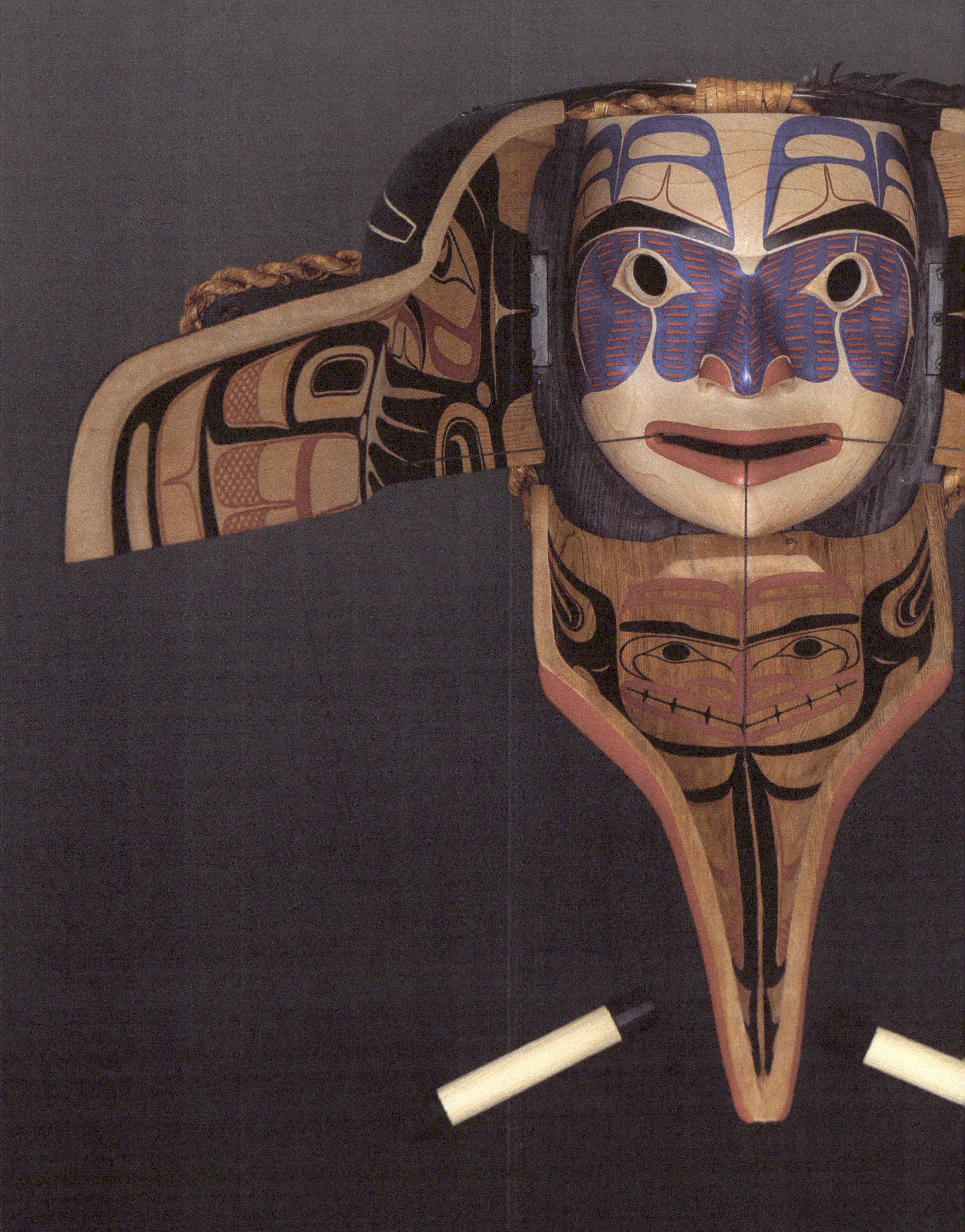

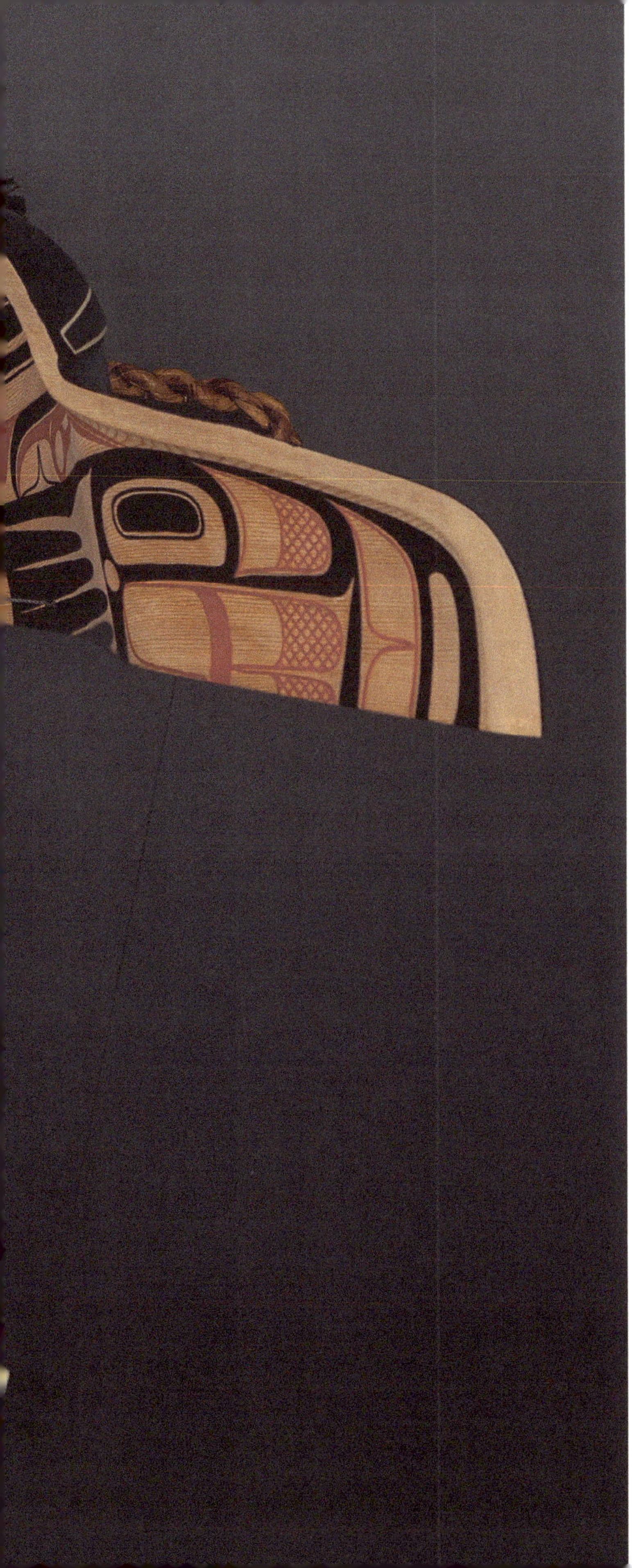

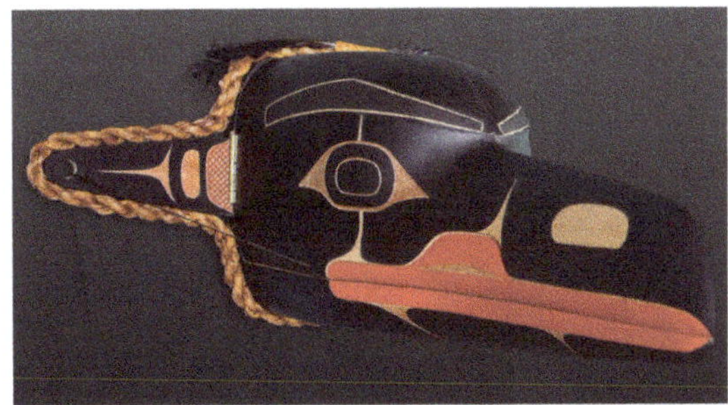

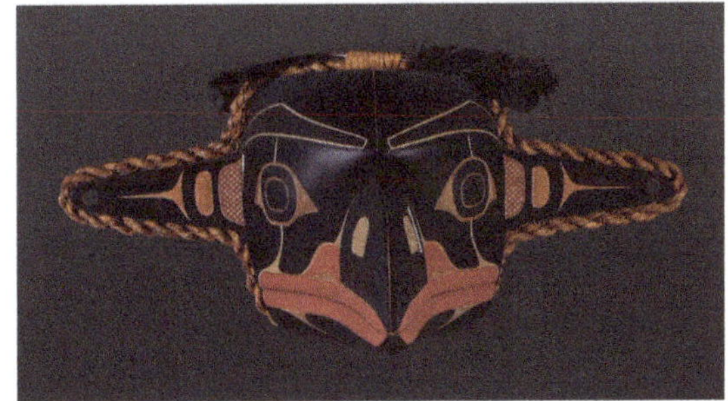

TRANSFORMATION MASKS

Transformation masks show the connection between the spirit world and the human world. It takes a lot of work to make two nesting masks that can be operated when worn to open and close.

There are people who believe every animal had a human spirit. That's one of the keys behind the transformation mask. You see the outside of the mask, that's the animal. When it opens up, that's the magical being.

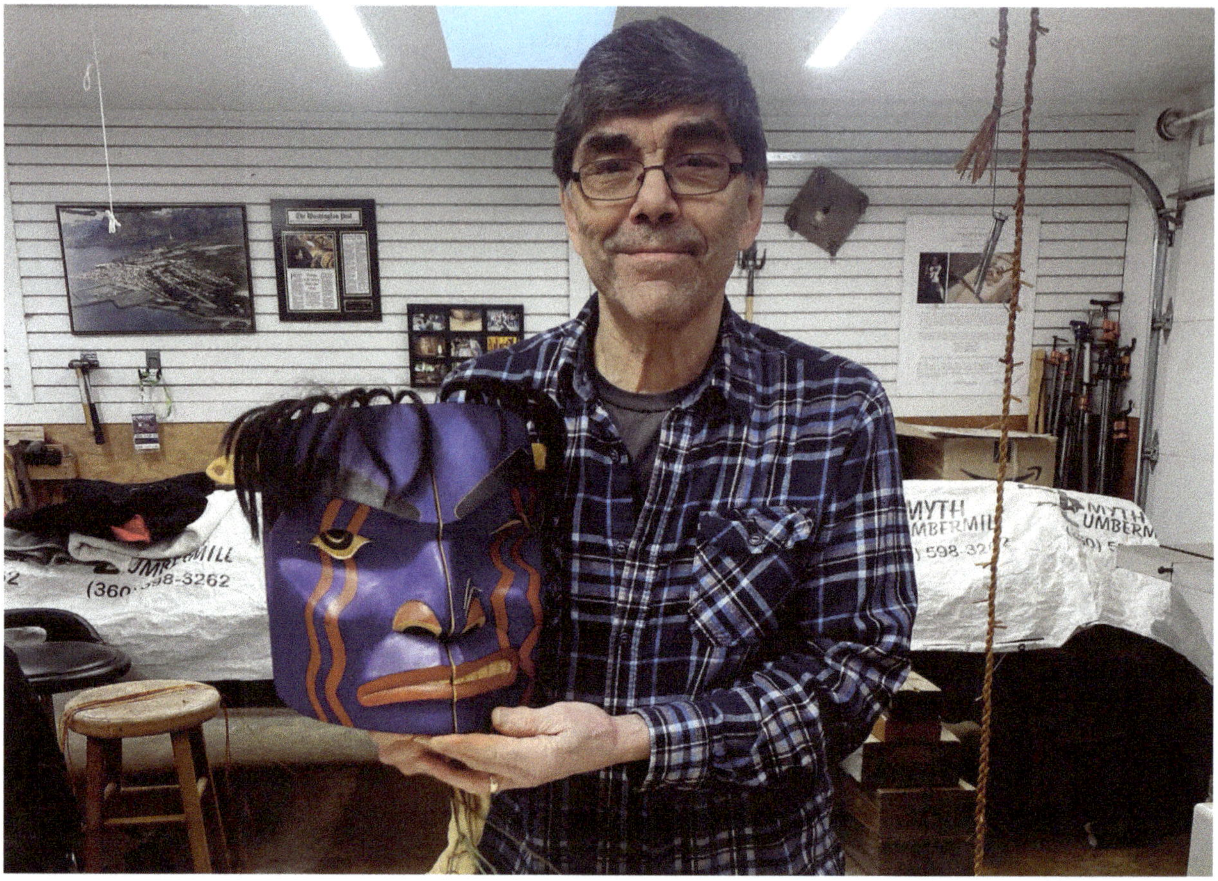

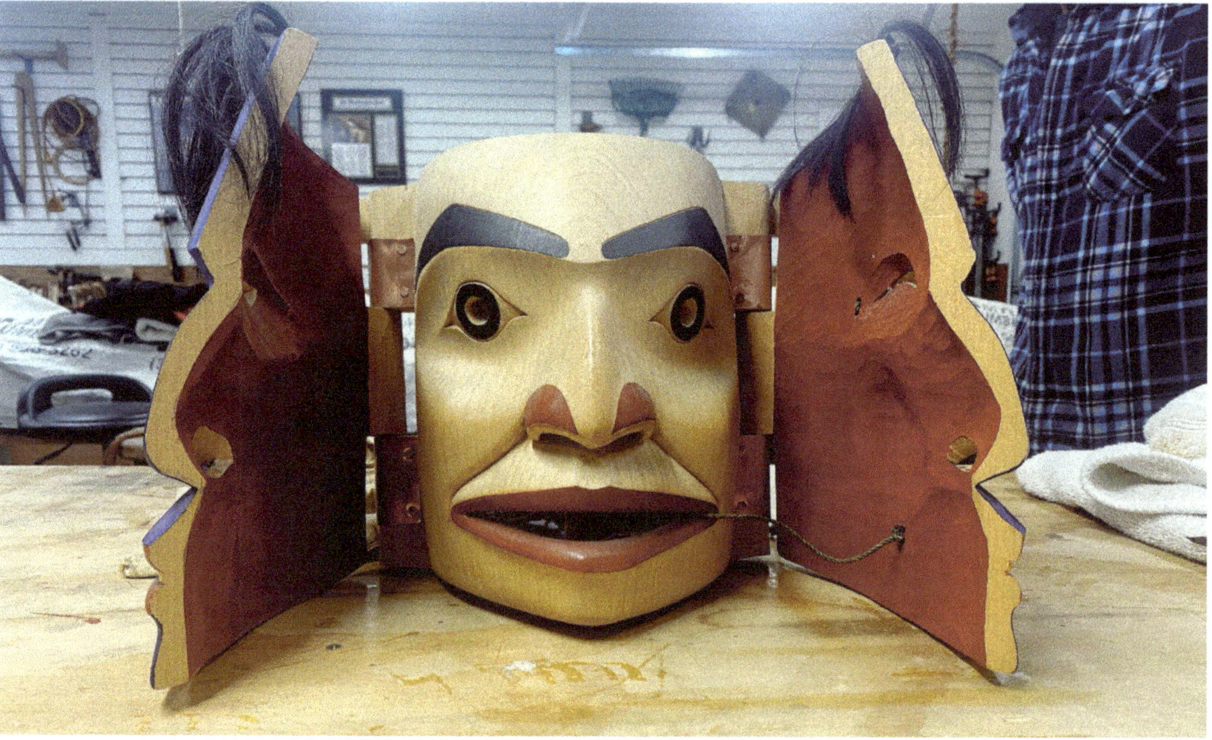

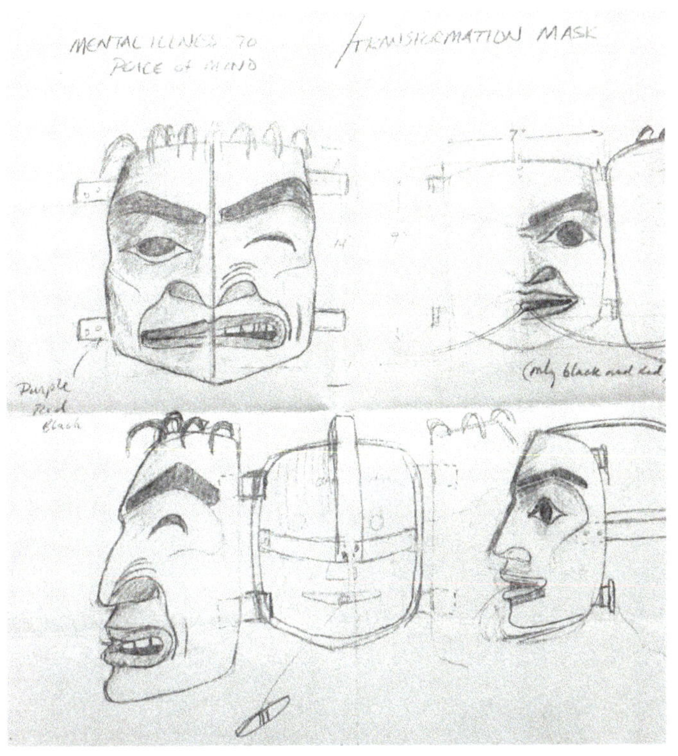

Pictured on the facing page is my first transformation mask. I made it before cell phones and email, I never met the woman who commissioned it. She was a counselor and wanted to have a mask that showed a person's outward appearance on the outer mask, someone going through the terrible stuff, which then opened to reveal calmness and healing. The hardest part of making the mask was the hinges.

Artists rarely ever get their old artworks back after they've sold them to somebody else. I've been fortunate enough to get art back from four different people. I was given the opportunity to buy this transformation mask back. She was moving, downsizing, and wanted to see if I knew someone who wanted to buy it. I was happy to be able to have it back after all this time.

The woman I sold the mask to was a mental health counselor. I was inspired by what she did for a living. That's why it has a split personality on the outside, and calmness or recovery on the inside. It really connected with me. That's what the words in the song speak to. I had been studying these old transformation masks in museums; they were really powerful. They told a story of a special power the masks had, so I wrote a song and put it on tape. She kept it all those years.

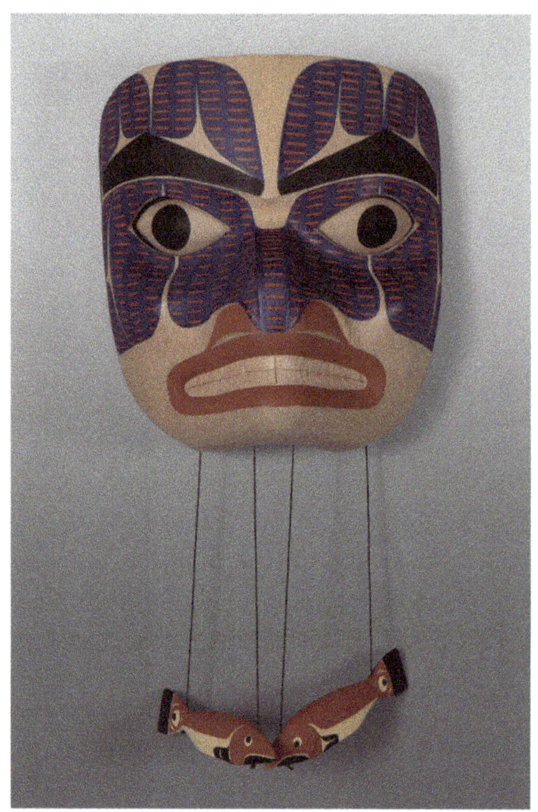

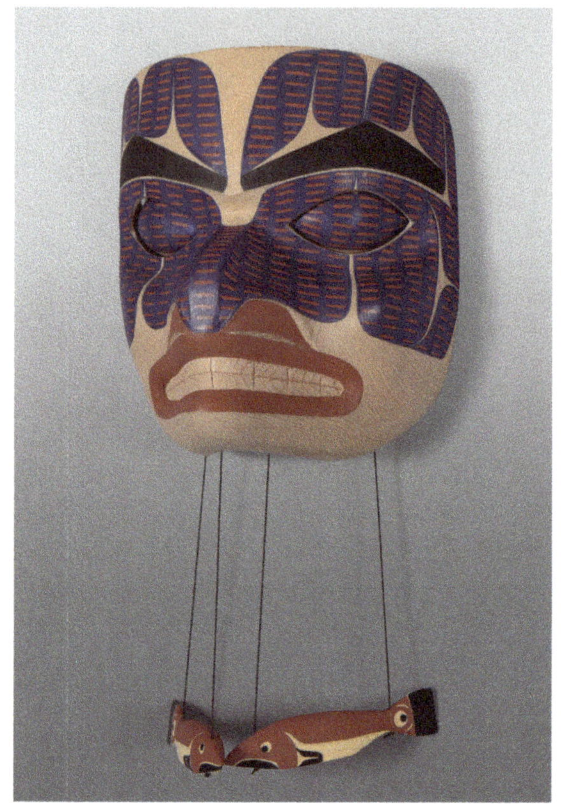

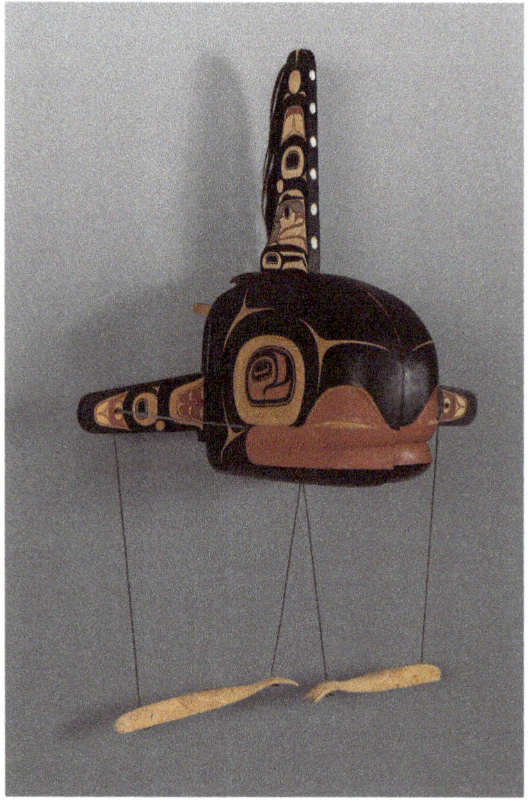

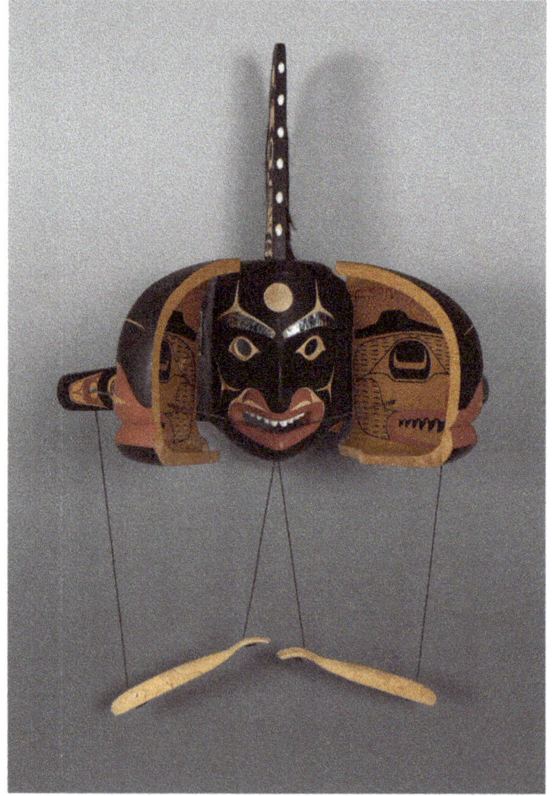

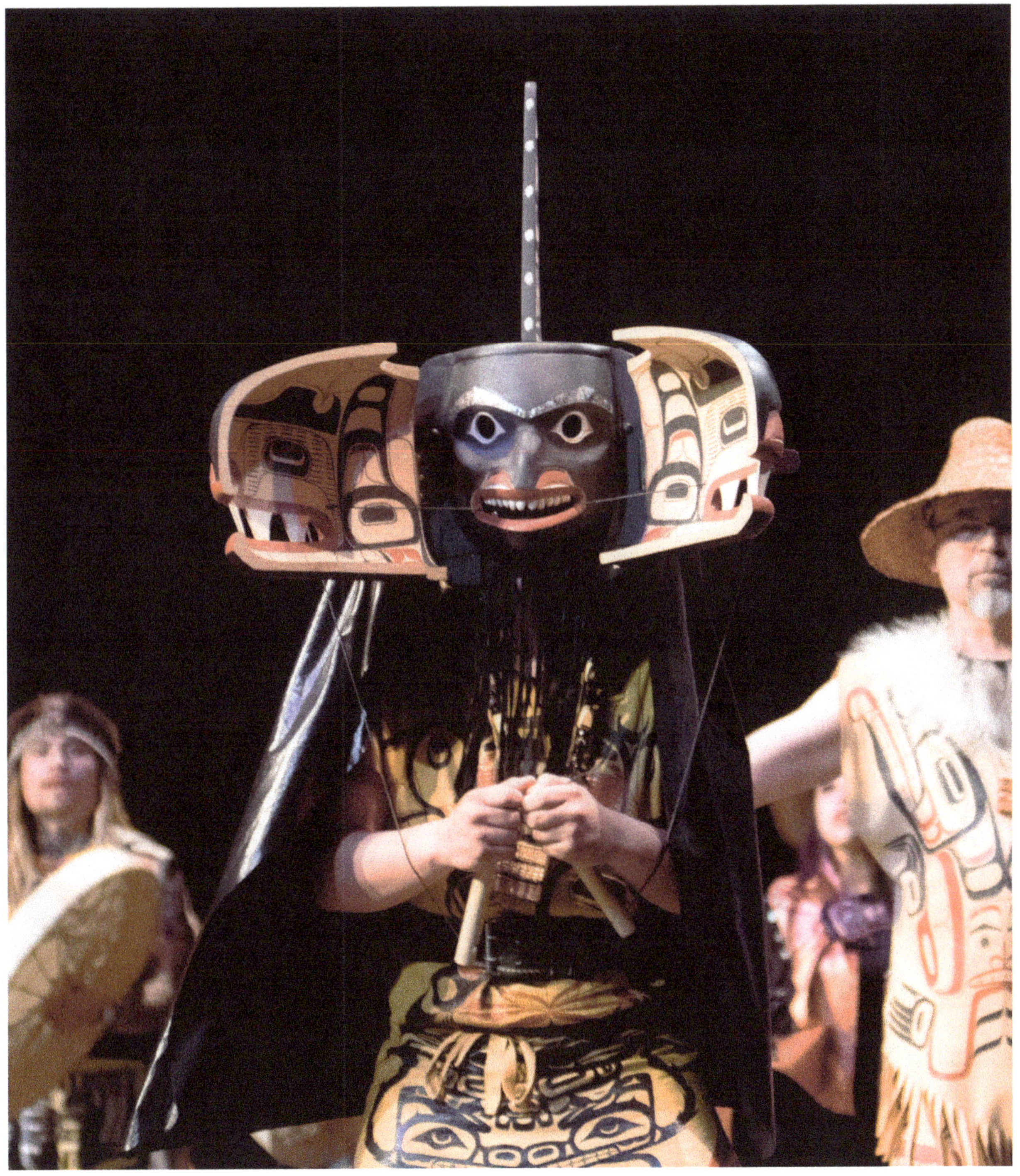

Transformation masks offer a dramatic moment during performances, like this one at Celebration 2016 in Juneau. The dancer is Jerome Nathan.

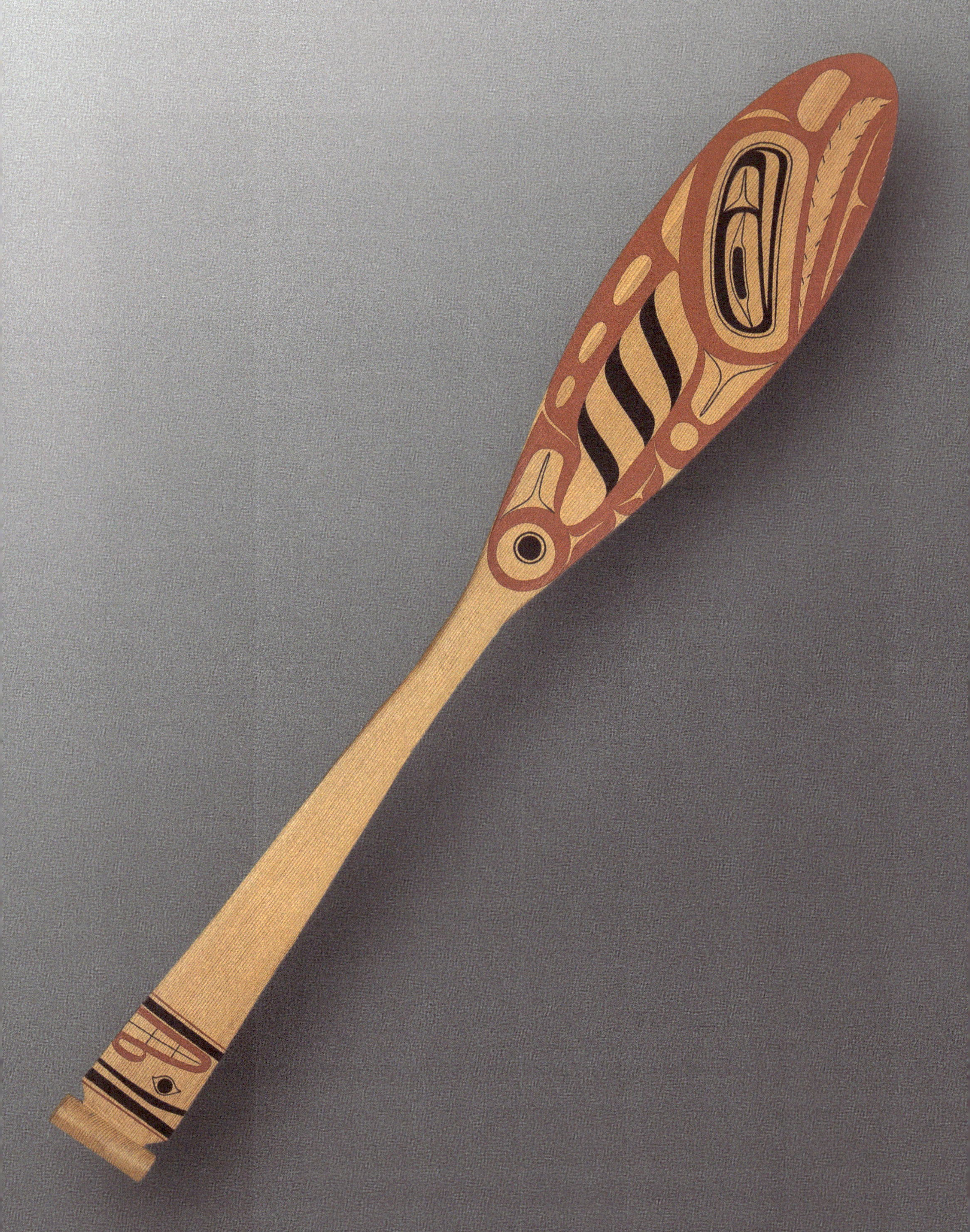

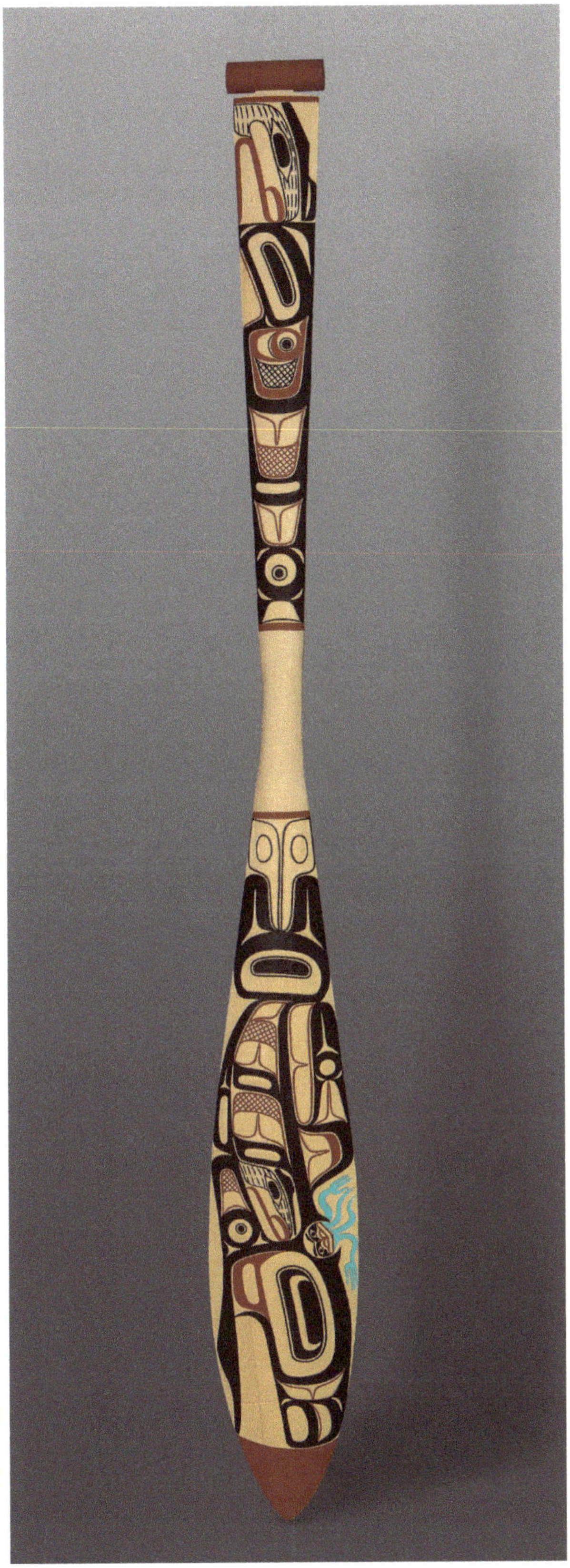

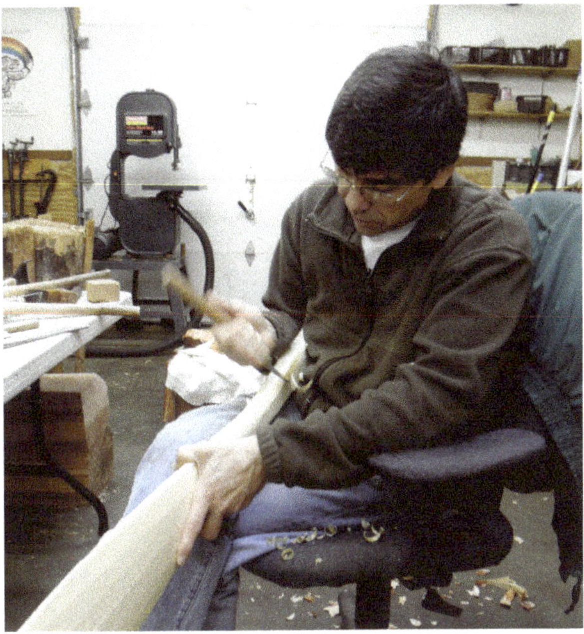

PADDLES

Paddles are a connection to our seagoing culture. They are one of those items that's easier to afford for some people or those who don't have a lot of room in their house.

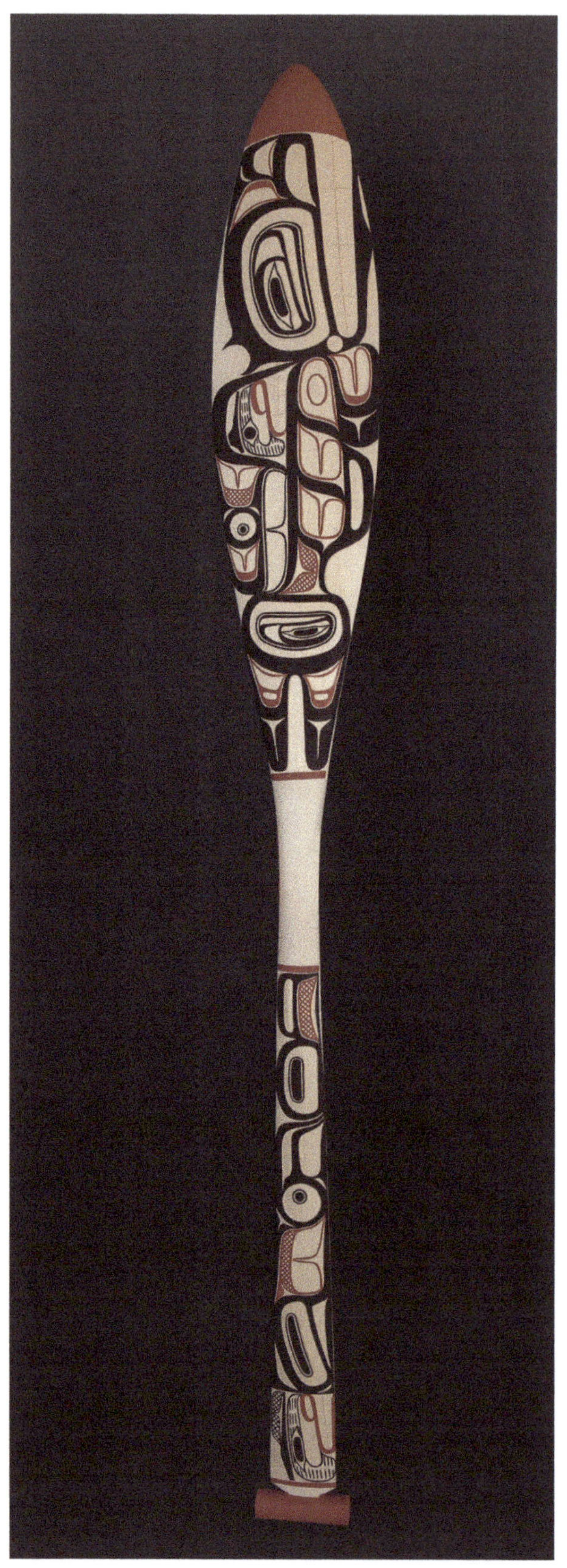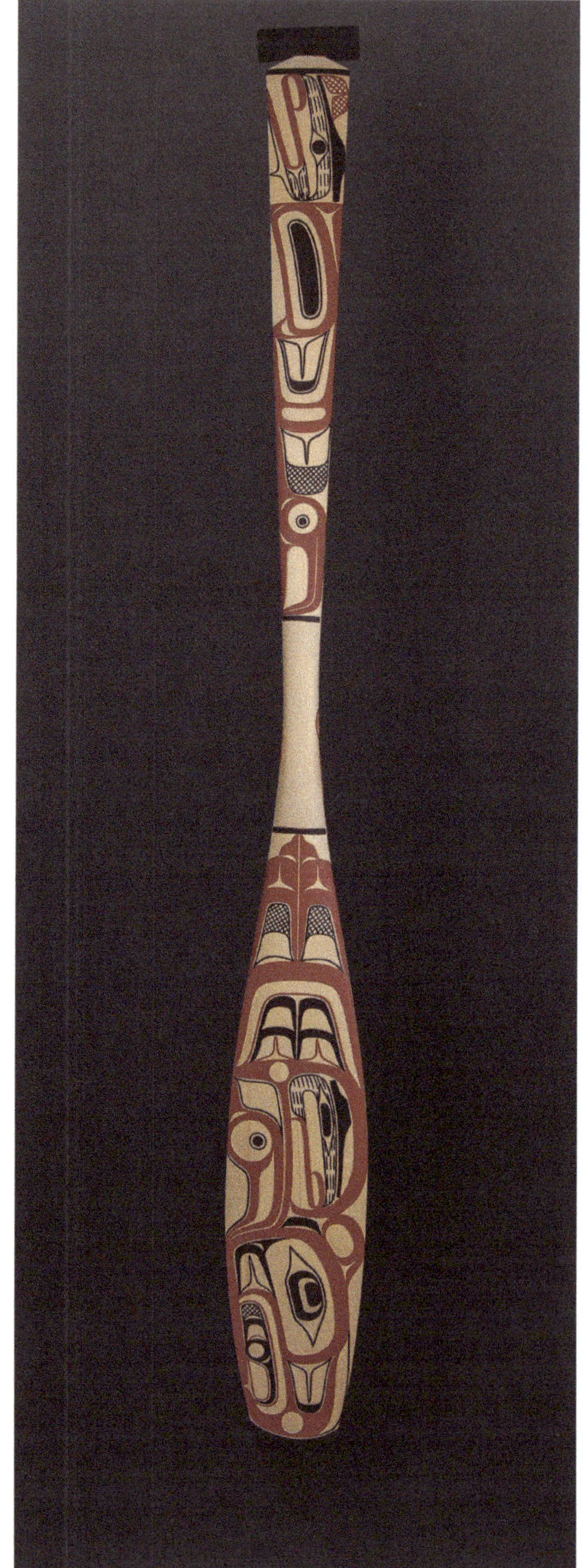

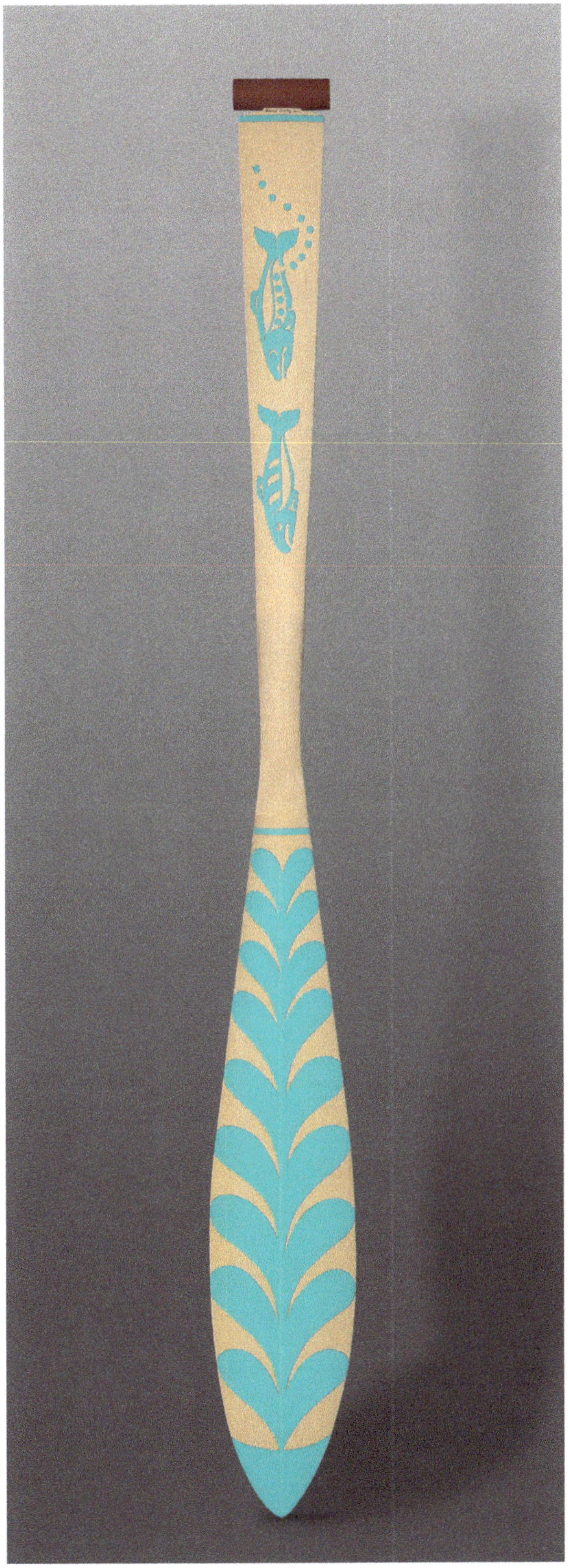

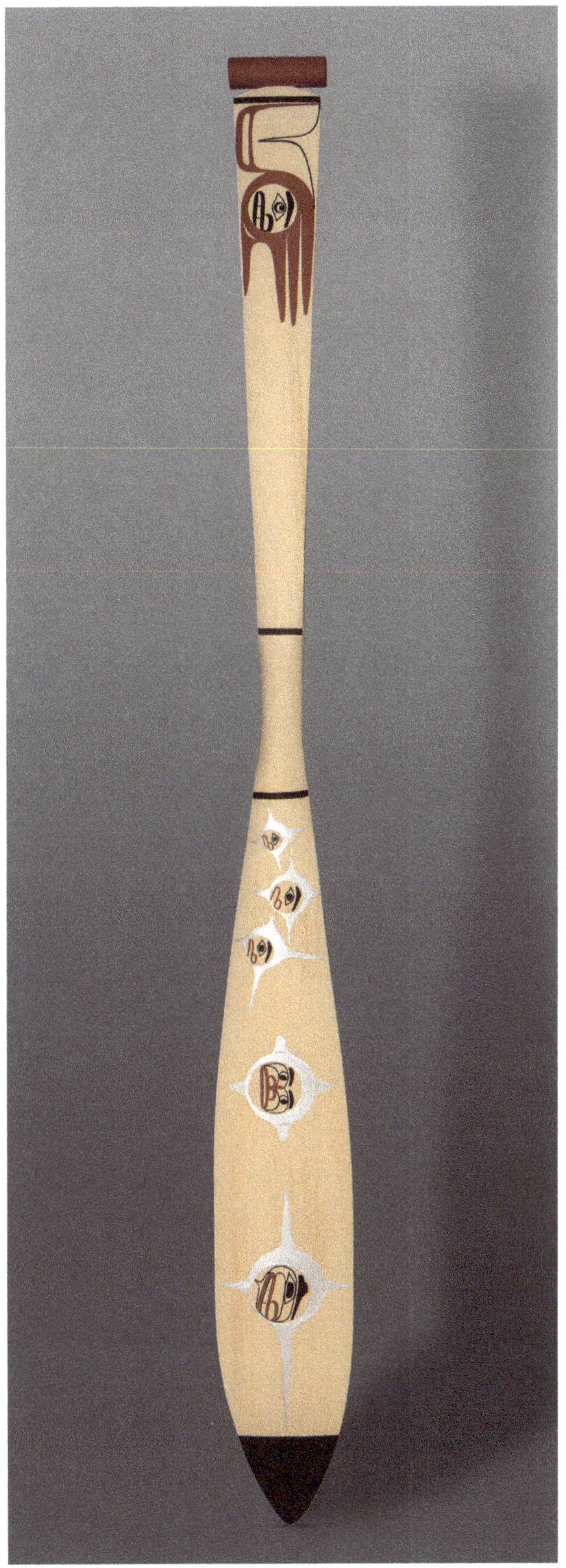

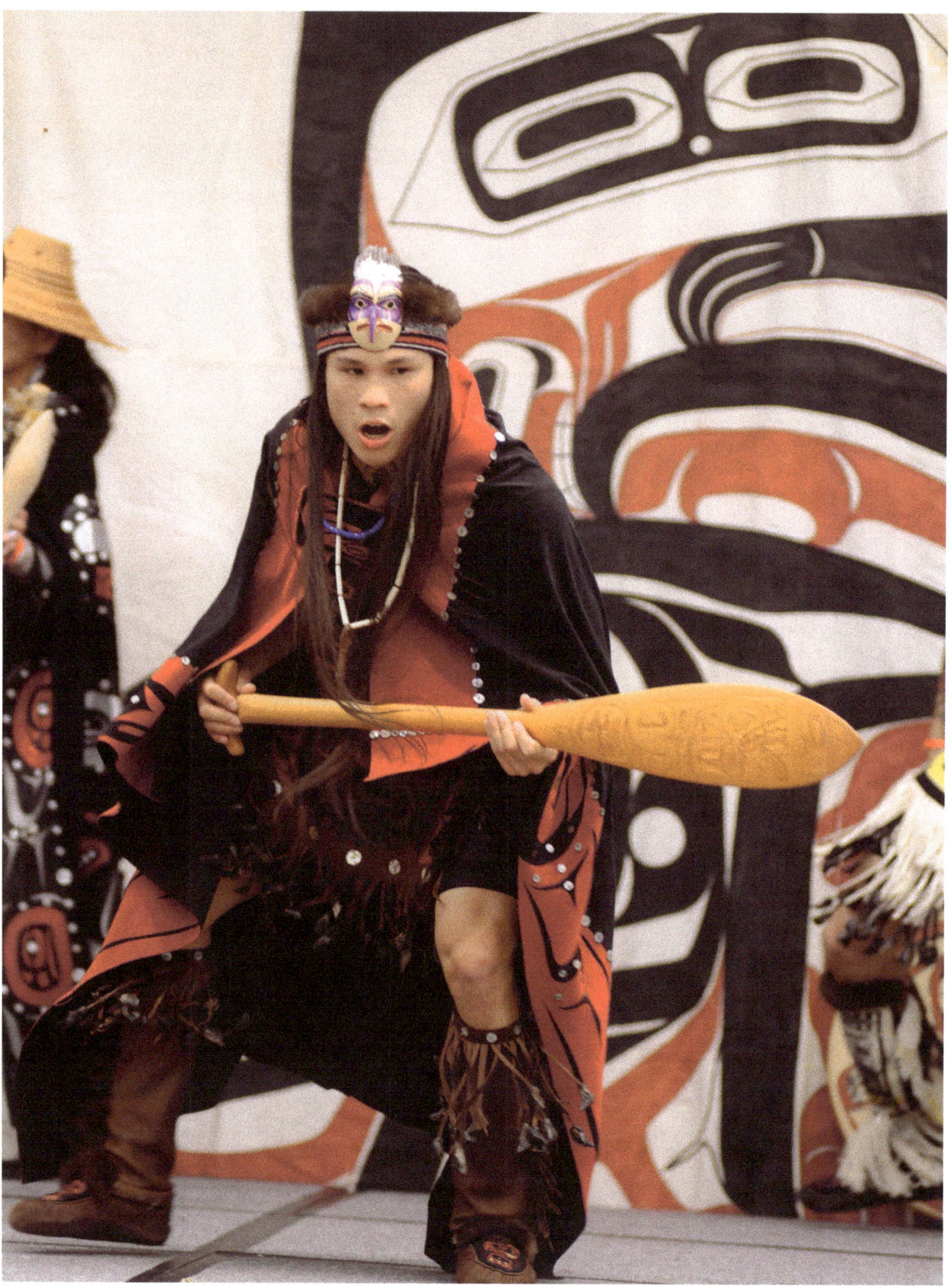

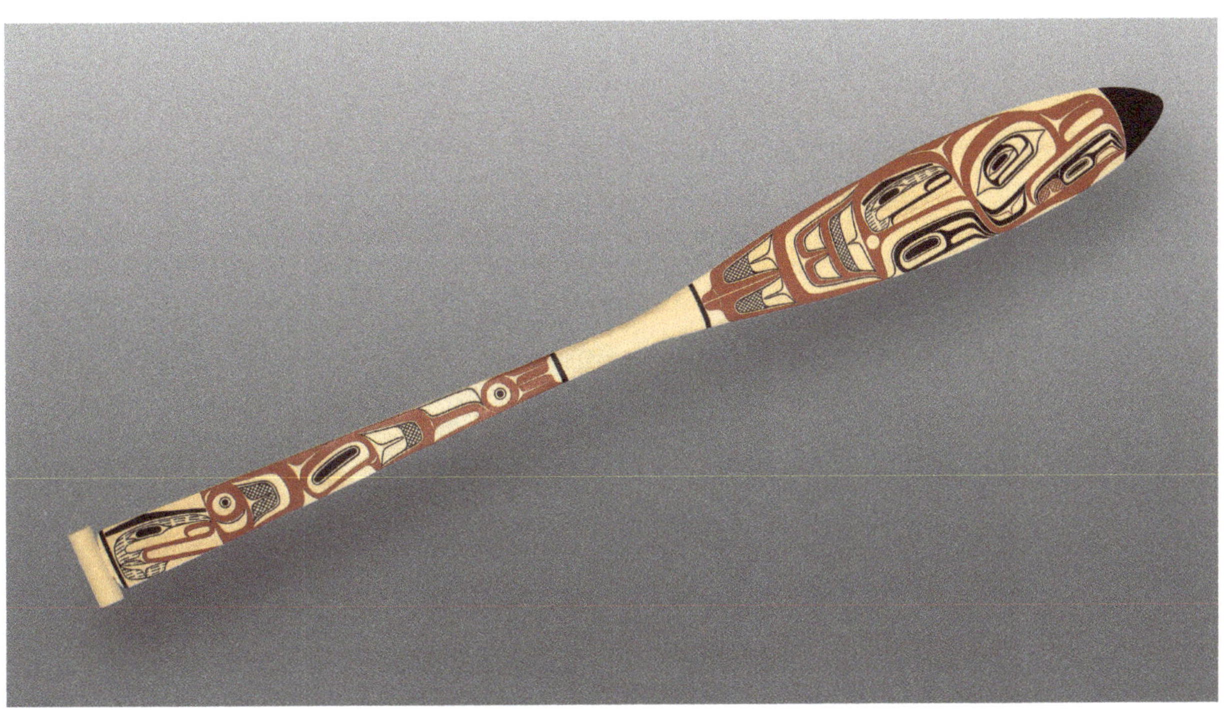

Paddles are also used in dance performances. These are eagle and killer whale paddles.

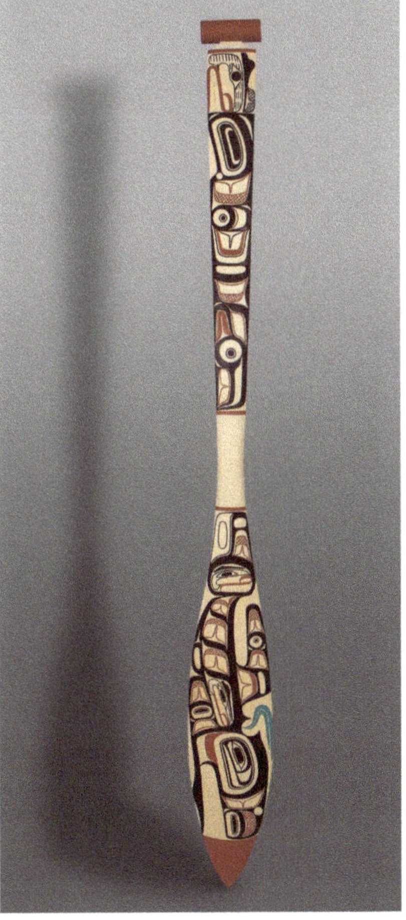

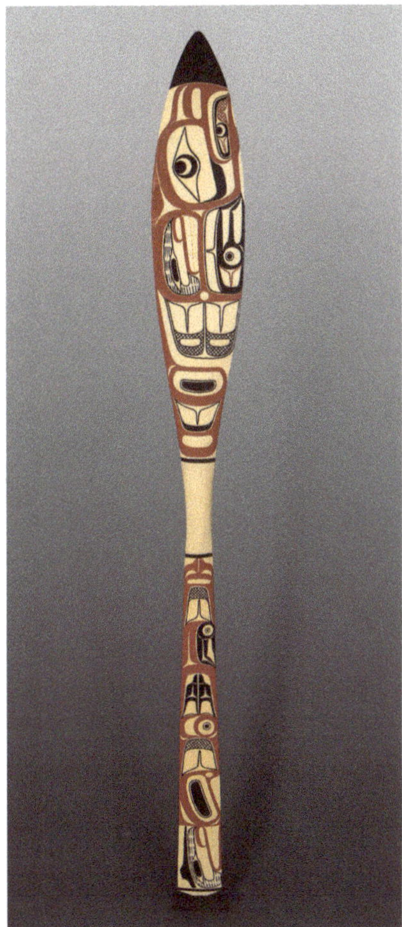

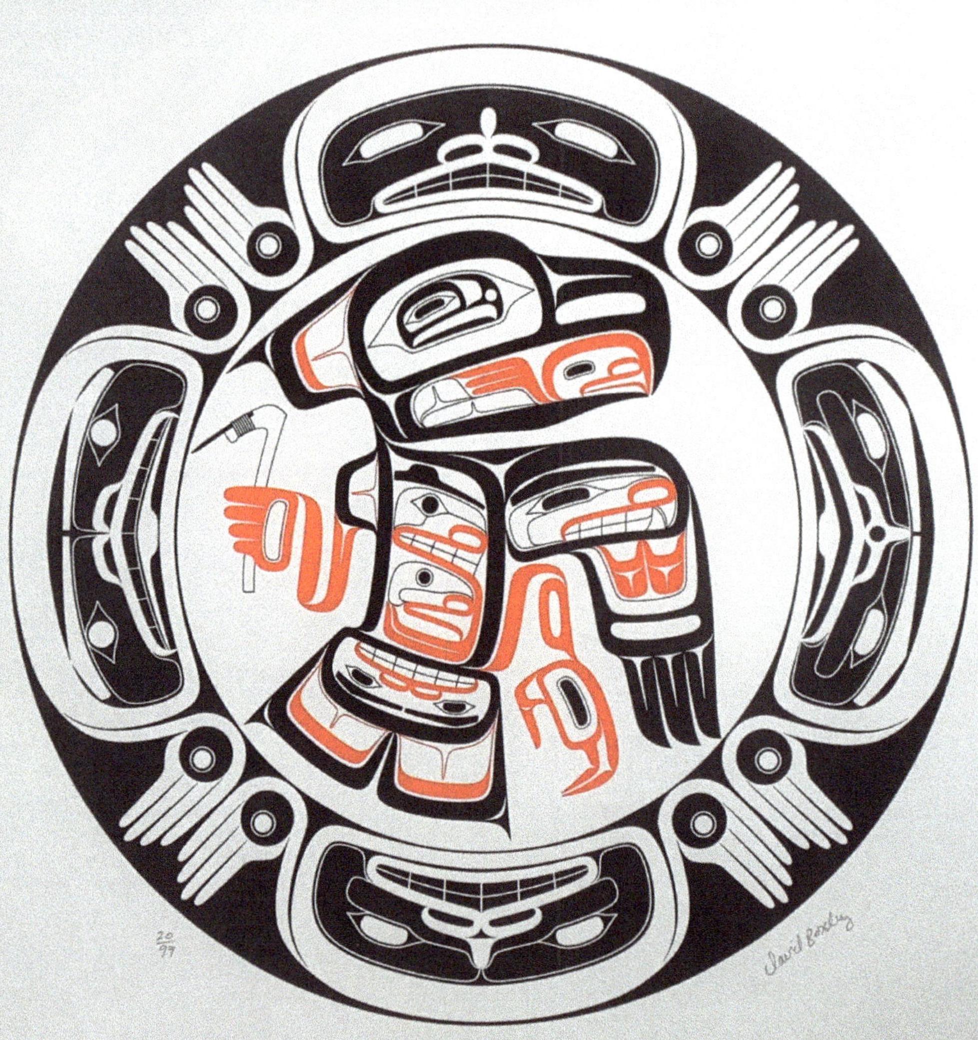
20/99
David Boxley
Fourty years

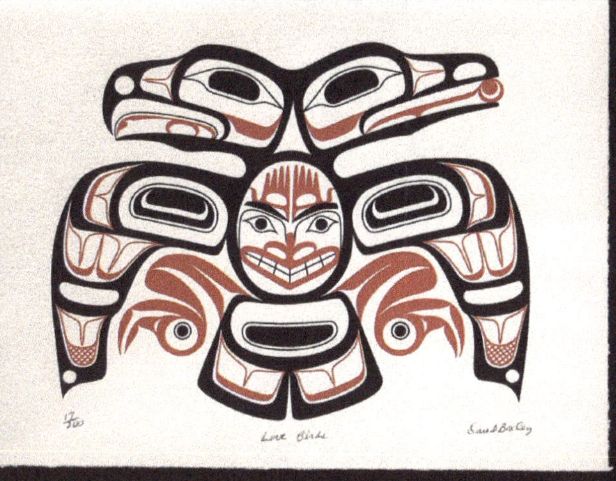

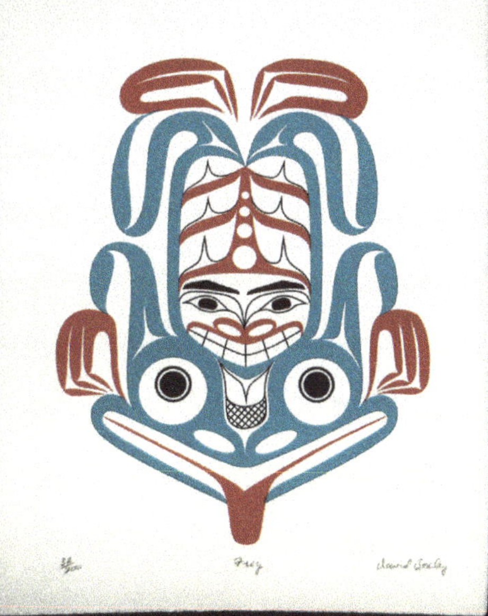

FORMLINE ANIMAL PRINTS

Like paddles, prints are ideal for people who want authentic Native art but can't afford to pay thousands of dollars. These are my drawings but most of these prints were hand-pulled silk screen prints by Paul Nicholson, who did the actual printing.

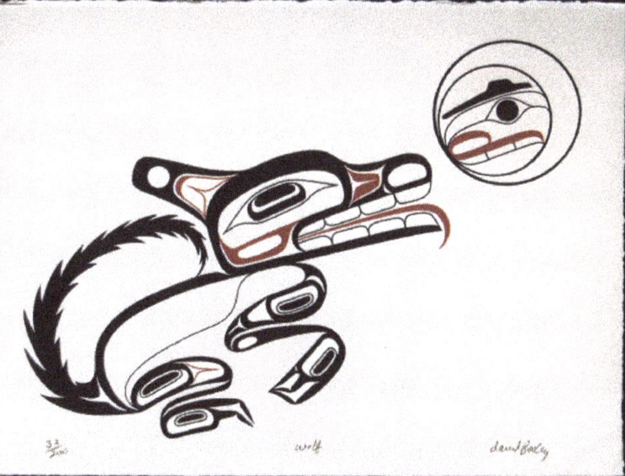

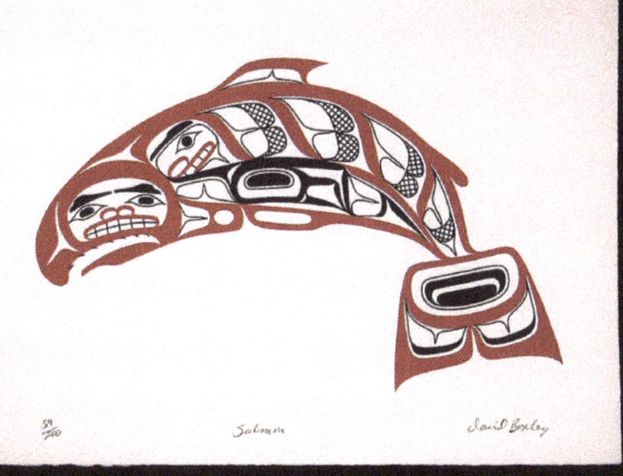

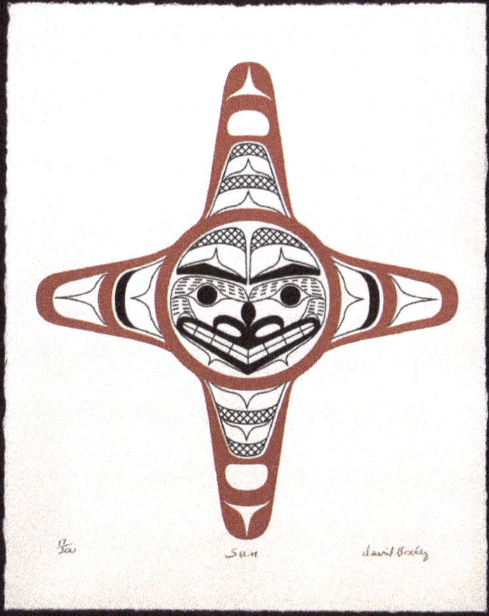

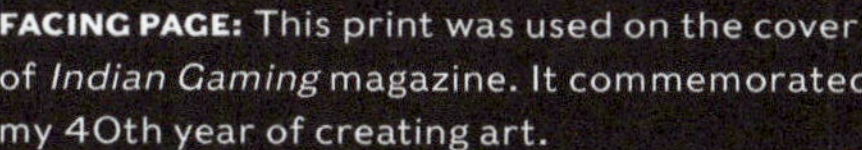

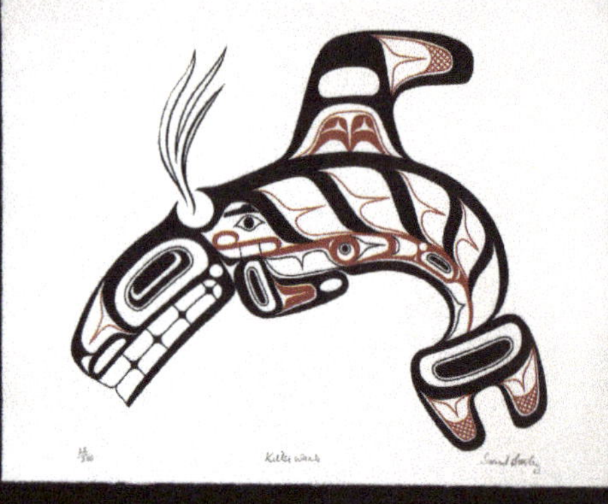

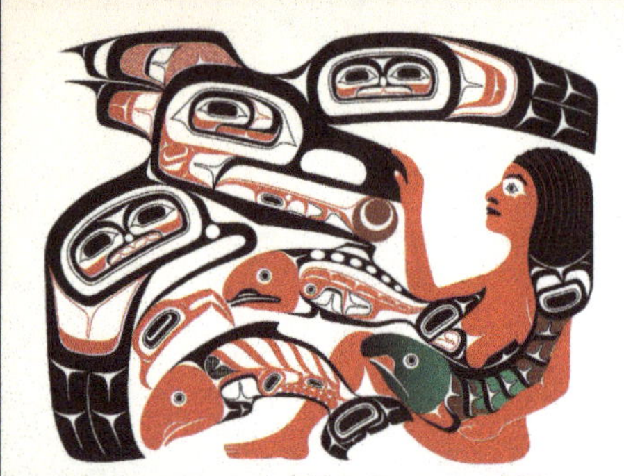

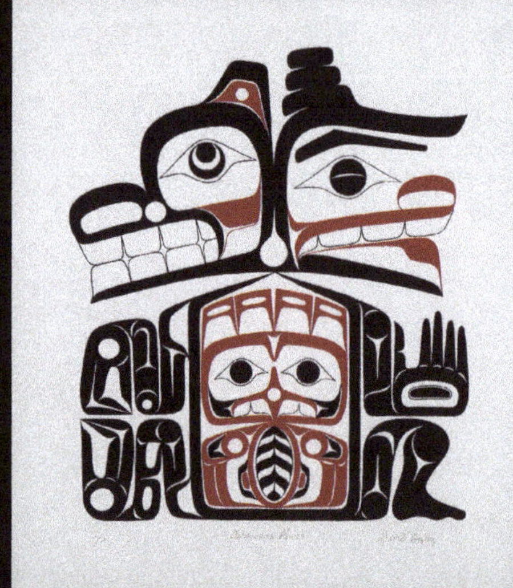

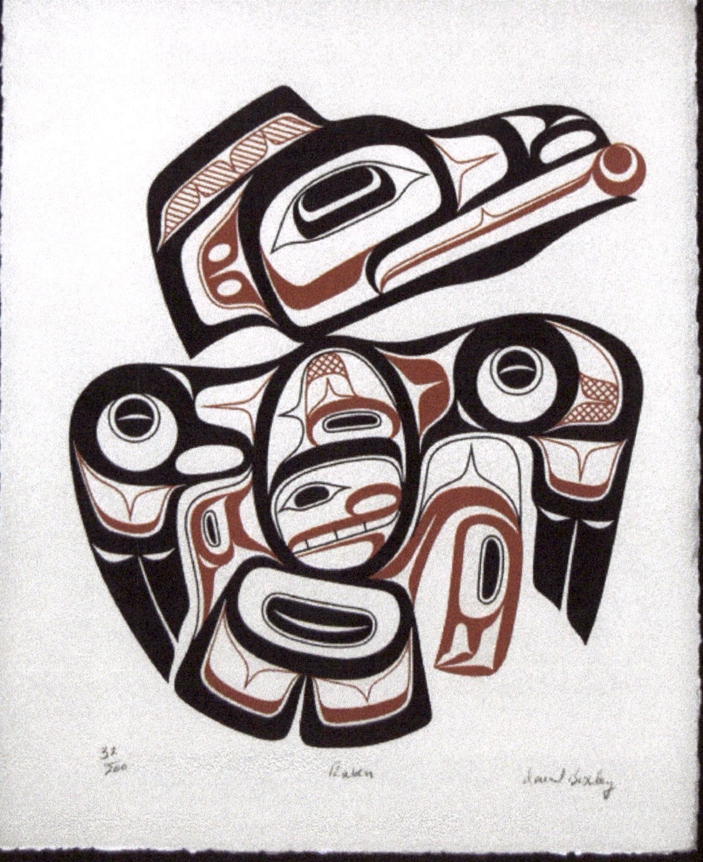

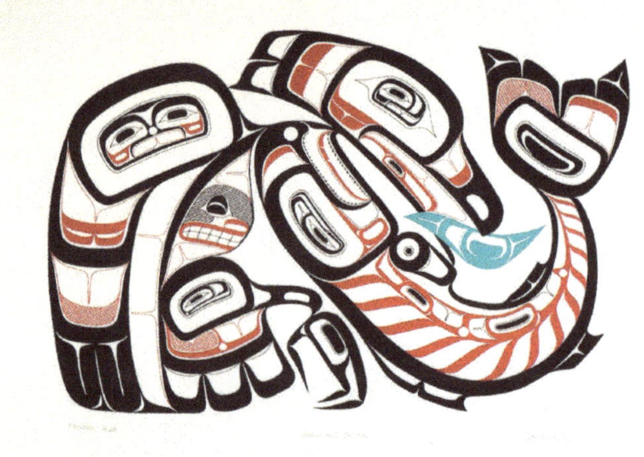

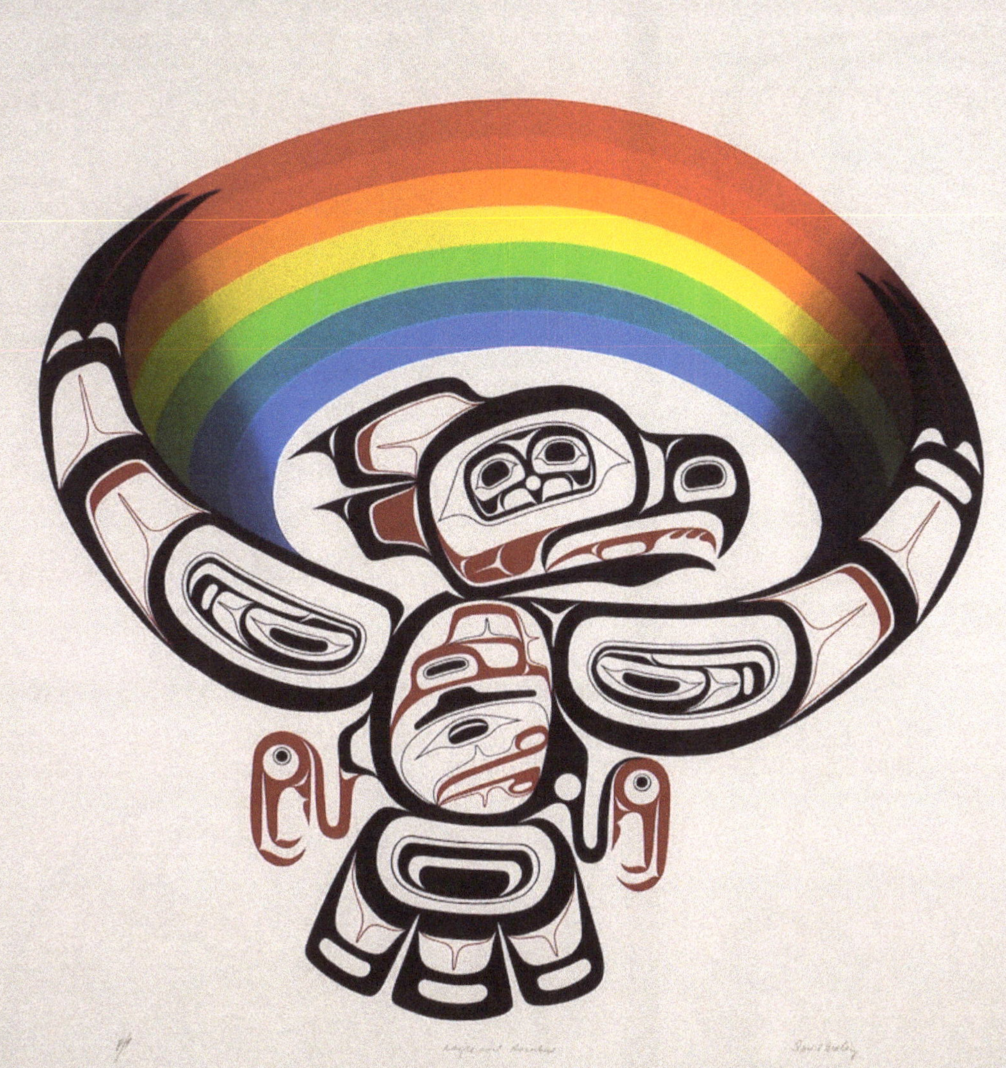

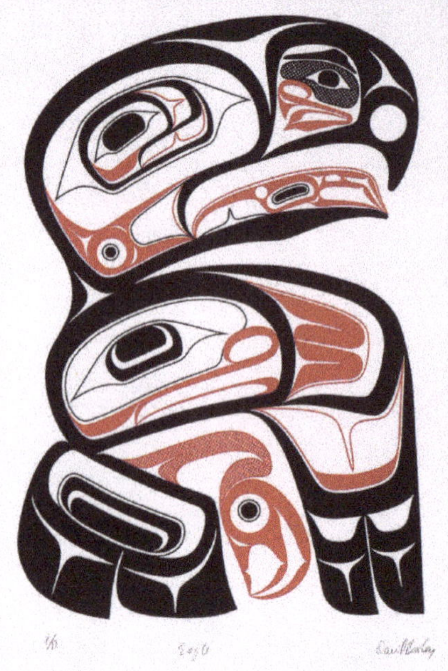

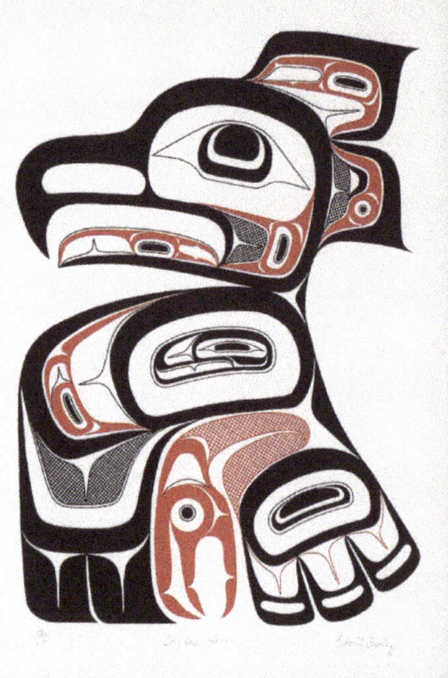

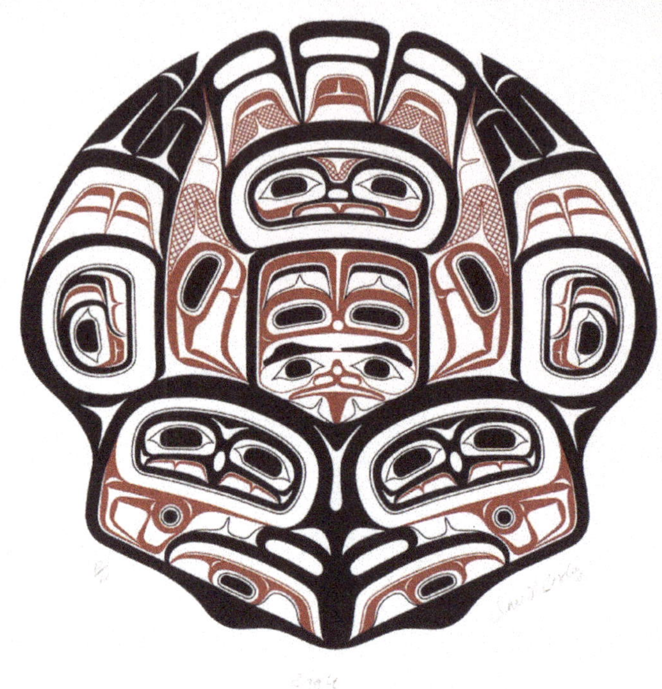

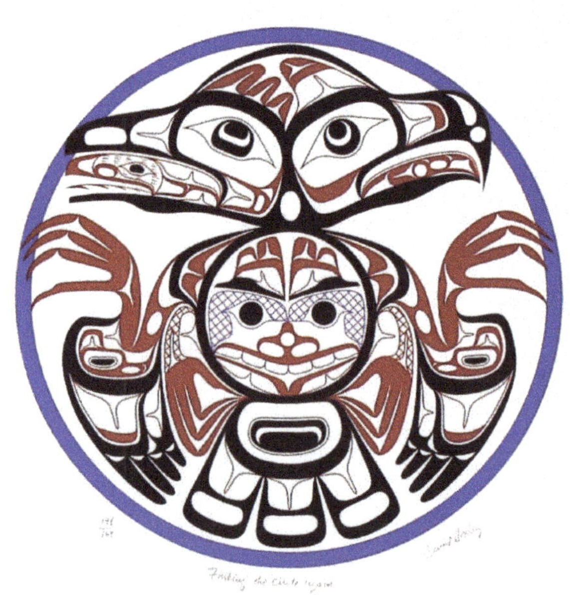

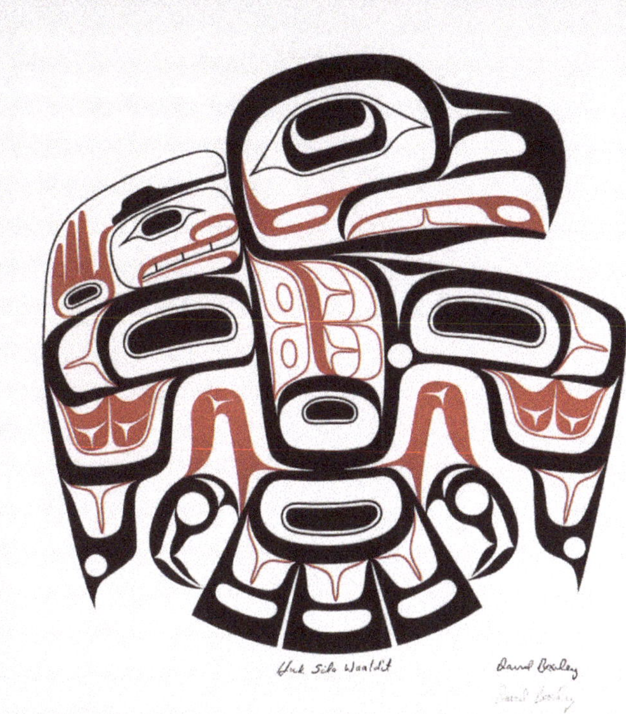
Huk Siha Waaldit
David Boxley
David Boxley

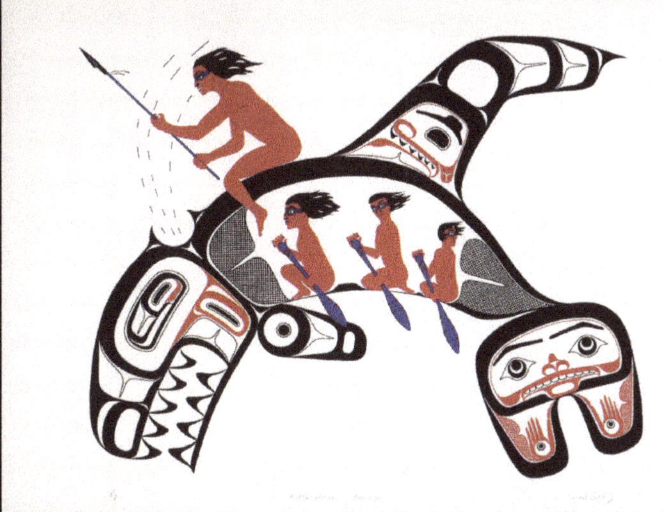

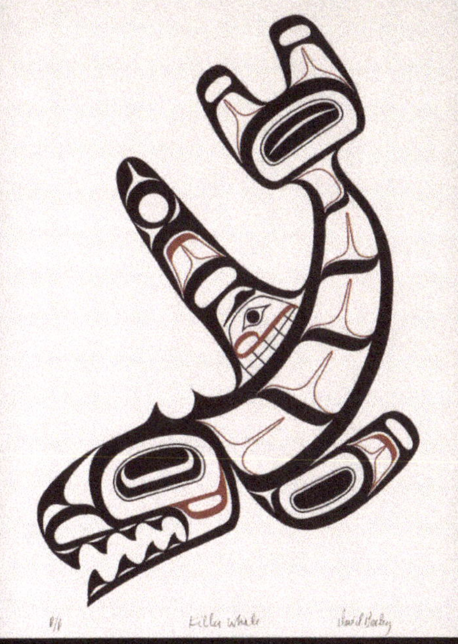
Killer Whale
David Boxley

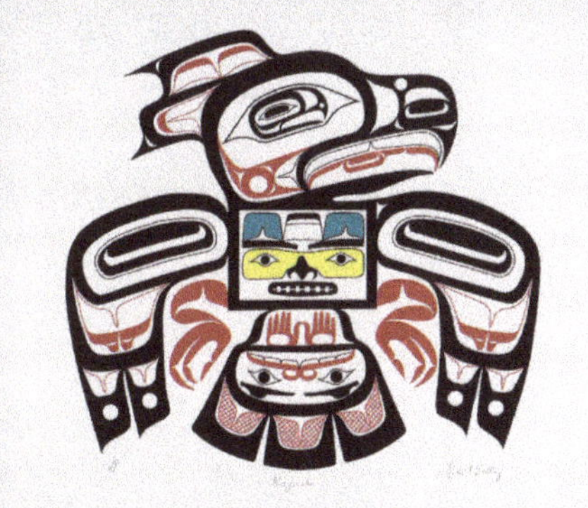

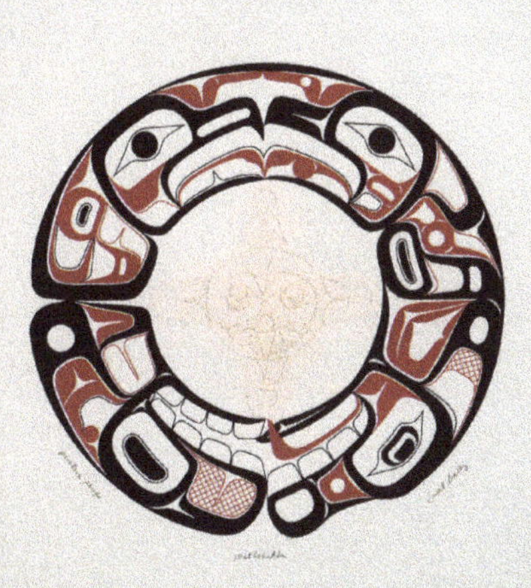

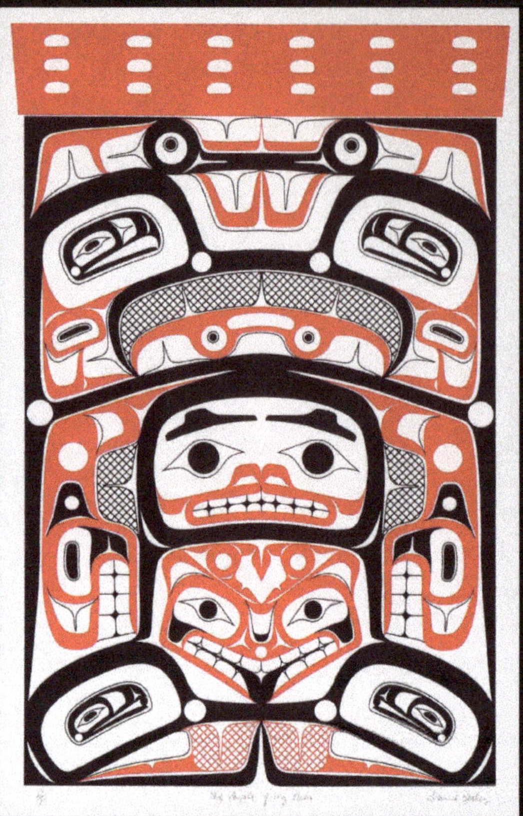

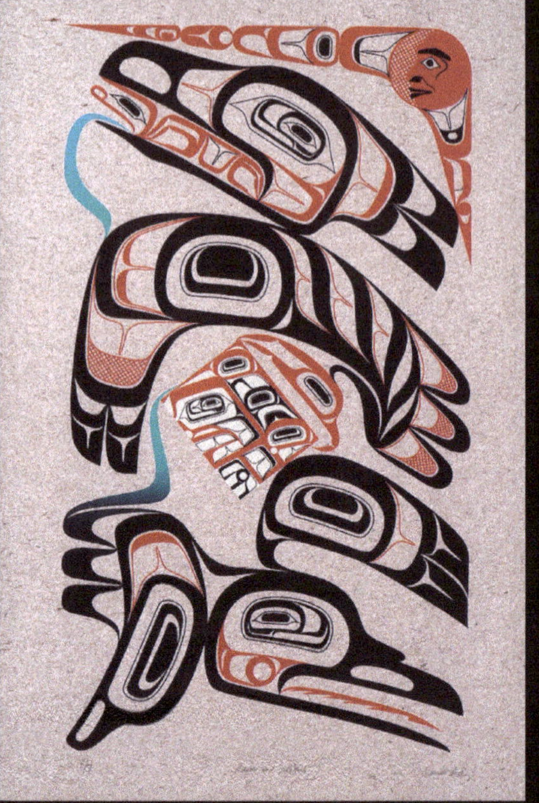

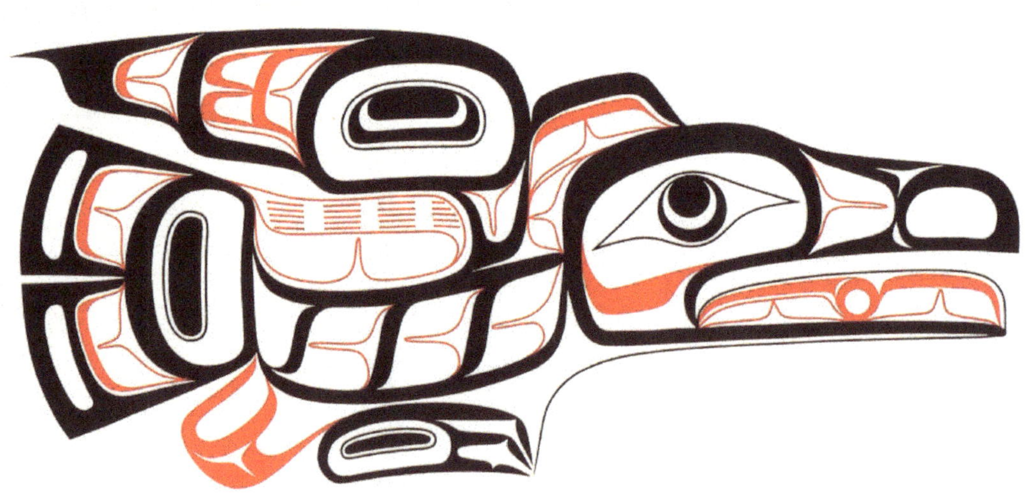

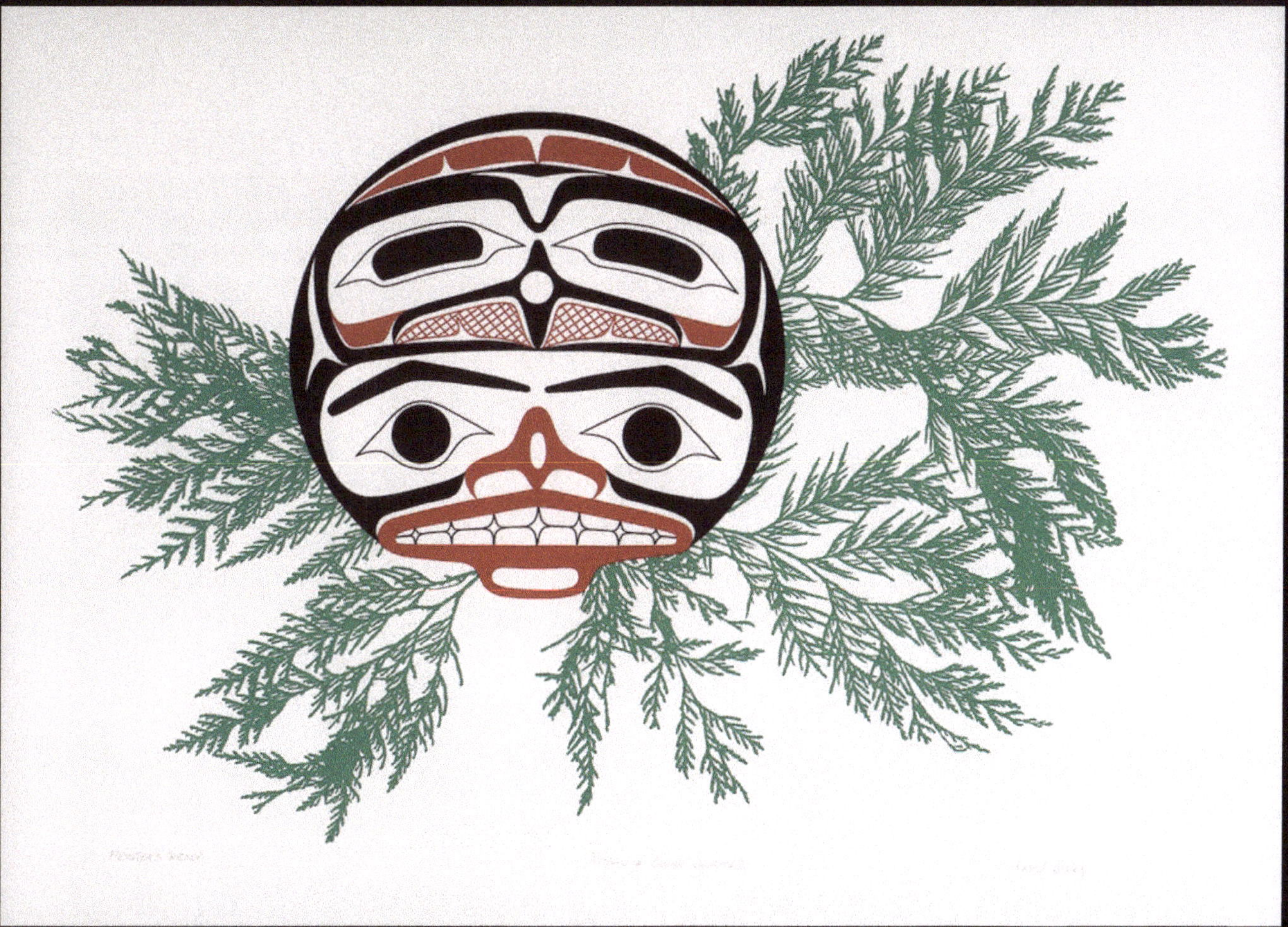

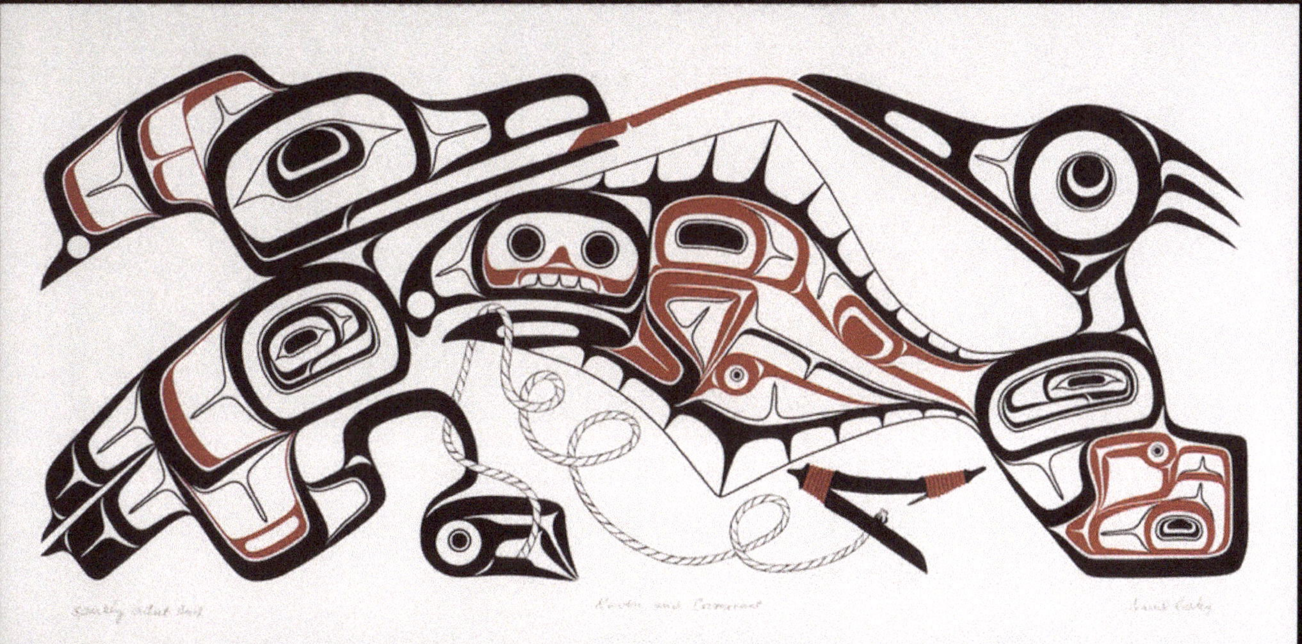

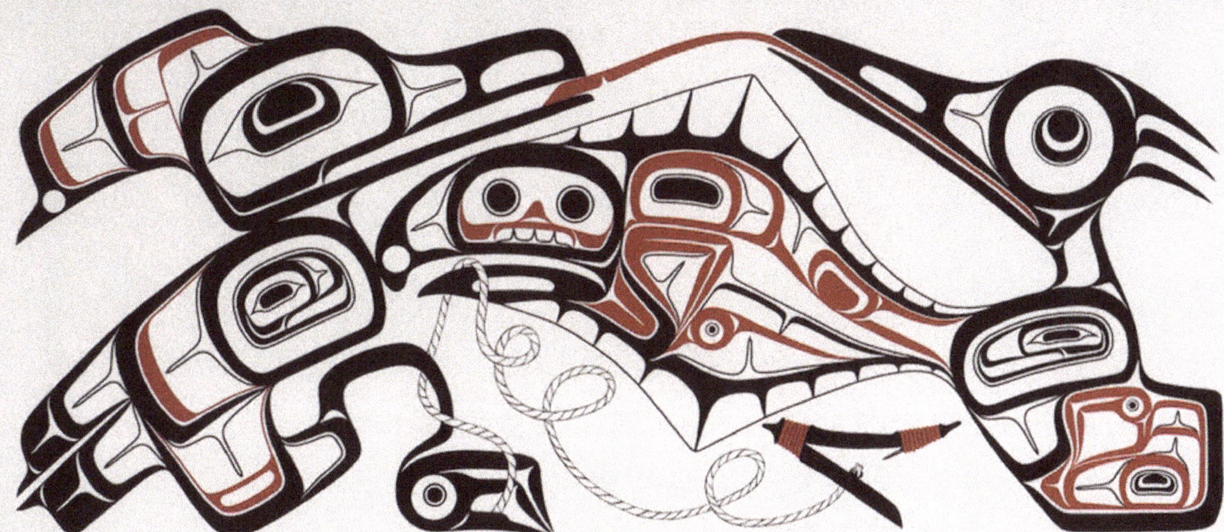

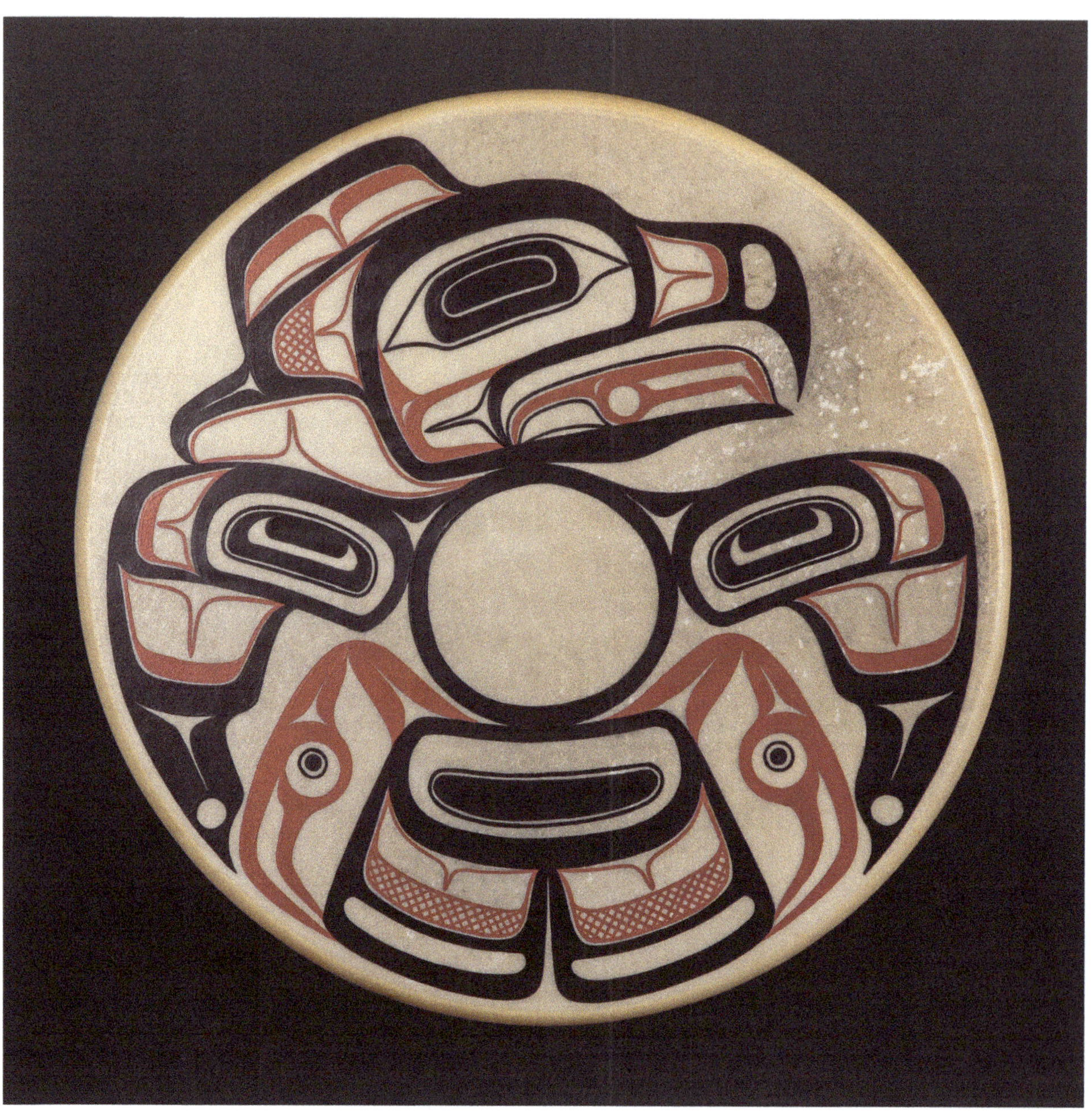

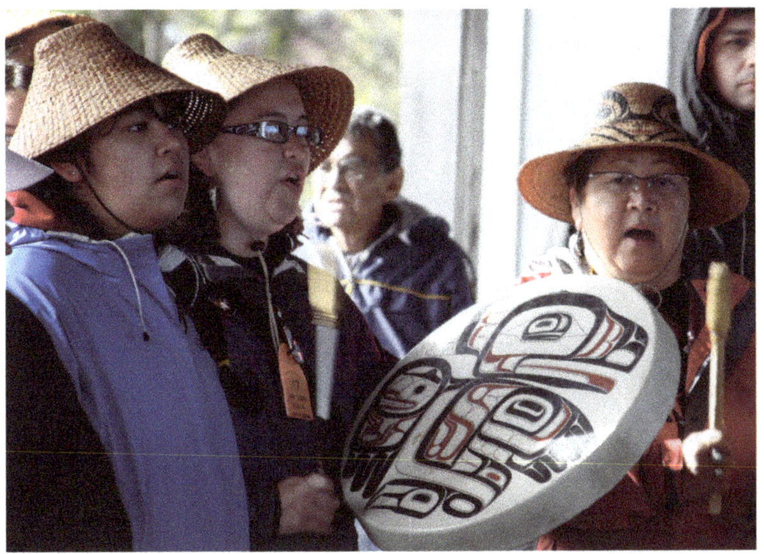

DRUMS

My son, Zach, has been my drum maker for years. He makes the drums and I design and paint them. Like other types of our art, drums have become so important up and down the Northwest coast as a part of our cultural revival. They are used by countless dance groups as well as art for display.

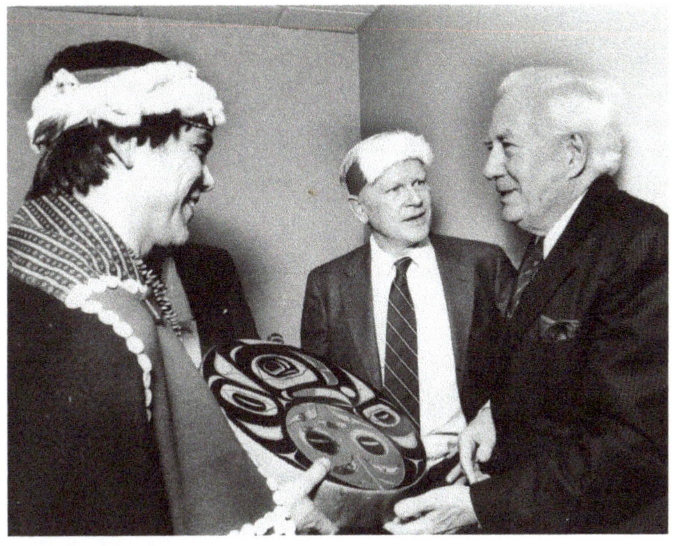

ABOVE: I'm holding one of my drums while meeting Chief Justice Earl Warren who came to a ceremony for an eight-foot pole carved for a Washington D.C. law firm, Hobbs, Straus, Dean & Walker.

LEFT: Drums featured during the final songs performed during the 2016 Celebration in Juneau, Alaska.

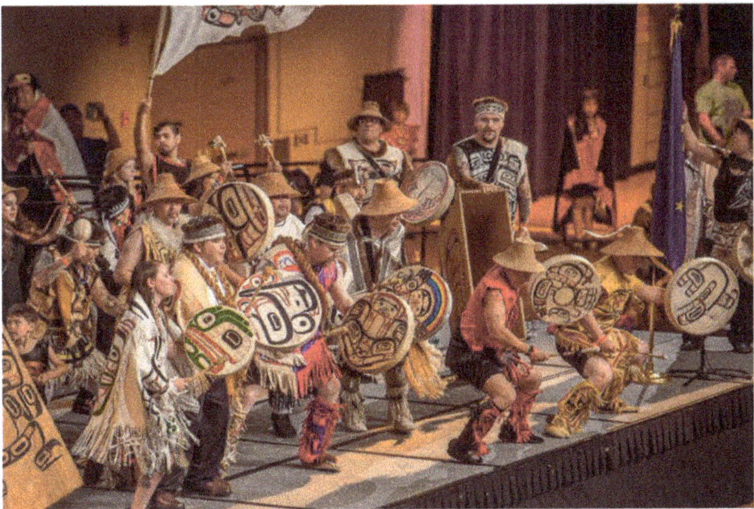

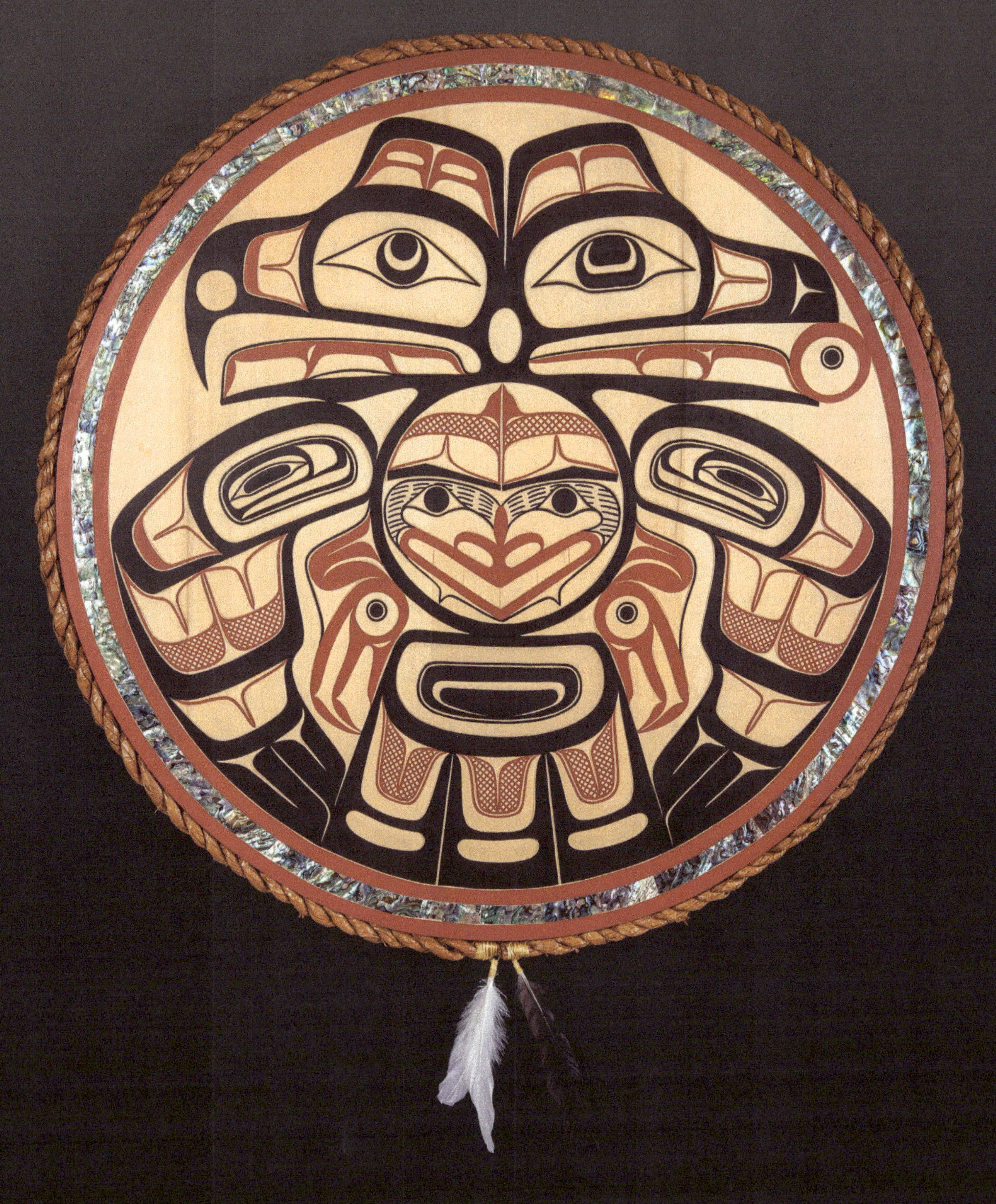

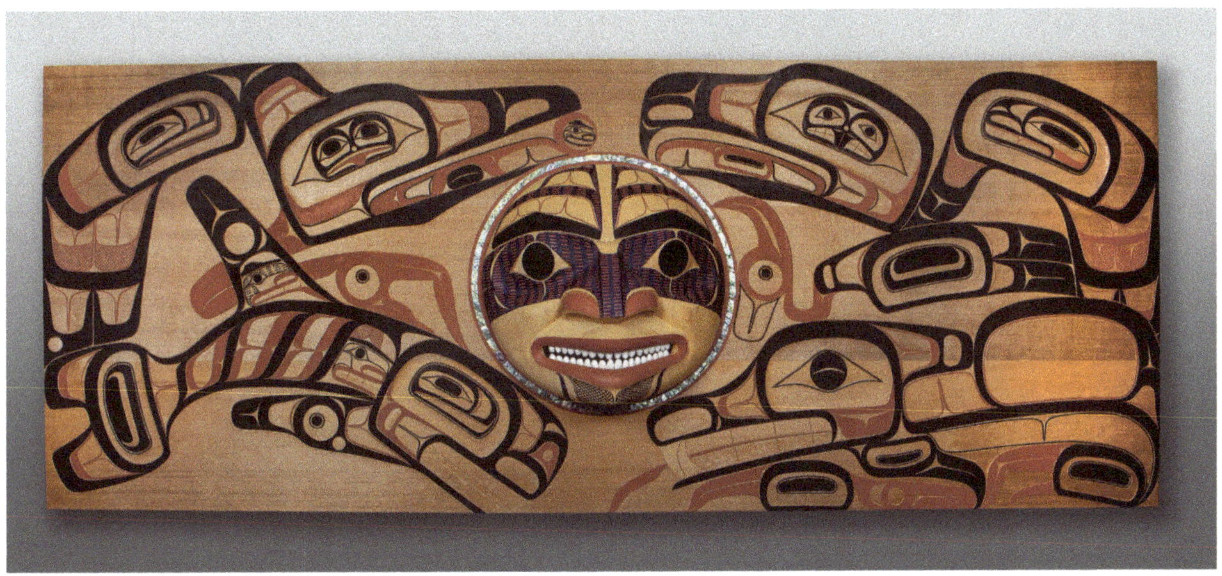

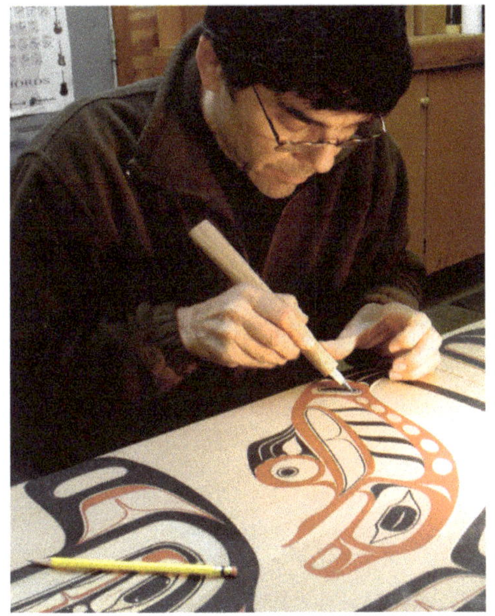

RELIEF PANELS

Much of my work is designs carved and painted onto flat wood panels. There are basically four types of cuts used to create two-dimensional carving such as these panels. Once a student learns those cuts and how the wood grain affects the cuts, their work grows and improves, and the details become cleaner.

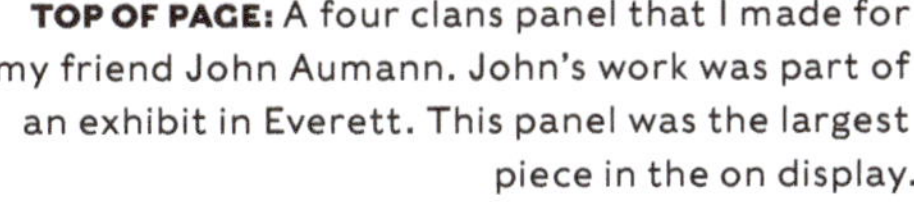

TOP OF PAGE: A four clans panel that I made for my friend John Aumann. John's work was part of an exhibit in Everett. This panel was the largest piece in the on display.

FACING PAGE: This round panel depicts the love birds, and the eagle and the raven are shown. Among the Tlingit and Haida, eagles and ravens traditionally would marry one another.

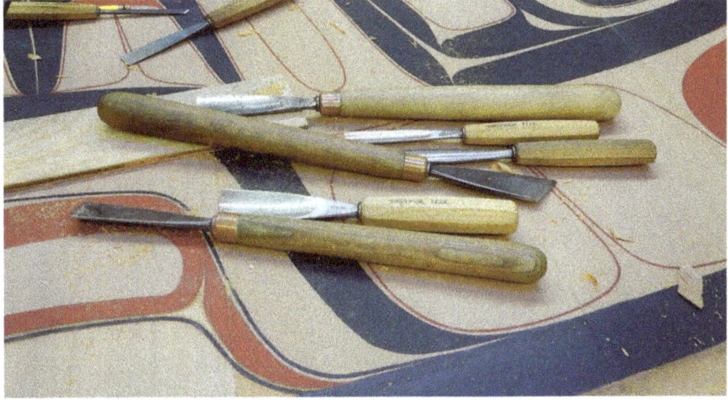

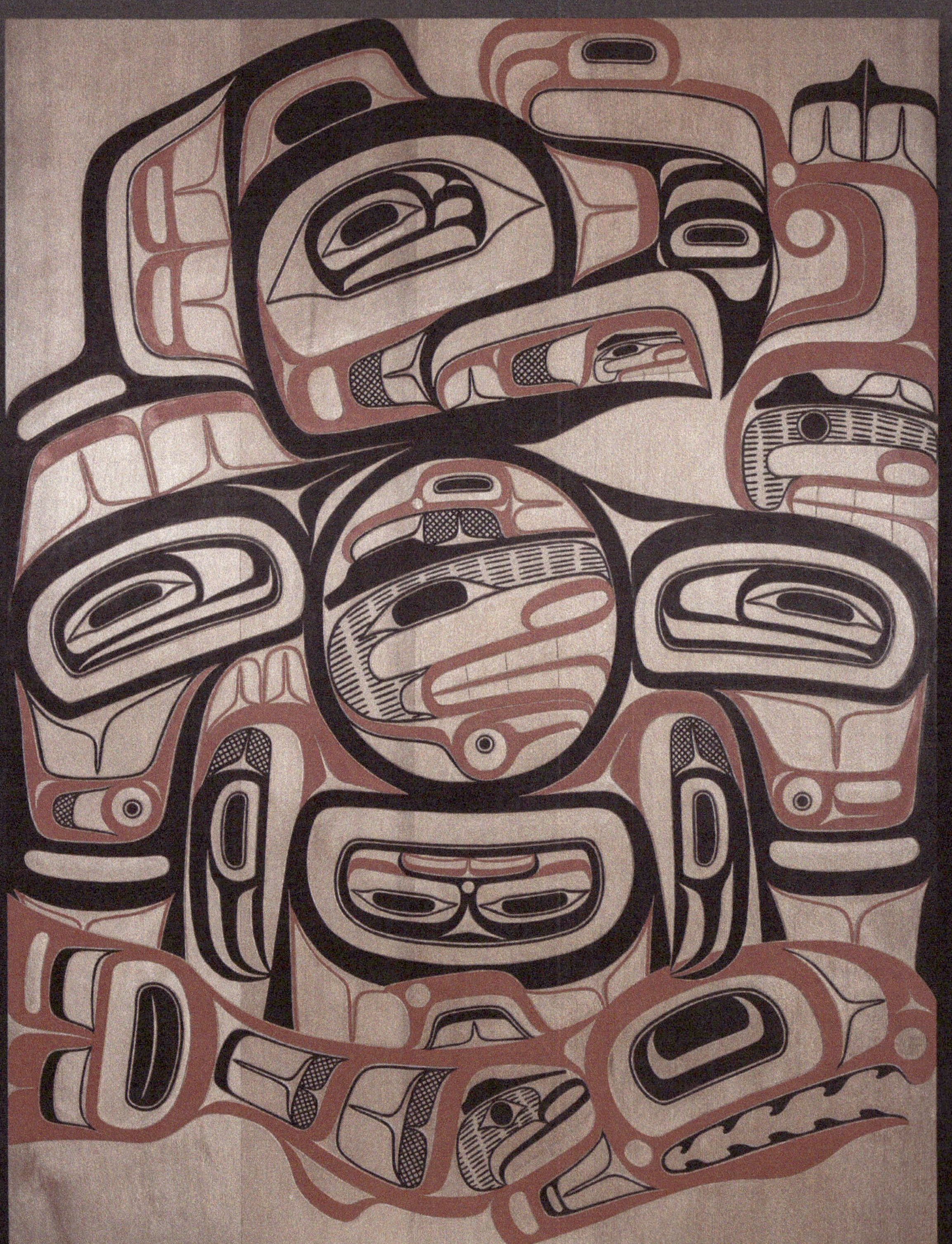

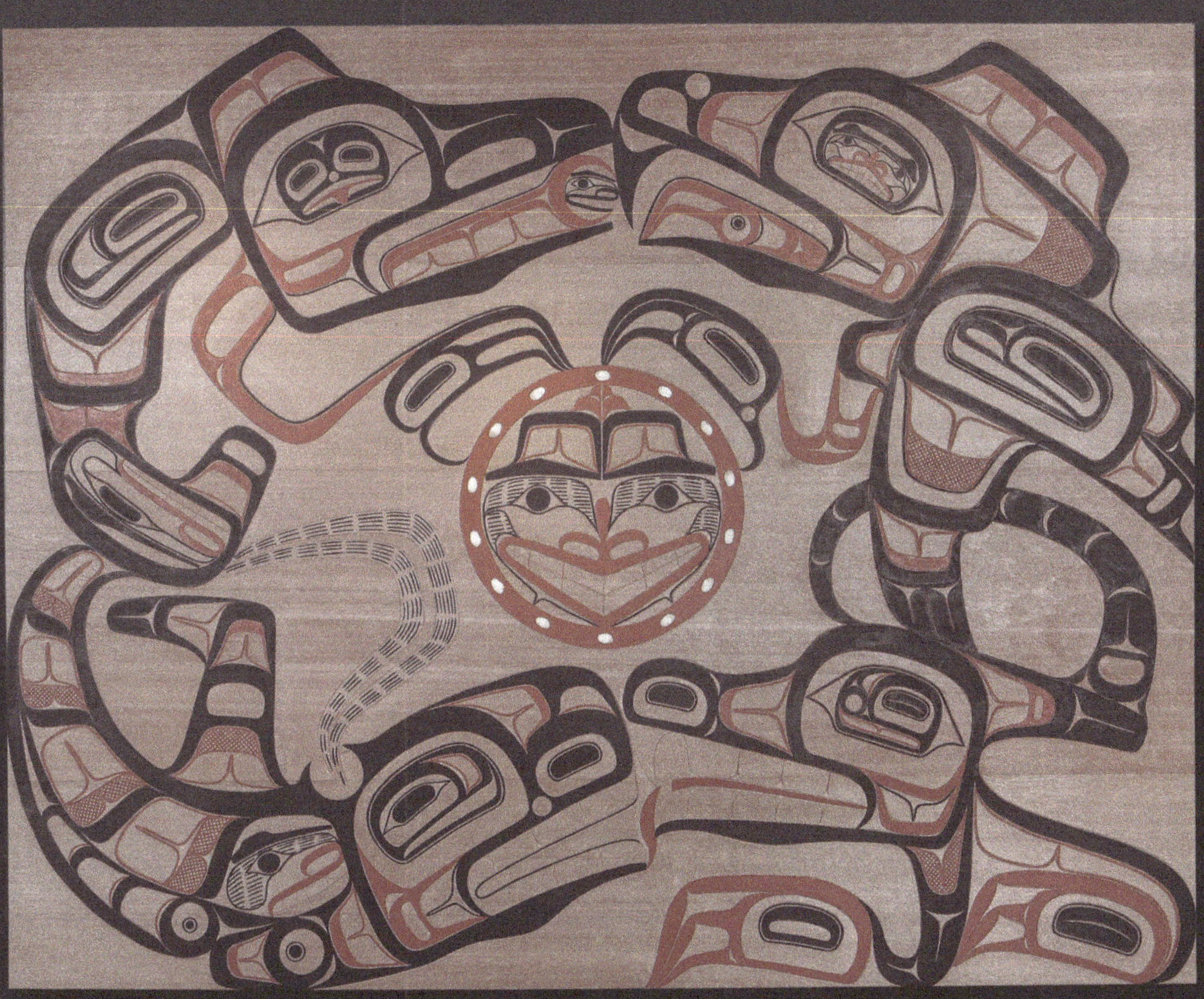

Another variation of the four clans panel, representing people and celebrating our culture with the happy face in the middle.

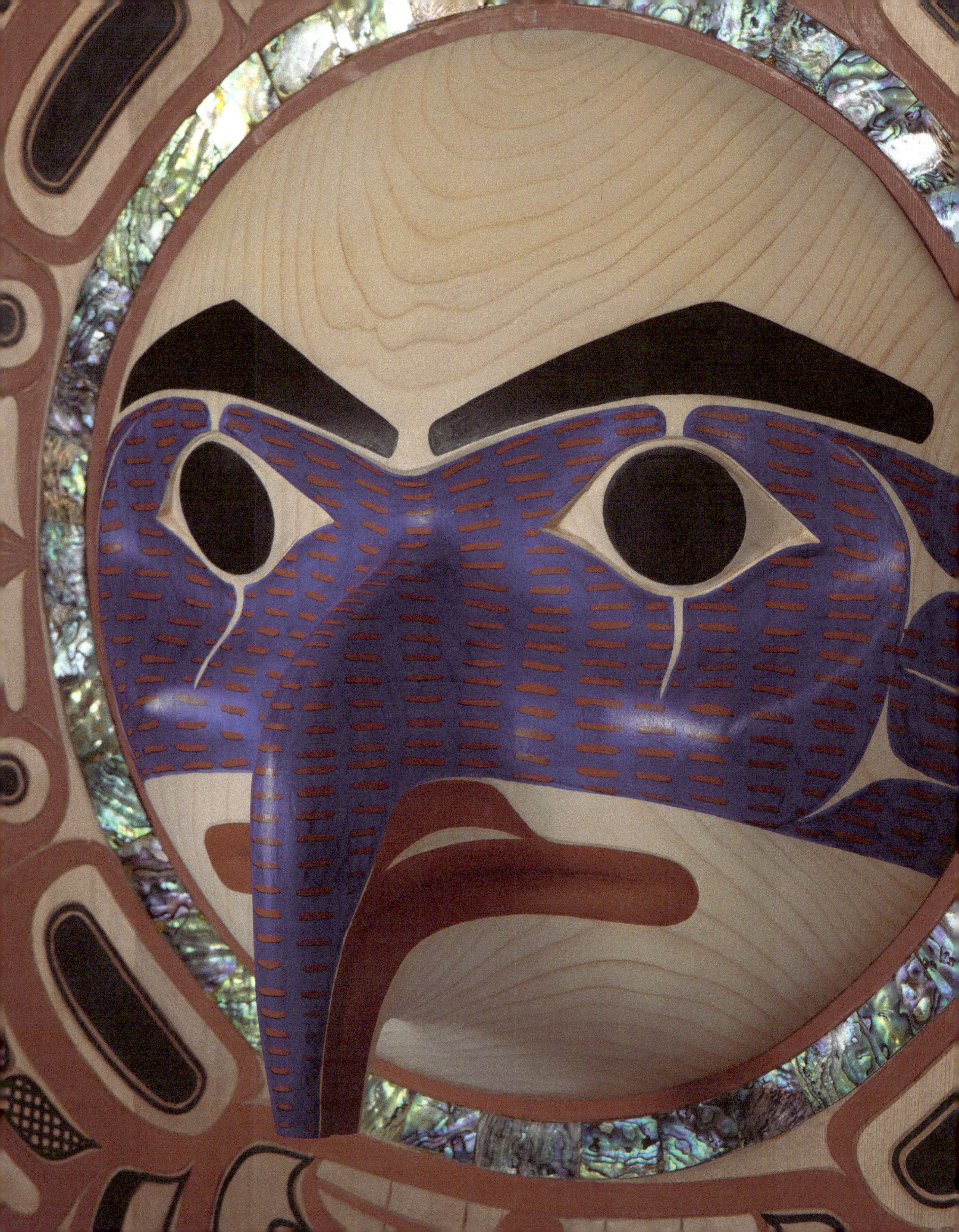

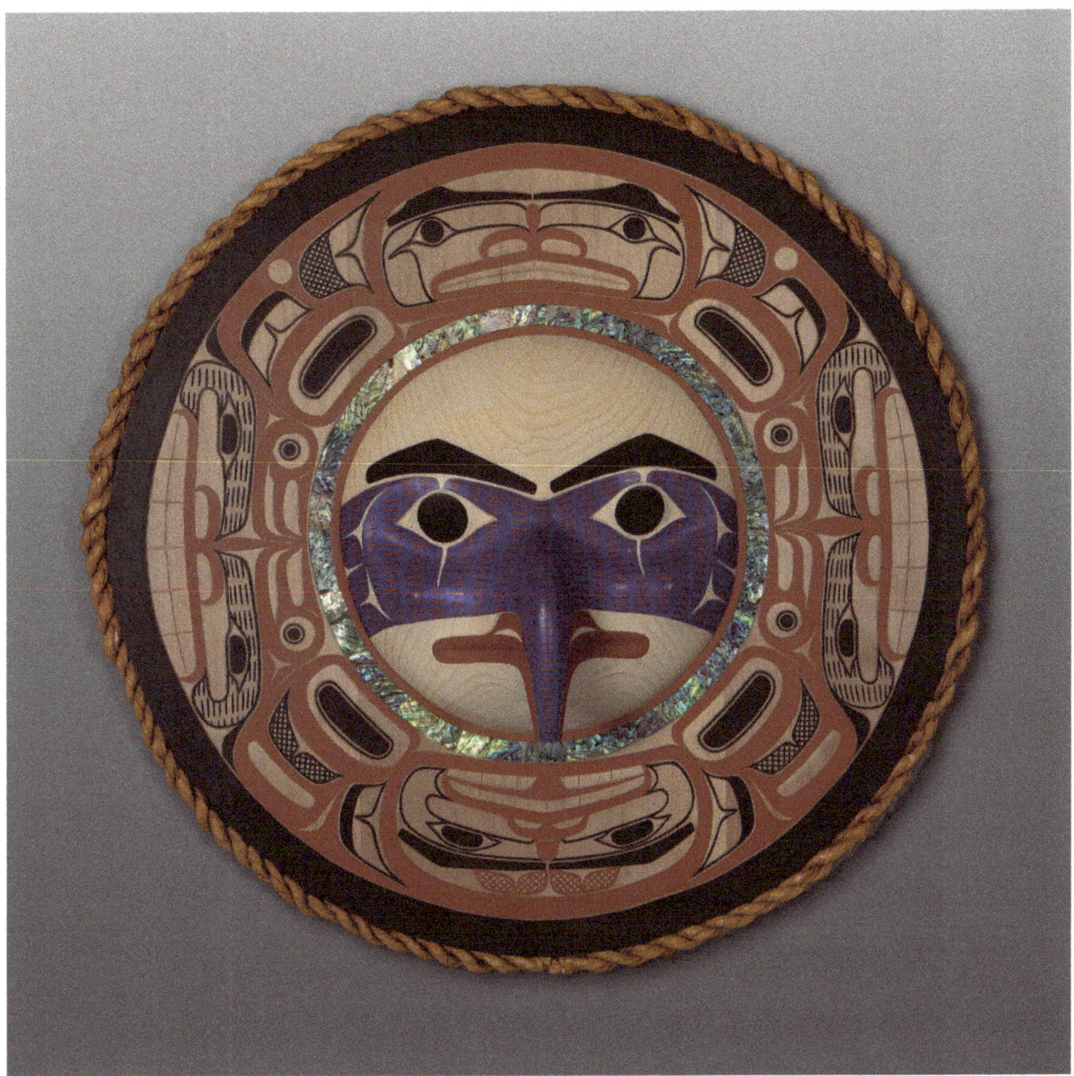

Sometimes I will add a mask to a panel. In this case, it illustrates the story of the eagle and the young chief. I put the story on masks and on totem poles and we dance that story all the time.

It's the story of a little boy who was walking down the beach and found an eagle trapped in a fish net. He took out his knife and cut the net, then the eagle flew away. He didn't realize he was releasing a spirit guardian.

Years later, the man became the chief of his village. He was walking along that same stretch of beach, worried because his people were starving as it had been a horrible fishing season. All of the sudden a large salmon fell at his feet. He looked up and there was that same eagle.

The eagle came back day after day and brought salmon, then he brought a seal, then a porpoise, and then a whale to pay the boy back for saving his life.

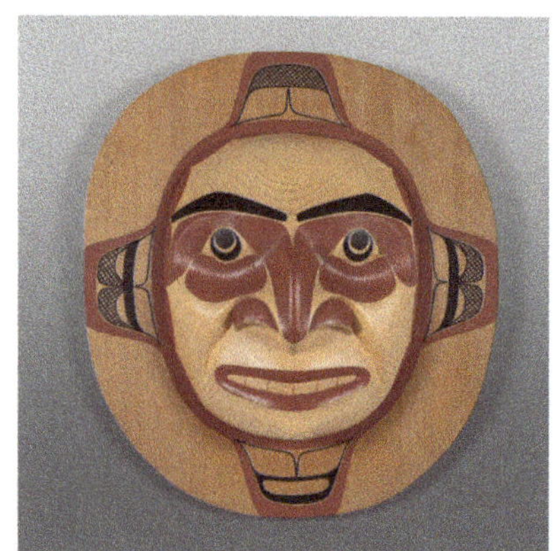
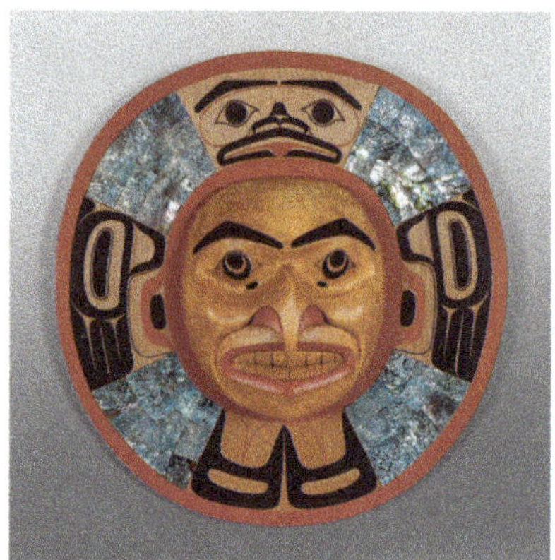
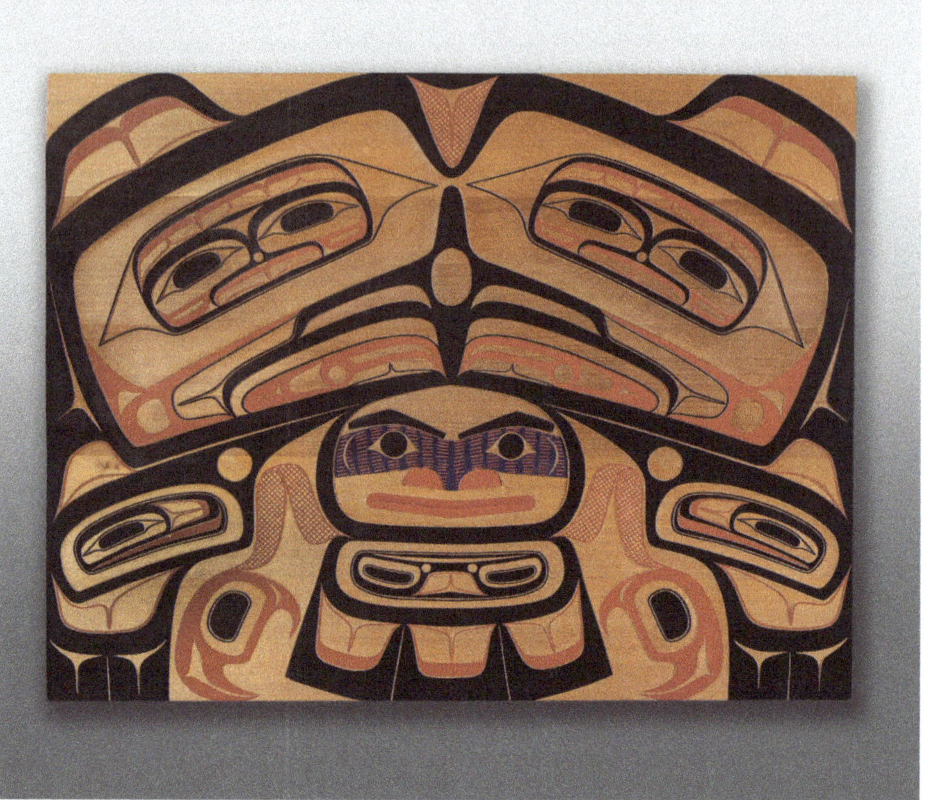
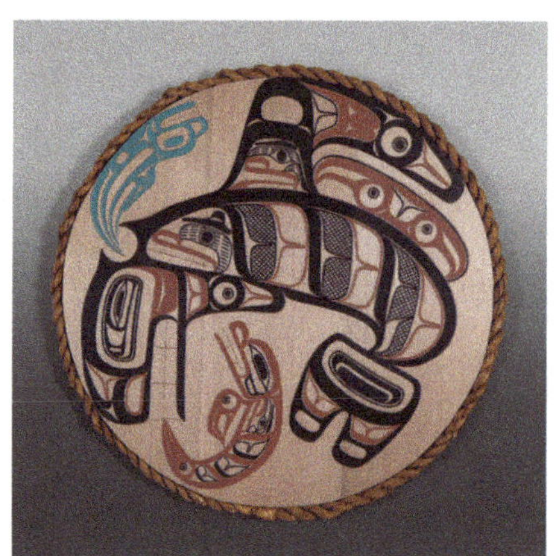
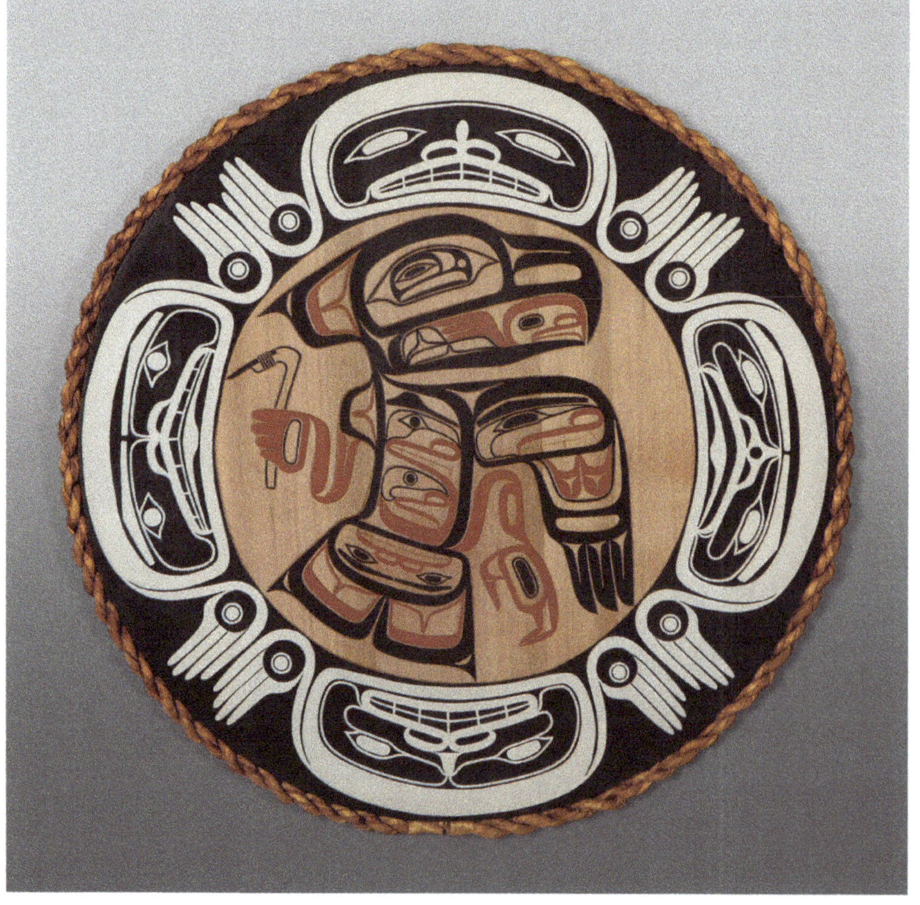

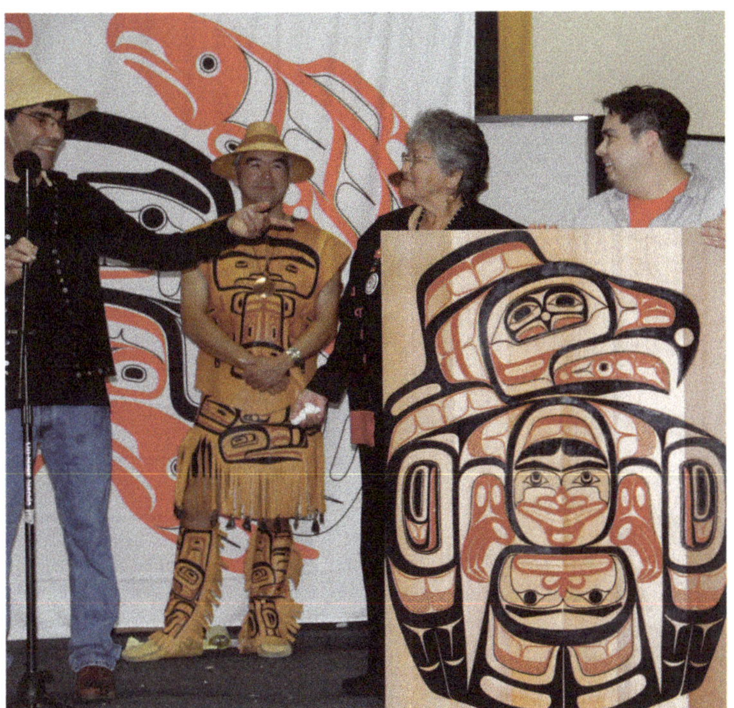

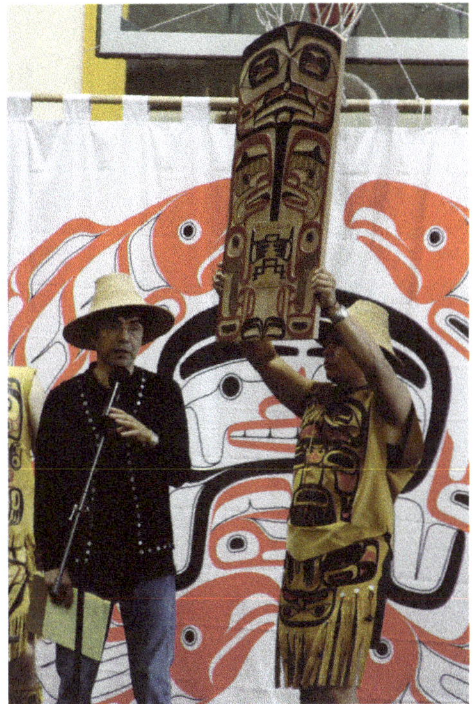

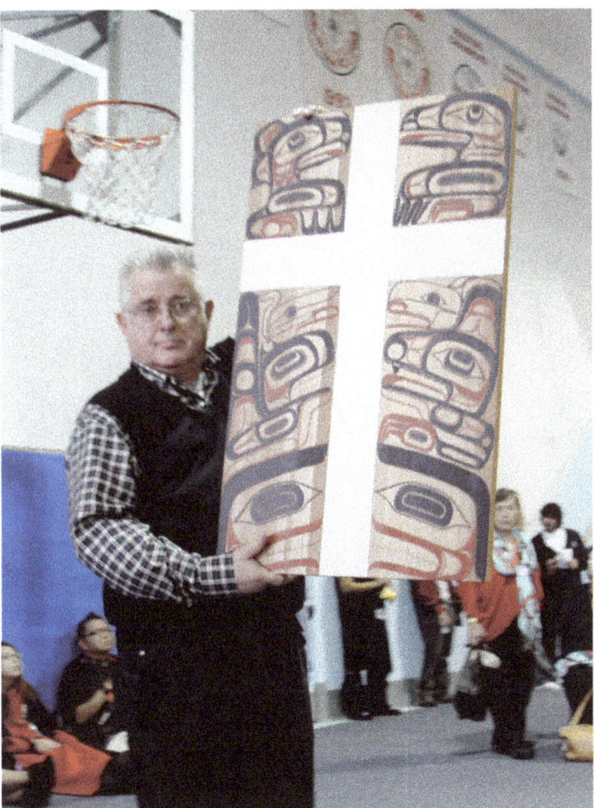

This panel went to the Presbyterian Church.
It was important that I thanked everyone
who was important in my mother's life.

In 2011, I gave away a lot of art at the potlatch for my mom Laverne Bolton Welcome, showing gratitude to the people who had assisted her while she was living and after she passed. People never forgot that potlach. That is the whole idea behind a potlatch—how it makes an impact on those who attend. You want to impress as much as possible with all the food and the gifts. Generosity is the hub of our culture's wheel.

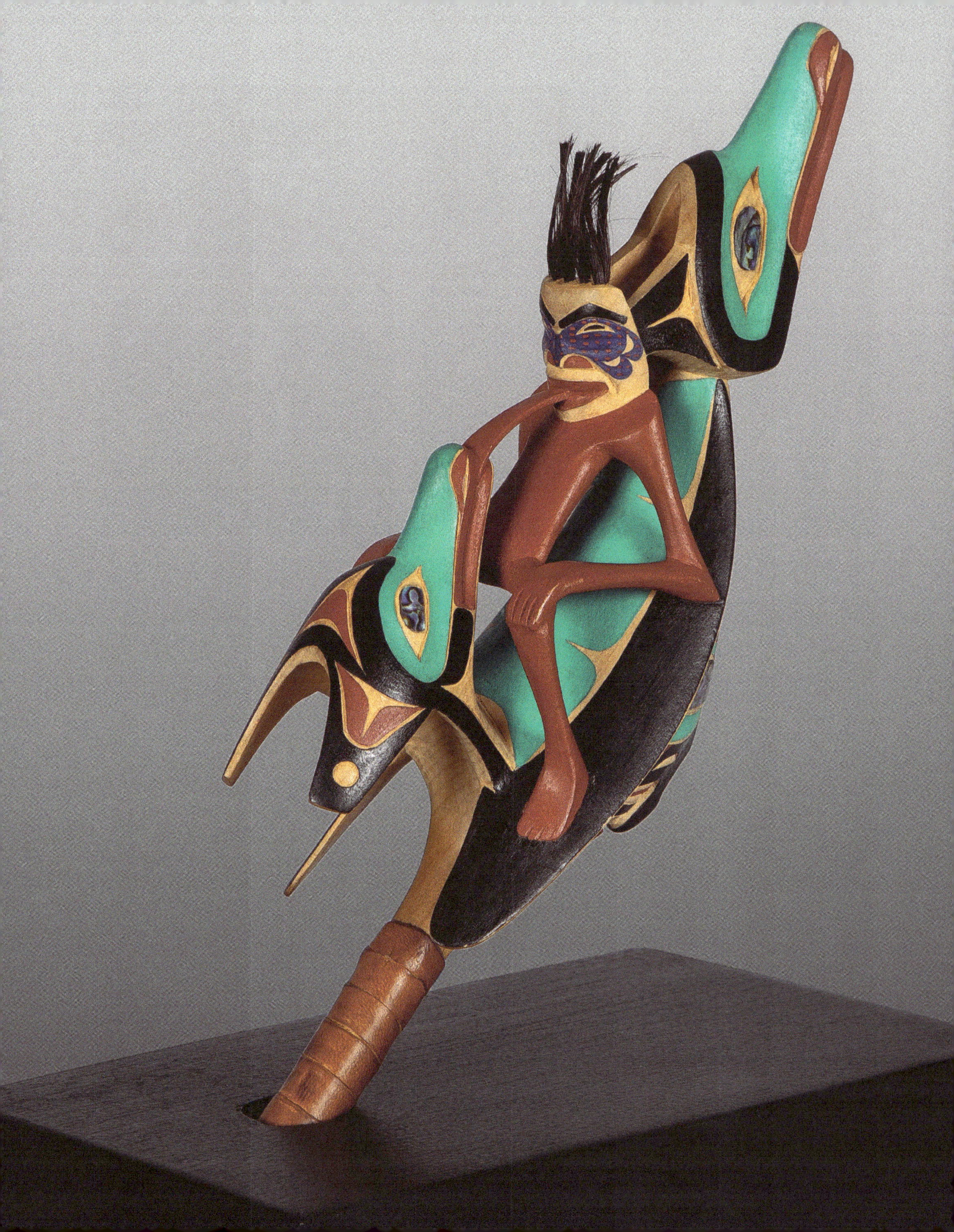

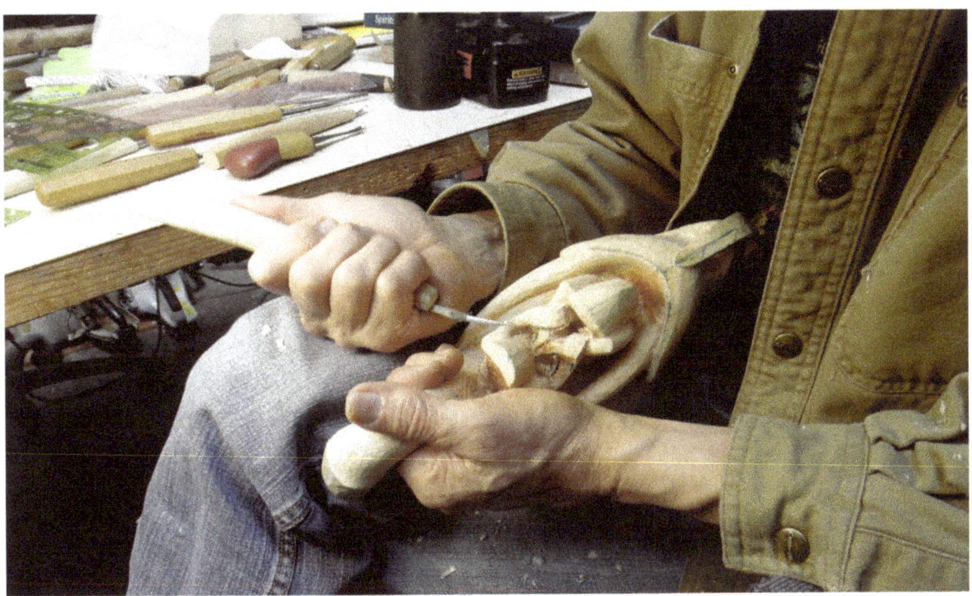

CARVED FIGURES & OBJECTS

My friends own a lot of my art. The figure below is owned by longtime friend and painter Chris Hopkins. It's called Waiting to Dance. I carved it and Davey did the design work.

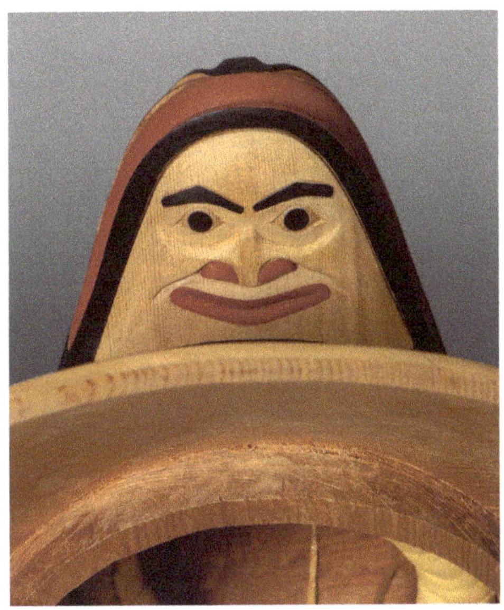

TOP OF PAGE: Carving a shaman's rattle.

ABOVE: A piece added to a wooden headdress.

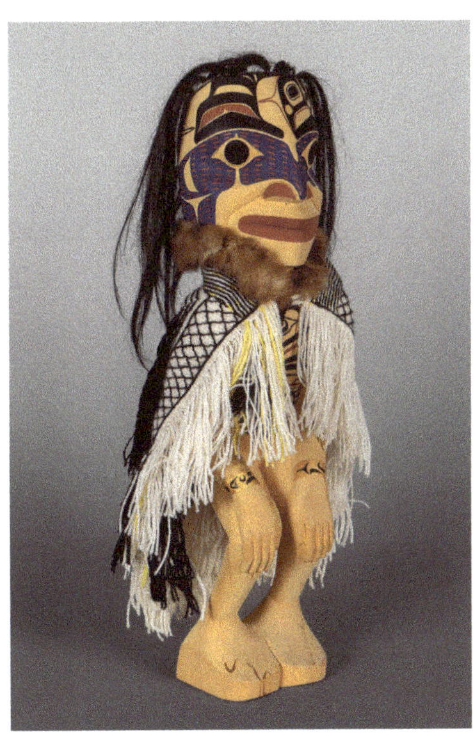

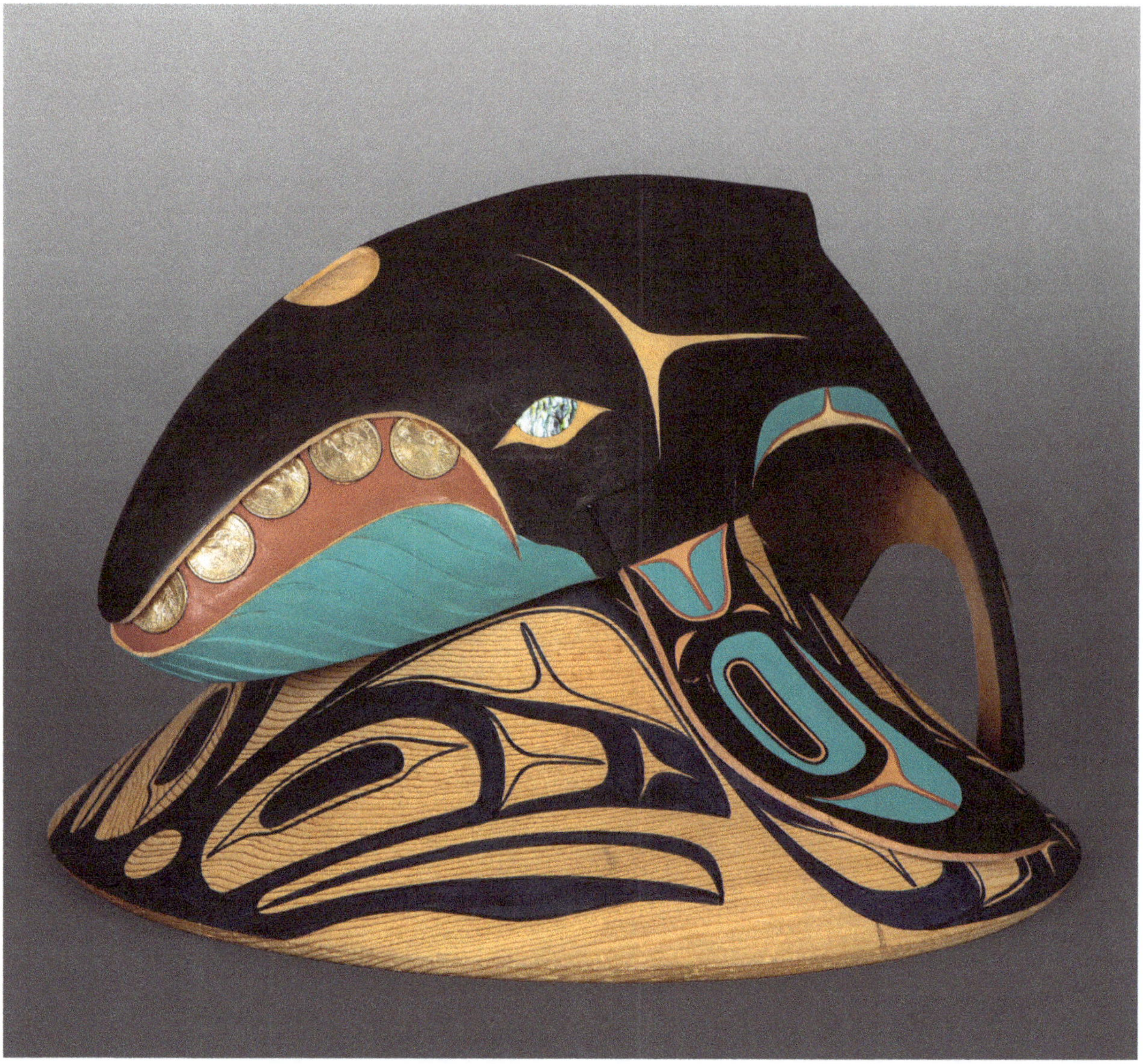

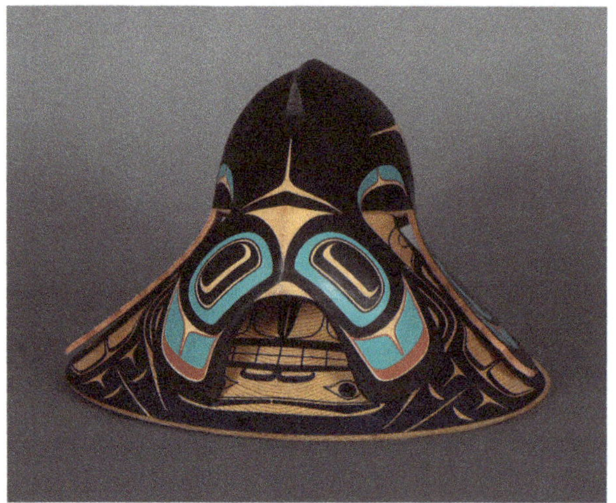

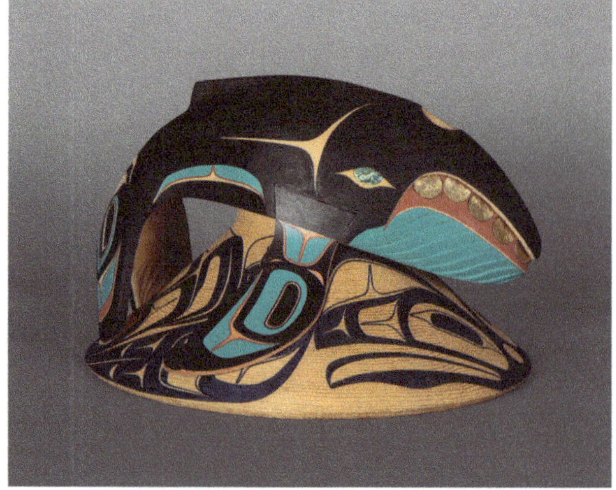

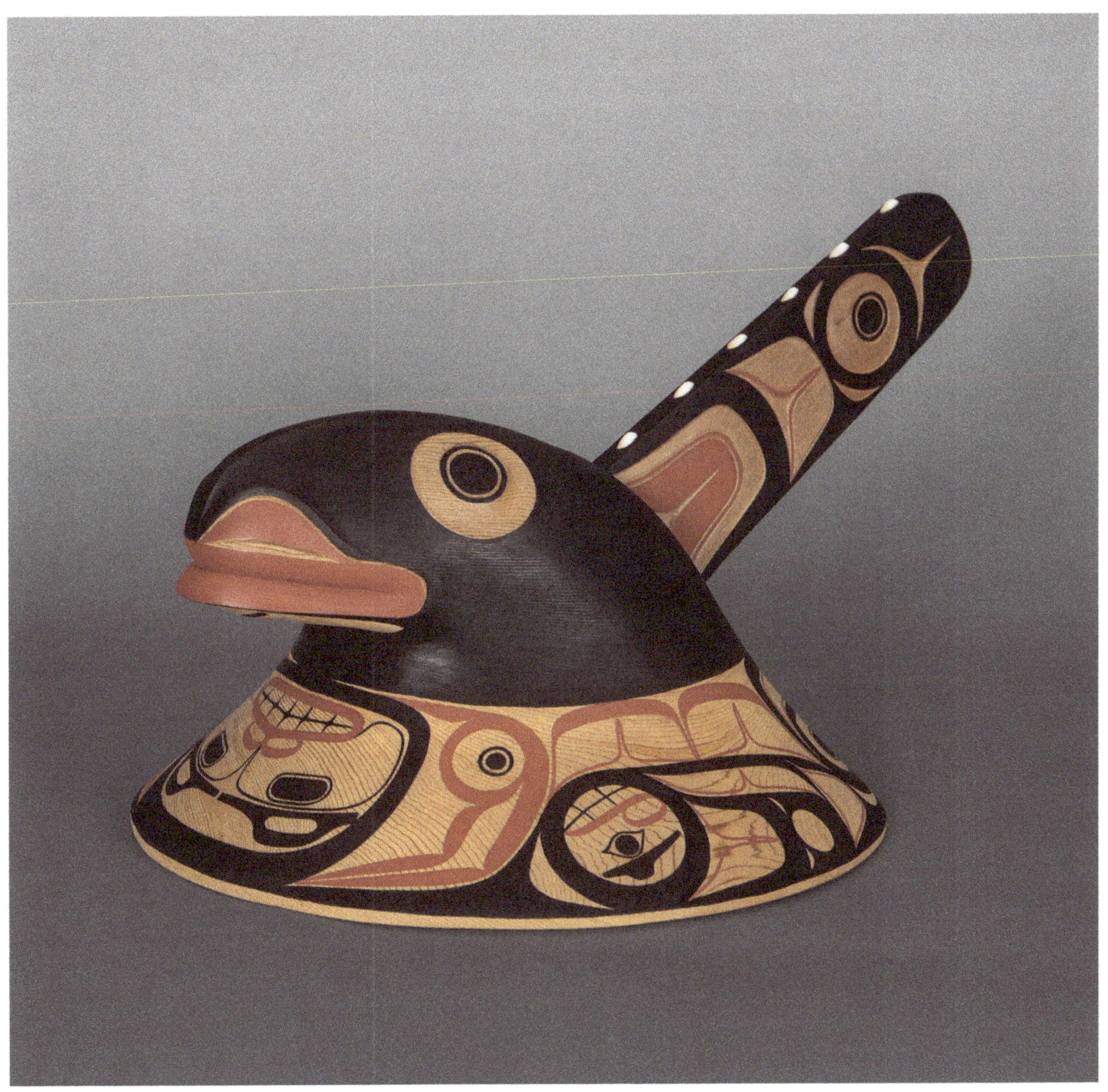

These are clan hats, also called helmets. Many are familiar with the blue hat on the facing page as it's worn by Tiny Barril, a Tlingit dance leader, during dance performances at Celebration.

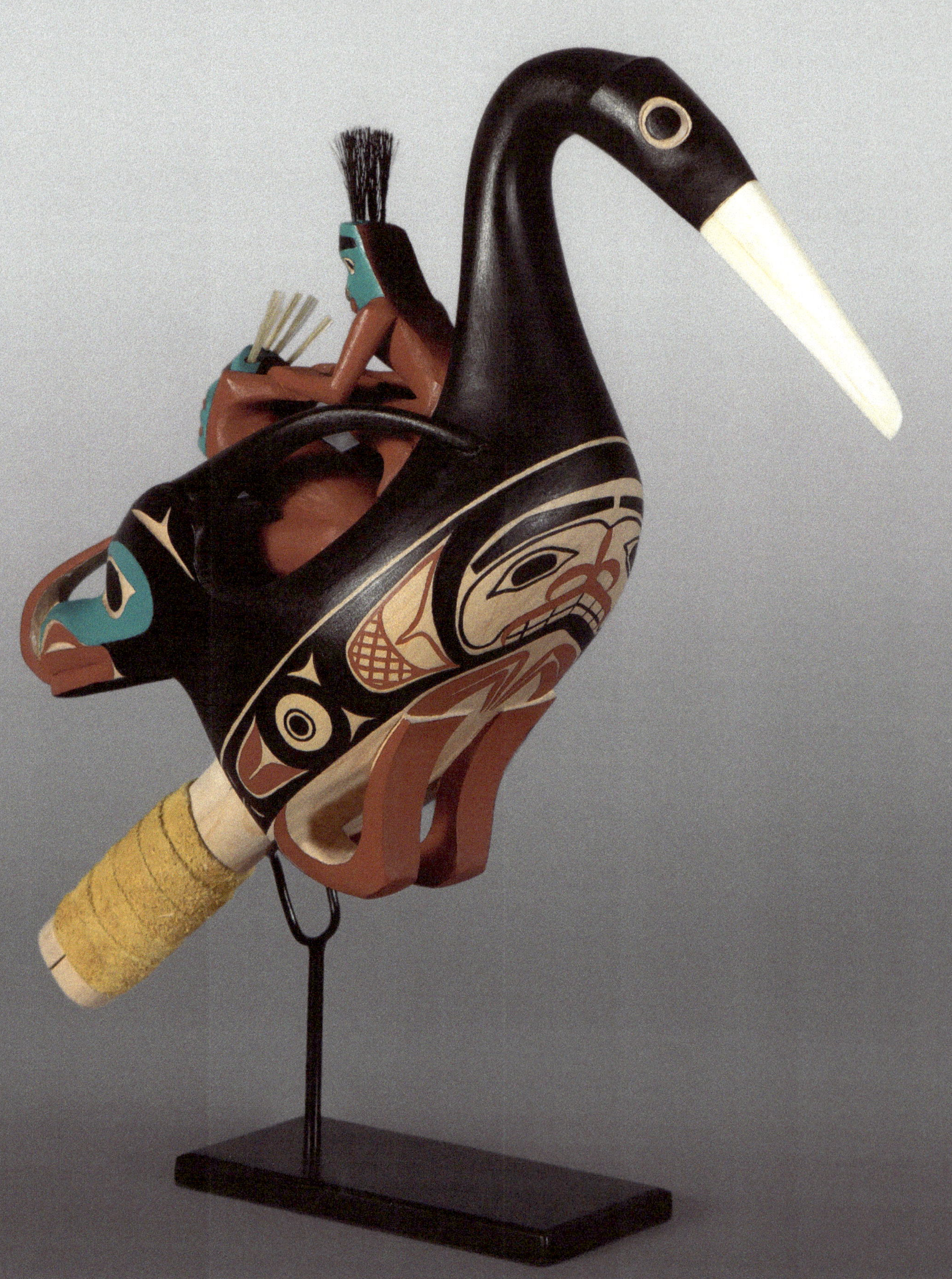

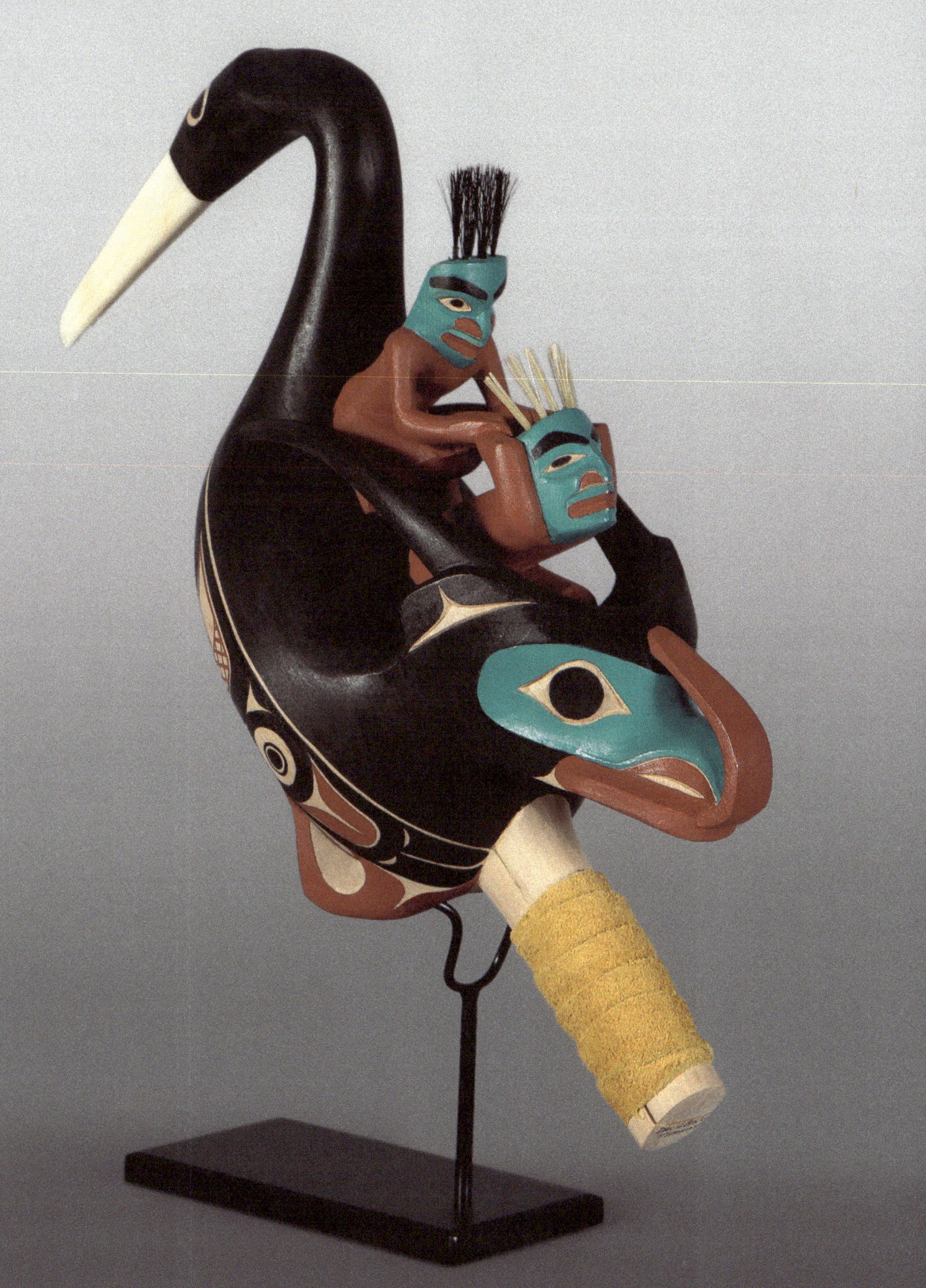

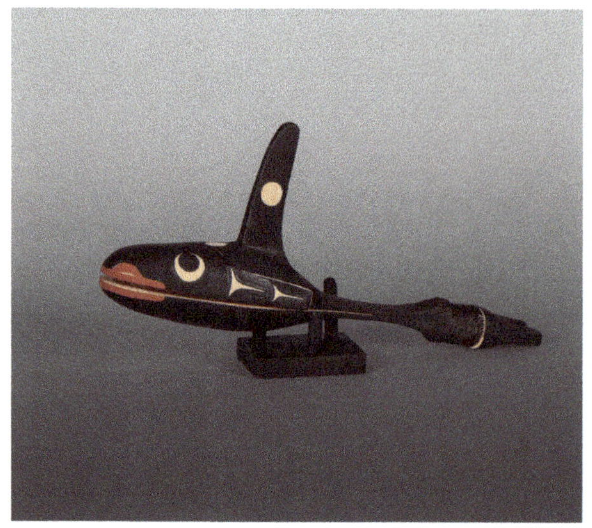

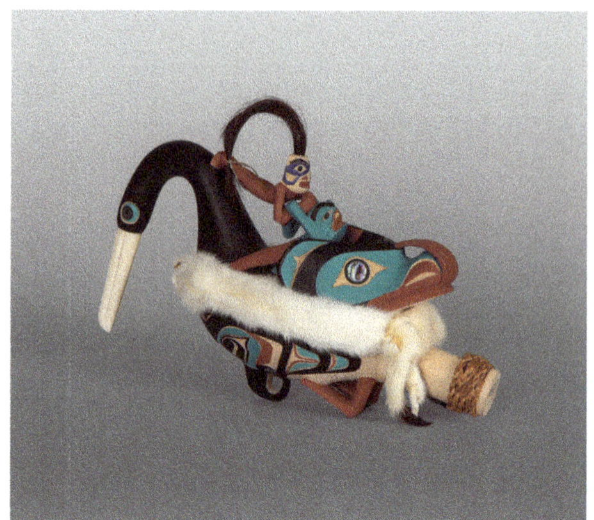

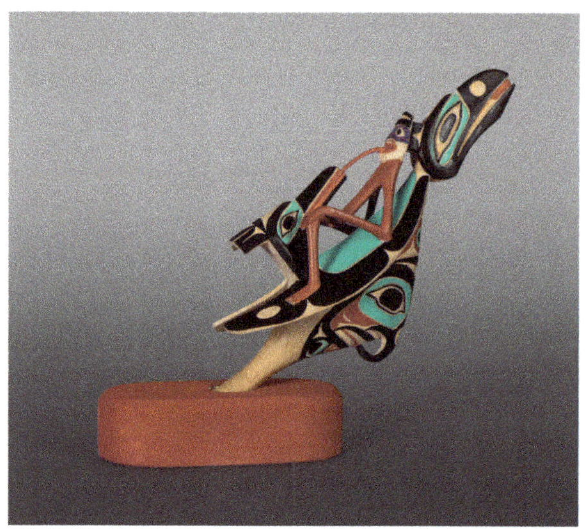

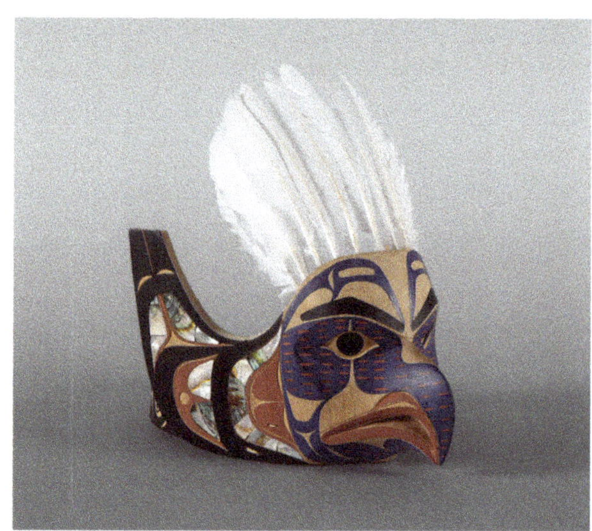

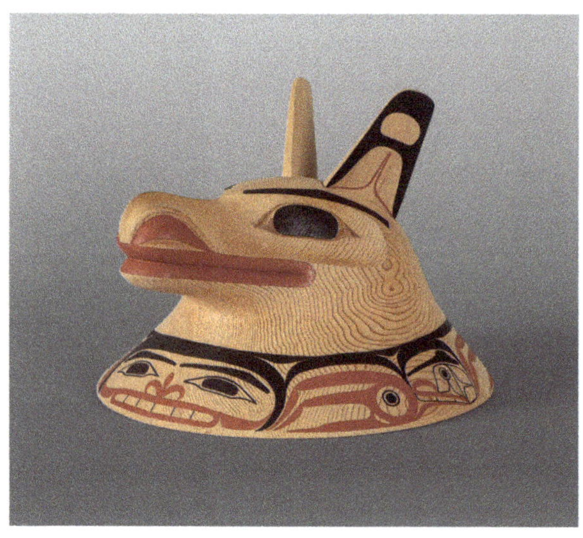

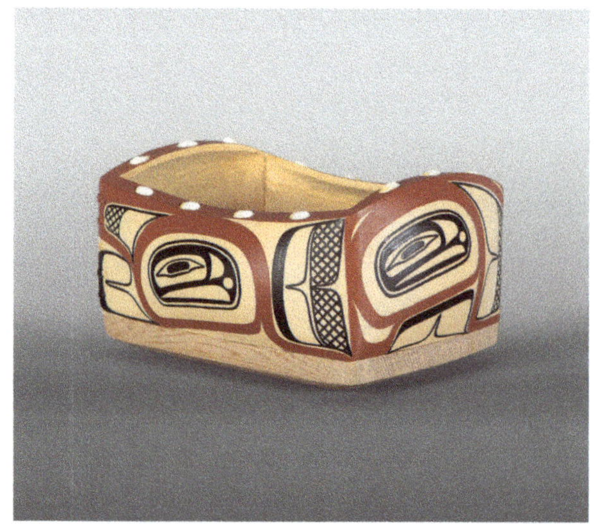

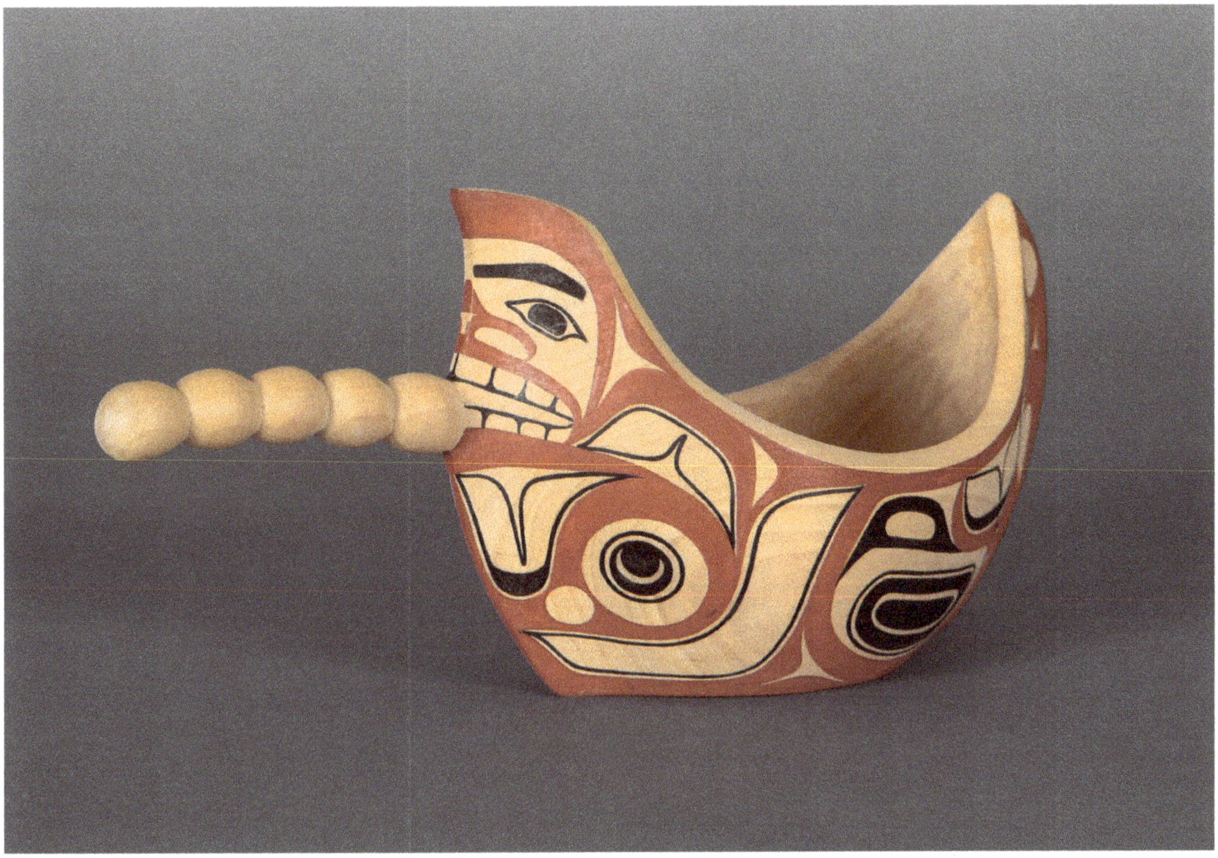

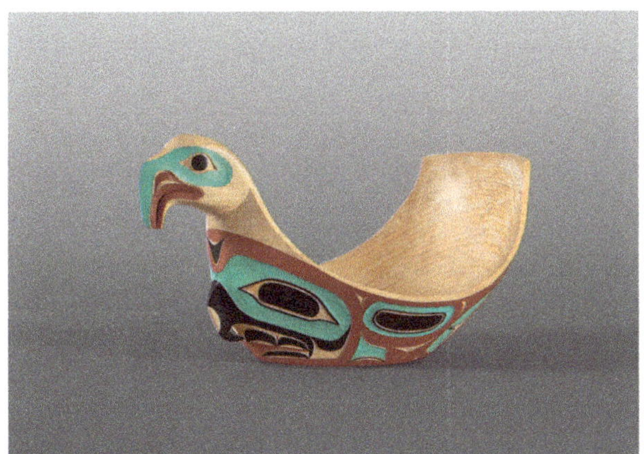

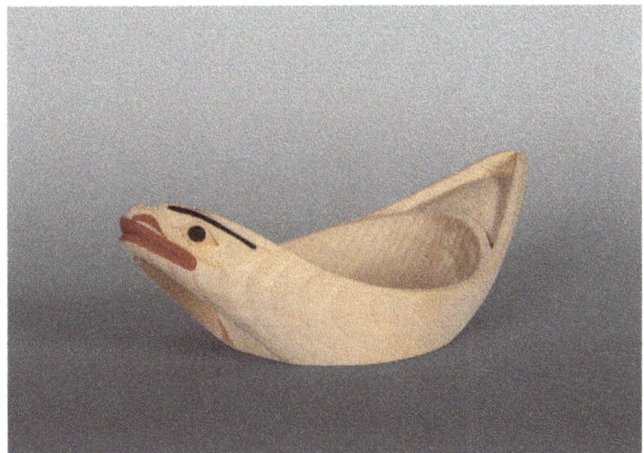

Feast bowls such as these were used at potlatches in the old days. Higher ranking folks would have ooligan oil or seal oil in them or serve food in them. If you look at examples of these in museums, some of the older ones still have oil permeating the wood.

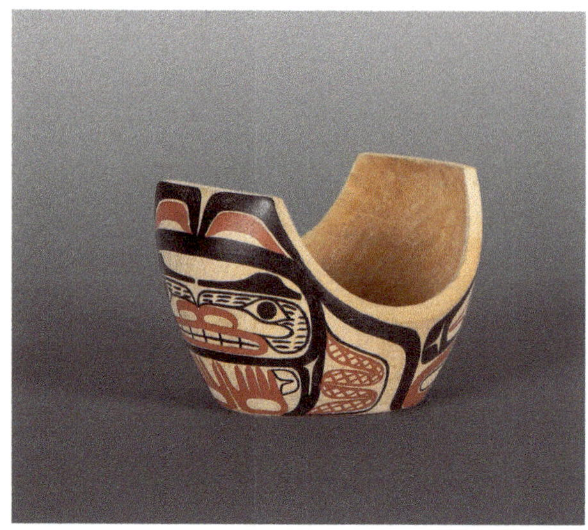

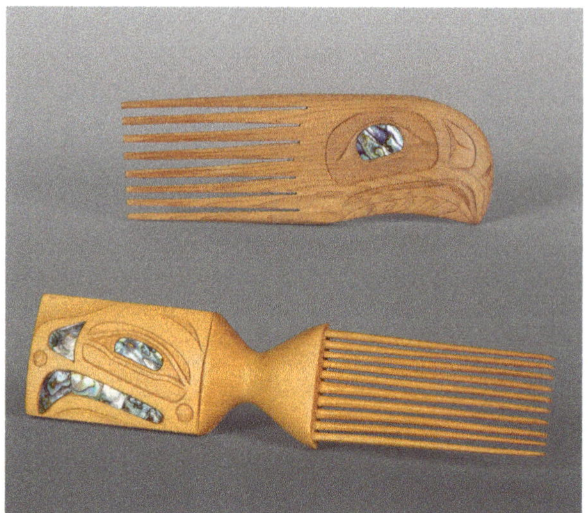

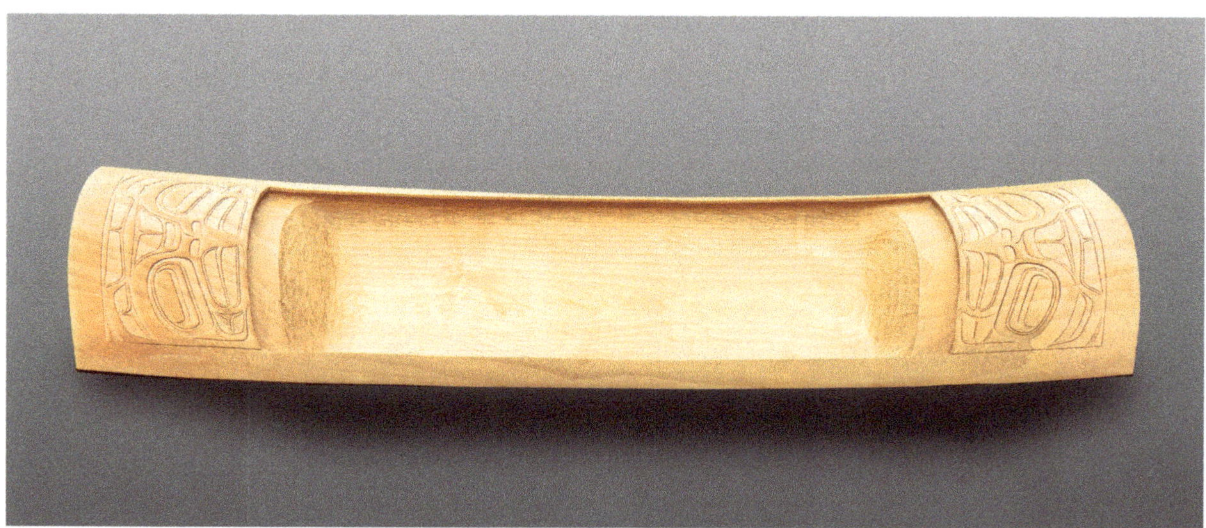

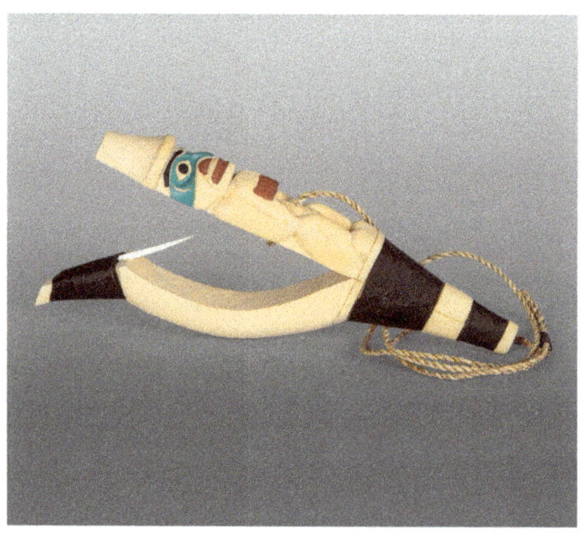

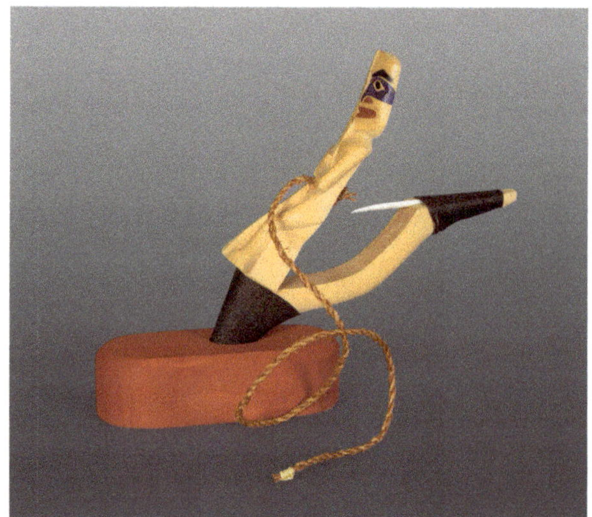

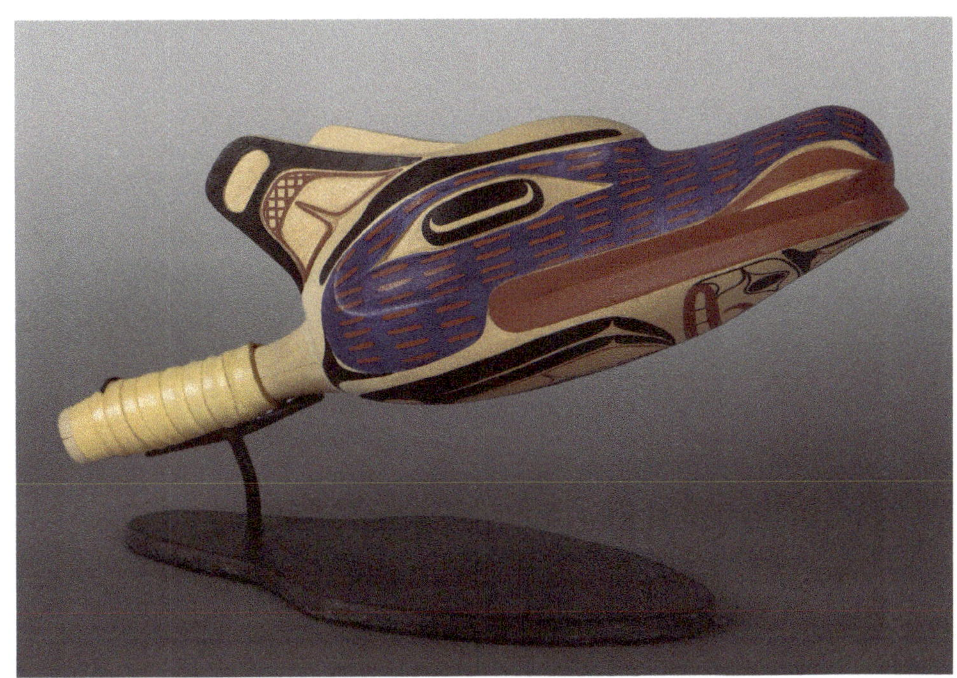

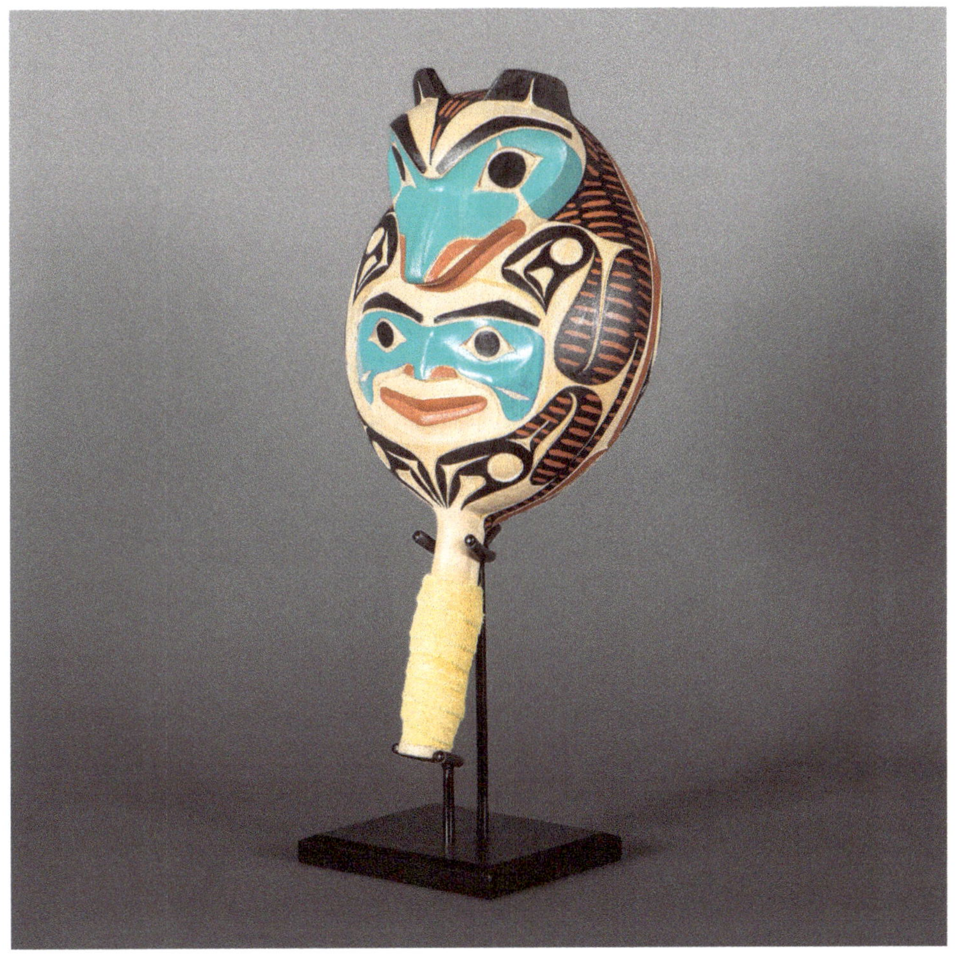

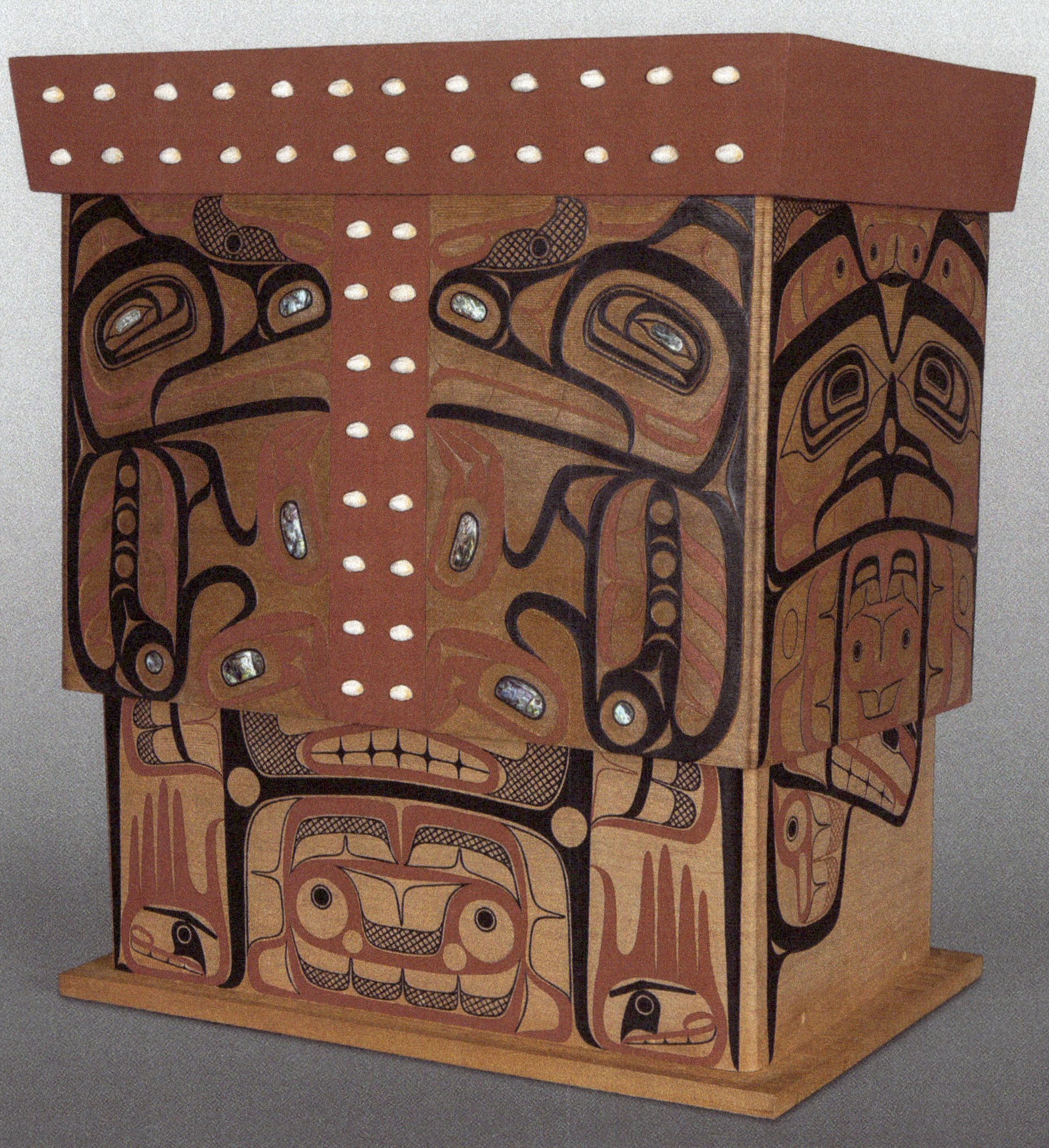

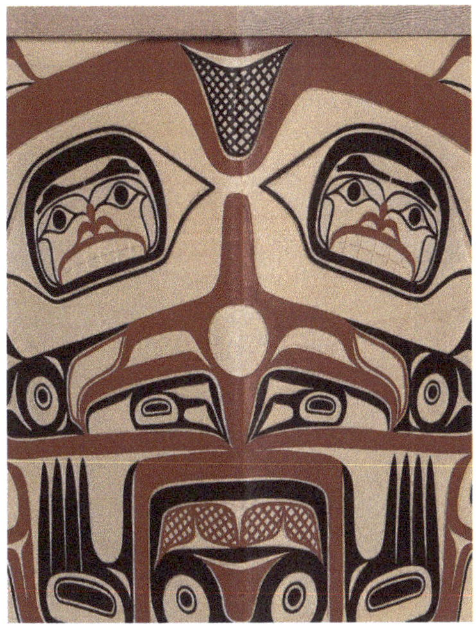

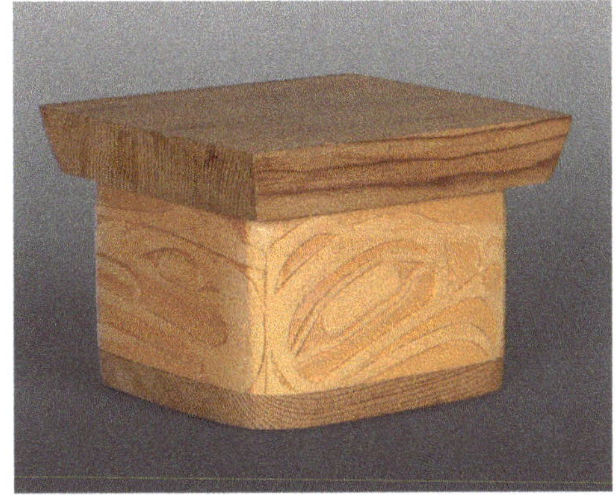

BENTWOOD BOXES

Bentwood boxes were one of the only items of furniture in the early, early days living in longhouses. They were used to store food and water and hold trade items. They were also used to hold remains of high-ranking people. Today, many people use bentwood boxes for loved ones' ashes.

I think bentwood boxes are one of the reasons two-dimensional Native art took off up and down the coast. It helped popularize this style of design.

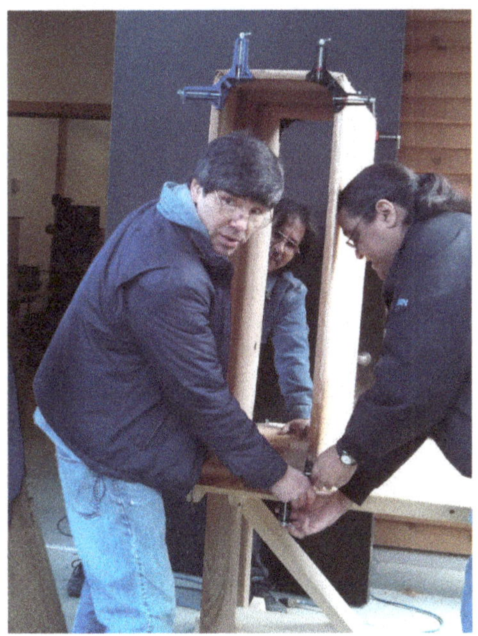

I've had the chance to teach box making classes throughout the Pacific Northwest. Here I'm teaching at Evergreen State College in Olympia.

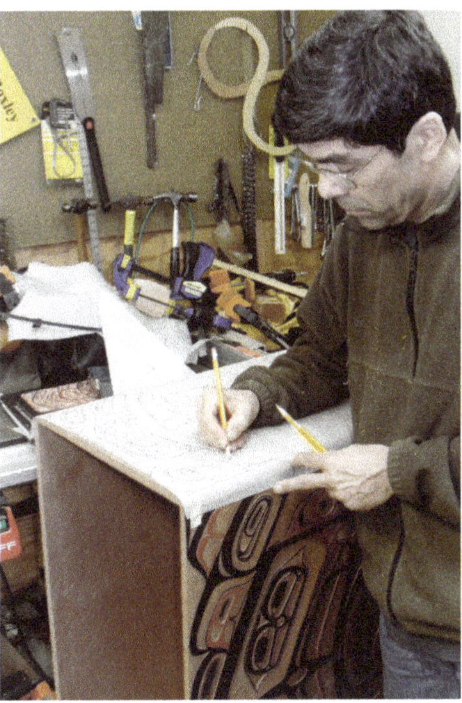

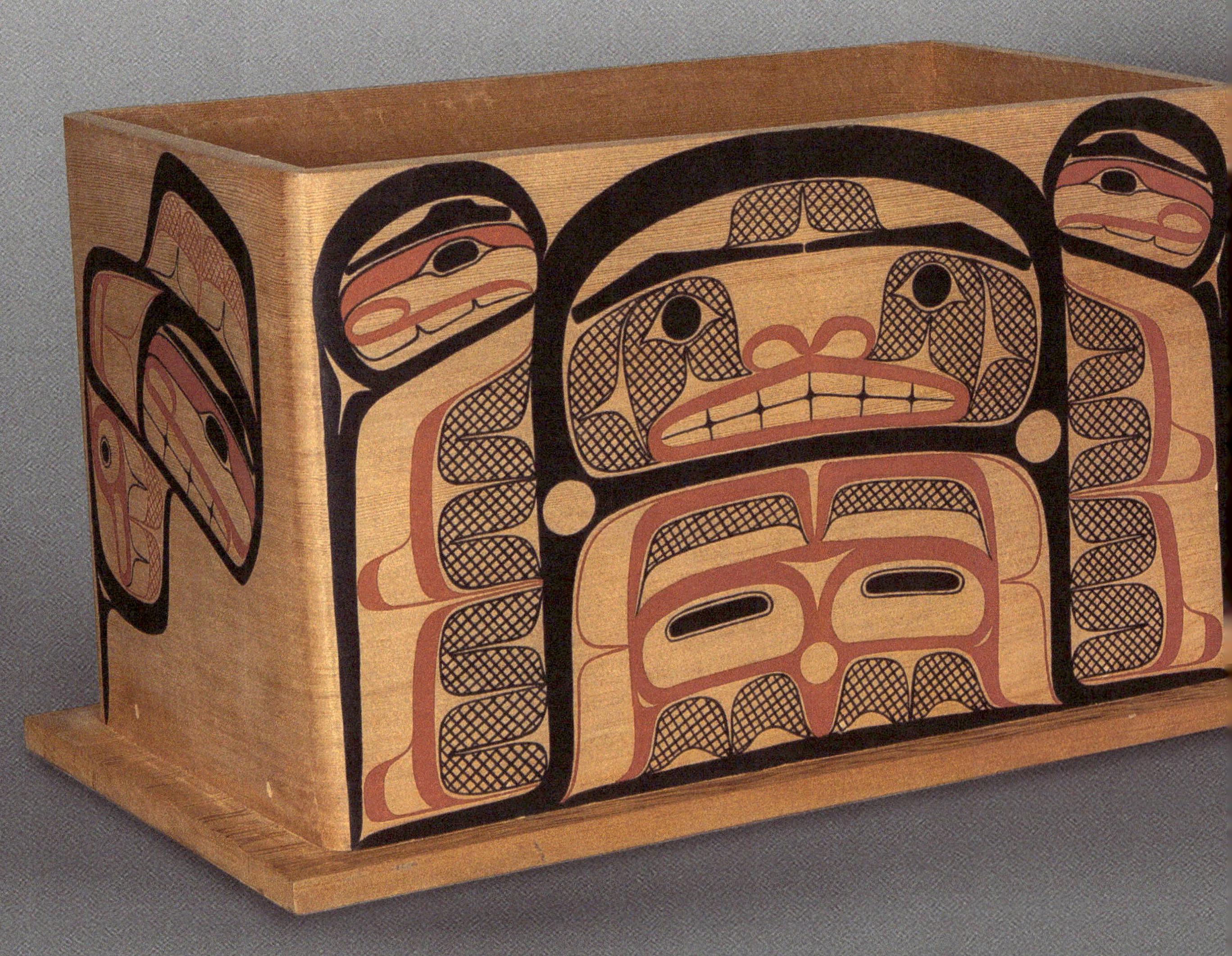

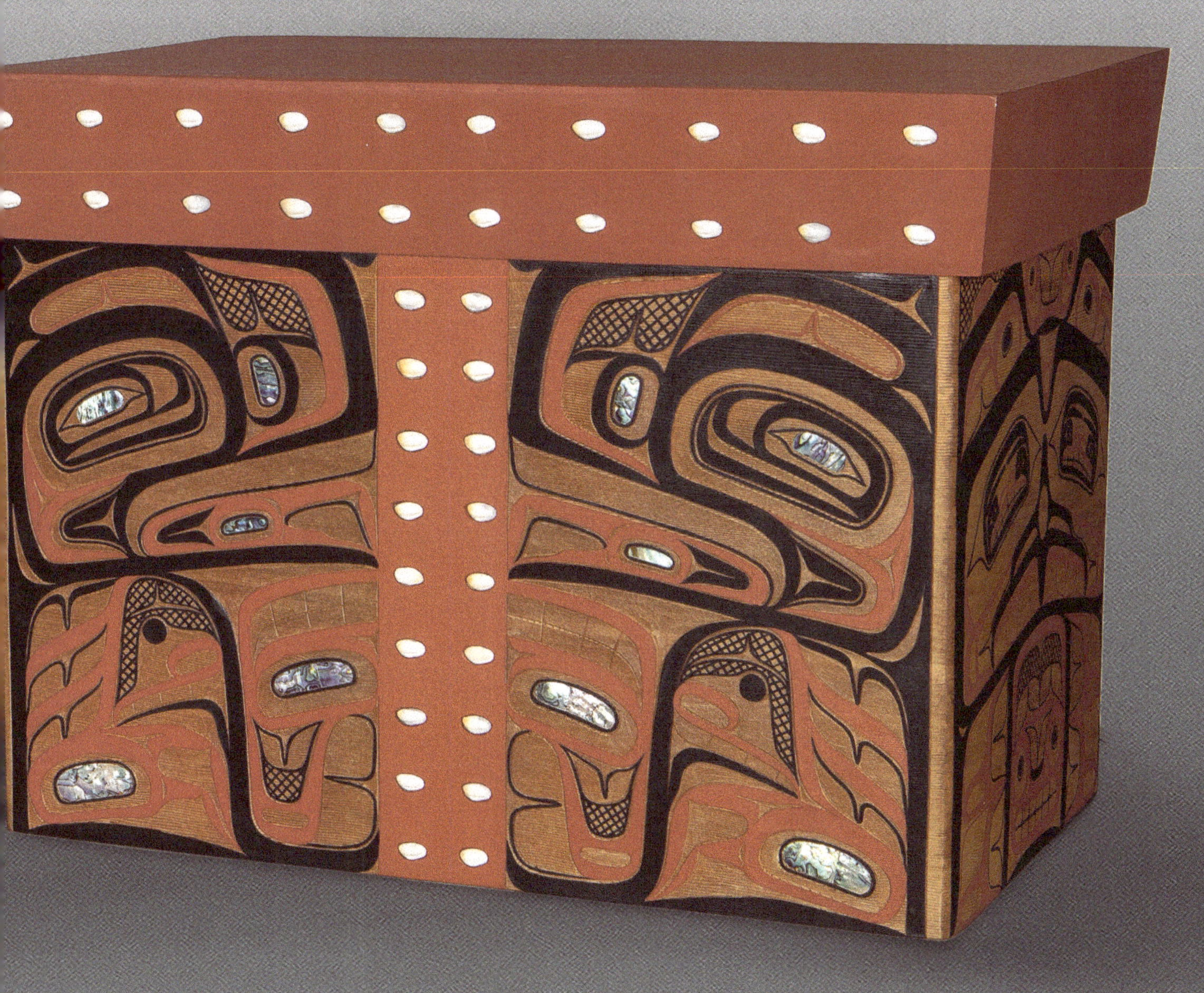

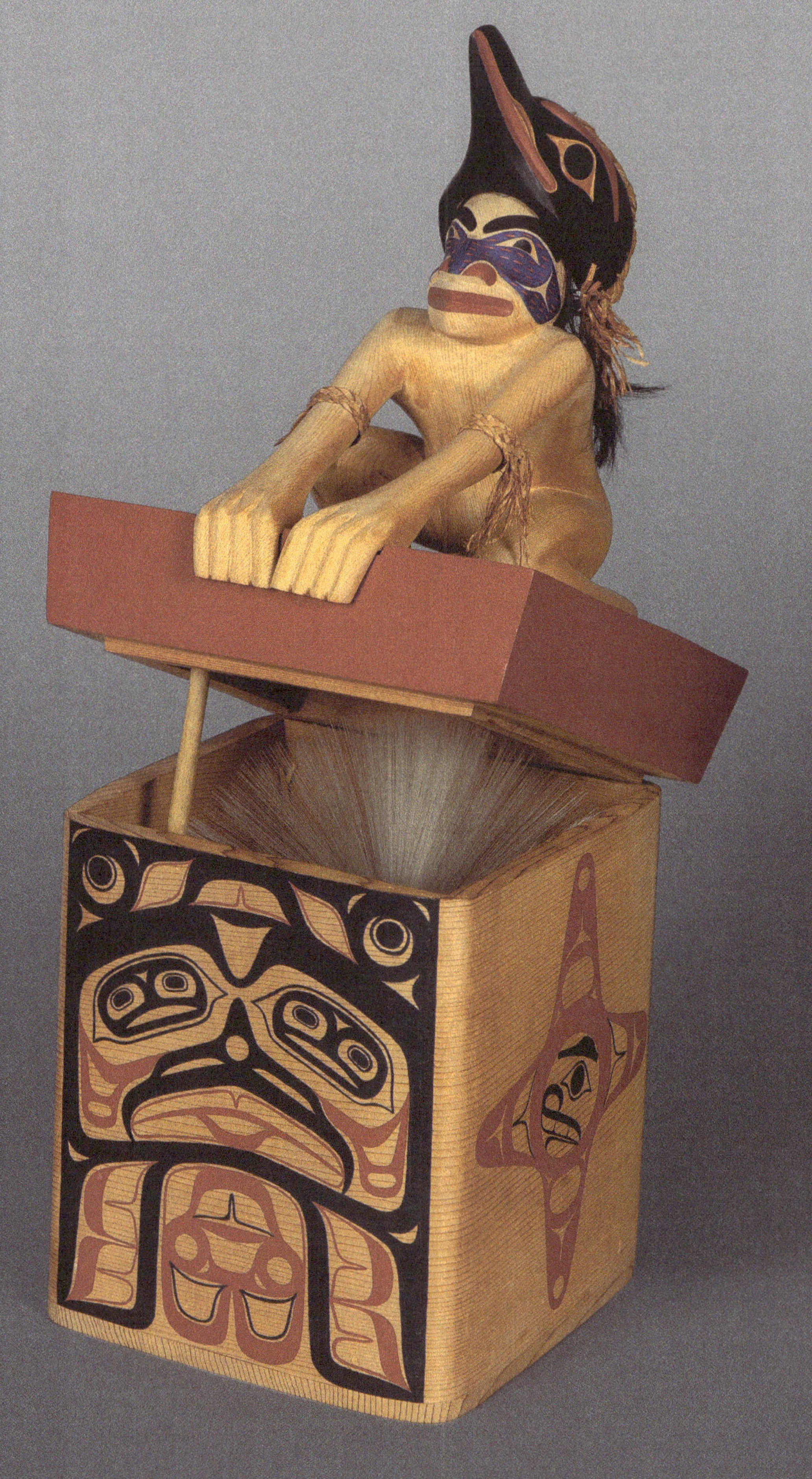

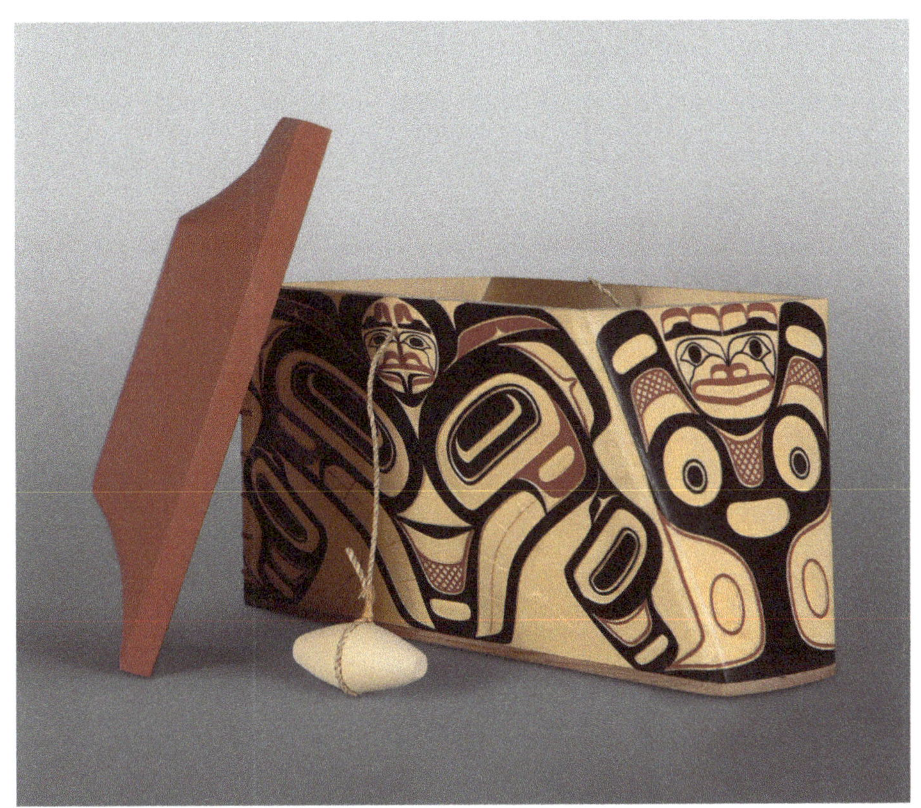

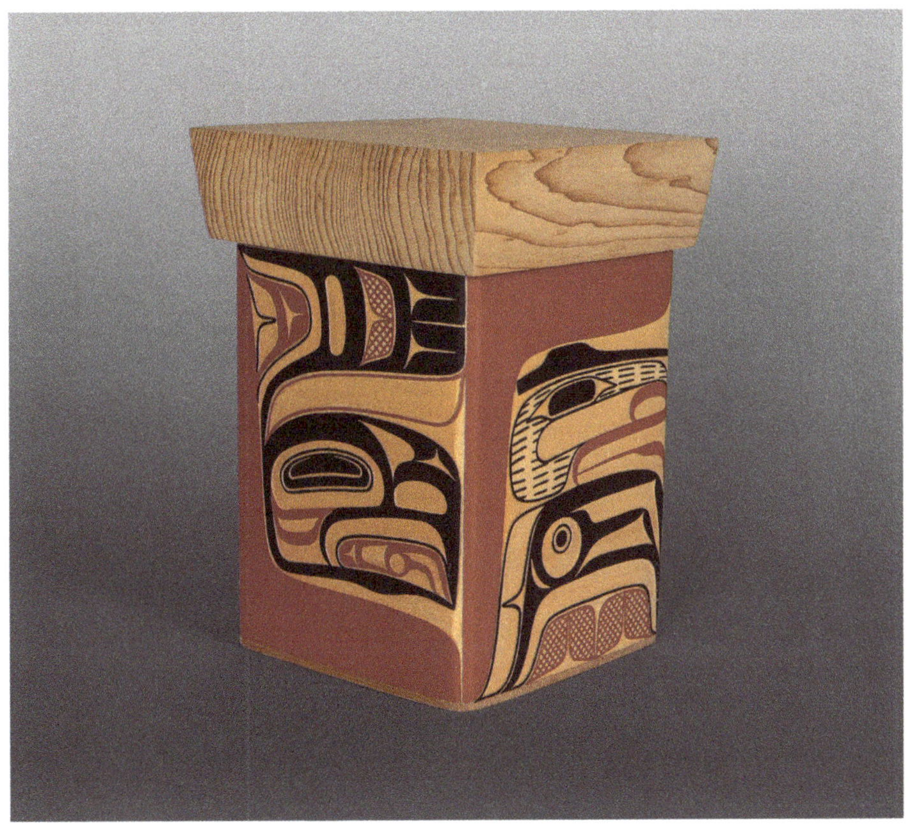

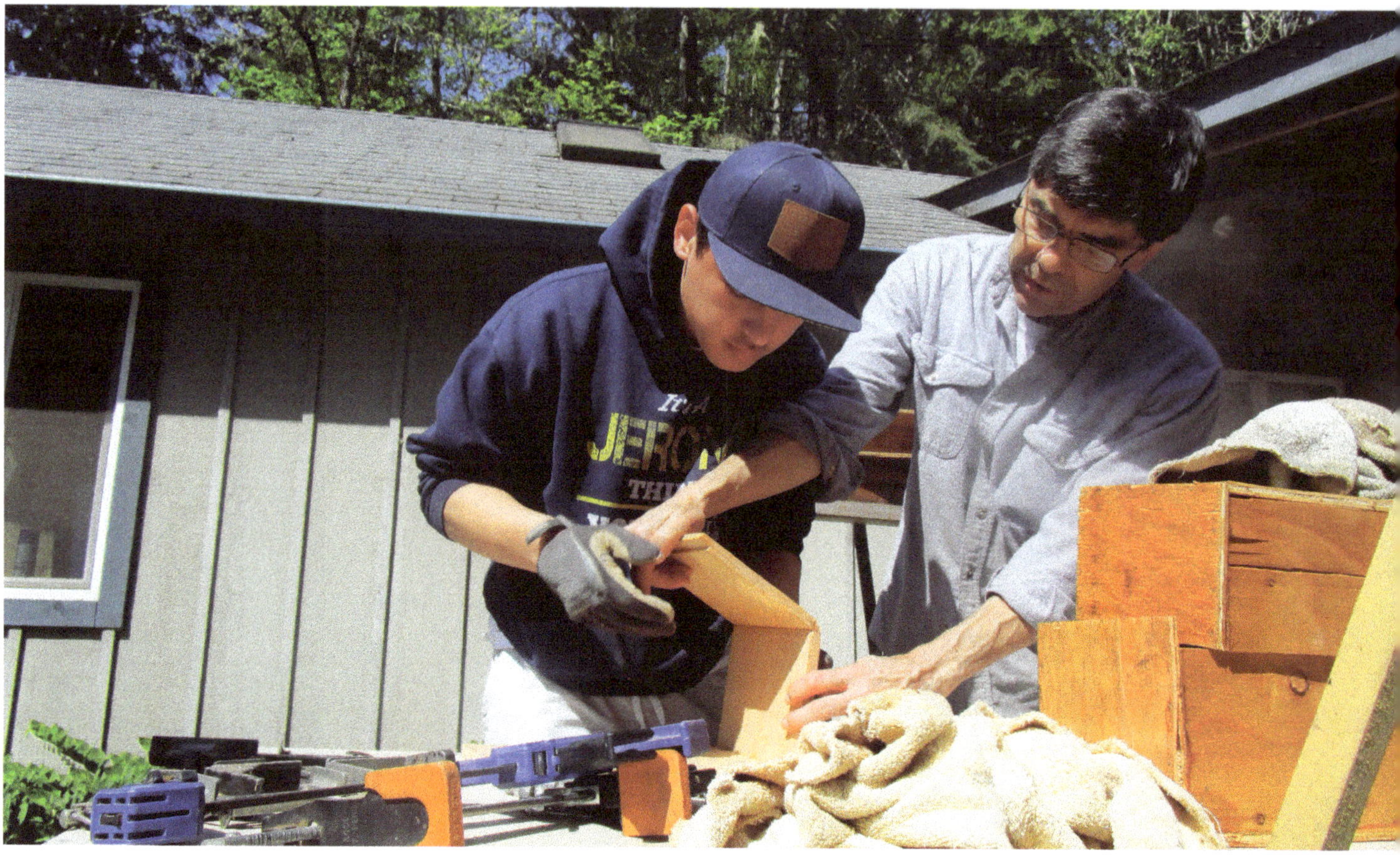

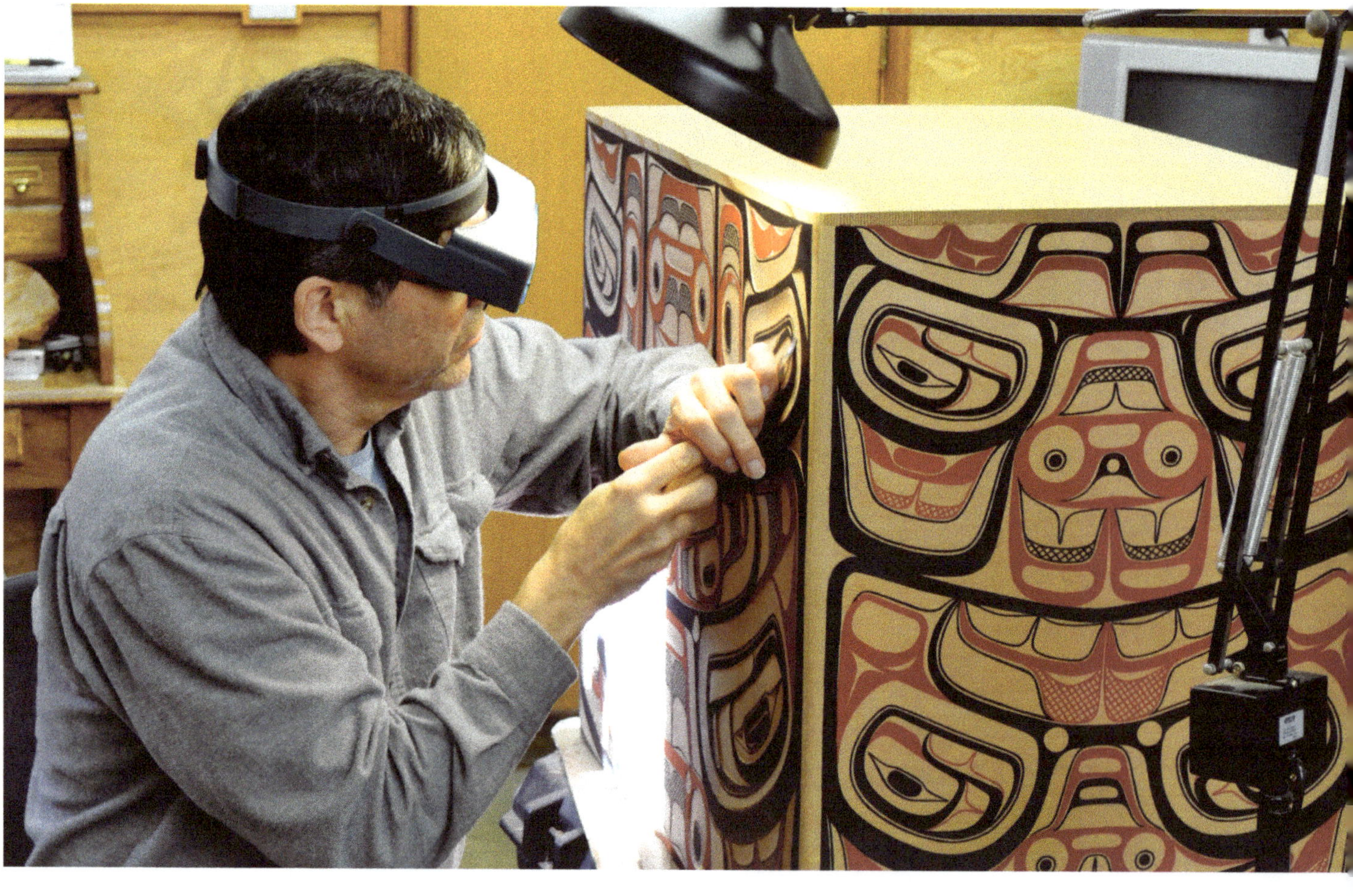

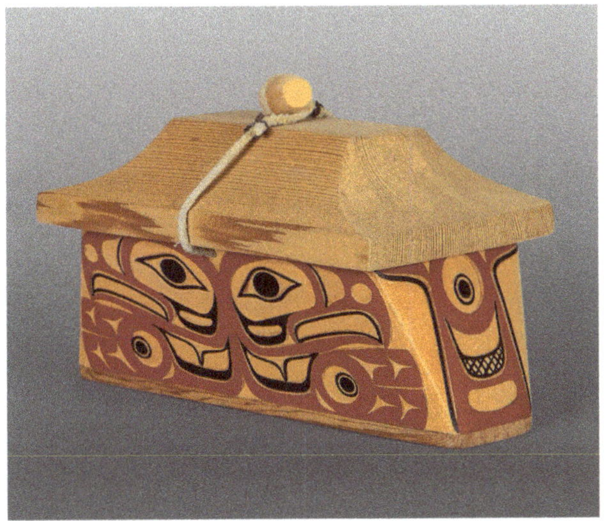 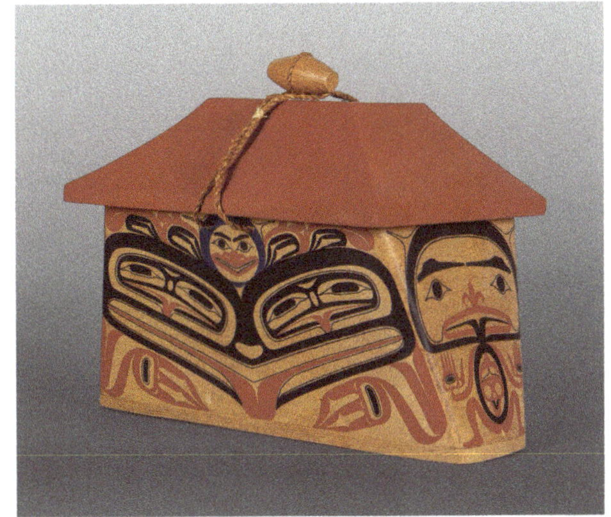

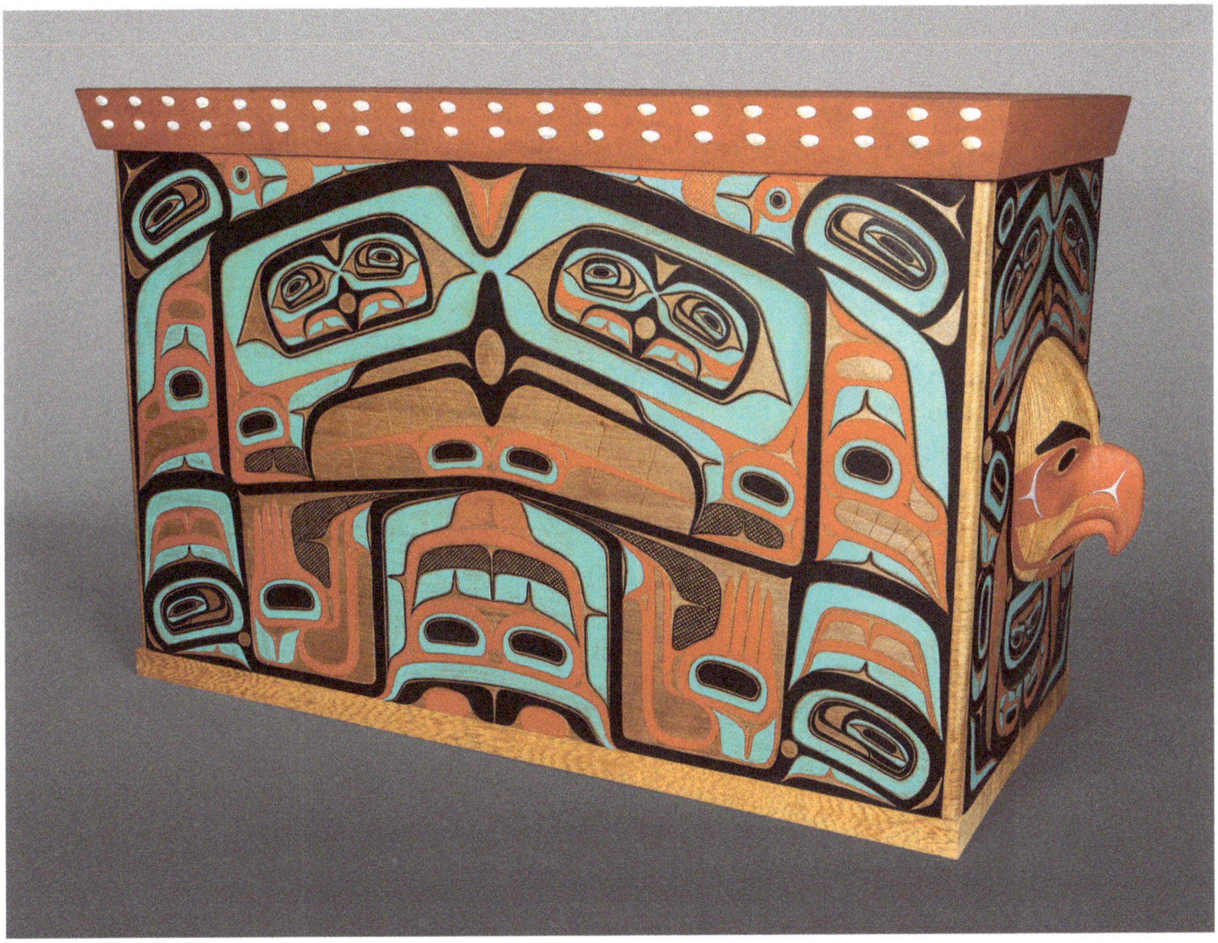

Small boxes are suitable for ashes, but others can be huge, and I've made a few chests like the one immediately above. In the old days, this would be a chief's chest. It's a place to keep regalia and other things that were not supposed to be seen until it was time to bring them out in a potlatch. This one is about 30" by 38" by 18". The scarcity of old growth cedar has already begun to affect making panels and bentwood boxes. You can't easily get wood with this tight grain to carve on anymore.

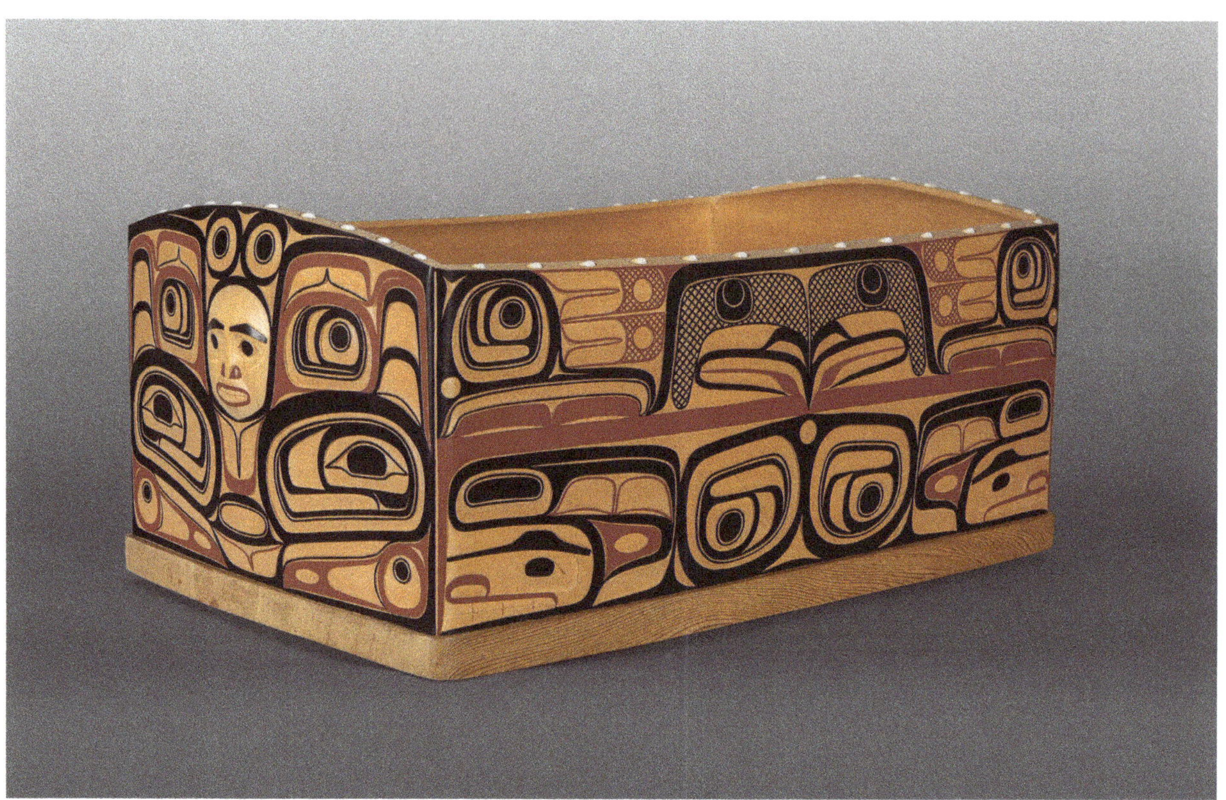

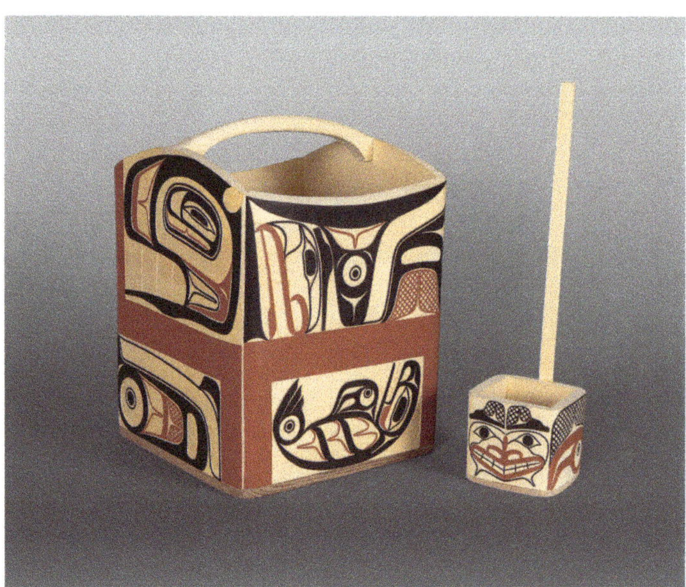

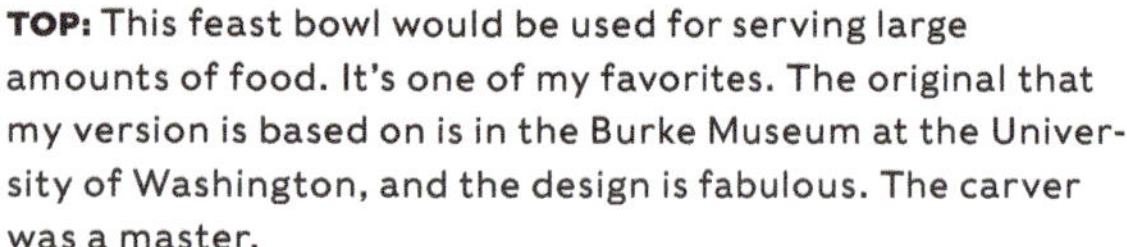

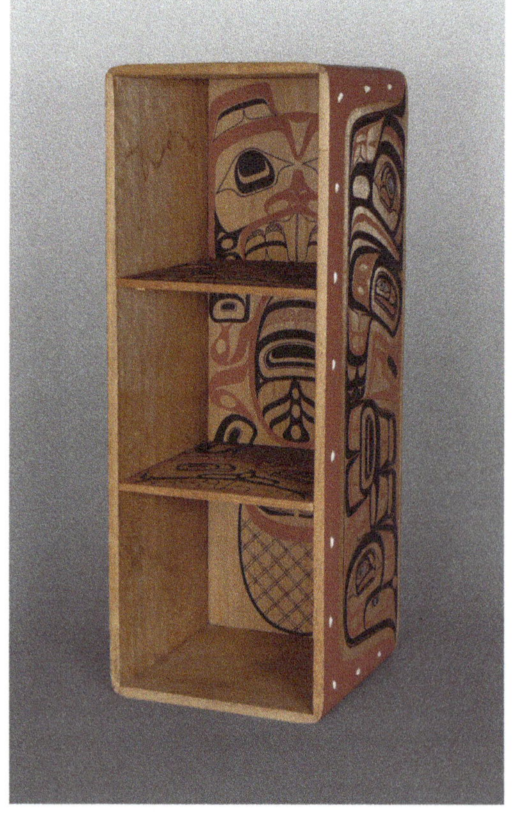

TOP: This feast bowl would be used for serving large amounts of food. It's one of my favorites. The original that my version is based on is in the Burke Museum at the University of Washington, and the design is fabulous. The carver was a master.

BOTTOM RIGHT: This bookshelf sits in my living room today.

BOTTOM LEFT: A water bucket and a ladle.

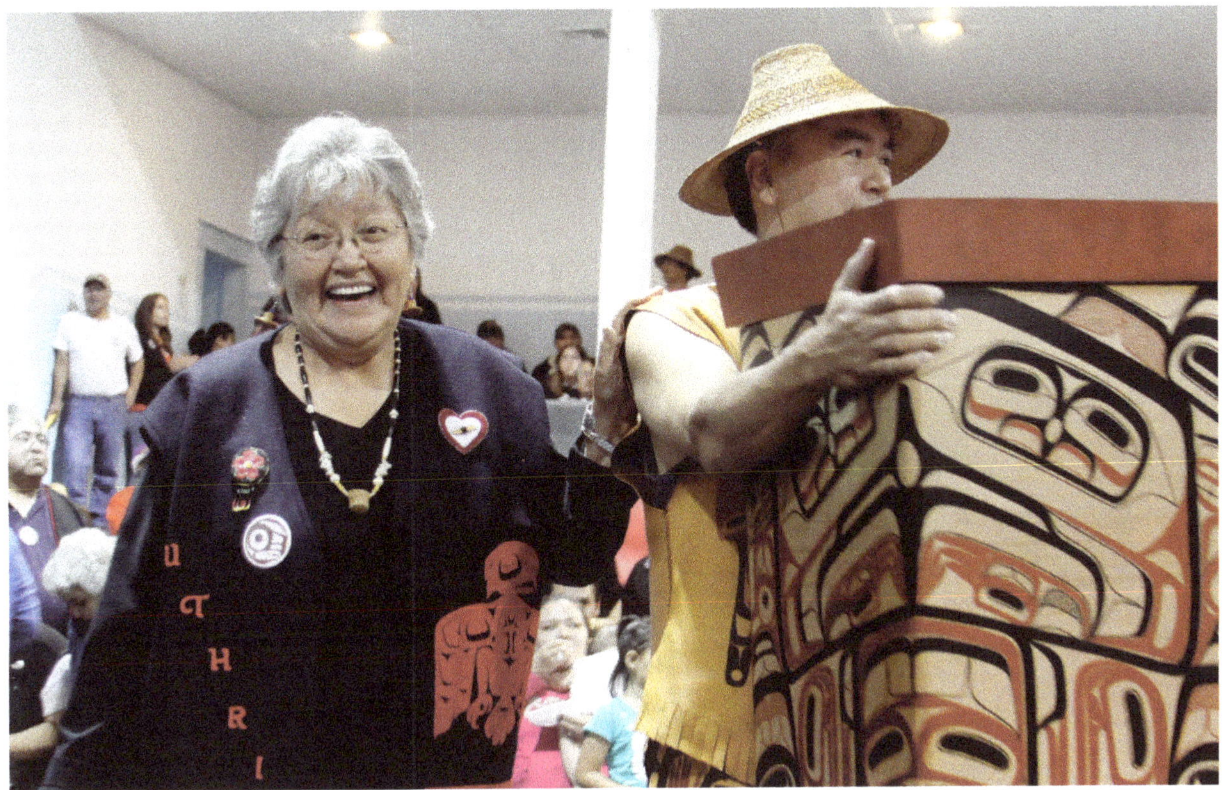

I gave away a lot of my art at my mother's potlatch. The boys and I worked for over a year making gifts for people who made a difference in my mother's life.

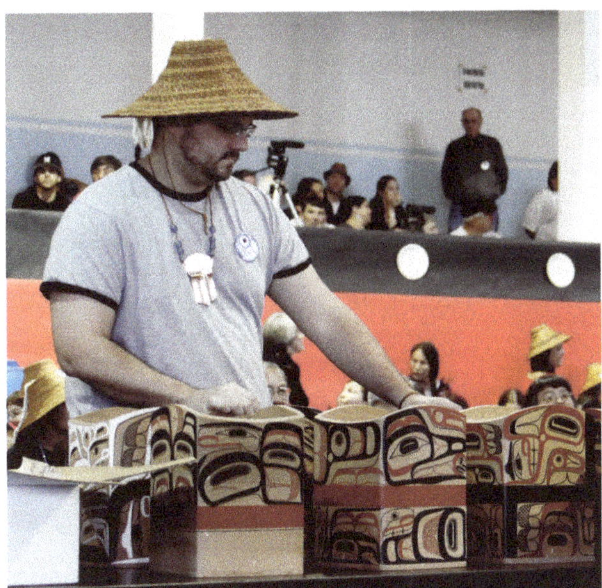

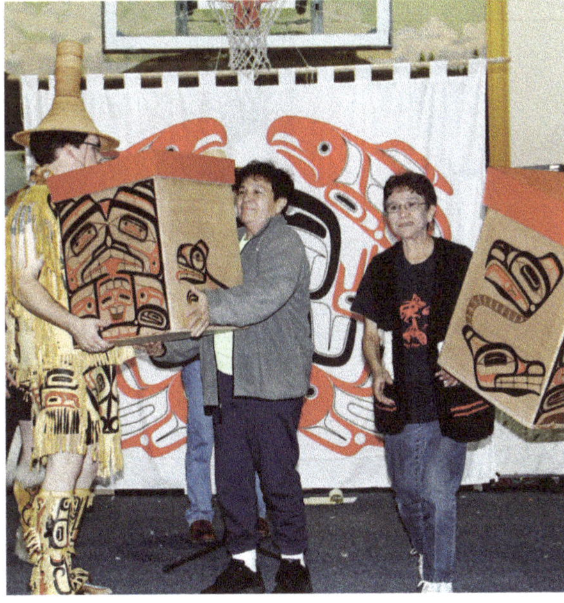

TOP: Janet Guthrie took care of my mother, and I wanted to thank her with this bentwood box held by one of my dancers, David Brendible.

BOTTOM LEFT: I gave these small boxes to people who either carried or helped raise the pole.

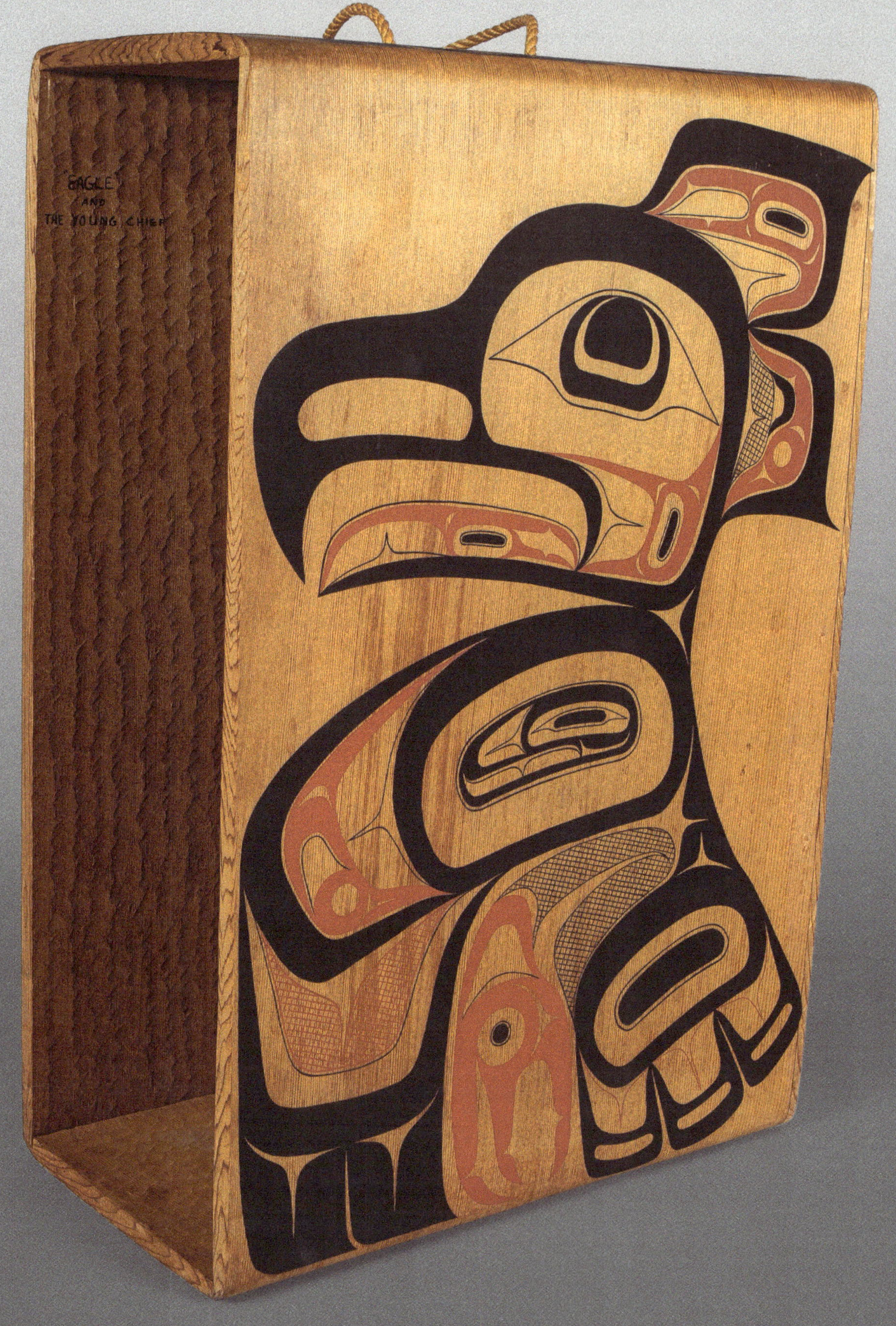
EAGLE
AND
THE YOUNG CHIEF

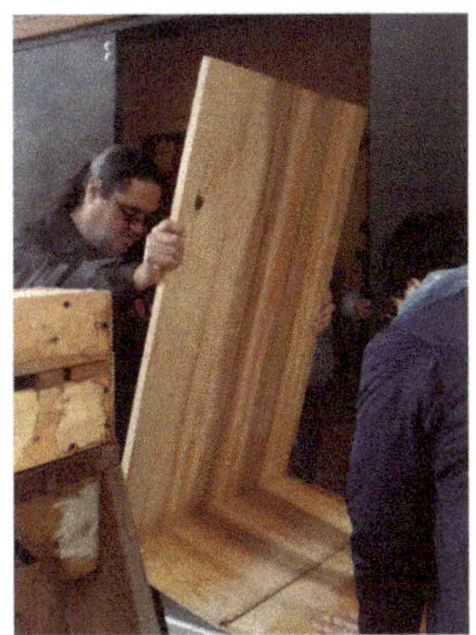
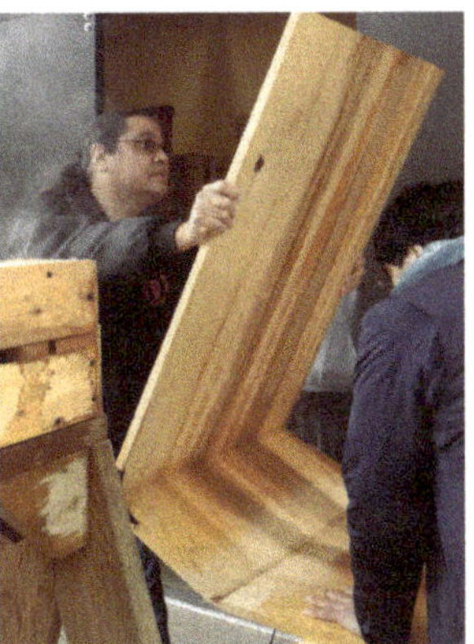
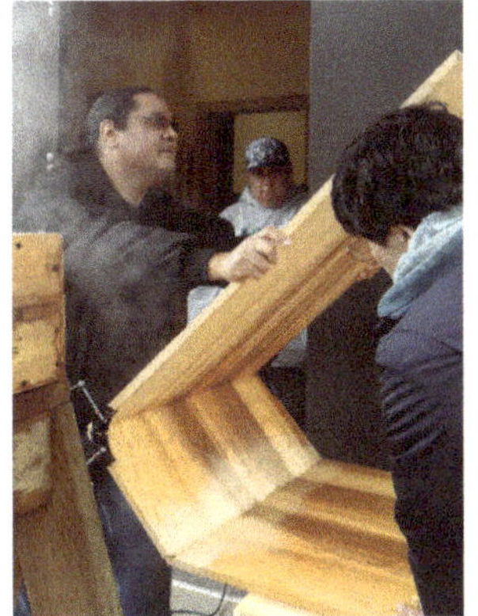
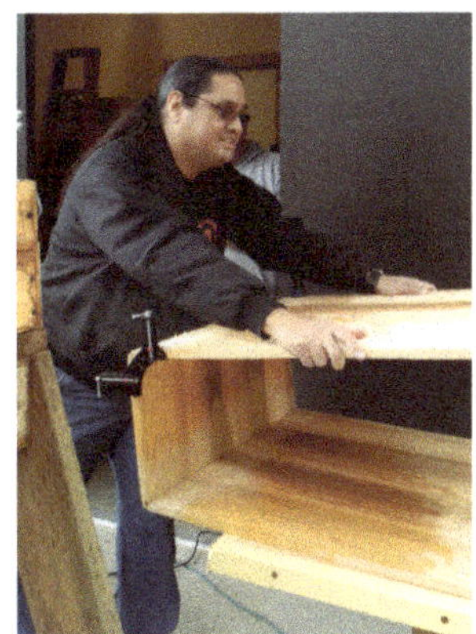

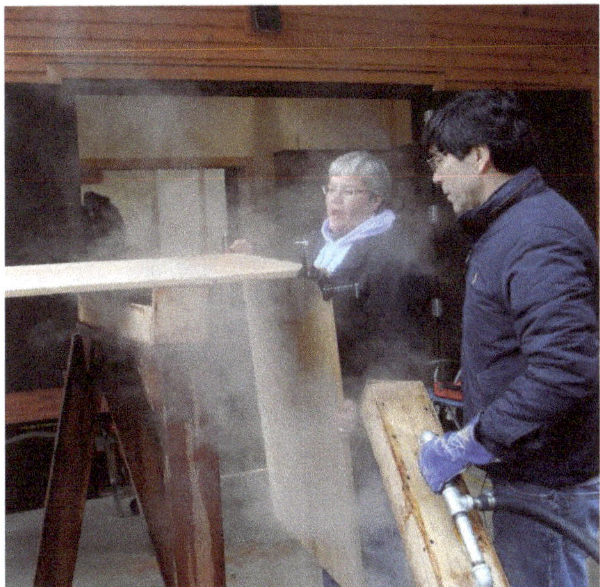

BOX DRUMS

At Olympia's Evergreen State College, I had the pleasure of teaching a wide variety of Natives in a box drum class: Salish people, Tlingits, Haidas, Tsimshian, easily four or five different tribes. The boards we used came from the Kitsap Peninsula.

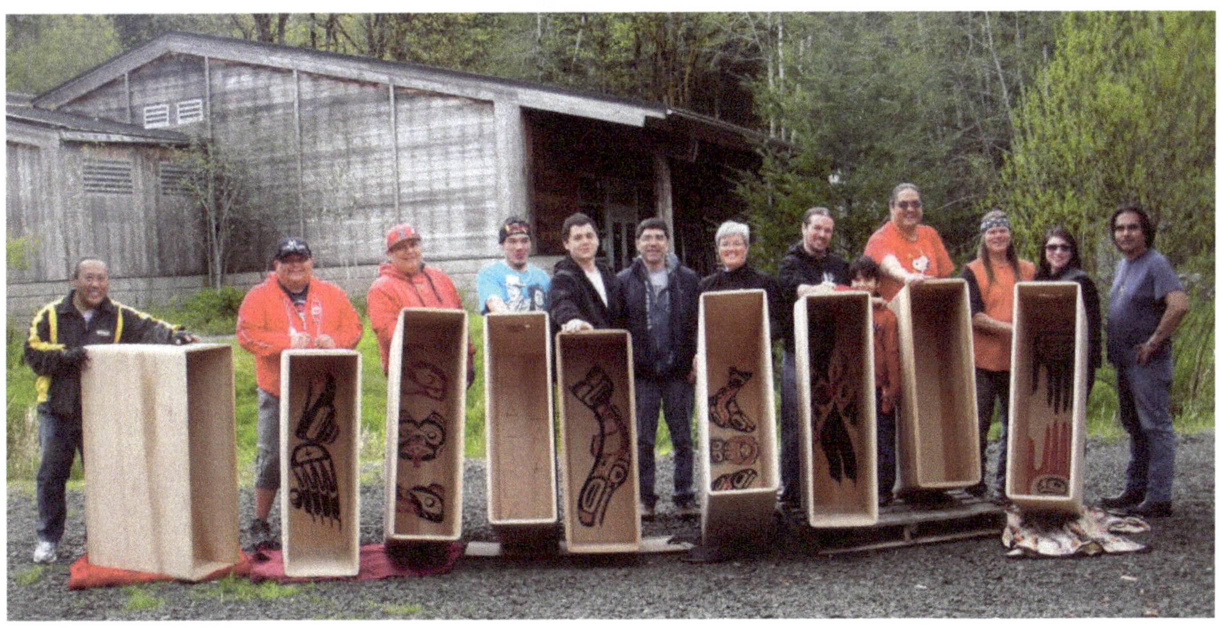

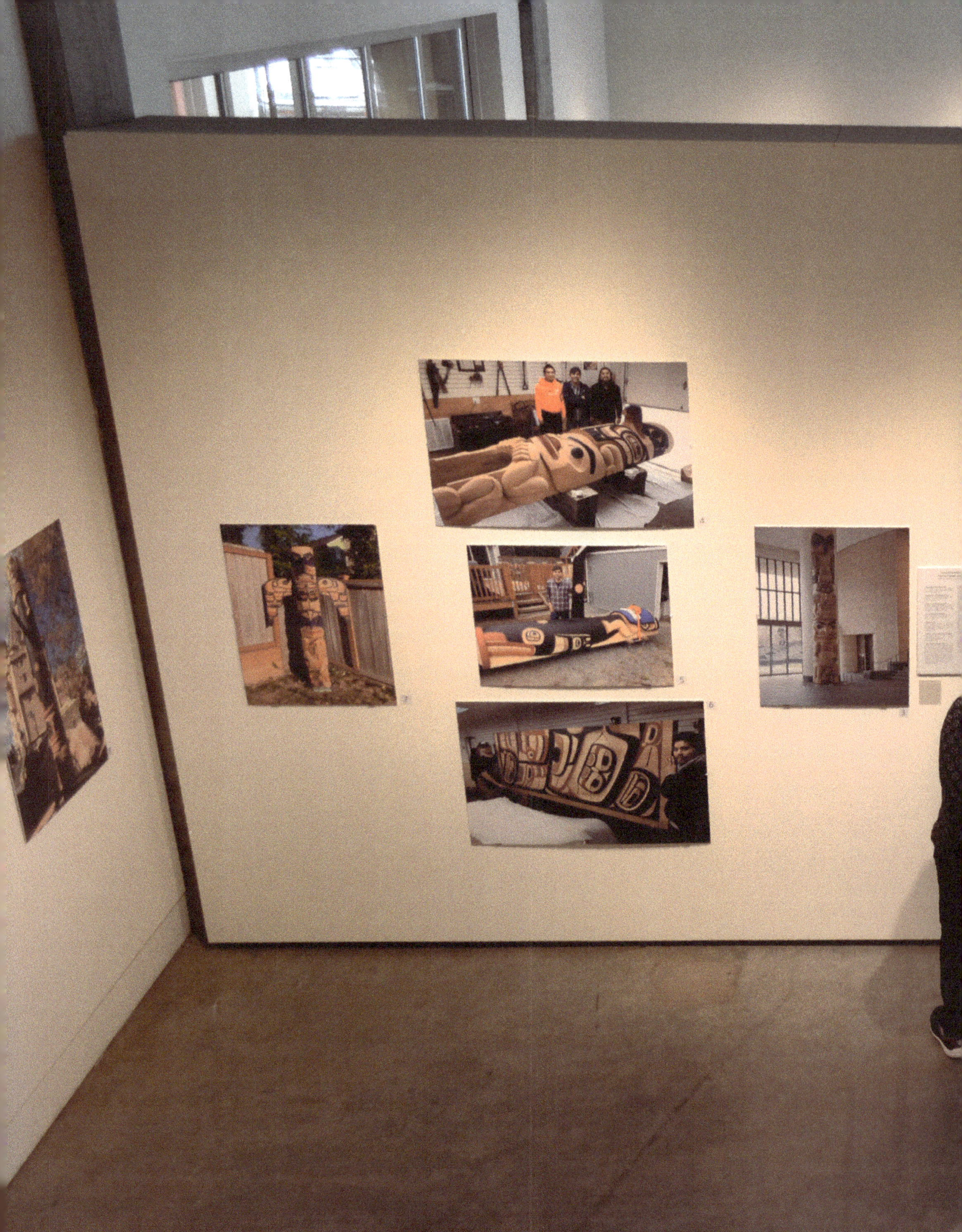

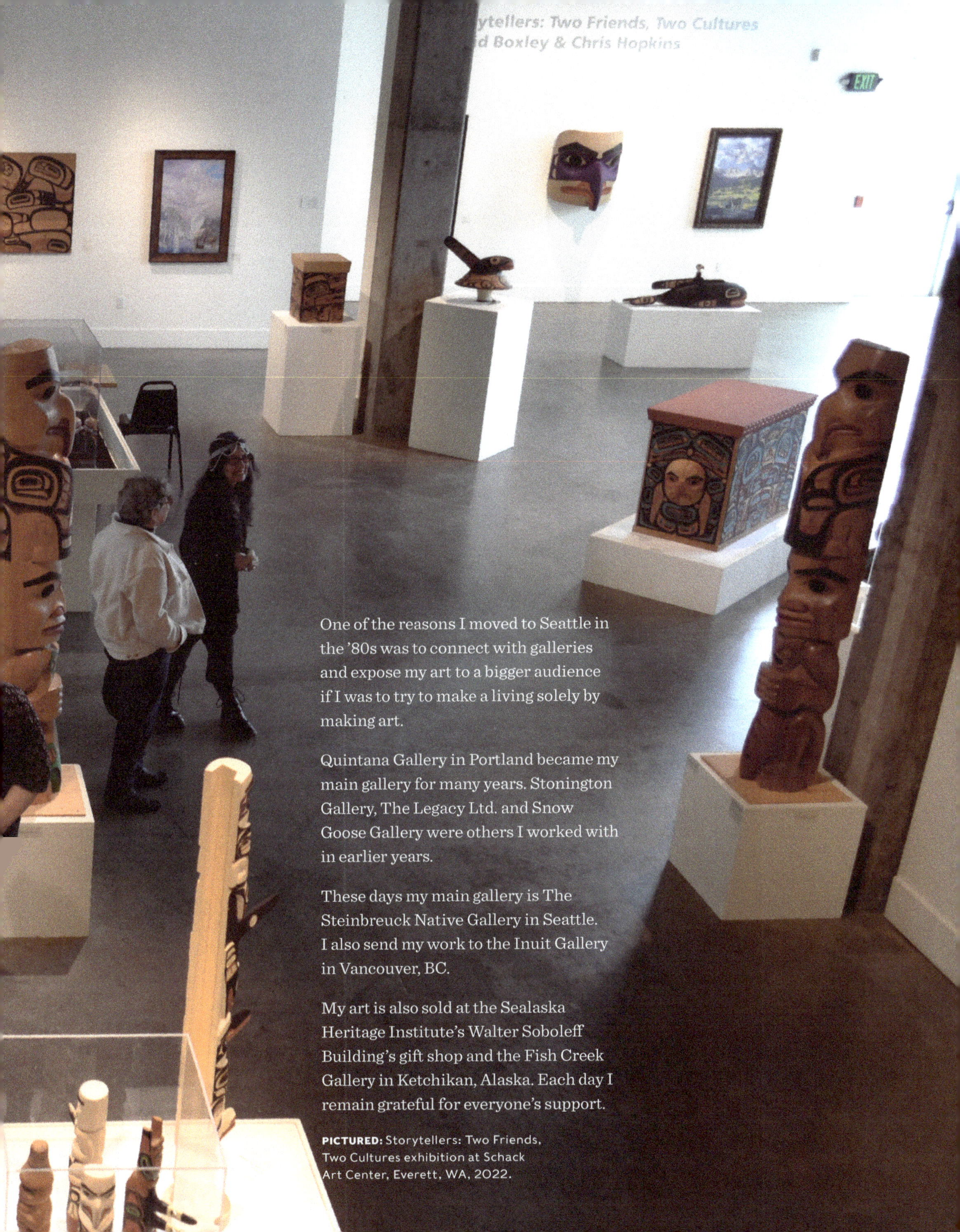

One of the reasons I moved to Seattle in the '80s was to connect with galleries and expose my art to a bigger audience if I was to try to make a living solely by making art.

Quintana Gallery in Portland became my main gallery for many years. Stonington Gallery, The Legacy Ltd. and Snow Goose Gallery were others I worked with in earlier years.

These days my main gallery is The Steinbreuck Native Gallery in Seattle. I also send my work to the Inuit Gallery in Vancouver, BC.

My art is also sold at the Sealaska Heritage Institute's Walter Soboleff Building's gift shop and the Fish Creek Gallery in Ketchikan, Alaska. Each day I remain grateful for everyone's support.

PICTURED: Storytellers: Two Friends, Two Cultures exhibition at Schack Art Center, Everett, WA, 2022.

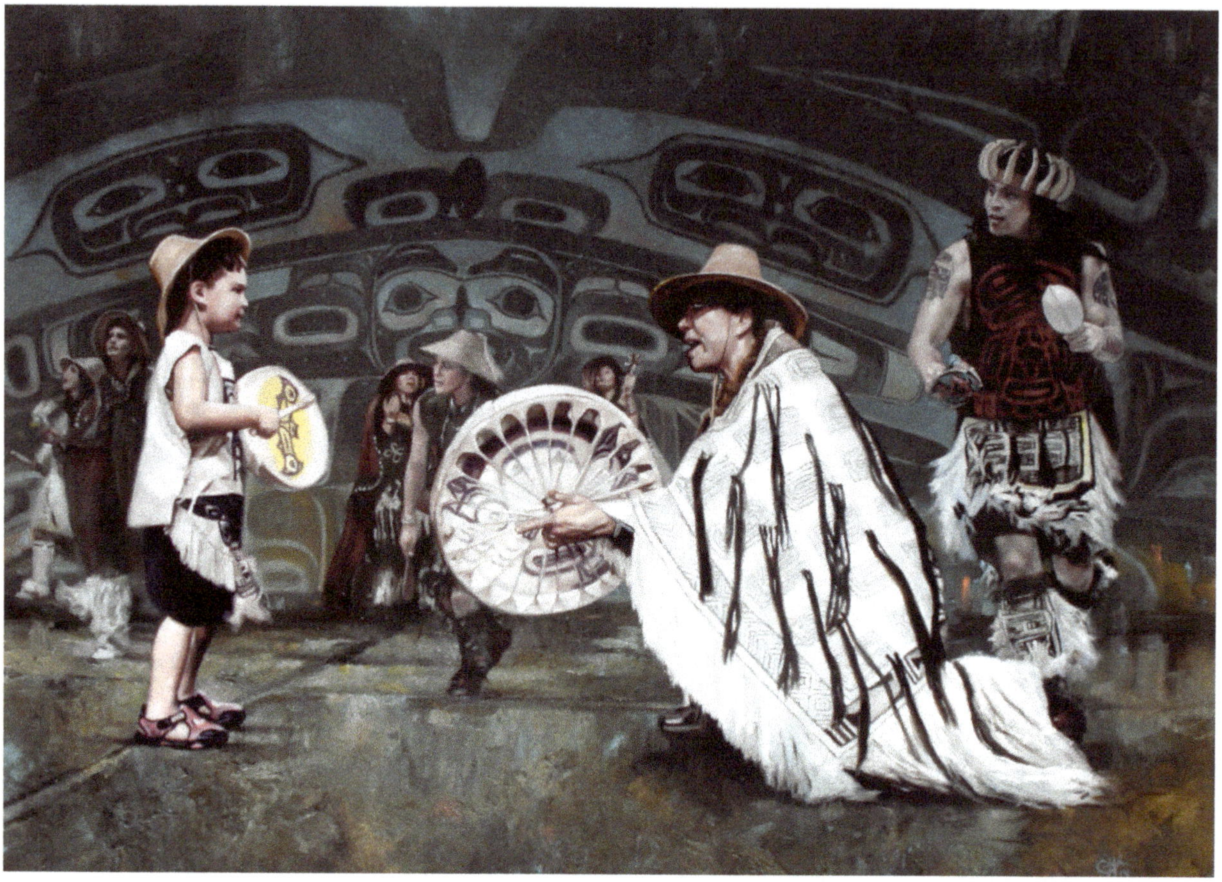

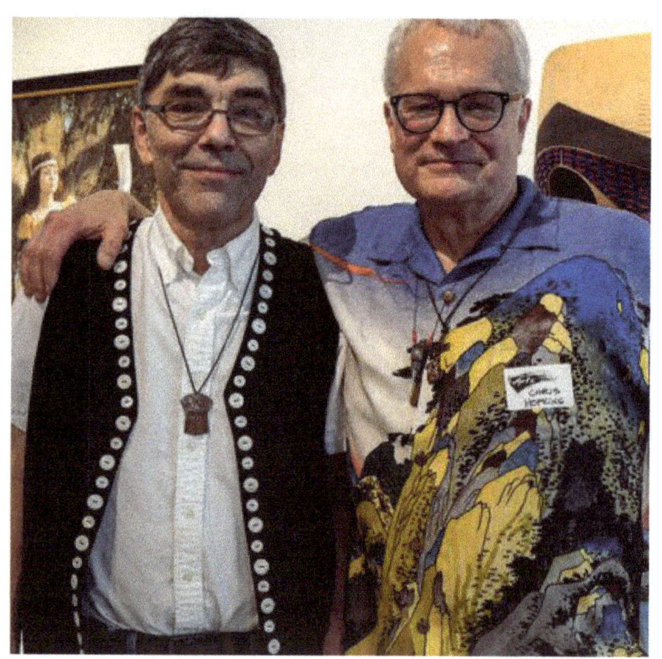

CHRIS HOPKINS

I shared the stage in a two-person retrospective exhibition at the Schack Art Center in Everett with my good friend and amazing artist Chris Hopkins, whose painting talents have portrayed different stages of my career. He made it possible for Davey to earn a four-year scholarship to Seattle's prestigious art school, Cornish College of the Arts. His paintings breathe life into his subjects. More important, his respect for my culture means a lot and illustrates how two people from such diverse backgrounds can become lasting friends.

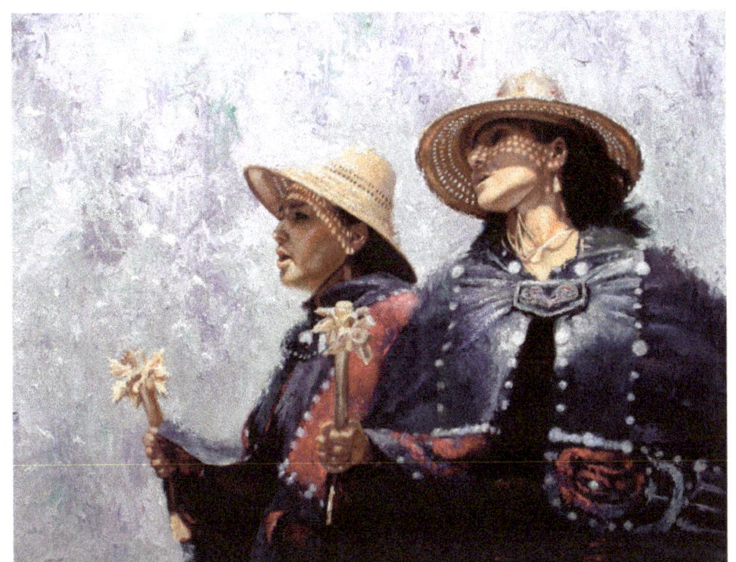

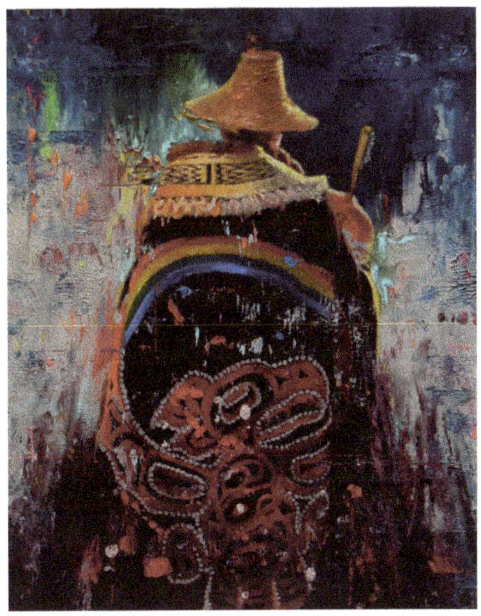

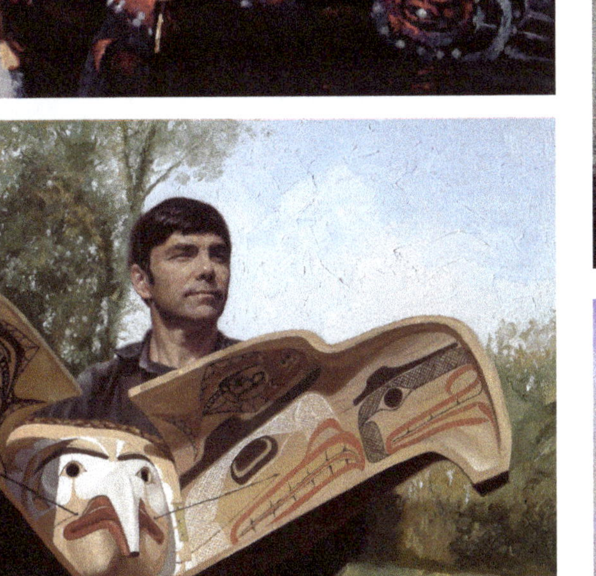

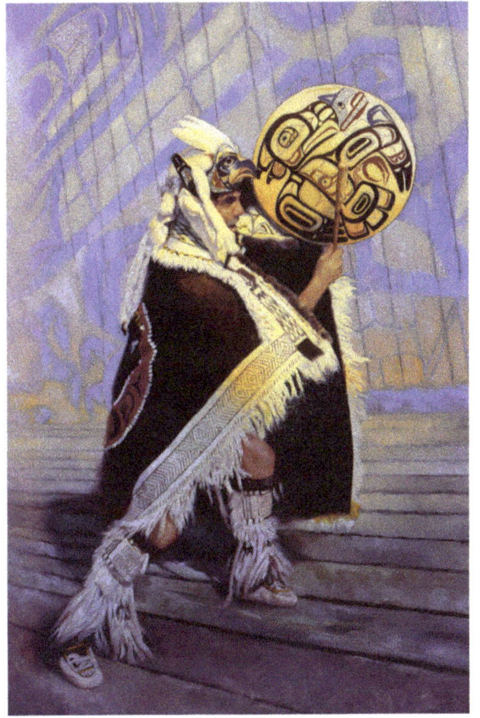

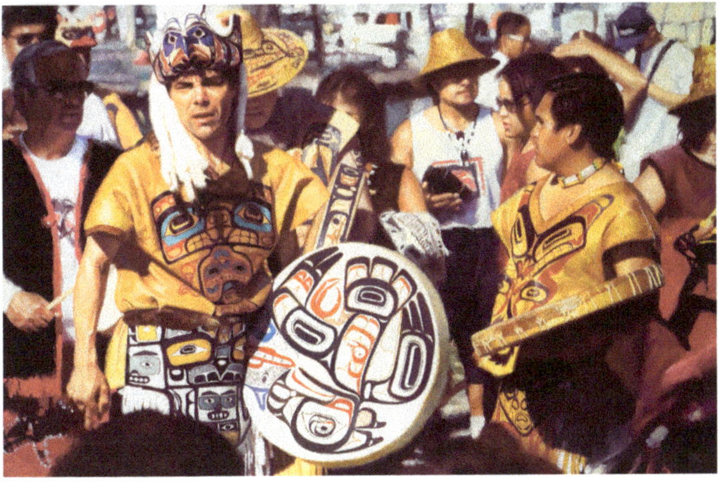

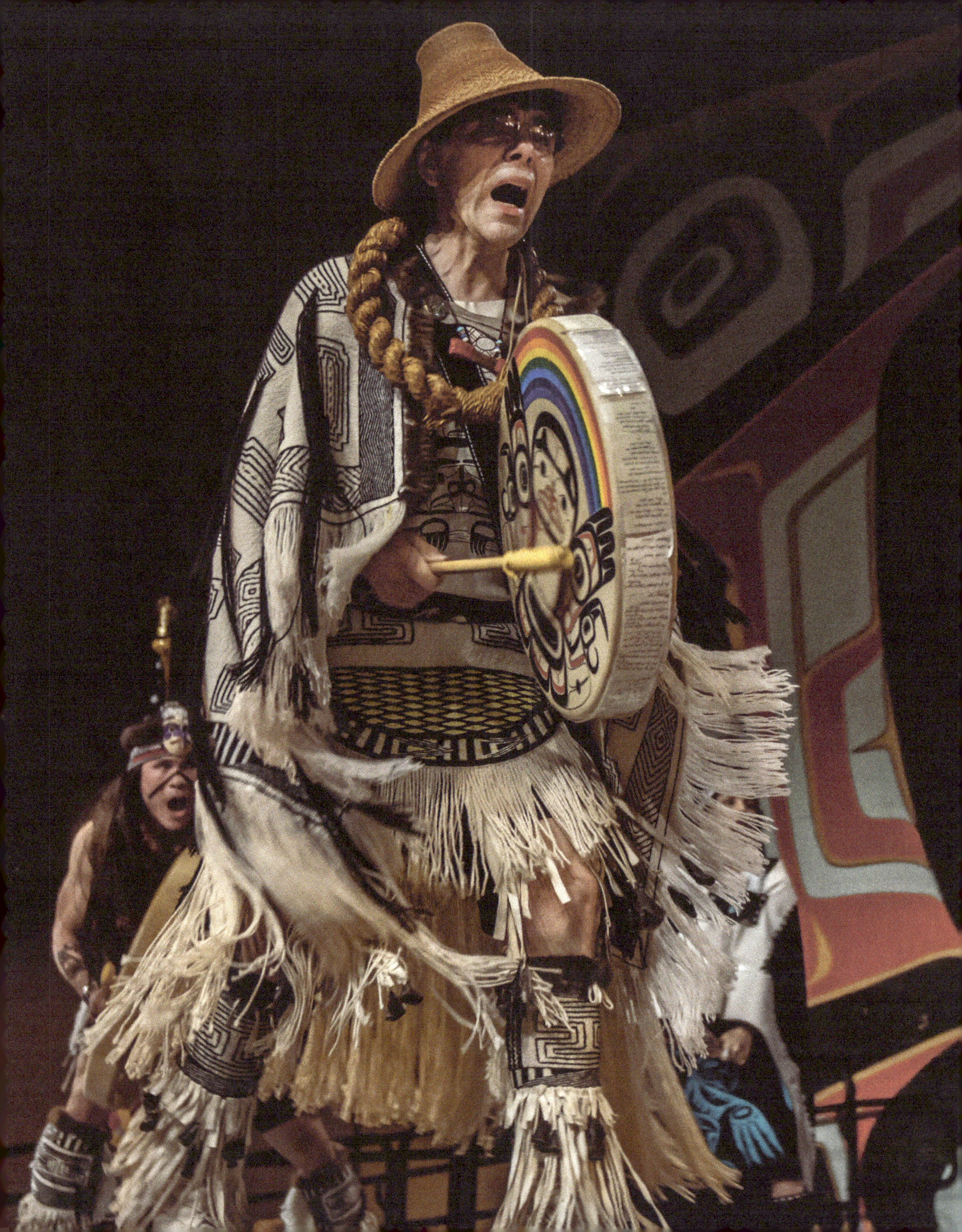

CHAPTER SIX

PEOPLE OF THE SALMON / *Git Hoan*

In 1973, while I was in college, my aunt Margaret Bolton invited Gitksan Chief Ken Harris and his wife, Margaret, to visit Metlakatla from British Columbia so they could teach Native songs and dances to the kids in our community.

The Chief's visit resulted in the formation of the Git Lax Likst'aa (People of the Island) Dancers. The original leaders who learned from Chief Harris were Yvonne Dundas, Barbara Fawcett, Elaine (Sissy) Guthrie, Sarah Booth, and Patsy Beal. Leadership has changed over time, but the group still performs to this day with new groups of children learning about their culture each year.

While home on break, I heard that something was going on at the gym, so I went down to check it out. I sat in the bleachers and watched them. It was pretty exciting. When they had an invitational dance—that's where the dance leader invites people to join the group for a song—I was the only adult who went on the floor with them. I didn't know what I was doing, but I was certainly excited. I was all jazzed up by what these kids were doing.

It reminded me of when I went to an all Black church in Seattle. Holy smokes, they get pretty jazzed up; the energy was so incredible that you just get excited. I had only five dollars in my pocket. I gave them the whole five dollars. After watching the kids dance, I realized we don't have to be on the outside watching the Tlingits and Haidas anymore. We can have our own groups.

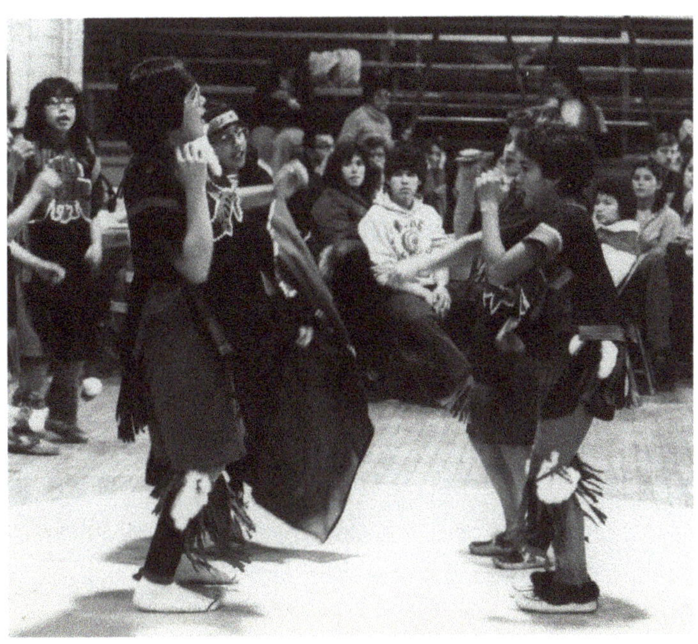

I really enjoyed watching the children's dance group Git Lax Likst'aa (People of the Island) perform at the 1982 potlatch.

I was so impressed when I saw the kids during that visit home from college. I didn't realize at the time just how significant it was. A beginning.

Today, I'm fortunate enough to lead a troupe called Git Hoan, The People of the Salmon, that melds high-energy song and dance, plus masks, into cultural performance art and storytelling. But, even with the children's inspiration, it still took decades before Tsimshian dance groups became a fixture in our culture.

Not long after I moved back to Washington to become a full-time artist in 1986, I had returned to Metlakatla one year before the village celebrated the Centennial arrival of its founders. That's almost ten years after I saw that dance troupe, and while we had a children's group, we still didn't have adults dancing. For culture day, I decided I would dance with a boombox. I sang my song—a chief's headdress song—into the boom-box. I danced all by myself to open the occasion. After that weekend was over, I went back to Seattle, and I got a call from my friend Theo Bayou. She said, "David, guess what? The adults decided to have an adult dance group. We had sixty people sign up. We don't want you to be dancing by yourself anymore."

For the next year, the community hired me to do a totem pole; it was sponsored by the senior citizens. I did the carving down in Washington, crated it up and shipped it to Metlakatla. We had a big pole-raising in front of the longhouse. The adult dance group performed for the first time in that longhouse. It was a neat occasion. A lot of people who never got to dance before finally had a chance. In the program I made, people had to dedicate their robe to someone before they danced. I don't know if we invented that or not, but that's what we did. Everybody had to get up and talk about their regalia, their robe, and say who it honors. There were a lot of people who got to shine that day. I was glad I got to back up into the shadows and watch people.

It was the first time for a lot of them to be proud of their culture. Today, there are four or five dance groups that are all offshoots of that original group. That was the start of the 4th Generation Dancers, who are still around today.

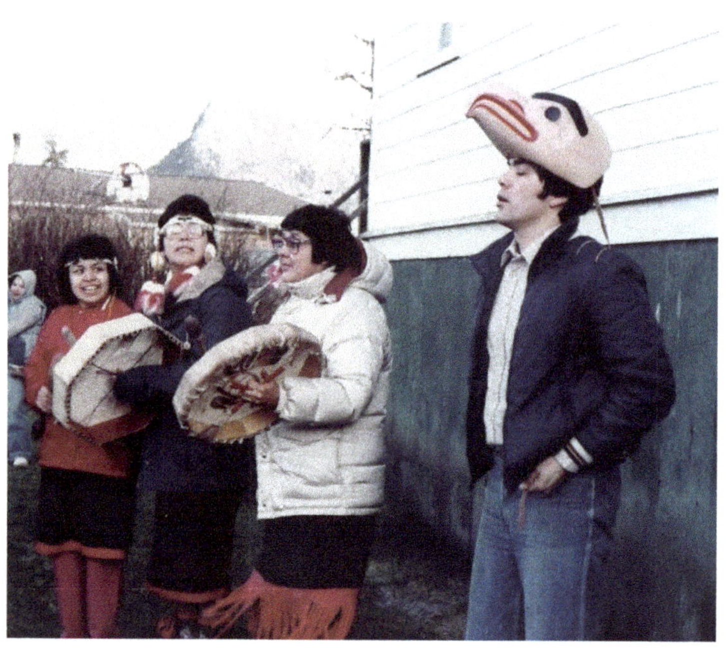

ABOVE: Patsy Beal, Sarah Booth, and Sissy Guthrie (from left to right) are three women who were cultural leaders in our village. They inspired me and sang for me at my grandmother's potlatch in 1982. This was the first time I danced and I didn't have any regalia. I danced the eagle dance with the children's dance group called Git Lax Likst'aa (People of the Island). See also **FACING PAGE, TOP**.

FACING PAGE, BOTTOM: A year before we celebrate the 100th year, I did a solo dance during a visit to Metlakatla. At that time, I had no one to sing for me. I recorded the chief's headdress song on to cassette tape. I had to put a microphone next to the boom box so people could hear it.

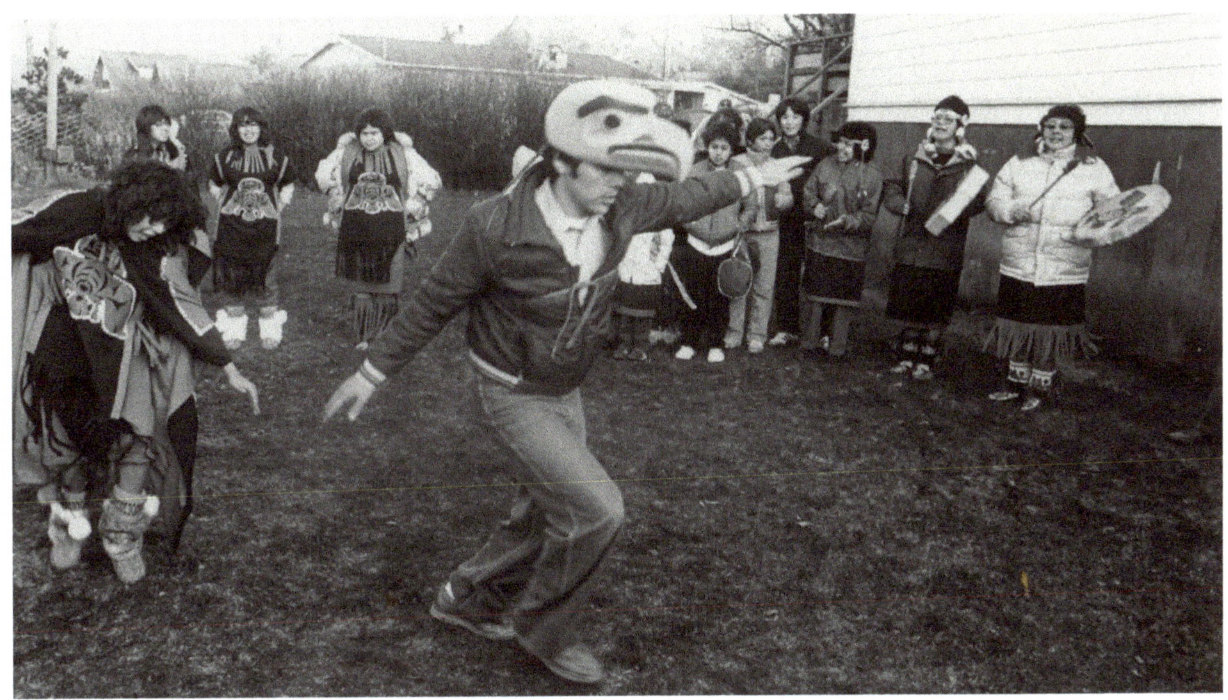

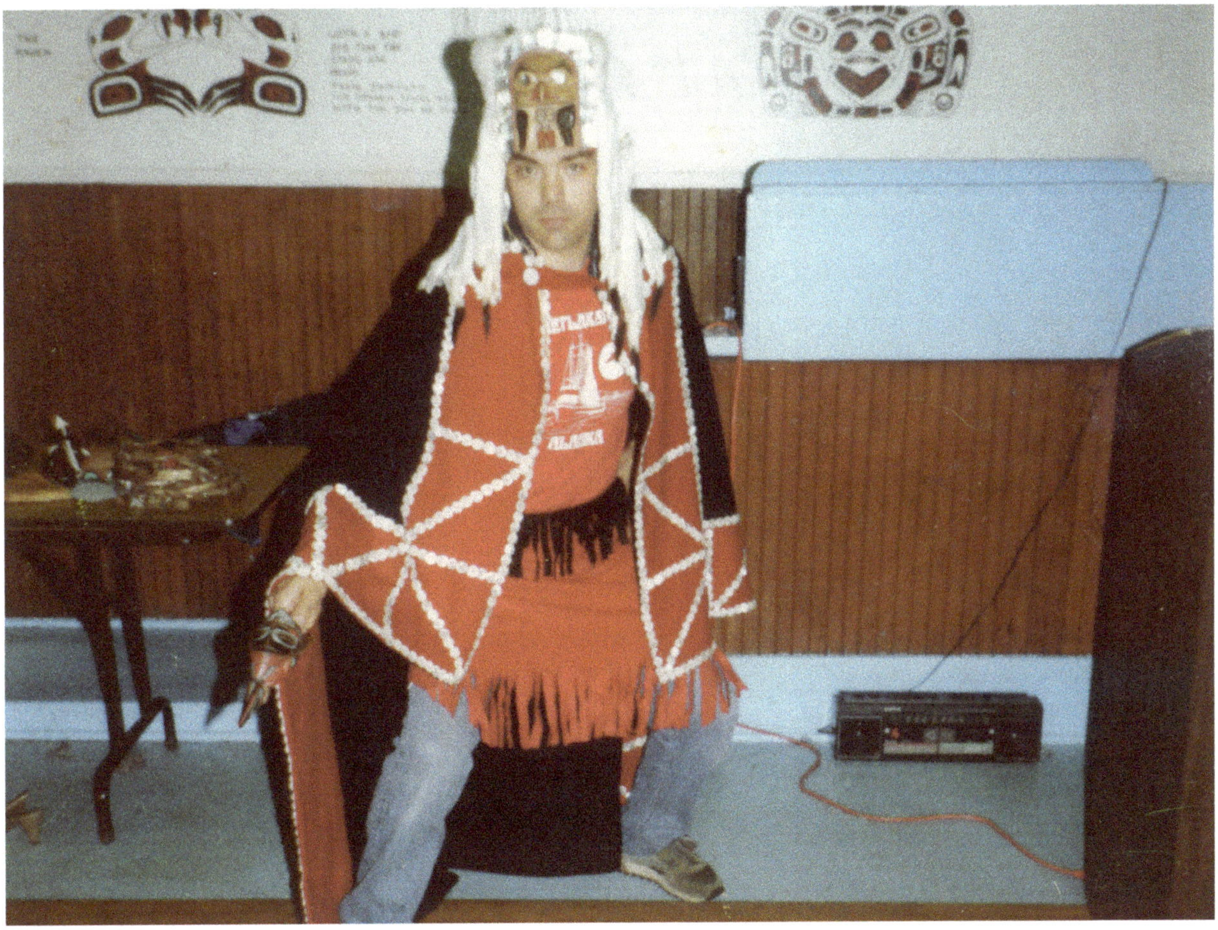

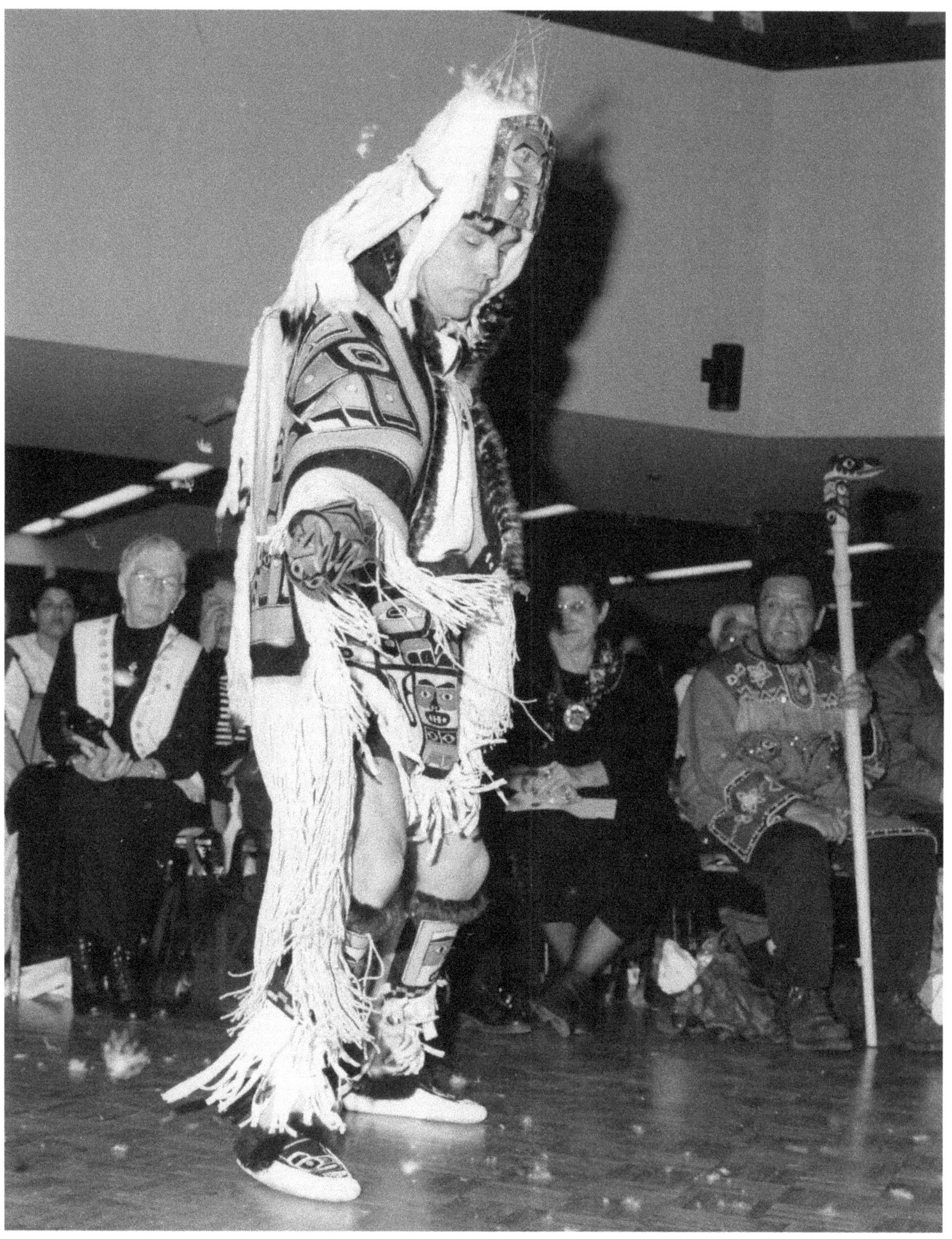

I sponsored a potlatch to celebrate Evelyn Vanderhoop's first chilkat robe,
and she asked me to dance wearing the robe at that feast.

It feels good that it's happening without me. That's the way it should be. Robert Davidson told me, "If you're always in charge, and no one else gets to do what you do, then what happens when you're not there?" The culture doesn't belong to me. It belongs to all of us. I'm just lucky enough to contribute.

*I*t was still another ten years before I found myself dancing with that same excitement the kids and adults showed in Metlakatla. In 1996, a couple of Tsimshian people came to me and asked if I would help set up a potlatch in Seattle. I agreed. The planning committee ended up being six or seven people, all of whom became part of a group called Tsimshian Haayuuk. I invited a bunch of Canadian and Alaskan groups. We put together this potlatch. We had gifts for everybody, food for everybody.

The participants were amazed. A lot of people who attended had never been to anything like that where they didn't have to pay to get in, where they were fed for free and received gifts for watching the performances. The Metlakatla group 4th Generation came down and helped us with the dancing.

People in this planning committee thought we should have a dance group. We grew from those six or seven people to fifty-five people in the next year in Tsimshian Haayuuk.

But a version of Git Hoan came before Haayuuk. The two people who asked me to help them with the potlatch, Robert Frederickson and Joyce Troyer Wilson, went with me to Ottawa. We spent six weeks out there dancing and researching. We put on nightly performances with the help of the museum and Director George McDonald. They had a million-dollar light and sound system. The people who worked there helped us make the props.

The show we put on in Ottawa was called People of the Salmon. We recorded all the songs and figured out what I was supposed to say in Seattle. The whole evening was pretty good and we performed at a place called Grand Hall. That museum is awesome. There are six longhouse facades in the main hall. We told the story of the first Tsimshian potlatch. I had to lip sync my own voice. The others had masks so they could mime as they were supposed to be talking and telling stories for those other tribes.

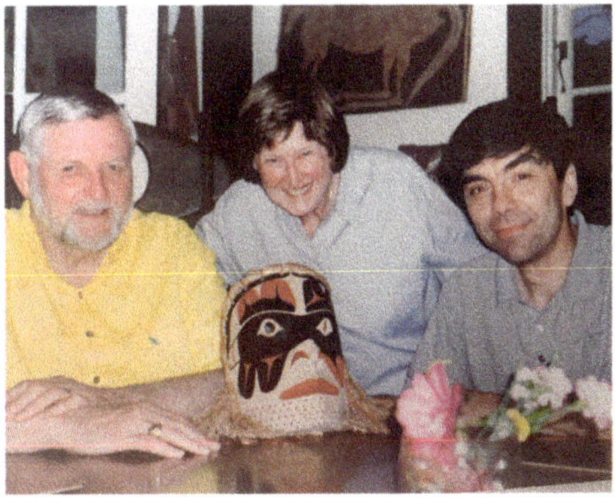

George McDonald was responsible for starting Git Hoan. He invited my group to Ottawa. The mask between him and his wife, Joanne, I made for him in appreciation for bringing us to Ottawa and giving Git Hoan its start.

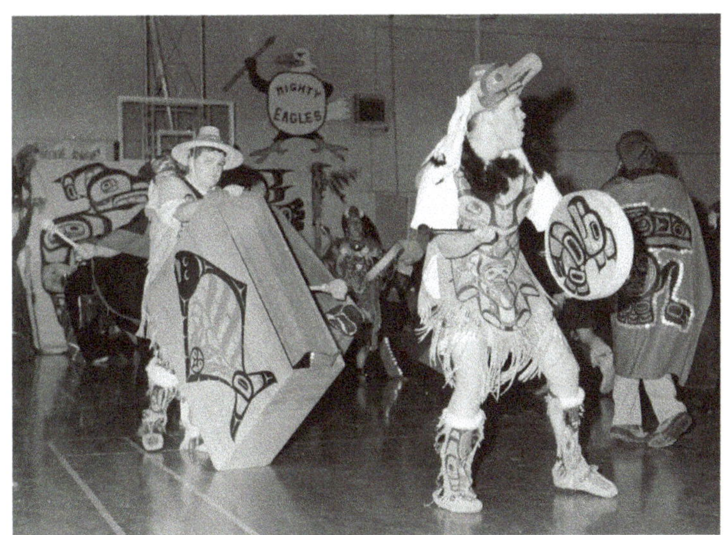

After I returned from Ottawa, I formed Tsimshian Haayuuk (Spirit of Tsimshian). Here, we're performing at Indian Heritage High School, where we held a potlatch in 1996.

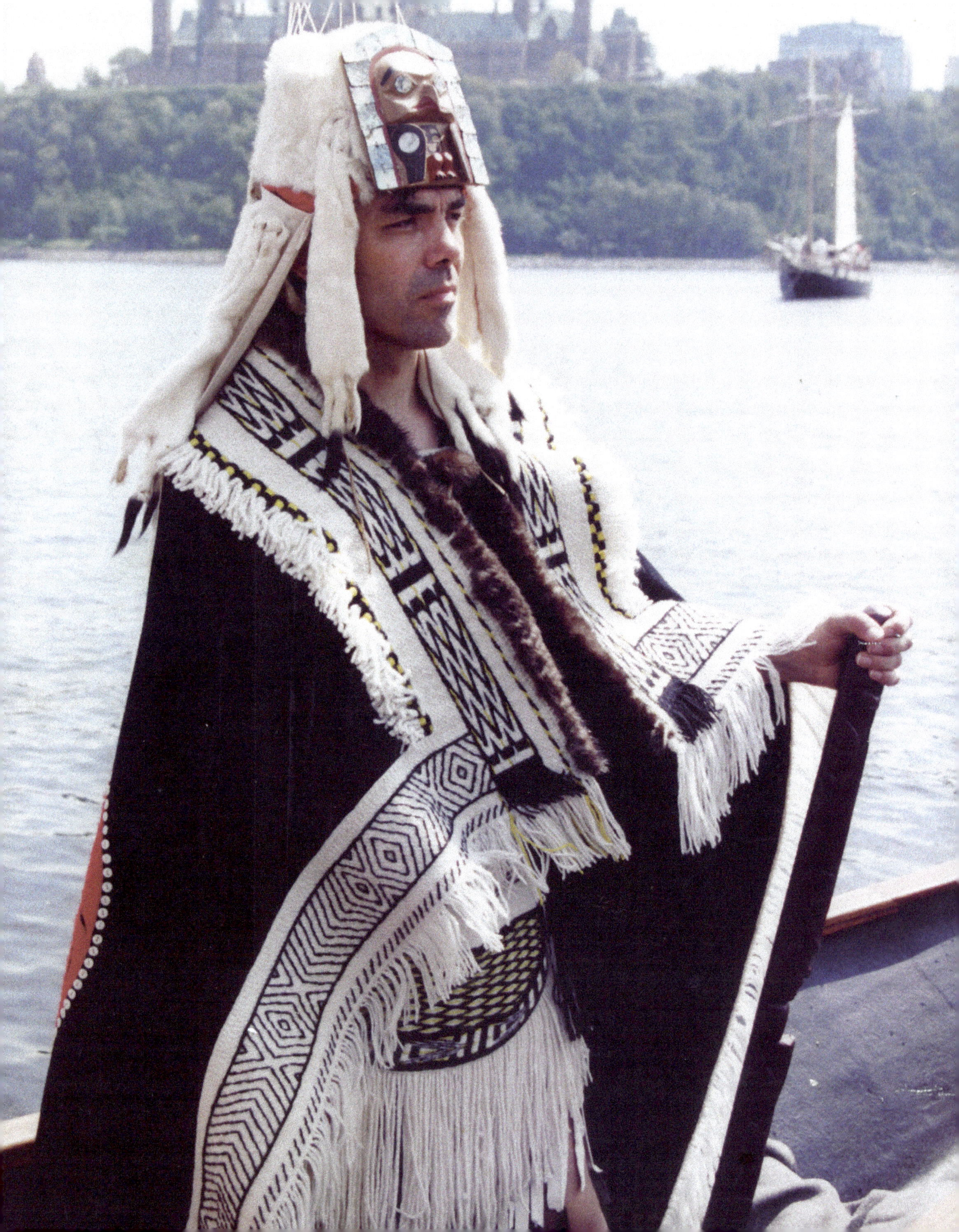

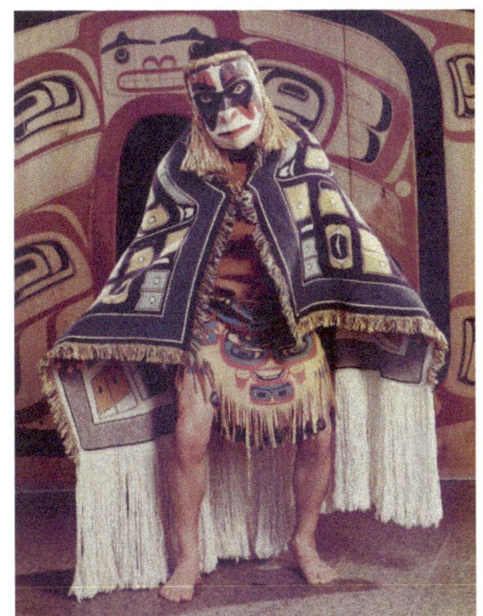
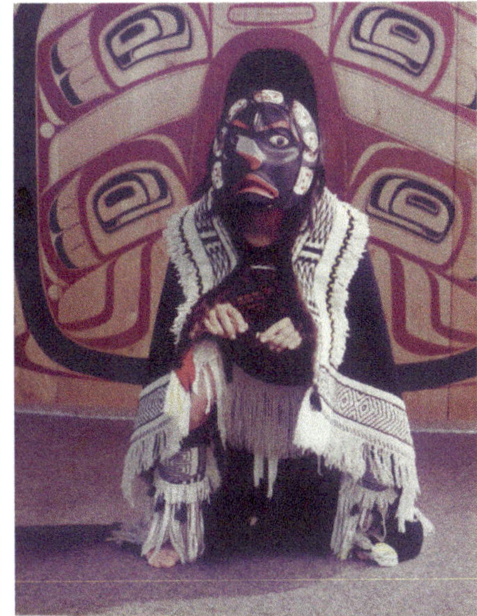
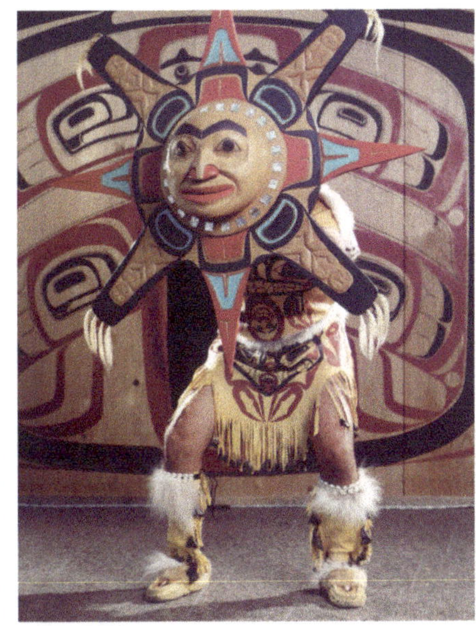
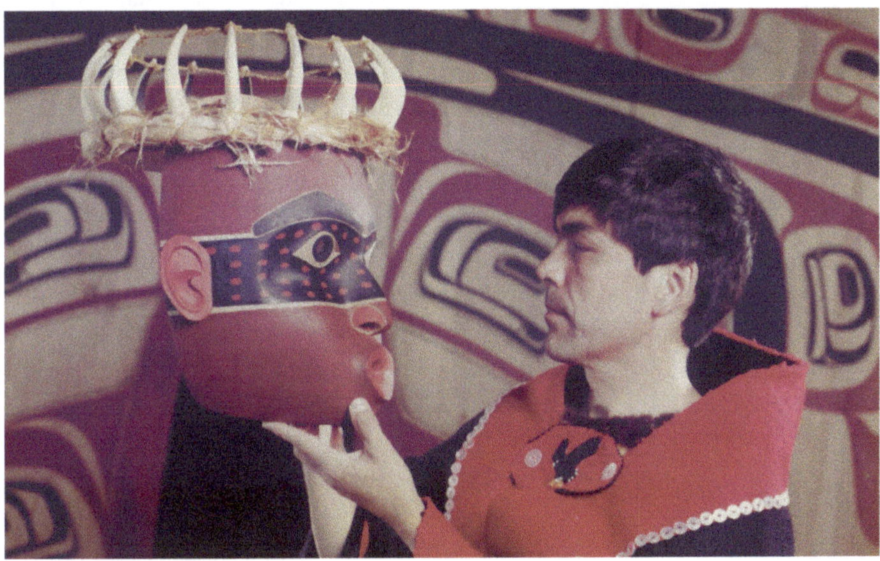
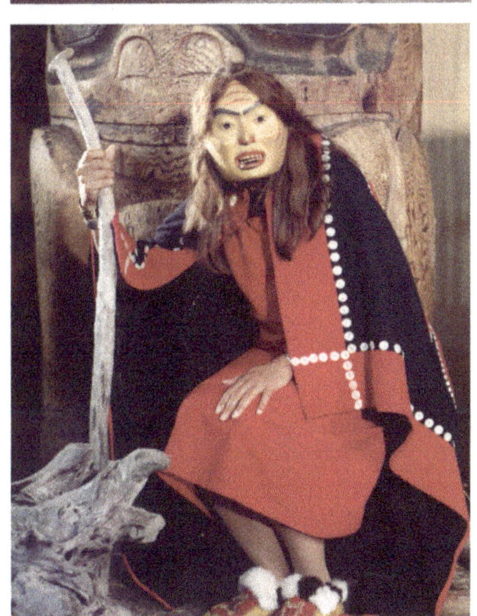

I made these masks during a six-week trip to Ottawa in 1996. I took five dancers there and it was the original forming of Git Hoan.

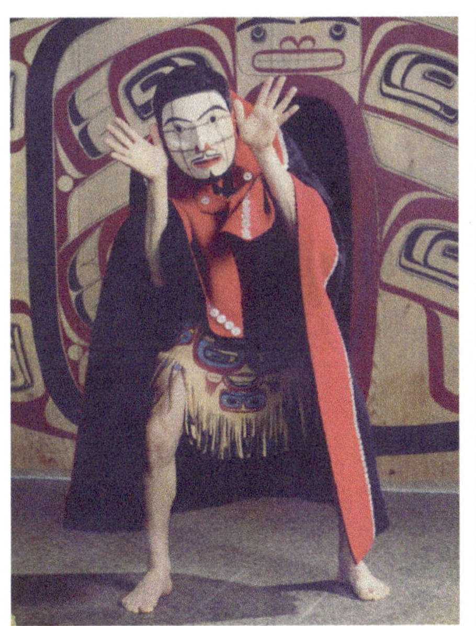
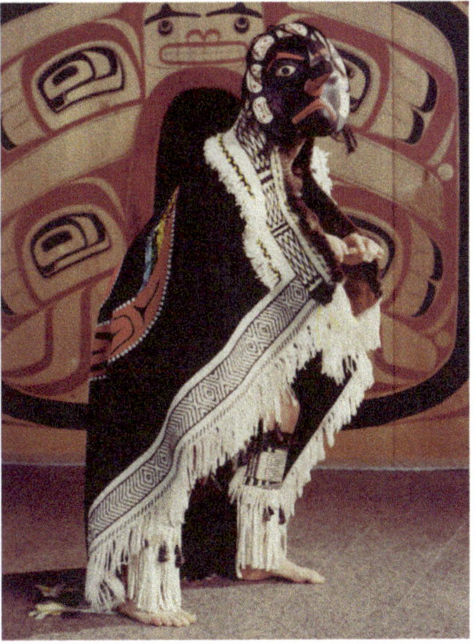
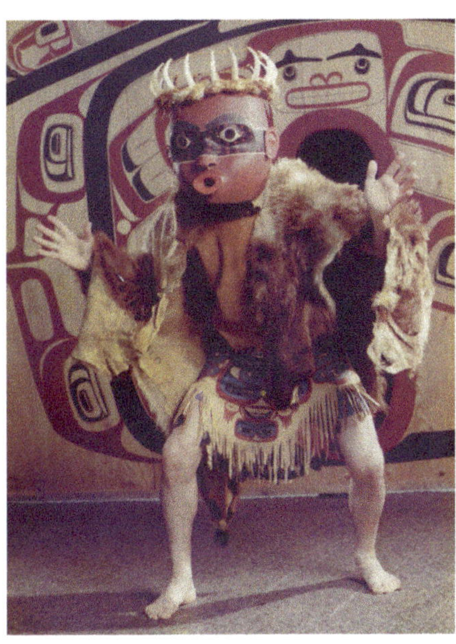

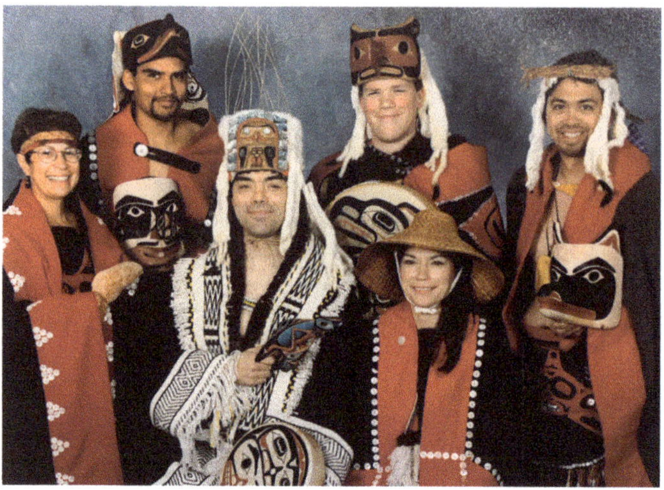

The original Git Hoan: Joyce Troyer Wilson, Robert Frederickson, my son Davey, Jerome Jainga, Evelyn Vanderhoop, and me.

It took a few days to get coordinated with those voices. After a while we got it all down. The museum itself was worth the trip. I got to do a lot of research. I got to do a couple of important replications of masks we still use in our performances. I saw them in their storage collections. I had wood with me. I was able to have the pieces in front of me, measure the wood, and then carve. The whole trip was very successful.

Tsimshian Haayuuk was formed the next year. No one had seen a group like ours, our style, the fast-paced, double-beat drumming, and all the masks. People still associate the double beat with my group, but I didn't invent that. I was influenced by the British Columbia dancers. I think it was a Nisga'a dance group that I saw performing with their box drums.

One of the reasons for Git Hoan's success is that we stay small. Tsimshian Haayuuk got too big too fast in the late 1990s. At the time, I also discovered my mother's health was failing. The doctors discovered she had dementia and colon cancer. It was time for me to leave the dance group. I took my cousin Elliott Nathan on a drive and told him I was turning the dance group over to him. The group still performs and remains under his strong leadership.

avey and I decided to revive Git Hoan, and we didn't want it to be Haayuuk Part II. I wrote new songs and made masks. For nearly twenty years, we've performed in Italy, Canada, and throughout the United States. Some of the most important dancing takes place at potlatches and totem pole raisings. But our favorite place to perform is at Celebration in Juneau, Alaska. It's a gathering that brings about fifty groups from Alaska, British Columbia, the Yukon Territory, and Washington State to Juneau for four days every other summer.

We enjoy a reunion with friends we haven't seen since the previous Celebration. We get to perform on two different stages, and, if the weather holds up, be part of a magnificent parade throughout the capital city's downtown. We've really been fortunate over the years to be asked to do extra performances and encores. There are not many groups who have been asked to do that. It pays you back for all those extra practices, all that travel, all the lugging of stuff.

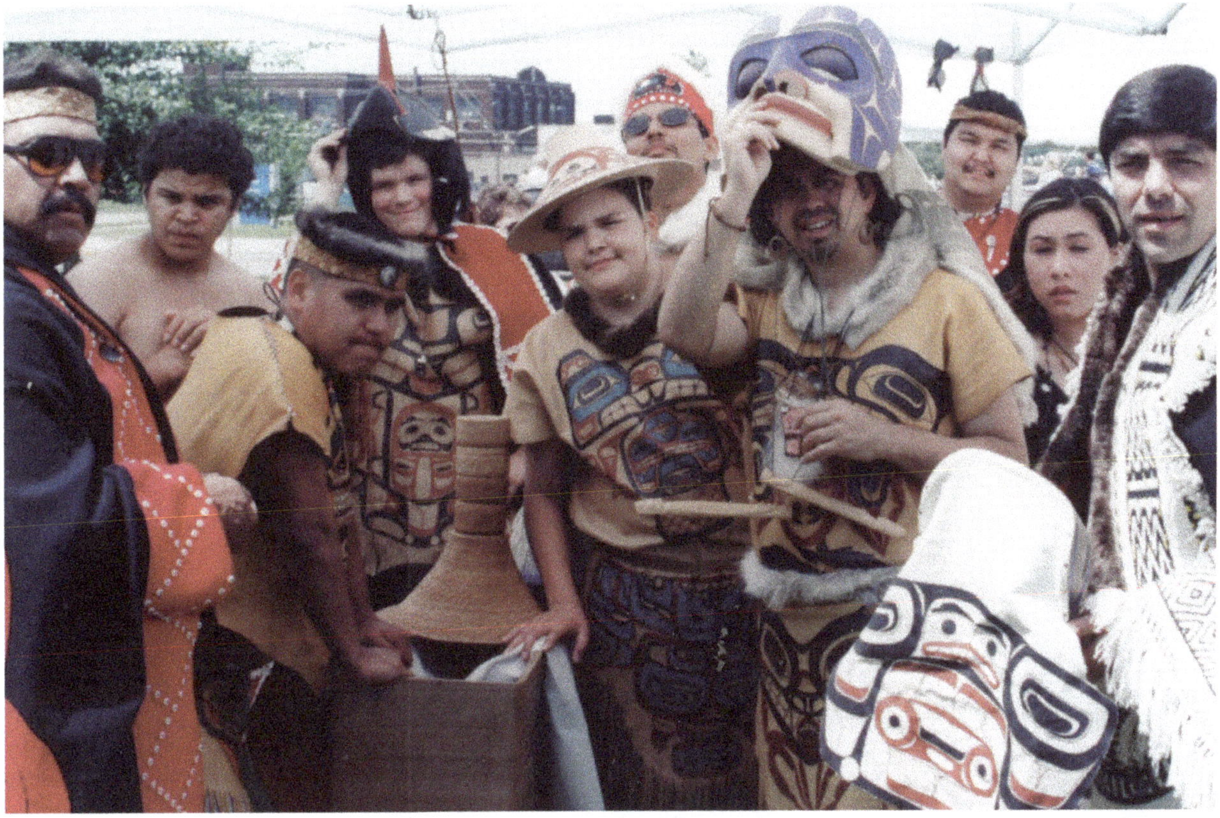

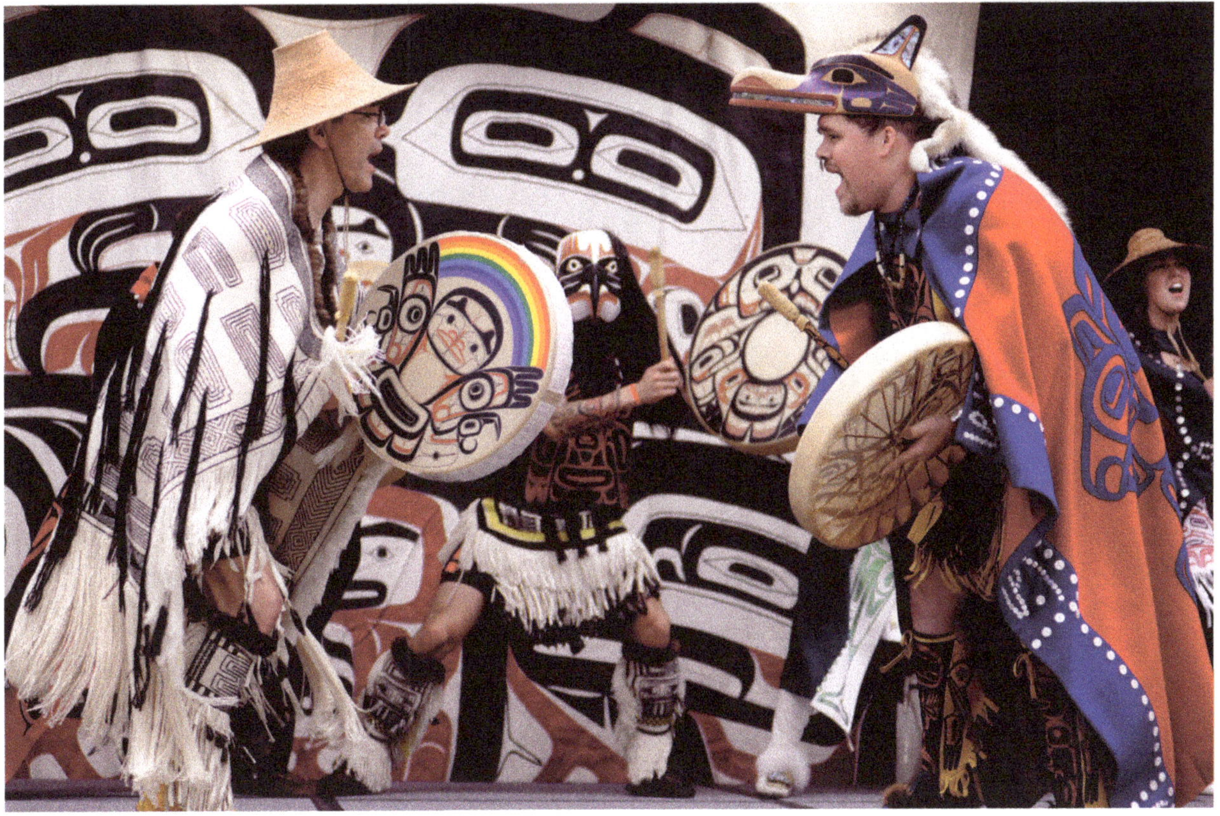

I've always told my group, "You need to be grateful. This is an opportunity that didn't exist when I was young." We do not brag about our success. What we are celebrating is that our culture is continuous. We are passing it on to the next generation. My generation growing up, we had nothing—I mean nothing. I really enjoy the fact that the young people are becoming the leaders today. So many of my generation and the one before, we were hesitant or afraid. Now, there is so much pride with these young people.

The people who sing the songs are learning the sounds of our language. When I teach songs to my groups over the years, we have meetings where all I do is go over the songs line by line, so they know what they are singing.

Back in 2010 at Celebration, Davey challenged every dance group to bring a new song to the next gathering two years later. This was not an easy challenge to issue, but it was critical. I understand how many have reverence toward the old songs, but every year there's a new group of people born and new experiences.

These songs were written to document people falling in love or a successful endeavor, or to show potlatch prerogative, rights and privileges. I'm somebody who believes we're a living culture and we need to produce songs relative to our lives right now—and we need to revere the songs that were written in the past. Where would I be if Davey and I didn't write all these songs for Tsimshian Haayuuk first and then Git Hoan, plus other songs I've written for other offshoot groups? I wouldn't have a group. The new songs say, "We're here, we're alive, we're here to document things that are happening."

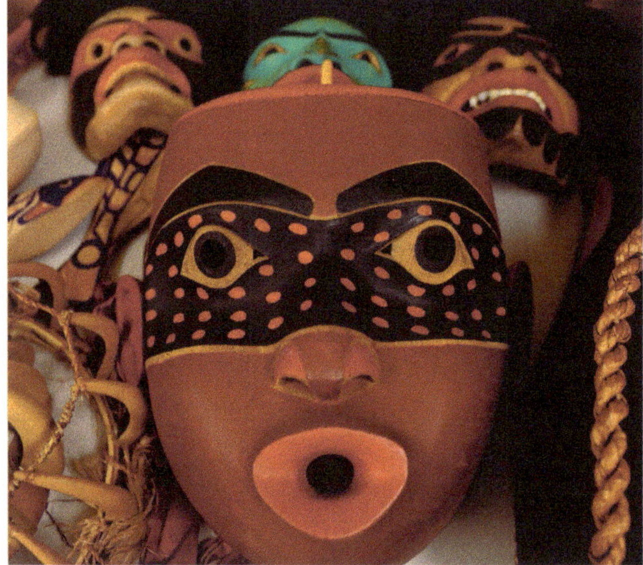

I enjoy carving masks for our group. This is a Shaman mask still used by Git Hoan, 27 years after I carved it. Behind the Shaman mask are the land otter masks.

One of our signature features is the use of masks. Before the 2016 performance, I was fortunate enough to get a grant to produce new masks for Celebration. All of the tribes in history have danced with masks. Fabulous masks have been used in intricately choreographed dances. Some carvers produced mechanical masks that help tell their stories. I've learned so much about masks by researching the archives and storage areas of different museums. For example, I've made shaman masks and spirit masks where the eyes blink. Those are directly

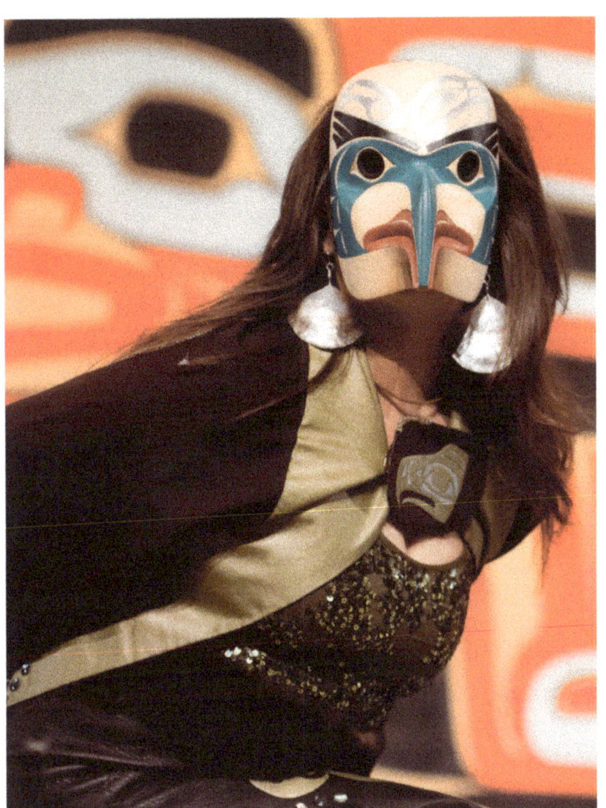

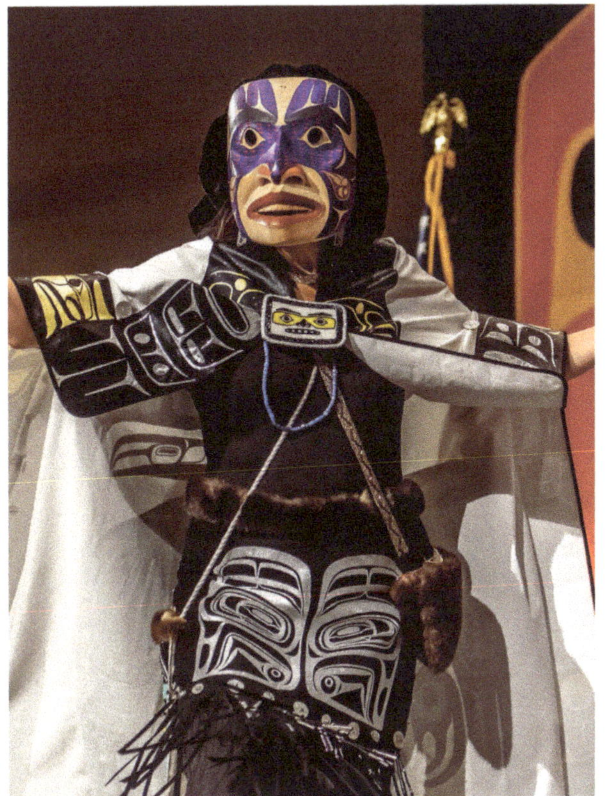

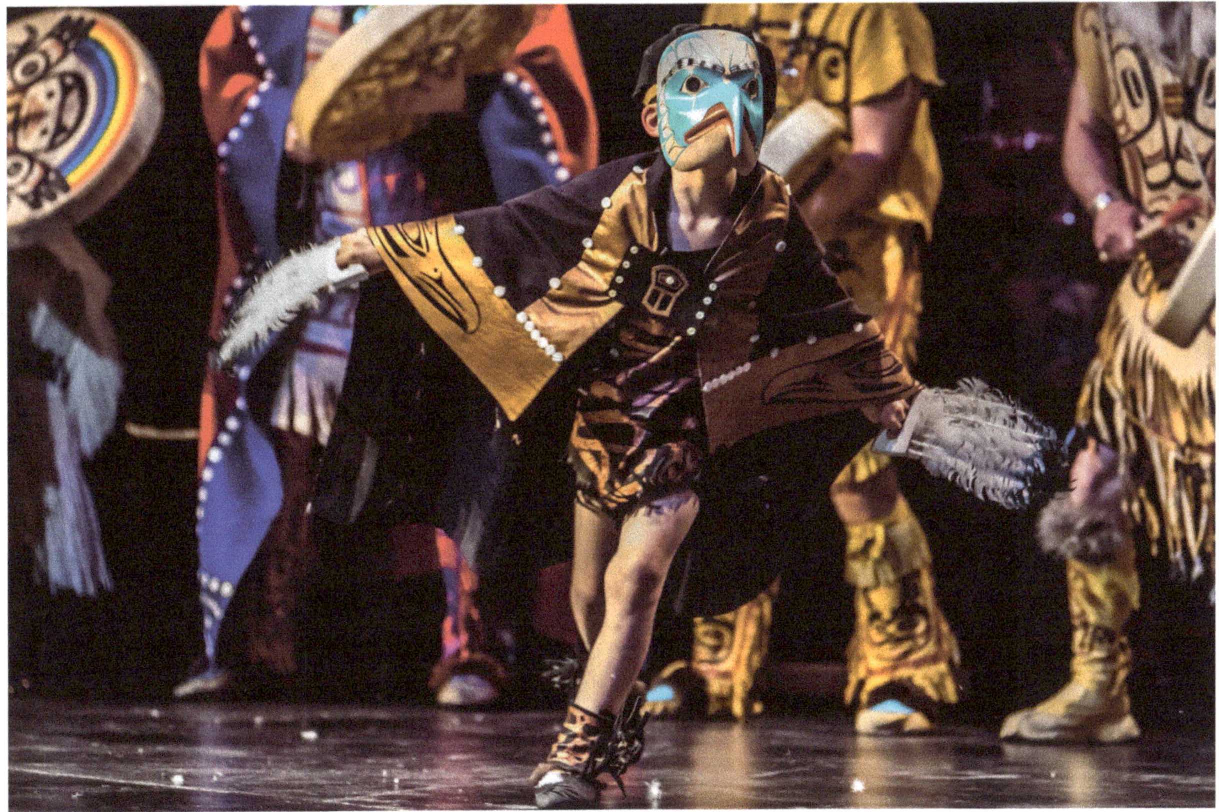

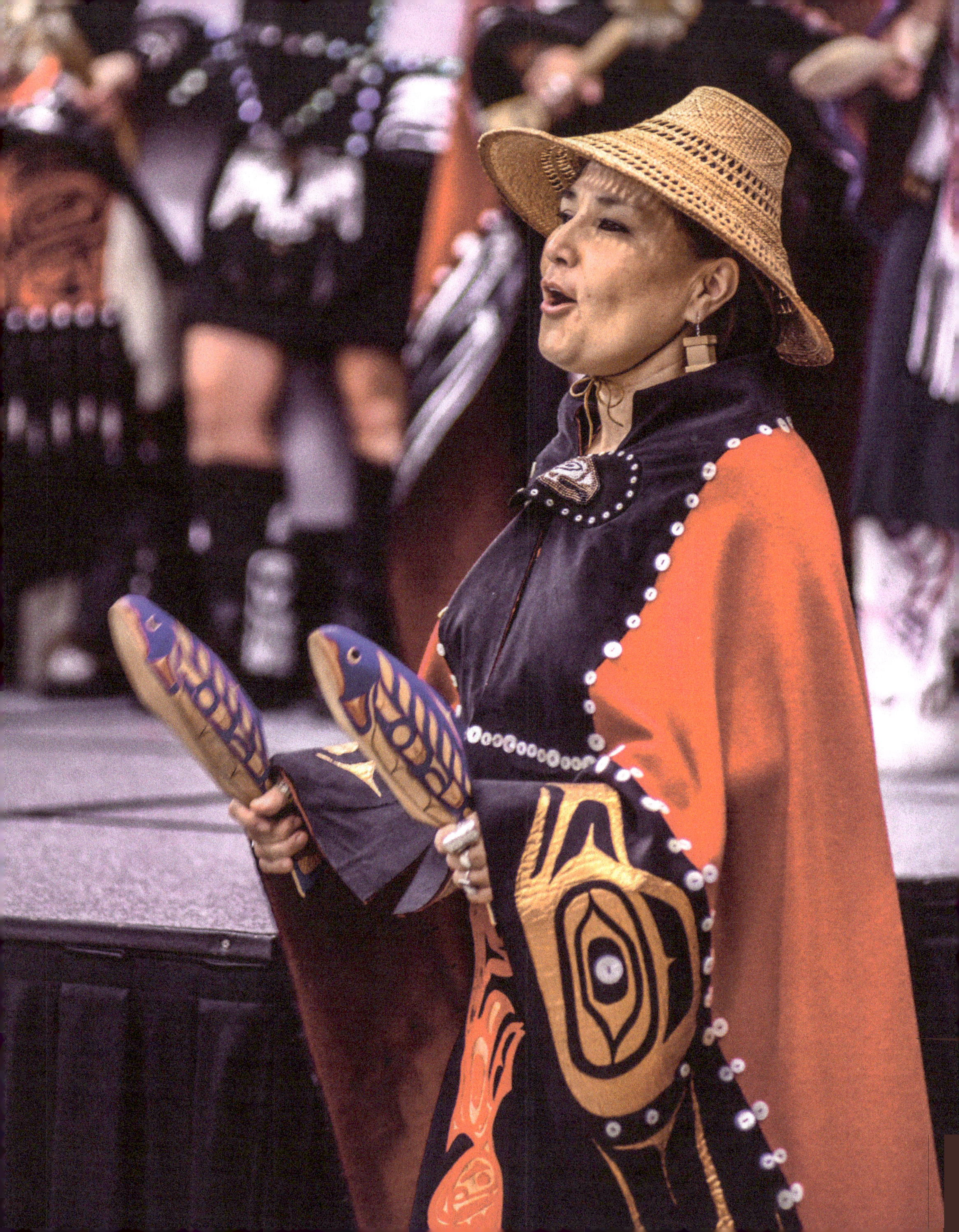

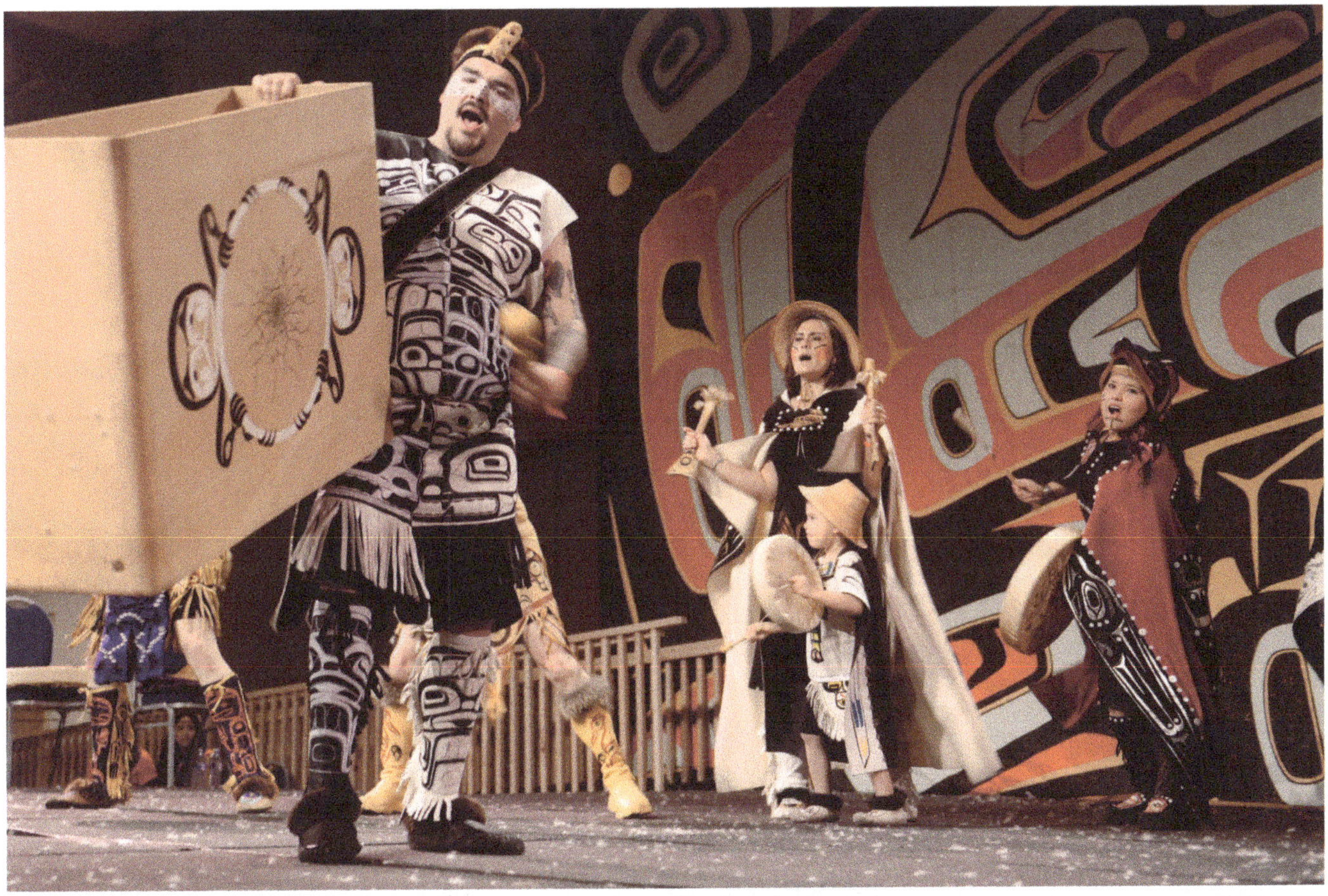

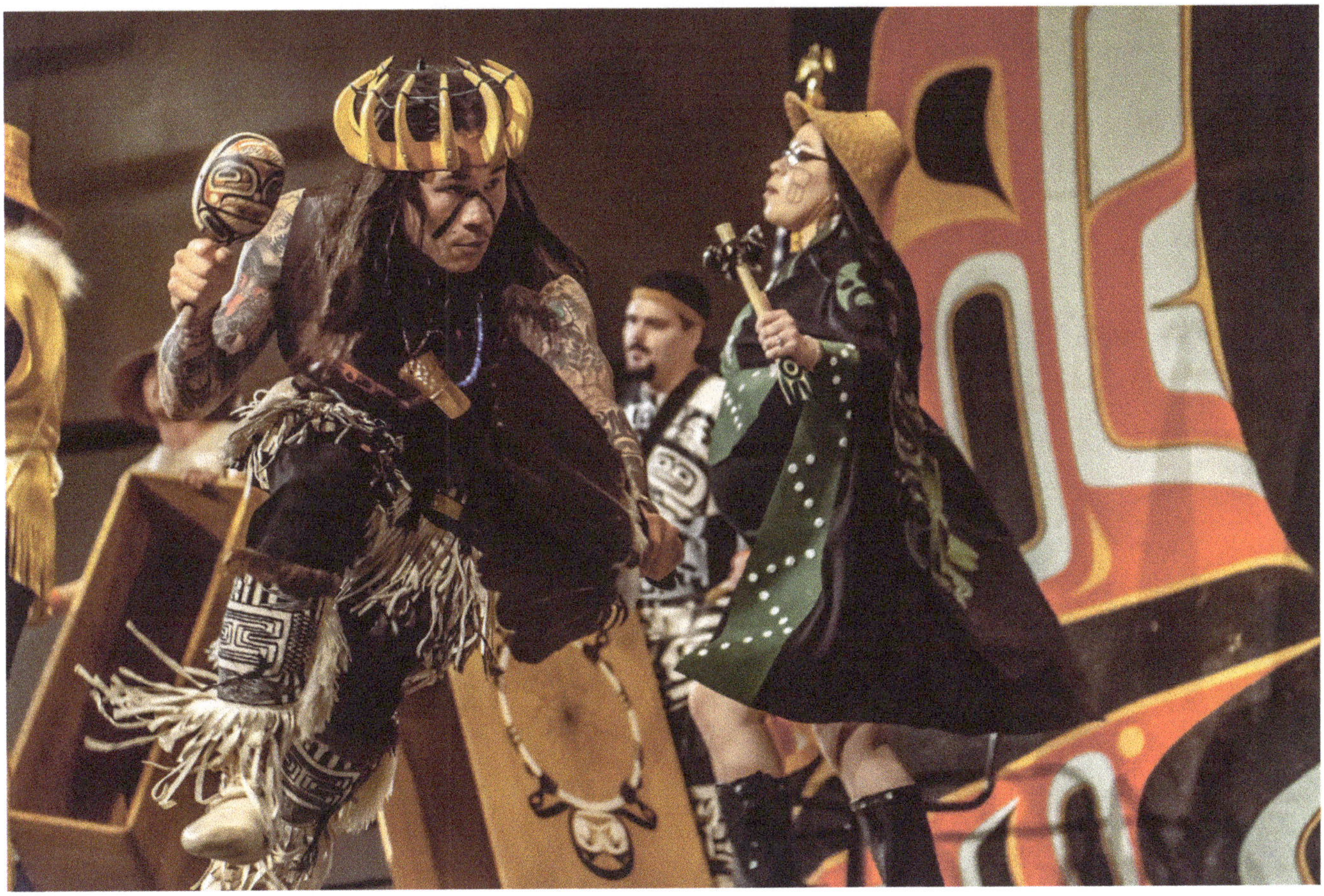

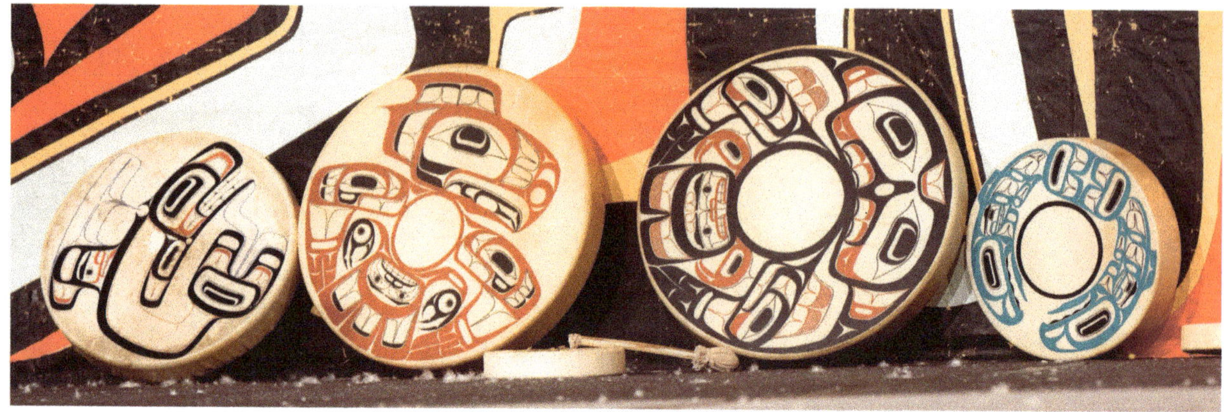

connected to my museum research.

These masks provide a solid connection to our past. If you look in natural history museums all over the world, they are chock full of the kinds of masks we use. One year, we were performing at the Smithsonian's National Museum of the American Indian in New York City where there was also an exhibit of masks and regalia. We were able to tell the school groups who were watching us, "Go to that exhibit and look. This is a living culture. It's not just in a case on a shelf." They could see us using the masks.

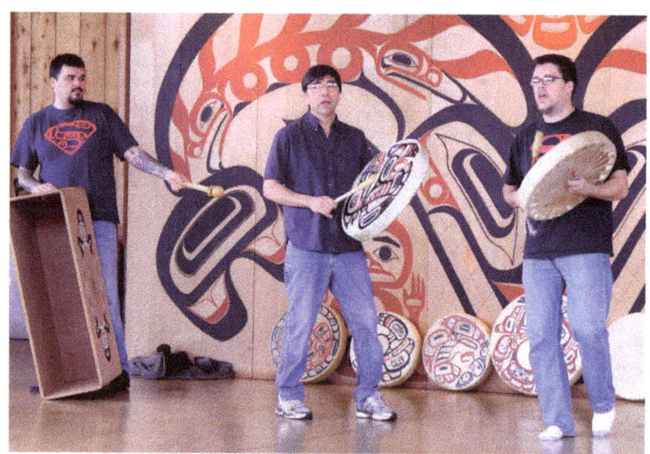

Robert Davidson once said, "The art is a reflection of the culture; it's helped bring back the culture. The song and the dance validate the art."

People say you can feel our performances in your body and soul. It's also a lot of hard work. That's why it's a proud thing for me to stand up there, especially with my boys, my wife, and her family standing next to me. It's a celebration every time we get together. Especially when Davey is here. He likes to have fun, but he wants us to be as sharp and as good as we can be.

I'm the authoritarian. I want people to have a good time, but I want them to make sure, when the drums start and we are in our regalia and there's an audience, we are all business. Cindy would tease me during our rehearsals. She would say, "God, you sure are bossy. Sometimes, I wish you weren't a basketball coach. But maybe that's why we're so good." I miss her.

I really don't know how much longer I'll lead this group. It's a lot of work hauling all of our regalia around, making rehearsals and traveling. It's also expensive. I have told Michelle on a number of occasions that I'm tired and I feel like I've done a lot and it may be time to step down. She says, "No, you're not tired. I don't believe you." I'm fortunate my health is good. I'm physically able to still do things. I figure I have ten more years. Watching these grandkids grow makes me want to live till ninety. Sage would be twenty-five then. If I haven't done it already by then—and I'm sure it's possible—I'll turn the group over to him. ❖

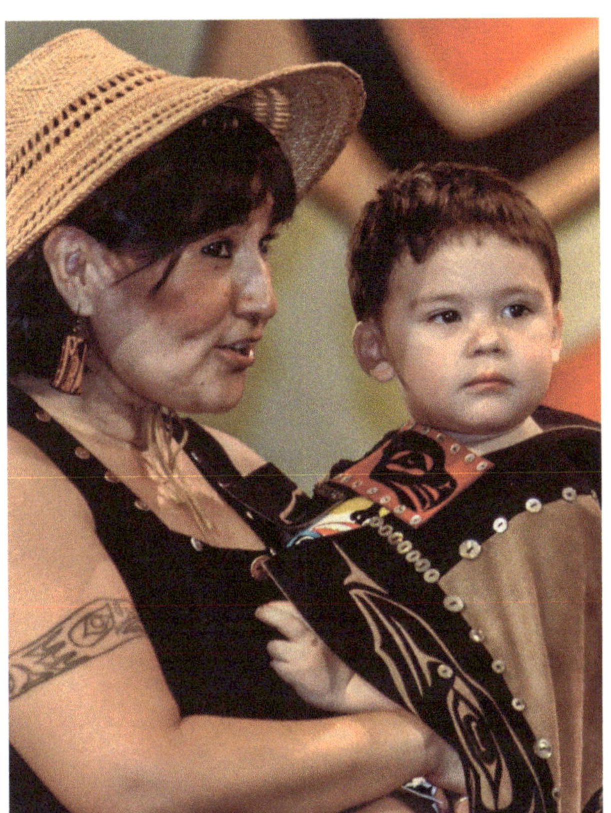

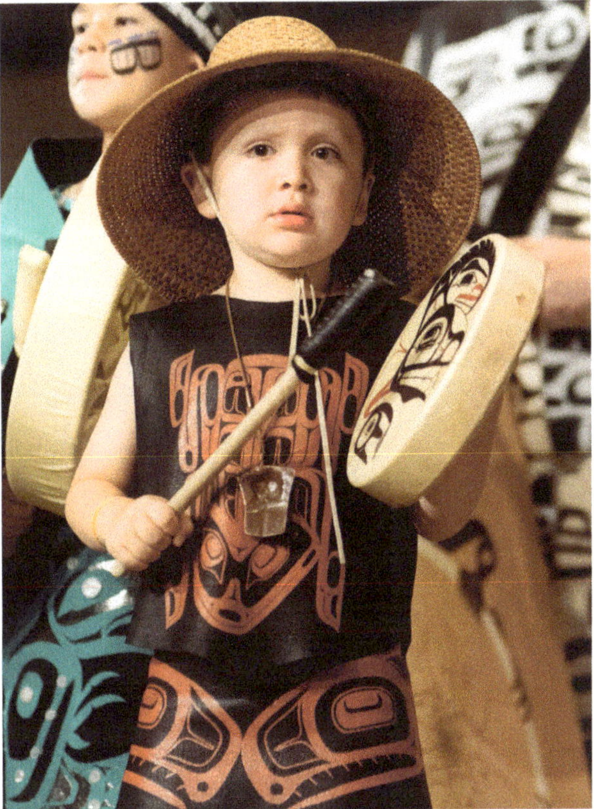

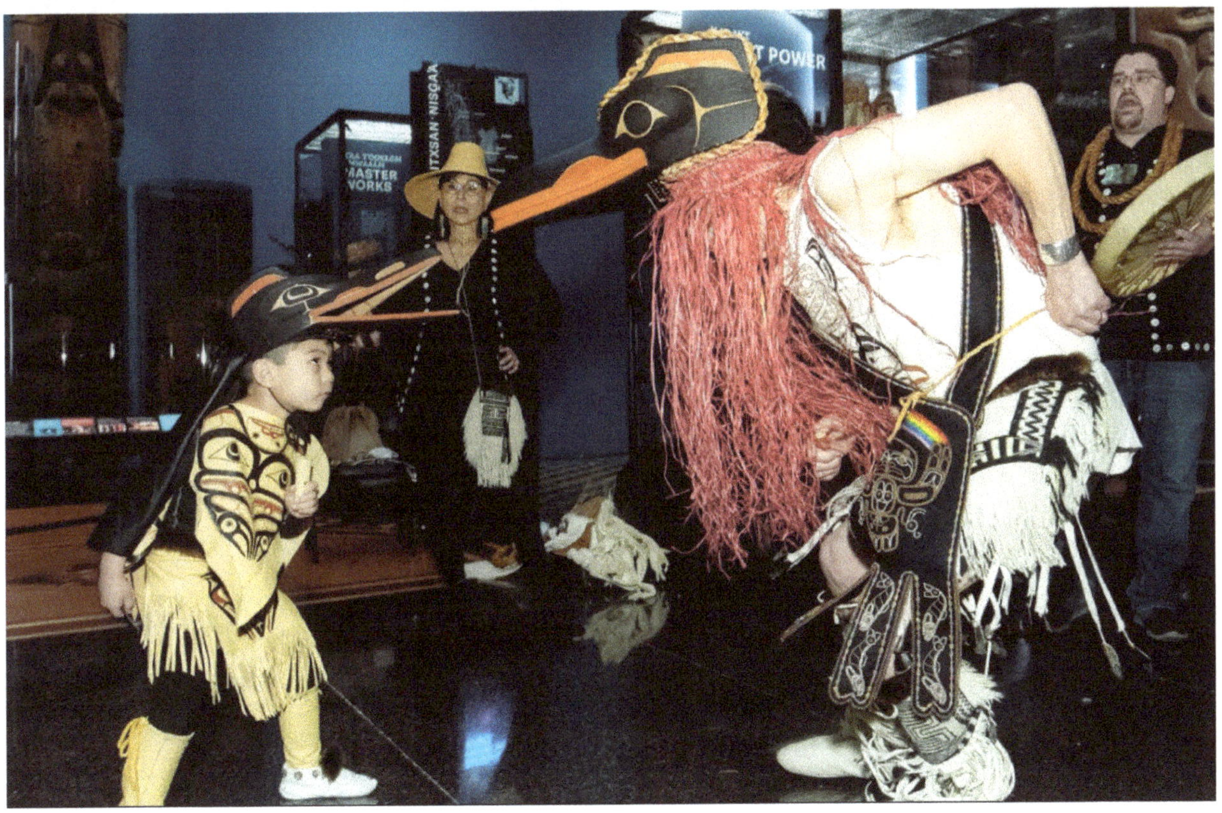

Git Hoan *at* The National Museum of the American Indian

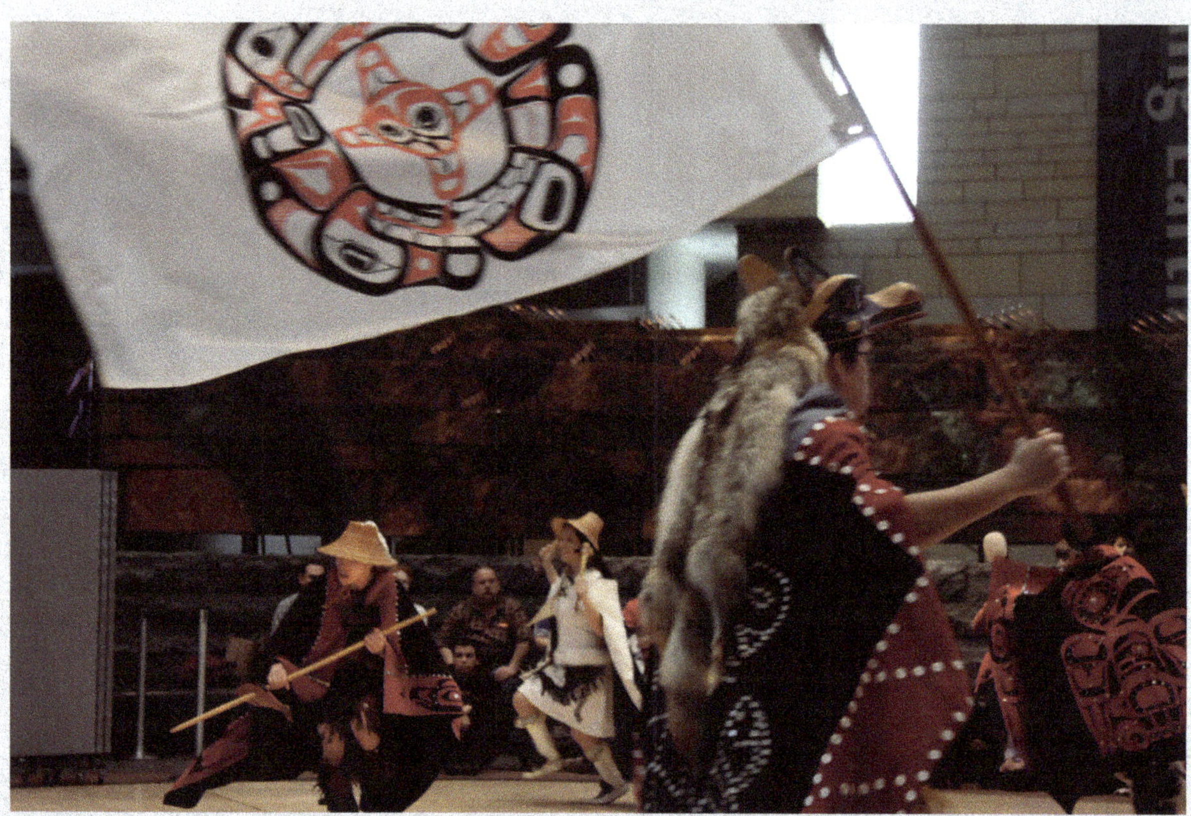

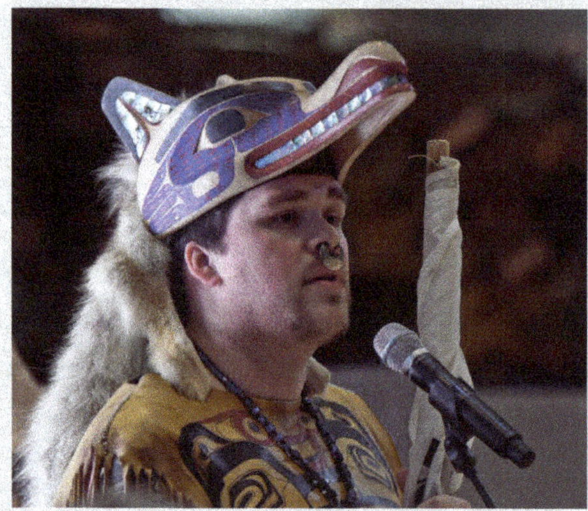

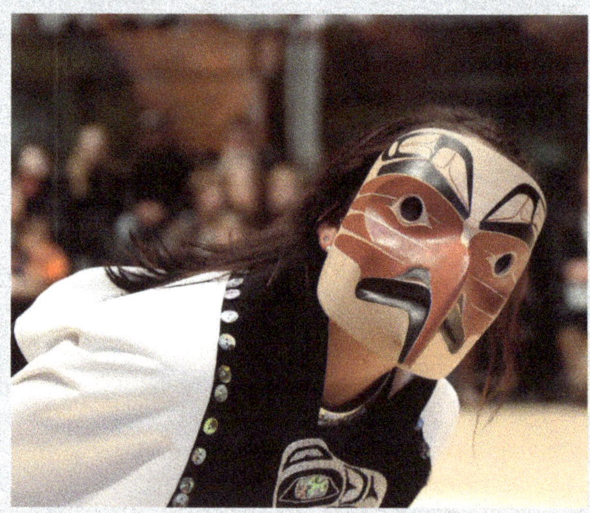

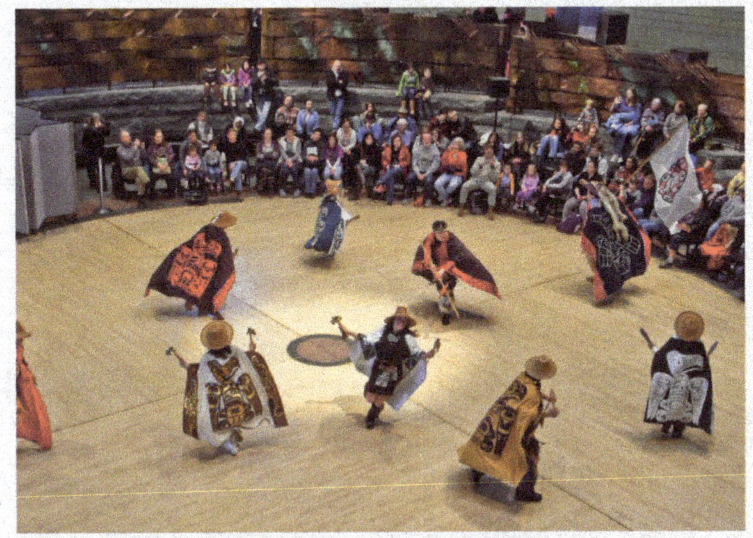
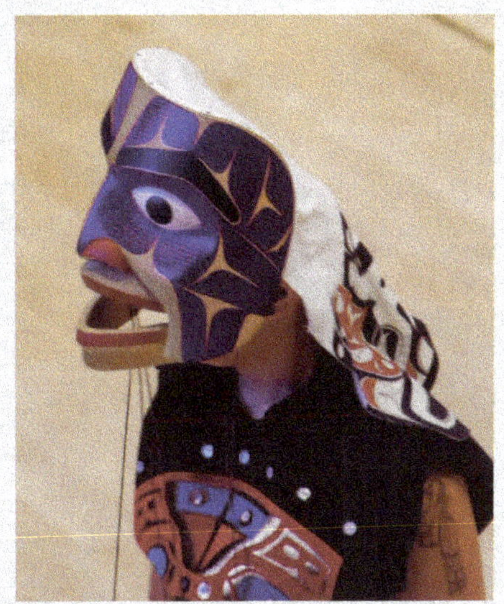
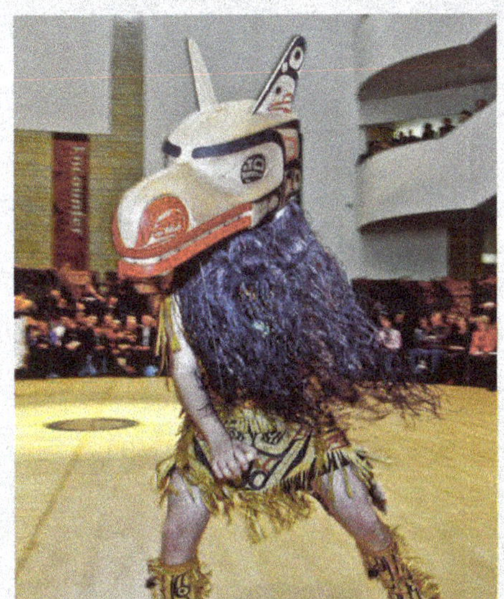
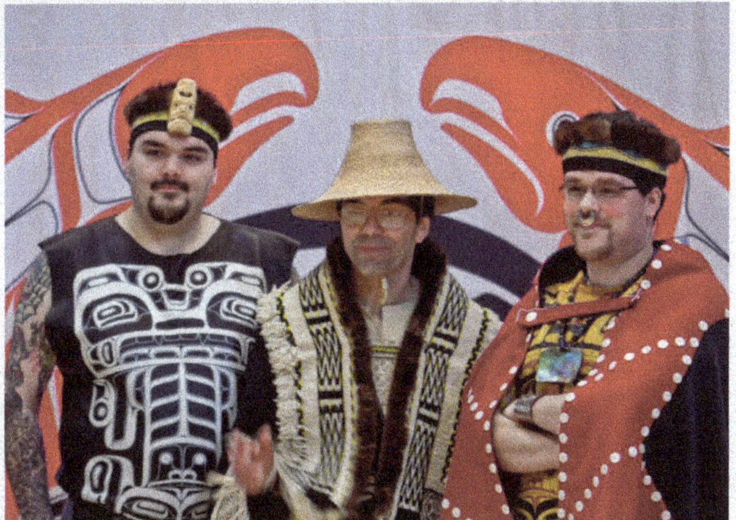
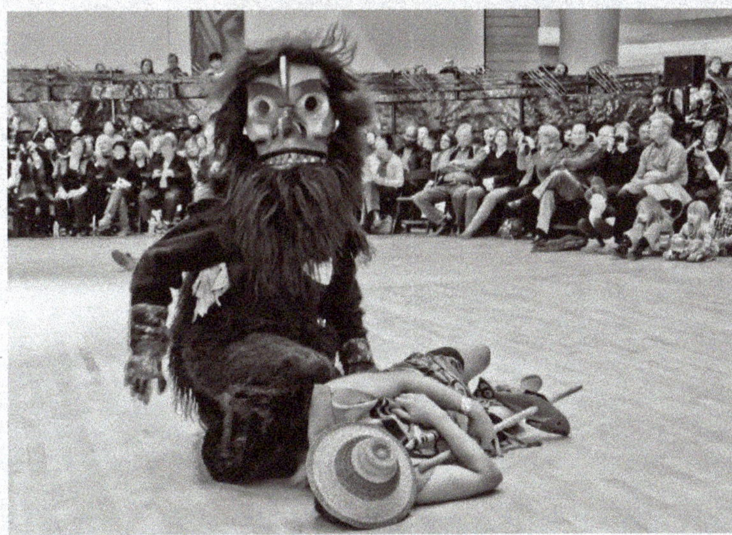
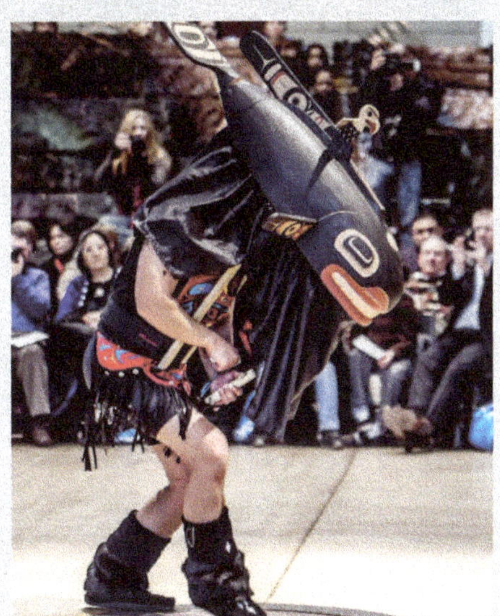

Git Hoan *at* Celebration 2016

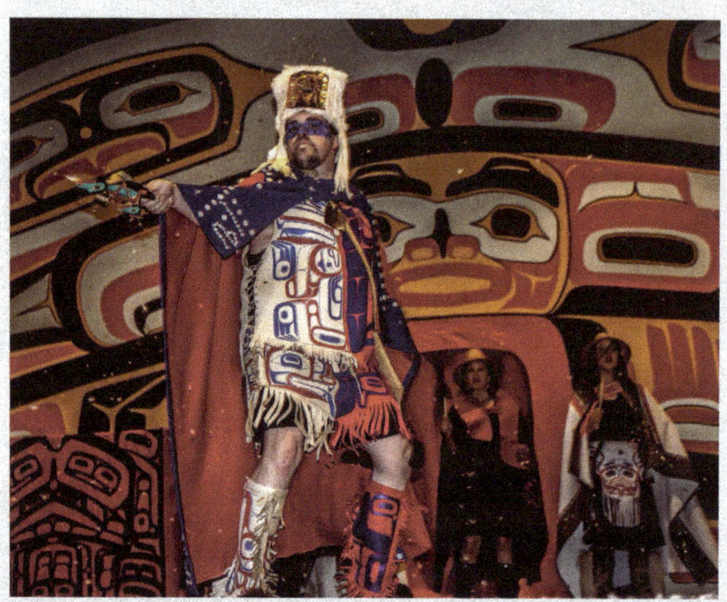

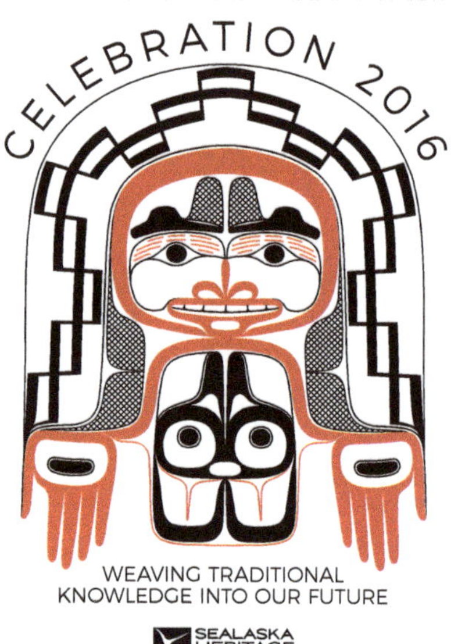

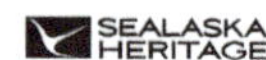

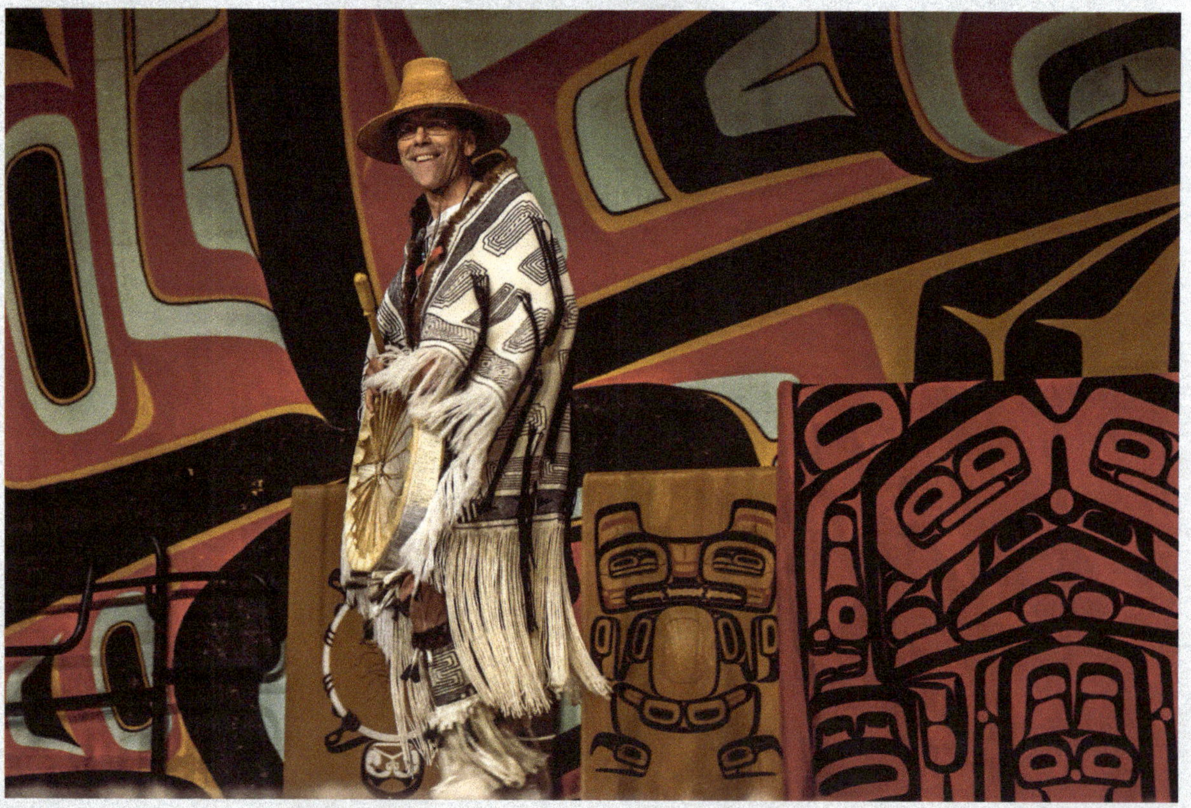

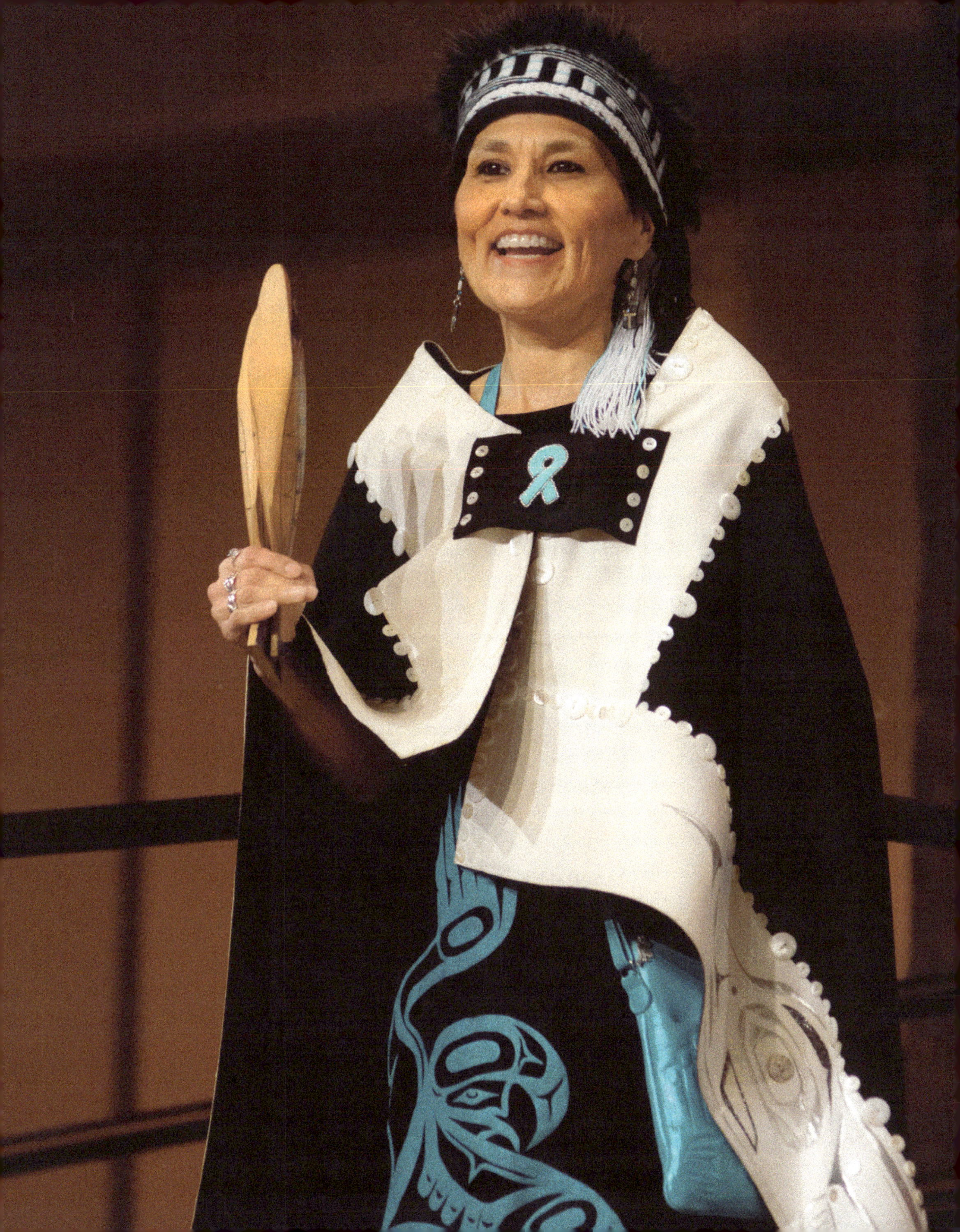

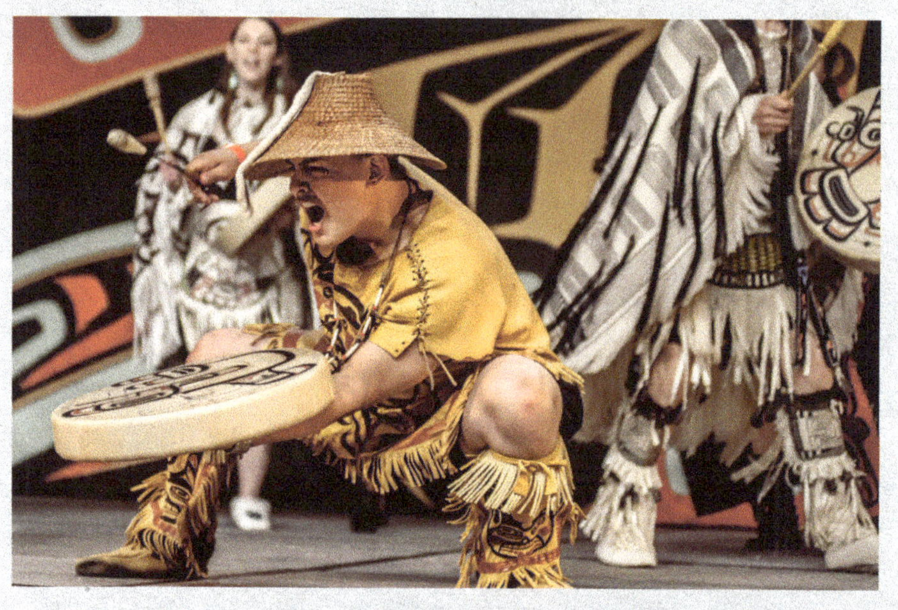

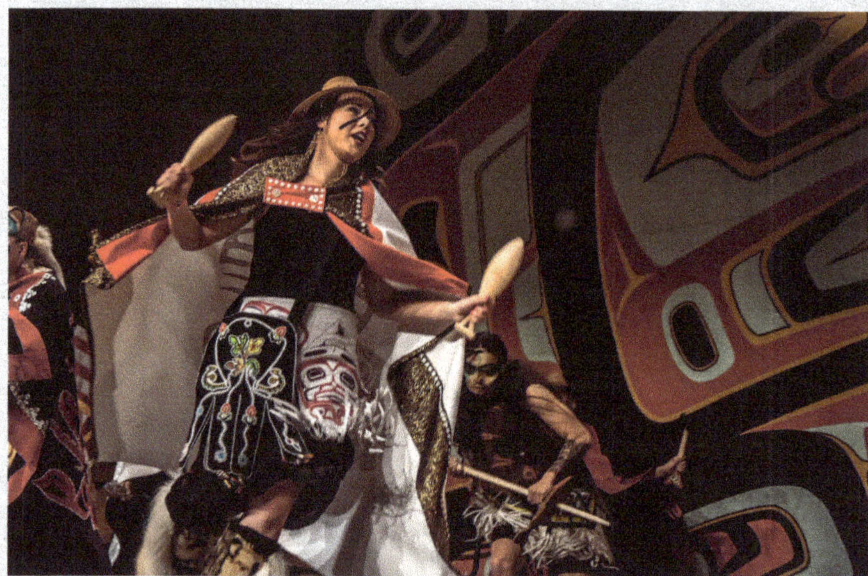

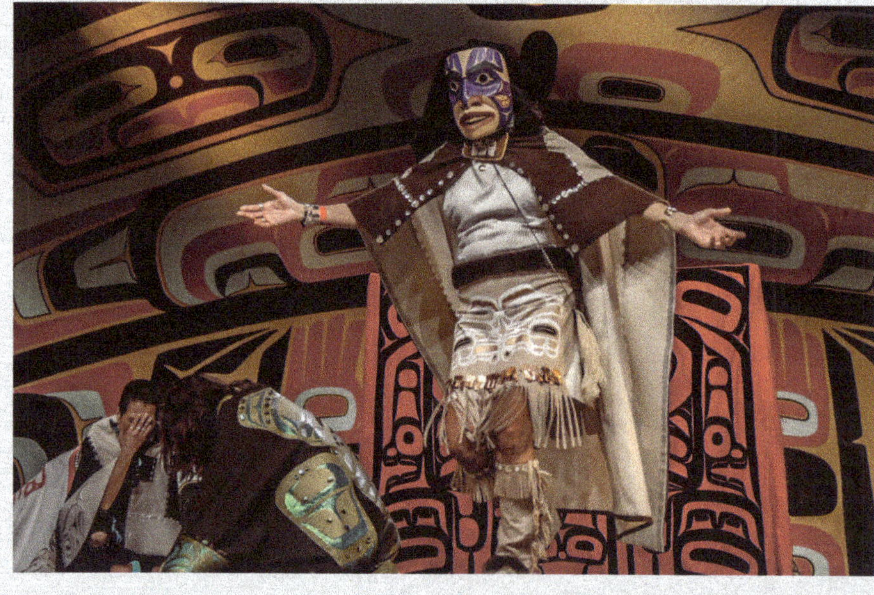

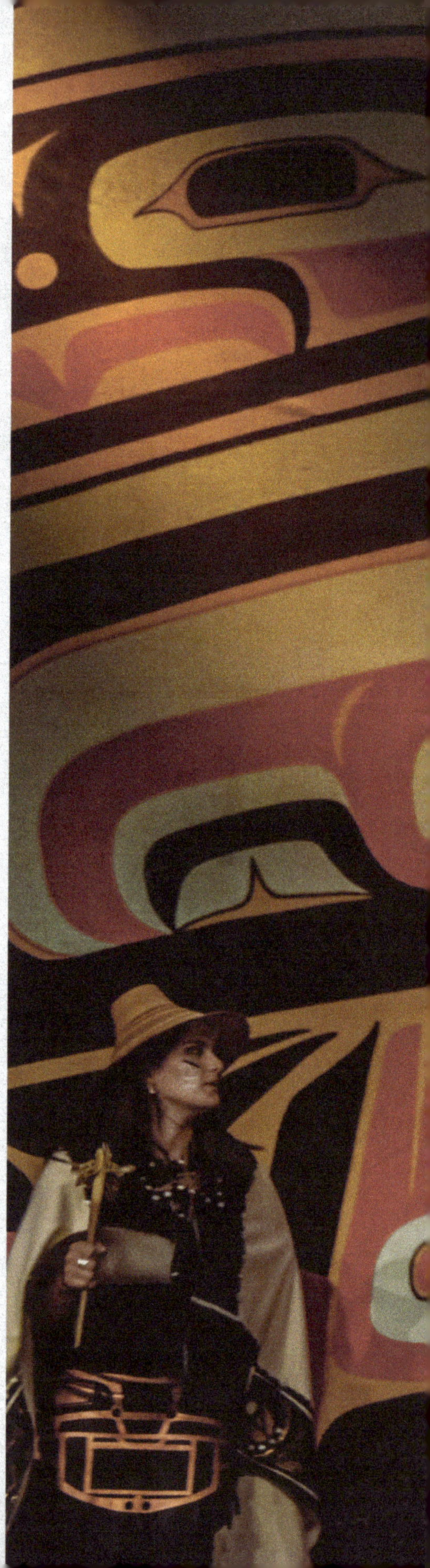

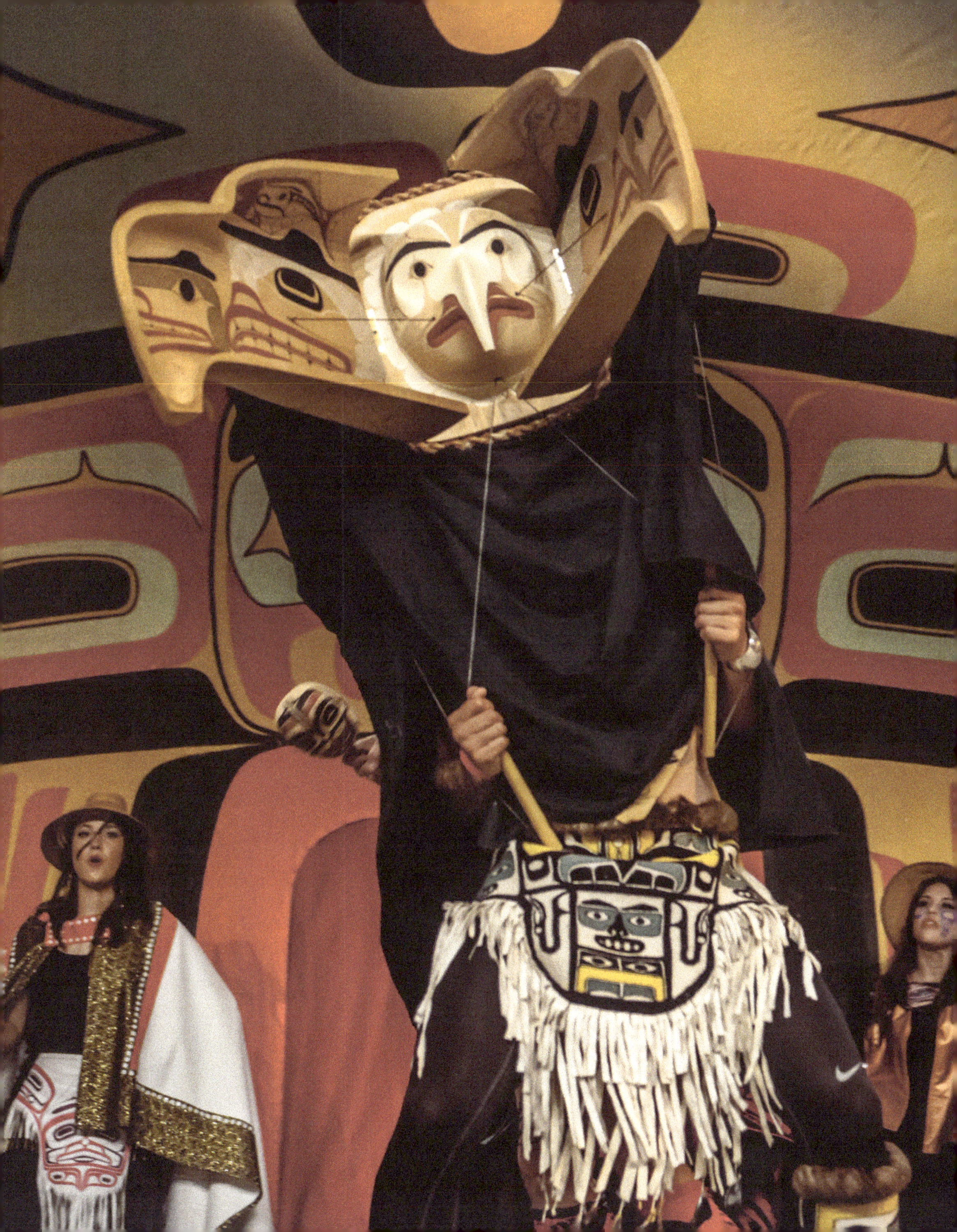

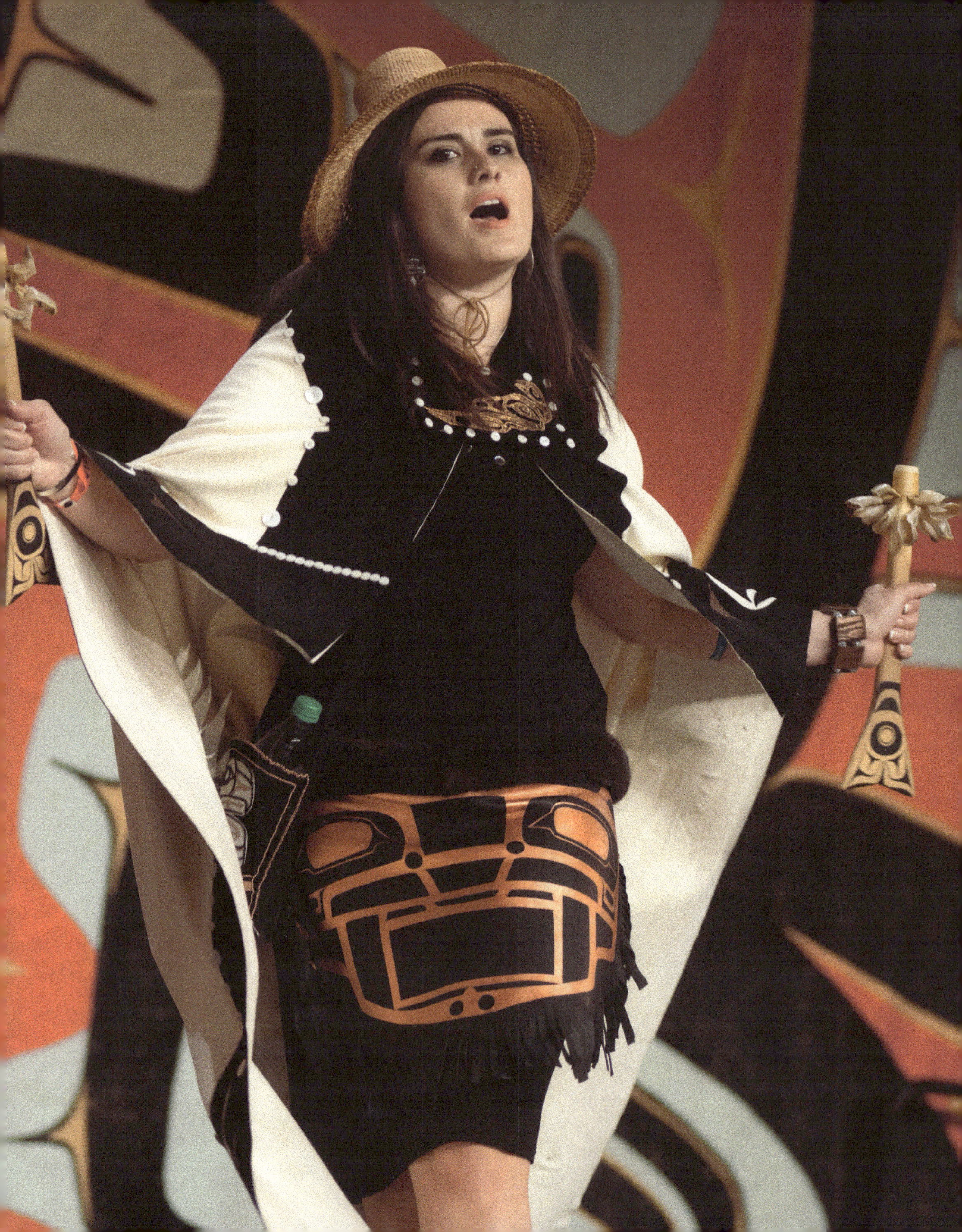

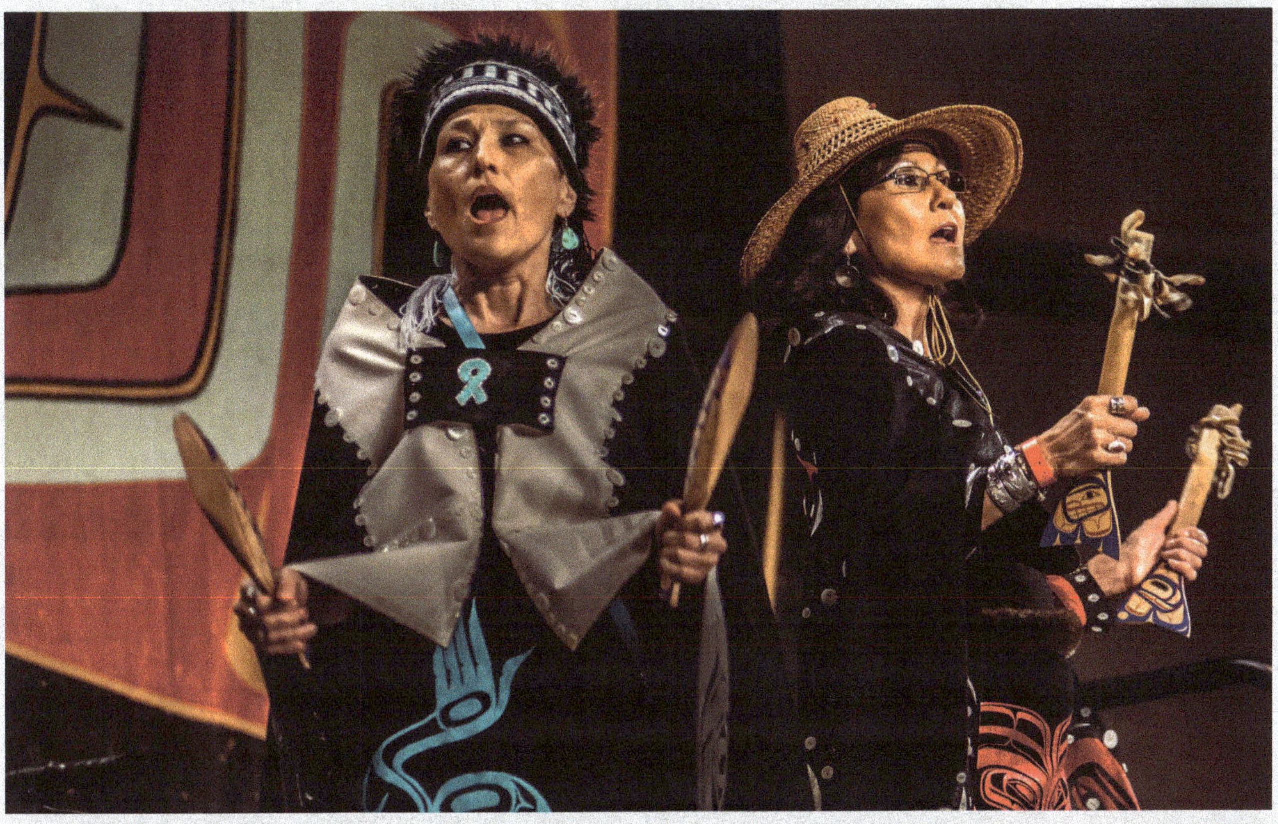

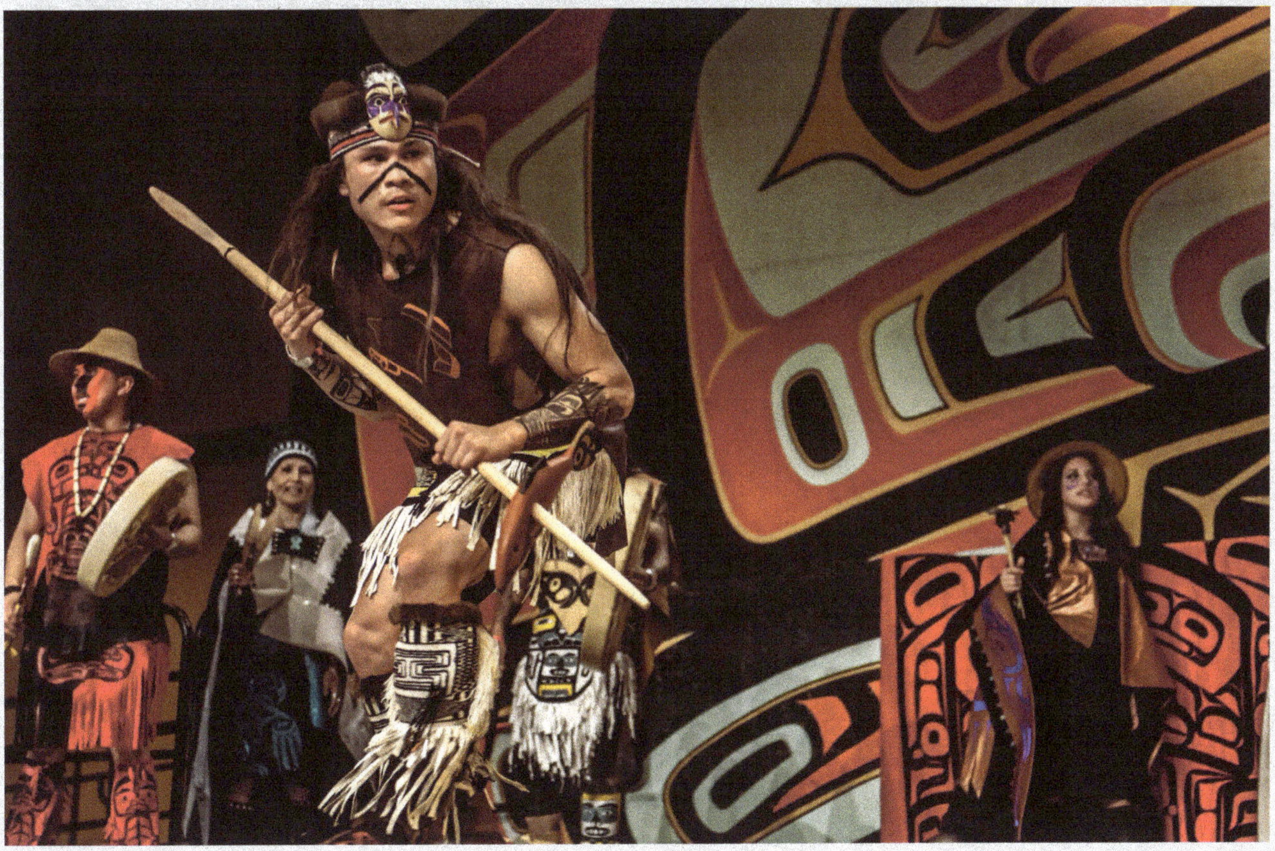

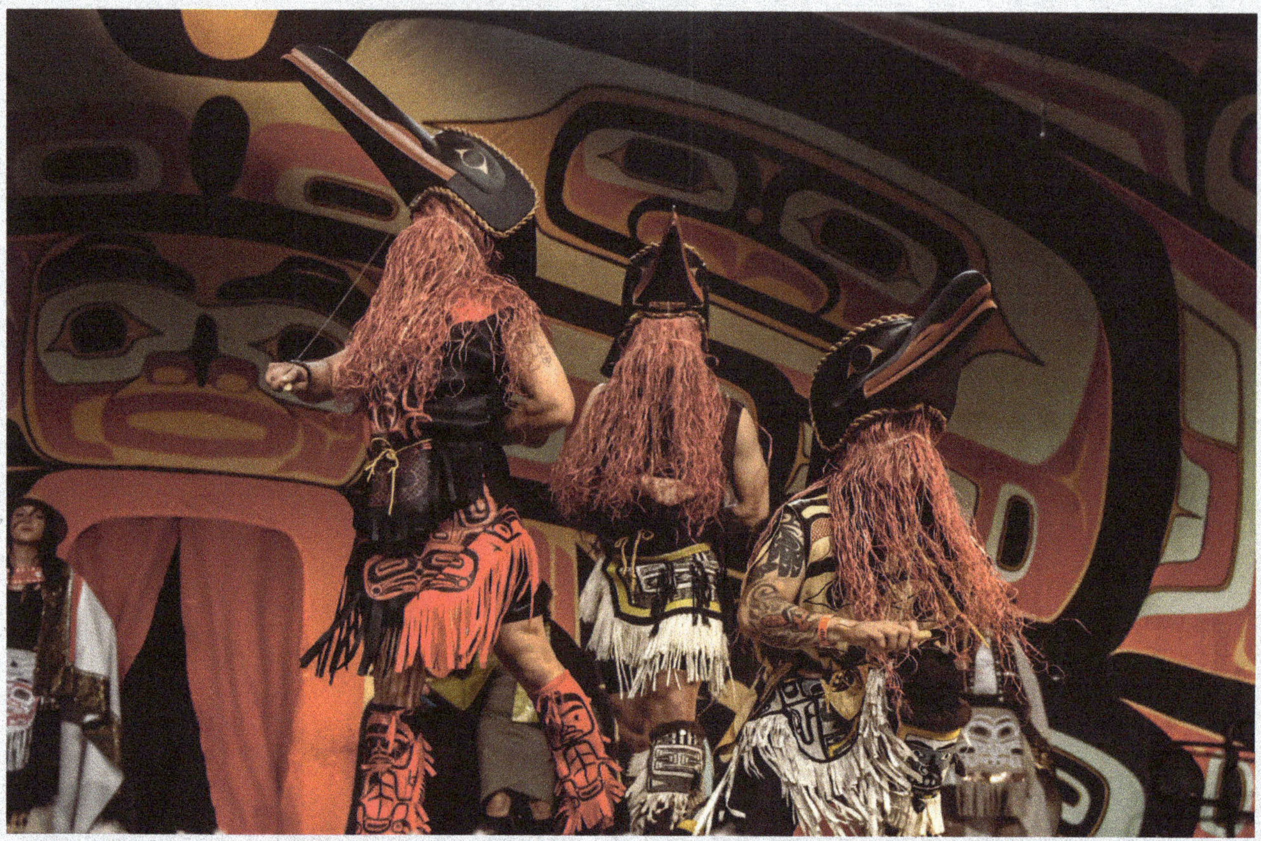

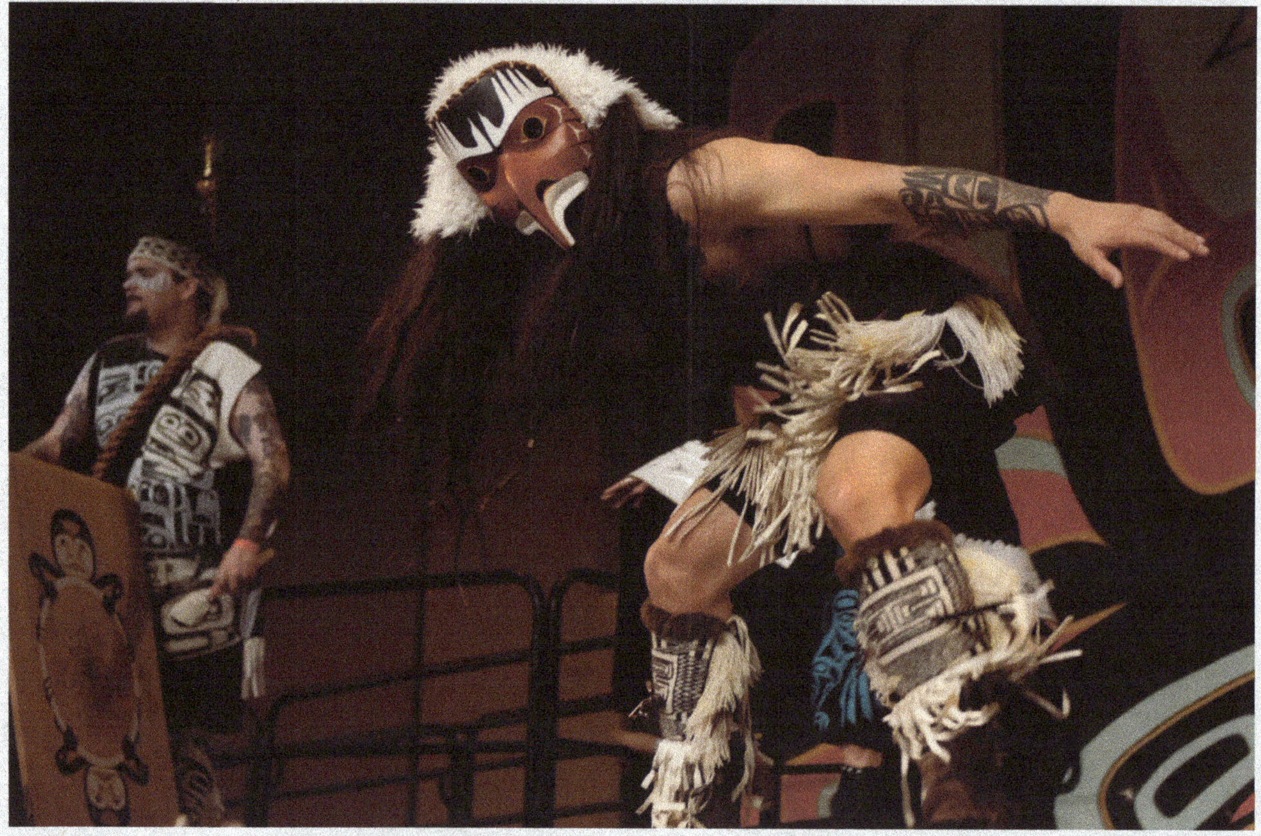

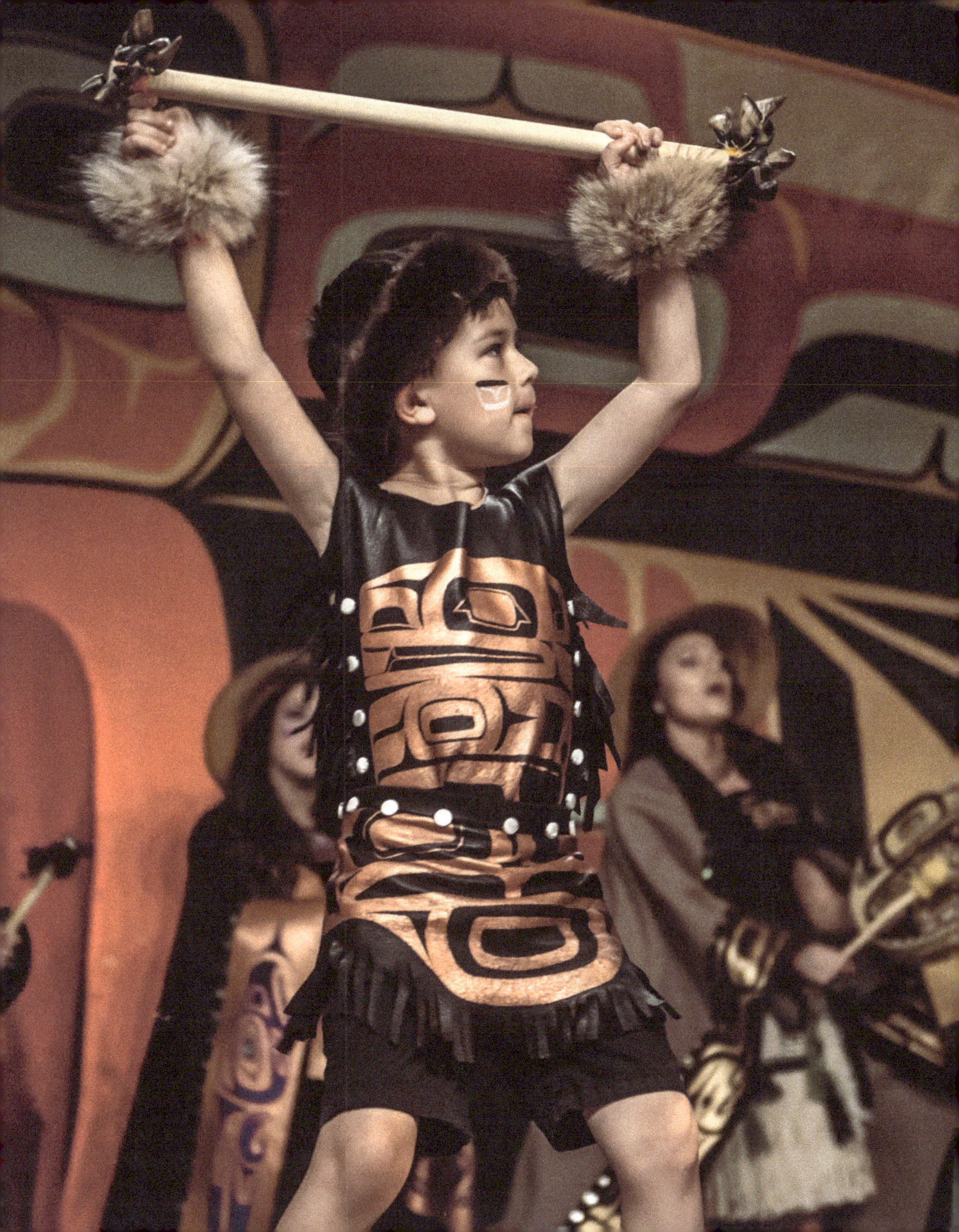

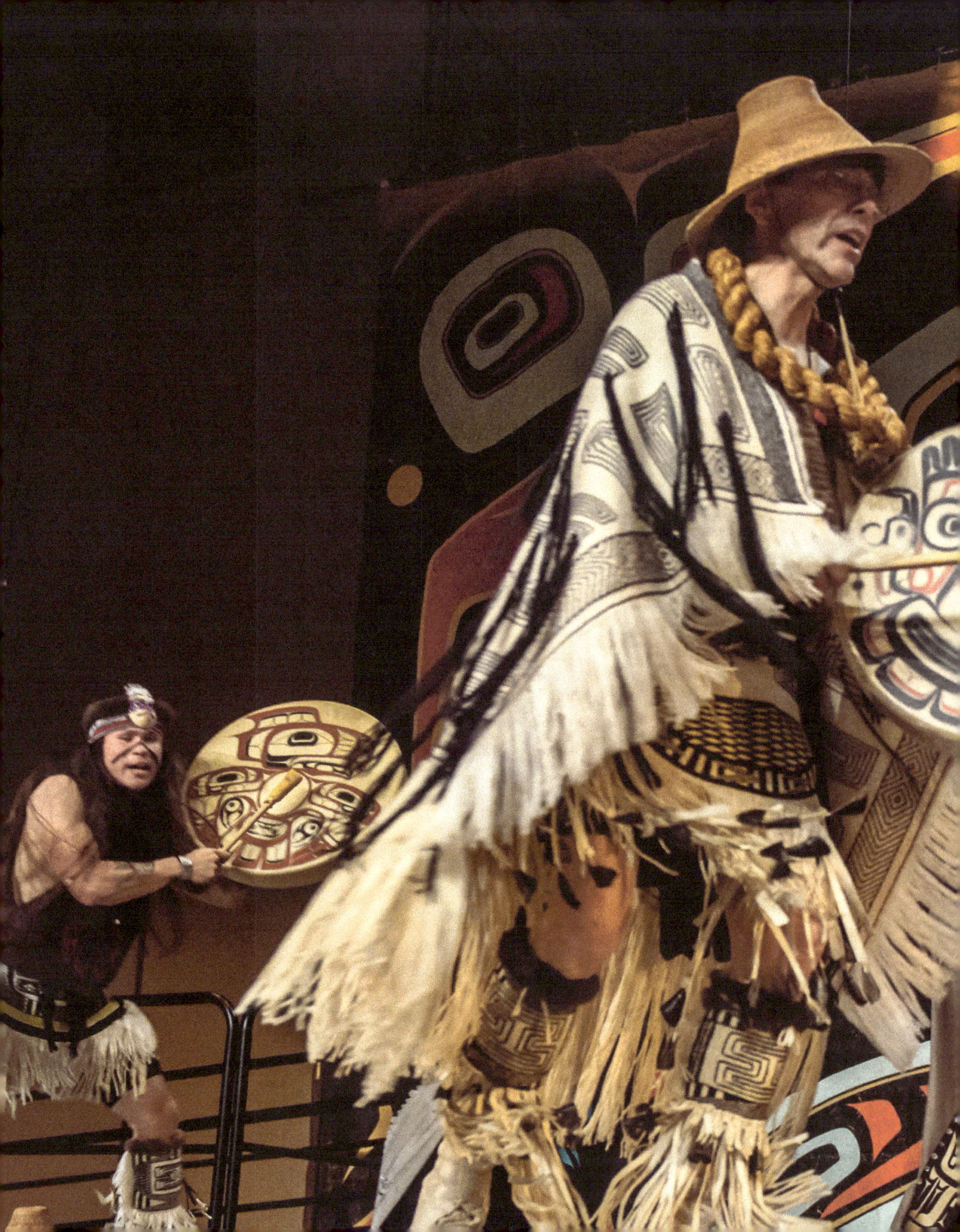

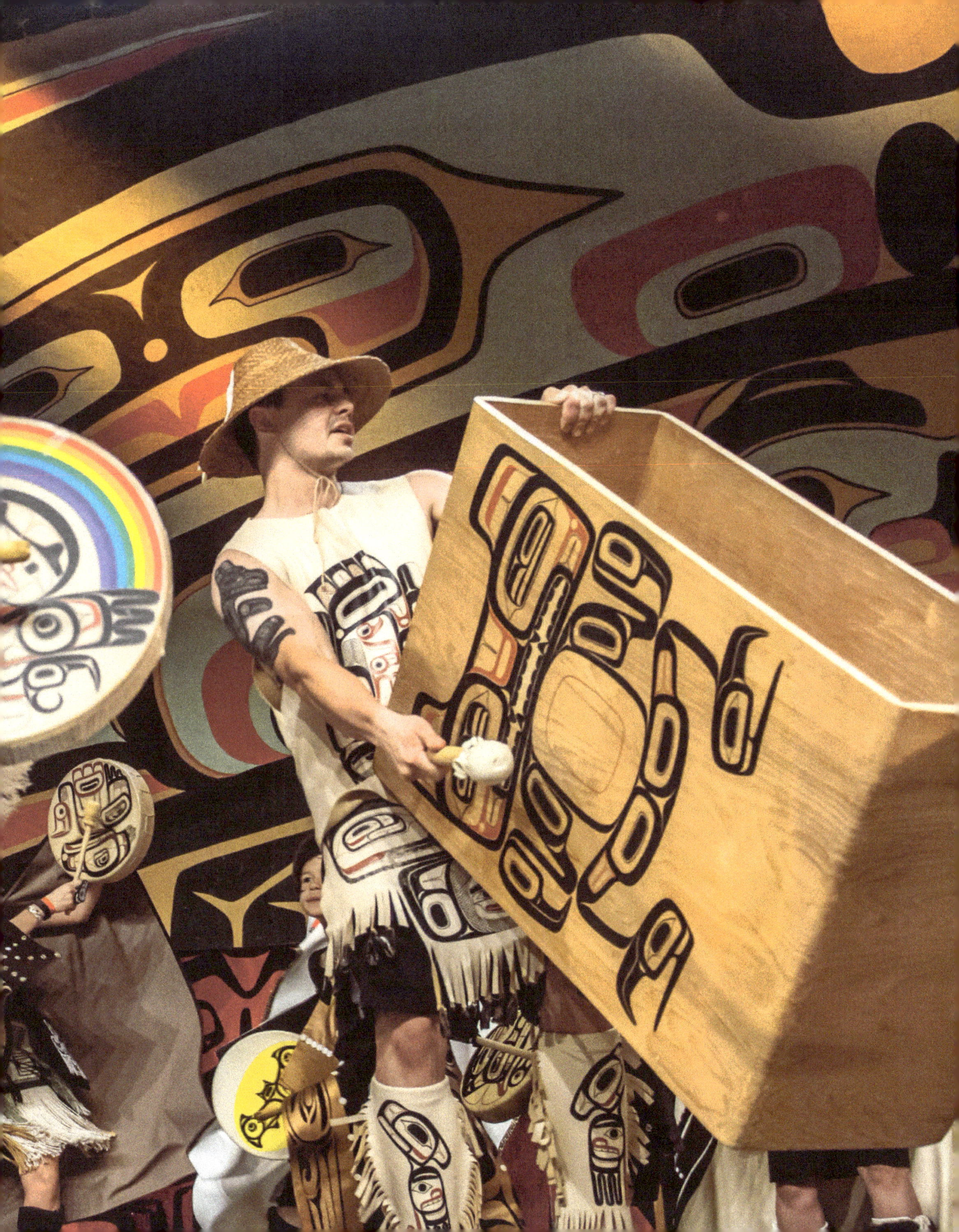

Git Hoan *in* Juneau

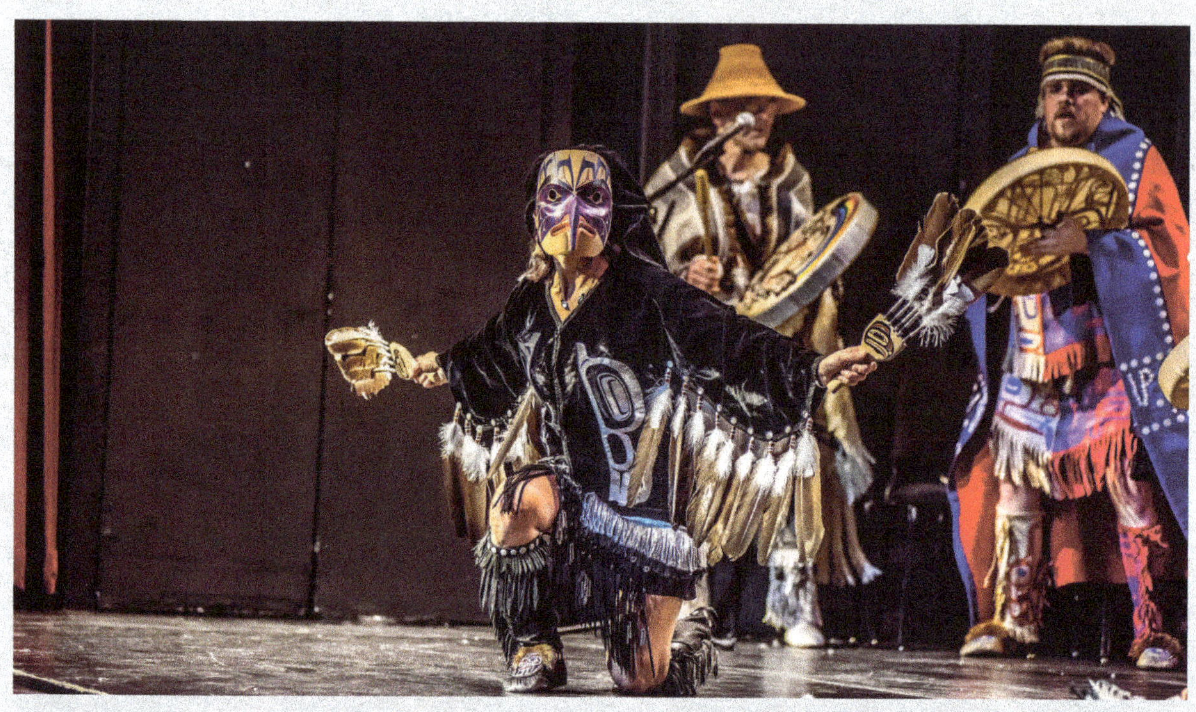

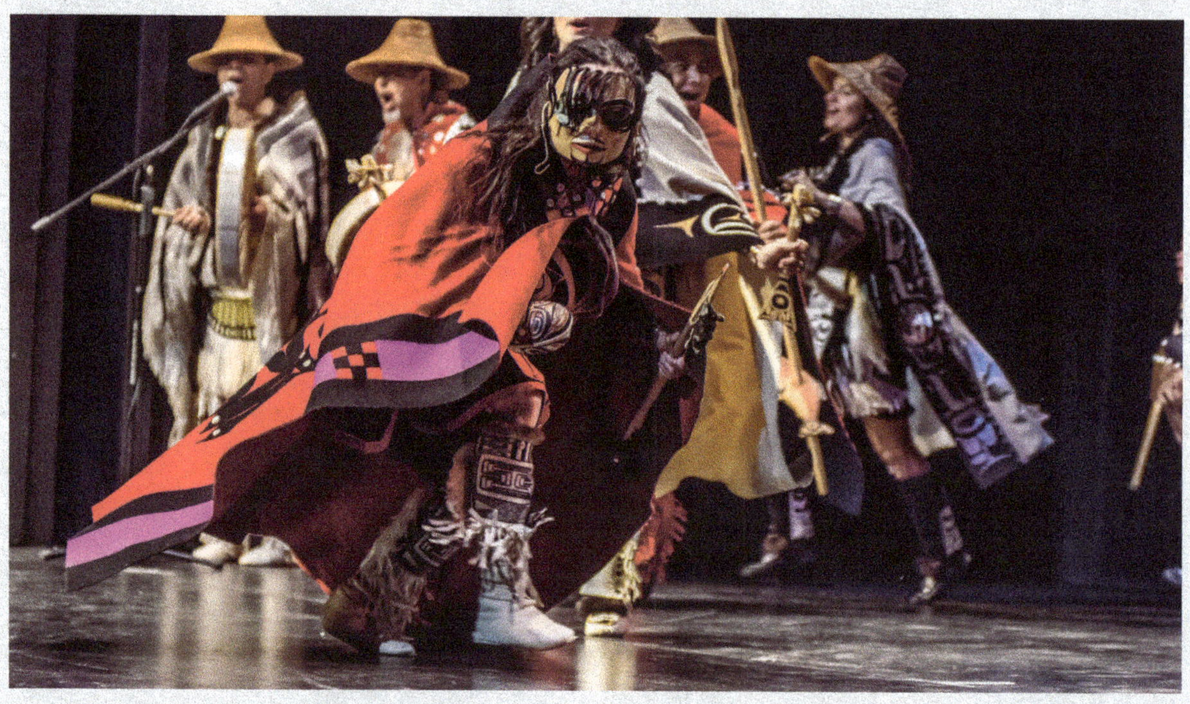

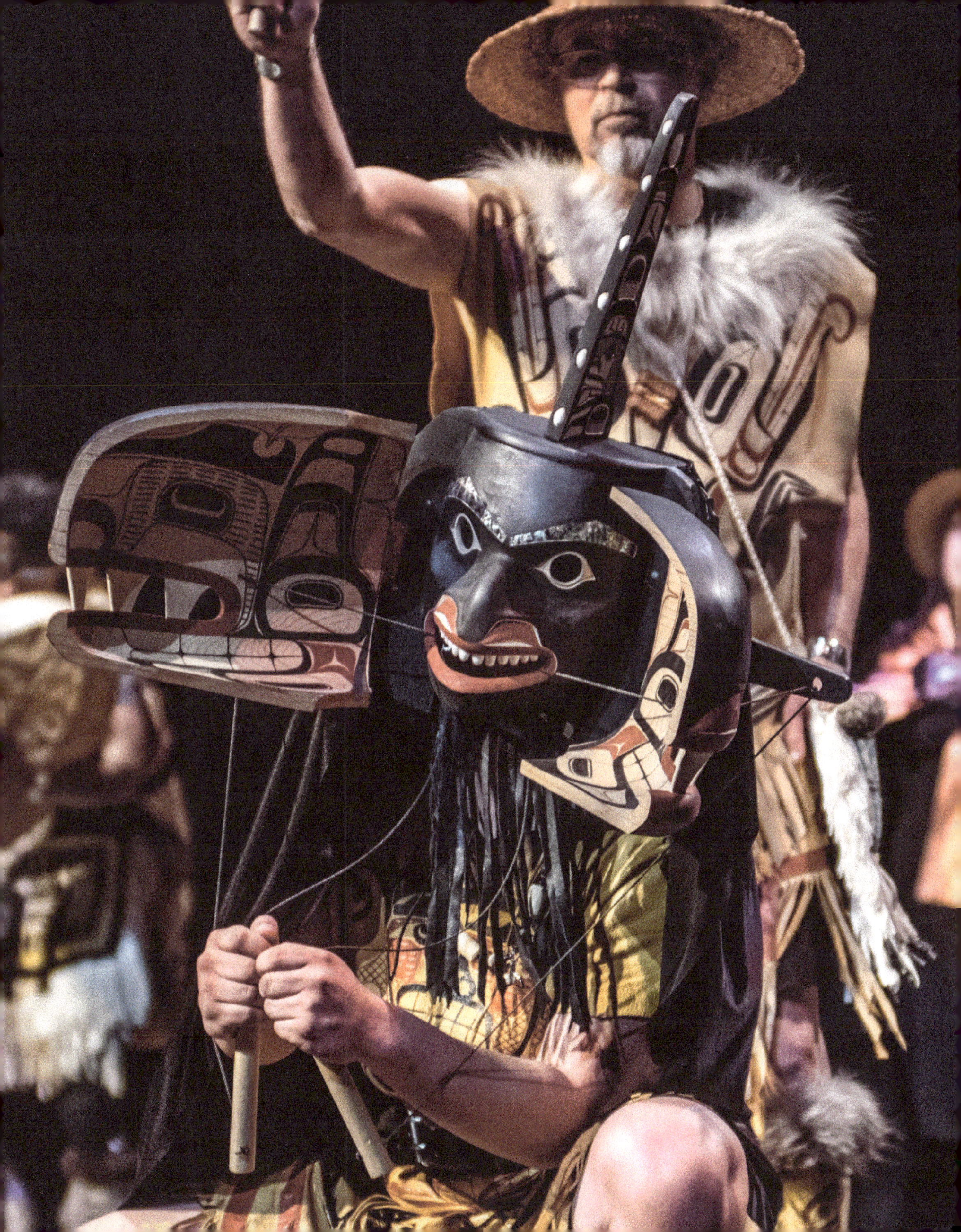

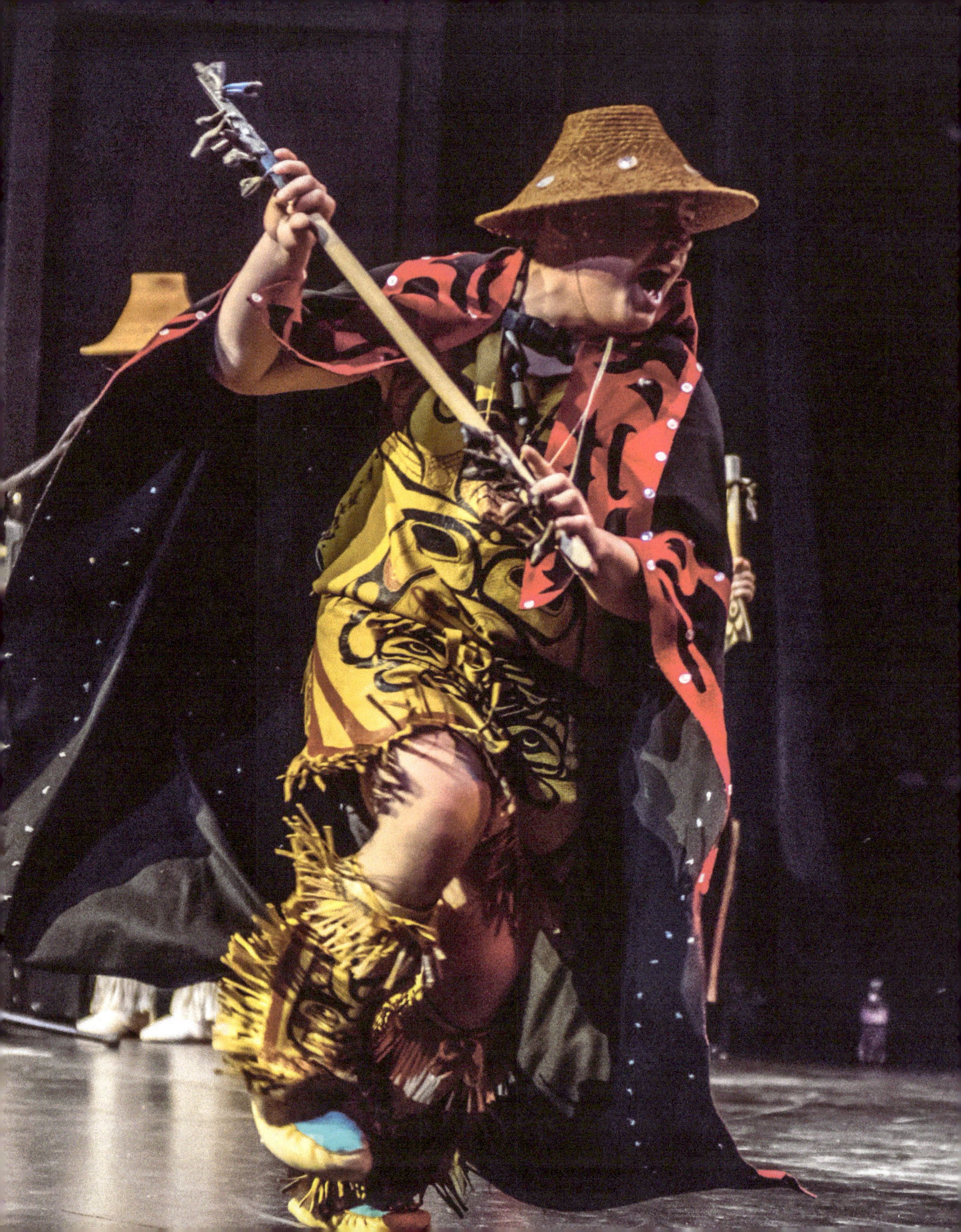

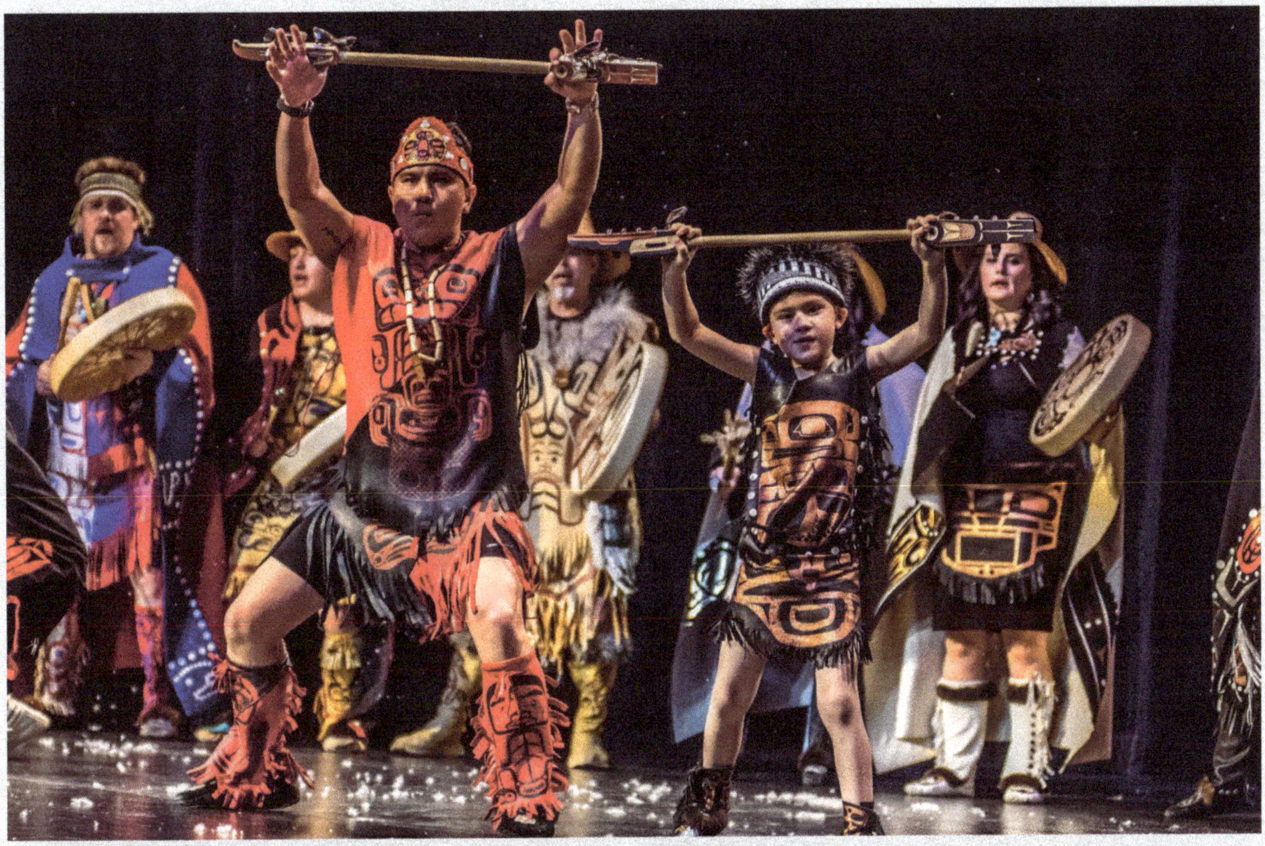

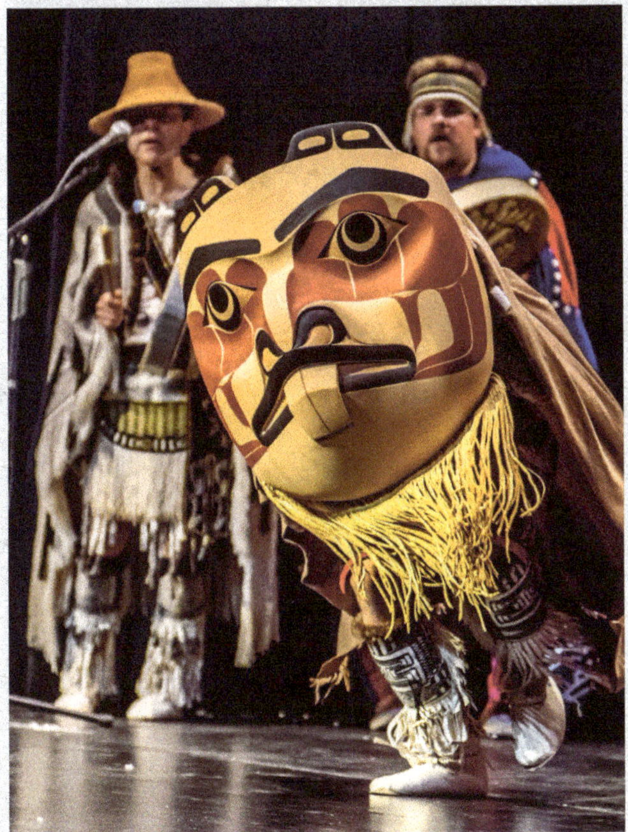

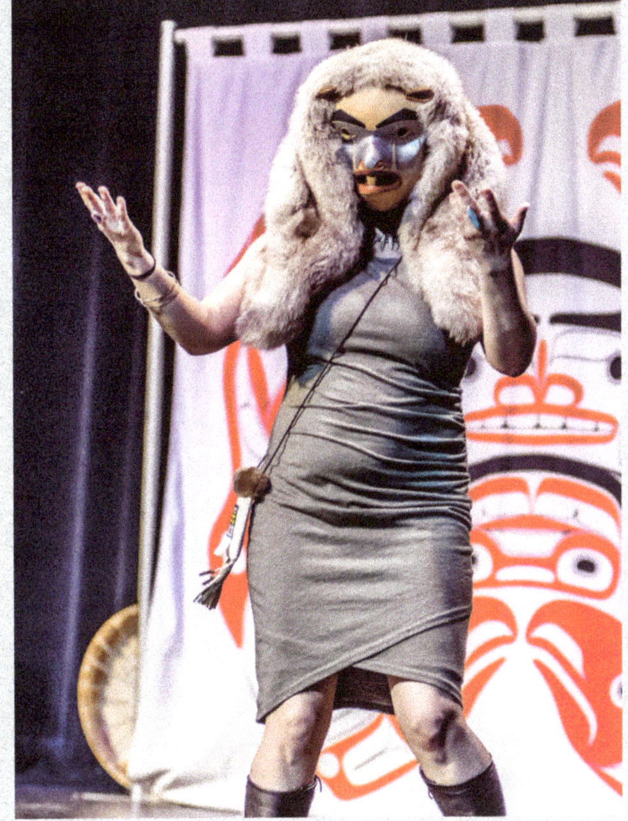

Git Hoan *at* Celebration 2018

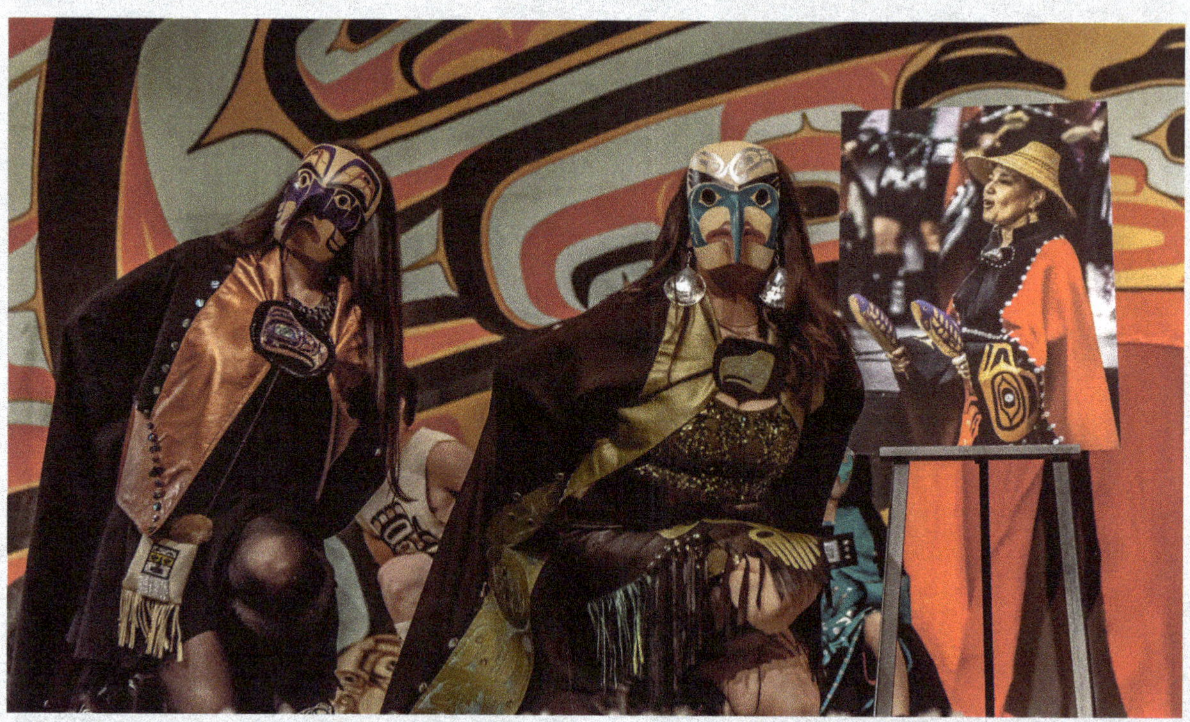

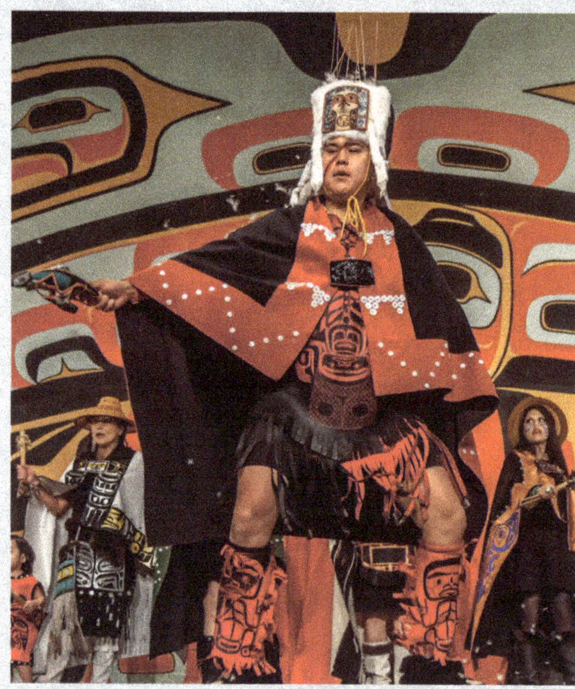

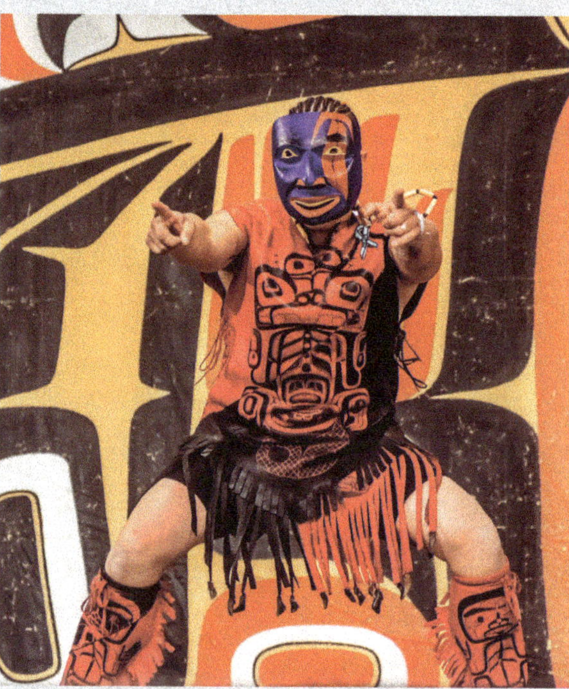

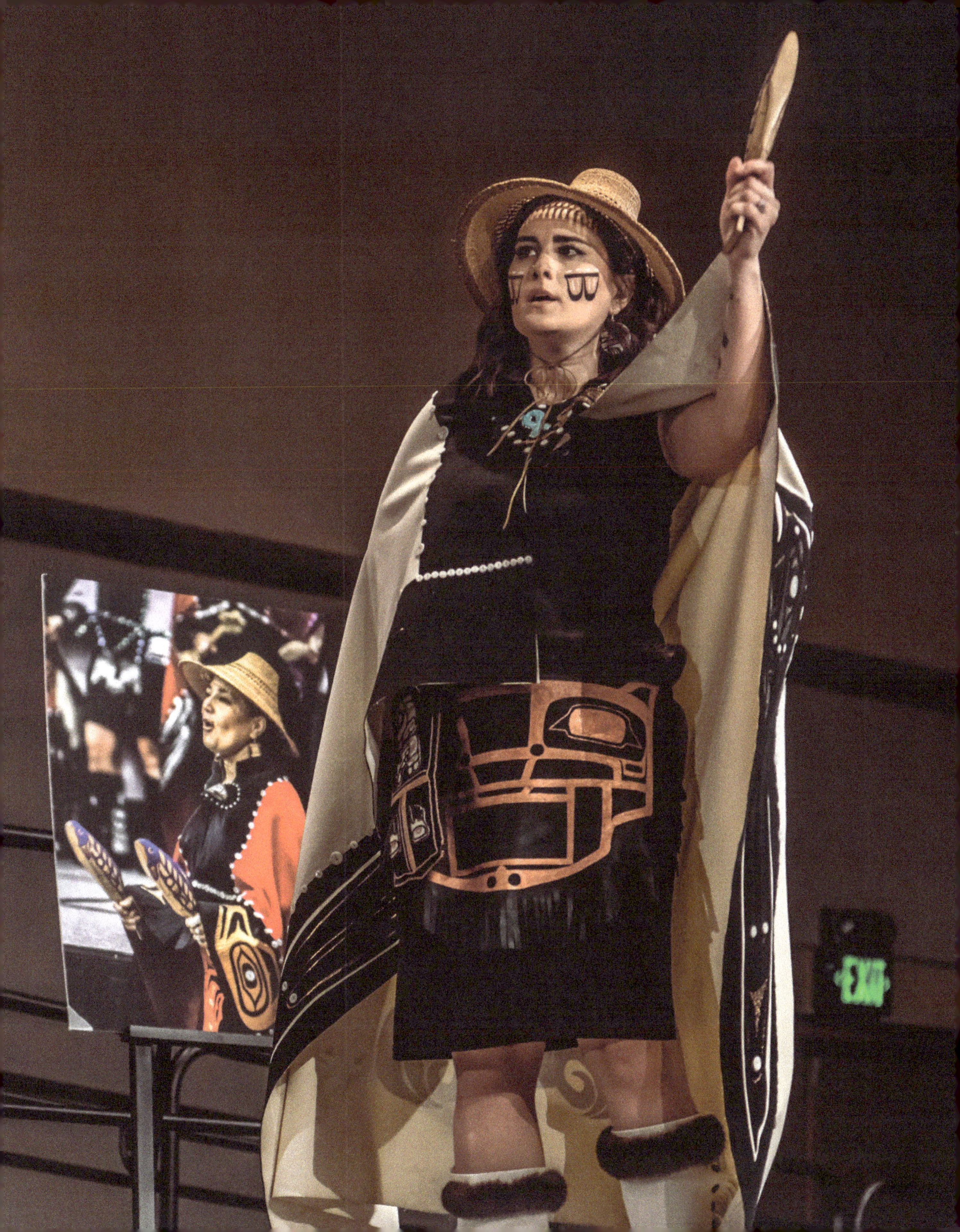

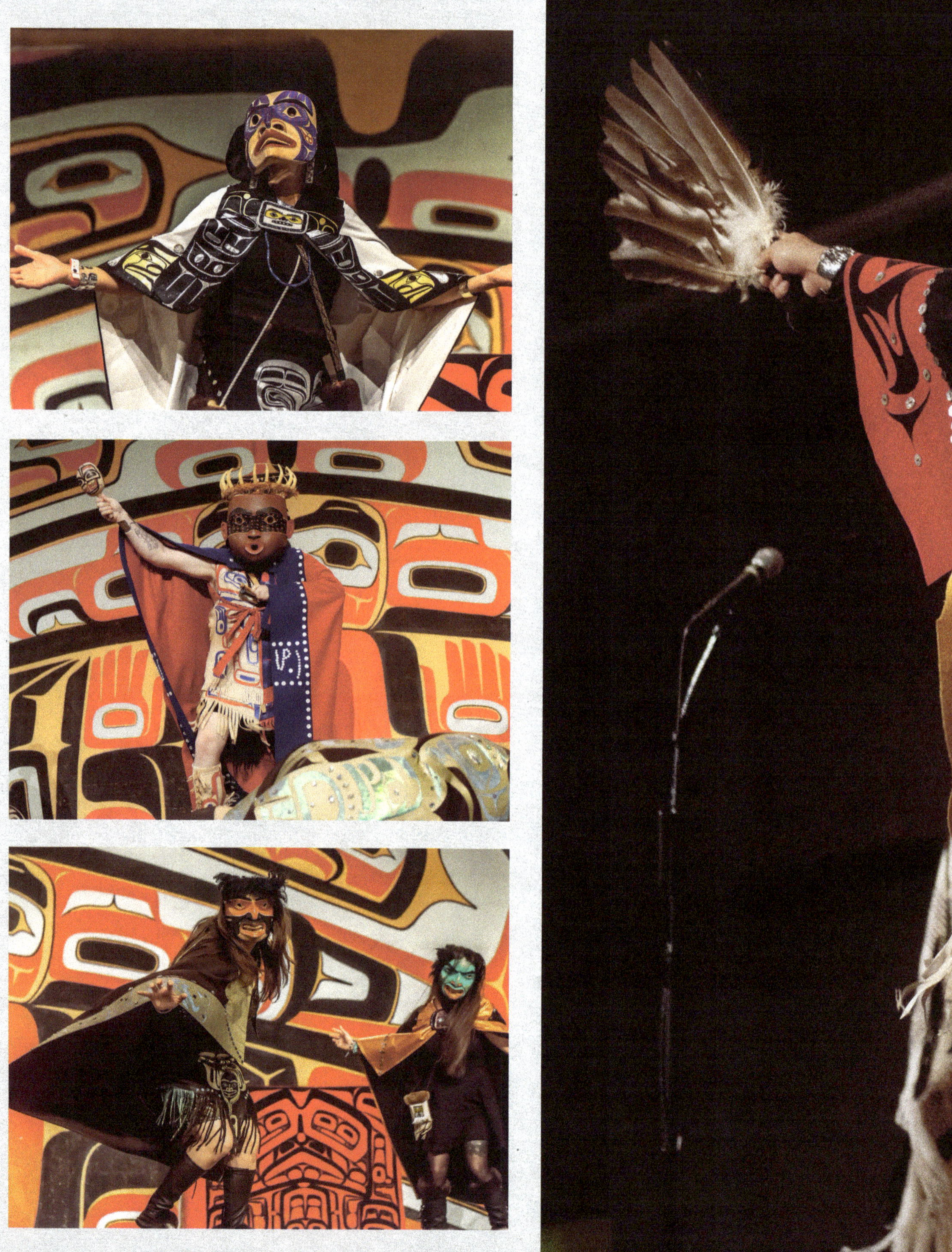

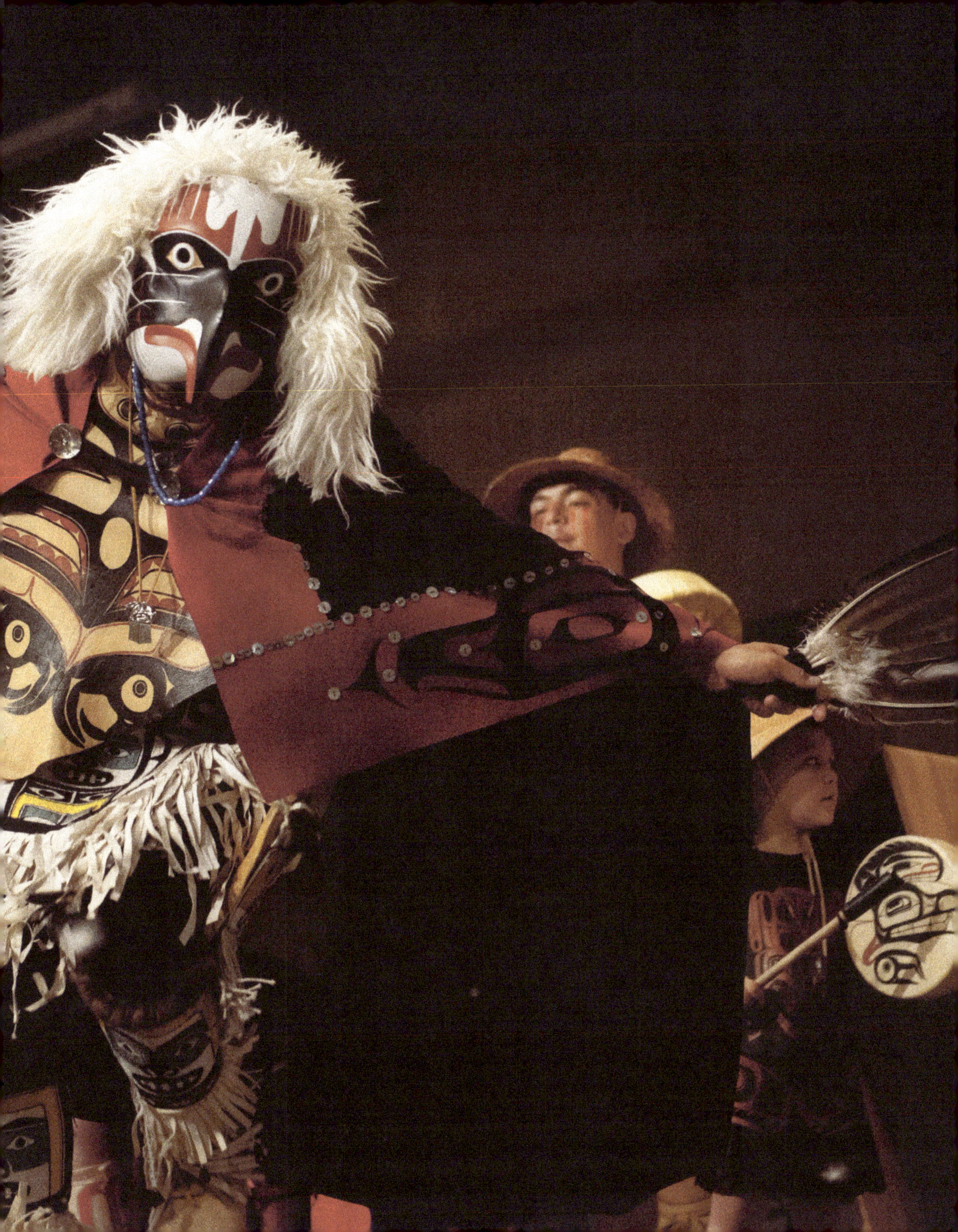

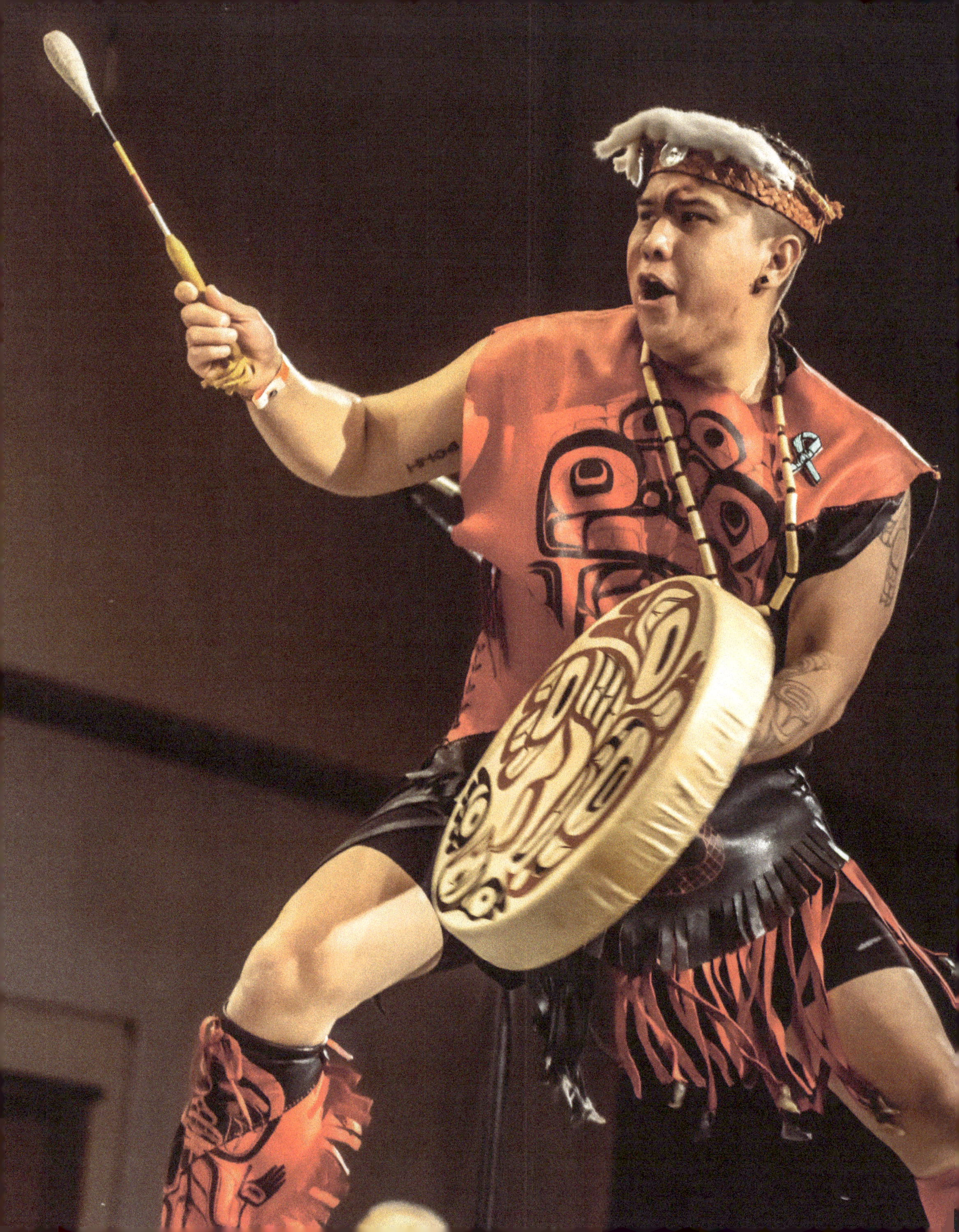

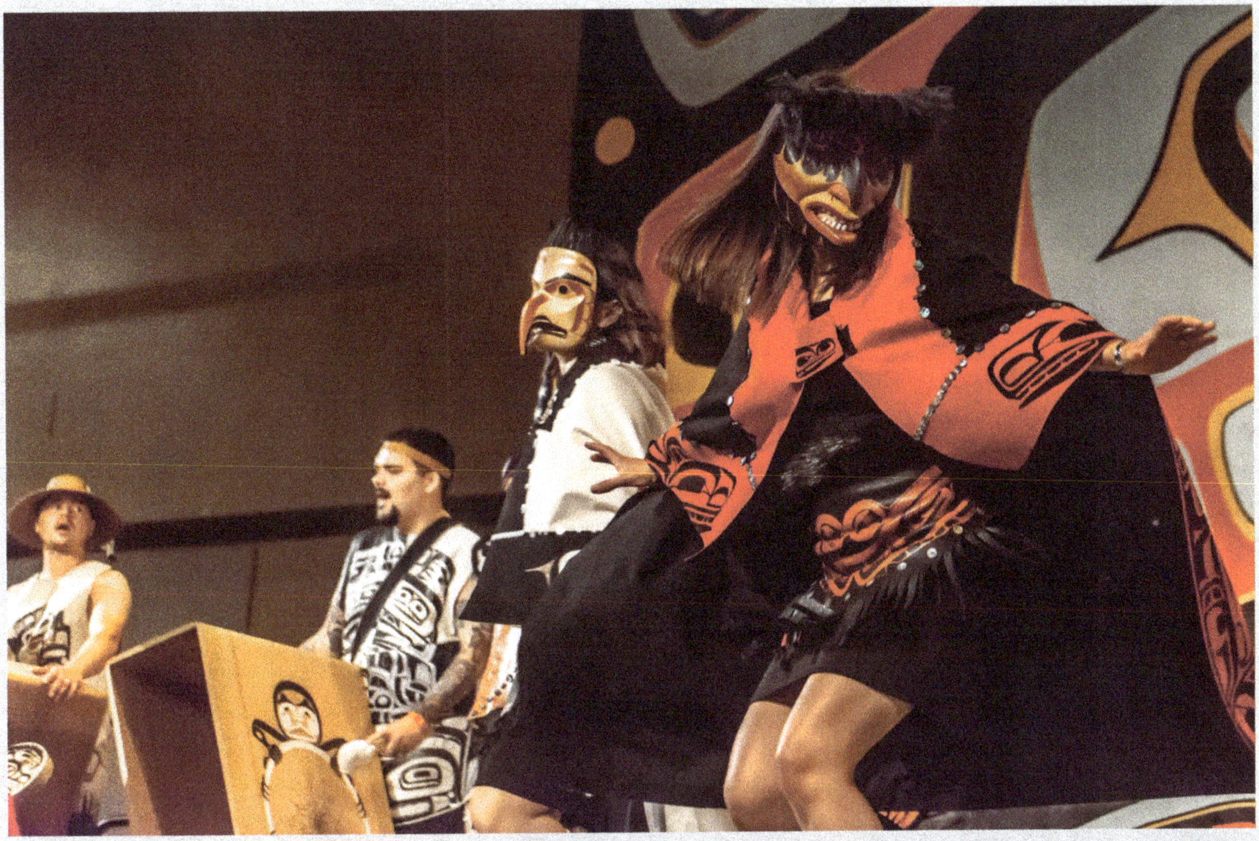

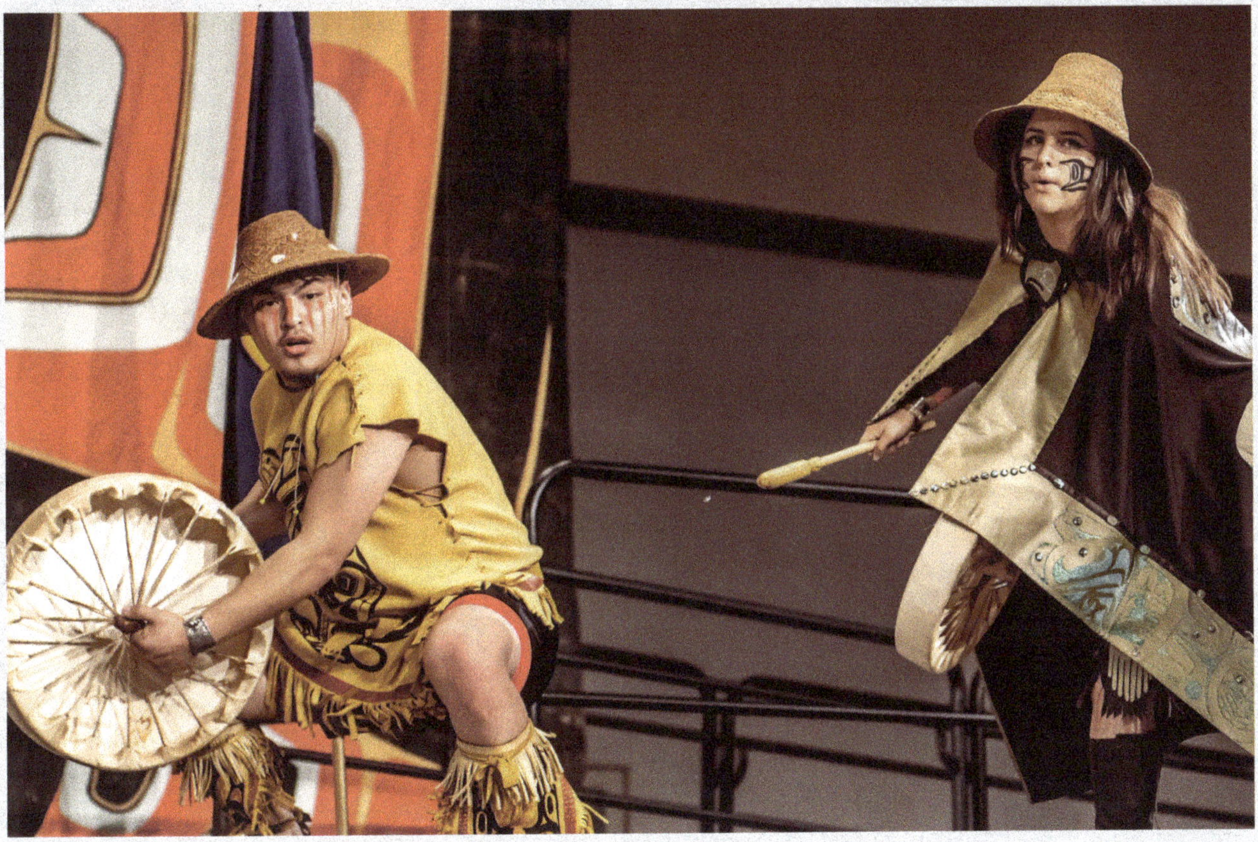

Git Hoan *at* Coastal Dance Festival

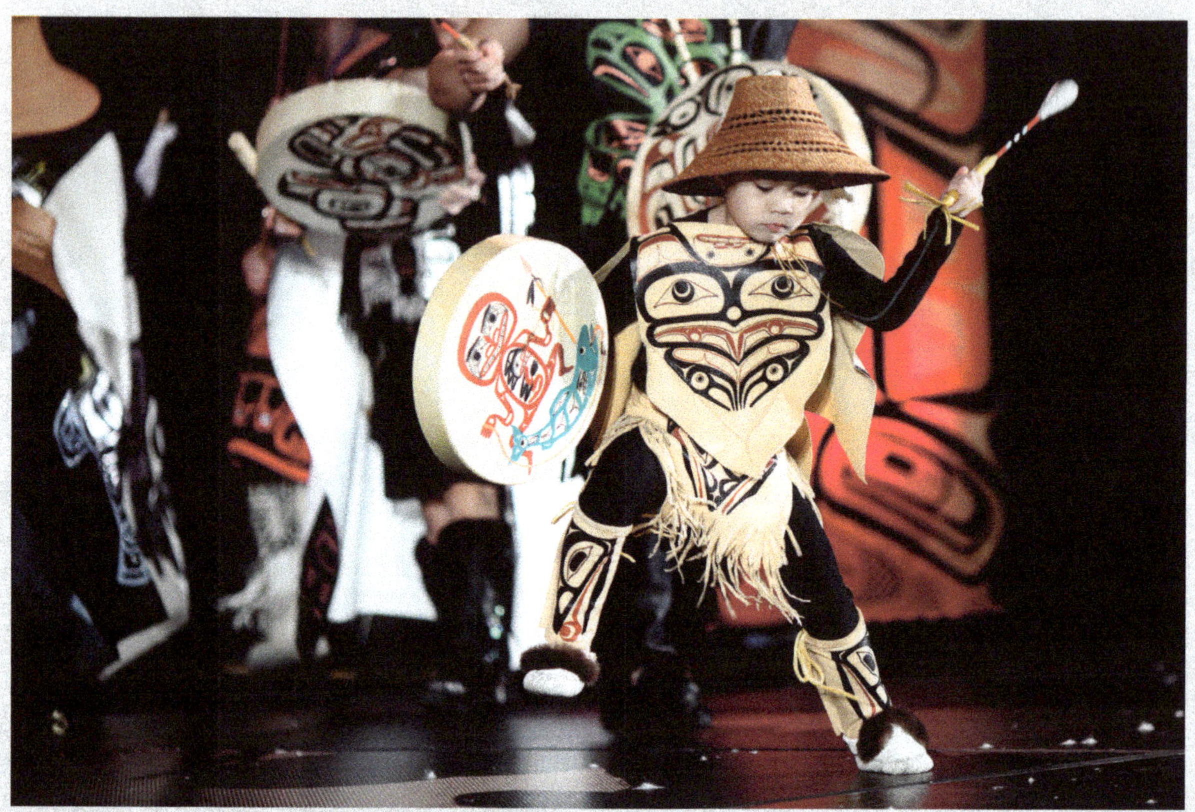

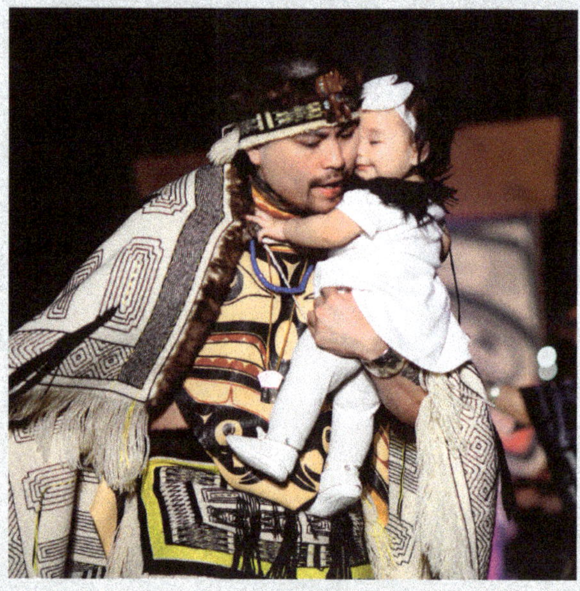

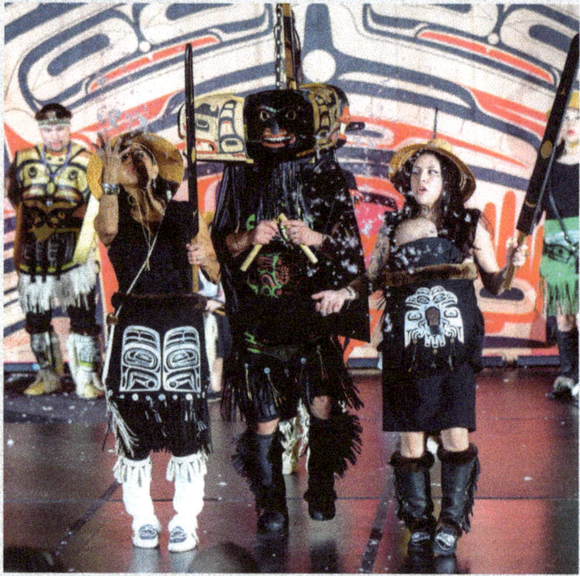

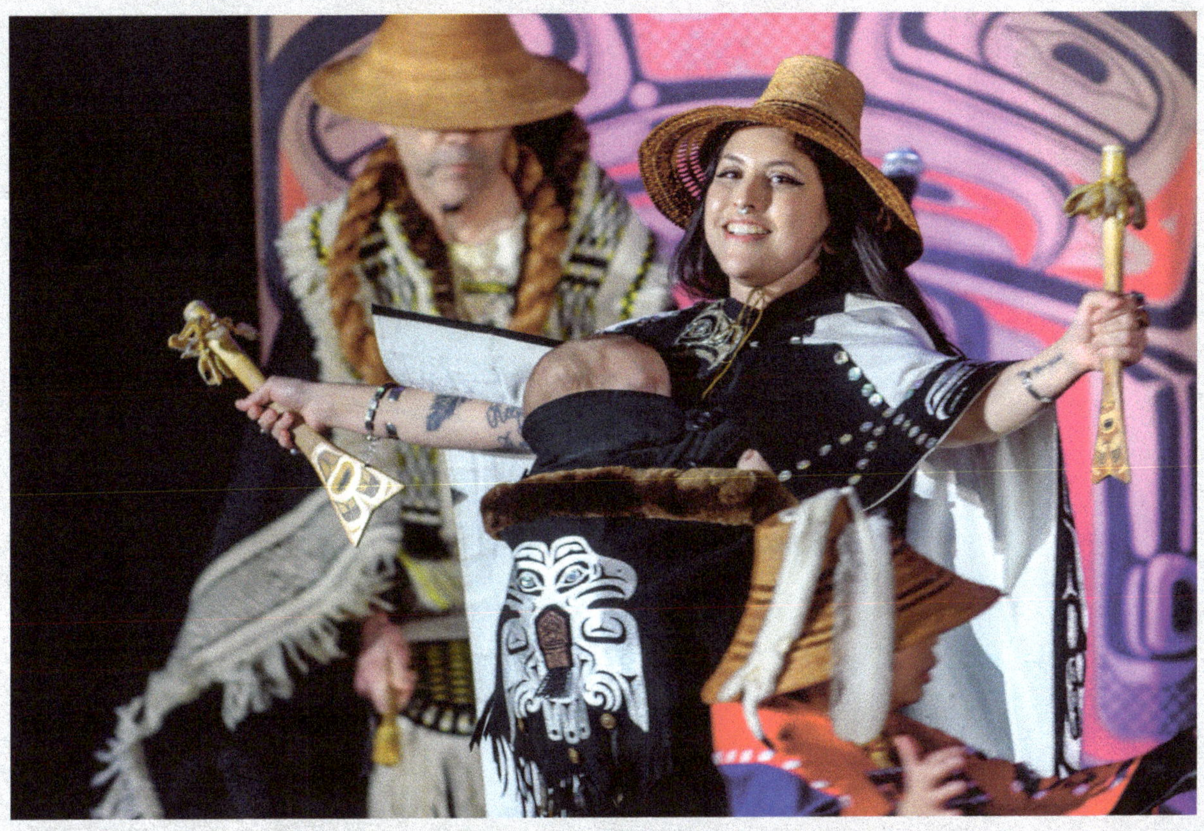

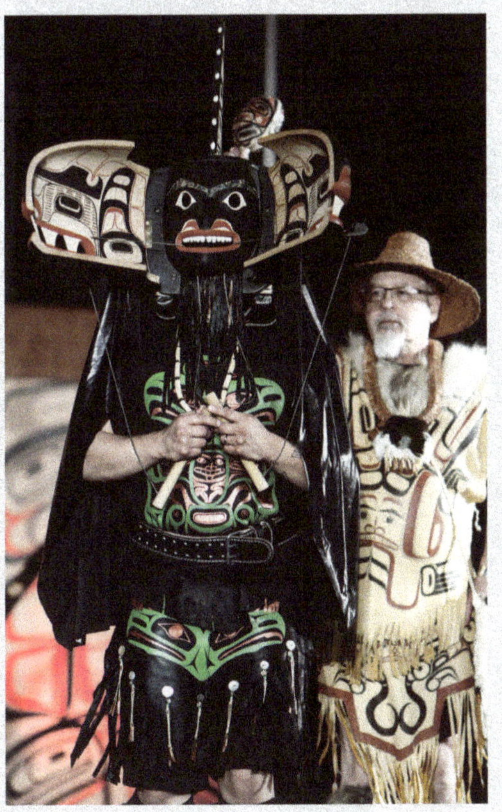

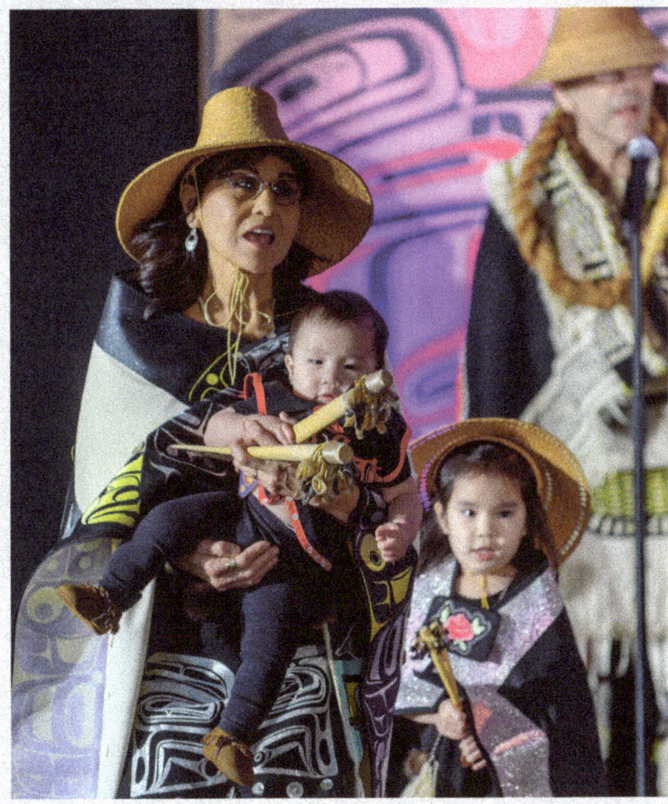

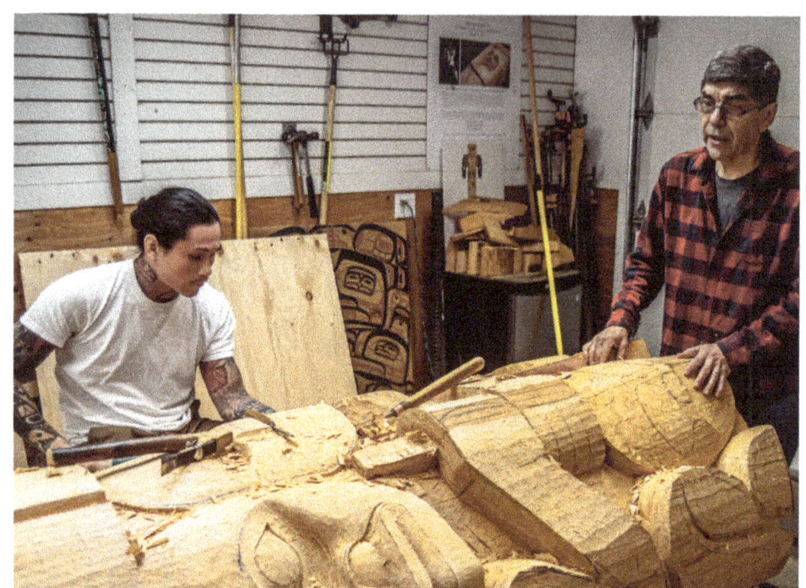
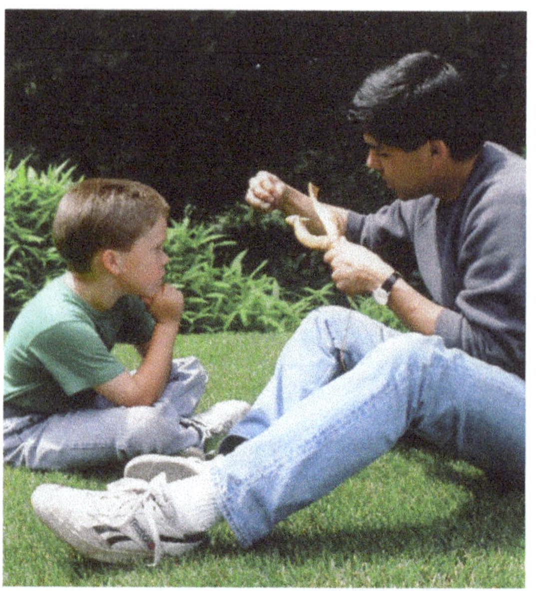
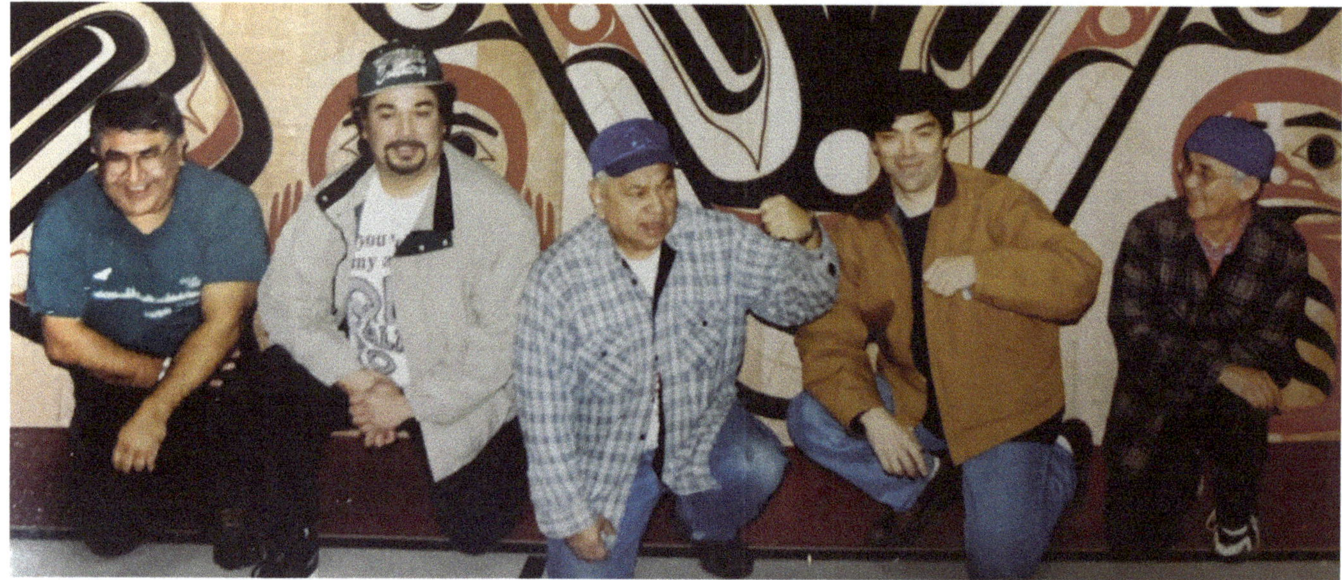
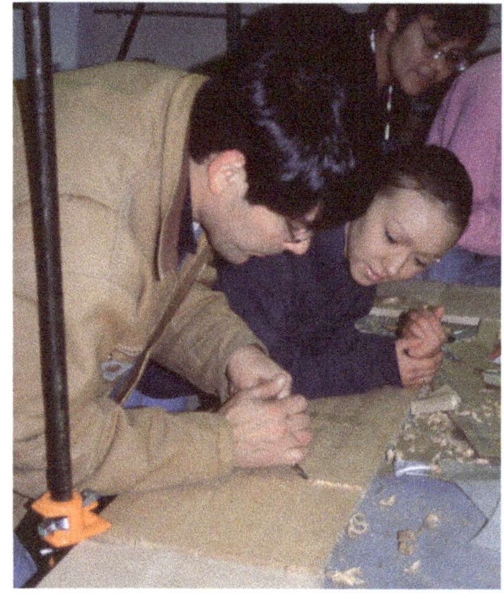
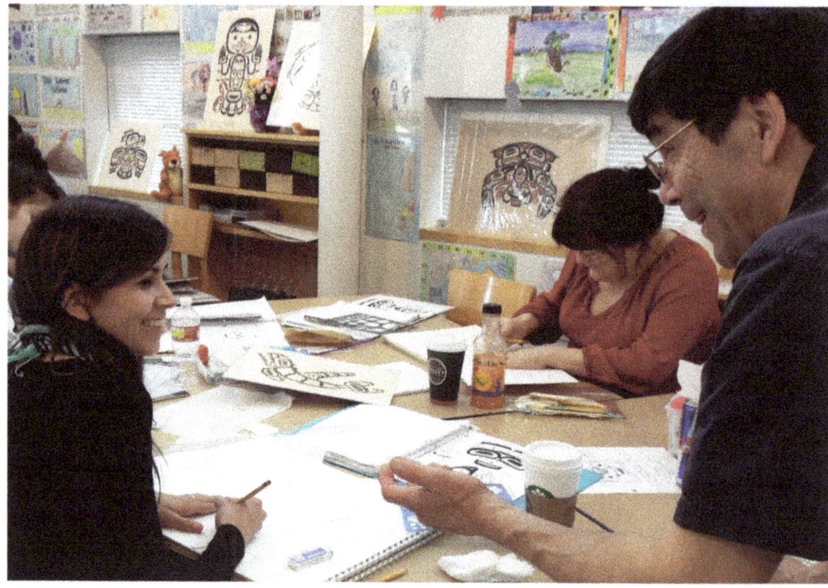

CHAPTER SEVEN

LEGACY / *Gugwilxya'ansk*

One hundred years from now, there is not going to be a person living who knows me. It's just a fact.

Human beings don't live that long. So, it's not as important to me that people remember me or remember my name or the things that I did. It's what I'm trying to do, or what I'm trying to hold onto or preserve or what I'm trying to keep alive that I want people to remember. That's a legacy I want to leave.

Our language, our singing, our dancing, our art, our history. Those are things I want to see survive. They survive by being passed to others who will do the same. I grew up in a village where none of that existed, and I wanted that to change. The only thing that I really remember culturally is subsistence living: fishing, hunting, and gathering. And hearing the old people speak the language. That's all we had.

When I left Metlakatla in 1986, I thought I left teaching for good. Turns out, I only left the school and classroom; I didn't stop teaching. My classroom is my shop, the dance stage, and conference rooms where I can speak our language with others who want to learn, then share it with others.

When teaching school, there are a certain percent of kids in the school who don't want to be there. But when somebody comes to me and wants to work with me, they want to be there. They have a vested interest in becoming a better artist, a better speaker.

I was always hungry for our culture even though I didn't know exactly what that meant at times. I was fascinated every time I was in a museum or saw some cultural event or performance.

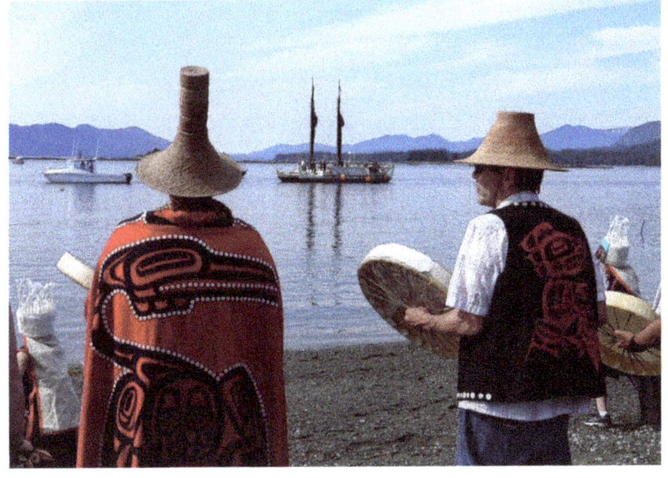

Davey and I stood along the shore to welcome the Hōkūle'a, which began its global journey in Alaska to celebrate the 50th anniversary of its maiden voyage. We were proud of how our tiny village could welcome the crew and celebrate our respective cultures with traditional food, dance and songs. It was a chance to share long-standing pride in my family, my home and our culture with the Hawaiian crew.

We grew up without singing, dancing, the potlaches and clans, rights and privileges.

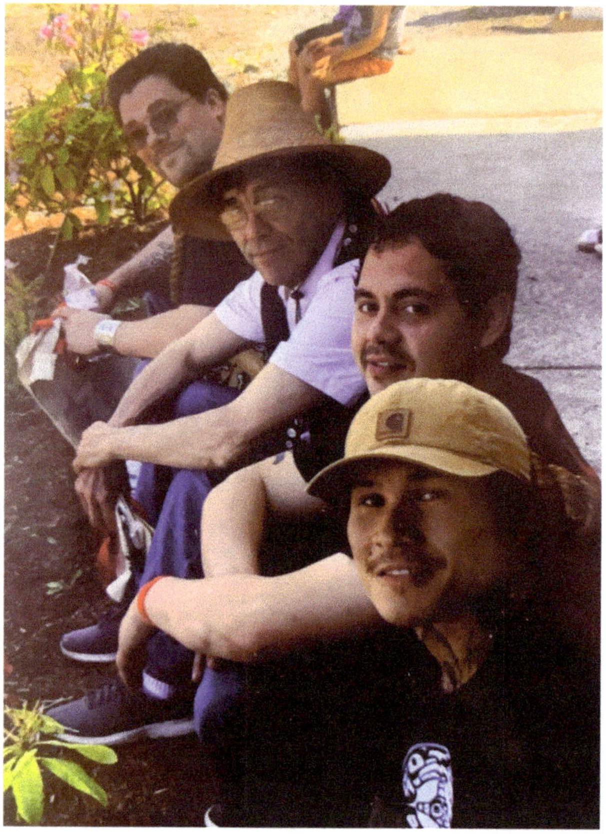

I tell my students, the culture belongs to you as much as it belongs to me. I know what little I know and I just want to share it. It's who we are. It pleases me when I see my own people—or even another tribe—celebrating who they are.

I teach two-dimensional art, carving, dance, and how it all goes together to allow us to tell our stories. But when you have nothing to draw from and no one to ask, it is daunting. When I teach, I take a chance. I am committed to share what I know because it doesn't belong to me, it belongs to our people.

When I get a chance to make things out of cedar and alder, I am aware that I'm doing the same thing that's been done for ten thousand years. What a feeling that is to know I'm continuing that. That's our ancestors' legacy. So, when I get a chance to teach others what I know, there is so much more to it than just making something they can sell. So many people don't see the value because they are trying to make it in this modern world. I'm trying to instill pride in our culture, our knowledge, our language. I struggle with it sometimes, but I accept the challenge with a purpose.

I'm sitting with our culture's future: Davey on my right and Clifton and Dylan on my left. All three wonderful artists.

⸺

I *don't have* a lot of regrets in my life, but one of them is not realizing that that my grandmother and grandfather would someday not be there and that I never pressed them to just speak the Tsimshian language, Sm'algyax, to me so I could be a fluent speaker. I didn't understand at the time that someday I would be sharing, with the few who are left speaking, the responsibility for teaching our language.

Losing our language is one of my biggest worries. On the planet, there are about a hundred fluent speakers left, mostly around Prince Rupert, British Columbia. My grandmother talked to me all the time in our language. I wish my grandfather talked to me in Sm'algyax when we were outside the house. I didn't know at the time to ask him to speak in our language.

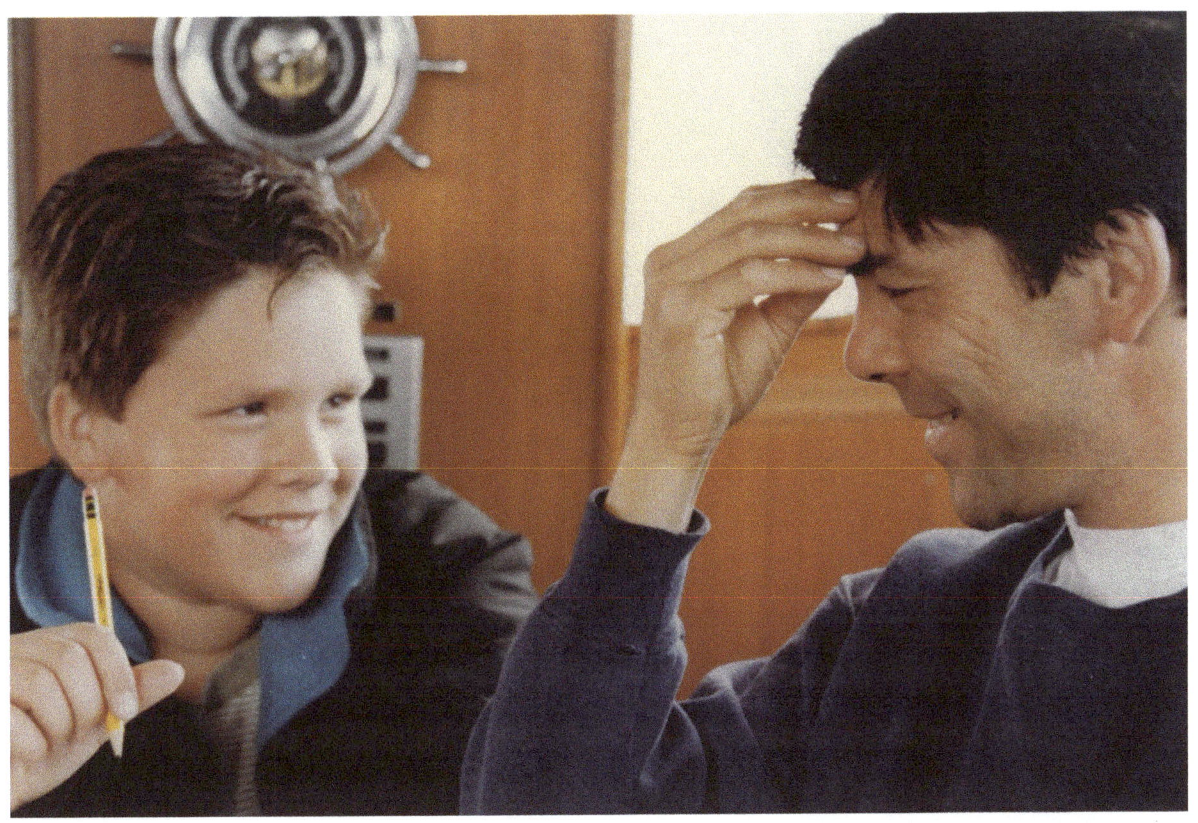

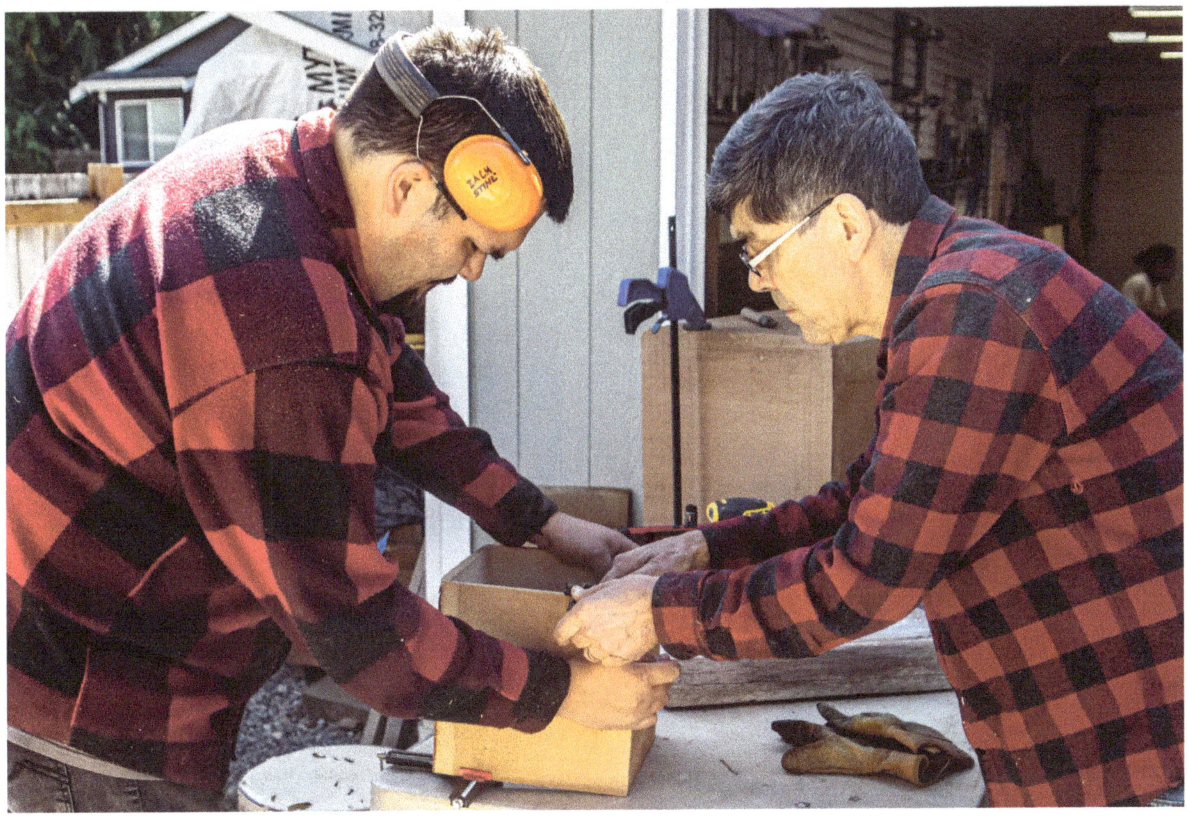

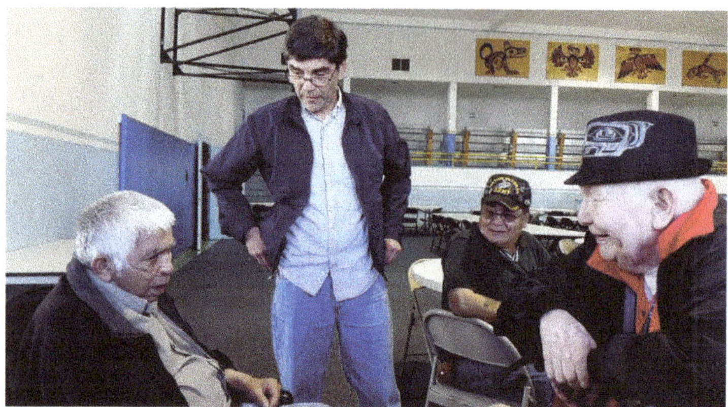

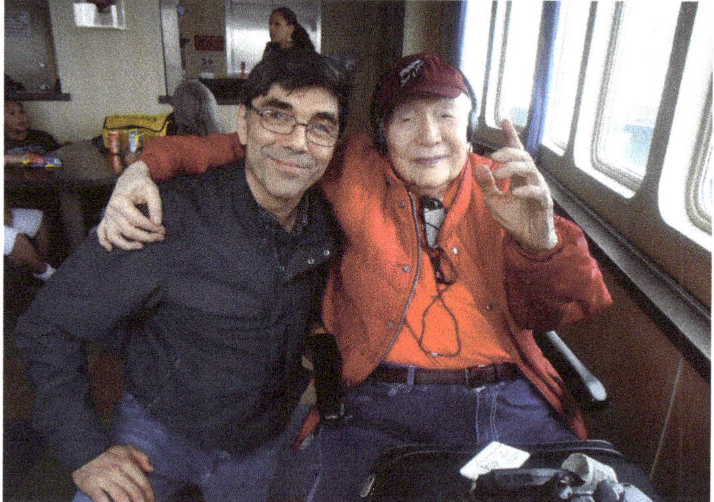

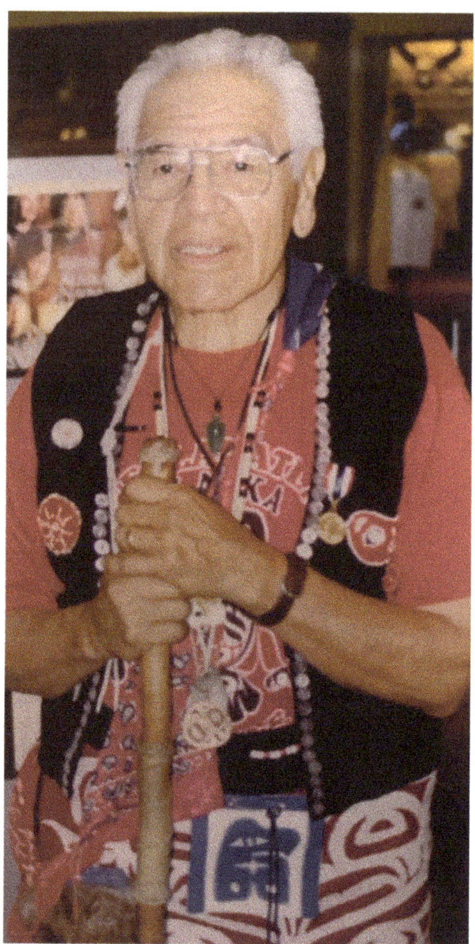

TOP LEFT: Orlando "Bossy" Bolton and John Reese were speaking Sm'algyax and
I was soaking it up.

BOTTOM LEFT: I'm not fluent, but I would always take time to learn from Orlando and John.

RIGHT: Arnold Booth was my 8th grade teacher. He was one of the people involved in trying to preserve our language and keep our culture alive in his elder years. He never stopped inspiring me.

I listened to them talk, and I can still hear their voices speaking this wonderful language. We didn't use it outside the house, but when I was a little boy all the way to the time I went to college, all I heard in the house was Sm'algyax, at least from my grandmother. I heard the old people using it all the time, and, for that, I was fortunate.

The Tsimshian language up and down the coast was always very well thought of. The Haidas have said their term for the Tsimshian language is "the beautiful language." We are all people of the salmon. We've all hunted in the woods for deer, caught salmon in the canoes. We all wear our regalia. We all follow the tribal protocols at potlatches.

The biggest difference between us and all the other tribes is our language: It's what makes us who we are. Everything revolves around it. I've said how the potlatch is the hub of our cultural wheel. The outer rim that holds it all together is our language. The places, the ideas, the concepts, the family

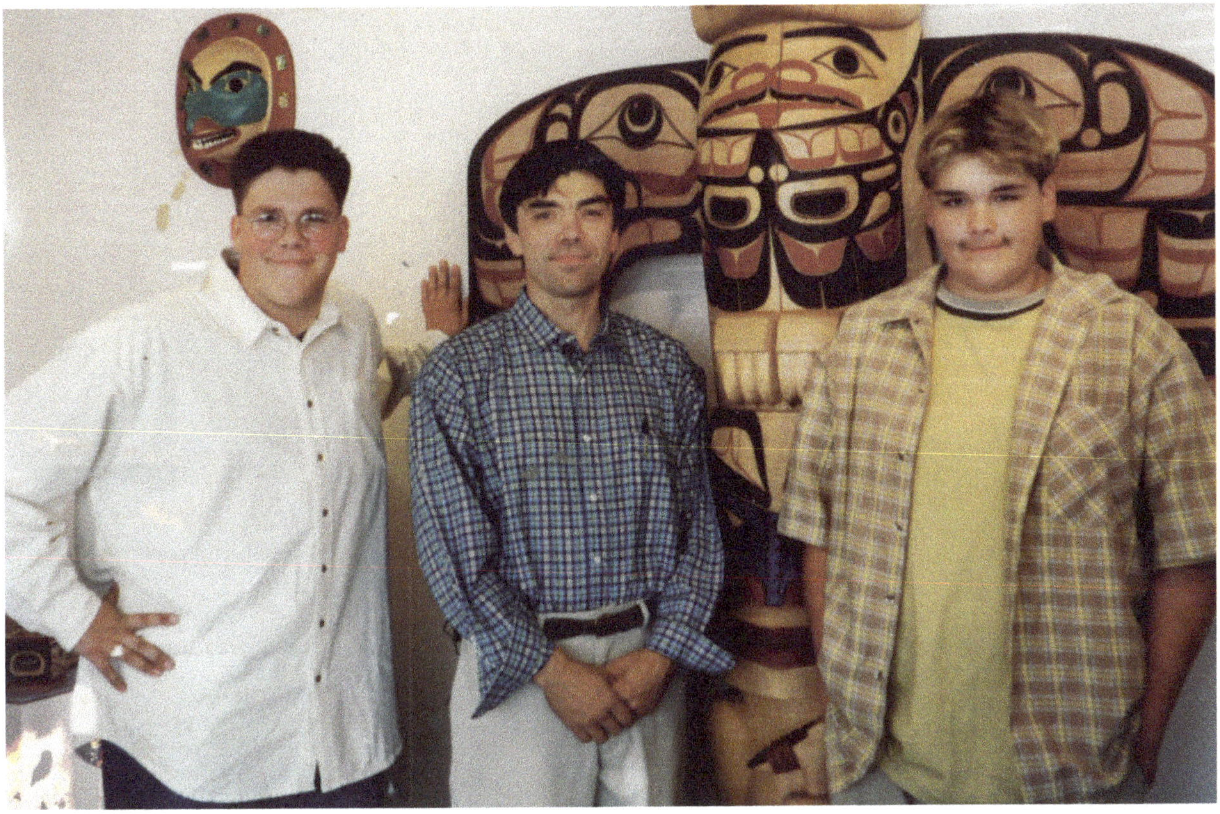

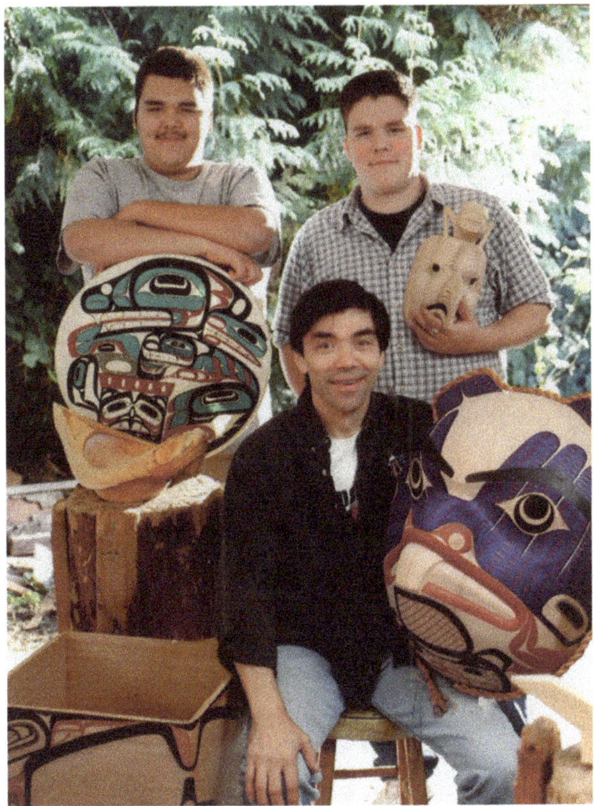

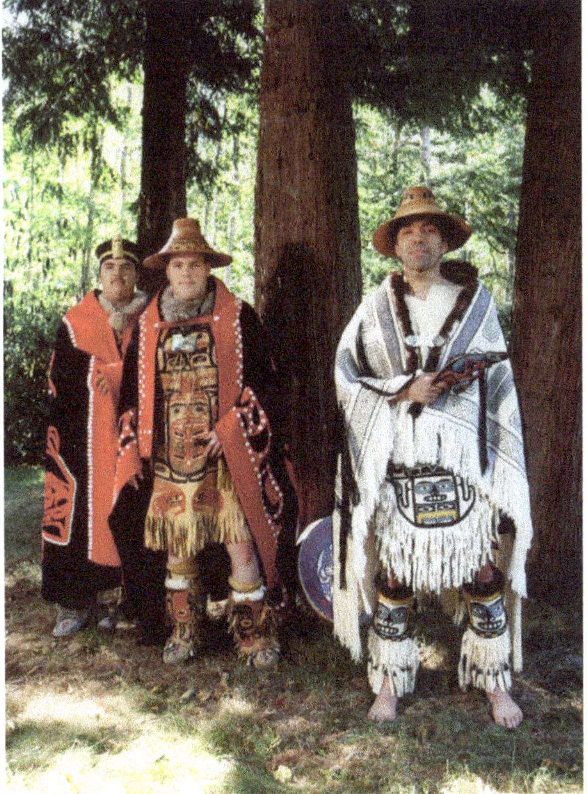

traditions, and the history are all oral. They aren't all tools of something somebody typed on a typewriter or computer. It was all passed on orally.

The thing about language is you don't get to any kind of fluency without immersion. It's just impossible. The language should be in the air. The more people who know it, the longer it will survive. My son has out stripped me by miles in his ability. He encourages me to call our friend in British Columbia, Theresa Louthir, who is Orlando "Bossy" Bolton's sister, whenever I need help with the language. He's really coming along. It's pretty amazing.

I'm real proud of what my son and his friends at Haayk Foundation are doing with the language. He and the others are going to be the ones that everybody goes to for help with our language. They are going to keep our language alive. But it's going to be up to the rest of our people to understand how important it is. You can't just learn to speak the language by taking a class once in a while.

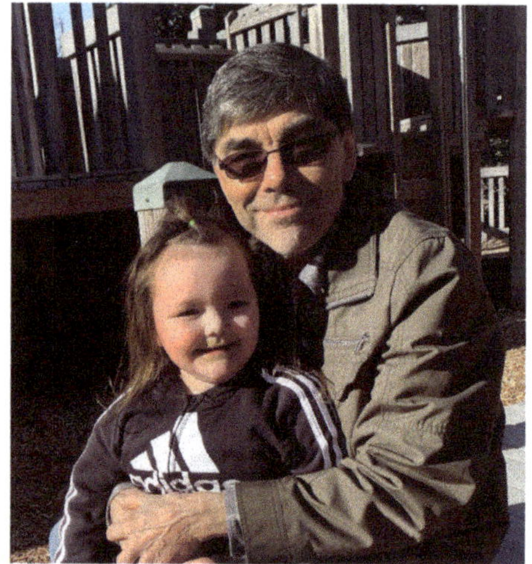

There's a story that I tell often because it's very appropriate—even today. I took my dance group to Cherokee, North Carolina. The night before we were going to dance, they had a gala where all the big shots from the tribes came. All the dance groups and presenters were going to have five minutes to show a snippet of what we could expect to see.

We were waiting our turn and the guy speaking right before me was from Telaqua, Oklahoma, from the western Cherokee, whose ancestors were part of the Trail of Tears. People in Cherokee hid away in the mountains and weren't removed. The guy was giving his talk and people were listening closely. At one point he said, "I really feel bad that there are only ten thousand Cherokee speakers left." You could hear my jaw hit the ground. I forgot everything I was going to say.

Instead of doing my regular protocol in my language, the first thing out of my mouth was, "Ten thousand?" Everybody laughed.

I said, "We don't have ten." And nobody laughed.

I still feel like I can do more. I think I made some mistakes because I was trying to gather in as many people as I could. I thought I could get more people excited about adoptions, namings, and regalia. I just wanted our culture to be alive again. I want our people to have something to be proud of. It's a beautiful culture: the language, the dancing, the art. It's worth working for. Every day. And I'm going to keep working. ❖

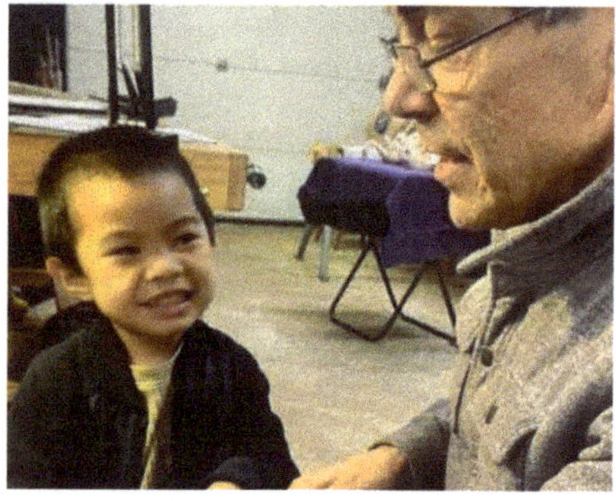

My grandchildren mean so much to me. Between my wife and me, we have 10 so far. They all know me as yaya. I just love holding Zach's daughter, Olivia Grace (**ABOVE**). Sage, the son to Michelle's eldest son (**BELOW**), has spent significant time with us since he was born. I think he is the genuine future of our culture.

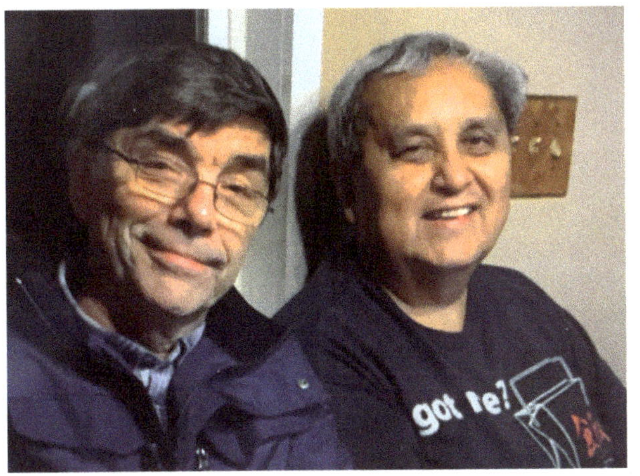

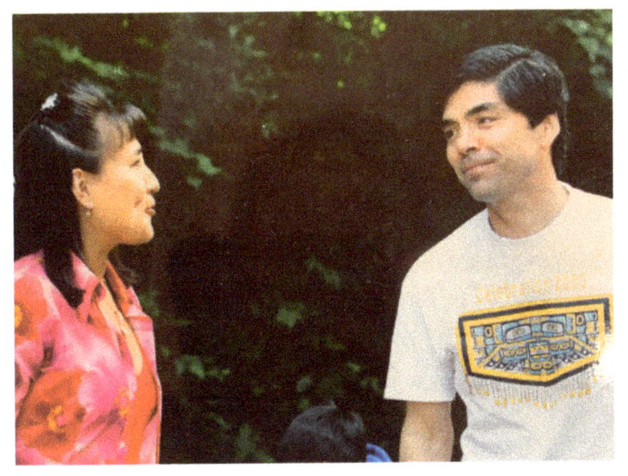

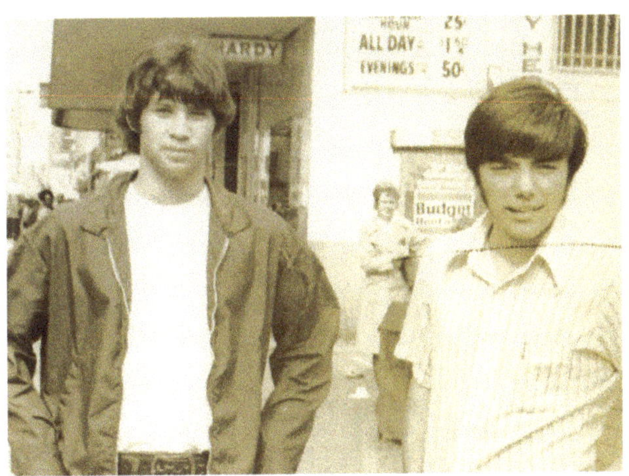

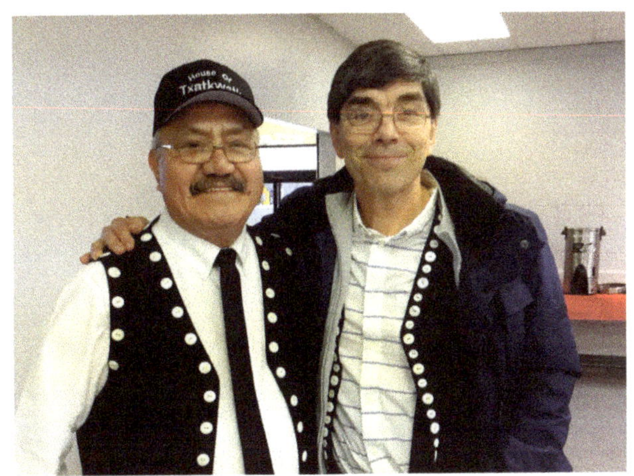

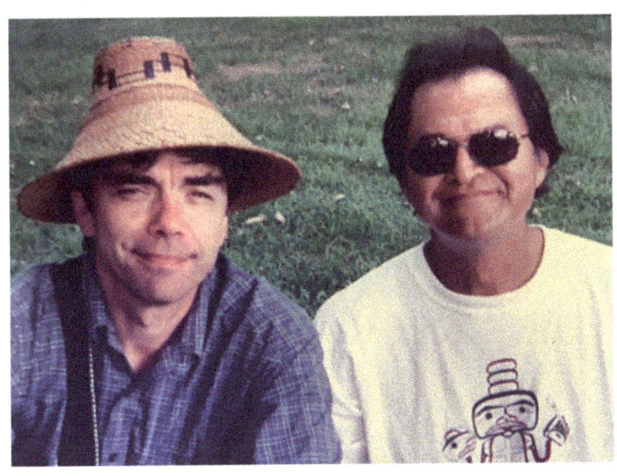

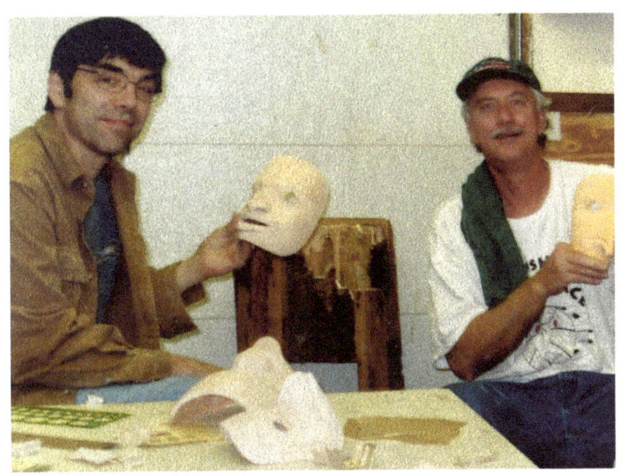

REMEMBERING FRIENDS

I miss these unique and special people. Each gave me real and lasting friendship.
They touched my heart and enriched my life.

TOP: Albert Kookesh • Cindy James **MIDDLE:** Dan Leask • Greg Buxton **BOTTOM:** Wayne Hewson • John Aumann

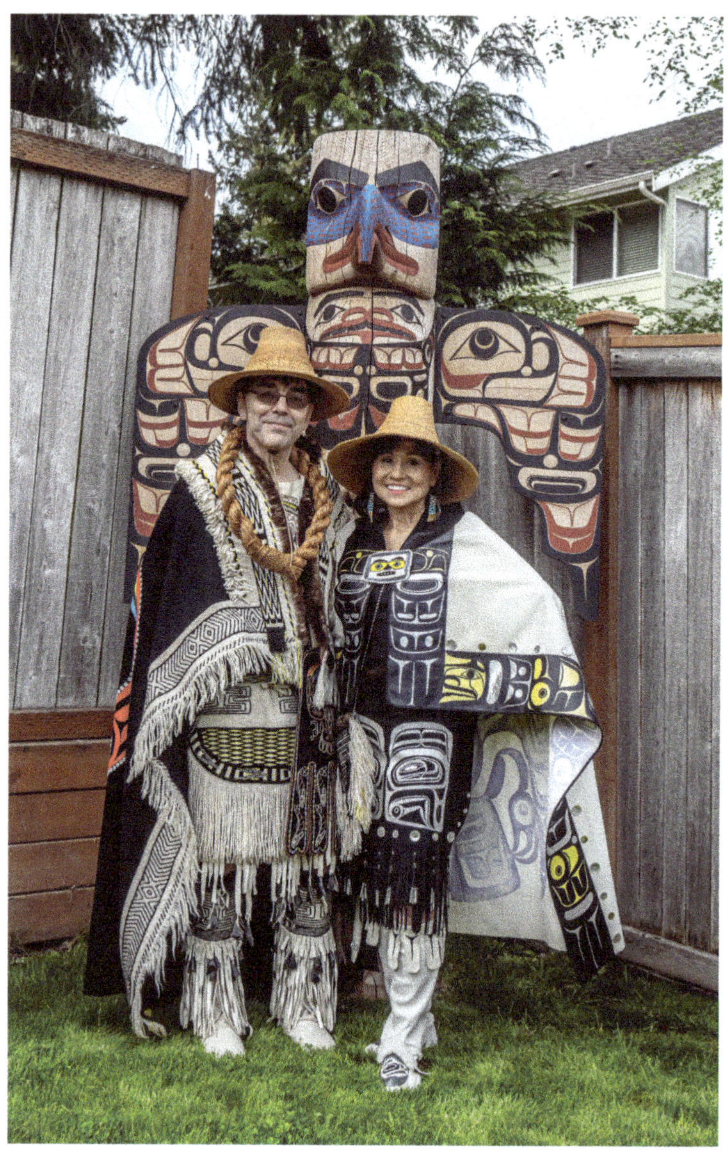

My wife, Michelle, is a genuine partner to me. She's my friend, my business partner, my dance partner who leads me in her own special way. She's an amazing artist who creates beautiful regalia for herself, for me and for our grandchildren.

SI'AAMŁ WAALSM

People call me a culture bearer because I've had the honor to influence my own people in a certain direction. I came along at just the right time, trying to pass on what little I know, and also trying to pass on the excitement. I've never said I was a fluent speaker; I've never said I know everything; I've never said I'm the best at anything. But I want to make sure that what we have doesn't go away—again.

I tell Davey, we're doing this for everybody, whether they agree with us or not. It doesn't belong to you or me; it belongs to all of us, even those who don't want it or don't know about it. It's important for us to do as much as we can.

Our culture is the center of who we are. Without it, we might as well be some other country, some other place.

My grandfather used to say, it's a good weight to be a teacher. One day we were just talking, and he put his hand on my shoulder. He looked at me and pushed down, and then he said, as closely as I can remember, "This is what it feels like to be responsible for your culture. It's a good weight. Feel that weight; never lose that feeling. It's a good weight."

We have a phrase in our language that's very important to me: "Si'aamł waalsm." It means, "May your names always be good." That's how we leave each other.

Si'aamł waalsm

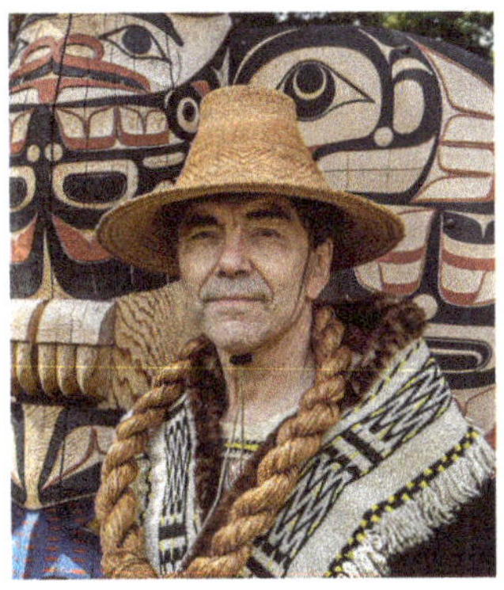

DAVID A. BOXLEY

Raised by his grandparents in the tiny village of Metlakatla, Alaska, David A. Boxley thought he was going to be a teacher and basketball coach. Already on that path, David faced a choice: leave a secure teaching job in his hometown or move to Seattle where he would pursue an uncharted path and become a full-time Tsimshian artist, ultimately leading a revival of cultural art, dance and song.

About his unusual path to becoming an artist, Boxley says, "It's strange. I had to move from my traditional village to become a traditional carver and cultural leader. It is so important that we as Native people hold on to and be proud of the beautiful culture we come from and more importantly, we are responsible to pass it on to the next generation. It belongs to all of us."

WWW.DAVIDBOXLEY.COM

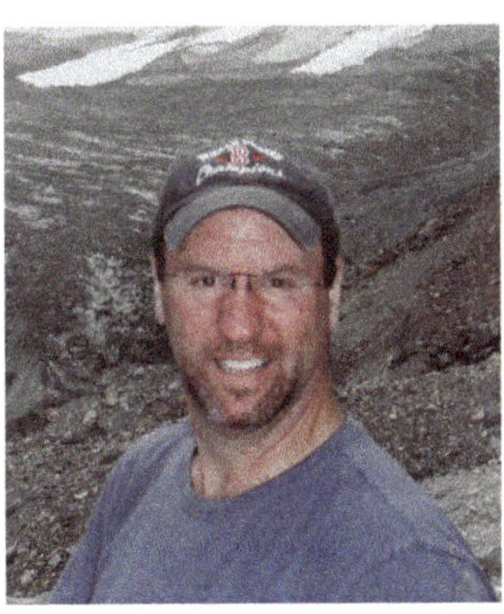

STEVE QUINN

Steve Quinn is a Seattle-based writer, who for 12 years worked in Juneau, Alaska, where he first met David Boxley and members of his dance group Git Hoan. who traveled from Seattle to perform in Juneau. He has won several magazine writing awards featuring Alaska Native culture.

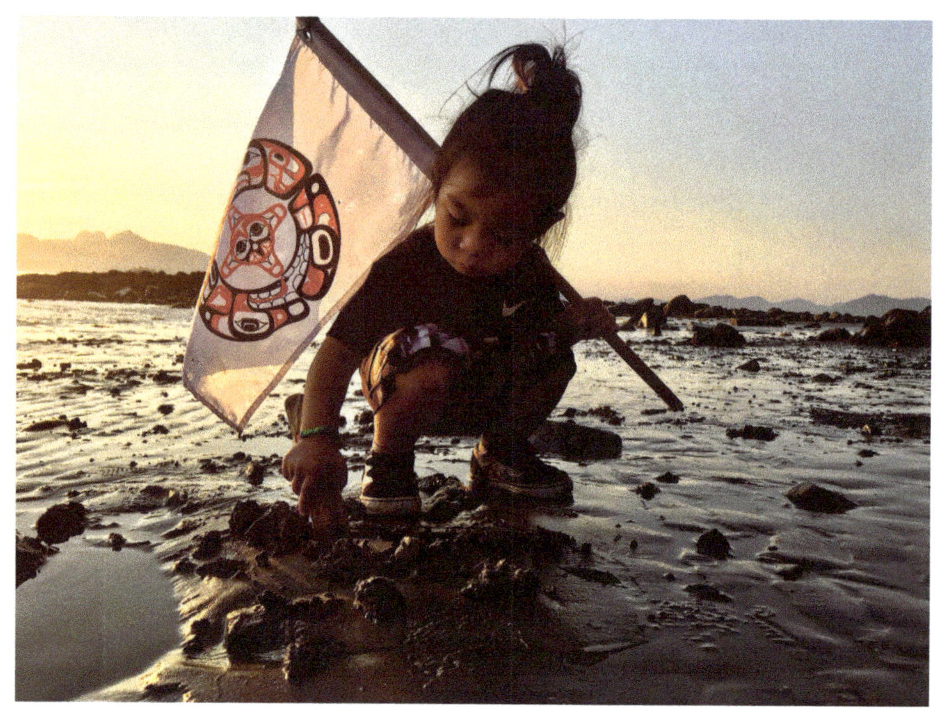

for FUTURE GENERATIONS

May the path I've walked and
the things I've left be of use.